Lecture Notes in Artificial Intelligence 12416

Subseries of Lecture Notes in Computer Science

More information about this series at http://www.springer.com/series/1244

Leszek Rutkowski · Rafał Scherer ·
Marcin Korytkowski · Witold Pedrycz ·
Ryszard Tadeusiewicz · Jacek M. Zurada (Eds.)

Artificial Intelligence and Soft Computing

19th International Conference, ICAISC 2020
Zakopane, Poland, October 12–14, 2020
Proceedings, Part II

 Springer

Editors
Leszek Rutkowski (iD)
Częstochowa University of Technology
Częstochowa, Poland

Marcin Korytkowski
Częstochowa University of Technology
Częstochowa, Poland

Ryszard Tadeusiewicz
AGH University of Science and Technology
Kraków, Poland

Rafał Scherer
Częstochowa University of Technology
Częstochowa, Poland

Witold Pedrycz
Electrical and Computer Engineering
University of Alberta
Edmonton, AB, Canada

Jacek M. Zurada
Electrical and Computer Engineering
University of Louisville
Louisville, KY, USA

ISSN 0302-9743   ISSN 1611-3349   (electronic)
Lecture Notes in Artificial Intelligence
ISBN 978-3-030-61533-8   ISBN 978-3-030-61534-5   (eBook)
https://doi.org/10.1007/978-3-030-61534-5

LNCS Sublibrary: SL7 – Artificial Intelligence

This Springer imprint is published by the registered company Springer Nature Switzerland AG
The registered company address is: Gewerbestrasse 11, 6330 Cham, Switzerland

Preface

This volume constitutes the proceedings of the 19th International Conference on Artificial Intelligence and Soft Computing (ICAISC 2020), held in Zakopane, Poland, during October 12–14, 2020. The conference was held virtually due to the COVID-19 pandemic and was organized by the Polish Neural Network Society in cooperation with the University of Social Sciences in Łódź, the Department of Intelligent Computer Systems at the Częstochowa University of Technology, and the IEEE Computational Intelligence Society, Poland Chapter. Previous conferences took place in Kule (1994), Szczyrk (1996), Kule (1997), and Zakopane (1999, 2000, 2002, 2004, 2006, 2008, 2010, 2012, 2013, 2014, 2015, 2016, 2017, 2018, and 2019) and attracted a large number of papers and internationally recognized speakers: Lotfi A. Zadeh, Hojjat Adeli, Rafal Angryk, Igor Aizenberg, Cesare Alippi, Shun-ichi Amari, Daniel Amit, Plamen Angelov, Albert Bifet, Piero P. Bonissone, Jim Bezdek, Zdzisław Bubnicki, Andrzej Cichocki, Swagatam Das, Ewa Dudek-Dyduch, Włodzisław Duch, Adel S. Elmaghraby, Pablo A. Estévez, João Gama, Erol Gelenbe, Jerzy Grzymala-Busse, Martin Hagan, Yoichi Hayashi, Akira Hirose, Kaoru Hirota, Adrian Horzyk, Eyke Hüllermeier, Hisao Ishibuchi, Er Meng Joo, Janusz Kacprzyk, Jim Keller, Laszlo T. Koczy, Tomasz Kopacz, Jacek Koronacki, Zdzisław Kowalczuk, Adam Krzyzak, Rudolf Kruse, James Tin-Yau Kwok, Soo-Young Lee, Derong Liu, Robert Marks, Ujjwal Maulik, Zbigniew Michalewicz, Evangelia Micheli-Tzanakou, Kaisa Miettinen, Krystian Mikołajczyk, Henning Müller, Ngoc Thanh Nguyen, Andrzej Obuchowicz, Erkki Oja, Witold Pedrycz, Marios M. Polycarpou, José C. Príncipe, Jagath C. Rajapakse, Šarunas Raudys, Enrique Ruspini, Jörg Siekmann, Andrzej Skowron, Roman Słowiński, Igor Spiridonov, Boris Stilman, Ponnuthurai Nagaratnam Suganthan, Ryszard Tadeusiewicz, Ah-Hwee Tan, Dacheng Tao, Shiro Usui, Thomas Villmann, Fei-Yue Wang, Jun Wang, Bogdan M. Wilamowski, Ronald Y. Yager, Xin Yao, Syozo Yasui, Gary Yen, Ivan Zelinka, and Jacek Zurada. The aim of this conference is to build a bridge between traditional artificial intelligence techniques and so-called soft computing techniques. It was pointed out by Lotfi A. Zadeh that "soft computing (SC) is a coalition of methodologies which are oriented toward the conception and design of information/intelligent systems. The principal members of the coalition are: fuzzy logic (FL), neurocomputing (NC), evolutionary computing (EC), probabilistic computing (PC), chaotic computing (CC), and machine learning (ML). The constituent methodologies of SC are, for the most part, complementary and synergistic rather than competitive." These proceedings present both traditional artificial intelligence methods and SC techniques. Our goal is to bring together scientists representing both areas of research. This volume is divided into four parts:

- Computer Vision, Image and Speech Analysis
- Data Mining

- Various Problems of Artificial Intelligence
- Agent Systems, Robotics and Control

The conference attracted a total of 265 submissions from 32 countries, and after the review process, 112 papers were accepted for publication.

I would like to thank our participants, invited speakers, and reviewers of the papers for their scientific and personal contribution to the conference. The following reviewers were very helpful in reviewing the papers:

M. Baczyński	P. Klęsk	G. Papa
Z. Boger	J. Kluska	A. Parkes
R. Burduk	A. Kołakowska	A. Paszyńska
C. Castro	M. Korytkowski	Y. Pei
P. Ciskowski	L. Kotulski	V. Piuri
M. Clerc	Z. Kowalczuk	Ł. Rauch
J. Cytowski	M. Kretowska	S. Rovetta
L. Diosan	E. Kucharska	A. Rusiecki
A. Dockhorn	P. Kudová	A. Sashima
P. Głomb	J. Kulikowski	R. Scherer
Z. Gomółka	J. Kwiecień	M. Sepesy Maucec
G. Gosztolya	M. Ławryńczuk	D. Słota
D. Grabowski	A. Marszałek	B. Starosta
C. Grosan	F. Masulli	N. Tsapanos
J. Grzymala-Busse	R. Matuk Herrera	M. Vajgl
F. Hermann	J. Mazurkiewicz	E. Volna
J. Ishikawa	J. Michalkiewicz	R. Vorobel
D. Jakóbczak	M. Morzy	J. Wąs
E. Jamro	H. Nakamoto	E. Weitschek
M. Jirina	G. Nalepa	J. Yeomans
A. Kasperski	A. Owczarek	A. Zamuda
E. Kerre	E. Ozcan	Q. Zhao
H. Kim	W. Palacz	

Finally, I thank my co-workers Łukasz Bartczuk, Piotr Dziwiński, Marcin Gabryel, Marcin Korytkowski, and Rafał Scherer, for their enormous efforts in making the conference a very successful event. Moreover, I would like to acknowledge the work of Marcin Korytkowski who was responsible for the Internet submission system.

October 2020   Leszek Rutkowski

Organization

ICAISC 2020 was organized by the Polish Neural Network Society in cooperation with the University of Social Sciences in Łódź and Department of Intelligent Computer Systems at Częstochowa University of Technology.

ICAISC Chairpersons

General Chair

Leszek Rutkowski, Poland

Area Chairs

Fuzzy Systems

Witold Pedrycz, Canada

Evolutionary Algorithms

Zbigniew Michalewicz, Australia

Neural Networks

Jinde Cao, China

Computer Vision

Dacheng Tao, Australia

Machine Learning

Nikhil R. Pal, India

Artificial Intelligence with Applications

Janusz Kacprzyk, Poland

International Liaison

Jacek Żurada, USA

ICAISC Program Committee

Shiro Usui, Japan
Deliang Wang, USA
Jun Wang, Hong Kong
Lipo Wang, Singapore
Paul Werbos, USA
Bernard Widrow, USA
Kay C. Wiese, Canada

Bogdan M. Wilamowski, USA
Donald C. Wunsch, USA
Ronald R. Yager, USA
Xin-She Yang, UK
Gary Yen, USA
Sławomir Zadrożny, Poland
Jacek Zurada, USA

ICAISC Organizing Committee

Rafał Scherer, Poland
Łukasz Bartczuk, Poland
Piotr Dziwiński, Poland
Marcin Gabryel (Finance Chair), Poland
Rafał Grycuk, Poland
Marcin Korytkowski (Databases and Internet Submissions), Poland

Contents – Part II

Computer Vision, Image and Speech Analysis

Data Mining

Various Problems of Artificial Intelligence

Contents – Part I

Pattern Classification

Artificial Intelligence in Modeling and Simulation

Computer Vision, Image and Speech Analysis

A New Approach to Detection of Abrupt Changes in Black-and-White Images

Tomasz Gałkowski[1]($\boxtimes$) and Adam Krzyżak[2,3]

[1] Institute of Computational Intelligence, Czestochowa University of Technology, Czestochowa, al. Armii Krajowej 36, 42-200 Częstochowa, Poland
tomasz.galkowski@pcz.pl
[2] Department of Computer Science and Software Engineering, Concordia University, Montreal, Quebec H3G 1M8, Canada
[3] Department of Electrical Engineering, Westpomeranian University of Technology, 70-310 Szczecin, Poland
krzyzak@cs.concordia.ca

Abstract. In data analysis one of the most important problems is to verify whether data observed or/and collected in time are genuine and stationary, i.e. the information sources did not change their characteristics. Nowadays, unprecedented amounts of heterogeneous data collections are stored, processed and transmitted via the Internet. There is a variety of data types: texts, ordinary numbers, images, audio or video files or streams, metadata descriptions, etc. All of them change in many ways. If the change happens then the interesting issue is what is the essence of this change and when and where the change has occurred. The main focus of this paper is detection of change in pictures. Many algorithms have been proposed to detect abnormalities and deviations in the data. We propose a new approach for abrupt changes detection based on the Parzen kernel estimation of the partial derivatives of the multivariate regression functions in presence of probabilistic noise. The proposed change detection algorithm is applied to one- and two-dimensional patterns to detect the abrupt changes.

Keywords: Edge detection · Nonparametric regression estimation

1 Introduction

There is a variety of data types processed, transmitted and stored in the Internet: texts, images, audio or video files or streams, metadata descriptions or just ordinary numbers. It is important to be convinced that these collected data are genuine, or reliable i.e., information sources did not change their characteristics in time. Let us note that we are not interested in the ordinary distortion of

A. Krzyżak—Part of this research was carried out by the second author during his visit of the Westpomeranian University of Technology while on sabbatical leave from Concordia University.

© Springer Nature Switzerland AG 2020
L. Rutkowski et al. (Eds.): ICAISC 2020, LNAI 12416, pp. 3–18, 2020.
https://doi.org/10.1007/978-3-030-61534-5_1

data (errors) by impulse noise, for instance. These types of problems are dealt by error correcting codes and/or digital filtering in telecommunications. We are interested in determining the essence of the changes if they occurred, and in knowing where or when they have arisen. The fundamental question is how to detect such changes automatically, i.e. by the appropriate use of a computer program.

The popular approaches for detecting abnormalities or deviations in the data are based on the probabilistic and statistical tests or model building. Such strategies are motivated by the lack of precise and complete mathematical description of the process generating the observed data, even if we apply the known physical, biological or medical principles and mathematical equations.

The following general types of changes may be of interest to us (see: [2]):

- anomalies: accidental, fortuitous, often single, less important aberration or simply error in observations caused e.g. by transmission channel noise, measurement inaccuracy or temporary disturbances. Their effect quickly passes away. Generally they are irrelevant and can be ignored. They can be easily removed from the data by appropriate filtering or corrections.

- abrupt, narrow changes, also called edges or jumps: significant deviation from the standard or model observed yet. They are important to the observer. They may indicate the problem which requires an urgent response. The abrupt changes in the stock market, abnormalities in physiological parameters of hospital patients, in imaging tomography, changes in geological processes, especially in seismology, cartography, and in several industrial processes - need the more attention. Sudden increase of network traffic flow including the web clickstreams, sensor data, phone calls quantities - can indicate possible hacker attack and general lack of information security and the system threats.

- trends or drifts: subtle shifts that cannot be easily detected manually. They proceed slowly, are hardly visible in the long period and more difficult to detect and classify as important. However, such changes can be of great qualitative importance and may indicate a profound change in the structure of the model. Examples: the changes in the global temperature of the earth's surface, the amount of underground water resources in certain areas, the gradual general degradation of air quality, changes in the earth magnetic field - all of them, in the long perspective, threaten the human civilization and even life on Earth.

2   A Short Overview of the Used Methodologies

There are several methods and algorithms developed to detect abnormalities or deviations in the data. The brief survey of the edge detection techniques in *2d-* image processing one can be found in, e.g., [2,59]. The authors described several approaches for abrupt changes detection via classical gradient-based methods using operations involving first order derivatives such as Sobel, Prewitt, Robert's [37] and Canny [4] edge detectors at which the distribution of intensity values in the neighborhood of given pixels determines the probable edges. The algorithms involving second order derivatives such as the Laplacian and Gaussian filtering used for detecting of zero-crossings also allow edge detection in images [34].

The common methodology relies on phenomena analysis by modelling the problems by multidimensional probability density functions in continuous d-dimensional spaces, and distributions in case of discrete series of random numbers representing statistical multidimensional processes. The natural approach is to model the data via densities or distributions [8]. The significant features could be compared using different sample sets by using mathematical statistics and the representative templates like means and simple models (e.g. linear regression). This comparison may result in the detection of a change in some parameters. More general criteria like mean square error can be also used to detect change. When a parameter of the process is estimated the so-called parametric approach is applied. The nonparametric approach is used when no assumptions on the functional form of data distributions have been made. Many statistical tests like the Kolmogorov-Smirnov test or Wilcoxon test have been applied in this problem, for instance (see [6]). The main approach is to compute a scalar function of the data (so-called test statistics) and compare the values to determine whether a significant change (defined before) has occurred. The relative entropy known as the Kullback-Leibler distance [30] is one of the most common distribution distance measures.

The methods cited above are effective when the data volumes are not very large, and they are usable off-line. So, for data streams, they are not applicable directly. The interesting results on various regression models for stream data mining are discussed in [12–14, 27, 36, 50–53].

The objects and/or processes in general can be described mathematically as a function $R(.)$ of the d-dimensional vector of random variable $\mathbf{X}$. Then the methods based on regression function analysis can be applied. An abrupt change of the function $R(.)$ value at point p may be recognized as a jump discontinuity of the function. In one dimensional case $(d = 1)$ it may be observed as a steep change in function value. The main problem is to determine the point p at which this occurs. In case $d > 1$ the change location (edge) takes form of a curve in d-dimensional space (across which R has jump discontinuity). It is more difficult to establish it and the calculation requires much more computational effort. One way of detecting change is to compare likelihood between the subsequent examples using adjacent sliding time-windows, for previous elements in the stream and the further ones. The point p could be estimated when we observe a decreasing likelihood.

The application of the Kulback-Leibler divergence one may find in e.g. [16]. The data in consecutive time-windows are clustered using k-means into K clusters. The discrete distribution is calculated where each cluster has a probability proportional to the number of examples it holds. If two distributions are identical the Kulback-Leibler divergence is 0, when they are substantially different the Kullback-Leibler divergence is close to 1.

A compromise between Hoteling (parametric detector) and non-parametric Kullback-Leibler divergence was one recently studied in [16] using, among others, the Mahalanobis distance and Gaussian mixture of distributions.

Another interesting approach is based on radial basis functions (RBF). The method described in [46] uses the scalable radial kernels in the form $K(\mathbf{x}, \mathbf{y}) := \Phi(\mathbf{x} - \mathbf{y})$ where Φ is a radial function, defined on R^d. It can be rewritten in the form $\Phi(r)$ where $r = \|.\|$ denotes the distance norm and $\Phi : [0, \infty) \to \Re$ - a function of a single non-negative real variable. The authors have chosen the Wendland kernels of polynomials with even order of smoothness. Kernels on R^d can be scaled by the positive factor delta in the following way: $K(\mathbf{x}, \mathbf{y}, \delta) := K\left(\frac{\mathbf{x}}{\delta}, \frac{\mathbf{y}}{\delta}\right), \forall \mathbf{x}, \mathbf{y} \in R^d$.

The parameter δ is called the shape or scale parameter and can be tuned by the experimenter (depending to the application). It controls the accuracy and the stability of the interpolation. The main task is to interpolate the data with the radial kernel functions, next calculating the set of the coefficients of this interpolation in some cardinal function. The main conclusion follows from the Gibbs phenomenon: when the approximated function has the discontinuity at the point p in the Fourier series the high frequency components arise, so the corresponding Fourier coefficients take larger absolute values in this region. A suitable thresholding strategy could be used to detect point p.

In this paper, we focus our attention on the challenge of abrupt change detection (also called edge detection problem) by presenting a new original approach. The main result is the method of edge detection derived from nonparametric approach based on Parzen kernel algorithms for estimation of unknown regression functions and their derivatives from the set of noisy measurements. The algorithms are developed for two-dimensional functions or patterns on the plane. Restricting our considerations to *2-dimensional* space allows to better understand the proposed approach, but by no means precludes its generalization to *d-dimensional* space.

This article concerns techniques useful in the wide range of fields such as classification, computer vision, diagnostics etc. (see e.g. [5, 9, 10, 23–25, 29, 42, 43, 57, 58, 60]). The approach based on regression analysis is developed as an attractive tool also in classification and modelling of objects (e.g. [32, 33]), forecasting of phenomena (e.g. [3, 28, 31, 40, 45]), and entire methodology of machine learning like neural networks, fuzzy sets, genetic algorithms (e.g. [7, 35, 54–56]). Nonparametric approach to analysis and modelling of various systems one may found e.g. in [41, 44, 47–49].

Edge detection technique based on Parzen kernel estimate has also been described by Qiu in [38, 39]. Unlike our algorithm the method presented in [39] is quite complicated and its performance in real applications has not been investigated. The algorithm described in [38] is significantly different from our approach and it uses derivatives computed in a very inefficient way. The algorithm has not been thoroughly tested in experiments. In our approach we compute the derivatives of the kernel itself which is a very simple and efficient process and our algorithms performs in satisfactory manner in numerical experiments. Furthermore, our algorithm can scale up and it does not require the samples to be uniformly spaced.

3   Algorithm for Abrupt Change Detection - One-Dimensional Case

The RBF methods described in Sect. 2 are one of the kernel-type methods. See [26] for theoretical analysis of Parzen and other nonparametric regression estimation techniques for so-called random design case.

The main goal of this paper is to introduce a new simple method of edge detection derived from the nonparametric approach based on multidimensional Parzen kernel algorithms for estimating unknown functions and their derivatives from the set of noisy measurements.

We consider the model of the object in the form:

$$y_i = R\left(\mathbf{x}_i\right) + \varepsilon_i, \, i = 1, ..., n \tag{1}$$

where $\mathbf{x}_i$ is assumed to be the d-dimensional vectors of deterministic input, $\mathbf{x}_i \in R^d$, y_i is the scalar random output, and ε_i is a measurement noise with zero mean and bounded variance. $R(.)$ is assumed to be completely unknown function. This is so-called fixed-design regression problem, see e.g. [15].

We start with estimator $\hat{R}_n\left(\mathbf{x}\right)$ of function $R(.)$ at point $\mathbf{x}$ based on the set of measurements y_i, $i = 1, ..., n$.

We use the Parzen kernel based algorithm of the integral type:

$$\hat{R}(\mathbf{x}) = h_n{}^{-d} \sum_{i=1}^{n} y_i \int_{D_i} \mathbf{K}\left(\frac{\|\mathbf{x} - \mathbf{u}\|}{h_n}\right) d\mathbf{u}, \tag{2}$$

where $\|\mathbf{x} - \mathbf{u}\|$ denotes a norm or the distance function defined for points $\mathbf{x}$ and $\mathbf{u}$ in d-dimensional space and D_i's are defined below.

Factor h_n depending on the number of observations n is called the smoothing factor.

Let us mention that in nonparametric approach we impose no constraints on either the shape of unknown function (like e.g. in the spline methods or linear regression) or on any mathematical formula with a certain set of parameters to be found (like in so-called parametric approach).

The domain area D (the space where function R is defined) is partitioned into n disjunctive nonempty sub-spaces D_i and the measurements $\mathbf{x}_i$ are chosen from D_i, i.e.: $\mathbf{x}_i \in D_i$.

For instance, in one-dimensional case let the $D = [0, 1]$, then $\cup D_i = [0, 1]$, $D_i \cap D_j = \emptyset$ for $i \neq j$, the points x_i are chosen from D_i, i.e.: $x_i \in D_i$.

The set of input values $\mathbf{x}_i$ (independent variable in the model (1) are chosen in the process of collecting data e.g., equidistant samples of ECG signal in time domain, or stock exchange information, or internet activity on specified TCP/IP port of the web or ftp server logs recorded in time. These data points should provide a balanced representation of function R in the domain D.

The standard assumption in theorems on convergence of (3) is that the maximum diameter of set D_i tends to zero if n tends to infinity (see e.g. [17, 18, 21]).

We may assume that in the set of pairs $(\mathbf{x}_i, \mathbf{y}_i)$ information (in some way *inscribed*) on essential properties of function R, like its smoothness is present.

The kernel function $\mathbf{K}$ in one-dimensional case $K(.)$ satisfies the following conditions:

$$K(t) = 0 \qquad t \notin (-\tau, \tau), \tau > 0$$
$$\int_{-\tau}^{\tau} K(t)dt = 1 \qquad\qquad (3)$$
$$\sup_t |K(t)| < \infty$$

We will use the following trigonometric cosine kernel satisfying (3)

$$K(t) = \begin{cases} \frac{\pi}{4} \cos\left(\frac{\pi}{2}t\right) & for\ t \in (-1, 1) \\ 0 & otherwise \end{cases} \qquad (4)$$

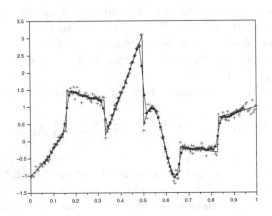

Estimated function with added noise

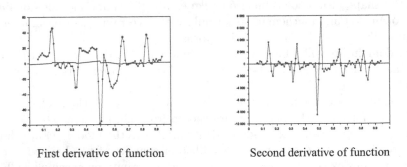

First derivative of function   Second derivative of function

Fig. 1. Simulation example - one-dimensional function. (Color figure online)

The algorithm for estimating the derivatives of order k is based on differentiation of the kernel function. Thus the kernel $K(.)$ must be differentiable function of order k. The trigonometric cosine kernel (4) fulfils this condition. The estimate of $k - th$ derivative of the regression function in point x can be defined as follows:

$$\hat{R}^{(k)}(x) = h_n^{-1} \sum_{i=1}^{n} y_i \int_{D_i} K^{(k)} \left(\frac{x - u}{h_n} \right) du \qquad (5)$$

The nonparameric approach in application to estimation of unknown functions and their derivatives was previously proposed and studied in univariate case in e.g. [19, 22].

The main idea of the paper is to deduce the dynamics of changes of any function by analysing the course of the first derivative estimated from sample. The more rapidly the change occurs - the higher the first derivative (or speed). The steeper the slope - the larger the tangent referring to horizon surface at a given point. These facts motivate us to propose as a detector of abrupt changes the nonparametric estimator of the derivatives described previously. The smoothing property of these algorithms makes it applicable when the observations are taken in the presence of random noise. The integral version of nonparametric kernel estimation algorithms (2), using the Parzen kernel (3), enables not only estimation of the value of the desired regression function, but also estimation of the value of its first derivative and higher order derivatives, too.

The appropriate strategy using the estimates of the first and the second derivatives of R for edge detection is proposed. Using only the first derivative we need the appropriate thresholding strategy to detect jumps in function R, however, applying the second derivative and finding its zero values lets us to determine edges directly.

Next we present simulation results for one-dimensional function. The function chosen for testing has five discontinuities (similar to this proposed by Romani et al. in [46] and not detailed here).

Figure 1 presents the simulation results for noised inputs generated. Diagrams show the original function and its 1-st and 2-nd derivative, respectively. The black solid lines - functions and derivatives, their nonparametric estimates - blue points and lines. Red pluses represent the noised measurements. The maxima of the first derivative (marked as red points) assign the points of probable jumps or abrupt changes. In the third row, we have the second derivative. By observing the zeros of this function in relation to the corresponding maxima of the first derivative we may deduce at which points the jumps have occurred.

The smoothing properties of the nonparametric algorithm of the Parzen kernel type depend on the parameter h_n. The choice of its value plays an important role in the interpretation of results. The bigger the h_n the bigger the level of smoothness, but then detection at which point the jump has occurred is more difficult. On the other hand, a too small value of h_n causes higher oscillations of the estimates of the derivatives and consequently, the bigger number of sharp peaks of the first derivative. Optimal choice of smoothing sequence or bandwidth is rather difficult and it is often data dependent, see [1, 11, 61]. Preliminary results on application of Parzen kernels to change detection have been shown in [20].

4　Detection of Edges in Two-Dimensional Patterns

In this section, we propose the multidimensional extension of the nonparametric method of edge detection. The simplicity and ease of application of product kernels make them more preferred in practice than the radial kernel, particularly when differentiation is needed.

We use the product kernel given by:

$$\mathbf{K}\left(\mathbf{x}, \mathbf{u}, h_n\right) = \prod_{p=1}^{d} K\left(\frac{|x_p - u_p|}{h_n}\right) = \mathbf{K}\left(\frac{\|\mathbf{x} - \mathbf{u}\|}{h_n}\right) \tag{6}$$

In the multidimensional case $(d > 1)$ the estimate of partial derivative of order k with respect to the coordinate variable x_j is given by:

$$\hat{R}_{x_j}^{(k)}(\mathbf{x}) = h_n^{-d} \sum_{i=1}^{n} y_i \int_{D_i} \frac{\partial^k}{\partial x_j^k} \mathbf{K}\left(\frac{\|\mathbf{x} - \mathbf{u}\|}{h_n}\right) d\mathbf{u} \tag{7}$$

It is clear that the estimation of particular derivative is obtained by the differentiation of the kernel function depending on the relative coordinate. Let us analyze the two-dimensional case.

The model of the two-dimensional object is now in the form:

$$y_i = R([x_1, x_2]_i) + \varepsilon_i, \, i = 1, ..., n \tag{8}$$

where the $2d$-vector of independent variable: $\mathbf{x}_i = [x_1, x_2]_i$.

The $2d$ Parzen kernel based estimator is defined by:

$$\hat{R}([x_1, x_2]) = h_n^{-2} \sum_{i=1}^{n} y_i \cdot \\ \cdot \int_{D_i} K\left(\frac{x_1 - u_1}{h_n}\right) \cdot K\left(\frac{x_2 - u_2}{h_n}\right) du_1 du_2 \tag{9}$$

By using the cosine kernel defined in unidimensional case by (4) we obtain the estimator based on product kernel in the form:

$$\hat{R}([x_1, x_2]) = \frac{\pi^2}{16} \cdot h_n^{-2} \sum_{i=1}^{n} y_i \cdot \\ \cdot \int_{D_i} \cos\left(\frac{\pi(x_1 - u_1)}{2h_n}\right) \cdot \cos\left(\frac{\pi(x_2 - u_2)}{2h_n}\right) du_1 du_2 \tag{10}$$

We can derive the estimators of the partial derivatives on coordinates x_1 and x_2, respectively - as follows:

$$\frac{\partial}{\partial x_1} \hat{R}([x_1, x_2]) = \frac{\pi^3}{32} \cdot h_n^{-3} \sum_{i=1}^{n} y_i \int_{D_i} \sin\left(\frac{\pi(u_1 - x_1)}{2h_n}\right) \cdot \\ \cdot \cos\left(\frac{\pi(x_2 - u_2)}{2h_n}\right) du_1 du_2 \tag{11}$$

$$\frac{\partial}{\partial x_2} \hat{R}([x_1, x_2]) = \frac{\pi^3}{32} \cdot h_n^{-3} \sum_{i=1}^{n} y_i \cdot$$
$$\cdot \int_{D_i} cos\left(\frac{\pi(x_1 - u_1)}{2h_n}\right) \cdot sin\left(\frac{\pi(u_2 - x_2)}{2h_n}\right) du_1 du_2 \quad (12)$$

The integrals in (11) and (12) are easy to calculate analytically, so we omitted this. The last requirement is to prepare the subsets D_i keeping in mind that the points x_i should be chosen from D_i, i.e.: $x_i \in D_i$. The natural solution is an equally spaced grid easy to construct but it is not detailed here.

5 Testing of the Algorithm Using Black-and-White Images

A series of simulation tests were carried out to assess the effectiveness of the proposed algorithms. We did it using five chosen pictures found in the internet. The original pictures were black-and-white grey scale JPG compressed images. The simulations were performed with application of the *python* programming language. Our nonparametric algorithm was preceded by increasing the contrast procedure (*python*, Pillow library, *ImageEnhance.Contrast()* procedure), and transformation to exclusively black and white pixels (*python*, *imgage.point()* procedure).

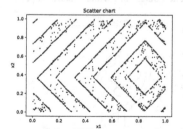

Black-and-white picture No. 1.

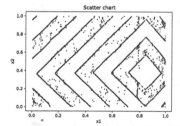

Sharpened black-and-white picture No. 1.

Edges detected by differentiation with respect to x1-coordinate

Edges detected by differentiation with respect to x2-coordinate

Fig. 2. Simulation - Sample 1: black-and-white picture edge detection

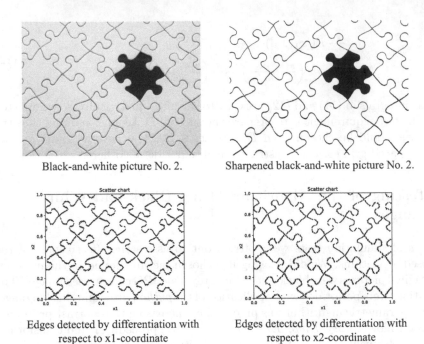

Black-and-white picture No. 2.   Sharpened black-and-white picture No. 2.

Edges detected by differentiation with   Edges detected by differentiation with
respect to x1-coordinate   respect to x2-coordinate

Fig. 3. Simulation - Sample 2: black-and-white picture edge detection

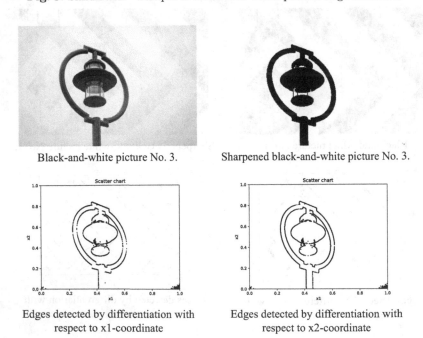

Black-and-white picture No. 3.   Sharpened black-and-white picture No. 3.

Edges detected by differentiation with   Edges detected by differentiation with
respect to x1-coordinate   respect to x2-coordinate

Fig. 4. Simulation - Sample 3: black-and-white picture edge detection

Black-and-white picture No. 4.   Sharpened black-and-white picture No. 4.

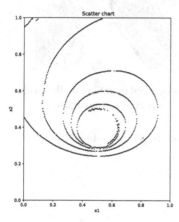
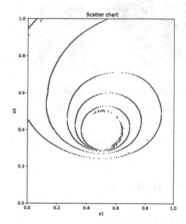

Edges detected by differentiation with   Edges detected by differentiation with
respect to x1-coordinate   respect to x2-coordinate

Fig. 5. Simulation - Sample 4: black-and-white picture edge detection

Resulting pictures are shown in the Figs. 2, 3, 4, 5 and 6 in the upper row, respectively: original and picture after transformation. The *scipy.signal.find_peaks* procedure was used to detect the local maxima of derivatives corresponding to jumps. In the lower row are presented results of detection of abrupt changes using our algorithm. The left picture in each Figure shows the scatter chart obtained when the derivative estimates, respective to coordinate x_1, were calculated; in the right side we see the scatter chart obtained using the derivative estimates respective to coordinate x_2.

Black-and-white picture No. 5.   Sharpened black-and-white picture No. 5.

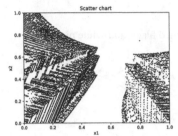 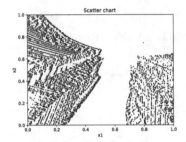

Edges detected by differentiation with   Edges detected by differentiation with
respect to x1-coordinate   respect to x2-coordinate

Fig. 6. Simulation - Sample 5: black-and-white picture edge detection

6   Conclusions

7   Conclusions

This paper considered the important problem of detection the abrupt or sudden change occurred in the data and where or when it happened - in application to black-and-white picture analysis. The proposed algorithm is derived from the nonparametric kernel regression estimation techniques with fixed-design of unknown functions and their partial derivatives in multidimensional space. The proposed two-dimensional algorithm is presented in detail. The algorithm is tested case of jump detections in black-and-white pictures. Simulation results showed in the series of diagrams confirmed utility of the proposed approach in practical cases. From the presented Figs. 1, 2, 3, 4, 5 and 6 one may conclude that the effectiveness of the method improves when the magnitude of the jump is higher. The extension of the edge detection algorithm to multivariate ($d > 2$) case is described and it directly follows from the presented methodology using the product-type of multidimensional kernel.

References

1. Berlinet, A., Biau, G., Rouviere, L.: Optimal L1 bandwidth selection for variable Kernel density estimates. Stat. Probab. Lett. **74**(2), 116–128 (2005). Elsevier
2. Bhardwaj, S., Mittal, A.: A survey on various edge detector techniques. Proc. Technol. **4**, 220–226 (2012). Elseiver, SciVerse ScienceDirect. 2nd International Conference on Computer, Communication, Control and Information Technology
3. Bustamam, A., Sarwinda, D., Ardenaswari, G.: Texture and gene expression analysis of the MRI brain in detection of Alzheimer's disease. J. Artif. Intell. Soft Comput. Res. **8**(2), 111–0120 (2018)
4. Canny, J.F.: A computational approach to edge detection. IEEE Trans. Pattern Anal. Mach. Intell. **8**(6), 679–698 (1986)
5. Cao, Y., Samidurai, R., Sriraman, R.: Stability and dissipativity analysis for neutral type stochastic markovian jump static neural networks with time delays. J. Artif. Intell. Soft Comput. Res. **9**(3), 189–204 (2019)
6. Corder, G.W., Foreman, D.I.: Nonparametric Statistics: A Step-by-Step Approach. Wiley, New York (2014)
7. Cpałka, K., Rutkowski, L.: Evolutionary learning of flexible neuro-fuzzy systems. In: Proceedings of the 2008 IEEE International Conference on Fuzzy Systems (IEEE World Congress on Computational Intelligence, WCCI 2008), Hong Kong, 1–6 June CD, pp. 969–975 (2008)
8. Dasu, T., Krishnan, S., Venkatasubramanian, S., Yi, K.: An information-theoretic approach to detecting changes in multi-dimensional data streams. In: Proceedings Symposium on the Interface of Statistics, Computing Science, and Applications (2006)
9. Davis, J.J., Lin, C.-T., Gillett, G., Kozma, R.: An integrative approach to analyze EEG signals and human brain dynamics in different cognitive states. J. Artif. Intell. Soft Comput. Res. **7**(4), 287–299 (2017)
10. Devi, V.S., Meena, L.: Parallel MCNN (PMCNN) with application to prototype selection on large and streaming data. J. Artif. Intell. Soft Comput. Res. **7**(3), 155–169 (2017)
11. Devroye, L., Lugosi, G.: Combinatorial Methods in Density Estimation. Springer, New York (2001). https://doi.org/10.1007/978-1-4613-0125-7
12. Duda, P., Jaworski, M., Rutkowski, L.: Convergent time-varying regression models for data streams: tracking concept drift by the recursive Parzen-based generalized regression neural networks. Int. J. Neural Syst. **28**(2), 1750048 (2018)
13. Duda, P., Jaworski, M., Rutkowski, L.: Knowledge discovery in data streams with the orthogonal series-based generalized regression neural networks. Inf. Sci. **460–461**, 497–518 (2018)
14. Duda, P., Rutkowski, L., Jaworski, M., Rutkowska, D.: On the Parzen kernel-based probability density function learning procedures over time-varying streaming data with applications to pattern classification. IEEE Trans. Cybern. **50**, 1–14 (2018)
15. Eubank, R.L.: Nonparametric Regression and Spline Smoothing, 2nd edn. Marcel Dekker, New York (1999)
16. Faithfull, W.J., Rodriguez, J.J., Kuncheva, L.I.: Combining univariate approaches for ensemble change detection in multivariate data. Inf. Fusion **45**, 202–214 (2019). Elseiver
17. Gałkowski, T., Rutkowski, L.: Nonparametric recovery of multivariate functions with applications to system identification. Proc. IEEE **73**, 942–943 (1985)

18. Gałkowski, T., Rutkowski, L.: Nonparametric fitting of multivariable functions. IEEE Trans. Autom. Control **AC–31**, 785–787 (1986)

19. Gałkowski, T.: On nonparametric fitting of higher order functions derivatives by the kernel method - a simulation study. In: Proceedings of the 5th International Symposium on Applied Stochastic Models and data Analysis, Granada, Spain, pp. 230–242 (1991)

20. Gałkowski, T., Krzyżak, A., Filutowicz, Z.: A new approach to detection of changes in multidimensional patterns. J. Artif. Intell. Soft Comput. Res. **10**(2), 125–136 (2020)

21. Gasser, T., Müller, H.-G.: Kernel estimation of regression functions. In: Gasser, T., Rosenblatt, M. (eds.) Smoothing Techniques for Curve Estimation. LNM, vol. 757, pp. 23–68. Springer, Heidelberg (1979). https://doi.org/10.1007/BFb0098489

22. Gasser, T., Müller, H.-G.: Estimating regression functions and their derivatives by the Kernel method. Scand. J. Stat. **11**(3), 171–185 (1984)

23. Grycuk, R., Scherer, R., Gabryel, M.: New image descriptor from edge detector and blob extractor. J. Appl. Math. Comput. Mech. **14**(4), 31–39 (2015)

24. Grycuk, R., Knop, M., Mandal, S.: Video key frame detection based on SURF algorithm. In: Rutkowski, L., Korytkowski, M., Scherer, R., Tadeusiewicz, R., Zadeh, L.A., Zurada, J.M. (eds.) ICAISC 2015. LNCS (LNAI), vol. 9119, pp. 566–576. Springer, Cham (2015). https://doi.org/10.1007/978-3-319-19324-3_50

25. Grycuk, R., Gabryel, M., Scherer, M., Voloshynovskiy, S.: Image descriptor based on edge detection and Crawler algorithm. In: Rutkowski, L., Korytkowski, M., Scherer, R., Tadeusiewicz, R., Zadeh, L.A., Zurada, J.M. (eds.) ICAISC 2016. LNCS (LNAI), vol. 9693, pp. 647–659. Springer, Cham (2016). https://doi.org/10.1007/978-3-319-39384-1_57

26. Györfi, L., Kohler, M., Krzyzak, A., Walk, H.: A Distribution-Free Theory of Nonparametric Regression. Springer, New York (2002). https://doi.org/10.1007/b97848

27. Jaworski, M., Duda, P., Rutkowski, L.: New splitting criteria for decision trees in stationary data streams. IEEE Trans. Neural Netw. Learn. Syst. **29**(6), 2516–2529 (2018)

28. Krell, E., Sheta, A., Balasubramanian, A.P.R., King, S.A.: Collision-free autonomous robot navigation in unknown environments Utilizing PSO for path planning. J. Artif. Intell. Soft Comput. Res. **9**(4), 267–282 (2019)

29. Korytkowski, M., Senkerik, R., Scherer, M.M., Angryk, R.A., Kordos, M., Siwocha, A.: Efficient image retrieval by fuzzy rules from boosting and metaheuristic. J. Artif. Intell. Soft Comput. Res. **10**(1), 57–69 (2020)

30. Kullback, S., Leibler, R.A.: On information and sufficiency. Ann. Math. Stat. **22**(1), 79–86 (1951)

31. Lam, M.W.Y.: One-match-ahead forecasting in two-team sports with stacked Bayesian regressions. J. Artif. Intell. Soft Comput. Res. **8**(3), 159–171 (2018)

32. Łapa, K., Cpałka, K., Przybył, A., Grzanek, K.: Negative space-based population initialization algorithm (NSPIA). In: Rutkowski, L., Scherer, R., Korytkowski, M., Pedrycz, W., Tadeusiewicz, R., Zurada, J.M. (eds.) ICAISC 2018. LNCS (LNAI), vol. 10841, pp. 449–461. Springer, Cham (2018). https://doi.org/10.1007/978-3-319-91253-0_42

33. Łapa, K., Cpałka, K., Przybył, A.: Genetic programming algorithm for designing of control systems. Inf. Technol. Control **47**(5), 668–683 (2018)

34. Marr, D., Hildreth, E.: Theory of edge detection. Proc. R. Soc. Lond. B Biol. Sci. **B–207**, 187–217 (1980)

35. Oded, K., Hallin, C.A., Perel, N., Bendet, D.: Decision-making enhancement in a big data environment: application of the K-means algorithm to mixed data. J. Artif. Intell. Soft Comput. Res. **9**(4), 293–302 (2019)
36. Pietruczuk, L., Rutkowski, L., Jaworski, M., Duda, P.: How to adjust an ensemble size in stream data mining? Inf. Sci. **381**(C), 46–54 (2017). Elsevier Science Inc.
37. Pratt, W.K.: Digital Image Processing, 4th edn. John Wiley Inc., New York (2007)
38. Qiu, P.: Nonparametric estimation of jump surface. Indian J. Stat. Ser. A **59**(2), 268–294 (1997)
39. Qiu, P.: Jump surface estimation, edge detection, and image restoration. J. Am. Stati. Assoc. **102**, 745–756 (2007)
40. Rahman, M.W., Zohra, F.T., Gavrilova, M.L.: Score level and rank level fusion for Kinect-based multi-modal biometric system. J. Artif. Intell. Soft Comput. Res. **9**(3), 167–176 (2019)
41. Rafajłowicz, E., Schwabe, R.: Halton and Hammersley sequences in multivariate nonparametric regression. Stat. Probab. Lett. **76**(8), 803–812 (2006)
42. Rafajłowicz, E., Wnuk, M., Rafajłowicz, W.: Local detection of defects from image sequences. Int. J. Appl. Math. Comput. Sci. **18**(4), 581–592 (2008)
43. Rafajłowicz, E., Rafajłowicz, W.: Testing (non-)linearity of distributed-parameter systems from a video sequence. Asian J. Control **12**(2), 146–158 (2010)
44. Rafajłowicz, W.: Nonparametric estimation of continuously parametrized families of probability density functions - Computational aspects. Wrocław University of Science and Technology, Wrocław, Preprint of the Department of Engineering Informatics (2020)
45. Rivero, C.R., Pucheta, J., Laboret, S., Sauchelli, V., Patino, D.: Energy associated tuning method for short-term series forecasting by complete and incomplete datasets. J. Artif. Intell. Soft Comput. Res. **7**(1), 5–16 (2017)
46. Romani, L., Rossini, M., Schenone, D.: Edge detection methods based on RBF interpolation. J. Comput. Appl. Math. **349**, 532–547 (2019)
47. Rutkowski, L.: Application of multiple Fourier-series to identification of multivariable non-stationary systems. Int. J. Syst. Sci. **20**(10), 1993–2002 (1989)
48. Rutkowski, L., Rafajłowicz, E.: On optimal global rate of convergence of some nonparametric identification procedures. IEEE Trans. Autom. Control **34**(10), 1089–1091 (1989)
49. Rutkowski, L.: Identification of MISO nonlinear regressions in the presence of a wide class of disturbances. IEEE Trans. Inf. Theory **37**(1), 214–216 (1991)
50. Rutkowski, L., Pietruczuk, L., Duda, P., Jaworski, M.: Decision trees for mining data streams based on the McDiarmid's bound. IEEE Trans. Knowl. Data Eng. **25**(6), 1272–1279 (2013)
51. Rutkowski, L., Jaworski, M., Pietruczuk, L., Duda, P.: Decision trees for mining data streams based on the Gaussian approximation. IEEE Trans. Knowl. Data Eng. **26**(1), 108–119 (2014)
52. Rutkowski, L., Jaworski, M., Pietruczuk, L., Duda, P.: The CART decision tree for mining data streams. Inf. Sci. **266**, 1–15 (2014)
53. Rutkowski, L., Jaworski, M., Pietruczuk, L., Duda, P.: A new method for data stream mining based on the misclassification error. IEEE Trans. Neural Netw. Learn. Syst. **26**(5), 1048–1059 (2015)
54. Rutkowski, T., Romanowski, J., Woldan, P., Staszewski, P., Nielek, R., Rutkowski, L.: A content-based recommendation system using neuro-fuzzy approach. In: International Conference on Fuzzy Systems: FUZZ-IEEE, pp. 1–8 (2018)

55. Rutkowski, T., Romanowski, J., Woldan, P., Staszewski, P., Nielek, R.: Towards interpretability of the movie recommender based on a neuro-fuzzy approach. In: Rutkowski, L., Scherer, R., Korytkowski, M., Pedrycz, W., Tadeusiewicz, R., Zurada, J.M. (eds.) ICAISC 2018. LNCS (LNAI), vol. 10842, pp. 752–762. Springer, Cham (2018). https://doi.org/10.1007/978-3-319-91262-2_66

56. Rutkowski, L., Jaworski, M., Duda, P.: Stream Data Mining: Algorithms and Their Probabilistic Properties. SBD, vol. 56. Springer, Cham (2020). https://doi.org/10.1007/978-3-030-13962-9

57. Rutkowski, T., Łapa, K., Nielek, R.: On explainable fuzzy recommenders and their performance evaluation. Int. J. Appl. Math. Comput. Sci. 29(3), 595–610 (2019)

58. Rutkowski, T., Łapa, K., Jaworski, M., Nielek, R., Rutkowska, D.: On explainable flexible fuzzy recommender and its performance evaluation using the akaike information criterion. In: Gedeon, T., Wong, K.W., Lee, M. (eds.) ICONIP 2019. CCIS, vol. 1142, pp. 717–724. Springer, Cham (2019). https://doi.org/10.1007/978-3-030-36808-1_78

59. Singh, S., Singh, R.: Comparison of various edge detection techniques. In: 2nd International Conference on Computing for Sustainable Global Development, pp. 393–396 (2015)

60. Tezuka, T., Claramunt, Ch.: Kernel analysis for estimating the connectivity of a network with event sequences. J. Artif. Intell. Soft Comput. Res. 7(1), 17–31 (2017)

61. Yatracos, Y.G.: Rates of convergence of minimum distance estimators and Kolmogorov's entropy. Ann. Stat. 13, 768–774 (1985)

Active Region-Based Full-Disc Solar Image Hashing

Rafał Grycuk[1] ⓘ, Kelton Costa[2] ⓘ, and Rafał Scherer[1(✉)] ⓘ

[1] Department of Intelligent Computer Systems, Częstochowa University
of Technology, Al. Armii Krajowej 36, 42-200 Częstochowa, Poland
{rafal.grycuk,rafal.scherer}@pcz.pl
[2] Department of Computing, São Paulo State University, Bauru, Brazil
kelton.costa@unesp.br
http://kisi.pcz.pl

Keywords: Solar activity analysis · Solar image description · CBIR ·
Solar hash

1 Introduction

The main components of the Solar activity are solar flares, coronal mass ejections, high-speed solar wind, and solar energetic particles. Solar flares impact the Earth when they occur on the side facing our planet. Coronal holes close to the solar equator cause winds impacting the Earth. Intense Sun activity can cause a geomagnetic storm which can disrupt technological infrastructure on the Earth. Therefore, it is crucial to gain knowledge and means to predict such phenomena. The Solar Dynamics Observatory (SDO, Fig. 1) is a 3-axis stabilized spacecraft with three main sensory instruments: Atmospheric Imaging Assembly (AIA), EUV Variability Experiment (EVE) and Helioseismic and Magnetic Imager (HMI). It provides massive data to research the connected Sun-Earth system and the impact of the Sun on living on the Earth. AIA provides continuous full-disk observations of the solar chromosphere and corona in seven extreme ultraviolet (EUV) channels with the 12-second cadence of high-resolution 4096 × 4096 pixel images. It is impossible to search and annotate manually such a waste collection of images. Moreover, this type of images is very repetitive and monotonous for humans, making the process even more troublesome. The AIA-produced, high resolution images are very similar to each other what causes problems with their retrieval [1].

To find similar images we have to compare them. Direct image content comparing is impractical in large databases. Therefore, we have to use more compact image representation allowing effectively retrieve and classify images. One of the possible solutions is hashing, i.e. creating low-dimensional, compact codes. Hashes can be created by a data-independent family of methods existing under umbrella of locality sensitive hashing (LSH) [3,5,6] or trained from data. In the paper, we use the second approach, that is we train hash function from domain-specific data. The idea is to use similarity in the original object space to compute relevant vectors in the hash coding space. A seminal work coined

L. Rutkowski et al. (Eds.): ICAISC 2020, LNAI 12416, pp. 19–30, 2020.
https://doi.org/10.1007/978-3-030-61534-5_2

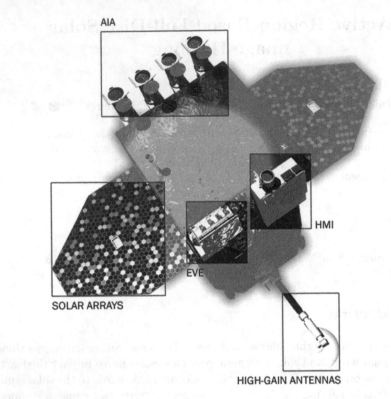

Fig. 1. The Solar Dynamics Observatory spacecraft with the main instruments (https://sdo.gsfc.nasa.gov/).

the term semantic hashing [10]. Another seminal technique was spectral hashing [13]. Image retrieval relies usually on finding objects or their features similar to the query image. As the hashes are much smaller, they accelerate the hash table lookup in nearest neighbour search. In [14] a hash is generated by a convolutional neural network where fully connected layers generate hashing vector. Desired hash is computed from a decomposed image similarity matrix. The matrix is decomposed approximately by a scalable coordinate descent algorithm. Later, most hashing approaches used convolutional autoencoders. Thus, motivated by the previous works on image hashing and by the enormousness of the SDO solar image collection, we propose deep learning solar image hashing, described in Sect. 2.

2   AR-Based Full-Disc Solar Hash

This section of the paper describes a new method for the solar image description. The proposed method can be used for image retrieval of solar images in large data sets. The images which we used for training and retrieving are taken from the SDO AIA module. They were extracted from SDO and later published in the form of Web API by the authors of [8]. We decided to use 2048×2048-pixel images. The presented method can be divided into three main steps: detecting active regions, learning and hash generation, and retrieval. In the first step of our method, we use filters, morphological operations and thresholding for detecting active regions (AR) in the solar images. In the next step, we use a convolutional autoencoder for learning compact hashes from the solar images. In the second step, we use only the encoding part of the autoencoder for the hash generation purposes. The last stage allows retrieving similar images to a given query image. The task is not trivial because we do not have any labels or any validation data; thus, we also propose a method for defining the similarity of the unlabeled solar images. Based on that, we can evaluate the accuracy of the proposed method.

2.1   Active Region Detection

Active Regions (AR, see Fig. 2) are places connected with solar activity. These regions can take various shapes, and due to Earth's rotation, their position on the consecutive images is shifted. This stage of the presented method determines active region positions and shapes. Active region detection process consists of several steps. At first, we convert the input image (obtained from SDO) to the 8-bit grayscale. Afterwards, the 11×11 Gaussian blur filter is applied in order to remove insignificant, small regions of the image; thus, in the next step, we can analyze only essential objects. The performed preprocessing allows us to move to the thresholding stage. In this step, we compare every pixel intensity with the provided threshold th value. If the value is greater or equal, we assume that the pixel is a part of the active region area. Every pixel above this value is treated as an active region. The value of th parameter was obtained empirically, and it was adjusted for the given type of solar images. The last two steps are applied to the thresholded image they are morphological operations, namely erosion and dilation [4,11]. The morphological erosion removes small objects so that only substantive objects remain. The dilation, on the other hand, makes objects more visible, fills in small holes in objects, thus, emphasize the only the important areas of the active regions. The process of active region detection is presented in the form of pseudo-code as Alg. 1. An example output image of the active region detection is presented in Fig. 3. The applied operations on the input DSO image allow detecting active regions. The location and shape of these regions are crucial to detecting the Coronal Mass Ejections (CME) and thus, to the solar flare prediction. In our experiments, we retrieve similar images.

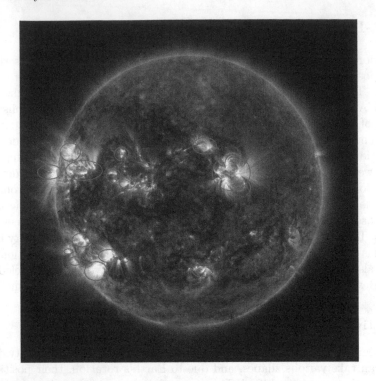

Fig. 2. Manually annotated solar active regions.

INPUT: *SolarImage*
OUTPUT: *ActiveRegionDetectedImg*
GrayScaleImg := *ConvertToGrayScale(SolarImage)*
BlurredImg := *Blur(GrayScaleImg)*
ThreshImg := *Threshold(BlurredImg)*
ErodedImg := *Erode(ThreshImg)*
ActiveRegionDetectedImg = *Dilate(ErodedImg)*
        Algorithm 1: Active region detection steps.

2.2   Learning and Hash Generation

The presented section describes the learning process, along with encoding. We used a convolutional autoencoder for learning active region images; afterwards, we use only encoding layers for the encoding process. The rationale behind the autoencoder is that it is an unsupervised convolutional neural network and does not require labelled data for training. The architecture of the autoencoder (network model) is presented in Table 1. We used an autoencoder with two convolutional layers with max-pooling, where *kernel_size* parameter is equal 2. *Kernel_size* parameter for convolutional layers is set to 3. After two convolutional layers with pooling, we have the latent space (a bottleneck layer), which output is the hash. In this way we reduce data volume from $1 \times 2048 \times 2048$ to

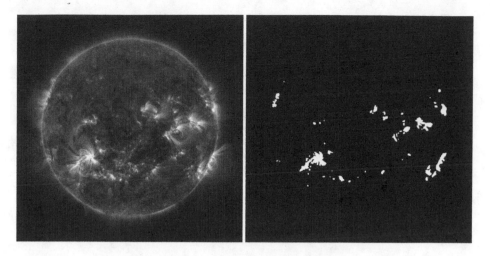

Fig. 3. Active region detection, left image is the input, right image is the output.

$8 \times 170 \times 170$. After encoding layers, we have convolutional decoding layers. The decoding layers are used only for training. For the hash generation, we only use the encoding layers. During the experiments, we used Python along with Pytorch tensor library. We split the SDO dataset into 90% learning and 10% testing. We applied the binary cross-entropy loss function. We empirically proved that 40 epochs are sufficient to obtain the required level of generalization and not cause the network over-fitting. After the learning process, every active region image is fed to the encoded layers of the autoencoder. As a result, the encoded solar image hash is obtained. The hash length is $231, 200$. Such hash can be used for content-based solar image retrieval applications (see Sect. 2.3).

2.3 Retrieval

In the last step of the presented method, we perform the image retrieval process. We assumed that every solar image has a hash assigned in our image database. The input in the image retrieval step is a query image; it is an image to which we will compare images stored in the database. In most cases the comparison will be performed by some distance measure. In the first step of this process, we need to create the same type of hash that we created for all images in the database. The image retrieval scheme is presented in Fig. 4. The generated hash for the query image is used for calculating the distance between an image in the database and the query image hash. The retrieval step requires to have a solar image database with a hash generated for every image. The next step allows us to calculate the distance between the query image hash and every hash in the database. The distance d is calculated by the cosine distance measure [7]

$$\cos(Q_j, I_j) = \sum_{j=0}^{n} \frac{(Q_j \bullet I_j)}{\|Q_j\| \, \|I_j\|}, \qquad (1)$$

Table 1. Tabular representation of the convolutional autoencoder model.

Layer (type)	Output Shape	Filters (in, out)	Kernel size	Params no.
$Input2d(InputLayer)$	[1, 2048, 2048]			
$Conv2d\_1(Conv2D)$	[16, 683, 683]	1,16	3	160
$ReLU\_1$	[16, 683, 683]			
$Max\_pooling2d\_1(MaxPool2D)$	[16, 341, 341]		2	
$Conv2d\_2(Conv2D)$	[8, 171, 171]	16,8	3	1160
$ReLU\_2$	[8, 171, 171]			
$Encoded(MaxPool2D)$	[8, 170, 170]		2	
$ConvTranspose2d\_1(ConvTranspose2D)$	[16,341,341]	8,16	3	1168
$ReLU\_4$	[16,341,341]			
$ConvTranspose2d\_2(ConvTranspose2D)$	[8, 1025, 1025]	8, 1	2	3208
$ReLU\_5$	[8, 1025, 1025]			
$ConvTranspose2d\_3(ConvTranspose2D)$	[1, 2048, 2048]	61, 1	2	33
$Decoded(Tanh)$	[1, 2048, 2048]			

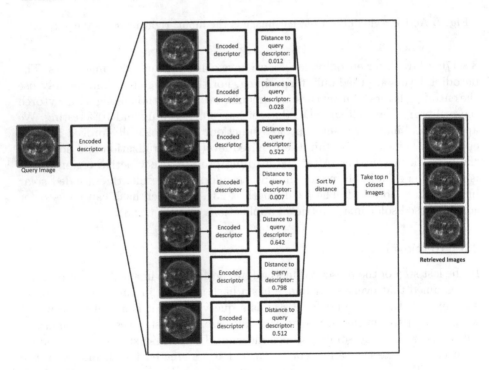

Fig. 4. The retrieval process scheme.

where • is dot product. The performed experiments proved that chosen distance measure is the most suitable for the proposed hash. We also supported our decision by analyzing similar methods [7]. After calculating the distances between all images and a query image, they are sorted in the ascending order by the distance d to the query. The last step allows us to take n images closest to the query. Those images are returned to the user as the retrieved images. Parameter n is provided during query execution along with the query image. The entire retrieval process is described by Algorithm 2.

INPUT: $Hashes, QueryImage, n$
OUTPUT: $RetrievedImages$
foreach $hash \in Hashes$ **do**
    $QueryImageHash = CalculateHash(QueryImage)$
    $D[i] = Cos(QueryImageHash, hash)$
end
$SortedDistances = SortAscending(D)$
$RetrievedHashes = TakeFirst(n)$
$RetrievedImages = GetCorrespondingImages(RetrievedHashes)$
Algorithm 2: Image retrieval steps.

3 Experimental Results

This section describes experimental results along with our approach to method evaluation of unlabelled images. The unlabelled data allowed to train the autoencoder, but there were no possibility to evaluate the retrieval accuracy by the proposed method. Therefore, we used Earth's rotation motion to determine the similarity of the images. The consecutive images within a small time window have similar active regions; thus, we can treat them as similar. These images should be slightly shifted relative to the previous image. We define the next and previous images by using their creation date by SDO. The provided API allows fetching solar images with a 6-minute window (cadence); therefore, we can assume the similarity of consecutive images. The only condition is adjusting the time window. During performed experiments, it was determined that a 48-hour window allows determining the similarity of the images. This process is presented in Table 2. Based on that, we performed a series of simulations in order to determine similar images (SI). Every experiment is composed of the following steps:

1. Execute image query and obtain the retrieved images.
2. For every retrieved image compare its timestamp with the query image timestamp.
3. If the timestamp is the 48-hour window, the image is similar to the query.

Obtaining the similar images (SI) and (NSI) allows us to define performance measures *precision* and *recall* [2,12]. They are defined using the following sets:

Table 2. Example series of solar images explaining image similarity.

Timestamp	SI (similar image)/NSI (not similar image)
2012-02-13, 23:54:00	NSI
2012-02-14, 00:00:00	SI
2012-02-14, 00:06:00	SI
2012-02-14, 00:12:00	SI
2012-02-14, 00:18:00	SI
2012-02-14, 00:24:00	SI
2012-02-14, 00:30:00	SI
....	SI
2012-02-15, 00:00:00	QI (query image)
....	SI
2012-02-15, 23:24:00	SI
2012-02-15, 23:30:00	SI
2012-02-15, 23:36:00	SI
2012-02-15, 23:42:00	SI
2012-02-15, 23:48:00	SI
2012-02-15, 23:54:00	SI
2012-02-16, 00:00:00	NSI

SI - set of similar images; RI - set of retrieved images for query; $PRI(TP)$ - set of positive retrieved images (true positive); $FPRI(FP)$ - false positive retrieved images (false positive); $PNRI(FN)$ - positive not retrieved images; $FNRI(TN)$ - false not retrieved images (TN). We use standard definitions of precision and recall to evaluate the method

$$precision = \frac{|PRI|}{|PRI + FPRI|}, \tag{2}$$

$$recall = \frac{|PRI|}{|PRI + PNRI|}. \tag{3}$$

The results on example periods presented in Tables 3 and 4 show that our method obtains a high value of the *precision* measure. Most of the images close to the query are correctly retrieved. The farther from the query, the more positive not retrieved images (PNRI) are retrieved. This is caused by the Earth's rotation motion and thus missing active regions. The significant active regions might change its position in the 48-hour window and because of that, significantly change the hash. Therefore, the distance to the query will be increased. Such a case was observed during the experiments. We can determine that lower values of *Recall* measure is caused by this phenomena. The presented simulation environment was created in Python using PyTorch [9]. The learning time took 12 h for 83,819 images. The hash creation process took 2 h. The average retrieval time is 800 ms.

Table 3. Experiment results of the proposed algorithm performed on a sample period of AIA images obtained from [8]. Due to lack of space, we present only a part of all queries.

Timestamp	RI	SI	PRI(TP)	FPRI(FP)	PNRI(FN)	Prec.	Recall
2017-01-01 00:00:00	216	241	169	47	72	0.78	0.70
2017-01-04 14:00:00	335	481	322	13	159	0.96	0.67
2017-01-11 07:00:00	351	481	321	30	160	0.91	0.67
2017-01-14 21:00:00	340	481	301	39	180	0.89	0.63
2017-01-17 07:00:00	358	481	326	32	155	0.91	0.68
2017-01-21 23:00:00	338	481	310	28	171	0.92	0.64
2017-01-25 15:00:00	337	481	327	10	154	0.97	0.68
2017-01-28 06:06:00	356	481	315	41	166	0.88	0.65
2017-02-04 18:06:00	369	481	324	45	157	0.88	0.67
2017-02-09 05:06:00	368	481	334	34	147	0.91	0.69
2017-02-13 01:06:00	349	481	342	7	139	0.98	0.71
2017-02-17 06:12:00	329	481	306	23	175	0.93	0.64
2017-02-22 08:18:00	319	481	295	24	186	0.92	0.61
2017-02-27 17:18:00	364	481	322	42	159	0.88	0.67
2017-03-07 04:18:00	356	481	325	31	156	0.91	0.68
2017-03-15 22:24:00	313	481	301	12	180	0.96	0.63
2017-03-18 19:24:00	367	481	321	46	160	0.87	0.67
2017-03-27 04:30:00	365	481	333	32	148	0.91	0.69
2017-04-01 06:36:00	362	481	331	31	150	0.91	0.69
2017-04-06 02:36:00	377	481	333	44	148	0.88	0.69
2017-04-11 15:36:00	349	481	316	33	165	0.91	0.66
2017-04-16 23:42:00	340	481	308	32	173	0.91	0.64
2017-04-18 09:42:00	334	481	320	14	161	0.96	0.67
2017-04-20 23:42:00	359	481	330	29	151	0.92	0.69
2017-04-23 10:42:00	340	481	305	35	176	0.90	0.63
2017-04-26 08:42:00	382	481	336	46	145	0.88	0.70
2017-05-02 18:48:00	358	481	316	42	165	0.88	0.66
2017-05-06 17:48:00	366	481	320	46	161	0.87	0.67
2017-05-13 23:48:00	357	481	321	36	160	0.90	0.67
2017-05-20 03:48:00	309	481	285	24	196	0.92	0.59
2017-05-25 15:54:00	366	481	321	45	160	0.88	0.67
2017-05-31 18:00:00	385	481	334	51	147	0.87	0.69
2017-06-06 21:06:00	327	481	305	22	176	0.93	0.63
2017-06-08 03:06:00	323	481	300	23	181	0.93	0.62
2017-06-10 22:12:00	381	481	340	41	141	0.89	0.71
2017-06-16 10:12:00	351	481	325	26	156	0.93	0.68
2017-06-21 11:18:00	349	481	318	31	163	0.91	0.66
2017-06-24 20:18:00	336	481	316	20	165	0.94	0.66
2017-06-29 22:18:00	343	481	331	12	150	0.97	0.69
2017-07-01 05:24:00	359	481	315	44	166	0.88	0.65
2017-07-05 01:30:00	351	481	325	26	156	0.93	0.68
2017-07-10 19:36:00	351	481	329	22	152	0.94	0.68
2017-07-13 08:42:00	346	481	319	27	162	0.92	0.66
2017-07-17 19:48:00	338	481	313	25	168	0.93	0.65
2017-07-21 05:54:00	362	481	311	51	170	0.86	0.65

Table 4. Experiment results of the proposed algorithm performed on a sample period of AIA images obtained from [8]. Due to lack of space, we present only a part of all queries.

Timestamp	RI	SI	PRI(TP)	FPRI(FP)	PNRI(FN)	Prec.	Recall
2015-01-01 00:00:00	219	241	170	49	71	0.78	0.71
2015-01-04 22:00:00	358	481	309	49	172	0.86	0.64
2015-01-08 11:06:00	377	481	330	47	151	0.88	0.69
2015-01-12 07:06:00	356	481	308	48	173	0.87	0.64
2015-01-18 05:06:00	366	481	319	47	162	0.87	0.66
2015-01-24 17:12:00	342	481	309	33	172	0.90	0.64
2015-01-27 20:18:00	343	481	327	16	154	0.95	0.68
2015-01-29 03:18:00	379	481	333	46	148	0.88	0.69
2015-02-03 03:18:00	371	481	325	46	156	0.88	0.68
2015-02-05 12:24:00	320	481	313	7	168	0.98	0.65
2015-02-12 07:24:00	346	481	326	20	155	0.94	0.68
2015-02-17 14:30:00	355	481	319	36	162	0.90	0.66
2015-02-23 22:30:00	350	481	329	21	152	0.94	0.68
2015-02-27 02:36:00	350	481	315	35	166	0.90	0.65
2015-03-02 18:42:00	348	481	319	29	162	0.92	0.66
2015-03-11 00:42:00	369	481	331	38	150	0.90	0.69
2015-03-13 19:42:00	364	481	312	52	169	0.86	0.65
2015-03-20 22:48:00	379	481	328	51	153	0.87	0.68
2015-03-28 09:48:00	349	481	329	20	152	0.94	0.68
2015-03-31 18:48:00	351	481	320	31	161	0.91	0.67
2015-04-07 02:48:00	341	481	319	22	162	0.94	0.66
2015-04-13 18:48:00	355	481	320	35	161	0.90	0.67
2015-04-21 06:54:00	371	481	349	22	132	0.94	0.73
2015-04-25 11:00:00	328	481	317	11	164	0.97	0.66
2015-05-02 19:06:00	335	481	317	18	164	0.95	0.66
2015-05-04 21:12:00	340	481	308	32	173	0.91	0.64
2015-05-11 05:12:00	348	481	307	41	174	0.88	0.64
2015-05-13 12:12:00	350	481	312	38	169	0.89	0.65
2015-05-17 10:12:00	340	481	306	34	175	0.90	0.64
2015-05-23 13:18:00	375	481	329	46	152	0.88	0.68
2015-05-26 02:24:00	371	481	343	28	138	0.92	0.71
2015-06-02 03:30:00	373	481	332	41	149	0.89	0.69
2015-06-05 12:30:00	365	481	318	47	163	0.87	0.66
2015-06-07 17:36:00	341	481	324	17	157	0.95	0.67
2015-06-11 01:42:00	371	481	335	36	146	0.90	0.70
2015-06-17 15:42:00	341	481	312	29	169	0.91	0.65
2015-06-22 11:42:00	369	481	327	42	154	0.89	0.68
2015-06-25 04:42:00	358	481	312	46	169	0.87	0.65
2015-06-28 18:42:00	355	481	309	46	172	0.87	0.64
2015-06-30 15:48:00	355	481	325	30	156	0.92	0.68
2015-07-09 14:48:00	329	481	310	19	171	0.94	0.64
2015-07-16 10:54:00	389	481	354	35	127	0.91	0.74
2015-07-17 23:00:00	322	481	313	9	168	0.97	0.65
2015-07-22 11:00:00	351	481	313	38	168	0.89	0.65
2015-07-31 04:06:00	353	481	328	25	153	0.93	0.68

4   Conclusions

We proposed a full-disc solar hash for content-based solar image retrieval. The method uses morphological operations for active regions detection. Afterwards, an unsupervised convolutional autoencoder is used to obtain the solar image hash. This process reduces the hash length more than 18 times compared to the active region image matrix. Reducing the hash length is significant for calculating the distances between hashes. The performed experiments and comparisons (see Tables 3 and 4) proved the efficiency of the proposed approach. The presented method has various potential applications. It can be used for searching and retrieving solar flares, which has crucial importance for many aspects of life on Earth.

References

1. Banda, J.M., Schuh, M.A., Wylie, T., McInerney, P., Angryk, R.A.: When too similar is bad: a practical example of the solar dynamics observatory content-based image-retrieval system. In: Catania, B., et al. (eds.) New Trends in Databases and Information Systems. AISC, vol. 241, pp. 87–95. Springer, Cham (2014). https://doi.org/10.1007/978-3-319-01863-8_10
2. Buckland, M., Gey, F.: The relationship between recall and precision. J. Am. Soc. Inf. Sci. **45**(1), 12 (1994)
3. Charikar, M.S.: Similarity estimation techniques from rounding algorithms. In: Proceedings of the Thiry-Fourth Annual ACM Symposium on Theory of Computing, pp. 380–388 (2002)
4. Dougherty, E.R.: An Introduction to Morphological Image Processing. SPIE, Bellingham (1992)
5. Gabryel, M., Grzanek, K., Hayashi, Y.: Browser fingerprint coding methods increasing the effectiveness of user identification in the web traffic. J. Artif. Intell. Soft Comput. Res. **10**(4), 243–253 (2020)
6. Indyk, P., Motwani, R.: Approximate nearest neighbors: towards removing the curse of dimensionality. In: Proceedings of the Thirtieth Annual ACM Symposium on Theory of Computing, pp. 604–613 (1998)
7. Kavitha, K., Rao, B.T.: Evaluation of distance measures for feature based image registration using alexnet. arXiv preprint arXiv:1907.12921 (2019)
8. Kucuk, A., Banda, J.M., Angryk, R.A.: A large-scale solar dynamics observatory image dataset for computer vision applications. Sci. Data **4**, 170096 (2017)
9. Paszke, A., et al.: Pytorch: an imperative style, high-performance deep learning library. In: Wallach, H., Larochelle, H., Beygelzimer, A., d' Alché-Buc, F., Fox, E., Garnett, R., (eds.) Advances in Neural Information Processing Systems, vol. 32, pp. 8024–8035. Curran Associates, Inc. (2019)
10. Salakhutdinov, R., Hinton, G.: Semantic hashing. Int. J. Approximate Reasoning **50**(7), 969–978 (2009). Special Section on Graphical Models and Information Retrieval
11. Serra, J.: Image Analysis and Mathematical Morphology. Academic Press, Inc., Orlando (1983)
12. Ting, K.M.: Precision and recall. In: Sammut, C., Webb, G.I. (eds.) Encyclopedia of Machine Learning. Springer, Boston (2011). https://doi.org/10.1007/978-0-387-30164-8_652

13. Weiss, Y., Torralba, A., Fergus, R.: Spectral hashing. In: Advances in Neural Information Processing Systems, pp. 1753–1760 (2009)
14. Xia, R., Pan, Y., Lai, H., Liu, C., Yan, S.: Supervised hashing for image retrieval via image representation learning. In: AAAI, vol. 1, p. 2 (2014)

Inferring Colors in Paintings of M.F. Husain by Using Cluster Analysis

Shailendra Gurjar$^{(\boxtimes)}$ (iD) and Usha Ananthakumar

Shailesh J. Mehta School of Management, Indian Institute of Technology Bombay, Mumbai, India
gurjar.s@iitb.ac.in, usha@som.iitb.ac.in

Abstract. Color plays a vital role in the creation and interpretation of paintings. While for an artist, color is a tool to express emotions and feelings and establish the tone of a painting, for a viewer color is one of the features that draws immediate attention. In this paper, we analyze paintings of Indian artist M.F. Husain to understand his choice of the color palette. We present a novel clustering approach to group paintings based on color similarity. The suggested approach uses the Earth Mover's Distance to compute similarity and Affinity Propagation algorithm to identify clusters. Also, using the same methodology, a diachronic analysis of the color palette used by M.F. Husain is performed.

Keywords: Paintings · Cluster analysis · Similarity measure · Color palette · Color similarity

1 Introduction

Recognised as one of the best and the most famous painters of India, M.F. Husain is known for his synthesis of stylistic elements of Western Modern Art with myths, motifs and themes from Indian culture. Disenchanted by the revivalist nationalism themes prevalent in Indian paintings, M.F. Husain along with F. N. Souza, S. H. Raza, K. H. Ara, H. A. Gade, and S. K. Bakre formed The Progressive Artists' Group in 1947. The Group sought to break away from the existing order and establish a new identity for Indian Art. However, unlike his fellow members of the progressive Group who dwell into themes of introspection, anger, or political statements, Husain drew inspiration from Indian epics, heritage, and popular culture.

Due to Husain's penchant for experimenting with colors, we focus on the role of color in his paintings and the evolution of his color palette. Though M.F. Husain's unique art style and his role in shaping the landscape of Indian art have been analyzed by art historians [1, 2], we believe the digitization of paintings and advancements in computer vision offers an opportunity to explore alternative approaches to understand Husain.

The rest of the paper is organized as follows. In Sect. 2, we briefly present the related research. Section 3 explains our approach. The experiment and results are explained in Sect. 4. We conclude in Sect. 5, with a discussion on the application of our research and possibilities for future research.

© Springer Nature Switzerland AG 2020
L. Rutkowski et al. (Eds.): ICAISC 2020, LNAI 12416, pp. 31–38, 2020.
https://doi.org/10.1007/978-3-030-61534-5_3

2 Related Works

The complexities involved in the creation, interpretation, and evaluation of paintings, render painting analysis one of the most challenging computer vision tasks. In the last two decades, there has been significant growth in research on the investigation of artwork. The majority of the research focuses on automation tasks such as, classifying artworks in different groups or identifying the creator of the artwork [3–7]. The color descriptor is often used in image retrieval system or image recoloration [8–11]. However, the use of color in painting analysis is rare.

No doubt valuable, but the majority of the existing research has limited applicability in enhancing our understanding of art and artists. We believe the research by [12] is closest to our work. In [12], authors provide a qualitative color descriptor and define a measure to calculate the color similarity of paintings. Moreover, there is a significant lack of research on art from the developing world. We have not come across any research that uses image processing to shed light on artworks by Indian artists.

3 Method

Any color-based clustering algorithm has two fundamental parts – 1. identify dominating colors in an image; 2. group images based on color similarity. The differences in algorithms arise from the number of colors identified, and the choice of the similarity measure. Our approach (Fig. 1) relies on the same fundamentals, and it consists of the following steps: 1. Convert images from RGB to CIEL*a*b space; 2. Extract color palette; 3. Measure similarity between color palettes; 4. Cluster images based on similarity measures from 3; 5. Diachronic analysis of paintings based on the color palette.

3.1 Color Space

The images are generally stored digitally in RGB color space. RGB color space works well for displaying images on digital screens, but it fails to resemble human perception. To match human perception, we convert images from RGB space to CIEL*a*b* space. Proposed by CIE in 1976 [13], CIEL*a*b* expresses color as three values: luminosity (L*) from black (0) to white (100), tone (a*) from red to green, and tone (b*) from yellow to blue. Since RGB is device-dependent, a direct conversion from RGB to L*a*b* is not possible. To convert, first, we transform RGB images to CIEXYZ space, and from CIEXYZ, we convert them to CIEL*a*b*. We use OpenCV for color space conversion. In OpenCV, the conversion is performed as:

$$\begin{bmatrix} X \\ Y \\ Z \end{bmatrix} = \begin{bmatrix} 0.412543 & 0.357580 & 0.180423 \\ 0.212671 & 0.715160 & 0.072169 \\ 0.019334 & 0.119193 & 0.950227 \end{bmatrix} \begin{bmatrix} R \\ G \\ B \end{bmatrix} \quad (1)$$

$$X \leftarrow \frac{X}{X_n}, where\, X_n = 0.950456 \quad (2)$$

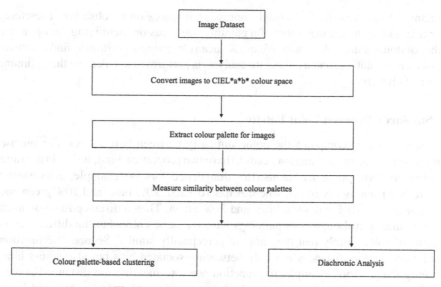

Fig. 1. Flow chart of the suggested approach

$$Z \leftarrow \frac{Z}{Z_n}, where\ Z_n = 1.088754 \tag{3}$$

$$L \leftarrow \begin{cases} 116 * Y^{\frac{1}{3}} - 16, & x > 0.008856 \\ 903.3 * Y, & x \le 0.008856 \end{cases} \tag{4}$$

$$a \leftarrow 500(f(X) - f(Y)) + delta \tag{5}$$

$$b \leftarrow 200(f(Y) - f(Z)) + delta \tag{6}$$

where,

$$f(t) \leftarrow \begin{cases} t^{1/3}, & t > 0.008856 \\ 7.787 * t + 16/116, & t \le 0.008856 \end{cases} \tag{7}$$

For 8 bits images, delta $= 128$ and the final converted values are given by,

$$L \leftarrow L * \frac{255}{100}$$
$$a \leftarrow a + 128 \tag{8}$$
$$b \leftarrow b + 128$$

3.2 Extraction of Color Palette

After converting images to CIEL*a*b space, either clustering or color histogram is used to find colors in an image. Although an image can have millions of colors, only a few dominant colors determine the visual impression it leaves on an observer. Therefore, rather than extracting all the colors of a painting, we focus on identifying the optimum number of dominating colors only. We use K-mean clustering algorithm to find dominating colors in a painting, and a silhouette analysis is performed to calculate the optimum number of clusters.

3.3 Similarity Between Color Palette

A distance function computes the color similarity between two images. For precise computation, the distance function needs to have two properties. First, it should measure not only color correspondence but also the strength of colors. For example, let us assume there are two paintings A and B, where A has 70% red, 20% blue, and 10% green and B is composed of 10% red, 40% blue, and 50% green. Then a distance function must recognize that even though both paintings have the same colors but the differences in strengths of colors imply that they are not perceptually similar. Second, the function should calculate the distances not only between associated bins but also across bins. Following the previous example, the function needs to measure the distance between red-red, blue-blue and green-green, and also between red-green, red-blue, blue-red, blue-green etc.

With this background, the choice of distance function is critical for meaningful clustering. Although a common approach is to use Euclidean distance and χ^2 distance, neither of these methods measures across bin distances. To alleviate this problem, we propose the use of Earth Mover's Distance (EMD). The EMD measures the minimal cost one has to pay to transform one distribution into another [14]. When two images have precisely the same color distribution, the EMD between them is 0. The higher the EMD, the higher the color distribution difference between them.

3.4 Color Palette Based Clustering

Though there are multiple clustering algorithms available, we use Affinity Propagation (AP) to cluster images [15]. Our choice is informed by the following reasons- first, unlike K-means or PAM, where the number of clusters has to be defined a-priori, AP drives the optimum number of clusters from the data itself. Second, while K-mean can be applied only when distance function is Euclidean, AP operate on any distance matrix. In our study, we make use of EMD matrix for clustering. Third, as shown in [15], AP generally finds better clustering solutions, and it is computationally faster. Motivated by graph theory, AP is based on message passing between nodes. It begins with considering every data point as a potential exemplar. After a series of message transfers among data points, AP converges to the optimum number of exemplars, where each exemplar functions as a representative of a cluster.

Formally, let us assume there are n data points from x_i and x_n, and s be a real-valued function that measures similarity between any two data points, then $s_{i,j}$ denotes similarity between data points x_i and x_j and $\{s_{i,j}\}$ is a real-valued similarity matrix. Each element of $\{s_{i,j}\}$ functions as a node of a graph. AP passes two types of messages between data points: responsibilities, and availability. A responsibility message from node i to k, $r(i, k)$, indicates the suitability of x_k to function as an exemplar of x_i when all other potential exemplars are taken into consideration. While an availability message from node k to i, $a(i, k)$, reflects how appropriate it would be for x_k to serve as an exemplar of x_i when considering other points' preference for x_k as an exemplar. Both responsibility and availability matrices are initialized to all zeros, and they are updated as follows:

$$r(i, k) \leftarrow s(i, k) - \max_{k' \neq k}\{a(i, k') + s(i, k')\} \tag{9}$$

$$a(i, k) \leftarrow \begin{cases} \dfrac{\sum_{i' \neq k} max(0, r(i', k)), \; for \; k = i}{\min\left(0, r(k, k) + \sum_{i' \notin \{i,k\}} \max(0, r(i', k))\right), \; for \; k \neq i} \end{cases} \tag{10}$$

$r(i, k)$ and $a(i, k)$ are updated till convergence and exemplars for data point i are found by calculating maximum of $r(i, k) + a(i, k)$. AP has two tuning parameters: diagonal of $\{s_{i,j}\}$ (preferences); and damping. While damping controls the convergence rate, preferences determine the number of clusters. A higher value of preference leads to a greater number of clusters, but a lower value gives a fewer number of clusters.

3.5 Diachronic Analysis of Color Palette

Other than clustering Husain's paintings, we are also interested in understanding how Husain's color palette has developed and evolved over his artistic career. In particular, we want to know whether Husain's color palette selection remained consistent throughout his life or it changed with time, or it saw wide variations for the entire duration of his career. We begin the analysis by calculating EMD of all the paintings from a reference painting. We assume that if all paintings share a color palette with the reference painting, then it will prove that he was very consistent, if not, otherwise. Though it is possible to use any painting as a reference painting, our choice of reference is solely based on the auction price. The painting selected as the reference is the most expensive of Husain's work in our dataset.

4   Experiment and Results

We collected painting data from Blouin Artinfo. Along with images of paintings, we also have their years of creation. After removing distorted images, we were left with 303 paintings created during 1950-2005. While no efforts are made to select paintings from a particular style, subject matter, or orientation, for the consistency of medium, all the paintings use oil on canvas.

As a result of multiple experiments and silhouette measures for a subset of images, we decided to extract three colors from a painting. In other words, the color palette for each image is composed of three dominating colors of that image. As described in Sect. 3, we compute similarity among color palette using EMD. In our experiment, the EMD matrix is a 303*303 symmetric matrix. In our final palette-based clustering by

Affinity Propagation, we use negative of EMD matrix as a similarity matrix, and the minimum value of negative EMD matrix is set as a preference.

From the analysis, we find that the paintings of M.F. Husain form 8 clusters [Fig. 2]. The maximum distance between two color palettes is 185.645, and the mean distance and standard deviation are 185.645, and 24.931 respectively. As can be seen from [Fig. 2], the clusters look well-formed. While the cluster one is dominated by black and brown, cluster 8 is predominantly red. Looking at [Fig. 2] carefully, we can observe that although Husain's palette is diverse, his choice of colors is not very wide. Husain often employed bright colors, such as black, brown, red, orange, green, and yellow color.

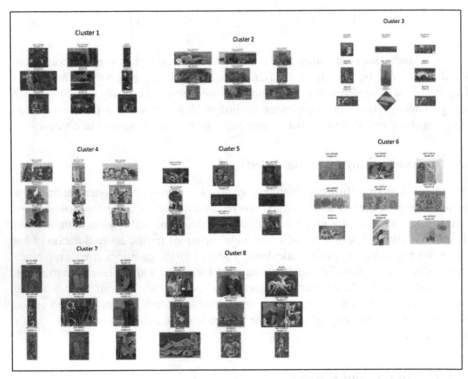

Fig. 2. Eight clusters identified in MF Husain paintings (Color figure online)

The results of the diachronic analysis are shown in Fig. 3. In the figure, X-axis is the time of painting creation, and the distance of a painting from the reference painting is shown on Y-axis. From the Fig. 3, we observe that there is high variation along the Y-axis for a fixed value of X; which implies that even within a single year, Husain's paintings are very different from each other in terms of the color palette used. Interestingly, our finding is consistent with the observations made by art historians [2].

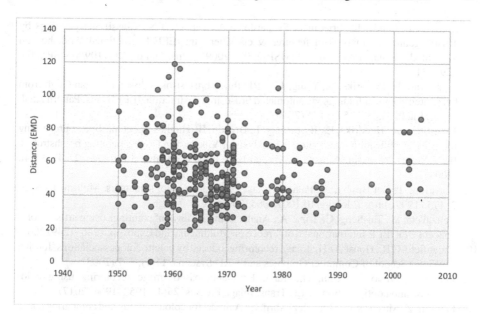

Fig. 3. Earth Mover's Distance between reference painting and all other paintings

5 Conclusion

In this work, we examined the choice of color palette employed by M.F. Husain. We leverage the existing techniques used in computer vision and image processing to propose a simple but effective approach to study the color signature of an artist. We also show how the distance matrix can be used to study the development and evolution of an artist's color palette. Our work contributes to the growing literature by being one of the very few works that identify the color signature of an artist and analyze the selection of colors throughout the artistic career. Besides, ours' is the first work to apply image processing and clustering to study paintings of an Indian artist.

We believe our research can be used by art galleries and museums to catalogue artworks. In addition, this work can also be extended to find the effect of color on the prices of artworks. In the future, we aim to extend this work to look deeper into the relationship of color with other features such as brushstrokes, texture.

References

1. Ramaswamy, S.: Barefoot across the Nation: M F Husain and the Idea of India. Routledge, London (2019)
2. Chandra, P.: M.F. Husain: A Pictorial Tribute. Niyogi Books, New Delhi (2012)
3. Shamir, L., Macura, T., Orlov, N., Eckley, D.M., Goldberg, I.G.: Impressionism, expressionism, surrealism: Automated recognition of painters and schools of art. ACM Trans. Appl. Percept. **7**(2), 8:1–8:17 (2010)
4. Jiang, S., Q., Ye, Q., Gao, W.: An effective method to detect and categorise digitised traditional chinese paintings. Pattern Recogn. Lett. **27**(7), 734–746 (2006)

5. Zujovic, J., Gandy, L., Friedman, S., Pardo, B.A., Pappas, T.N.: Classifying paintings by artistic genre: An analysis of features & classifiers. In: IEEE International Workshop on Multimedia Signal Processing, MMSP 2009 (2009). https://doi.org/10.1109/MMSP.2009.5293271

6. Li, J., Yao, L., Hendriks, E., Wang, J.Z.: Rhythmic brushstrokes distinguish van Gogh from his contemporaries: findings via automated brushstroke extraction. IEEE Trans. Pattern Anal. Mach. Intell. **34**(6), 1159–1176 (2010)

7. Johnson, C.R., Hendriks, E., Berezhnoy, I., Brevdo, E., Hughes, S., et al.: Image processing for artist identification - computerised analysis of Vincent van Gogh's painting brushstrokes. IEEE Signal Processing Magazine, Special Issue on Visual Cultural Heritage. **25**(4), 37–48 (2008)

8. Corridoni, J., Del Bimbo, A., Pala, P.: Image retrieval by color semantics. Multimedia Syst. **7**, 175 (1999). https://doi.org/10.1007/s005300050120

9. Yelizaveta, M., Tat-Seng, C., Irina, A.: Analysis and retrieval of paintings using artistic color concepts. In: IEEE International Conference on Multimedia and Expo, pp. 1246–1249 (2005)

10. Greenfield, G.R., House, D.H.: Image recoloring induced by palette color associations. Journal of Winter School of Computer Graphics and CAD Systems. **11**(1), 3–7 (2003)

11. Zhang, Q., Xiao, C., Sun, H., Tang, F.: Palette-based image recoloring using color decomposition optimization. IEEE Trans. Image Process. **26**(4), 1952–1964 (2017)

12. Falomir, Z., Museros, L., Gonzalez-Abril, L.: A model for colour naming and comparing based on conceptual neighbourhood. An application for comparing art compositions. Knowl.-Based Syst. **81**, 1–21 (2015)

13. McLaren, K.: The development of the CIE 1976 (L* a* b*) uniform colour space and colour difference formula. J. Soc. Dyers Colour. **92**, 338–341 (1976)

14. Rubner, Y., Tomasi, C., Guibas. L.J.: The earth mover's distance as a metric for image retrieval. Int. J. Comput. Vision **40**, 99–121 (2000)

15. Frey, B.J., Dueck, D.: Clustering by passing messages between data points. Science **315**(5814), 972–976 (2007)

Data Augmentation Using Principal Component Resampling for Image Recognition by Deep Learning

Olusola Oluwakemi Abayomi-Alli[1] (iD), Robertas Damaševičius[1,2] (iD),
Michał Wieczorek[2], and Marcin Woźniak[2(✉)] (iD)

[1] Department of Software Engineering, Kaunas University of Technology, Kaunas, Lithuania
{olusola.abayomi-alli,robertas.damasevicius}@ktu.edu
[2] Faculty of Applied Mathematics, Silesian University of Technology, Gliwice, Poland
michal_wieczorek@hotmail.com, marcin.wozniak@polsl.pl

Abstract. Image recognition by deep learning usually requires many sample images to train. In case of a small number of images available for training, data augmentation techniques should be applied. Here we propose a novel image augmentation technique based on a random permutation of coefficients of within-class principal components obtained after applying Principal Component Analysis (PCA). After reconstruction, newly generated surrogate images are employed to train a deep network. In this study, we demonstrated the applicability of our approach on training a custom convolutional neural network using the CIFAR-10 image dataset. The experimental results show an improvement in terms of classification accuracy and classification ambiguity.

Keywords: Image recognition · Convolutional neural network · Principal component analysis · Data augmentation · Small data · Deep learning

1 Introduction

The neural network (NN) is considered as one of main models of deep learning. The advantage of NN is the ability to effectively learn useful domain features in diverse areas such as image and signal processing [1]. This ability enables the neural network to learn deep models on domain data, which have proven successful in numerous areas of Artificial Intelligence (AI) such as object detection, defect recognition, speech recognition, voice evaluation, remote sensing, and medical decision support. Convolutional neural networks (CNNs) have been popularly used in computer vision and other related fields [2]. Recently, a lot of very large-scale deep CNN models were proposed such as VGG and ResNet. However, previous studies showed that despite increase in accuracy, oversized deep neural network models contribute to generate a lot of redundant features which are either the shifted version of one another or are closely related or display slight or no variations, thus resulting in redundant computations [3]. However, many parameters to be trained can be a disadvantage when training is performed on a limited amount of data available.

L. Rutkowski et al. (Eds.): ICAISC 2020, LNAI 12416, pp. 39–48, 2020.
https://doi.org/10.1007/978-3-030-61534-5_4

Data augmentation can be applied for training of neural network models to enhance the classification accuracy and model performance. The main idea of data augmentation is that the transformations applied to the already labeled data result in new, surrogate training data. Image augmentation techniques include geometric image transforms, mixing images, color space transforms, feature space augmentation, kernel filters, random erasing, etc. [4]. Data augmentation is relevant in case of small data problem [5], when a dataset is too small to train a deep neural network effectively.

The aim of this paper is to propose a novel image augmentation technique based on random permutation of coefficients of within-class principal components (PCs) obtained after Principal Component Analysis (PCA). The remaining parts of the paper are as follows: related work is presented in Sect. 2, while Sect. 3 discusses the proposed methods with detailed description. Section 4 discusses results and compares with known state-of-the-art methods. Finally, the paper concludes in Sect. 5.

2   Related Work

The use of data augmentation techniques has been considered in several recent papers. Leng et al. [6] presented joint Bayesian analysis for augmenting, while Chen et al. [7] proposed fuzzy operation rules for developing new data attributes and increasing data dimensionality for the small dataset learning. Truong et al. [8] presented augmentation methods based on 2D image sequence and 3D transformation. The classification model used was cascaded fully convolutional neural architecture. Li et al. [9] suggested to pair adjacent pixels and to use their combinations as additional data for hyperspectral image classification with deep CNN. Haut et al. [10] used random occlusions to generate new images for training of CNN for hyperspectral image classification. Finally, our proposed method has similarity to method for microscopy images proposed by Drivinskas et al. [11], however they use a different (multiplication) based scheme to modify principal components for augmentation. Similarly in [21] Najgebauer et al. proposed also deep learning based microscopic image processing for special sampling. Some other examples of data augmentation were given in [22] and [23]. Despite their usefulness, the existing data augmentation methods have limitations such as over-fitting, high computational time, poor accuracy of models, etc. In this article, a novel image augmentation technique based on a random permutation of coefficients of within-class PCs obtained after PCA. After image reconstruction, new images are used to train a deep network.

3   Proposed Method

This section presents a detailed description of the neural network models and the data augmentation techniques used in this study as depicted in Fig. 1.

3.1   Neural Network

This study focuses on small data [5] and tiny neural networks [12] for object recognition, these restrictions were applied for the design of the neural network. We do not use the

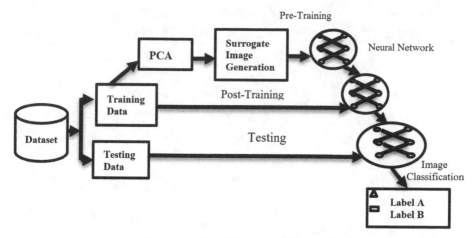

Fig. 1. Outline of the proposed method

ensemble models [13] and focus on a simpler structure. We did not adopt long training with more than 300 epochs (as suggested in [14]) due to hardware and time limitations. Different from very large very deep network models, we focused on a simple custom model allowing to demonstrate the advantages of data augmentation.

A 15-layer CNN with one input layer followed by 13 hidden layers and one output layer was designed (Fig. 2). The input layer consists of $32 \times 32 \times 3$ pixel images, i.e. it has 3072 neurons. The first hidden layer is the convolution layer 1 which is responsible for feature extraction from an input data. This layer performs convolution operation to small localized areas by convolving a $5 \times 5 \times 3$ filter with the previous layer. Rectified linear unit (ReLU) is used as an activation function at the end of each convolution layer to enhance the performance of the model. The next max pooling layers are used after each ReLU layer to reduce the output from the convolution layer and diminish the complexity of the model. The layer is followed by the convolution layer 2, ReLU layer 2 and pooling layer 2, operate in the same way except for their feature maps and kernel size varies. These are followed by a third set of layers (convolution layer 3, ReLU layer 3 and pooling layer 3). A fully connected layer FC 1 with 576 inputs and 64 outputs is followed by the final ReLU layer 4 and final fully connected layer FC 2 with 64 inputs and 10 outs, each corresponding to the target class. Using the FC layers is essential for the wider datasets, which have fewer examples per class for training [15]. Finally, softmax was employed as predictor to distinguish the classes. For optimization, we used the stochastic gradient descent with momentum (SGDM) optimizer with a learning rate of $\alpha = 0.001$, a learning rate drop factor of 0.1 and learning rate drop period of 8. The network is trained for 40 epochs.

3.2 Data Augmentation

In this study, we use a lower-dimensional representation of images obtained using Principal Component Analysis (PCA). PCA performs data decomposition into multiple orthogonal principal components (PCs) using the variance criterion. The PCs are the

	Name	Type	Activations	Learnables
1	imageinput 32x32x3 images with 'zerocenter' normalization	Image Input	32×32×3	-
2	conv_1 32 5x5x3 convolutions with stride [1 1] and padding [2 2 2 2]	Convolution	32×32×32	Weights 5×5×3×32 Bias 1×1×32
3	relu_1 ReLU	ReLU	32×32×32	-
4	maxpool_1 3x3 max pooling with stride [2 2] and padding [0 0 0 0]	Max Pooling	15×15×32	-
5	conv_2 32 5x5x32 convolutions with stride [1 1] and padding [2 2 2 2]	Convolution	15×15×32	Weights 5×5×32×32 Bias 1×1×32
6	relu_2 ReLU	ReLU	15×15×32	-
7	maxpool_2 3x3 max pooling with stride [2 2] and padding [0 0 0 0]	Max Pooling	7×7×32	-
8	conv_3 64 5x5x32 convolutions with stride [1 1] and padding [2 2 2 2]	Convolution	7×7×64	Weights 5×5×32×64 Bias 1×1×64
9	relu_3 ReLU	ReLU	7×7×64	-
10	maxpool_3 3x3 max pooling with stride [2 2] and padding [0 0 0 0]	Max Pooling	3×3×64	-
11	fc_1 64 fully connected layer	Fully Connected	1×1×64	Weights 64×576 Bias 64×1
12	relu_4 ReLU	ReLU	1×1×64	-
13	fc_2 10 fully connected layer	Fully Connected	1×1×10	Weights 10×64 Bias 10×1
14	softmax softmax	Softmax	1×1×10	-
15	classoutput crossentropyex with 'airplane' and 9 other classes	Classification Output	-	-

Fig. 2. Architecture of neural network and its parameters

projections of the data along the eigenvectors of the covariance matrix of a dataset. The first PC is the axis with the most variance and each subsequent PC is calculated in the order of decreasing variance. The first PCs are the most significant, while the last ones are considered to represent only the "noise".

First, PCA discovers the eigenvectors and their matching eigenvalues of the covariance matrix of a data set and the eigenvectors are sorted by their decreasing eigenvalues. Given a dataset $\chi = \{x_1, \ldots, x_M\}$ of samples drawn from a data source representing a specific class $\mathbb{C}$, and the covariance matrix C of the data set; the eigenvectors E are found by solving equation

$$CE = \lambda E, \tag{1}$$

here λ is the eigenvalue that matches E. Each eigenvector e_i can be expressed as

$$e_i = \sum_j \alpha_j^i x_j, \tag{2}$$

The original data can be reconstructed by multiplying principal components with their loadings W as follows:

$$\hat{X} = WE \tag{3}$$

Now each eigenvector e_i represents a specific independent aspect of data samples belonging to the class $\mathbb{C}$. Next, we perform random reshuffling of these values:

$$\hat{W} = \Gamma W, \tag{4}$$

where Γ is a random permutation operator applied with a specific probability of p.

Then the modified image dataset is reconstructed using the reshuffled loadings $\tilde{W}$ and eigenvectors E. Note that in order to avoid excessive variability in the surrogate images, we did not perform permutation of loading on first two PCs, which encode the most essential information of image class. The outcomes of image augmentation are illustrated in Fig. 3 and the image augmentation method is summarized as:

Fig. 3. Illustration of image augmentation: original images (left) and surrogate (augmented) images (right)

1. Compute PCs for each class in dataset using classical PCA.
2. Perform random permutations of the PC loadings (with a predefined probability) starting from the loading representing the third principal component.
3. Construct surrogate images using the randomly permuted loadings.
4. Use the surrogate image dataset to perform pre-training of a neural network.
5. Freeze the learned weights of the selected layers of the neural network and perform post-training using the original (unchanged) training dataset.

The computational complexity of the method is determined by the calculation of PCA, which is $O\left(min\left(p^3, n^3\right)\right)$, here p is the number of pixels in an image, and n is the number images. For our experiments we construct different surrogate image datasets using 2%, 3%, 4%, 5%, 7%, 10%, 15%, 20%, 25% and 30% of permutations of the PC loadings. We generated 1000 new images for each image class and used them for network pre-training. For final training, we used the original images from the training set, while we explored different training scenarios: 1) Freeze only the first convolutional layer (CL) conv_1; 2) Freeze two first CLs conv_1 and conv_2; 3) Freeze all CLs conv_1 and conv_2, conv_3.

4   Experimental Results

We use the CIFAR-10 dataset [16], which is a known benchmark dataset in image classification and recognition domain. The dataset has 60,000 32 × 32 color images between 10 different classes, which represent the images of both natural (birds, cats, deer, dogs, frogs, horses) and artificial (airplanes, cars, ships, and trucks) objects. The dataset has 6,000 images of each class. The training set has 50,000 images (equally balanced), while a testing set has 10,000 images (1,000 images of each class). The classes do not overlap and they are fully mutually exclusive.

We evaluated the performance using accuracy and uncertainty of classification based on ambiguity, i.e. the ratio of the second-largest probability to the largest probability of the softmax layer activations. The ambiguity is between zero (nearly certain classification) and 1 (the network is unsure of the class due to inability to learn the differences between them). We also evaluated the mean value of accuracy and ambiguity over the testing image set and the results are depicted in Tables 1 and 2.

Table 1. Accuracy improvement with image augmentation using CIFAR-10 dataset (larger values are better, best value is shown in bold). All improvement values are given with respect to the accuracy of baseline network on testing data without any image augmentation applied

PC loadings reshuffled, %	Accuracy improvement, % (first CL frozen)	Accuracy improvement, % (first two CLs frozen)	Accuracy improvement, % (all CLs frozen)
2	3.6600	−0.4900	−3.0900
3	6.5400	4.2400	2.9900
4	6.1200	4.3900	2.7500
5	3.5500	1.2800	−0.6100
6	4.7300	2.2900	0.5000
7	6.0100	2.4100	0.9600
10	3.7200	1.1700	−0.1600
15	4.9200	1.8700	0.4400
20	6.3700	5.3100	3.9100
25	**7.1800**	4.8500	3.0500
30	5.8200	5.0700	3.6700
Mean	5.3291	2.9445	1.3100
Std. dev	1.2795	1.9260	2.1679

The results show that best improvement in accuracy is achieved using a neural network pretrained with surrogate images generated with 25% of principal component loadings reshuffled and then post-trained with the weights of the first CL frozen (the improvement is significant at $p < 0.001$ using one-sample t-test). In terms of classification ambiguity, the best results are also obtained with the weights of only the first CL frozen (the reduction is significant at $p < 0.001$ using one-sample t-test).

The results are also summarized in Fig. 4. Note that here we presented the reduction of error rate instead of the improvement of accuracy for better comparison. These results show that larger shuffling rates lead to better results, while the best results are achieved by leaving the first CL frozen while retraining other layers.

For visualization of the activation maps, we use t-distributed stochastic neighbor embedding (t-SNE). The method uses a nonlinear map that attempts to preserve distances and maps network activations in a layer to two dimensions. See the results for the fully

Table 2. Classification ambiguity with image augmentation using CIFAR-10 dataset (smaller values are better, best value is shown in bold)

PC loadings shuffled,%	Ambiguity (first CL frozen)	Ambiguity (first two CLs frozen)	Ambiguity (all CLs frozen)
2	0.1552	0.2408	0.3206
3	0.0811	0.1102	0.1612
4	0.0871	0.1088	0.1632
5	0.1367	0.1714	0.2348
6	0.1202	0.1533	0.2035
7	0.0929	0.1408	0.1890
10	0.1319	0.1782	0.2456
15	0.1210	0.1476	0.2252
20	0.0883	0.1054	0.1499
25	**0.0788**	0.1014	0.1554
30	0.0901	0.0974	0.1366
Mean	0.1076	0.1414	0.1986
Std. dev	0.0262	0.0438	0.0547

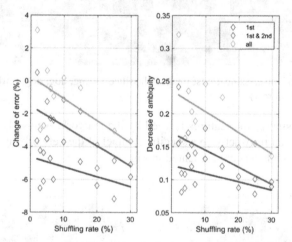

Fig. 4. Classification error and ambiguity vs principal component shuffling rate with trend lines. The results are shown after the network was post-trained with original training dataset with its 1st, 1st and 2nd, and all convolutional layers frozen, respectively.

connected fc2 layer in Fig. 5. One can see that the network tends to put natural and artificial object classes closer. This may mean that any misclassifications arise due to the similarity of semantically close classes such as dogs and cats.

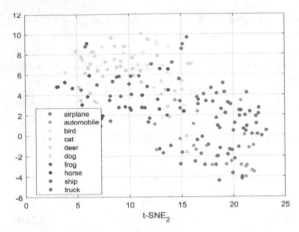

Fig. 5. Activation visualization of the final fully connected layer using t-SNE

The examples of misclassification by the neural network are presented in Fig. 6. They confirm that most misclassifications are between similar classes such as dog and cat images.

Fig. 6. Examples of misclassifications: images classified as dog, dog, dog, bird (top row), bird, frog, cat, deer (bottom row)

In order to visualize the features learned by the network, we use DeepDream [17] to obtain images that fully activate a specific channel of the network layers. The results for conv2 and conv3 layers are presented in Fig. 7.

Fig. 7. Feature visualization of outputs from convolutional layers conv2 and conv3

Finally, a comparison of the results of our approach with the results of other authors in Table 3. Our results compare well in the context of other state-of-the art methods, considering that we used a smaller neural network with only 15 layers.

Table 3. Comparison with other works using CIFAR-10 dataset

Method description	Error rate (%)	Reference
Maxout Networks	9.38	[18]
Densely Connected CNN-BC (100-layer DenseNet)	6.3	[19]
CNN with PCA based data augmentation	5.34	This paper
16-layer-deep Wide Residual Network	3.8	[20]

5 Conclusion

This paper presents a novel image data augmentation technique based on the random permutation of coefficients of within-class principal component scores obtained after Principal Component Analysis (PCA). After reconstruction, the newly generated surrogate images are used to pretrain a deep network (we used a custom 15-layer convolutional neural network). Then one or more convolutional layers of the neural network were frozen and the final training was performed using the original images.

This study also showed the practical applicability of our approach on training the custom-made neural network using CIFAR-10 image dataset. The approach allowed both to improve accuracy (up to 7.18%) and reduce ambiguity of classification. Thus, it can be used for addressing the small data problem, when there is only a small number of images available for training a neural network.

In future work, we will examine and compare our approach with other types of image dataset augmentation approaches. Also, we will explore the use of dropout and batch regularization to improve the accuracy of the custom neural network.

Acknowledgments. Authors acknowledge contribution to this project of the Program "Best of the Best 4.0" from the Polish Ministry of Science and Higher Education No. MNiSW/2020/43/DIR/NN4.

References

1. Schmidhuber, J.: Deep learning in neural networks: an overview. Neural Netw. **61**, 85–117 (2015). https://doi.org/10.1016/j.neunet.2014.09.003
2. Rawat, W., Wang, Z.: Deep convolutional neural networks for image classification: a comprehensive review. Neural Comput. **29**(9), 2352–2449 (2017)
3. Ayinde, B.O., Inanc, T., Zurada, J.M.: Regularizing deep neural networks by enhancing diversity in feature extraction. IEEE Trans. Neural Netw. Learning Syst. **30**(9), 2650–2661 (2019). https://doi.org/10.1109/TNNLS.2018.2885972

4. Shorten, C., Khoshgoftaar, T.M.: A survey on image data augmentation for deep learning. J. Big Data **6**(1), 1–48 (2019). https://doi.org/10.1186/s40537-019-0197-0

5. Qi, G.-J., Luo, J.: Small data challenges in big data era: a survey of recent progress on unsupervised and semi-supervised methods. CoRR abs/1903.11260 (2019)

6. Leng, B., Yu, K., Jingyan, Q.I.N.: Data augmentation for unbalanced face recognition training sets. Neurocomputing **235**, 10–14 (2017)

7. Chen, H.Y., Li, D.C., Lin, L. S.: Extending sample information for small data set prediction. In: 2016 5th IIAI International Congress on Advanced Applied Informatics (IIAI-AAI), pp. 710–714 (2016)

8. Truong, T.N., Dam, V.D., Le, T.S.: Medical images sequence normalization and augmentation: improve liver tumor segmentation from small dataset. In: 3rd International Conference on Control, Robotics and Cybernetics (CRC), pp. 1–5 (2018)

9. Li, W., Chen, C., Zhang, M., Li, H., Du, Q.: Data augmentation for hyperspectral image classification with deep CNN. IEEE Geosci. Remote Sens. Lett. **16**(4), 593–597 (2019)

10. Haut, J.M., Paoletti, M.E., Plaza, J., Plaza, A., Li, J.: Hyperspectral image classification using random occlusion data augmentation. IEEE Geosci. Remote Sens. Lett. **16**(11), 1751–1755 (2019). https://doi.org/10.1109/LGRS.2019.2909495

11. Dirvanauskas, D., Maskeliūnas, R., Raudonis, V., Damaševičius, R., Scherer, R.: Hemigen: human embryo image generator based on generative adversarial networks. Sensors **19**(16), 3578 (2019)

12. Womg, A., Shafiee, M.J., Li, F., Chwyl, B.: Tiny SSD: a tiny single-shot detection deep convolutional neural network for real-time embedded object detection. In: 15th Conference on Computer and Robot Vision (CRV), Toronto, ON, pp. 95–101 (2018)

13. Zhou, Z.-H., Wu, J., Tang, W.: Ensembling neural networks: Many could be better than all. Artif. Intell. **137**(1–2), 239–263 (2002). https://doi.org/10.1016/s0004-3702(02)00190-x

14. Amory, A.A., Muhammad, G., Mathkour, H.: Deep convolutional tree networks. Future Generation Comput. Syst. **101**, 152–168 (2019). https://doi.org/10.1016/j.future.2019.06.010

15. Basha, S.H.S., Dubey, S.R., Pulabaigari, V., Mukherjee, S.: Impact of fully connected layers on performance of convolutional neural networks for image classification. Neurocomputing **378**, 112–119 (2019). https://doi.org/10.1016/j.neucom.2019.10.008

16. Krizhevsky, A.: Learning multiple layers of features from tiny images. Master's thesis, Department of Computer Science, University of Toronto, Canada (2009)

17. Mordvintsev, A., Olah C., Tyka, M.: Inceptionism: Going deeper into neural networks. Google research blog (2015)

18. Goodfellow, I.J., Warde-Farley, D., Mirza, M., Courville, A., Bengio, Y.: Maxout networks. arXiv:1302.4389 (2013)

19. Huang, G., Liu, Z., Weinberger, K. Q., van der Maaten, L.: Densely connected convolutional networks. arXiv preprint arXiv:1608.06993 (2016)

20. Zagoruyko, S., Komodakis, N.: Wide residual networks. arXiv:1605.07146 (2016)

21. Najgebauer, P., Grycuk, R., Rutkowski, L., Scherer, R., Siwocha, A.: Microscopic sample segmentation by fully convolutional network for parasite detection. In: Rutkowski, L., Scherer, R., Korytkowski, M., Pedrycz, W., Tadeusiewicz, R., Zurada, Jacek M. (eds.) ICAISC 2019. LNCS (LNAI), vol. 11508, pp. 164–171. Springer, Cham (2019). https://doi.org/10.1007/978-3-030-20912-4_16

22. Aizenberg, I., Luchetta, A., Manetti, S., Piccirilli, M.C.: A MLMVN with arbitrary complex-valued inputs and a hybrid testability approach for the extraction of lumped models using FRA. J. Artif. Intell. Soft Comput. Res. **9**(1), 5–19 (2019)

23. Costa, M., Oliveira, D., Pinto, S., Tavares, A.: Detecting driver's fatigue, distraction and activity using a non-intrusive Ai-based monitoring system. J. Artif. Intell. Soft Comput. Res. **9**(4), 247–266 (2019)

Multi-agent Architecture for Internet of Medical Things

Dawid Połap[1]([✉])[iD], Gautam Srivastava[2][iD], and Marcin Woźniak[1][iD]

[1] Faculty of Applied Mathematics, Silesian University of Technology,
Kaszubska 23, 44-101 Gliwice, Poland
{Dawid.Polap,Marcin.Wozniak}@polsl.pl
[2] Department of Mathematics and Computer Science, Brandon University,
Brandon R7A 6A9, Canada
SrivastavaG@brandonu.ca

Abstract. The technological advancements in recent years has enabled the creation of the Internet of Medical Things, i.e. solutions where medical devices can communicate with each other and exchange data. The guiding idea is to model solutions that can reduce the amount of expected time for analysis of examination results, quick response in the case of diseases as well as assist doctors. In this paper, we propose a solution based on a multi-agent system, where agents are adapted to use classifiers based on artificial intelligence techniques. In the proposed model, we also analyze patient data security and describe the solution so that it is possible to use data in training classifiers without affecting their patient identity. Our approach has been tested on solution simulations based on the most popular technique of artificial intelligence – convolutional neural network.

Keywords: Multi-agent · Internet of Medical Things · Artificial intelligence

1 Introduction

Technological development and faster implementation of the 5G infrastructure means that more and more devices can use the Internet. This makes data exchange between devices efficient and fast. Besides, the huge potential of artificial intelligence (AI) techniques finds its place in data analysis and management. The combination of all these solutions enabled the creation of the Internet of Things, which is already visible within smart cities, homes or any other smart infrastructures.

Also, the narrowing of devices to the medical environment has created the Internet of Medical Things (IoMT), which enables the exchange of data and their processing during various examinations. The main idea of such infrastructure is to reduce the waiting time for the results of medical tests, as well as to assist doctors in making decisions. Moreover, information about patients' state can be

© Springer Nature Switzerland AG 2020
L. Rutkowski et al. (Eds.): ICAISC 2020, LNAI 12416, pp. 49–58, 2020.
https://doi.org/10.1007/978-3-030-61534-5_5

gathered by some sensors [15]. In [6], the idea of creating a t-shirt composed of sensors to monitor the health state of patients was described. The authors analyzed the possible creation and made a basic model. Nowadays, we are using smartwatches, bands that can be used for monitoring our pulse, or blood pressure and this information might help some doctors to analyze this data for a long time around the clock [14].

Smart Things can be used in some infrastructures to monitor health as was shown in [17]. One of the actual problems in this solution is how to model such an infrastructure. Edge computing is becoming a very promising solution, where collected data are processed and analyzed by devices which gathered them or in other but placed close [10]. Another problem is how to process data to obtain strong results. An increasing amount of data requires tools for splitting the data and clustering the data into classes. In [11], the authors proposed a new algorithm of clustering data in IoMT using fuzzy logic. After clustering, there is a need to obtain some features from this data for classification purposes. Neural networks are very useful tools for classification as can be seen in [12]. In this paper, a solution for classification features of ovarian cancer was described in detail. Again in [24], the authors showed a technique for fusion of medical data. Another major issue is privacy of patient data [5]. There is great risk in storing data without proper levels of security. Large amounts of data must be stored in databases located on servers or in the clouds. However, blockchain technology is becoming very popular, which can enable data security due to a decentralized database [8].

In this paper, we propose using a multi-agent system as a basic solution in IoMT. Our proposal offers a great flexibility of using artificial intelligence techniques, as also protection of data by the use of blockchain to store some information. This approach was modelled and tested by some factors like time of processing data, possible communication of agents and applying some classification methods.

The rest of the paper is organized as follows. In Sect. 3, we present our proposed architecture. Next, in Sect. 4 we give details experiments on our methodology and architecture. Finally, we end with some concluding remarks in Sect. 5.

2   Related Work

Blockchain architecture is increasingly used in practice because of the numerous advantages that are primarily related to decentralization, security, and authorization. It is particularly important to use elliptic curve cryptography as described in [9], where Dinh *et al.* point to the flow of information in this technology and analyze the possibilities of use. In [13], Gordon *et al.* introduce the idea of using such safeguards in health care and outline its advantages and disadvantages. Also available solutions in this area are evaluated and compared what can be seen in [18].

Parallel research is being carried out on classifiers to increase their effectiveness as well reduce training time. In [2], Albahar *et al.* show using a convolutional neural network (CNN) effective classification of skin marks. These types of experiments may not only allow classification but also possible prediction of metastases. The idea of prognosis for pancreatic cancer treatment was described and analyzed by using an artificial neural networks (ANN) in [20] or others types of classifier [3, 4, 22].

Scientists from around the world are trying to combine the advantages of both technologies, which is visible in such works as [21]. Winnicka *et al.* proposed a new technique model to obtain the best weights configuration in ANN. As a reward for performing tasks in the chain, the given device received a certain number of points indicating its consumption due to the use of computing power to perform this task. Again in [23], Xu *et al.* described using the crowd-intelligence ecosystem for mobile edge computing by apply blockchain ideas.

3 Proposed Architecture

The proposed solution is based on building an architecture that can be used in IoMT. Particular attention during system modelling was given to the need to use AI methods, which are increasingly finding their practical implementations in many different areas. Moreover, such systems are built on devices that primarily perform tests on patients, so all patient data and collected data must remain confidential. To keep these comments, we suggest a multi-agent architecture that will use blockchain to store all confidential information.

3.1 Agent Architecture

Medical Things should perform several operations. In this paper, the basic procedure is simplified to performing examinations and saving any and all acquired information. Unfortunately, such data is quite often signed by a given patient. The agent [1, 16] should, therefore, be able to encrypt this information and delete it from the data.

The data obtained by such devices can take mainly two forms - numerical data and graphical data. For numeric values, deleting them is not a complicated process. In the case of a graphical data however, the removal consists of placing a black rectangle on the image in place of the data. Deleting data from the image does not delete the data from the device. This data is processed using the patient's ID and assigning a new ID to the study. Such a pair of data $(id_{patient}, id_{examination})$ is placed in the blockchain. Patient data after encryption (for example, using AES) is placed in a classic database – if such a record does not exist. Otherwise, the patient ID is retrieved.

This step protects patient data, but test results still needs to be addressed. Test results are placed in a database as $id_{examination}$. This operation is performed without the need for any encryption. Placing medical data in this form allows it to be used for other processing needs. Let us assume that each agent may have

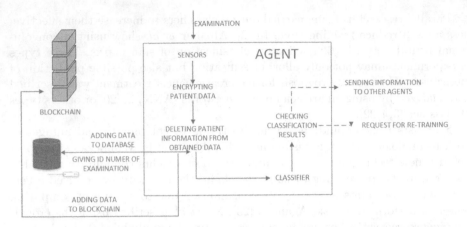

Fig. 1. Visualization of the agent architecture corresponding to a given device on the Internet of Medical Things.

a module that classifies and analyzes data obtained using sensors embedded in a given device. The result of the classification without distinguishing the technique will always be written as a numerical vector, where each value is the probability of belonging to a particular class. It is worth noting that unresolved results may be ambiguous, i.e. membership values will fluctuate in similar values. This type of operation should quite often be the reason for re-training the classifier. However, this is not always possible due to low computing power or even a time factor. During the retraining of the classifier, the device will not be available. For this reason, we suggest implementing a system that analyzes whether the classifier should be overtrained. Such a need will arise if the condition that the classification results are ambiguous is met. Of course, another device on the network could be trained for such data, so the classifier is updated through communication between agents.

Determining whether results are unambiguous can be performed using a technique with data correlation. Suppose than obtained results are given as a vector $[x_0, x_1, \ldots, x_{n-1}]$, where index indicates the given class of disease (which can be defined as a vector $[y_0, y_1, \ldots, y_{n-1}]$). The proposed approach is based on calculating Pearson correlation coefficient using covariation $\mathrm{cov}(\cdot)$ and average values as Sd_x and Sd_y following equations

$$\mathrm{cov}(x,y) = \frac{\sum(x_i - \overline{x})(x_i - \overline{y})}{n}, \tag{1}$$

$$Sd_x = \sqrt{\frac{\sum(x_i - \overline{x}_x)^2}{n}}, \tag{2}$$

$$Sd_y = \sqrt{\frac{\sum(y_i - \overline{x}_y)^2}{n}}, \tag{3}$$

where $\overline{x}$ and $\overline{y}$ are the average of all values of a given variable. The above formula for correlation can be presented as

$$
\begin{aligned}
r_{xy} &= \frac{\text{cov}(x,y)}{Sd_x \cdot Sd_y} = \frac{\sum (x_i - \overline{x})(x_i - \overline{y})}{n} \cdot \frac{n}{\sqrt{\sum (x_i - \overline{x}_x)^2}\sqrt{\sum (y_i - \overline{x}_y)^2}} \\
&= \frac{\sum (x_i - \overline{x})(x_i - \overline{y})}{\sqrt{\sum (x_i - \overline{x}_x)^2}\sqrt{\sum (y_i - \overline{x}_y)^2}}.
\end{aligned}
\tag{4}
$$

The correlation coefficient for the classification results will be in the range of $\langle -1, 1 \rangle$, which will mean, respectively, a lack of relationship between the ideal classification results and the obtained one. In the case of correlation at the level of the middle of the range (i.e. when the level of the coefficient r_{xy} is close to 0), the agent sends information with a request to re-train the classifier. If the agent has enough computing power, it can perform overtraining using data in the database. However, a simpler solution due to practical application is to send a request to another agent on the network to do this overtraining.

If the correlation result is close to 1, it means that the patient is ill with one of the diseases, so the information must be sent to the doctor to inform him. If the value is negative, it means that the patient does not have any of the classified diseases. A visualization of the agent's architecture is shown in Fig. 1.

3.2   System Architecture

Each Thing in the IoMT network is associated with an agent. Depending on various applications, it is possible to create a system based only on agents, but practical use in medicine causes that the amount of data is huge, so there is a need to extend the architecture with additional components. The general scheme of operation is shown in Fig. 2.

The proposed architecture assumes that there will be at least one database where medical data will be stored and a second database with encrypted patient information. Additionally, a blockchain system will be existing, thanks to which data about connecting patient information and examination will be stored. The system is based on the idea of a decentralized database which increases the security of information. The main advantage of this approach is the fact that medical data is in a database that all agents have access to, so adding new agents with new classifiers allows the use of ready resources in training processes. Especially if we take into account the fact that artificial intelligence techniques are data-hungry algorithms. Also, the proposed solution can be implemented even with a defect, which is the low efficiency of classifiers, because thanks to the classification analysis mechanism, it will force re-training on the current database, which is constantly increasing. With the condition that in a situation where the correlation coefficient described by the Eq. (4) is close to 1, then the data in the database will be described by the approximate result of the classification by rounding probabilities to whole numbers.

Agents communicate with each other primarily in two ways – in blockchain technique to store data on the connection of medical data with patients and

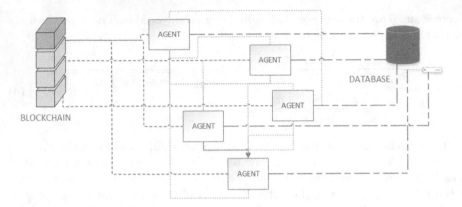

Fig. 2. Simplified visualization of multi-agent system architecture. Blue lines indicate the possibility of connecting to the database, all agents form a blockchain system (which is also added as an element), and communication between agents is indicated using the yellow lines.

by sending information about the classification of data that is to be sent to the device's screen to notify about the analyzed situation or with a request to overtrain the classifier. If there is a possibility of having high computing power it is possible to re-training on this device, if not the agent sends a request to everyone else. Message has four elements – $id_{examination}$, r_{yx}, identification of agent and machine type. The machine type indicates who is the recipient of the information. Each agent who has the same machine takes data from a database and classifies it. If the obtained result is better, it sends classifier configuration to the agent by its identification number. If the next agent has retraining options, then he performs it. However, in order not to duplicate the same information, the agent (which cannot do it) does not send information asking for retraining, but waits for other agents.

In the proposed system it may turn out that none of the agents will be able to re-train the classifier, in this case, there will be an impasse. All agents update the status of classifiers using the best one. This choice is illustrated by the following equation

$$\min\left(r_{yx}^{(0)}, r_{yx}^{(1)}, \ldots, r_{yx}^{(k-1)}\right), \tag{5}$$

where k is the number of all agents with the same machine type.

4   Experiments

Our solution was modeled to analyze basic performance. We used a database called HAM10000, ISIC 2018 Lesion Diagnosis Challenge [7,19], which has seven classes of image representing skin marks and different diseases contained in seven classes.

Table 1. Average time [s] for response after 100 tests using random image form set.

	Agents			
	1	2	3	4
x	0	1223	1318
0	x	1536	1456
0	0	x (932)	0
0	0	0	x (1231)

To show potential in our proposed system, 4 instances of the same program with an implemented agent with the classic convolutional neural network were used. Each network has been trained separately using Inception architecture by 10 epochs. A simple blockchain architecture was created using four instances of programs and one, sample patient. Then, we added a single image to the sample agent to see the operation. In our test, we assumed, that only two instances can train a network. During these experiments, we measured the average response time, the amount of time needed to complete this task, and the training coefficient r_{xy} that has been achieved by trained instances.

Four used instances were numbered from 1 to 4, where 3 and 4 have a possibility of re-training. In Table 1, a result of average time response after 100 test is presented. An instance that gets an image and should send a request is marked as x. We notice, that sending a request is received in each instance that can re-train and in all cases, this process is made. in a situation, when the system will have a large number of agents, it might be very problematic to make so many unnecessary calculations. To prevent this, it would be worth adding some mechanism to provide information on who trains. This result shows that lower time to calculate new weights in networks is obtained when there is no need to send a request. The increased time is caused by an additional load such as taking the last image from the database, recalculating r_{xy}, and then re-training.

Table 2. Average time [s] for complete classification task after 100 tests using random image from each class.

Instance	Class						
	1	2	3	4	5	6	7
1	1052	1034	1123	1363	1367	1973	1672
2	1023	1219	1289	1102	1319	1863	1783
3	983	1123	1167	1209	1293	1753	1665
4	1010	945	983	1023	1245	1653	1561

After testing the response time, the average classification time of a random image from each class was measured. The results are presented in Table 2.

In most cases, a better time was obtained when an image was received to an agent which could re-train. However, it can be noticed, that for classes 5–7, time was much longer than for the previous ones. Additionally, in this experiment, we measured also the Pearson coefficients when an agent needs re-training and after getting better weights configuration. This is presented in Fig. 3. The value was changed to receive at least 0,5, which can indicate one of the classes. This result shows, that this approach can be very promising not on the Internet of Medical Things but also in other solutions. Proposed architecture is very flexible because of the simple implementation, possibility of using different techniques of classification and protection of data by deleting data from the medical image and store confidential information in the blockchain.

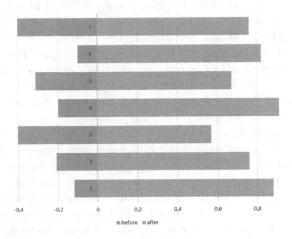

Fig. 3. Average Pearson coefficient before/after classification of random image from each sample after 100 tests.

5   Conclusion

Architecture of solutions in the Internet of Things based on a multi-agent system can be used everywhere. The described approach enables simple implementation in practice and great freedom in modelling artificial intelligence techniques that play a key role here. As part of our research, we modelled this solution based on the classification of lung and skin diseases. We used several artificial intelligence models to indicate the approximate response time as well as the possibilities of these techniques.

In future works, we plan to focus more on the security level of such a system to improve this approach. Moreover, we plan to analyze a model composed of a different type of agent and their communication.

References

1. Abdulghafor, R., Turaev, S., Zeki, A., Abubaker, A.: Nonlinear convergence algorithm: structural properties with doubly stochastic quadratic operators for multi-agent systems. J. Artif. Intell. Soft Comput. Res. **8**(1), 49–61 (2018)
2. Albahar, M.A.: Skin lesion classification using convolutional neural network with novel regularizer. IEEE Access **7**, 38306–38313 (2019)
3. Alkhazaleh, S., Hazaymeh, A.A.: N-valued refined neutrosophic soft sets and their applications in decision making problems and medical diagnosis. J. Artif. Intell. Soft Comput. Res. **8**(1), 79–86 (2018)
4. Alshamlan, H.M., Badr, G.H., Alohali, Y.A.: Abc-svm: artificial bee colony and svm method for microarray gene selection and multi class cancer classification. Int. J. Mach. Learn. Comput **6**(3), 184 (2016)
5. Alsubaei, F., Abuhussein, A., Shiva, S.: Security and privacy in the Internet of medical things: taxonomy and risk assessment. In: 2017 IEEE 42nd Conference on Local Computer Networks Workshops (LCN Workshops), pp. 112–120. IEEE (2017)
6. Balestrieri, E., et al.: The architecture of an innovative smart t-shirt based on the Internet of medical things paradigm. In: IEEE International Symposium on Medical Measurements and Applications (MeMeA), pp. 1–6. IEEE (2019)
7. Codella, N.C., et al.: Skin lesion analysis toward melanoma detection: a challenge at the 2017 international symposium on biomedical imaging (isbi), hosted by the international skin imaging collaboration (isic). In: 2018 IEEE 15th International Symposium on Biomedical Imaging (ISBI 2018), pp. 168–172. IEEE (2018)
8. Dilawar, N., Rizwan, M., Ahmad, F., Akram, S,.: Blockchain: securing Internet of medical things (iomt). Int. J. Adv. Compu.t Sci. Appl. **10**(1), 82–89 (2019)
9. Dinh, T.T.A., Liu, R., Zhang, M., Chen, G., Ooi, B.C., Wang, J.: Untangling blockchain: a data processing view of blockchain systems. IEEE Trans. Knowl. Data Eng. **30**(7), 1366–1385 (2018)
10. Dubey, H., et al.: Fog computing in medical Internet-of-Things: architecture, implementation, and applications. In: Khan, S.U., Zomaya, A.Y., Abbas, A. (eds.) Handbook of Large-Scale Distributed Computing in Smart Healthcare. SCC, pp. 281–321. Springer, Cham (2017). https://doi.org/10.1007/978-3-319-58280-1_11
11. El-Zeheiry, H., Elmogy, M., Elaraby, N., Barakat, S.: Fuzzy c-mean and density-based spatial clustering for internet of things data processing. In: Hassanien, A.E., Dey, N., Borra, S. (eds.) Med. Big Data Internet Med. Things, pp. 161–187. CRC Press, Boca Raton (2018)
12. Elhoseny, M., Bian, G.B., Lakshmanaprabu, S., Shankar, K., Singh, A.K., Wu, W.: Effective features to classify ovarian cancer data in Internet of medical things. Comput. Netw. **159**, 147–156 (2019)
13. Gordon, W.J., Catalini, C.: Blockchain technology for healthcare: facilitating the transition to patient-driven interoperability. Comput. Struct. Biotechn. J. **16**, 224–230 (2018)
14. Lamonaca, F., et al.: An overview on Internet of medical things in blood pressure monitoring. In: IEEE International Symposium on Medical Measurements and Applications (MeMeA), pp. 1–6. IEEE (2019)
15. Magsi, H., Sodhro, A.H., Chachar, F.A., Abro, S.A.K., Sodhro, G.H., Pirbhulal, S.: Evolution of 5g in Internet of medical things. In: 2018 International Conference on Computing, Mathematics and Engineering Technologies (iCoMET), pp. 1–7. IEEE (2018)

16. Mizera, M., Nowotarski, P., Byrski, A., Kisiel-Dorohinicki, M.: Fine tuning of agent-based evolutionary computing. J. Artif. Intell. Soft Comput. Res. **9**(2), 81–97 (2019)
17. Suganthi, M.V., Elavarasi, M.K., Jayachitra, M.J.: Tele-health monitoring system in a rural community through primary health center using Internet of medical things. Int. J. Pure Appl. Math. **119**(14), 695–703 (2018)
18. Tang, H., Shi, Y., Dong, P.: Public blockchain evaluation using entropy and TOPSIS. Expert Syst. Appl. **117**, 204–210 (2019)
19. Tschandl, P., Rosendahl, C., Kittler, H.: The ham10000 dataset, a large collection of multi-source dermatoscopic images of common pigmented skin lesions. Sci. Data **5**, 180161 (2018)
20. Walczak, S., Velanovich, V.: Improving prognosis and reducing decision regret for pancreatic cancer treatment using artificial neural networks. Decis. Support Syst. **106**, 110–118 (2018)
21. Winnicka, A., Kesik, K.: Idea of using blockchain technique for choosing the best configuration of weights in neural networks. Algorithms **12**(8), 163 (2019)
22. Xu, G., Zhang, M., Zhu, H., Xu, J.: A 15-gene signature for prediction of colon cancer recurrence and prognosis based on SVM. Gene **604**, 33–40 (2017)
23. Xu, J., Wang, S., Bhargava, B., Yang, F.: A blockchain-enabled trustless crowd-intelligence ecosystem on mobile edge computing. IEEE Trans. Industr. Inf. **15**, 3538–3547 (2019)
24. Zhang, W., Yang, J., Su, H., Kumar, M., Mao, Y.: Medical data fusion algorithm based on Internet of Things. Pers. Ubiquit. Comput. **22**(5–6), 895–902 (2018). https://doi.org/10.1007/s00779-018-1173-y

Automatic Visual Quality Assessment of Biscuits Using Machine Learning

Mardlla de Sousa Silva[1] (ID), Luigi Freitas Cruz[1] (ID), Pedro Henrique Bugatti[1] (ID), and Priscila Tiemi Maeda Saito[1,2(✉)] (ID)

[1] Department of Computing, Federal University of Technology - Paraná, Cornélio Procópio, Curitiba, Brazil
{mardlla,luigicruz}@alunos.utfpr.edu.br
{pbugatti,psaito}@utfpr.edu.br
[2] Institute of Computing, University of Campinas, Campinas, Brazil

Abstract. Considering the great competition among industries, one of the main factors that make companies market leaders is the quality of their products. However, the techniques applied to quality control are often flawed or inefficient, due to the great dependence on the human factor, which leads to a tiresome process and highly susceptible to errors. Besides that, in the context of the industry 4.0 the use of technologies to improve the evaluation of these products becomes increasingly essential. Hence, this work aims to find the most appropriate automatic classification method of non-standard food products allowing its deployment in a real biscuit industry. To do so, we evaluate different image descriptors and classifiers, based on deep learning (end-to-end and deep features) and traditional techniques (handcrafted features). From the obtained results, we can see that the proposed methodology can provide more effective quality control for the company, reaching an accuracy of up to 99%. This testifies that it can avoid offering non-compliant products in the market, improving the credibility of the brand with the consumer, its profitability and consequently its competitiveness.

Keywords: Image classification · Computer vision · Machine learning · Deep learning · Food industry

1 Introduction

Nowadays, any manufacturing process aims to make use of the most effective machine/information technology, mainly taking advantage of machine learning methods. Hence, there is great potential for improvement of the production activity to provide higher quality products. From the increasingly automated production process, it becomes important to have a more efficient process of checking non-standard quality products to keep up with the advances and the speed of the large-scale production.

In the food industry, the bakery sector can be considered one of the most important [23]. It includes the production of biscuits, pasta and bread. However,

L. Rutkowski et al. (Eds.): ICAISC 2020, LNAI 12416, pp. 59–70, 2020.
https://doi.org/10.1007/978-3-030-61534-5_6

to keep the sector constantly growing, technological innovation is essential in the production process. The quality of what is produced becomes vital, because it is intrinsically linked to customers' satisfaction, which is the key to the success or failure of a company. Non-standard products (i.e. regarding color, size, texture or flavor) can generate consumer complaints [14]. Consumers disappointed with the quality of products can generate losses and compromise the competitiveness of the company.

The great problem is that many quality control procedures are performed through human analysis (e.g. visual analysis). The visual quality analysis performed by employees is inefficient and unfeasible, considering that a large number of products are produced daily in an industry.

In this context, automating the quality inspection processes to provide higher quality products may require technological investments and, consequently, it demands increased costs. In this sense, it is important to evaluate the most appropriate automatic learning strategies capable to providing good and reliable results.

Taking into account the described scenario, this work aims to learn descriptors and pattern classifiers, improving the classification and the quality control of biscuits in a real food industry. Hence, in summary, our contributions in this paper are twofold: (i) we introduced an approach based on transfer learning capable of better identifying biscuits corresponding (or not) to the standards required by the company; (ii) we performed an extensive comparison between handcrafted and deep features with several traditional supervised classifiers, and against end-to-end state-of-the-art convolutional neural network architectures.

2 Background

It is extremely important to automate the process of identifying products that do not meet the standards established by the company. In these cases, the use of computer vision techniques has presented significant results for the classification of products [5,9,19,22,27,28]. According to [22] one of the main problems, regarding to the biscuit classification in real time, refers to the high volume of computing at high speed, which requires high performance computing vision techniques. Although there are many papers in the literature related to food quality inspection [8,18,27], few of them can be used in high-speed product classification.

In [22,23,28] the authors analyze only one type of defect (e.g. detection of cracks) in a specific kind of biscuit (only one type). Differently, our work deals with not only the classification of different types of biscuits, but also with their standard or non-standard quality.

2.1 Image Description and Classification

Ideally, image descriptors should perform the extraction of relevant characteristics of a given image in a similar manner to a human observer. However, despite some advances, there is still much to be explored and improved, given the current knowledge regarding vision, cognition and human emotion.

Among the most used features to describe an image are those defined as primitive (low-level) derived from three fundamental elements of the image: distribution of intensities (colors), texture and shape.

Color-based features are widely used in numerous applications, due to low computational cost and invariance to operations such as rotations and translations. The color description is usually used to build a color histogram. In spite of presenting linear cost w.r.t. the number of *pixels*, histograms present reduced discrimination capacity and do not provide information about the spatial distribution of colors in an image.

Several proposals have been made to address such problem, including a combination of color and texture features. Unlike color, texture occurs over a certain region rather than a point (*pixel*). In addition, since it has a certain periodicity and scale, it can be described in terms of direction, roughness, contrast, among others. The shape-based features, although in general involve non-trivial processes (which can generate a higher computational cost), are also interesting when used in some application domains.

All the aforementioned image description processes (i.e. feature extraction) are based on the so-called handcrafted features (i.e. they are intrinsically bounded to the problem's context). Hence, they can present some generalization issues. To diminish such problem, nowadays, there is an expansion of image description methods based on deep learning architectures like convolutional neural networks (CNN) [21]. This kind of architecture is capable of learning the features regarding a problem through an hierarchical representation of features from low-level to high-level ones.

It can be used not only to generate "generic" visual features (deep features), but also to perform the classification step at the same process (end-to-end learning). However, the computational cost of such techniques (requiring great computational power and volume of data) can impairs their use in some real scenarios. There are different CNN architectures in the literature. For instance, ResNet [24] presents residual blocks to reduce the training time. It introduces a "shortcut" connection, which skips one or more layers. Another one is Inception-v3 [26] that applies the so-called bottlenecks' layers also trying to reduce the cost.

Besides the aforementioned possibilities of cost reduction, there is the transfer learning technique. Through this process we can reuse a CNN that was pretrained in a "generic" context (e.g. ImageNet dataset [29]) and apply it to solve a more specific problem. To do so, we just need to retrain a considerably smaller portion of the original architecture (e.g. dense layers) and freeze the remaining ones (e.g. convolutional layers).

3   Proposed Methodology

In this section, we present our proposed methodology for classification and quality control in a food industry focused on the production of biscuits. For this, it is important to obtain the best learning approaches for description and classification. Then, different feature extractors and classifiers should be analyzed both for i-) identification of biscuits corresponding (or not) to the standards required by the company (i.e. binary classification), and ii-) identification of different types of biscuits (i.e. multiclass classification). Figure 1 illustrates the pipeline of our proposed methodology.

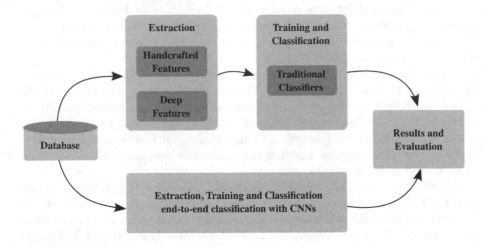

Fig. 1. Pipeline of the proposed methodology.

Initially, we obtained the image database from a production line in an industry. After organizing the datasets (see description in Sect. 4.1), there are two main flows. Through the first flow, it is possible to perform the extraction of (handcrafted and deep) features, using the traditional and the CNN architectures, respectively. Considering the deep features, we can obtain them from a given layer (generally the last dense layer) or fine-tune the pre-trained CNN model to work with a new domain. Different CNN architectures can be used. In this case, we applied the transfer learning technique and used the pre-trained models, which generally were trained on a bigger dataset from a general domain (i.e. not related to biscuits). We considered the learned weights (i.e. trainable parameters) from the CNNs as deep features. Therefore, these (handcrafted and deep) extracted features can be evaluated by the traditional classifiers.

Regarding the second flow, in the fine-tuning step, we evaluated the end-to-end classification process. In this case, we retrain the fully connected layer and replace the final classification layer (e.g. softmax) to output the correct number of probabilities, according to our dataset.

Afterwards, our methodology enables performing analyses between different types of extractors and classifiers, and evaluating the more appropriate setting (pair extractor/classifier) to the classification of biscuits. Algorithm 1 presents details of our methodology.

Algorithm 1: Proposed methodology

---

    input   : image dataset $\mathcal{D}$
    output   : best learning model M^Ω obtained through maximum accuracies
    auxiliaries: E: set of feature extractors; H: set of pre-trained CNN
            architectures; Feats: hand-crafted and deep feature sets; TrainSets
            and TestSets: training and test sets; perTrain and perTest:
            percentages of the training and test sets; nsplits: number of splits;
            $\mathcal{C}$: set of traditional classifiers; ModelSets: learning model sets;
            AccSets: mean accuracies; TrainSetIds and TestSetIds: identifiers of
            the training and testing samples from each split, $MeanAcc^\Omega$:
            maximum accuracies.

 1 HandCraftedFeatures $\leftarrow$ getHCFeatures($\mathcal{D}$, E);
 2 DeepFeatures $\leftarrow$ getDeepFeatures($\mathcal{D}$, H);
 3 Feats $\leftarrow$ HandCraftedFeatures $\bigcup$ DeepFeatures;
 4 **for** *each $i \in$ Feats$_i$, $i = 1, ..., nf$* **do**
 5   TrainSets$_i$, TestSets$_i$ $\leftarrow$ stratifiedSplits(Feats$_i$, perTrain, perTest, nsplits);
 6   **for** *each $j \in \mathcal{C}_j$* **do**
 7   ModelSets$_{ij}$ $\leftarrow$ generateModels(TrainSets$_i$, $\mathcal{C}_j$);
 8   AccSets$_{ij}$ $\leftarrow$ testModels(TestSets$_i$, ModelSets$_{ij}$);
 9   **end**
10 **end**
11 **for** *each $i \in H_i$, $i = 1, ..., nh$* **do**
12   AccSets $\leftarrow$ AccSets $\bigcup$ end2end(TrainSetIds, TestSetIds, H$_i$);
13 **end**
14 MeanAcc$^\Omega$ $\leftarrow$ findMaxAcc(AccSets);

---

4 Experiments

4.1 Dataset Description

The initial stage of this work was to build the image dataset. To do so, we chose different types of biscuits (e.g. strawberry, vanilla, among others) presenting standard and non-standard quality according to the factory policy. The dataset was divided into 8 classes, regarding each biscuit flavor and its quality level (standard or non-standard). We collected $1,000$ samples for each class, composing a set of $8,000$ samples for the experiment. All samples were preprocessed changing the background of the image from white to blue background, which simulates the color of the treadmill used in the manufacturing process. Table 1 shows each image class and its respective description and number of samples.

    Employees of the production line were needed to collect these biscuits, since it is not possible to frequently visit the production line by unauthorized people. The employees collected the samples once a week, because the biscuits are produced on demand. Thus, a given type of biscuit are not produced every day. The image acquisition was performed using an 8 megapixel camera with a resolution of 3264×2448 pixels Full HD (1920×1080 pixels) with 60 fps. Figure 2 shows

image examples of the dataset's classes (each type of biscuit and its quality level
- standard and non-standard).

Table 1. Description of the biscuit dataset.

Class	Description	Total
C_1	Standard Vanilla	1000
C_2	Non-standard Vanilla	1000
C_3	Standard Chocolate	1000
C_4	Non-standard Chocolate	1000
C_5	Standard Candy	1000
C_6	Non-standard Candy	1000
C_7	Standard Strawberry	1000
C_8	Non-standard Strawberry	1000

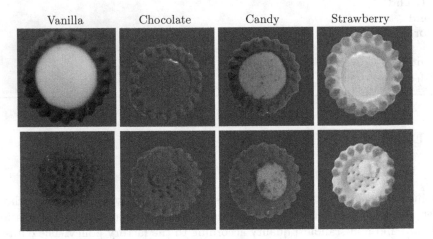

Fig. 2. Biscuit samples from each class. Upper images correspond to standard samples
and lower images refer to non-standard samples.

4.2   Scenarios

To perform the experiments we extracted handcrafted features using traditional
image descriptors and deep features from two different state-of-the-art CNN
architectures, called Inception-v3 [2,26] and Resnet-v2 [24]. We applied the
transfer learning technique for both of them (pre-trained on ImageNet dataset
[29]). This provides a considerable reduction of data and training cost. We used

Table 2. Description of the extractors of handcrafted and deep features.

Extractor	Category	Features
ACC [13]	Color	768
BIC [3]	Color	128
CEDD [7]	Color	144
FCTH [6]	Color and Texture	192
Gabor [30]	Texture	60
GCH [32]	Color	255
Haralick [20]	Texture	14
JCD [17]	Color and Texture	336
LBP [12]	Texture	256
LCH [32]	Color	135
Moments [30]	Texture	4
MPO [10]	Texture	6
MPOC [10]	Texture	18
PHOG [33]	Texture	40
RCS [31]	Color	77
Tamura [15]	Texture	18
Inception-v3 [29]	Generic	2048
ResNet-v2 [24]	Generic	1536

both architectures not only to extract deep features from our image dataset, but also to perform the end-to-end process (retraining just the dense layers and freezing the others). Table 2 shows the traditional extractors that we used, with their respective types (e.g. color, texture, generic) and number of features.

Moreover, we used different traditional supervised classifiers considering each type of features (handcrafted and deep ones), and compared them against the end-to-end process with transfer learning. To the evaluation process we used the hold-out protocol. To do so, we split our dataset into 80% for training and 20% for testing. We generated 10 stratified splits. Regarding the traditional supervised classifiers we used k-NN [25], J48 [1], RF [4] and SVM [11], all of them with their default literature parameters.

Considering the Inception-v3 and ResNet-v2 architectures, as required by them, the images were resized to 299 × 299 pixels. Both were trained using 50 epochs, and we used a batch size of 32 samples, an initial learning rate of 10^{-4}, a learning rate decay factor equal to 0.7, a number of epochs before decay of 2, and the Adam optimizer [16].

4.3 Results

Table 2 shows the results obtained by each combination of feature extractor and traditional classifiers. From the results, it is possible to observe and obtain the

Table 3. Mean accuracies ± standard deviation presented by descriptors and classifiers.

	k-NN	J48	RF	SVM
ACC	**98.75 ± 0.40**[*]	97.56 ± 0.58	**99.03 ± 0.37**[*]	85.28 ± 1.09
BIC	**98.88 ± 0.42**[*]	97.83 ± 0.60	**99.33 ± 0.28**[*]	85.47 ± 2.24
CEDD	**97.84 ± 0.55**	96.08 ± 0.70	**98.69 ± 0.37**[*]	90.81 ± 0.96
FCTH	**96.43 ± 0.55**	94.29 ± 0.74	**96.66 ± 0.51**	85.67 ± 1.03
Gabor	**96.33 ± 0.67**	90.70 ± 2.00	**96.21 ± 0.58**	66.82 ± 1.26
GCH	**99.08 ± 0.38**[*]	97.59 ± 0.56	**99.20 ± 0.34**[*]	84.66 ± 2.55
Haralick	**96.56 ± 0.54**	94.43 ± 1.29	**96.97 ± 0.54**	52.41 ± 6.04
JCD	**98.23 ± 0.50**	96.70 ± 0.60	**99.07 ± 0.36**[*]	91.17 ± 0.95
LBP	**98.56 ± 0.44**[*]	95.36 ± 0.82	**98.10 ± 0.40**	98.20 ± 0.52
LCH	**98.95 ± 0.41**[*]	97.29 ± 0.61	**99.17 ± 0.35**[*]	**98.55 ± 0.40**[*]
Moments	95.04 ± 0.80	94.88 ± 0.90	**97.14 ± 0.62**	65.63 ± 4.17
MPO	**97.50 ± 0.57**	96.07 ± 0.69	**97.95 ± 0.54**	66.74 ± 4.46
MPOC	**98.23 ± 0.48**	96.72 ± 0.62	**98.40 ± 0.40**	82.91 ± 2.79
PHOG	93.45 ± 0.72	89.53 ± 0.96	**96.08 ± 0.61**	60.72 ± 1.35
RCS	**97.82 ± 0.53**	96.34 ± 0.67	**98.16 ± 0.52**	69.45 ± 1.23
Tamura	**96.50 ± 0.67**	94.73 ± 0.67	**97.28 ± 0.47**	78.75 ± 1.49
Inception-v3	**98.92 ± 0.38**[*]	96.92 ± 0.68	**99.04 ± 0.40**[*]	**99.24 ± 0.34**[*]
Resnet-v2	**98.65 ± 0.41**[*]	96.12 ± 0.65	**98.84 ± 0.37**[*]	**99.09 ± 0.36**[*]

best feature extractor for each classifier (see underlined values, Table 3). For example, using the k-NN classifier, the most appropriate extractors were ACC, BIC, GCH, LBP, LCH, Inception-v3 and Resnet-v2. LCH and Inception-v3 were the best extractors for all classifiers.

Analyzing each extractor, the most suitable classifiers (bold values) were RF, k-NN and SVM. The RF classifier presented the best accuracies for all feature extractors. It is also possible to observe the best combinations (extractor and classifier pairs) through the highest accuracy results (highlighted by an asterisk).

The best combinations were ACC using k-NN and RF; BIC using k-NN and RF; CEDD using RF; GCH using k-NN and RF; JCD using RF; LBP using k-NN; LCH using k-NN, RF and SVM; Inception-v3 using k-NN, RF and SVM; Resnet-v2 using k-NN, RF and SVM. Such pairs have equivalent results in terms of accuracy. However, analyzing the dimensionality of the feature vectors, we can see that the best pairs would be BIC with kNN and BIC with RF. The BIC extractor enables to obtain high (or equivalent) accuracies with a smaller number of features than the others.

We also compared the best result obtained by (handcrafted or deep) features combined with traditional classifiers, against the results achieved by the end-to-end classification process. Regarding the traditional classifiers, the best accuracy was up to 99.33% obtained by the BIC extractor with the RF classifier (see Table 3). The end-to-end classification processes reached accuracies of 99.89%

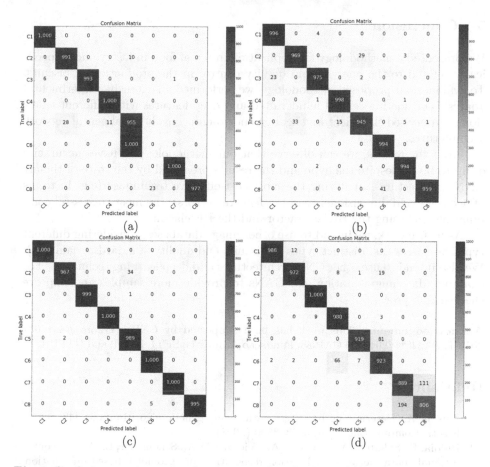

Fig. 3. Confusion matrices using the extractor-classifier pairs: (a) GCH-k-NN, (b) BIC-J48, (c) BIC-RF, (d) Inception-v3-SVM.

and 99.71% by the Inception-v3 and Resnet-v2, respectively. However, they are more costly because they have to learn a higher number of weights.

Analyzing the confusion matrices (Figs. 3(a)–(d)), it is possible to note that all pairs (descriptor/classifier) presented good behavior. The confusion matrix using the BIC extractor and the RF classifier (see Fig. 3(c)) shows one of the best results. There is still some confusion between classes C_2 (Non-standard Vanilla) and C_5 (Standard Candy) as presented by the other matrices, but in overall its accuracy is more robust (i.e. higher concentration of values in the main diagonal of the matrix). For instance, Fig. 3(a) (pair GCH/k-NN) predicted wrong all samples from the C_6 class (i.e. Non-standard Candy, labeling them as class C_5 – Standard Candy). Other matrices like the one illustrated in Fig. 3(d) presented confusion between classes ($trueLabel - predictedLabel$), such as: C_7-C_8, C_5-C_6, C_6-C_4. However, these were minor misclassifications (i.e. few samples among one thousand) and we were capable of obtaining good accuracies.

5   Conclusion

We presented a methodology for application in a real food industry, more specifically related to the analysis and quality control in the production of biscuits. To evaluate our proposed methodology, we performed an extensive experimental analysis considering several handcrafted and deep features with different traditional supervised classifiers, and against end-to-end convolutional neural network architectures.

From the results, we can observe that our methodology achieves accuracies of up to 99%. Despite the hype and the results presented by the state-of-the-art CNN architectures, analyzing the most cost-effective techniques (e.g. in terms of accuracy and dimensionality of the feature vectors), the most successful combination was using the BIC extractor and the RF classifier.

As future work, we intend to use other image databases, considering different types of classes (i.e. distinct types of biscuits and quality standards - damages). We also intend to use other CNN architectures and deep learning techniques. For example, data augmentation and GANs to provide more samples and improve the learning process.

Acknowledgements. This work has been supported by CNPq (grants #431668/2016-7, #422811/2016-5); CAPES; Fundação Araucária; SETI; PPGI; and UTFPR.

References

1. Arwan, A.: Determining basis test paths using genetic algorithm and J48. Int. J. Electr. Comput. Eng. **8**(5), 3333–3340 (2018)
2. Bidoia, F., Sabatelli, M., Shantia, A., Wiering, M.A., Schomaker, L.: A deep convolutional neural network for location recognition and geometry based information. In: Proceedings of the 7th International Conference on Pattern Recognition Applications and Methods, pp. 27–36. SciTePress (2018)
3. Biship, C.M.: Pattern Recognition and Machine Learning (Information Science and Statistics), 1st edn. Springer, New York (2007)
4. Breiman, L.: Random forests. Mach. Learn. **45**(1), 5–32 (2001). https://doi.org/10.1023/a:1010933404324
5. Brosnan, T., Sun, D.-W.: Improving quality inspection of food products by computer vision-a review. J. Food Eng. **61**(1), 3–16 (2004)
6. Chatzichristofis, S.A., Boutalis, Y.S.: Fcth: fuzzy color and texture histogram - a low level feature for accurate image retrieval. In: 9th International Workshop on Image Analysis for Multimedia Interactive Services, pp. 191–196 (2008)
7. Chatzichristofis, S.A., Boutalis, Y.S.: CEDD: color and edge directivity descriptor: a compact descriptor for image indexing and retrieval. In: Gasteratos, A., Vincze, M., Tsotsos, J.K. (eds.) ICVS 2008. LNCS, vol. 5008, pp. 312–322. Springer, Heidelberg (2008). https://doi.org/10.1007/978-3-540-79547-6_30
8. Cubeddu, A., Rauh, C., Delgado, A.: Hybrid artificial neural network for prediction and control of process variables in food extrusion. Innov. Food Sci. Emerg. Technol. **21**, 142–150 (2014)

9. Davidson, V.J., Ryks, J., Chu, T.: Fuzzy models to predict consumer ratings for biscuits based on digital image features. IEEE Trans. Fuzzy Syst. **9**(1), 62–67 (2001)
10. Gunaydin, H.: Probabilistic approach to generating MPOs and its application as a scoring function for CNS drugs. ACS Medicinal Chem. Lett. **7**(1), 89–93 (2016)
11. He, Z., Xia, K., Niu, W., Aslam, N., Hou, J.: Semisupervised SVM based on cuckoo search algorithm and its application. Math. Probl. Eng. **1–13**, 2018 (2018)
12. Huang, D., Shan, C., Ardabilian, M., Wang, Y., Chen, L.: Local binary patterns and its application to facial image analysis: a survey. IEEE Trans. Syst. Man Part C (Appl. Rev.) **41**(6), 765–781 (2011)
13. Huang, J., Kumar, S.R., Mitra, M., Zhu, W.J., Zabih, R.: Image indexing using color correlograms. In: IEEE Conference on Computer Vision and Pattern Recognition, pp. 762–768 (1997)
14. Juran, J.M.: Juran's Quality Control Handbook, 4th edn. Mcgraw-Hill, New York (1974)
15. Karmakar, P., Teng, S.W., Zhang, D., Liu, Y., Lu, G.: Improved tamura features for image classification using kernel based descriptors. In: International Conference on Digital Image Computing: Techniques and Applications, pp. 1–7 (2017)
16. Kingma, D.P., Ba, J.: Adam: a method for stochastic optimization. In: International Conference on Learning Representations, pp. 1–15 (2015)
17. Kumar, P.P., Aparna, D.K., Rao, K.V.: Compact descriptors for accurate image indexing and retrieval:fcth and cedd. Int. J. Eng. Res. Technol. (IJERT) **1**, 10 (2012)
18. Lemanzyk, T., Anding, K., Linss, G., Hernández, J.R., Theska, R.: Food safety by using machine learning for automatic classification of seeds of the South-American incanut plant. J. Phys: Conf. Ser. **588**, 012036 (2015)
19. Lu, Y.: Food image recognition by using convolutional neural networks (CNNs). CoRR, abs/1612.00983 (2016)
20. Löfstedt, T., Brynolfsson, P., Asklund, T., Nyholm, T., Garpebring, A.: Gray-level invariant haralick texture features. PLoS ONE **14**(2), 1–18 (2019)
21. Mosavi, A.: Deep learning: a review. Adv. Intell. Syst. Comput. **1**, 11 (2017)
22. Nashat, S., Abdullah, A., Abdullah, M.Z.: Machine vision for crack inspection of biscuits featuring pyramid detection scheme. J. Food Eng. **120**, 233–247 (2014)
23. Nashat, S., Abdullah, A., Aramvith, S., Abdullah, M.Z.: Support vector machine approach to real-time inspection of biscuits on moving conveyor belt. Comput. Electron. Agric. **75**(1), 147–155 (2011)
24. Nguyen, L.D., Lin, D., Lin, Z., Cao, J.: Deep CNNs for microscopic image classification by exploiting transfer learning and feature concatenation. In: IEEE International Symposium on Circuits and Systems, pp. 1–5 (2018)
25. Rani, P., Vashishtha, J.: An appraise of KNN to the perfection. Int. J. Comput. Appl. **170**(2), 13–17 (2017)
26. Wahed, R.B.: Comparative analysis between inception-v3 and other learning systems using facial expressions detection. In: Department of Computer Science & Engineering BRAC UNIVERSITY, p. 35 (2016)
27. Sivakumar, B., Srilatha, K.: A survey on computer vision technology for food quality evaluation. Res. J. Pharm. Biol. Chem. Sci. **7**, 365–373 (2016)
28. Srivastava, S., Boyat, S., Sadistap, S.: A robust machine vision algorithm development for quality parameters extraction of circular biscuits and cookies digital images. J. Food Process. **2014**, 13 (2014)
29. Szegedy, C., Vanhoucke, V., Ioffe, S., Shlens, J., Wojna, Z.: Rethinking the inception architecture for computer vision. CoRR, abs/1512.00567 (2015)

30. Vinayak, V., Jindal, S.: CBIR system using color moment and color auto-correlogram with block truncation coding. Int. J. Comput. Appl. **161**(9), 1–7 (2017)
31. Wang, J., Zhang, P., Zhang, X., Luo, L.: Evaluation of color similarity descriptors for human action recognition. In: International Conference on Internet Multimedia Computing and Service, pp. 197–200. ACM (2014)
32. Wang, S.: A Robust CBIR Approach Using Local Color Histograms [microform]. Thesis (M.Sc.)-University of Alberta (2001)
33. Zhang, H., Sha, Z.: Product classification based on SVM and PHOG descriptor. Int. J. Comput. Sci. Netw. Secur. **13**, 4 (2013)

Classifying Image Series with a Reoccurring Concept Drift Using a Markov Chain Predictor as a Feedback

Magda Skoczeń[ID], Wojciech Rafajłowicz[ID], and Ewaryst Rafajłowicz[(✉)][ID]

Faculty of Electronics, Wrocław University of Science and Technology,
Wrocław, Poland
{magda.skoczen,wojciech.rafajlowicz,ewaryst.rafajlowicz}@pwr.edu.pl

Abstract. We consider the problem of classifying images, ordered in a sequence (series), to several classes. A distinguishing feature of this problem is the presence of a slowly varying, reoccurring concept drift which results in the existence of relatively long subsequences of similar images from the same class. It seems useful to incorporate this knowledge into a classifier. To this end, we propose a novel idea of constructing a Markov chain (MC) that predicts a class label for the next image to be recognized. Then, the feedback is used in order to modify slightly a priori probabilities of class memberships. In particular, the a priori probability of the class predicted by the MC is increased at the expense of decreasing the a priori probabilities of other classes.

The idea of applying an MC predictor of classes with the feedback to a priori probabilities is rather general. Thus, it can be applied not only to images but also to vectors of features arising in other applications. Additionally, this idea can be combined with any classifier that is able to take into account a priori probabilities. We provide an analysis when this approach leads to the reduction of the classification errors in comparison to classifying each image separately.

As a vehicle to elucidate the idea we selected a recently proposed classifier (see [23, 25]) that is based on assuming matrix normal distribution (MND) of classes. We use a specific structure of the MND's covariance matrix that can be estimated directly from images without feature extraction.

The proposed approach was tested on simulated images as well as on an example of the sequence of images from an industrial gas burner's flames. The aim of the classification is to decide whether natural gas contains a sufficient amount of methane (the combustion process is proper, lower air pollution) or not.

Keywords: Classification of ordered images · Reoccurring concept drift · Generalized matrix normal distribution · Classifier with feedback · Markov chain predictor

© Springer Nature Switzerland AG 2020
L. Rutkowski et al. (Eds.): ICAISC 2020, LNAI 12416, pp. 71–84, 2020.
https://doi.org/10.1007/978-3-030-61534-5_7

1 Introduction

A large number of examples can be pointed out when images should be considered as a series (i.e., a sequence of images that are ordered in time). This is of particular importance when we want to observe and classify selected features over time. We assume that the features of interest can fluctuate over a long time intervals without changing their class membership of subsequent images. At unknown time instants, the observed features can change (abruptly or gradually), leading to the change of their classification for a longer period. Then, the next parts of the series can return to previously visited class memberships. We shall name such sequences *image series with a slow reoccurring concept drift*. The assumption that we are faced with an image series with a slow reoccurring concept drift is crucial for this paper. The reason is that we can use this fact in order to increase the classification accuracy by predicting a class label of the next image and incorporating this a priori knowledge into a classifier.

The following examples of such image series can be pointed out.

- Quality control of manufacturing processes monitored by cameras. The following two cases can be distinguished:
  1. Separate items are produced and classified as proper or improper (conforming to requirements or not). One can expect long sequences of conforming items and shorter sequences of non-conforming ones.
  2. Production is running continuously in time (e.g., molding and rolling of copper, other metals or steel alloys). Here also slow changes of the quality can be expected, while the proper classification of a product is crucial for economic efficiency.
- Combustion processes monitored by a camera (see [20, 29] and the bibliography cited therein).
- Automated Guided Vehicles (AGV) are more and more frequently monitored by cameras and/or other sensors. Most of the time they operate in an environment which is well defined and built-in into their algorithms, but sometimes it happens that they meet other AVG's or other obstacles to be recognized.

For simplicity of the exposition we impose the following constraints on an image series:

- it is not required that class labels of subsequent images strictly form a Markov chain (MC), but if it is possible to indicate the corresponding MC, then the proposed classification algorithm has a stronger theoretical justification,
- images are represented as matrices, i.e., only their grey levels are considered,
- an image series has slow reoccurring concept drift in the sense explained above,
- the probability density functions (p.d.f.'s) of images in each class have covariance structures similar to that of matrix normal distributions (MND's).

The last assumption will be stated more formally later. We usually do not have enough learning images to estimate the full covariance matrix of large images. An alternative approach, that is based projections is proposed in [26].

The paper is organized as follows:

- in the section that follows we provide a short review of the previous works,
- in Sect. 3, we state the problem more precisely,
- in the next sections, we provide a skeletal algorithm, then its exemplifications and the results of testing are discussed.
- an example of classifying flames of an industrial gas burner is discussed in the section before last.

Notice that we place an emphasis on classifying images forming a time series, but avoiding a tedious (and costly) features extraction step (an image is considered as an entity).

2 Previous Work

We start from papers on the bayesian classifiers that arise in cases when the assumption that class densities have the MND distribution holds. This assumption will be essentially weakened in this paper, but it cannot be completely ignored when one wants to avoid the feature extraction step without having millions of training and testing images.

Then, we briefly discuss classic papers on classifying images when their class labels form a Markov chain. We also indicate the differences in using this information in classic papers and here.

As mentioned in [25], "The role of multivariate normal distributions with the Kronecker product structure of the covariance matrix for deriving classifiers was appreciated in [15], where earlier results are cited. In this paper the motivation for assuming the Kronecker product structure comes from repeated observations of the same object to be classified."

It was also documented in [22,23] and [24] that the classifier based on the MND's assumption is sufficiently efficient for classifying images without features extraction. Furthermore, in [25] it was documented that an extended version of such classifiers is useful for recognizing image sequences, considered as whole entities.

The second ingredient that is used in the present paper is a Markov chain based predictor of class labels, which is used as feedback between the classifier output and a priori class probabilities for classifying the next image in a sequence. This idea was proposed by the first author (see Fig. 1 for a schematic view of the overall system).

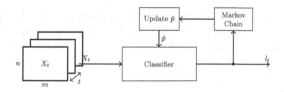

Fig. 1. A general scheme of classifying an image series.

The idea of using the assumption that class labels form a Markov structure has a long history [13] and its usefulness is appreciated up to now (see, e.g., [14,28]). In these and many other papers, the Markov chain assumption was used in order to improve the classification accuracy of a present pattern using its links to the previous one. Here, we use a Markov chain differently, namely, it serves in the feedback as a predictor of the next class label.

A recurrence in neural networks has reappeared several times. A well-known class is Elman networks (see the original paper [9] and [4] for a learning process of Elman's networks which is so laborious that it requires parallel computing tools). In Elman's networks, an input vector is extended by stacking values of all the outputs from the previous iteration.

Hopfield neural networks (HNN) have even a more complicated structure. Their learning is also rather laborious, since after presenting an input vector the HNN internally iterates many times until a stable output is attained. We refer the reader to [18] for the description of the HNN that is dedicated to change detection between two images and to [2] for the HNN designed to classify temporal trajectories.

In the context of Elman's and Hopfield's nets, our feedback can be called weak, for the following reasons:

1. only limited information (class labels) is transmitted back to the recognizer,
2. the transmission is done once per image to be recognized (there are no inner loop iterations),
3. feedback information does not influence an input image, but provides only an outer context for its classification, by modifying a priori class probabilities.

The problem of dealing with reoccurring concept drift has been intensively studied in recent years. We refer the reader to [8,10] and the bibliography cited therein. We adopt the following definition from [8]: "We say that the changes are reoccurring if we know that the concept can appear and disappear many times during processing the stream." We agree also with the following opinion: "Many methods designed to deal with concept-drift show unsatisfactory results in this case [3]."

Our approach can also be used for data streams, but after a learning phase that is based on long historical sequences of images. We shall not emphasise this aspect here. We refer the reader to [12] for the recent survey paper on learning for data stream analysis.

3   Problem Statement

In this section, we first recall the pattern recognition problem for matrices in the Bayesian setting. Then, we specify additional assumptions concerning a series of images and reoccurring concept drift.

3.1   Classic Bayesian Classification Problem for Random Matrices

A sequence of ordered images $\mathbf{X}_k$, $k = 1, 2, \ldots, K$ is observed one by one. Grey level images are represented by $m \times n$ real-valued[1] matrices.

Each image $\mathbf{X}_k$, $k = 1, 2, \ldots, K$ can be classified to one of $J > 1$ classes, labeled as $j = 1, 2, \ldots, J$. The following assumptions apply to all J classes.

As 1) Each $\mathbf{X}_k$ is a random matrix, which was drawn according to one of the probability density functions (p.d.f.'s), denoted further by $f_j(\mathbf{X})$, $j = 1, 2, \ldots, J$, of the $m \times n$ matrix argument $\mathbf{X}$

As 2) Random matrices $\mathbf{X}_k$, $k = 1, 2, \ldots, K$ are mutually independent (this does not exclude stochastic dependencies between elements of matrix $\mathbf{X}_k$).

As 3) Each matrix $\mathbf{X}_k$ is associated with class label $j_k \in \mathcal{J}$, $k = 1, 2, \ldots, K$, where $\mathcal{J} \overset{def}{=} \{j : 1 \leq j \leq J\}$.

Labels j_k's are random variables, but – as opposed to the classic problem statement – they are not required to be mutually independent. When new matrix (image) $\mathbf{X}_0$ has to be classified to one of the classes from $\mathcal{J}$, then the corresponding label j_0 is not known. On the other hand, when ordered pairs $(\mathbf{X}_k, j_k)$, $k = 1, 2, \ldots, K$ are considered as a learning sequence, then both images $\mathbf{X}_k$'s and the corresponding labels j_k's are assumed to be known exactly, which means that a teacher (an expert) properly classified images $\mathbf{X}_k$'s.

As 4) We assume that for each class there exists a priori probability $p_j > 0$ that $\mathbf{X}$ and $\mathbf{X}_k$'s were drawn from this class. Clearly $\sum_{j=1}^{J} p_j = 1$. Notice that here a priori probabilities are interpreted in the classic way, namely, as the probabilities drawing some of $\mathbf{X}_k$'s from j-th class. In other words, in specifying p_j's we do not take into account the fact that $\mathbf{X}_k$'s form an image series with possible concept drift. Later, we modify this assumption appropriately.

As 5) **(optional)** In some parts of the paper we shall additionally assume that class densities $f_j(\mathbf{X})$'s have matrix normal distributions $\mathcal{N}_{n,m}(\mathbf{M}_j, U_j, V_j)$, i.e., with the expectation matrices $\mathbf{M}_j$ and U_j as $n \times n$ inter-rows covariance matrices and V_j as an $m \times m$ covariance matrix between columns, respectively. We refer the reader to [23] and the bibliography cited therein for the definition and basic properties of MND's.

It is well-known (see, e.g., [7]) that for the 0–1 loss function the Bayes risk of classifying $\mathbf{X}$ is minimized by the following classification rule:

$$j^* = \arg \max_{1 \leq j \leq J} p_j f_j(\mathbf{X}), \tag{1}$$

since a posteriori probabilities $P(j|\mathbf{X})$ of $\mathbf{X}$ being from class $j \in \mathcal{J}$ are proportional to $p_j f_j(\mathbf{X})$, $j \in \mathcal{J}$ for each fixed $\mathbf{X}$.

In [23] particular cases of (1) were derived under assumption As 5).

---

[1] In implementations, grey levels are represented by integers from the range 0 to 255, but for theoretical considerations we consider them to be real numbers.

3.2 Classification of Images in a Series

Consider a discrete-time and discrete states Markov chain (MC) that is represented by $J \times J$ matrix $\mathcal{P}$ with elements $p_{jj'} \geq 0$, $j, j' \in \mathcal{J}$, where $p_{jj'}$ is interpreted as the probability that the chain at state j moves to state j' at the next step. States of the MC are further interpreted as labels attached to $\mathbf{X}$'s. Clearly, $\mathcal{P}$ must be such that $\sum_{j' \in \mathcal{J}} p_{jj'} = 1$ for each $j \in \mathcal{J}$. Additionally, the MC is equipped with column vector $\bar{q}_0 \in R^J$ with nonnegative elements that sum up to 1. The elements of this vector are interpreted as the probabilities that the MC starts from one of the states from $\mathcal{J}$. According to the rules governing Markov chains, vectors $\bar{q}_k$ of the probabilities of the states in subsequent steps are given by $\bar{q}_k = \mathcal{P}\,\bar{q}_{k-1}$, $k = 1, 2, \ldots, K$. At each step k a particular state of the MC is drawn at random according to the probabilities in $\bar{q}_k$.

As 6) Class labels j_k in series of images $(\mathbf{X}_k, j_k)$, $k = 1, 2, \ldots, K$ are generated according to the above described Markov chain scheme.

In order to assure that the MC $\mathcal{P}$ is able to model reoccurring concept drifts, represented by changes of j_k's, we impose the following requirements on $\mathcal{P}$:

As 7) The MC $\mathcal{P}$ possesses the following properties: all the states are communicating and recurrent, the MC is irreducible and aperiodic.

In the Introduction (see also the section before last) it was mentioned that our motivating example is the combustion process of natural gas, which can have slowly varying contents of methane modelled here as slowly varying, reoccurring concept drift. Similar concept drift changes can be observed in drinking water and the electricity supply networks in which concept drifts appear as changes of parameters of a supplied medium (e.g., the purity of water or the voltage of the current).

The ability of MC to generate long sequences of the same labels is guaranteed by the following assumption.

As 8) Transition matrix $\mathcal{P}$ of the MC has strongly dominating diagonal elements (by strong dominance we mean the diagonal elements are about 5–10 times larger than other entries of $\mathcal{P}$.

Mimicking decision rule (1) for images in a series, under assumptions A1)-A4) and A6)-A8), it is expedient to consider the following sequence of decision rules:

$$j_k^* = \arg \max_{1 \leq j' \leq J} \left[p_{j_{(k-1)}^* \, j'} \, f_{j'}(\mathbf{X}_k) \right], \quad k = 1, 2, \ldots, K, \tag{2}$$

where it is assumed that at step $(k-1)$ it was decided that j_{k-1}^* is the label maximizing the same expression (2), but at the previous step.

Under assumptions As 1) - As 4) and As 6) - As 8), our aim in this paper is the following:

1. having learning sequences of images: $(\hat{\mathbf{X}}_k, \hat{j}_k)$, $k = 1, 2, \ldots, \hat{K}$
2. and assuming proper classifications $\hat{j}_k$ to one of the classes
3. to construct an empirical classifier that is based on (2) decision rules.

and to test this rule on simulated and real data.

4   A General Idea of a Classifier with the MC Feedback

Decision rules (2) suggest the following empirical version of decision rules: $\mathbf{X}'_k$ is classified to class $\tilde{j}_k$ at k-th step if

$$\tilde{j}_k = \arg \max_{1 \leq j' \leq J} \left[\tilde{p}_{\tilde{j}_{(k-1)} j'} \, \hat{f}_{j'}(\mathbf{X}'_k) \right], \quad k = 1, 2, \ldots, K, \tag{3}$$

where $\tilde{j}_{(k-1)}$ is the class indicated at the previous step, while:

1. $\hat{f}_{j'}(\mathbf{X}_k)$, $j' \in \mathcal{J}$ are estimators of p.d.f.'s $f_{j'}(\mathbf{X}_k)$ that are based on the learning sequence.
2. $\tilde{p}_{\tilde{j}_{(k-1)} j'}$, $j' \in \mathcal{J}$ plays the role of the a priori class probabilities at k-th step. Possible ways of updating them are discussed below.

As estimators in 1) one can select either

– parametric families with estimated parameters (an example will be given in the next section),
– nonparametric estimators, e.g., from the Parzen-Rosenblat family or apply another nonparametric classifier that allows specifying a priori class probabilities, e.g., the support vector machine (SVM) in which class densities are not explicitly estimated (see an example in the section before last).

The key point of this paper is the way of incorporating the fact that we are dealing with an image series with a reoccurring concept drift into the decision process. As already mentioned (see Fig. 1), the idea of a decision process is to modify a priori class probabilities taking into account the result of classifying the previous image by giving preferences (but not a certainty) to the latter class.

This idea can be formalized in a number of ways. We provide two of them that were tested and reported in this paper.

Skeletal classifier for image series with the MC feedback

Step 0 Initial learning phase: select estimators $\hat{f}_{j'}(\mathbf{X})$, $j' \in \mathcal{J}$ and calculate them from the learning sequence, estimate the original a priori class probabilities $\tilde{p}^0_{j'}$, $j' \in \mathcal{J}$ as the frequencies of their occurrence in the learning sequence. Then, set

$$\tilde{p}_{\tilde{j}_0 j'} = \tilde{p}^0_{j'}, \quad \text{for all } j' \in \mathcal{J} \tag{4}$$

for the compatibility of the notations in further iterations, where for $k = 0$ we select $\tilde{j}_0 = \arg \max_{1 \leq j \leq J} [\tilde{p}^0_j]$ as the maximum a priori probability. Estimate transition matrix $\hat{P}$ of the MC from the labels of the learning sequence. Select $\gamma \in [0, 1]$ and $\Delta_p \in [0, 1)$ as parameters of the algorithm (see remarks after the algorithm for explanations). Set $k = 1$ and go to Step 1.

Step 1 Decision: acquire the next image in the series $\mathbf{X}'_k$ and classify it to class

$$\tilde{j}_k = \arg \max_{1 \le j' \le J} \left[\tilde{p}_{\tilde{j}_{(k-1)} \, j'} \, \hat{f}_{j'}(\mathbf{X}'_k) \right]. \tag{5}$$

Step 2 Prediction: run one step ahead of the MC $\hat{\mathcal{P}}$, starting from the initial state: $[0, 0, \ldots, \underbrace{1}_{\tilde{j}_k}, \ldots, 0, 0]$. Denote by $\check{j}_k$ the label resulting from this operation.

Step 3 Update the probabilities in (5) as follows:

$$\tilde{p}_{\tilde{j}_k \, j'} = \check{p}_{\tilde{j}_k \, j'} \bigg/ \sum_{j=1}^{J} \check{p}_{\tilde{j}_k \, j} \text{ for all } j' \in \mathcal{J}, \tag{6}$$

where $\check{p}_{\tilde{j}_k \, j'}$'s are defined as follows: if $j' \ne \check{j}_k$, then for all other $j' \in \mathcal{J}$

$$\check{p}_{\tilde{j}_k \, j'} = (1 - \gamma) \, \tilde{p}_{j'}^0 + \gamma \, \tilde{p}_{\tilde{j}_{(k-1)} \, j'}, \tag{7}$$

otherwise, i.e., for $j' = \check{j}_k$

$$\check{p}_{\tilde{j}_k \, j'} = (1 - \gamma) \, \tilde{p}_{j'}^0 + \gamma \, \tilde{p}_{\tilde{j}_{(k-1)} \, j'} + \Delta_p. \tag{8}$$

Step 4 If $\mathbf{X}'_k$ is not the last image in the series (or if $\mathbf{X}'_k$'s form a stream), then set $k := k + 1$ and go to Step 1, otherwise, stop.

The following remarks are in order.

1. In (7) and (8) parameter $\gamma \in [0, 1]$ influences the mixture of the original a priori information and information gathered during the classification of subsequent images from the series.
2. Parameter $\Delta_p \in [0, 1)$ is added only to the probability of the predicted class $\check{j}_k$ in order to increase its influence on the next decision. The necessary normalization is done in (6). In the example presented in the section before last the influence of Δ_p on the classification accuracy is investigated.

5   Classifying Series of Images Having Matrix Normal Distributions

In this section, we exemplify and test the skeletal algorithm when As 5) is in force. In more details, for $m \times n$ images (matrices) $\mathbf{X}$ class distributions have the MND's of the following form (see [17]):

$$f_j(\mathbf{X}) = \frac{1}{c_j} \exp\left[-\frac{1}{2} \text{tr}[U_j^{-1}(\mathbf{X} - \mathbf{M}_j) \, V_j^{-1} \, (\mathbf{X} - \mathbf{M}_j)^T] \right], \, j \in \mathcal{J}, \tag{9}$$

where it is assumed that $n \times n$ matrices U_j's and $m \times m$ matrices V_j's are assumed to be nonsingular, while $n \times m$ matrices $\mathbf{M}_j$'s denote the class means. The normalization constants c_j's are defined as follows:

$$c_j \overset{def}{=} (2\pi)^{0.5\,n\,m} \det[U_j]^{0.5\,n} \det[V_j]^{0.5\,m}, \; j \in \mathcal{J}. \tag{10}$$

As one can observe, (9) has a special structure of the covariance matrix, namely, U_j's are the covariance matrices between rows only, while V_j's between columns only, which makes it possible to estimate them from learning sequences of reasonable lengths. This is in contrast to a general case when the full covariance matrix would have $m\,n \times m\,n$ elements, which is formidable for estimation even for small images $m = n = 100$. We refer the reader to [16,27] for the method of estimating U_j's and V_j's from the learning sequence. Further on we denote these estimates by $\hat{U}_j$'s and $\hat{V}_j$'s, respectively. Analogously, we denote by $\hat{\mathbf{M}}_j$'s the estimates of the expectations of f_j's that are obtained as the mean values of the corresponding matrices from the learning sequence, taking into account, however, that the entries of $\mathbf{X}_k$'s are contained either in [0, 255] or [0 1], depending on the convention.

Matrix Classifier with a Markov Chain Feedback (MCLMCF)

Step 0: Select $0 < \kappa_{max} \leq 100$. Select $\Delta_p \in (0,1)$.

Step 1: Initial learning phase: estimate $\hat{\mathbf{M}}_j$, $\hat{U}_j$, $\hat{V}_j$, $\hat{c}_j$ for $j \in \mathcal{J}$ from a learning sequence. Select $c_{min} = min(\hat{c}_j)$, estimate the original a priori class probabilities $\tilde{p}_j^0$, $j \in \mathcal{J}$ as class occurrence frequencies in a learning sequence. Calculate $\check{j}_0 = max(\tilde{p}_j^0)$. Set $k = 1$. Estimate $\hat{\mathcal{P}}$ based on the learning sequence. If $\hat{\mathcal{P}}$ has an absorbing state then use MCL [23]), otherwise go to step 2.

Step 2: Verify whether the following conditions hold:

$$\frac{\lambda_{max}(\hat{U}_j)}{\lambda_{min}(\hat{U}_j)} < \kappa_{max}, j \in \mathcal{J} \quad \text{and} \quad \frac{\lambda_{max}(\hat{V}_j)}{\lambda_{min}(\hat{V}_j)} < \kappa_{max}, j \in \mathcal{J} \tag{11}$$

If so, go to step 3a, otherwise, go to step 4.

Step 3a: Classify new matrix $\mathbf{X}_k'$ to class, according to (12). Go to step 3b.

$$\check{j}_k = \text{argmin}_{0<j'\leq J} \left[\frac{1}{2} tr[\hat{U}_{j'}{}^{-1}(\mathbf{X}_k' - \hat{\mathbf{M}}_{j'})\hat{V}_{j'}{}^{-1}(\mathbf{X}_k' - \hat{\mathbf{M}}_{j'})^T] \right] \tag{12}$$

$$- \log(\tilde{p}_{\check{j}_{(k-1)}j'}/c_{min})$$

Step 3b: Update estimate of a priori probability $\tilde{p}$, using the following procedure:

(a) Select class $\check{j}$, according to probabilities in $\check{j}_k$ row of transition matrix $\hat{\mathcal{P}}$.

(b) Set $\tilde{p}_{\check{j}_k\check{j}} = \tilde{p}_{\check{j}_{(k-1)}\check{j}}$.

(c) For every $j' \neq \check{j}, j' \in \mathcal{J}$ check if $\tilde{p}_{\check{j}_{(k-1)}j'} - \frac{\Delta_p}{J-1} > 0$, if so then update $\tilde{p}_{\check{j}_kj'}$ and $\tilde{p}_{\check{j}_k\check{j}}$ according to (13), else $\tilde{p}_{\check{j}_kj'}$ and $\tilde{p}_{\check{j}_k\check{j}}$ remain unchanged.

$$\tilde{p}_{\tilde{j}_k j'} = \tilde{p}_{\tilde{j}_{(k-1)} j'} - \frac{\Delta_p}{J-1} \quad \text{and} \quad \tilde{p}_{\tilde{j}_k \tilde{j}} = \tilde{p}_{\tilde{j}_k \tilde{j}} + \frac{\Delta_p}{J-1} \tag{13}$$

Set $k = k + 1$. If $k \leq K$ then go to step 3a else stop.

Step 4: Classify new matrix $\mathbf{X}'_k$ according to the nearest mean rule. Add the current result $(\mathbf{X}'_k, \tilde{j}_k)$ to the training set, then update the estimates of $\tilde{p}_{j_0}$, $\hat{\mathbf{M}}_j$, $\hat{U}_j$, $\hat{V}_j$, $\hat{c}_j$ and select c_{min} for $j \in \mathcal{J}$ in the same manner, as described in step 1. Set $k = k + 1$. If $k \leq K$ then go to step 2, otherwise stop.

6   Experiments on Simulated Data

In this section, we present the results of experiments performed on simulated data for the evaluation of the proposed classifier performance. We generated 486 sequences, each consisting of 300 matrices. Matrices were randomly generated according to one of the three matrix normal distributions, which represents three classes. MNDs parameters are presented in Table 1, where J_8 is an 8×8 matrix of ones and D_8 is an 8×8 tridiagonal matrix with 2 at the main diagonal and 1 along the bands running above and below the main diagonal. The order of classes in the sequence was modeled by the MC with transition probability matrix $\mathcal{P}$ (see Eq. (14)). In the conducted experiments, the data were divided into a training and testing set in the following manner: the first 100 matrices of a sequence were used as a training set for classifiers, the remaining matrices were used as a test set. Then Gaussian noise with ($\sigma = 0.05$) was added to matrices in the test set.

Table 1. Parameters of MND for each class and transition matrix $\mathcal{P}$.

Class	M	U	V
1	$0.1J_8$	I_8	D_8
2	$0.2J_8$	D_8	I_8
3	$0.5J_8$	D_8	D_8

$$\mathcal{P} = \begin{bmatrix} 0.9 & 0.1 & 0 \\ 0.1 & 0.8 & 0.1 \\ 0 & 0.15 & 0.85 \end{bmatrix} \tag{14}$$

In order to analyze the impact of value of parameter Δ_p on the MCLMCF performance, we performed tests for $\Delta_p = [0.01, 0.02, 0.05, 0.1, 0.2, 0.5]$. Table 2, which presents the results obtained with the MCL and MCLMCF with different Δ_p parameter, reveals that increasing the value of Δ_p improves the classification performance of the MCLMCF. We can observe that the proposed classifier outperforms the MCL. We also analyzed the characteristics of sequences in the test set. We divided sequences into two groups: the first group (improved or the same) contains 411 sequences that were classified with higher or same accuracy with the use of MCLMCF with $\Delta_p = 0.5$, the second group (worse) comprises 75 sequences that were better classified with the MCL. Then we measured the

Table 2. Left panel – the results of the experiments for different values of Δ_p. Right panel – the lengths of homogeneous class sub-sequences in the test set.

Classifier	Mean acc	Var of acc
$\Delta_p = 0.5$	0.7757	0.0142
$\Delta_p = 0.2$	0.7627	0.0154
$\Delta_p = 0.01$	0.7237	0.0167
MCL	0.7212	0.0142
$\Delta_p = 0.1$	0.7190	0.0199
$\Delta_p = 0.05$	0.7165	0.0185
$\Delta_p = 0.02$	0.6913	0.0206

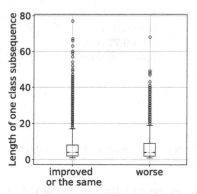

lengths of the homogeneous class subsequences (Table 2 - right panel). Our analysis shows that the proposed classifier performs better than MCL on sequences that contain long subsequences of the same class.

7   Case Study – Classifying an Image Series of Gas Burner Flames

The proposed approach was also tested on an image series of industrial gas burner flames. The contents of methane in natural gas fluctuate over longer periods of time, leading to proper, admissible or improper combustion that can be compensated by regulating the air rate supply. Thus, the contents of methane in the gas have all the features of the reoccurring concept drift. The mode of the combustion is easy to classify by an operator simply by visual inspection since the flame is either blue, blue and yellow, but still laminar or only yellow with a turbulent flow (see [19] and [20] for images and more details). It is however more difficult to derive an image classifier that works properly in heavy industrial conditions.

In order to test the Skeletal algorithm with the MC predictor, we selected the support vector machine (SVM) as the classifier in Step 1. The learning sequence consisted of 90 images in the series while the testing sequence length was 55. Having such a small testing sequence, we decided to extend it by adding 100 of its repetitions with the noise added (see [1] for the survey of methods of testing classifiers and to [11] for handling possibly missing data). The noise was rather heavy, namely, it was uniformly distributed in $[-0.25, 0.25]$ for grey level images represented in $[0, 1]$ interval.

In this study, we apply the estimated transition matrix shown in Fig. 2(left panel). Properties of the MC with matrix $\hat{\mathcal{P}}$ are listed in Table 3(right panel). Alternatively, one can consider the optimization of this matrix so as to attain better classification accuracy. This is however not such an easy task because we

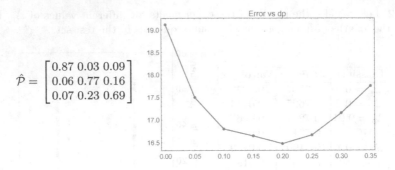

$$\hat{\mathcal{P}} = \begin{bmatrix} 0.87 & 0.03 & 0.09 \\ 0.06 & 0.77 & 0.16 \\ 0.07 & 0.23 & 0.69 \end{bmatrix}$$

Fig. 2. Left panel – estimated $\mathcal{P}$ matrix of the MC. Right panel – the classification error vs Δ_p.

Table 3. Left panel – the fraction of the mean occupation time (fMOT) for the labels of the learning system (2nd column) and for the states of MC $\mathcal{P}$ (3rd column) Right panel – basic properties of MC $\mathcal{P}$.

State	fMOT L.S.	fMOT MC $\mathcal{P}$
1	0.367	0.365
2	0.344	0.365
3	0.289	0.270

"Communicating", [1, 2, 3],
"RecurrentClasses", [1, 2, 3],
"Irreducible", True,
"Aperiodic", True

have to take into account many constraints (see [21] for a global search algorithm that is able to handle complicated constraints).

The mean occupation time (MOT) of the MC state is the number of discrete times (steps of the MC) that are spent by the MC in a given state. We apply this notion also to the labels of the learning sequence. By the fraction of the MOT (fMOT) we understand MOT's of the states divided by the length of the observations or the length of the learning sequence, respectively. The comparison of the second and the third columns of Table 3 shows a very good agreement of the fMOT's, which justifies the usage of our prediction model.

Then the Skeletal algorithm with $\gamma = 0.5$ and SVM as the basic classifier was run 100 times for Δ_p varying from 0 (i.e., there is no feedback from the MC predictor) to 0.35. As one can observe in Fig. 2 (right panel), for properly selected $\Delta_p = 0.2$ we can reduce the classification error by about 3 % in comparison to the case when the MC feedback is not applied. For long runs of industrial gas burners, the improvements of the decisions by 3 % may lead to essential savings. On the other hand, the same figure indicates the optimum is rather flat and selecting Δ_p in the range for 0.1 to 0.25 provides similar improvements.

8   Concluding Remarks

The problem of classifying a series of images with a reoccurring concept drift was considered. The class of algorithms for such problems was proposed and tested both on simulated and industrial images. The idea of introducing feedback from the MC predictor of class labels to a priori class probabilities occurred to be fruitful in both cases, leading to the reduction of the classification error by about 3%, especially when we observe a long series of images from the same class.

Possible applications of the proposed approach include a long image series arising in the medical diagnostics (see, e.g., [5]). One can also combine the idea of the MC predictor with classifiers that are based on deep neural networks, e.g., in the version that was proposed in [6].

References

1. Anguita, D., Ghelardoni, L., Ghio, A., Ridella, S.: A survey of old and new results for the test error estimation of a classifier. J. Artif. Intell. Soft Comput. Res. 3(4), 229–242 (2013)
2. Bersini, H., Saerens, M., Sotelino, L.G.: Hopfield net generation, encoding and classification of temporal trajectories. IEEE Trans. Neural Netw. 5(6), 945–953 (1994)
3. Bifet, A.: Classifier concept drift detection and the illusion of progress. In: Rutkowski, L., Korytkowski, M., Scherer, R., Tadeusiewicz, R., Zadeh, L.A., Zurada, J.M. (eds.) ICAISC 2017. LNCS (LNAI), vol. 10246, pp. 715–725. Springer, Cham (2017). https://doi.org/10.1007/978-3-319-59060-8_64
4. Bilski, J., Smoląg, J.: Parallel realisation of the recurrent Elman neural network learning. In: Rutkowski, L., Scherer, R., Tadeusiewicz, R., Zadeh, L.A., Zurada, J.M. (eds.) ICAISC 2010. LNCS (LNAI), vol. 6114, pp. 19–25. Springer, Heidelberg (2010). https://doi.org/10.1007/978-3-642-13232-2_3
5. Bruździński, T., Krzyżak, A., Fevens, T., Jeleń, Ł.: Web-based framework for breast cancer classification. J. Artif. Intell. Soft Comput. Res. 4(2), 149–162 (2014)
6. Chang, O., Constante, P., Gordon, A., Singana, M.: A novel deep neural network that uses space-time features for tracking and recognizing a moving object. J. Artif. Intell. Soft Comput. Res. 7(2), 125–136 (2017)
7. Devroye, L., Gyorfi, L., Lugosi, G.: A Probabilistic Theory of Pattern Recognition. Springer, Berlin (2013). https://doi.org/10.1007/978-1-4612-0711-5
8. Duda, P., Jaworski, M., Rutkowski, L.: On ensemble components selection in data streams scenario with reoccurring concept-drift. In: 2017 IEEE Symposium Series on Computational Intelligence (SSCI), pp. 1–7. IEEE (2017)
9. Elman, J.L.: Finding structure in time. Cogn. Sci. 14, 179–211 (1990)
10. Jaworski, M., Duda, P., Rutkowski, L.: Concept drift detection in streams of labelled data using the restricted Boltzmann machine. In: 2018 International Joint Conference on Neural Networks (IJCNN), pp. 1–7. IEEE(2018)
11. Jordanov, I., Petrov, N., Petrozziello, A.: Classifiers accuracy improvement based on missing data imputation. J. Artif. Intell. Soft Comput. Res. 8(1), 31–48 (2018)
12. Krawczyk, B., Minku, L.L., Gama, J., Stefanowski, J., Woźniak, M.: Ensemble learning for data stream analysis: a survey. Inf. Fusion 37, 132–156 (2017)
13. Kurzynski, M., Zolnierek, A.: A recursive classifying decision rule for second-order Markov chains. Control Cybern. 9(3), 141–147 (1980)
14. Kurzynski, M., Majak, M.: Meta-Bayes classifier with Markov model applied to the control of bioprosthetic hand. In: Czarnowski, I., Caballero, A.M., Howlett, R.J., Jain, L.C. (eds.) Intelligent Decision Technologies 2016. SIST, vol. 57, pp. 107–117. Springer, Cham (2016). https://doi.org/10.1007/978-3-319-39627-9_10

15. Krzyśko, M., Skorzybut, M.: Discriminant analysis of multivariate repeated measures data with a Kronecker product structured covariance matrices. Stat. Pap. **50**(4), 817–835 (2009)

16. Manceur, A.M., Dutilleul, P.: Maximum likelihood estimation for the tensor normal distribution: algorithm, minimum sample size, and empirical bias and dispersion. J. Comput. Appl. Math. **239**, 37–49 (2013)

17. Ohlson, M., Ahmad, M.R., Von Rosen, D.: The multilinear normal distribution: introduction and some basic properties. J. Multivar. Anal. **113**, 37–47 (2013)

18. Pajares, G.: A Hopfield neural network for image change detection. IEEE Trans. Neural Netw. **17**(5), 1250–1264 (2006)

19. Rafajłowicz, E., Pawlak-Kruczek, H., Rafajłowicz, W.: Statistical classifier with ordered decisions as an image based controller with application to gas burners. In: Rutkowski, L., Korytkowski, M., Scherer, R., Tadeusiewicz, R., Zadeh, L.A., Zurada, J.M. (eds.) ICAISC 2014. LNCS (LNAI), vol. 8467, pp. 586–597. Springer, Cham (2014). https://doi.org/10.1007/978-3-319-07173-2_50

20. Rafajłowicz, E., Rafajłowicz, W.: Image-driven decision making with application to control gas burners. In: Saeed, K., Homenda, W., Chaki, R. (eds.) CISIM 2017. LNCS, vol. 10244, pp. 436–446. Springer, Cham (2017). https://doi.org/10.1007/978-3-319-59105-6_37

21. Rafajłowicz, W.: Method of handling constraints in differential evolution using Fletcher's filter. In: Rutkowski, L., Korytkowski, M., Scherer, R., Tadeusiewicz, R., Zadeh, L.A., Zurada, J.M. (eds.) ICAISC 2013. LNCS (LNAI), vol. 7895, pp. 46–55. Springer, Heidelberg (2013). https://doi.org/10.1007/978-3-642-38610-7_5

22. Rafajłowicz, E.: Data structures for pattern and image recognition with application to quality control. Acta Polytechnica Hungarica Informatics **15**(4), 233–262 (2018)

23. Rafajłowicz, E.: Classifiers for matrix normal images: derivation and testing. In: Rutkowski, L., Scherer, R., Korytkowski, M., Pedrycz, W., Tadeusiewicz, R., Zurada, J.M. (eds.) ICAISC 2018. LNCS (LNAI), vol. 10841, pp. 668–679. Springer, Cham (2018). https://doi.org/10.1007/978-3-319-91253-0_62

24. Rafajłowicz, E.: Robustness of raw images classifiers against the class imbalance – a case study. In: Saeed, K., Homenda, W. (eds.) CISIM 2018. LNCS, vol. 11127, pp. 154–165. Springer, Cham (2018). https://doi.org/10.1007/978-3-319-99954-8_14

25. Rafajłowicz, E.: Classifying image sequences with the Markov chain structure and matrix normal distributions. In: Rutkowski, L., Scherer, R., Korytkowski, M., Pedrycz, W., Tadeusiewicz, R., Zurada, J.M. (eds.) ICAISC 2019. LNCS (LNAI), vol. 11508, pp. 595–607. Springer, Cham (2019). https://doi.org/10.1007/978-3-030-20912-4_54

26. Skubalska-Rafajłowicz, E.: Sparse random projections of camera images for monitoring of a combustion process in a gas burner. In: Saeed, K., Homenda, W., Chaki, R. (eds.) CISIM 2017. LNCS, vol. 10244, pp. 447–456. Springer, Cham (2017). https://doi.org/10.1007/978-3-319-59105-6_38

27. Werner, K., Jansson, M., Stoica, P.: On estimation of covariance matrices with Kronecker product structure. IEEE Trans. Signal Process. **56**(2), 478–491 (2008)

28. Wozniak, M.: Markov chains pattern recognition approach applied to the medical diagnosis tasks. In: Oliveira, J.L., Maojo, V., Martín-Sánchez, F., Pereira, A.S. (eds.) ISBMDA 2005. LNCS, vol. 3745, pp. 231–241. Springer, Heidelberg (2005). https://doi.org/10.1007/11573067_24

29. Wójcik, W., Kotyra, A.: Combustion diagnosis by image processing. Photonics Lett. Poland **1**(1), 40–42 (2009)

Explainable Cluster-Based Rules Generation for Image Retrieval and Classification

Paweł Staszewski[1], Maciej Jaworski[1(✉)] (iD), Leszek Rutkowski[1,2] (iD), and Dacheng Tao[3] (iD)

[1] Department of Computational Intelligence, Czestochowa University of Technology, Czestochowa, Poland
{pawel.staszewski,maciej.jaworski,leszek.rutkowski}@pcz.pl
[2] Information Technology Institute, University of Social Sciences, Łódź, Poland
[3] UBTECH Sydney AI Centre, School of Computer Science, Faculty of Engineering, The University of Sydney, Sydney, Australia
dacheng.tao@sydney.edu.au

Abstract. In this paper, we propose a method for rules generation for images, which can be further used to enhance the classification accuracy of a convolutional neural network as well as to increase the level of explainability of neural network decisions. For each image from the training set, a descriptor is created based on the information contained in the convolutional layers of the network. The descriptors of images of the same class are then used to create a single-class prototype, which is characteristic of that class. The prototypes of different but semantically similar prototypes are then grouped into major categories using the DBSCAN algorithm. The analysis is carried out using the ILSVRC dataset and the VGG16 net is used. The experimental verification performed on the validation set demonstrated the validity and general nature of the rules obtained using the proposed method.

Keywords: Image retrieval · Explainable AI · Convolutional neural network.

1 Introduction

In recent years the subject of various image processing techniques receives much attention from machine learning researchers. Examples of the most challenging issues of this type are image classification or content-based image retrieval (CBIR). In the image classification, a model is built on the supervised training dataset of images, which is further used to classify formerly unseen images. The CBIR algorithms focus on analyzing the objects on the image as well as their surroundings, textures, or backgrounds, in order to find similar images in the database. In the literature, there are many effective methods of CBIR [2,4,8,9,21]. Almost all of the modern techniques of various image processing tasks are based on deep learning [6] and the convolutional neural networks

© Springer Nature Switzerland AG 2020
L. Rutkowski et al. (Eds.): ICAISC 2020, LNAI 12416, pp. 85–94, 2020.
https://doi.org/10.1007/978-3-030-61534-5_8

(CNN). Their effectiveness and accuracy are relatively high. However, there is still some room for improvement. Moreover, the models learned by the CNNs are hardly understandable for the users, i.e. they are not explainable. For the mentioned reasons, in this paper, we propose a method for rules generation, which could be used to support the classification of query images. Each rule has assigned a group of different but semantically similar classes, where all of these classes belong to the same major category. If a newly observed query image matches one of the rules, this information can be incorporated in the classification process and tilt the final decision of the CNN towards the classes contained in the rule. Additionally, the rules will increase the explainability of the learned models since the rules can receive 'human-friendly' names given by the expert. The process of rules construction can be divided into three steps, which are described in more detail in Sect. 2. The first step aims at constructing a proper descriptor, containing the characteristic features of single images. The proper descriptors construction is a very important in many tasks of image processing [7,12,20]. The descriptors based on the activations of CNN neurons are commonly applied in various methods of the CBIR [14,16,17,19]. Most of them use the information contained in the fully connected layers, which are placed on top of the convolutional part of the CNN. This approach is, for example, applied in the neural codes proposed in [1]. Such descriptors are very effective in the tasks where the semantic classes are the most important. However, it should be noted that there is a lot of additional information contained in the activations of convolutional layers. Descriptors based in such a way are useful in tasks where the features like textures or background play an important role [3,10,11,18]. In our approach, we decided to construct descriptors using activations of the last convolutional layer, i.e. the one just before the fully connected layers. The second step of our approach is to construct a class prototype descriptor, which would summarize the knowledge gathered in descriptors of images belonging to the same class. We proposed to define such a prototype simply as an arithmetic average over all descriptors of images belonging to the considered class. In the third step, we apply the DBSCAN clustering algorithm [5] to group the class prototypes obtained in the second step. We observed that the descriptors of semantically similar classes tend to form clusters and can be assigned to a major common category. The obtained clusters are then considered as rules for query images. Although the method can be applied to any kind of CNN, in this paper we worked with the VGG16 neural network. Its detailed structure is presented in Fig. 1. The VGG16 net is relatively simple, allowing as to verify our intuitions fast and straightforwardly. The rest of this paper is organized as follows. Section 2 describes the process of cluster-based rules generation, which takes into account the knowledge gathered in activations of the convolutional layer feature maps. In Sect. 3, the experimental verification of the validity of the rules is performed based on the ILSVRC validation set. Section 4 concludes the paper and points out some possible directions for future research.

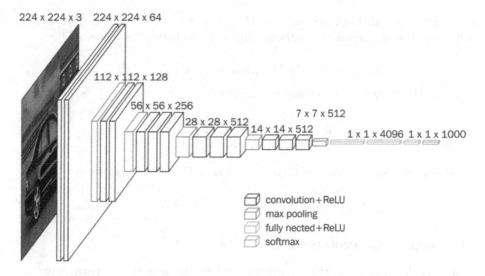

Fig. 1. The structure of the VGG16 neural network.

2 Rules Generation Method

The proposed method of rules generation consists of three steps. First, for each image a descriptor is created, which uses the information contained in the convolutional part of the CNN. In the second step, single-class prototypes are created. The prototype summarizes knowledge about the most characteristic features of the considered class. Then, the single-class prototypes are grouped together using a clustering algorithm to generate rules in their final shape.

2.1 Descriptor Construction

Let us assume that the training dataset consists of N elements, each belonging to one of K classes. Let x_n denote the n-th image and let $y_n, \in \{1, \ldots, K\}$, be the class assigned to it. The training dataset can be divided into K disjoint subsets

$$S_k = \{x_n : y_n; \ n = 1, \ldots, N\}. \tag{1}$$

To generate the descriptor, we focus on the activations generated in the convolutional part of the network. As can be seen in Fig. 1, the VGG16 net consists of five blocks of convolutional layers. Each block ends with a max-pooling layer which downsizes the width and the height of feature maps. We want to construct a descriptor that would summarize the knowledge gathered in the convolutional blocks. We take into account only the last block which contains D feature maps. The max-pooling layer of the last convolutional block is of size $W \times H \times D$. Since we apply the VGG16 net, the parameters are equal to $W = 7$, $H = 7$, and $D = 512$. Let us denote the activations of the d-th feature map after processing the n-th data elements as $M(x_n)_{ijd}$, $i = 1, \ldots, W$, $j = 1, \ldots W$. In each feature map, we take activations with values above some threshold τ

$$I(x_n)_d = \{(i, j) : M(x_n)_{ijd} > \tau\}, \ d = 1, \ldots, D. \tag{2}$$

Next, their arithmetic average is computed

$$h(x_n)_k = \frac{\sum_{(i,j) \in I(x_n)_k} M(x_n)_{ijk}}{\sum_{(i,j) \in I(x_n)_k} 1}. \tag{3}$$

The descriptor for image x_n is then defined as a D-dimensional vector

$$h(x_n) = [h(x_n)_1, \ldots, h(x_n)_D], \tag{4}$$

2.2 Single-Class Prototypes

Analyzing descriptors for the exemplary ILSVRC dataset [15], it turns out that descriptors of images of the same class have significant similarities. This fact points out that it is possible to establish a set of rules, which would help to interpret the class of a query image based only on its descriptor. Although the descriptors are similar, it still may be a hard task to invent the proper rules. Therefore, we decided to make it in a simple way, by calculating the arithmetic average of descriptors belonging to the considered class

$$\overline{h}_k = \frac{\sum_{x_n \in S_k} h(x_n)}{|S_k|}, \tag{5}$$

where $|S_k|$ denotes the cardinality of set S_k. After this step, we have K different D-dimensional representative prototype rules, one for each class. Newly created average-descriptors $\overline{h}_k$ can be used to help in determining the class of a query image by comparing the distances of its descriptor with all the prototypes.

2.3 Cluster-Based Rules

The fact that descriptors for images of the same class have similar features might be quite expectable. However, it also turns out to be true that the descriptors of different classes also demonstrate some similarities. For example, we might expect that descriptors for various animals share common characteristics and therefore, should lie in their neighborhood in the D-dimensional feature space. To visualize it, we focused on the previously mentioned ILSVRC dataset, for which $K = 1000$. To reduce the data dimensionality, we applied the t-SNE algorithm [13] on 1000 prototypes given by (5). The t-SNE algorithm reduces data from a high-dimensional space into a lower-dimensional one, while keeping distances between the original and projected data as much as possible. We projected descriptors $\overline{h}_k$ into a 2-dimensional space

$$H_k = tSNE(\overline{h}_k), \tag{6}$$

where $tSNE()$ is a table-valued function, which links the $\overline{h}_k$ descriptor with the corresponding 2-dimensional vector H_k obtained using the t-SNE algorithm. The parameters of the t-SNE were set to: perplexity = 30, early exaggeration = 12.0, learning rate = 200.0. Distribution of H_k vectors, which Visualizes the distribution of the single-class prototypes $\overline{h}_k$ in a 2-dimensional space, is shown in Fig. 2. Each vector H_k is represented by a thumbnail of an image $X_k \in S_k$, for which the descriptor was the closest to the prototype h_k.

Fig. 2. Distribution of H_k vectors, which visualizes the distribution of the single-class prototypes $\overline{h}_k$ in a 2-dimensional space, obtained using the t-SNE algorithm. The picture in the high resolution can be found at https://github.com/pstaszewski/2020_06/blob/master/tsne_vizualization.png.

As can be seen, the descriptors of images with semantically similar classes tend to appear close to each other. They form groups of classes to which a parent class could be assigned, e.g. animals, fruits, or meals. It should be noted that the ILSVRC dataset originally contains a hierarchy of classes, however, we did not use this information in our analysis. This hierarchy can be found at http://image-net.org/explore – we encourage the readers to compare it with the result presented in Fig. 2. Summarizing, each class contains a set of features typical for it, but some features are common also for other classes, which are grouped together in a parent category.

To group precisely the prototypes $H_1, \ldots, H_K$, we applied the DBSCAN clustering algorithm [5]. This algorithm has two advantages, i.e. it does not require to fix the number of clusters a priori, and it founds clusters of arbitrary shapes. In our analysis, we obtained 19 clusters, which are visualized in Fig. 3. We denote these clusters as $G_j, j = 1, \ldots, 19$. It should be noted that clusters G_j can be considered either as groups of prototypes H_k or $\overline{h}_k$ since there is a one-to-one correspondence between the high and low-dimensional prototypes. Groups G_j play the role of rules, which could be further used to enhance the classification process for query images and explainability of the obtained results.

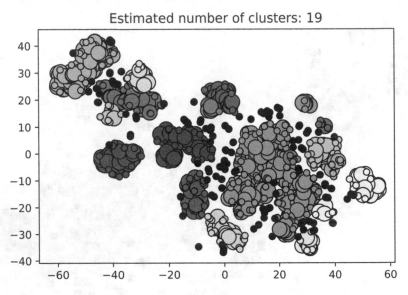

Fig. 3. Groups of 2-dimensional single-class prototypes obtained using the DBSCAN algorithm.

3   Experimental Verification

As it was previously mentioned, our model was created and analyzed using the ILSVRC training dataset. To verify it, we will use the ILSVRC validation set. It contains images that were not used for the construction of single-class prototypes and cluster-based rules presented in Subsects. 2.2 and 2.3.

In the beginning, we chose five exemplary clusters obtained by the DBSCAN algorithm. These clusters contain descriptors of images, for which we can assign the following major categories: Dogs ($G1$), Birds ($G2$), Fruit and Vegetables ($G3$), Vehicles ($G4$), and Buildings ($G5$). The clusters of H_k descriptors and the thumbnails of images corresponding to them are presented in Table 1.

To investigate the usability of the obtained cluster-based rules in enhancing the classification or explainability of query images, we performed simulations based on the ILSVRC validation set $V = \{y_1, \ldots, y_{N_V}\}$. We checked whether the query images descriptors match the clusters containing descriptors of images of the same or similar classes. To this end, we performed two slightly different

Table 1. Five exemplary clusters obtained using the DBSCAN algorithm. Each cluster contains descriptors of images of different (but semantically similar) classes, belonging to one common parent category

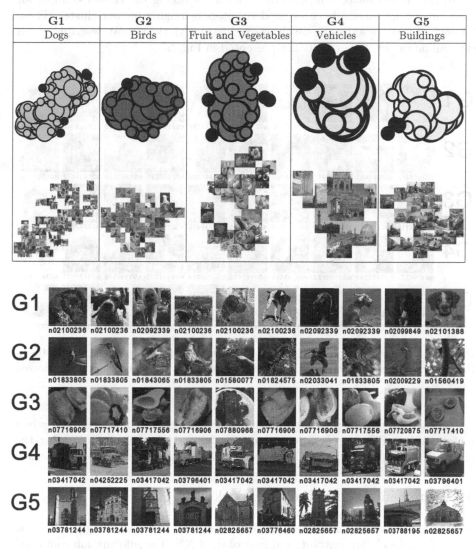

Fig. 4. The top-10 images from the validation set with the shortest distance between their descriptors and corresponding cluster centers.

computations. In the beginning, for each data element y from the validation set, we calculated the descriptor $h(y)$ using (4). Then, for each cluster $G_1, \ldots, G_5$ computed their centers $c_1, \ldots, c_5$. Then, for each cluster center, we found the top-10 images from the validation set, whose descriptors are the closest to this center. The obtained results are presented in Fig. 4. As can be seen, the images are very similar to the images corresponding to the cluster center, since their distances are very small.

In the second set of computations, instead of taking the cluster centers, for each cluster, we randomly chose 10 descriptors belonging to that cluster. Then, for each of these descriptors, we chose one image with the closest descriptor from the validation set. The results are presented in Fig. 5.

Fig. 5. Images retrieved from the validation set with the shortest distance between their descriptor and descriptors of 10 images randomly chosen from the considered cluster.

As can be seen, the presented results demonstrate that the presented method for cluster-based rule generation is very useful and can help in enhancing the classification process of query images or can be applied in explainability issues.

4   Conclusions and Future Work

In this paper, we presented a method of rules generation for images, based on the activations of the convolutional part of the CNN. The information contained in convolutional layers was used to construct descriptors of images. Then, the descriptors were used to create single-class prototype rules, which characterize features of the classes. We observed that these prototypes tend to create groups with classes that are semantically similar to each other. Therefore, we applied the DBSCAN algorithm to create cluster-based rules. The experiments demonstrated that the rules are also valid for images from the validation set. These rules can be further use to upgrade the classification process of query images. In this paper, we worked with the VGG16 net, for which the top-1 accuracy is 74.4%, whereas the top-5 accuracy is equal to 91.9%. Hence, there is still a lot of room for improvement. We expect that the rules generated using our approach can enhance the classification accuracy of query images, what we plan to verify in our future work. Another possible research direction is the application of more advanced CNN than the VGG16. Moreover, more sophisticated descriptors could be proposed, which use the knowledge gathered in all convolutional layers of the network, not only the last one. Other clustering algorithms for rules generation could also be tested. Finally, the presented method could also be used in increasing the explainability of the neural network decisions.

Acknowledgment. This work was supported by the Polish National Science Centre under Grant no. 2017/27/B/ST6/02852.

References

1. Babenko, A., Slesarev, A., Chigorin, A., Lempitsky, V.: Neural codes for image retrieval. In: Fleet, D., Pajdla, T., Schiele, B., Tuytelaars, T. (eds.) ECCV 2014. LNCS, vol. 8689, pp. 584–599. Springer, Cham (2014). https://doi.org/10.1007/978-3-319-10590-1_38

2. Chauhan, S.S., Batra, S.: Efficient layer-wise feature incremental approach for content-based image retrieval system. J. Electron. Imaging **28**(2), 023038 (2019)

3. Dong, R., Liu, M., Li, F.: Multilayer convolutional feature aggregation algorithm for image retrieval. Math. Probl. Eng. **2019** (2019). https://www.hindawi.com/journals/mpe/2019/9794202/

4. Dubey, D., Suryawanshi, V., Prajapati, G.: Interactive content based image retrieval system: survey and overview. Int. Res. J. Eng. Technol. **3**, 1239–1245 (2016)

5. Ester, M., Kriegel, H.P., Sander, J., Xu, X.: A density-based algorithm for discovering clusters in large spatial databases with noise. In: Proceedings of the Second International Conference on Knowledge Discovery and Data Mining, KDD 1996, pp. 226–231. AAAI Press (1996)

6. Goodfellow, I., Bengio, Y., Courville, A.: Deep Learning. MIT Press, Cambridge (2016). http://www.deeplearningbook.org

7. Grycuk, R., Najgebauer, P., Kordos, M., Scherer, M.M., Marchlewska, A.: Fast image index for database management engines. J. Artif. Intel. Soft Comput. Res. **10**(2), 113–123 (2020). https://doi.org/10.2478/jaiscr-2020-0008

8. Gu, Y., Wang, Y., Li, Y.: A survey on deep learning-driven remote sensing image scene understanding: scene classification, scene retrieval and scene-guided object detection. Appl. Sci. **9**(10), 2110 (2019)

9. Ismail, M.M.B.: A survey on content-based image retrieval. Int. J. Adv. Comput. Sci. Appl. (IJACSA) **8**(5), 159–170 (2017)

10. Jose, A., Lopez, R.D., Heisterklaus, I., Wien, M.: Pyramid pooling of convolutional feature maps for image retrieval. In: 2018 25th IEEE International Conference on Image Processing (ICIP), pp. 480–484. IEEE (2018)

11. Jun, H., Ko, B., Kim, Y., Kim, I., Kim, J.: Combination of multiple global descriptors for image retrieval. arXiv preprint arXiv:1903.10663 (2019)

12. Long, C., Collins, R., Swears, E., Hoogs, A.: Deep neural networks in fully connected crf for image labeling with social network metadata. In: 2019 IEEE Winter Conference on Applications of Computer Vision (WACV), pp. 1607–1615. IEEE (2019)

13. Maaten, L.v.d, Hinton, G.: Visualizing data using T-SNE. J. Mach. Learn. Res. **9**, 2579–2605 (2008)
14. Radenović, F., Tolias, G., Chum, O.: CNN image retrieval learns from BoW: unsupervised fine-tuning with hard examples. In: Leibe, B., Matas, J., Sebe, N., Welling, M. (eds.) ECCV 2016. LNCS, vol. 9905, pp. 3–20. Springer, Cham (2016). https://doi.org/10.1007/978-3-319-46448-0_1
15. Russakovsky, O., et al.: ImageNet large scale visual recognition challenge. Int. J. Comput. Vis. **115**(3), 211–252 (2015). https://doi.org/10.1007/s11263-015-0816-y
16. Saritha, R.R., Paul, V., Kumar, P.G.: Content based image retrieval using deep learning process. Cluster Comput. **22**(2), 4187–4200 (2018). https://doi.org/10.1007/s10586-018-1731-0
17. Somasundaran, B.V., Soundararajan, R., Biswas, S.: Robust image retrieval by cascading a deep quality assessment network. Sig. Process. Image Commun. **80**, 115652 (2020)
18. Tzelepi, M., Tefas, A.: Deep convolutional learning for content based image retrieval. Neurocomputing **275**, 2467–2478 (2018)
19. Wu, Z., Yu, J.: A multi-level descriptor using ultra-deep feature for image retrieval. Multimedia Tools Appl. **78**(18), 25655–25672 (2019). https://doi.org/10.1007/s11042-019-07771-2
20. Zhou, W., Deng, X., Shao, Z.: Region convolutional features for multi-label remote sensing image retrieval. arXiv preprint arXiv:1807.08634 (2018)
21. Zhou, W., Li, H., Tian, Q.: Recent advance in content-based image retrieval: a literature survey. arXiv preprint arXiv:1706.06064 (2017)

SURF Algorithm with Convolutional Neural Network as Face Recognition Technique

Alicja Winnicka$^{(\boxtimes)}$, Karolina Kęsik, Dawid Połap⬤, and Marcin Woźniak⬤

Faculty of Applied Mathematics, Silesian University of Technology, Kaszubska 23,
44-100 Gliwice, Poland
Alicja.Lidia.Winnicka@gmail.com, Karola.Ksk@gmail.com,
{Dawid.Polap,Marcin.Wozniak}@polsl.pl

Abstract. Recent developments in technology need the methods to become more efficient in various conditions. We can see this situation is much visible in multimedia and verification, where biometrics are used to recognize somebody from images, both as detections of suspicious behaviors and user verification. The paper presents proposed technique for face verification by the use of hybrid method based on SURF and neural network classifier. On the input image SURF is searching for potential key points, for which it creates special maps. These descriptors are forwarded to neural network for analysis and verification. Proposed solution works well and experimental results show good efficiency.

Keywords: Feature extraction · Identity verification · Neural networks

1 Introduction

In many systems we grant access based on verification of some credentials. There are many ways to do that. First and the most classic one is password check. Second, which becomes much more popular due to technology boost, is verification of bio-metric features. Some systems use fingerprint authentication, another use iris pattern, but also face recognition is very popular. New high definition cameras take images where objects are visible in many details, what makes them useful for precise detection.

New systems analyze face details by comparing them to the pattern, however it is not easy task mainly because of big problems with obtaining user-specific features. Classic approaches use graphics processing algorithms to extract bio features distances between eyes, position of mouth and nose, relation in distance to ears, contours of face. These are most appropriate, since features like hair may easily change over time. Actually also biologic features may differ over time so the most important for correct classification is adjusting to possible changes in outlook.

Identity verification research can be divided into various stages: extraction of features and classification. For extraction the most specific characteristics are used to describe entire set of samples. In [1], the idea of extraction features for hyperspectral images was described, while in [2] was presented robust discriminant regression. Acquired features are used in large biometric systems which are described in [3]. The authors analyzed

© Springer Nature Switzerland AG 2020
L. Rutkowski et al. (Eds.): ICAISC 2020, LNAI 12416, pp. 95–102, 2020.
https://doi.org/10.1007/978-3-030-61534-5_9

biometric security in cloud computing. Systems based on the analysis of the person's signature are also often created [4]. As tool for classification artificial intelligence algorithms are created. An example are fuzzy rough rule based systems [5], classic neural networks [6, 7] and convolutional ones [8]. The large use of these techniques is in the development of block chain mechanisms where authorization is important step on the way to payment confirmation [9]. Big achievements are also obtained in the field of holding and searching in large databases [10]. Various approaches use deep learning and mixed features to solve decision making. In [11] an idea of pattern matching by graph structures was proposed, while [12, 13] proposed pattern matching of various inputs by advanced neural processing approaches.

In this paper, we proposed an idea of combing classic algorithm for key-points search and after processing of obtained data samples by the use of convolutional neural network. As final effect we have a system which is trained to classify selected bio-metric features. Proposed solution is developed to evaluate biometric features which have the lowest possibility to have big changes over time. We have examined our idea using two different feature extraction matrices. The results have shown good efficiency in both cases and potential of our proposition for development.

2 Face Recognition Technique

First the input image is filtered and after we have a search procedure for key points. These locations are used to compose feature maps forwarded for verification purposes by the use of convolutional neural network.

2.1 Feature Extraction for the Purpose of Classification

For extraction from images we need to define simple object features which will be searched for by selected method. The input in a form of a color image is very complex so first step will be simplification. At the beginning the image will be filtered for simplification of unimportant elements. Simplified elements should be not important for classification, what means this would be no influence on work of the algorithm. Filtered image will be easier to proceed for the algorithm which searches for key points. We have used an image matrix:

$$\begin{bmatrix} P_{1,1} \ P_{1,2} & \cdots & P_{1,n-1} \ P_{1,n} \\ P_{2,1} \ P_{2,2} & & P_{2,n-1} \ P_{2,n} \\ \vdots & \ddots & \vdots \\ P_{m-1,1} \ P_{m-1,2} & \cdots & P_{m-1,n-1} \ P_{m-1,n} \\ P_{m,1} \ \ P_{m,2} & & P_{m,n-1} \ \ P_{m,n} \end{bmatrix}$$

where $P_{i,j}$ is the color the pixel presented in RGB model (Red-Green-Blue), where coordinates of pixels are (i,j) for $i \in \langle 1, m \rangle$ and $j \in \langle 1, n \rangle$ and $m \times n$ are dimensions of the image.

The first filter is used to binarize an image, what changes pixel color to white or black according to the formula:

$$P_{ij} = \begin{cases} 1, & if \ \frac{R(P_{i,j})+G(P_{i,j})+B(P_{i,j})}{3} < t/2, \\ 0, & if \ \frac{R(P_{i,j})+G(P_{i,j})+B(P_{i,j})}{3} \geq t/2 \end{cases}$$

where $R(P_{i,j})$, $G(P_{i,j})$ and $B(P_{i,j})$ represent red, green and blue, while $P_{i,j}$ is the pixel, t is the threshold value $\langle 0, 255 \rangle$. Standard threshold is $t = 255$ since we divide possible values of colors for two equal parts. Presented filtering technique allows to eliminate colorful clothes or hair but also helps to find face elements, because usually they are darker than the rest of the picture. At the end the simplified image is ready for key points searching, or this task Speeded Up Robust Features (SURF) was implemented. them. Proposed SURF algorithm uses Hessian matrix $H(x, y, \omega)$ for each pixel:

$$H(x, \omega) = \begin{bmatrix} L_{xx}(x, \omega) \ L_{xy}(x, \omega) \\ L_{yx}(x, \omega) \ L_{yy}(x, \omega) \end{bmatrix}$$

where each partial we understand as

$$L_{xx}(x, y, \omega) = I(x)\frac{\partial^2}{\partial x^2}g(\omega)$$

$$L_{yy}(x, y, \omega) = I(x)\frac{\partial^2}{\partial y^2}g(\omega)$$

$$L_{xy}(x, y, \omega) = L_{yx}(x, y, \omega) = I(x)\frac{\partial^2}{\partial x\partial y}g(\omega).$$

where $L_{xx}(x, y, \omega)$, $L_{yy}(x, y, \omega)$, $L_{xy}(x, y, \omega)$ and $L_{yx}(x, y, \omega)$ are convolutions of the image from second derivative, $g(\omega)$ is a kernel and (x, y) are pixels coordinates. Integrated image $I(x)$ is composed by formula:

$$I(x) = \sum_{k=0}^{k \leq x} \sum_{l=0}^{l \leq y} I(k, l).$$

SURF searches for pixels where determinant of Hessian matrix is the biggest

$$\det(H_{xy}) = L_{xx}(x, y, \omega) * L_{yy}(x, y, \omega) - (L_{xy}(x, y, \omega))^2.$$

Pixels of highest values are recognized as key points. Then, around them we make squares 5×5 and check if 80% of this square is black or white. If yes, the pixel is deleted from key points since surrounding does not show much features. Later the algorithm analyzes our image by region of interest. It takes these points, which are in the middle of the image with help of Hough transform. We choose only 25 key points which should be useful and for each of them create a square 3×3, connecting them into the one image 15×15 pixels. This image is the input to Convolutional Neural Network.

2.2 Convolutional Neural Network

Convolutional Neural Networks are developed for image analyzing. First working layers, which are not fully connected layers are called convolution and pooling layers.
The combination of convolution and polling layers can be duplicated many times. The
convolution layer consists of small filters, which are treated as a matrix and the name
"convolution" was taken from this. In a discrete form it works like normal multiplication
of matrices, what means that this filter multiplies pixels and move further. The pooling
layer reduces dimensions of the image. For example in case of 3x3 matrix, it takes only
one value (usually the maximum). In the next step this matrix moves one pixel further
and do it again for new values. The fully-connected layer is classical neural network
layer, where each neuron in one layer is connected with each neuron in next layer.

We used Adam algorithm to train the network. It took its name from "adaptive
moment estimation", which is important part of its working. The algorithm is a combination of two stochastic algorithms: Adaptive Gradient Algorithm (AdaGrad) and Root
Mean Square Propagation (RMSProp) and takes advantages from both of them. Adam
uses estimation of the first and second moment of gradient to modify learning rate for
all weights in the neural network. The moment is chosen randomly and n-th moment is
defined as:

$$m_n = E[x^n].$$

where m is the moment and x is the random variable. The first and second moments are
mean and uncentered variance respectively. To estimate them Adam changes moving
averages computed by formulas:

$$m_t = \beta_1 m_{t-1} + (1 - \beta_1)g_t$$

$$v_t = \beta_2 v_{t-1} + (1 - \beta_2)g_t^2$$

where m_t and v_t are moving averages, g is a gradient and β_1, β_2 are the hyper-parameters
in range (0, 1). Default value are $\beta_1 = 0,9$ and $\beta_2 = 0,999$. These values are connected
with moment:

$$E[m_t] = E[g_t]$$

$$E[v_t] = E[g_t^2]$$

These expected estimators should be equal to parameter we are trying to estimate by
formula for m_t:

$$m_t = (1 - \beta_1) \sum_{i=0}^{t} \beta_1^{t-i} g_i$$

and

$$E[m_t] = E[g_1](1 - \beta_1^t) + \sigma.$$

Because of approximation σ is the probable error. After calculating these values, we need to find better estimator:

$$\bar{m}_t = \frac{m_t}{1 - \beta_1^t}$$

$$\bar{v}_t = \frac{v_t}{1 - \beta_2^t}$$

Now we just need to move averages to adjust the learning rate for each parameter. The weight update is presented by following formula:

$$w_t = w_{t-1} - \mu \frac{\bar{m}_t}{\sqrt{\bar{v}_t} + \epsilon}$$

where w_t is the $t - th$ weight and μ is the step size, which depends on iteration. After certain number of iterations neural network is learned.

3 Face Recognition as a Mechanism for Identity Verification

Our algorithm can be used for verification of people, in situations when we i.e. verify identity of somebody without documents. Photo of this person is taken as input to the algorithm. The first step is filtering, which helps in later key points searching. The purpose of filtering is to simplify the image and eliminate potential pixels, which could be useless key points, for example the cloth with complex pattern or colorful hair. Binarization eliminates colors and even shades of gray, so picture consists of only white and black pixels. It is highly probable to delete majority of useless potential key points.

After filtering, the image should be as simple as possible to use it as the input for key points search algorithm (like SURF). The algorithm finds certain number of key points, which should be important parts of face like eyes or mouth, and connect them to one

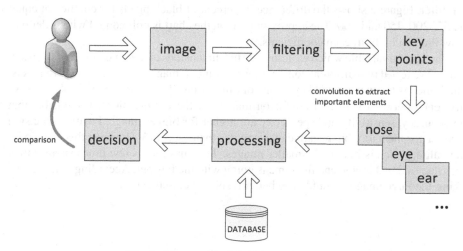

Fig. 1. The model of the proposed method

smaller image. This image is important for the next step, because it is used as the input to convolutional neural network. The network compares this image to database and as the result gives us the identity, which is the most similar to the image elements as shown in Fig. 1.

4 Experiments

As our database we use 100 images of 15 individuals and neural network, which architecture is shown in Table 1. The neural network was trained in proportion 70:30 for learning to classification images and was learning for 200 iterations. Later we expand the database about next 30 images for better verification of effectiveness.

Table 1. Used classifier architecture.

Type of Layer	Output Shape
Convolution 2 × 2	(14, 14, 64)
Max pooling 2 × 2	(7, 7, 64)
Convolution 2 × 2	(14, 14, 64)
Max pooling 2 × 2	(7, 7, 64)
Flatten	288
Dense	128
Dense	96
Dense	15

We tested different values for few variables. The first one is coefficient t in binarization filter. Figure 2 shows the difference in percent of black pixels for coefficient equal to 255, 200, 150 and 100. The approximation on the chart is polynomial with order 6 to show the similarity in each coefficients.

The second variable which we tested are the dimensions of the image created from key points. We tested two different constructions, for input image 35×35 and 15×15 pixels, which means that we created key points of dimensions 7×7 and 3×3. Table 2 shows difference between values of confusion matrix for these dimensions. It is visible that the accuracy, sensitivity and specificity are higher for bigger image. Positive precision is better for them too, but negative one is worse than for 3×3. However this is the only one value, which is better for smaller images. The miss rate is few times smaller than miss rate of 3×3 image and the same is going with the fall-out. According to this table, taking the large images should have better results of classification.

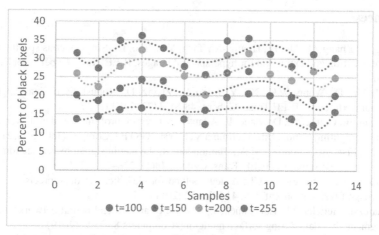

Fig. 2. Comparisons for different coefficient in binarization

Table 2. The values for two different dimensions of images

Measure	For 3 × 3 images	For 7 × 7 images
Accuracy	0.743	0.882
Sensitivity	0.875	0.973
Specificity	0.261	0.577
Precision	0.812	0.884
Negative predictive value	0.366	0.866
Miss rate	0.124	0.026
Fall-out	0.738	0.422
False discovery rate	0.187	0.115
False omission rate	0.633	0.133
F1 score	0.842	0.926

5 Conclusions

In this paper we used combination of key points search algorithm and Convolutional Neural Network for face recognition algorithm. The whole algorithm can be used in real time to verify identities of the people in the crowded places like airport. The results are good, however in its initial proposition the key points searching still finds some points, which are useless for further verification. This aspect will be eliminated in our future research. Except of this disadvantage, the algorithm is effective in real time verification.

Acknowledgments. Authors acknowledge contribution to this project of the Program "Best of the Best 4.0" from the Polish Ministry of Science and Higher Education No. MNiSW/2020/43/DIR/NN4.

References

1. Zhang, L., Zhang, Q., Du, B., Huang, X., Tang, Y.Y., Tao, D.: Simultaneous spectral-spatial feature selection and extraction for hyperspectral images. IEEE Trans. Cybern. **48**(1), 16–28 (2016)
2. Lai, Z., Mo, D., Wong, W.K., Xu, Y., Miao, D., Zhang, D.: Robust discriminant regression for feature extraction. IEEE Trans. Cybern. **48**(8), 2472–2484 (2017)
3. Al-Bayati, B., Clarke, N., Dowland, P.: Adaptive behavioral profiling for identity verification in cloud computing: a model and preliminary analysis. GSTF J. Comput. (JoC) **5**(1), 21 (2016)
4. Diaz, M., Fischer, A., Ferrer, M.A., Plamondon, R.: Dynamic signature verification system based on one real signature. IEEE Trans. Cybern. **48**(1), 228–239 (2016)
5. Nowicki, R.K., Starczewski, J.T.: A new method for classification of imprecise data using fuzzy rough fuzzification. Inf. Sci. **414**, 33–52 (2017)
6. Wlodarczyk-Sielicka, M., Lubczonek, J.: The use of an artificial neural network to process hydrographic big data during surface modeling. Computers **8**(1), 26 (2019)
7. Nourani, V., Mousavi, S., Dabrowska, D., Sadikoglu, F.: Conjunction of radial basis function interpolator and artificial intelligence models for time-space modeling of contaminant transport in porous media. J. Hydrol. **548**, 569–587 (2017)
8. Nowak, J., Korytkowski, M., Scherer, R.: Classification of computer network users with convolutional neural networks. In: 2018 Federated Conference on Computer Science and Information Systems (FedCSIS), pp. 501–504. IEEE, September 2018
9. Malik, N., Nanda, P., Arora, A., He, X., Puthal, D.: Blockchain based secured identity authentication and expeditious revocation framework for vehicular networks. In: 2018 17th IEEE International Conference On Trust, Security And Privacy In Computing And Communications/12th IEEE International Conference On Big Data Science And Engineering (TrustCom/BigDataSE), pp. 674–679. IEEE, August 2018
10. Marszałek, Z.: Parallel fast sort algorithm for secure multiparty computation. J. UCS **24**(4), 488–514 (2018)
11. Horzyk, A., Czajkowska, A.: Associative pattern matching and inference using associative graph data structures. In: Rutkowski, L., Scherer, R., Korytkowski, M., Pedrycz, W., Tadeusiewicz, R., Zurada, J.M. (eds.) ICAISC 2019. LNCS (LNAI), vol. 11509, pp. 371–383. Springer, Cham (2019). https://doi.org/10.1007/978-3-030-20915-5_34
12. Nobukawa, S., Nishimura, H., Yamanishi, T.: Pattern classification by spiking neural networks combining self-organized and reward-related spike-timing-dependent plasticity. J. Artif. Intell. Soft Comput. Res. **9**(4), 283–291 (2019)
13. de Souza, G.B., da Silva Santos, D.F., Pires, R.G., Marana, A.N., Papa, J.P.: Deep features extraction for robust fingerprint spoofing attack detection. J. Artif. Intell. Soft Comput. Res. **9**(1), 41–49 (2019)

Grouping Handwritten Letter Strokes Using a Fuzzy Decision Tree

Michał Wróbel[1]($^{(\boxtimes)}$) (iD), Janusz T. Starczewski[1] (iD), and Christian Napoli[2] (iD)

[1] Department of Intelligent Computer Systems,
Czestochowa University of Technology, Czestochowa, Poland
`michal.wrobel@iisi.pcz.pl`
[2] Department of Computer, Control and Management Engineering,
Sapienza University of Rome, Roma, Italy

Abstract. This paper presents an algorithm for grouping strokes. This method includes two stages. Firstly, a set of strokes is transformed into a set of hypotheses that a group of strokes matches the pattern. For this purpose, a method for comparing small groups of strokes is proposed. Then, the set of hypotheses is selected with the use of a decision tree to get a proposition of a word.

Keywords: Handwritten letter recognition · Fuzzy decision tree

1 Introduction

An off-line handwriting recognition is the ability of a computer to read handwritten text from a static image, for example, a document scan. This issue is more complex than printed text recognition. In the basic handwriting style, called a cursive script, the letters are connected to each other (see [5]). Therefore, the extraction of a single letter to compare it with a pattern is difficult.

To tackle this, an approach based on stroke extraction is introduced. The stroke is defined as a basic fragment of a letter created by a single move of a hand. Using this method the problem is decomposed into separate stages. Firstly, the strokes must be extracted from a picture. Then, letter patterns must be found in the set of strokes. This paper focuses on the second stage of this approach.

We need a method for comparing two small groups of strokes. One of them is a pattern of a letter (or generally of a small fragment of the text), second is a group selected from the set of extracted strokes. The similarity of the two groups is not a binary value in general, therefore a fuzzy logic approach is useful (see [1,7,8,15]).

Each comparison creates a hypothesis that this group of stokes matches the pattern. Of course, a single stroke may belong to many hypotheses. Therefore, we have to design an algorithm for selection to get a set of non-exclusive hypotheses.

In this paper, we propose a method for comparing small groups of strokes (including one or two elements) and a compatible method for selection of

© Springer Nature Switzerland AG 2020
L. Rutkowski et al. (Eds.): ICAISC 2020, LNAI 12416, pp. 103–113, 2020.
https://doi.org/10.1007/978-3-030-61534-5_10

hypotheses. It makes possible to transform the set of strokes into a word. The method also enables to get more word hypothesis to select the proper one using a decision system.

2   Input Data

First of all, we need to have a set of extracted strokes. Stroke extraction is not a topic of this paper, therefore we can use an algorithm proposed in [14] or [6]. In this paper, the set of extracted strokes set is called *the dataset*.

As discussed in [12], an extracted stroke can be represented by a couple of polynomials

$$x(t) = a_3t^3 + a_2t^2 + a_1t + a_0$$
$$y(t) = b_3t^3 + b_2t^2 + b_1t + b_0$$

(1)

where

$$t \in [0, 1].$$

Using these polynomials we can get the vector of coefficients

$$\vec{v} = (a_3, a_2, a_1, a_0, b_3, b_2, b_1, b_0).$$

(2)

An algorithm described in this paper requires two input objects: the dataset and the set of patterns. In both cases, each stroke should be represented in the vector form (2).

As defined in [13], the pattern may contain one or more strokes. In this paper, to reduce complexity, we analyze patterns composed of one or two strokes. If the pattern is larger we can select two most important strokes.

3   Pattern Recognition

3.1   Comparing One Stroke with the Pattern

The idea of comparing the single stroke with the pattern is presented in [12]. As described, if we want to measure the similarity between two strokes, we are only interested in its shape. Values a_0 and b_0 in the vector (2) represent only localization of the stroke, not a shape, so we can omit these two elements. Hence, the stroke is described by a vector

$$\vec{s} = (a_3, a_2, a_1, b_3, b_2, b_1).$$

Let us notice that the same stroke may be represented by two different vectors, since both endpoints can be treated as the beginning of the stroke. Accordingly, the two following functions represent the shape of the same stroke:

$$x(t) = a_3t^3 + a_2t^2 + a_1t + a_0$$
$$x'(t) = a_3(1-t)^3 + a_2(1-t)^2 + a_1(1-t) + a_0$$

If we have vector $\vec{s}$, we can calculate its alternative vector $\vec{s'}$

$$\vec{s} = (a_3, a_2, a_1, b_3, b_2, b_1)$$
$$\vec{s'} = (a'_3, a'_2, a'_1, b'_3, b'_2, b'_1)$$

where

$$\begin{array}{ll}
a'_3 = -a_3, & b'_3 = -b_3, \\
a'_2 = 3a_3 + a_2, & b'_2 = 3b_3 + b_2, \\
a'_1 = -3a_3 - 2a_2 - a_1, & b'_1 = -3b_3 - 2b_2 - b_1.
\end{array} \tag{3}$$

Both vectors $\vec{s}$ and $\vec{s'}$ should be normalized due to the fact that we do not interest in a stroke size at this stage of the algorithm.

$$\vec{\hat{s}} = \frac{\vec{s}}{\|\vec{s}\|}, \vec{\hat{s'}} = \frac{\vec{s'}}{\|\vec{s'}\|}$$

Let the vector $\vec{p}$ represent the stroke in the pattern. We can express the difference between this vector and the vector $\vec{s}$ just by the euclidean distance between them. Both vectors are unit, so the distance between them belongs to $[0, 2]$. We must remember, that each stroke can be expressed by two vectors. Hence, the real difference between two strokes can be expressed by

$$D(s,p) = min(\|\vec{\hat{s}} - \vec{\hat{p}}\|, \|\vec{\hat{s'}} - \vec{\hat{p}}\|, \|\vec{\hat{s}} - \vec{\hat{p'}}\|, \|\vec{\hat{s'}} - \vec{\hat{p'}}\|)$$

and the fuzzy measure for two strokes similarity equals

$$F(s,p) = 1 - \frac{1}{2}D(s,p). \tag{4}$$

3.2   Comparing Two Strokes with the Pattern

Comparing a pattern of two strokes is a bit more complex. We must consider not only the similarity of each stroke pair, but also their size and location relative to each other.

Let the strokes in the pattern be represented by the vectors $\vec{p_1}$, $\vec{p_2}$, and the corresponding strokes in the dataset be represented by the vectors $\vec{s_1}$, $\vec{s_2}$. Using (4), we get similarity value $F(s_1, p_1)$ and $F(s_2, p_2)$.

Let us take into consideration stroke sizes. To calculate the stroke length, we need to transform the polynomial representation of the stroke into a list of points. Each point can be calculated by

$$P_{s,i} = (x(T_i), y(T_i)) \tag{5}$$

where $x(t)$, $y(t)$ are defined by (1) and

$$T = [0, 0.01, 0.02, ..., 0.99, 1].$$

The stroke length is equal to the sum of distances between successive points

$$L_s = \sum_{i=2}^{|T|} |P_{s,i-1}P_{s,i}|.$$

We expect that the relation between lengths of the strokes $\vec{s_1}$ and $\vec{p_1}$ is similar to the relation between $\vec{s_2}$ a $\vec{p_2}$. Hence, we can calculate their similarity by the formula

$$L = \frac{\min(L_1, L_2)}{\max(L_1, L_2)}$$

where

$$L_1 = \frac{L_{s_1}}{L_{p_1}}, L_2 = \frac{L_{s_2}}{L_{p_2}}.$$

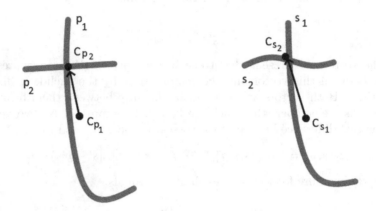

Fig. 1. Vectors connecting mass centers of the strokes

Finally, let us define a measure for the similarity of the relative location of the strokes. Let C_{s_1} be a center of mass of the stroke $\vec{s_1}$. Coordinates of this point are actually average coordinates of all points introduced in (5). We assume that the vector $\overrightarrow{C_{s_1}C_{s_2}}$ is similar to the vector $\overrightarrow{C_{p_1}C_{p_2}}$. This case is presented in Fig. 1. Therefore, the vector

$$\vec{d} = \overrightarrow{C_{s_1}C_{s_2}} - \overrightarrow{C_{p_1}C_{p_2}}$$

should be short (its length should be close to zero). Of course, for larger patterns this length could be relatively bigger, hence, a measure for the similarity of the location must depend on the average stroke length. It can be expressed by

$$C = 1 - tanh(\frac{|\vec{d}|}{L_{avg}})$$

where

$$L_{avg} = \frac{1}{4}(L_{s_1} + L_{s_2} + L_{p_1} + L_{p_2}).$$

To sum up, the fuzzy measure for the similarity of two sets containing two strokes equals

$$F(s_1, s_2, p_1, p_2) = \frac{1}{4} \left(F(s_1, p_1) + F(s_2, p_2) + L + C \right). \tag{6}$$

3.3 Preparing the Set of Hypotheses

If the pattern contains one stroke, we obtain one hypothesis for each stroke in the dataset. The hypothesis is true if the stroke exactly matches the pattern. A probability of this is defined by (4). Matching one line is more likely than matching a complex pattern, so this value is squared.

If a pattern contains two strokes, we get one hypothesis for each combination of two elements from the dataset. A number of them equal $N(N-1)$ where N is the size of the dataset. A probability that the hypothesis is true (the stroke matches the pattern) is defined by (6). For each combination, we can get two hypotheses, because we can assign $\vec{p_1}$ and $\vec{p_2}$ to two ways. It does not make sense to store both hypotheses, therefore, we chose the one with a greater probability. Summarizing, the quality measure of the hypothesis is defined by the formula

$$f_i = \begin{cases} F^2(s, p) & : \{s\} \\ F(s_1, s_2, p_1, p_2) & : \{s_1, s_2\}. \end{cases} \tag{7}$$

This way we receive a set of hypotheses. Each hypothesis contains a probability and a set of one or two stroke datasets. The time complexity of this part of the algorithm is $O(N^2 P)$ where N is the number of strokes in the dataset and P is the number of patterns.

To reduce the total number of received hypotheses, we can set the maximum number of hypotheses created for one pattern, e.g. on $\frac{1}{2}N$. For each pattern, the list of received hypothesis should be in descending order with respect to the fuzzy measure F with removing the poorest ones, if necessary.

4 Selection of Hypotheses

Let $A = \{h_1, h_2, \ldots, h_{|A|}\}$ be the set of all hypotheses generated by the algorithm presented in the previous section. Each hypothesis h_i has got assigned the following values:

- a set S_i containing such strokes from the dataset that are covered by the pattern,
- a fuzzy measure f_i defined by (7),
- a letter (or, generally, a small fragment of text) represented by the pattern.

Our goal is to create such subset $R \subset A$ that each stroke belongs to at least one hypothesis. This subset represents a proposition of the recognized word. The quality of this proposition may be defined as an average fuzzy measure of all hypotheses in R.

$$Q(R) = \frac{1}{|R|} \sum_{h_i \in R} f_i$$

We can assume that $Q(\emptyset) = 1$.

4.1   A Greedy Method

An easy approach to get a subset R is a greedy method:

1. Set $R = \emptyset$.
2. Sort A descending by the f_i.
3. Pop the hypothesis h_0 with the highest f_i.
4. Add h_0 into R.
5. Remove from A the hypotheses having any common strokes with h_0.
6. If $A \neq \emptyset$, go back to step 3.

4.2   A Decision Tree Method

The greedy method does not guarantee to receive the result with the highest quality measure $Q(R)$. To get more variants of R we propose to use a decision tree. The result of this approach is a family of sets $\mathcal{R}$. In each node of the tree, we have to make a decision which hypothesis should be added to R. The first option is the one with the highest f_i, similarly to the greedy method. Let us denote this hypothesis as h_i. Other options are the hypotheses that have at least one common stroke with h_i.

The recursive procedure for building the decision tree is presented below. In the beginning, $R = \emptyset$ and A includes all the hypotheses.

1. Pop the hypothesis h_0 with the highest f_i.
2. Create a subset $T \subset A$ where each element $h_t \in T$ has at least one common stroke with h_0.
3. For each $h_t \in T$:
   (a) Create a set $R_t = R \cup \{h_t\}$.
   (b) Create a set $A_t \in A$ by removing from A all the hypotheses having any common strokes with h_t.
   (c) If $A_t = \emptyset$, add the set R_t into $\mathcal{R}$. Otherwise, invoke this procedure recursively with $R = R_t$, $A = A_t$

This algorithm generates many variants $R_t \in \mathcal{R}$. Of course, the number of them may be huge, so this algorithm is hard to use in practical cases. To reduce time complexity significantly, it should be modified as follows. Let L be the list of pairs (A_t, R_t) sorted descending by $Q(R_t)$. At the beginning of the algorithm, this list contains only one pair $(A, \emptyset)$. Let l_{max} be the maximum number of pairs in L and r_{max} be the maximum number of variants in $\mathcal{R}$. Then, the modified algorithm is given by:

Fig. 2. An example of the input dataset

1. Pop the pair (A_0, R_0) from L with the highest $Q(R_i)$, remove it from the list.
2. Pop the hypothesis h_0 from A_0 with the highest f_i.
3. Create a subset $T \subset A_0$ where each element $h_t \in T$ has at least one common stroke with h_0.
4. For each $h_t \in T$:
   (a) Create a set $R_t = R \cup \{h_t\}$.
   (b) Create a set $A_t \in A$ by removing from A all the hypotheses having any common strokes with h_t.
   (c) If $A_t = \emptyset$, add the set R_t into $\mathcal{R}$. Otherwise, add a pair (R_t, A_t) into sorted list L.
5. If the number of stored pairs $|L|$ is greater than l_{max}, remove the poorest ones.
6. If the number of sets R_t is lower than r_{max} and L is not empty, return to step 1.

4.3   An Example

Let the dataset include three strokes, as in Fig. 2. Let us assume that the set of hypotheses presented in Table 1 is generated for this dataset. A similar example is presented in [13].

Table 1. The set of hypotheses

Hypothesis	Included strokes	Letter	Quality
h_1	s_3	i	0.9
h_2	s_1	c	0.8
h_3	s_1, s_2	a	0.7
h_4	s_2, s_3	u	0.6
h_5	s_2	i	0.5

The decision tree built by the algorithm is presented in Fig. 3. Three different text variants of the text have been generated: "ai" ($Q = 0.80$), "cii" ($Q = 0.73$), and "cu" ($Q = 0.80$). The greedy method selects a subset $R = \{h_1, h_2, h_5\}$ with quality $Q = 0.73$. It can be observed that the algorithm using the decision tree is able to generate a variant with a higher quality measure than the greedy method.

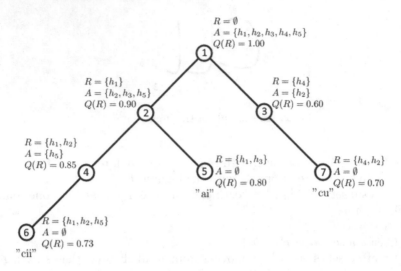

$R = \emptyset$
$A = \{h_1, h_2, h_3, h_4, h_5\}$
$Q(R) = 1.00$

①

$R = \{h_1\}$
$A = \{h_2, h_3, h_5\}$
$Q(R) = 0.90$
②

$R = \{h_4\}$
$A = \{h_2\}$
$Q(R) = 0.60$
③

$R = \{h_1, h_2\}$
$A = \{h_5\}$
$Q(R) = 0.85$
④

$R = \{h_1, h_3\}$
⑤ $A = \emptyset$
$Q(R) = 0.80$
"ai"

$R = \{h_4, h_2\}$
⑦ $A = \emptyset$
$Q(R) = 0.70$
"cu"

⑥ $R = \{h_1, h_2, h_5\}$
$A = \emptyset$
$Q(R) = 0.73$
"cii"

Fig. 3. Decision tree

Figure 3 presents the full decision tree. The numbers inside the nodes mean the order in which the nodes were created. An optimized version of the algorithm would skip some nodes to avoid poorly promising paths.

5   Implementation and Results

The algorithm has been implemented in Python 3. The set of input strokes and the set of patterns have been stored in CSV files. A stroke is represented by a specific class, so some computations, like (3) and (5), may be calculated once, during loading the input files.

The set of patterns is shown in Fig. 5 is used for experiments. Figure 4 presents the input dataset. The results are presented in Table 2. The column "distance" shows the Levenshtein distance between the correct word and the recognized word.

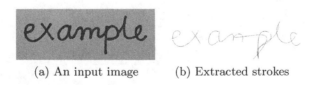

(a) An input image   (b) Extracted strokes

Fig. 4. An input dataset

Table 2. The results for the input dataset presented in Fig. 4

h_i	Distance	Recognized word
0.969	8	Slenscgm
0.969	8	Slenscwm
0.968	8	Slenscgd
0.967	8	Slenscwd
0.967	8	Sslenscgn
0.967	8	Slenscwn
0.966	8	Slenscgu
0.966	8	Slenscwu
0.961	8	Slenscgex
0.961	8	Slenscwex
0.956	8	Slenscgk
0.955	8	Slenscwk
0.944	7	Cemsgap
0.944	7	Ncmsgap
0.944	6	Cemsglep
0.944	6	Ncmsglep

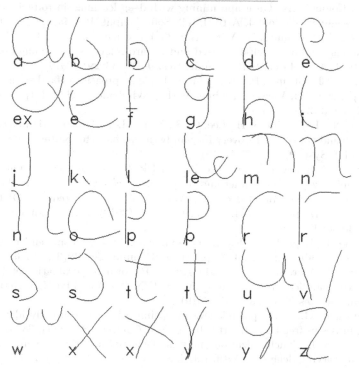

Fig. 5. An example set of 36 patterns

6   Conclusions and Future Works

The algorithm equipped with the decision tree can generate variants with better $Q(R)$ value than the greedy method. Additionally, we are able to generate a set of variants and choose the best one using a separate decision system. This system should use some additional knowledge, for instance, a dictionary, as it is implemented in bag-of-words models (see e.g. [2]). Other improvement can be introduced by identifying syntactic in text as in [10]. Consequently, our future works will focus on the optimization of the algorithm presented in this paper and the creation of the decision system to choose the best variant. At the top level of our method, we aim to employ particular forms of artificial neural networks as spiking [4] or memristive [11] neural networks. We expect our method to outperform standard approaches using deep neural networks [3,9].

References

1. D'Aniello, G., Gaeta, M., Loia, F., Reformat, M., Toti, D.: An environment for collective perception based on fuzzy and semantic approaches. J. Artif. Intell. Soft Comput. Res. **8**(3), 191–210 (2018)
2. Gabryel, M.: The bag-of-words method with different types of image features and dictionary analysis. J. UCS **24**(4), 357–371 (2018)
3. Hou, Y., Holder, L.B.: On graph mining with deep learning: introducing model r for link weight prediction. J. Artif. Intell. Soft Comput. Res. **9**(1), 21–40 (2019)
4. Nobukawa, S., Nishimura, H., Yamanishi, T.: Pattern classification by spiking neural networks combining self-organized and reward-related spike-timing-dependent plasticity. J. Artif. Intell. Soft Comput. Res. **9**(4), 283–291 (2019)
5. Ostrowski, D.J., Cheung, P.Y.K.: A Fuzzy Logic Approach to Handwriting Recognition, pp. 299–314. Vieweg+Teubner Verlag, Wiesbaden (1996). https://doi.org/10.1007/978-3-322-88955-3_10
6. Phan, D., Na, I.-S., Kim, S.-H., Lee, G.-S., Yang, H.-J.: Triangulation based skeletonization and trajectory recovery for handwritten character patterns. KSII Trans. Internet Inf. Syst. **9**, 358–377 (2015)
7. Rutkowski, T., Łapa, K., Jaworski, M., Nielek, R., Rutkowska, D.: On explainable flexible fuzzy recommender and its performance evaluation using the Akaike information criterion. In: Gedeon, T., Wong, K.W., Lee, M. (eds.) ICONIP 2019. CCIS, vol. 1142, pp. 717–724. Springer, Cham (2019). https://doi.org/10.1007/978-3-030-36808-1_78
8. Rutkowski, T., Łapa, K., Nielek, R.: On explainable fuzzy recommenders and their performance evaluation. Int. J. Appl. Math. Comput. Sci. **29**(3), 595–610 (2019)
9. Shewalkar, A., Nyavanandi, D., Ludwig, S.A.: Performance evaluation of deep neural networks applied to speech recognition: RNN, lSTM and GRU. J. Artif. Intell. Soft Comput. Res. **9**(4), 235–245 (2019)
10. Tambouratzis, G.: Using particle swarm optimization to accurately identify syntactic phrases in free text. J. Artif. Intell. Soft Comput. Res. **8**(1), 63–67 (2018)
11. Wei, R., Cao, J.: Synchronization analysis of inertial memristive neural networks with time-varying delays. J. Artif. Intell. Soft Comput. Res. **8**(4), 269–282 (2018)

12. Wróbel, M., Nieszporek, K., Starczewski, J.T., Cader, A.: A fuzzy measure for recognition of handwritten letter strokes. In: Rutkowski, L., Scherer, R., Korytkowski, M., Pedrycz, W., Tadeusiewicz, R., Zurada, J.M. (eds.) ICAISC 2018. LNCS (LNAI), vol. 10841, pp. 761–770. Springer, Cham (2018). https://doi.org/10.1007/978-3-319-91253-0_70
13. Wróbel, M., Starczewski, J.T., Napoli, C.: Handwriting recognition with extraction of letter fragments. In: Rutkowski, L., Korytkowski, M., Scherer, R., Tadeusiewicz, R., Zadeh, L.A., Zurada, J.M. (eds.) ICAISC 2017. LNCS (LNAI), vol. 10246, pp. 183–192. Springer, Cham (2017). https://doi.org/10.1007/978-3-319-59060-8_18
14. Wróbel, M., Starczewski, J.T., Nieszporek, K., Opiełka, P., Kaźmierczak, A.: A greedy algorithm for extraction of handwritten strokes. In: Rutkowski, L., Scherer, R., Korytkowski, M., Pedrycz, W., Tadeusiewicz, R., Zurada, J.M. (eds.) ICAISC 2019. LNCS (LNAI), vol. 11509, pp. 464–473. Springer, Cham (2019). https://doi.org/10.1007/978-3-030-20915-5_42
15. Zhao, Y., Liu, Q.: A continuous-time distributed algorithm for solving a class of decomposable nonconvex quadratic programming. J. Artif. Intell. Soft Comput. Res. 8(4), 283–291 (2018)

Data Mining

A Density-Based Prototype Selection Approach

Joel Luís Carbonera$^{(\boxtimes)}$ and Mara Abel

UFRGS, Porto Alegre, Brazil
{jlcarbonera,marabel}@inf.ufrgs.br

Abstract. Due to the increasing size of the datasets, prototype selection techniques have been applied for reducing the computational resources involved in data mining and machine learning tasks. In this paper, we propose a density-based approach for selecting prototypes. Firstly, it finds the density peaks in each dimension of the dataset. After that, it builds clusters of objects around these peaks. Finally, it extracts a prototype that represents each cluster and selects the most representative prototypes for including in the final reduced dataset. The proposed algorithm can deal with some crucial weak points of approaches that were previously proposed regarding the setting of parameters and the capability of dealing with high-dimensional datasets. Our method was evaluated on 14 well-known datasets used in a classification task. The performance of the proposed algorithm was compared to the performances of 8 prototype selection algorithms in terms of accuracy and reduction rate. The experimental results show that, in general, the proposed algorithm provides a good trade-off between reduction rate and the accuracy with reasonable time complexity.

Keywords: Prototype selection · Data reduction · Data mining · Machine learning · Big data

1 Introduction

Prototype selection is a data-mining (or machine learning) pre-processing task that consists of producing a smaller representative set of instances from the total available data, which can support a data mining task *with no performance loss* (or, at least, a reduced performance loss) [11]. Thus, every prototype selection strategy faces a *trade-off* between the *reduction rate* of the dataset and the resulting *classification quality* (accuracy) [10].

Most of the proposed algorithms for prototype selection, such as [2, 14–16, 18, 19] have a *high time complexity*, which is an undesirable property for algorithms that should deal with big volumes of data. Other approaches, such as [6–9], have a low complexity time, but require the setting of parameters whose values are not easy to select. In this paper, we propose an algorithm for prototype

© Springer Nature Switzerland AG 2020
L. Rutkowski et al. (Eds.): ICAISC 2020, LNAI 12416, pp. 117–129, 2020.
https://doi.org/10.1007/978-3-030-61534-5_11

selection, called DPS (*Density-based Prototype Selection*)[1]. The algorithm has three main steps: (I) it finds the *density peaks* in each dimension of the dataset (using kernel-density estimation), (II) it aggregates instances in clusters that are built around the *density peaks* identified in the previous step and (III) it extracts prototypes from the clusters that are more representative of each class of the dataset. The method provides to the user the capability of defining the number of prototypes that are generated, as a percentage of the total number of instances in the dataset. This level of control is not common in most of the approaches for prototype selection.

The proposed approach is inspired by the PSDSP algorithm, proposed in [8]. The main advantages of DPS over PSDSP are:

- It is guided by the *intrinsic properties* of the data for spliting the dataset in sets of similar instances, avoiding the necessity of an *arbitrary* setting of parameters, as in the case of PSDSP.
- It is more suitable than PSDSP algorithm for dealing with high-dimensional datasets, as it will be discussed in Sect. 4.

Our approach was evaluated on 14 well-known datasets and its performance was compared with the performance of 8 important algorithms provided by the literature, according to 2 different performance measures: *accuracy* and *reduction*. The accuracy was evaluated considering two classifiers: SVM and KNN. The results show that, when compared to the other algorithms, DPS provides a good trade-off between accuracy and reduction, while presents a reasonable time complexity.

Section 2 presents some related works. Section 3 presents the notation that will be used throughout the paper. Section 4 presents our approach. Section 5 discusses our experimental evaluation. Finally, Sect. 6 presents our main conclusions and final remarks.

2   Related Works

The *Condensed Nearest Neighbor* (CNN) algorithm [13] and *Reduced Nearest Neighbor* algorithm (RNN) [12] are some of the earliest proposals for instance selection. Both can assign noisy instances to the final resulting set, are dependent on the order of the instances and have a high time complexity. The *Edited Nearest Neighbor* (ENN) algorithm [19] removes every instance that does not agree with the label of the majority of its k nearest neighbors. This strategy is effective for removing noisy instances, but it does not reduce the dataset as much as other algorithms. In [18], the authors present 5 approaches, named the *Decremental Reduction Optimization Procedure* (DROP). These algorithms assume that those instances that have x as one of their k nearest neighbors are called the *associates* of x. Among the proposed algorithms, DROP3 has the best

---

[1] The source code of the algorithm is available in https://www.researchgate.net/publication/339883322_Density-based_prototype_selection_DPS_algorithm.

trade-off between the reduction of the dataset and the classification accuracy. It applies a noise-filter algorithm such as ENN. Then, it removes an instance x if its associates in the original training set can be correctly classified without x. The main drawback of DROP3 is its high time complexity. The *Iterative Case Filtering algorithm* (ICF) [2] is based on the notions of *Coverage set* and *Reachable set*. The coverage set of an instance x is the set of instances in T whose distance from x is less than the distance between x and its nearest enemy (instance with a different class). The Reachable set of an instance x, on the other hand, is the set of instances in T that have x in their respective coverage sets. In this method, a given instance x is removed from S if $|Reachable(x)| > |Coverage(x)|$. This algorithm also has a high running time. In [14], the authors adopted the notion of *local sets* for designing complementary methods for instance selection. In this context, the local set of a given instance x is the set of instances contained in the largest hypersphere centered on x such that it does not contain instances from any other class. The first algorithm, called *Local Set-based Smoother* (LSSm) uses two notions for guiding the process: *usefulness* and *harmfulness*. The usefulness $u(x)$ of a given instance x is the number of instances having x among the members of their local sets, and the harmfulness $h(x)$ is the number of instances having x as the nearest enemy. For each instance x in T, the algorithm includes x in S if $u(x) \geq h(x)$. Since the goal of LSSm is to remove harmful instances, its reduction rate is lower than most of the instance selection algorithms. The author also proposed the *Local Set Border selector* (LSBo). Firstly, it uses LSSm to remove noise, and then, it computes the local set of every instance $\in T$. Then, the instances in T are sorted in the ascending order of the cardinality of their local sets. In the last step, LSBo verifies, for each instance $x \in T$ if any member of its local set is contained in S, thus ensuring the proper classification of x. If that is not the case, x is included in S to ensure its correct classification. The time complexity of the two approaches is $O(|T|^2)$. In [4], the authors proposed the *Local Density-based Instance Selection* (LDIS) algorithm. This algorithm selects the instances with the highest density in their neighborhoods. It provides a good balance between accuracy and reduction and is faster than the other algorithms discussed here. The literature provides some extensions to the basic LDIS algorithm, such as [3,5]. In [6–9] the authors propose a family of algorithms that are based on the notion of *spatial partition*, which is a hyperrectangle that encompasses a specific set of instances in the whole data space of a given dataset. In an overview, these algorithms split the dataset in a set of non-overlapping spatial partitions (with the same volume) and select representative instances or prototypes from the most representative ones. These algorithms are very efficient and provide a good trade-off between accuracy and reduction. The main drawback of these approaches is the necessity of providing the number of segments in which each dimension will be split. This is an *arbitrary* choice that can produce results of low quality. The DPS algorithm presented in this paper is based on some intuitions underlying these approaches, but adopting a mathematically sound criterion based on kernel-density estimation for splitting the dataset into clusters of similar instances.

3   Notations

In this section, we introduce a notation adapted from [4] that will be used throughout the paper.

- $T = \{o_1, o_2, ..., o_n\}$ is the non-empty set of n instances (or data objects), representing the original dataset to be reduced in the prototype selection process.
- $D = \{d_1, d_2, ..., d_m\}$ is a set of m dimensions (that represent features, or attributes), where each $d_i \subseteq \mathbb{R}$.
- Each $o_i \in T$ is an $m - tuple$, such that $o_i = (o_{i1}, o_{i2}, ..., o_{im})$, where o_{ij} represents the value of the j-th feature (or dimension) of the instance o_i, for $1 \leq j \leq m$.
- $val \colon T \times D \to \mathbb{R}$ is a function that maps a data object $o_i \in T$ and a dimension $d_j \in D$ to the value o_{ij}, which represents the value in the dimension d_j for the object o_i.
- $L = \{l_1, l_2, ..., l_p\}$ is the set of p class labels that are used for classifying the instances in T, where each $l_i \in L$ represents a given class label.
- $l \colon T \to L$ is a function that maps a given instance $x_i \in T$ to its corresponding class label $l_j \in L$.
- $c \colon L \to 2^T$ is a function that maps a given class label $l_j \in L$ to a given set C, such that $C \subseteq T$, which represents the set of instances in T whose class is l_j. Notice that $T = \bigcup_{l \in L} c(l)$. In this notation, 2^T represents the *powerset* of T, that is, the set of all subsets of T, including the empty set and T itself.

4   The DPS Algorithm

In this paper, we propose the DPS (*Density-based Prototype Selection*) algorithm, which can be viewed as a specific variation of the general schema represented in [6] and that is inspired in the PSDSP algorithm [8]. The main difference regarding the PSDSP and DPS algorithms lies in the way that both algorithms split the datasets in sets of instances that are similar to each other. In PSDSP algorithm, the dataset is separated in a set of non-overlapping hyperrectangles with the same volume called *spatial partitions*. The number of hyperrectangles created by the algorithm is indirectly defined by a parameter n that *globally* defines the number of segments in that each dimension will be split. Thus, the total number of hyperrectangles created by the algorithm is $|L|.|D|^n$, that is, $|D|^n$ partitions for each class of objects in the datasets. Notice that the value of n is chosen by the user *arbitrarily*, without considering any *intrinsic property* of the dataset. Due to this, selecting a suitable value for n can be a challenge. Besides that, high-dimensional datasets can be a challenge for this approach, since some cases the number of spatial partitions (that depends on the number of dimensions of the dataset) can be equal or greater than the total number of instances in the dataset. In these cases, the partitioning procedure would be *useless*. In addition, in most of the cases, there is no justification for splitting all dimensions in an equal number of segments, since each dimension has its specific statistical properties. The DPS algorithm, on the other hand, splits the set of instances of each class according to the *density* of the data in each dimension. Due to this, DPS algorithm avoids the necessity of arbitrary choices made by the user regarding the way of splitting the dataset in sets of similar instances. Moreover, it uses *intrinsic properties* (density) of the dataset for guiding the identification of sets of similar instances. This allows the proposed algorithm to deal with high-dimensional datasets in a mathematically sound way, since that, in general, the resulting sets of instances identified by the algorithm is lower than the number of instances in the dataset.

In an abstract overview, the DPS algorithm (formalized in Algorithm 1) has the following steps: for each class, firstly, it identifies a set of *density peaks* of data in each dimension of the dataset, after it identifies clusters of instances that are built around these peaks, and finally, it extracts prototypes from the *densest* clusters.

The DPS algorithm takes as input a set of data objects T, a value $p \in [0, 1]$, which determines the expected number of prototypes that should be selected, as a percentage of the total number of instances ($|T|$) in the dataset; and a value λ which defines the bandwidth used by the *kernel-density estimation* method estimating the density of each value in each dimension of the dataset. The algorithm initializes P as an empty set and, for each $l \in L$, it:

1. Determines the number k of objects in $c(l)$ that should be included in P, in a way that $k = |c(l)|.p$;
2. Determines the set C of clusters of objects within $c(l)$. The set C is produced by the function *partitioning*, represented in Algorithm 2, which takes as input the set $c(l)$ of instances classified by l and the bandwidth λ.
3. Sorts the set C in descending order, according to the number of instances included by each cluster $c_i \in C$. Thus, after this step, the first cluster in C would represent the *densest* cluster, that is, the cluster in C that includes the *greatest number of instances*.
4. Extracts k prototypes, from the first k sets in C, and includes them in the resulting set P. Notice that when $|C| < k$, only $|C|$ prototypes are included.

Algorithm 1: DPS algorithm

Input: A set instances T, a value $p \in [0, 1]$, which is the number of prototypes, as a
       percentage of $|T|$; and a value λ that represents the bandwidth.
Output: A set P of prototypes.
begin
    $P \leftarrow \emptyset$;
    foreach $l \in L$ **do**
        $k \leftarrow p \cdot |c(l)|$;
        $C \leftarrow partitioning(c(l), \lambda)$;
        Sorting C in descending order, according to the number of instances included by
           each set $c_i \in C$;
        $i \leftarrow 0$;
        while $i \leq |C|$ *and* $i \leq k$ **do**
           $prot \leftarrow extractsPrototype(c_i)$;
           $P \leftarrow P \cup \{prot\}$;
           $i \leftarrow i + 1$;
    return P;

The function *partitioning*, on the other hand, is formalized by Algorithm 2. This algorithm takes as input a set of instances H and a value λ that represents the *bandwidth* used for estimating the density of each value in each dimension and, therefore, for identifying the *density peaks* in each dimension. It results in a set C of clusters of instances. Initially, the algorithm defines C as an empty set. After, for each dimension $d_i \in D$, the algorithm identifies the list DP, where each $DP_i \in DP$ is a list of *density peaks* of the dimension d_i, and each $dp_{ij} \in DP$ represents the j-th density peak of the i-th dimension in d. After, the algorithm considers *clusters* as a hash table whose keys are $|D|$-tuples in the form of $(x_1, x_2, ..., x_m)$, where each x_i is the index that identifies one of the peaks of the $i-th$ dimension in D. In addition, for each key x, *clusters* stores a set of objects, such that $clusters[x] \subseteq H$. Notice that a key of this hash table can be viewed as the identification of a given cluster. After, for each object $o \in H$, the algorithm:

1. Considers x as an empty $|D|$-tuple.
2. Assigns to $x_i \in x$, the index j that identifies the nearest peak $d_{ij} \in DP_i$ of the value $val(o, d_i)$ (the value of the dimension d_i of the object o). At the end of this process, each $x_i \in x$ identifies a density peak in the i-th dimension.
3. Includes o as an element of $region[x]$.

After, for each different key x of *region*, the algorithm includes the set $region[x]$ in C as element. Thus, each element of C is a cluster of objects that is built around a set of density peaks (one for each dimension). Finally, the algorithm returns C.

Algorithm 2: Partitioning

Input: A set instances H and a value λ
Output: A set C of sets of instances.
begin
    $C \leftarrow \emptyset$;
    Let DP an empty list;
    foreach $d_i \in D$ **do**
        $DP_i \leftarrow$ a list of density peaks of the dimension d_i, considering the instances in H and the bandwidth λ, where each dp_{ij} is the j-th density peak of the i-th dimension;
    Let *region* be a hash table whose keys are $|D|$-tuples in the form of $(x_1, x_2, ..., x_m)$ and where, for each key x, *region* stores a set of objects, such that $region[x] \subseteq H$.;
    foreach $o \in H$ **do**
        Let x be an empty $|D|$-tuple.;
        foreach $d_i \in D$ **do**
            $x_i \leftarrow$ the index j of the density peak dp_{ij}, such that $dp_{ij} - val(o, d_i)$ has its minimum value, among all the density peaks in DP_i;
        $region[x] \leftarrow region[x] \cup \{o\}$;
    foreach *key x of region* **do**
        C includes $region[x]$ as its element;
    return C;

Finally, the function *extractsPrototype*, adopted by Algorithm 1, takes as input a set of instances $H \subseteq T$ and produces a $|D|$-tuple that represents the centroid (the average point) of the objects in H. This is the same strategy used by [6] for extracting prototypes.

Notice that the algorithm extracts prototypes of the k *densest* spatial partitions because it assumes that the *density* of a spatial partition indicates the *amount of information* that it represents, and that the resulting set of prototypes should include the prototypes that abstract a richer amount of information.

Besides that, given a specific dataset, the DPS algorithm generates, at most, a total of

$$\sum_{l \in L} \prod_{d_i \in D} |peaks(d_i, c(l))| \tag{1}$$

clusters, where $peaks(d_i, c(l))$ represents the set of peaks identified in the dimension d_i for the set of objects $c(l)$ of the class $l \in L$. Notice that this number cam be lower than this limit, since only clusters that include at least one object are created. In general, the number of clusters generated by DPS algorithm is lower than the number of spatial partitions that are generated by the PSDSP algorithm.

Assuming that $kde(d_i, H)$ represents the time taken for estimating the probability density of the dimension d_i, considering the set of objects H, the temporal complexity of DPS algorithm is:

$$\sum_{l \in L} \left(\sum_{d_i \in D} kde(d_i, c(l)) \right) + |D|.|c(l)| \tag{2}$$

That is, the temporal complexity of DPS algorithm is dominated by the cost of kernel-density estimation method.

5   Experiments

For evaluating our approach, we compared the DPS algorithm in a *classification* task, with 8 important prototype selection algorithms[2] provided by the literature: DROP3, ENN, ICF, LSBo, LSSm, LDIS, ISDSP and PSDSP. We considered 14 well-known datasets with numerical dimensions: cardiotocography, diabetes, E. Coli, glass, heart-statlog, ionosphere, iris, landsat, letter, optdigits, page-blocks, parkinson, segment, spambase and wine. All datasets were obtained from the UCI Machine Learning Repository[3].

We use two standard measures to evaluate the performance of the algorithms: *accuracy* and *reduction*. Following [4,14], we assume: $accuracy = |Sucess(Test)|/|Test|$ and $reduction = (|T| - |S|)/|T|$, where $Test$ is a given set of instances that are selected for being tested in a classification task, and $|Success(Test)|$ is the number of instances in $Test$ correctly classified in the classification task.

For evaluating the classification *accuracy* of new instances in each respective dataset, we adopted a SVM and a KNN classifier. For the KNN classifier, we considered $k = 3$, as assumed in [4,14]. For the SVM, following [1], we adopted the implementation provided by Weka 3.8, with the standard parametrization

---

[2] All algorithms were implemented by the authors.
[3] http://archive.ics.uci.edu/ml/.

($c = 1.0$, *toleranceParameter* $= 0.001$, *epsilon* $= 1.0E - 12$, using a polynomial kernel and a multinomial logistic regression model with a ridge estimator as calibrator). For performing the kernel density estimation in DPS algorithm, we adopted the SMILE (Statistical Machine Intelligence & Learning Engine) library[4], adopting a gaussian kernel.

Besides that, following [4], the accuracy and reduction were evaluated in an *n-fold cross-validation* scheme, where $n = 10$. Thus, firstly a dataset is randomly partitioned in 10 equally sized subsamples. From these subsamples, a single subsample is selected as validation data (*Test*), and the union of the remaining 9 subsamples is considered the *initial training set* (*ITS*). Next, a prototype selection algorithm is applied for reducing the *ITS*, producing the *reduced training set* (*RTS*). At this point, we can measure the *reduction* of the dataset. Finally, the *RTS* is used as the training set for the classifier, which is used for classifying the instances in *Test*. At this point, we can measure the accuracy achieved by the classifier, using *RTS* as the training set. This process is repeated 10 times, with each subsample used once as *Test*. The 10 values of accuracy and reduction are averaged to produce, respectively, the *average accuracy* (*AA*) and *average reduction* (*AR*). Tables 1, 2 and 3 report, respectively, for each combination of dataset and prototype selection algorithm: the resulting *AA* achieved by the SVM classifier, *AA* achieved by the KNN classifier, and the *AR*. The best results for each dataset is marked in bold typeface.

In all experiments, following [4], we adopted $k = 3$ for DROP3, ENN, ICF, and LDIS. For the PSDSP and ISDSP algorithms, following [7,8], we adopted $n = 5$ and $p = 0.1$. For the DPS algorithm we have adopted $p = 0.1$ (the same preservation rate adopted by PSDSP and ISDSP), while the parameter

Table 1. Comparison of the *accuracy* achieved by the training set produced by each algorithm, for each dataset, adopting a SVM classifier.

Algorithm	DROP3	ENN	ICF	LSBO	LSSM	LDIS	ISDSP	PSDSP	DPS	Average
Cardiotocography	0.64	**0.67**	0.64	0.62	**0.67**	0.62	0.59	0.59	0.60	0.63
Diabetes	0.75	**0.77**	0.76	0.75	**0.77**	0.75	0.73	0.71	0.74	0.75
E.Coli	0.81	0.82	0.78	0.74	**0.83**	0.77	0.78	0.81	0.78	0.79
Glass	0.47	0.49	0.49	0.42	**0.55**	0.50	0.51	0.48	0.51	0.49
Heart-statlog	0.81	0.83	0.79	0.81	**0.84**	0.81	0.78	0.82	0.83	0.81
Ionosphere	0.81	0.87	0.58	0.45	**0.88**	0.84	0.86	0.86	0.82	0.77
Iris	0.94	**0.96**	0.73	0.47	**0.96**	0.81	0.80	0.84	0.87	0.82
Landsat	0.86	**0.87**	0.85	0.85	**0.87**	0.84	0.84	0.84	0.81	0.85
Optdigits	0.98	0.98	0.97	0.98	**0.99**	0.96	0.97	0.97	0.94	0.97
Page-blocks	0.93	**0.94**	0.93	0.92	**0.94**	**0.94**	0.91	0.91	0.92	0.93
Parkinsons	0.85	**0.87**	0.85	0.82	**0.87**	0.82	0.85	0.85	0.80	0.84
Segment	0.91	**0.92**	0.91	0.80	0.91	0.89	0.88	0.87	0.88	0.89
Spambase	**0.90**	**0.90**	**0.90**	**0.90**	**0.90**	0.89	0.87	0.87	0.88	0.89
Wine	0.93	0.95	0.94	0.96	**0.97**	0.94	0.93	0.95	0.93	0.94
Average	0.83	**0.85**	0.79	0.75	**0.85**	0.81	0.81	0.81	0.81	0.81

---

[4] Available in https://github.com/haifengl/smile.

λ was estimated according to the Silverman's heuristic [17], commonly used in statistics, where $\lambda = 1.06.\sigma.n^{-\frac{1}{5}}$, where σ is the standard deviation of the sample and n is the sample size. Besides that, for the algorithms that use distance (dissimilarity) function, we adopted the standard *Euclidean* distance.

Tables 1 and 2 show that LSSm achieves the highest *accuracy* in most of the datasets, for both classifiers. This is expected, since that LSSm was designed for removing noisy instances and does not provide high reduction rates. Besides that, for most of the datasets, the difference between the accuracy of DPS and the accuracy achieved by the other algorithms is not big. The average accuracy achieved by DPS is similar to the average accuracy of LDIS, ISDSP and PSDSP, which are considered efficient algorithms. In cases where the achieved accuracy is lower than the accuracy provided by other algorithms, this can be compensated by a higher reduction produced by DPS and by a reasonable running time. Table 3 shows that DPS achieves the highest *reduction* in most of the datasets, and achieves also the highest average reduction rate. Regarding the reduction rate, PSD has the same performance of ISDSP and PSDSP. This table also shows that, in some datasets (such as parkinson and segment), the DPS algorithm achieved a reduction rate that is significantly higher than the reduction achieved by other algorithms, with a similar accuracy.

We also carried out experiments for evaluating the impact of the parameters p and λ in the performance of DPS. The Table 4 represents the accuracy achieved by an SVM classifier (with the standard parametrization of Weka 3.8), as a function of the parameters λ and p. In this experiment, we considered λ assuming the values 2.0, 5.0, 10.0, 20.0 and also a value that is estimated specifically for each dataset according to the Silverman's heuristic. On the other hand, we considered p assuming the values 0.05, 0.1 and 0.2. We also considered the 10-fold cross validation schema in this experiment. Notice that the table presents

Table 2. Comparison of the *accuracy* achieved by the training set produced by each algorithm, for each dataset, adopting a KNN classifier.

Algorithm	DROP3	ENN	ICF	LSBO	LSSM	LDIS	ISDSP	PSDSP	DPS	Average
Cardiotocography	0.63	0.64	0.57	0.55	**0.67**	0.54	0.50	0.50	0.51	0.57
Diabetes	0.72	0.72	0.72	**0.73**	0.72	0.68	0.65	0.69	0.70	0.70
E.Coli	0.84	0.84	0.79	0.79	**0.86**	0.82	0.82	0.79	0.79	0.82
Glass	0.63	0.63	0.64	0.54	**0.71**	0.62	0.55	0.51	0.52	0.59
Heart-statlog	**0.67**	0.64	0.63	0.66	0.66	**0.67**	0.63	0.65	0.63	0.65
Ionosphere	0.82	0.83	0.82	**0.88**	0.86	0.85	0.85	0.86	0.86	0.85
Iris	**0.97**	**0.97**	0.95	0.95	0.96	0.95	0.95	0.94	0.95	0.95
Landsat	0.88	**0.90**	0.83	0.86	**0.90**	0.87	0.86	0.85	0.80	0.86
Optdigits	0.97	**0.98**	0.91	0.91	**0.98**	0.95	0.94	0.94	0.87	0.94
Page-blocks	0.95	**0.96**	0.93	0.94	0.96	0.94	0.77	0.72	0.93	0.90
Parkinsons	0.86	**0.88**	0.83	0.85	0.85	0.74	0.79	0.76	0.76	0.81
Segment	0.92	**0.94**	0.87	0.83	**0.94**	0.88	0.89	0.86	0.88	0.89
Spambase	0.79	0.81	0.79	0.81	**0.82**	0.75	0.77	0.74	0.76	0.78
Wine	0.69	0.66	0.66	0.74	0.71	0.69	**0.75**	0.67	0.67	0.69
Average	0.81	0.81	0.78	0.79	**0.83**	0.78	0.77	0.75	0.76	0.79

Table 3. Comparison of the *reduction* achieved by each algorithm, for each dataset.

Algorithm	DROP3	ENN	ICF	LSBO	LSSM	LDIS	ISDSP	PSDSP	DPS	Average
Cardiotocography	0.70	0.32	0.71	0.69	0.14	0.86	**0.90**	**0.90**	**0.90**	0.68
Diabetes	0.77	0.31	0.85	0.76	0.13	**0.90**	**0.90**	**0.90**	**0.90**	0.71
E.Coli	0.72	0.17	0.87	0.83	0.09	**0.92**	0.90	0.90	0.90	0.70
Glass	0.75	0.35	0.69	0.70	0.13	**0.90**	**0.90**	**0.90**	**0.90**	0.69
Heart-statlog	0.74	0.35	0.78	0.67	0.15	**0.93**	0.90	0.90	0.90	0.70
Ionosphere	0.86	0.15	**0.96**	0.81	0.04	0.91	0.90	0.90	0.90	0.71
Iris	0.70	0.04	0.61	0.92	0.05	0.87	**0.90**	**0.90**	**0.90**	0.65
Landsat	0.72	0.10	0.91	0.88	0.05	**0.92**	0.90	0.90	0.90	0.70
Optdigits	0.72	0.01	**0.93**	0.92	0.02	0.92	0.90	0.90	0.90	0.69
Page-blocks	0.71	0.04	0.95	**0.96**	0.03	0.87	0.90	0.90	0.90	0.70
Parkinsons	0.72	0.15	0.80	0.87	0.11	0.83	**0.90**	**0.90**	**0.90**	0.69
Segment	0.68	0.05	0.79	**0.90**	0.05	0.83	**0.90**	**0.90**	**0.90**	0.67
Spambase	0.74	0.19	0.79	0.82	0.10	0.82	**0.90**	**0.90**	**0.90**	0.68
Wine	0.80	0.30	0.82	0.75	0.11	0.88	**0.90**	**0.90**	**0.90**	0.71
Average	0.74	0.18	0.82	0.82	0.09	0.88	**0.90**	**0.90**	**0.90**	0.69

the measures grouped primarily by the parameter λ, and within each value of λ, they present the results for each value of p.

The experiment shows that the parameter λ does not have too much impact in the performance of the algorithm. However, the best average results are achieved using the λ estimated according to the Silverman's heuristic. This suggest that it is possible to consider this heuristic as a standard parametrization of the algorithm. On the other hand, in most of the cases, as the value of p increases, considering a fixed value of λ, the accuracy increases. This is expected, since as p increases, the total number of prototypes selected by the algorithm also increases. Since each prototype abstracts the local information of a specific cluster of instances, in most of the cases, increasing the value of p allows the resulting set of prototypes to capture more local information of the dataset. These additional prototypes the classifier to use the additional information to make more fine-grained distinctions in the classification process.

We also carried out a comparison of the running times of the prototype selection algorithms considered in our experiments. In this comparison, we applied the 9 prototype selection algorithms to reduce the 3 biggest datasets considered in our tests: *page-blocks*, *optdigits* and *spambase*. We adopted the same parametrizations that were adopted in the first experiment. We performed the experiments in an Intel® Core™ i5-5200U laptop with a 2.2 GHz CPU and 8 GB of RAM. The Fig. 1 shows that, considering these datasets, the DPS algorithm is not so efficient as the PSDSP algorithm (that is the main inspiration underlying PSD algorithm). This result is a consequence of the fact that PSDSP algorithm has a linear time complexity (ensured by its naive approach for splitting the dataset) while the time complexity of PSD algorithm is dominated by the computational cost of kernel density estimation. However, in this context, it is important to notice that, although PSD algorithm is not so efficient than PSDSP, it is mathematically well-founded, using probability estimation for splitting the dataset

Table 4. Comparison of the accuracy achieved by an SVM classifier trained with prototype selected by DPS with different values of p and λ. The estimated bandwidth was obtained for each dataset according to the Silverman's heuristic.

Bandwidth	Estimated			2.0			5.0			10.0			20.0			Average
Percentage	0.05	0.10	0.20	0.05	0.10	0.20	0.05	0.10	0.20	0.05	0.10	0.20	0.05	0.10	0.20	
Cardiotocography	0.59	0.60	0.61	0.58	0.60	**0.62**	0.58	0.61	0.61	0.60	0.61	0.63	0.60	0.59	0.61	0.60
Diabetes	**0.76**	0.74	0.73	0.71	0.73	0.74	0.74	0.74	0.75	0.73	0.74	**0.76**	0.74	0.75	0.75	0.74
E.Coli	0.73	**0.78**	**0.78**	0.75	**0.78**	**0.78**	0.75	**0.78**	0.77	0.75	**0.78**	**0.78**	0.75	**0.78**	**0.78**	0.77
Glass	0.55	0.51	**0.53**	0.43	0.50	0.51	0.46	0.48	0.51	0.44	0.52	0.49	0.50	0.52	0.50	0.50
Heart-statlog	0.77	**0.83**	**0.83**	0.78	0.80	**0.83**	0.80	0.79	0.80	0.79	0.81	0.82	0.75	0.81	**0.83**	0.80
Ionosphere	0.83	0.82	0.86	0.81	0.86	0.85	0.85	0.85	0.85	0.80	0.84	0.86	0.81	0.85	**0.87**	0.84
Iris	0.84	**0.87**	0.85	0.85	0.88	0.85	0.83	0.83	0.84	**0.87**	0.83	0.86	0.83	0.83	0.84	0.85
Landsat	0.81	0.81	0.78	**0.83**	0.82	0.80	0.79	0.76	0.75	0.76	0.71	0.70	0.75	0.72	0.71	0.77
Optdigits	**0.94**	**0.94**	0.93	0.92	0.91	0.92	0.92	0.92	0.92	0.92	0.91	0.92	0.92	0.92	0.92	0.92
Page-blocks	0.92	0.92	0.92	0.92	0.92	**0.93**	0.92	0.92	**0.93**	0.92	**0.93**	0.92	0.92	**0.93**	0.92	0.92
Parkinsons	0.71	0.80	0.79	0.79	0.82	0.82	0.81	0.81	0.85	0.78	0.78	0.84	0.80	0.82	**0.86**	0.81
Segment	0.84	0.88	**0.91**	0.84	0.88	0.90	0.84	0.87	0.90	0.85	0.87	**0.91**	0.85	0.87	0.90	0.87
Spambase	0.86	0.88	**0.89**	0.86	0.88	0.88	0.86	0.88	**0.89**	0.86	0.88	**0.89**	0.86	0.88	**0.89**	0.88
Wine	0.91	0.93	0.93	0.89	0.93	**0.95**	0.91	0.90	0.93	0.89	0.94	**0.95**	0.88	**0.95**	**0.95**	0.92
Average	0.79	**0.81**	**0.81**	0.78	**0.81**	**0.81**	0.79	0.80	**0.81**	0.78	0.80	**0.81**	0.78	0.80	**0.81**	0.80

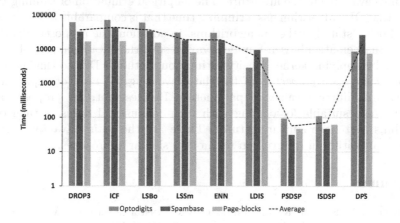

Fig. 1. Comparison of the running times of 9 prototype selection algorithms, considering the three biggest datasets. Notice that the time axis uses a logarithmic scale.

according to *intrinsic properties* of the data, avoiding the necessity of trying different parameters for finding suitable results, as in the case of PSDSP and ISDSP algorithms.

In summary, the experiments show that DPS presents the highest reduction rates, while preserves a good accuracy, which is similar to the accuracy achieved by other algorithms, such and LDIS, ISDSP and PSDSP. Besides that, the running time of DPS is lower than the running time of classic algorithms such as DROP3 and ICF, but is higher than the running time of LDIS, ISDSP and PSDSP. However, it is important to notice that DPS also has other advantages over ISDSP and PSDSP: it splits the dataset in sets of similar instances in a mathematically well-founded way (through kernel-density estimation), according to intrinsic properties of the data, avoiding the experimental tuning of parameters that is needed for applying PSDSP, for example. In addition, DPS is less prone than the PSDSP algorithm to split the dataset in a number of sets that is equal to or greater than the number of instances. As a consequence, DPS is suitable for dealing with high-dimensional datasets.

6   Conclusion

In this paper, we proposed an efficient algorithm for prototype selection, called DPS (Density-based Prototype Selection). It builds clusters of similar instances around the density peaks of each dimension and extracts prototypes of the more representative clusters. The resulting algorithm provides control to the user regarding the size of the reduced dataset. This is not a common feature in the prototype selection algorithms provided in the literature.

Our experiments show that DPS provides a good balance between accuracy and reduction, with a reasonable time complexity, when compared with other algorithms available in the literature. The empirical evaluation of running times showed that DPS algorithm has a running time that is comparable to the running times of other stated-of-the-art algorithms. In addition, the proposed algorithm adopts a mathematically well-founded way to split the dataset in sets of similar instances by applying kernel density estimation methods. Due to this, it is able to explore *intrinsic properties* of the data, avoiding the need of experimental evaluation of different values of parameters. Besides that, the proposed algorithm is more suitable for dealing with high-dimensional datasets than other algorithms that have similar features. These are the main advantages of the proposed algorithm in comparison with other similar approaches.

References

1. Anwar, I.M., Salama, K.M., Abdelbar, A.M.: Instance selection with ant colony optimization. Procedia Comput. Sci. **53**, 248–256 (2015)
2. Brighton, H., Mellish, C.: Advances in instance selection for instance-based learning algorithms. Data Min. Knowl. Disc. **6**(2), 153–172 (2002)
3. Carbonera, J.L.: An efficient approach for instance selection. In: Bellatreche, L., Chakravarthy, S. (eds.) DaWaK 2017. LNCS, vol. 10440, pp. 228–243. Springer, Cham (2017). https://doi.org/10.1007/978-3-319-64283-3_17
4. Carbonera, J.L., Abel, M.: A density-based approach for instance selection. In: 2015 IEEE 27th International Conference on Tools with Artificial Intelligence (ICTAI), pp. 768–774. IEEE (2015)
5. Carbonera, J.L., Abel, M.: A novel density-based approach for instance selection. In: 2016 IEEE 28th International Conference on Tools with Artificial Intelligence (ICTAI), pp. 549–556. IEEE (2016)
6. Carbonera, J.L., Abel, M.: Efficient prototype selection supported by subspace partitions. In: 2017 IEEE 29th International Conference on Tools with Artificial Intelligence (ICTAI), pp. 921–928. IEEE (2017)

7. Carbonera, J.L., Abel, M.: Efficient instance selection based on spatial abstraction. In: 2018 IEEE 30th International Conference on Tools with Artificial Intelligence (ICTAI), pp. 286–292. IEEE (2018)
8. Carbonera, J.L., Abel, M.: An efficient prototype selection algorithm based on dense spatial partitions. In: Rutkowski, L., Scherer, R., Korytkowski, M., Pedrycz, W., Tadeusiewicz, R., Zurada, J.M. (eds.) ICAISC 2018. LNCS (LNAI), vol. 10842, pp. 288–300. Springer, Cham (2018). https://doi.org/10.1007/978-3-319-91262-2_26
9. Carbonera, J.L., Abel, M.: An efficient prototype selection algorithm based on spatial abstraction. In: Ordonez, C., Bellatreche, L. (eds.) DaWaK 2018. LNCS, vol. 11031, pp. 177–192. Springer, Cham (2018). https://doi.org/10.1007/978-3-319-98539-8_14
10. Chou, C.H., Kuo, B.H., Chang, F.: The generalized condensed nearest neighbor rule as a data reduction method. In: 18th International Conference on Pattern Recognition. ICPR 2006, vol. 2, pp. 556–559. IEEE (2006)
11. García, S., Luengo, J., Herrera, F.: Data Preprocessing in Data Mining. Springer, New York (2015). https://doi.org/10.1007/978-3-319-10247-4
12. Gates, G.W.: Reduced nearest neighbor rule. IEEE Trans. Inf. Theor. 18(3), 431–433 (1972)
13. Hart, P.E.: The condensed nearest neighbor rule. IEEE Trans. Inf. Theor. 14, 515–516 (1968)
14. Leyva, E., González, A., Pérez, R.: Three new instance selection methods based on local sets: a comparative study with several approaches from a bi-objective perspective. Pattern Recogn. 48(4), 1523–1537 (2015)
15. Lin, W.C., Tsai, C.F., Ke, S.W., Hung, C.W., Eberle, W.: Learning to detect representative data for large scale instance selection. J. Syst. Softw. 106, 1–8 (2015)
16. Nikolaidis, K., Goulermas, J.Y., Wu, Q.: A class boundary preserving algorithm for data condensation. Pattern Recogn. 44(3), 704–715 (2011)
17. Silverman, B.W.: Density Estimation for Statistics and Data Analysis. Routledge, London (2018)
18. Wilson, D.R., Martinez, T.R.: Reduction techniques for instance-based learning algorithms. Mach. Learn. 38(3), 257–286 (2000)
19. Wilson, D.L.: Asymptotic properties of nearest neighbor rules using edited data. IEEE Trans. Syst. Man Cybern. SMC 2(3), 408–421 (1972)

FlexTrustRank: A New Approach to Link Spam Combating

Dariusz Czerski[1]([⊠]) [iD], Paweł Łoziński[1] [iD], Mieczysław Alojzy Kłopotek[1] [iD], Bartłomiej Starosta[1] [iD], and Marcin Sydow[1,2] [iD]

[1] Institute of Computer Science, Polish Academy of Sciences, Warsaw, Poland
`dariusz.czerski@ipipan.waw.pl`
[2] Polish-Japanese Academy of Information Technology, Warsaw, Poland

Abstract. The quality of search engine service relies on its capability to rank the webpages related to the user query in order of their intrinsic value. PageRank constituted a break-through as a method of webpage evaluation and was in use since then for multiple web search engines. This concept has been subject to attacks by malicious web linkage. As an counteraction, the so-called TrustRank was developed that instead of trusting all webpage developers it trusts only a handful of them that were manually selected. This approach has however a number of deficiencies: (1) it affects mainly the pages close to the manually selected pages, (2) it punishes other worthful webpages, (3) it leaves still a margin of manipulation on webpages with topics distant from those selected manually.

Therefore, we developed a new approach to webpage ranking, based on the trustrank concept, which attempts to annihilate the mentioned deficiencies via (1) restricting the number of links that can impact the pagerank (2) allowing for multistep linkage to be taken into account. The preliminary experiments on a large scale search engine data confirm the value of this new approach.

Keywords: Pagerank · Trustrank · Webmining

1 Introduction

The quality of search engine service relies on its capability to rank the webpages related to the user query in accordingly to their intrinsic value. Many initial efforts on webpage ranking concentrated on the page content itself. It turned out that such measures like rich vocabulary, following grammar rules or design rules may be easily manipulated by local page designers (for an overview see e.g. [1,12]). PageRank [9] constituted a break-through as a method of webpage evaluation and was in use since then for multiple web search engines. It relied on the assumption that a webpage creator links to another webpage if he finds it interesting for his topic of interest and has valuable content. A model of a random walker was proposed that walks from webpage to webpage via web links by selecting one of the outgoing links of a webpage with uniform probability.

© Springer Nature Switzerland AG 2020
L. Rutkowski et al. (Eds.): ICAISC 2020, LNAI 12416, pp. 130–139, 2020.
https://doi.org/10.1007/978-3-030-61534-5_12

With some probability it gets bored and jumps to any webpage with uniform probability. Then the PageRank of a webpage is computed as the stationary distribution $\mathbf{r}$ of a Markovian process over the (transposed) transition probability matrix P, columns of which sum up to 1, with the probability distribution $\mathbf{s}$ of jump when bored, and with probability γ of getting bored. Hence

$$\mathbf{r} = (1 - \gamma)P\mathbf{r} + \gamma\mathbf{s} \tag{1}$$

s was assumed to be a uniform distribution and $\gamma \leq 0.15$ This concept was initially a great success, but it has become subject to attacks by malicious web linkage. As an example counteraction, the so-called TrustRank [3] was developed that instead of trusting all webpage developers it trusts only a handful W_T of them that were manually selected. This concept led to modification of the above formula by setting s to zero for webpages not in W_T and to $\frac{1}{|W_T|}$ for those in W_T.

This approach has however a number of deficiencies: (1) it affects mainly the pages that are topologically close to the manually selected pages, (2) it punishes other valuable webpages, (3) it leaves still a margin of manipulation on webpages with topics distant from those selected manually (4) last but not least it requires manual inspection of a number of webpages.

Therefore, we developed a new approach to webpage ranking, based on the trustrank concept, which attempts to overcome the mentioned problems via (1) restricting the number of links that can impact the ranking (2) allowing for multistep linkage to be taken into account. We were able to abandon the step of manual selection of trusted webpages. Instead we used the set of root pages of the web domains. The preliminary experiments on a large scale search engine data confirm the value of this new approach.

2   Related Work

2.1   PageRank

The PageRank [9] has been used as a (main or supplementary) measure of importance of webpages. For various purposes different interpretations of PageRank have been explored. They include random walk, flow of authority as well as stationary Markov process. Its success led to broadening of its application areas to client and seller ranking, clustering, classification of web pages, social network analysis, word sense disambiguation, spam detection, detection of dead pages, etc. The new application areas as well as some deficiencies discovered when applying the original concept, led to development of numerous variants of the basic algorithm. For a thorough review of various methods and approaches see [7,8].

It has been perceived as a deficiency that the PageRank is used in the mode "one size fits all", without considering personal preferences of the user. The personalized PageRank [4] was elaborated to take into account the fact that user visited some pages in the past and he seeks content similar to that visited earlier.

Another concern was that many webpages are related to multiple topical areas and may have value different in those areas. To handle this, the approach called topic-sensitive PageRank [5] was elaborated. The Query-Dependent PageRank [2] may be considered as a refinement of that idea assuming that the webpage relevance measure should discern between webpages that are hit by user's query and those that are not. The idea of random walker neglects the fact that links out of the given webpage may have different degree of relevance to the topic of a given webpage. Intelligent Surfer idea was developed therefore in [10] that makes preferences for jumps towards topically related pages. A further criticism with respect to basic PageRank was that it does not reflect the true behavior of a surfer who uses "back" button from time to time. Ranking with Back-step [14] was developed therefore that proved to be more resilient to so-called surfer traps that were used as a method of link spamming and to better model the real behaviour of web surfers than classic PageRank [13]. Other modifications of PageRank try to take into account the age of a web page (from its creation and/or last modification), the page update frequency, etc. to properly estimate its value.

The idea of PageRank had a number of important advantages when it comes to combating the problem of spam on the Web. PageRank does not rely on the content of a single page. It takes into account opinions of many web content creators. No linguistic analysis is necessary.

However, the practice showed that it is vulnerable to some specific spamming attacks, like link farms, spider traps, that may unjustly increase the PageRank of a selected webpage or may be used to defame a web page by associating with malicious concepts. It turned out to be possible also to issue attacks decreasing the PageRank of some pages, by linking in from low rank (bad) pages.

2.2   TrustRank

In order to counteract the aforementioned spamming attacks, the concept of TrustRank, DeadRank and BadRank were invented.

DeadRank and BadRank operate on the inverted webgraph, that is one obtained by inverting the links. DeadRank deals with the issue of dangling links, that is links leading to pages that have been removed (or not yet crawled) from the network. "DeadPages" are assigned non-zero probability in the s vector, while the other have zero probability, and the rank computation is performed as for the ordinary PageRank. The higher the DeadRank, the lower quality of the webpage (as nobody is caring for it). While DeadRank does not handle deliberate spam, it nonetheless combats the web pages that belong to trash. BadRank [6] makes use of a list of webpages that have been considered as of bad content (collected by some community, e.g. parents). They play then the same role as dead pages in DeadRank.

The inventors of TrustRank [3] intended to create a system that would assign webpages values between 0 and 1 meaning the probability that a webpage is a good one (not a spamming page). It is assumed that a costly but reliable "oracle" is available with which we can evaluate a set of pages for their goodness.

Based on these, they propose to use the PageRank method described by Eq. (1) to compute the trust by assuming not the uniform s vector but rather one in which positive probabilities are assigned to the webpages that the oracle marked as good pages. They suggest to use one of three types of oracles: (1) manual evaluation, (2) webpages with high original PageRank, (3) pages with high pagerank in an inverted web graph. As an additional amendment they propose not to use the original Web graph but as a graph where nodes are linked if they are reachable from one another within a defined number of steps. The TrustRank algorithm exploits the PageRank so-called power computational method, however, they constrain themselves to a limited number of steps (instead of striving for convergence).

2.3 Other Approaches to Spam Combating

[11] provides a broader overview of methods of combating link spams. Five major groups of detection of link farms are distinguished there:

1. based on label propagation
2. based on link pruning and re-weighting
3. based on classifiers using link-related features
4. based on graph regularization

TrustRank and our method presented below belong to the first mentioned group.

3 Our Approach

The method of link spam elimination proposed in this paper, termed **Flex-TrustRank** (**Flex**ible **Trust**ed Set **Rank**) is based on similar intuition as the one that underlies TrustRank. The trust of a page p, however, is not modeled as a numeric value, but as a collection of top-k ranked pages that link to p in n hops. Such a back-link structure is a basis for computing a new ranking in the next iteration. The outline of the method is listed as Algorithm 1.

- $G = (V, E)$-host graph
- k-the number of top hosts used to compute the algorithm
- $idx(v)$-represents the position of a host v in the ranking (1 is the best)
- $r(v)$-final ranking of the vertex v
- $\mathcal{B}(n, v)$-the subset of k-top vertices in the current ranking, distinct from v that link to v in n hops (for which there exists a path of length n linking to v) , $\mathcal{B}(0, v) = \emptyset$,
- $I(n, v) = \sum_{b \in \mathcal{B}(n,v)}[k - idx(b)]$- aggregated information of positions of vertices from $\mathcal{B}(n, v)$ in the ranking
- N-the number of back-hops taken into account when computing the ranking
- $pagerank : V \rightarrow [0, 1]$-"classic" PageRank value for host $v \in V$
- c_{max}-maximum number of algorithm iteration.

Algorithm 1. FlexTrustRank Algorithm

1: **Input:** G - the web-graph, k - the limit on the rank of the considered page, and N
    - the number of backsteps;
2: Initially, idx is the position in the ranking according to the "classic" PageRank
    function
3: $c \leftarrow 0$;
4: $K_c \leftarrow \{v \in V : idx(v) <= k\}$;
5: **repeat**
6:     **for all** $v \in V$, $i = 1, \ldots, N$ **do**
7:        computation of $\mathcal{B}(i, v)$ based on G;
8:     **end for**
9:     **for all** $v \in V$ **do**
10:        based on $\{\mathcal{B}(i, v) : i = 1, \ldots, N\}$ and on K_c compute $r(v)$; {Examples of
          particular methods for computing $r(v)$ are discussed in Sect. 4.1.}
11:     **end for**
12:     The function $idx()$ returns the position in the ranking computed by function r;
13:     $c \leftarrow c + 1$;
14:     $K_c \leftarrow \{v \in V : idx(v) <= k\}$;
15: **until** $|K_c \setminus K_{c-1}| < \delta \wedge c < c_{max}$
16: **Output:** the function idx returns the final host ranking.

FlexTrustRank's steps:

1. compute "classic" PageRank on the host graph
2. select top-k PageRank hosts
3. compute FlexTrustRank initialized by the top-k PageRank
4. update the escape vector based on the updated rank of some hosts (i.e., the hosts that dropped in the ranking have lowered jump-in probabilities)
5. repeat the steps 1–4 above using the new escape vector

4   Evaluation

4.1   Configuration

The search engine NEKST.pl limits the impact of spamming websites by computing the pagerank not of a single webpage but rather of a single domain. The "Domain Rank" is then distributed among the pages in that domain. However, as NEKST team communicated us, this measure proved to be insufficient and that fact lead us to the design of the FlexTrustRank which is presented in this paper, to create a better domain ranking. Therefore, our experiments were not performed on the network of webpages, but rather on the network of domains.

     The graph of Polish Web domains (consisting of over 700,000 nodes after deduplication) was used as a testbed for the experiments. Domain A links into domain B, if there exists a webpage $p_A \in A$ that links to a webpage $p_B \in B$. The graph was collected and made available by the courtesy of the search engine NEKST.pl team to whom we are grateful.

Various variants of the Algorithm 1 were applied to the above graph and the ranks obtained by the identified spamming domains were tracked.

In all experiments, the initial selection of trusted domains was based on the domain PageRank top elements. But the number of top trusted domains k was varied. Also the method of computation of rank r was varied. The following r functions were considered (notation from the Sect. 3 is used):

- without taking the ranks of backlinks into account:
  - without taking into account the dynamics of backlink spreading:

$$r(v) = \sum_{i=1}^{N} |\mathcal{B}(i, v)|^{p_i}. \tag{2}$$

where p_i are fixed for $i = 1 \ldots N$.
  - with taking into account the dynamics of backlink spreading:

$$r(v) = \sum_{i=1}^{N} (|\mathcal{B}(i, v)| - |\mathcal{B}(i - 1, v)|) \cdot |\mathcal{B}(i, v)|. \tag{3}$$

- with taking the ranks of backlinks into account (counting the good domains pointing to a given domain):
  - without taking into account the dynamics of backlink spreading:

$$r(v) = \sum_{i=1}^{N} I(i, v)^{p_i}. \tag{4}$$

where p_i are fixed for $i = 1 \ldots N$.
  - with taking into account the dynamics of backlink spreading:

$$r(v) = \sum_{i=1}^{N} (I(i, v) - I(i - 1, v)) \cdot I(i, v). \tag{5}$$

The formula (3), given $N = 1$, expresses the intuition that the more non-spamming pages are pointing at a given page, the more likely the page is not spamming. For $N > 1$, we take into account also pages that do not link directly to a given page, but rather in two or more steps, but taking into account that the further the trusted page is, the less the indirect pointing is reliable.

While the formula (3) treats the weight of pages i steps away from the page v in isolation from the weight of pages $i - 1$ and less away from the page v, the formula (3) demotes tightly coupled top-ranking pages.

The formula (4) differs from the formula (2) in that not only the fact of belonging to the k top ranking pages counts, but also the actual ranking among those k best pages. The closer to the top are the pointing pages, the higher the rank of the pointed page.

A similar difference is visible when comparing the formula (5) differs from the formula (3)

4.2   Evaluation Results

In this subsection we report on the anti-spam capabilities with respect to all spamming domains that were ranked too high (into top k pages) by the traditional PageRank. As a measure of success, we present the comparison of the number of spamming pages among those returned as top-ranking by PageRank and by FlexTrustRank, as well as the average position change of the spamming domains. The measures are computed at the completion of the algorithm.

We used two sets of spamming pages, called BAD1 and BAD2.

The spamming domains of the set termed BAD1 were defined as ones containing "seo" or "katalog" strings in their domain names. Though strictly speaking they are not always spamming domains, but due to their content they are useless from the point of view of queries to a search engine. This kind of domains are very often used as a tool designed to artificially optimize PageRank score of other domains.

The second set of spamming domains, called here BAD2, was obtained as follows: the set BAD1top is constructed as those domains from BAD1 that PageRank qualified into top k domains. Then BAD2 is constructed as the set of all domains linked to by domains from BAD1top (so to say linked to by most suspicious bad pages). Note that BAD1top and BAD2 are obtained separately for each k, while BAD1 is the same in each experiment.

The Tables 1, 2 present the results. The columns have the following meaning:

K –the k parameter of the algorithm (how many domains are considered as top k domains)

Rank fun –the ranking function; $r999$-according to formula (2), where the digits mean p_1, p_2, p_3 resp., $r999Wgt$-according to formula (4), where the digits mean p_1, p_2, p_3 resp., $rDynl$-according to formula (3), $rDynlWgt$-according to formula (5).

P –the set of spam domains among top-k domains returned by PageRank

F –the set of spam domains among top-k domains returned by FlexTrustRank

P_2 –the set of spam domains among the second top-k domains returned by PageRank (ranked $k + 1 \ldots 2k$)

Avg jump –the average rank jump of spamming domains from top k of PageRank (negative means that the ranking after FlexTrustRank was worse than after PageRank)

Up –how many spamming domains from top k of PageRank got better ranks after FlexTrustRank

Down –how many spamming domains from top k of PageRank got worse ranks after FlexTrustRank

As one may expect, with increase of k, the number of spamming pages increases among top k domains as well as among top $2k$ domains of PageRank (the columns $|P|, |P_2|$ in both tables).

The Table 1 presents the anti-spam results assuming BAD1 set as spamming domains, that is domains with names containing "seo" or "katalog". As visible, the algorithm version r210Wgt leads consistently to the most significant decrease

Table 1. Experimental results of application of FlexTrustRank for BAD1 spamming set. Notation explained in the text.

K	Rank fun	$|P|$	$|F|$	$|P \cap F|$	$|F \setminus P|$	$|P \setminus F|$	$|F \cap P_2|$	$|P_2|$	Avg jump	Up/Down
1000	r110	3	0	0	0	3	0	3	−13959	0/3
	r111Wgt	3	1	0	1	3	1	3	−7726	0/3
	r210	3	0	0	0	3	0	3	−16516	0/3
	r210Wgt	3	0	0	0	3	0	3	−51793	0/3
	rDyn1	3	1	0	1	3	1	3	−6336	0/3
	rDyn1Wgt	3	1	0	1	3	1	3	−6314	0/3
2000	r110	6	2	2	0	4	0	17	−14715	1/5
	r111Wgt	6	3	2	1	4	1	17	−10217	1/5
	r210	6	2	1	1	5	1	17	−17490	0/6
	r210Wgt	6	2	1	1	5	1	17	−63175	0/6
	rDyn1	6	4	2	2	4	1	17	−8391	1/5
	rDyn1Wgt	6	4	2	2	4	1	17	−8321	1/5
5000	r110	28	13	7	6	21	4	29	−64993	4/24
	r111Wgt	28	19	11	8	17	4	29	−44032	5/23
	r210	28	5	2	3	26	2	29	−72407	1/27
	r210Wgt	28	5	2	3	26	2	29	−109457	1/27
	rDyn1	28	22	14	8	14	5	29	−34850	7/21
	rDyn1Wgt	28	24	14	10	14	5	29	−34240	7/21
10000	r110	57	32	24	8	33	4	35	−87000	10/47
	r111Wgt	57	35	26	9	31	4	35	−69369	11/46
	r210	57	19	11	8	46	3	35	−98467	4/53
	r210Wgt	57	19	11	8	46	3	35	−114587	4/53
	rDyn1	57	40	27	13	30	4	35	−65795	14/43
	rDyn1Wgt	57	43	28	15	29	4	35	65424	16/41

of rank of spamming pages. Furthermore, r210Wgt together with r210 remove the largest number of spamming domains from top k and promotes the lowest number of spamming pages from the second top k to top k. rDyn1Wgt seems to perform worst. But all the proposed variants demote BAD1 domains from top k and promote fewer domains from the second top k to the top k.

The Table 2 presents the anti-spam results assuming BAD2 as the set of spamming domains, that is ones pointed by most suspicious BAD1 domains.

Again, the algorithm version r210Wgt leads consistently to the most significant decrease of rank of spamming pages. Furthermore, r210Wgt together with r210 remove the largest number of spamming domains from top k and promotes the lowest number of spamming pages from second top k to top k. For all algorithm versions, the number of demoted spamming pages exceeds the number of promoted ones.

The versions rank210 and rank210Weighted proved to be superior to the other versions. However, starting with $k = 5000$ the performance in terms of the number of spamming pages in the top k set is worse than that of PageRank. This may be attributed to two factors (1) BAD2 set does not consist of clear spamming domains, (2) the number of bad domains in the initial set (returned by PageRank) is too high to be combated by information obtained from good domains.

Table 2. Experimental results of application of FlexTrustRank for BAD2 spamming set. Notation explained in the text.

K	Rank fun	$|P|$	$|F|$	$|P \cap F|$	$|F \setminus P|$	$|P \setminus F|$	$|F \cap P_2|$	$|P_2|$	Avg jump	Up/Down
1000	r110	49	28	20	8	29	6	50	−12838	16/33
	r111Wgt	49	36	22	14	27	9	50	−6134	16/33
	r210	49	23	19	4	30	4	50	−13847	14/35
	r210Wgt	49	24	18	6	31	5	50	−24400	13/36
	rDyn1	49	41	23	18	26	10	50	−4709	16/33
	rDyn1Wgt	49	41	23	18	26	10	50	−4698	16/33
2000	r110	133	106	67	39	66	26	134	−6305	45/88
	r111Wgt	133	127	69	58	64	29	134	−4373	47/86
	r210	133	77	54	23	79	17	134	−7844	35/98
	r210Wgt	133	72	53	19	80	13	134	−13654	35/98
	rDyn1	133	145	71	74	62	28	134	−3808	46/87
	rDyn1Wgt	133	146	71	75	62	28	134	−3796	46/87
5000	r110	920	981	505	476	415	193	726	−10267	286/634
	r111Wgt	920	1079	530	549	390	204	726	−8963	304/616
	r210	920	712	440	272	480	131	726	−12673	204/716
	r210Wgt	920	689	433	256	487	123	726	−15721	199/721
	rDyn1	920	1159	541	618	379	205	726	−8682	329/591
	rDyn1Wgt	920	1266	556	710	364	228	726	−8676	340/580
10000	r110	2095	3159	1247	1912	848	517	1662	−16244	702/1393
	r111Wgt	2095	3238	1267	1971	828	548	1662	−14481	747/1348
	r210	2095	3109	1125	1984	970	444	1662	−19569	598/1497
	r210Wgt	2095	3038	1104	1934	991	429	1662	−22888	595/1500
	rDyn1	2095	3223	1272	1951	823	551	1662	−14093	764/1331
	rDyn1Wgt	2095	3414	1299	2115	796	571	1662	−14036	803/1292

5   Conclusions

In this paper a new link spam combating algorithm for domain ranking was presented. It exhibits anti-spam properties superior to the broadly known PageRank algorithm when the number of spamming domains is low among top-ranked domains identified by PageRank.

These preliminary results appear to be encouraging and urge for an investigation to what extent our spamming/non-spamming behavior assumptions can be really confirmed by human investigators. We attest the success of the algorithm to the following assumptions: the authoritative pages/domains that enter into the top k pages of PageRank get there at least partially because other authoritative pages/domains point at them. If a website gets onto the top list that is supported only by low-ranking pages then one can suspect that this gain in authority results from a link spamming process. So it is worth investigating whether or not the websites staying high in the ranking are really authoritative ones. It is also worth investigating if the losing websites are really the ones that gain their authority from spamming. An alternative hypothesis may be that for example such a webpage is authoritative on a very narrow topic so that other authoritative websites that could point at it do not exist. Should this alternative hypothesis turn to be true, then still the algorithm may be used to get deeper insights into the contents of the Web.

As further research goals we consider comparisons to other anti-spam algorithms as well as an investigation why the specific version of our algorithm outperforms the other in order to extend its benefits.

References

1. Arora, N., Govilkar, S.: Survey on different ranking algorithms along with their approaches. Int. J. Comput. Appl. **135**(10), 8887 (2016)
2. Geng, X., Liu, T.Y., Qin, T., Arnold, A., Li, H., Shum, H.Y.: Query dependent ranking using k-nearest neighbor. In: Proceedings 31st Annual International ACM SIGIR Conference on Research and Development in Information Retrieval, pp. 115–122. ACM (2008)
3. Gyongyi, Z., Garcia-Molina, H., Pedersen, J.: Combating web spam with trustrank. Technical Report 2004–17, Stanford InfoLab, March 2004
4. Haveliwala, T., Kamvar, S., Jeh, G.: An analytical comparison of approaches to personalizing PageRank. Technical Report 2003–35, Stanford InfoLab, June 2003. http://ilpubs.stanford.edu:8090/596/
5. Haveliwala, T.H.: Topic-sensitive PageRank: a context-sensitive ranking algorithm for web search. IEEE Trans. Knowl. Data Eng. **15**(4), 784–796 (2003)
6. Kolda, T.G., Procopio, M.J.: Generalized badrank with graduated trust. No. SAND2009-6670. Sandia National Laboratories (2009)
7. Langville, A.N.: An annotated bibliography of papers about Markov chains and information retrieval (2005). http://www.cofc.edu/langvillea/bibtexpractice.pdf
8. Langville, A.N., Meyer, C.D.: Google's PageRank and Beyond: The Science of Search Engine Rankings. Princeton University Press, Jersey (2006)
9. Page, L., Brin, S., Motwani, R., Winograd, T.: The pagerank citation ranking: Bringing order to the web (1999)
10. Richardson, M., Domingos, P.: The intelligent surfer: probabilistic combination of link and content information in PageRank. In: Advances in Neural Information Processing Systems, vol. 14. MIT Press (2002). http://citeseer.ist.psu.edu/460350.html
11. Spirin, N., Han, J.: Survey on web spam detection: principles and algorithms. SIGKDD Explor. Newsl. **13**(2), 50–64 (2012)
12. Sudhakar, P., Poonkuzhali, G., Kumar, R.: Content based ranking for search engines. In: Proceedings International MultiConference of Engineers and Computer Scientists, Hong Kong, vol. 1 (2012)
13. Sydow, M.: Can link analysis tell us about web traffic? In: Special Interest Tracks and Posters of the 14th International Conference on World Wide Web. WWW'2005, Association for Computing Machinery, New York, NY, USA, pp. 954–955 (2005). https://doi.org/10.1145/1062745.1062815
14. Sydow, M.: Random surfer with back step. Fundamenta Informaticae **68**(4), 379–398 (2005)

A Comparative Analysis of Similarity Measures in Memory-Based Collaborative Filtering

Mara Renata Deac-Petruşel[✉]

Babeş-Bolyai University, Faculty of Mathematics and Computer Science,
Cluj-Napoca, Romania
mara@cs.ubbcluj.ro

Abstract. Recommendation Systems are powerful tools generating relevant suggestions for customers, as support in the decision-making process. The most sensitive step in the recommendation process is the choice of the similarity measure. The goal of this article is to present a detailed analysis of similarity measures applied to memory-based collaborative filtering techniques. Several experiments have been conducted, considering various similarity-based scenarios, to determine which measure fits best in the user-based or item-based context. Moreover, the characteristics of similarity measures and data sets (sparsity, dimensionality) are explored to determine their impact on the recommendation process. Besides, this study provides valuable information that can be used to sustain the choice of similarity measure, which can lead to improved performance of the recommendation system.

Keywords: Recommendation systems · Collaborative filtering · Similarity measures

1 Introduction

Due to the continuous growth of available information, it is getting much harder to search and find those high-quality trustworthy items and services. Moreover, friends' opinions and feelings about an item have a great influence on the user's decisions and beliefs. Additionally, when exploring the available item offers, it is highly appreciated to be presented with a list of items generated by a recommendation system, as this not only saves time and money but also consists only of those items that best suit the users' preferences.

In the process of producing satisfying recommendations, the most important step is determining the similarity between the target user and his peers, respectively between certain items.

In this context, the goal of the proposed approach is to compare the performances of various similarity measures applied to memory-based collaborative filtering algorithms: the *user-based collaborative filtering* and the *item-based collaborative filtering*, through several numerical experiments. Several data sets,

© Springer Nature Switzerland AG 2020
L. Rutkowski et al. (Eds.): ICAISC 2020, LNAI 12416, pp. 140–151, 2020.
https://doi.org/10.1007/978-3-030-61534-5_13

which are different in terms of sparsity and dimensionality, are used in the experimental setup.

The remaining of this paper has been structured in the following manner: the second chapter offers an overview of both traditional and newly designed similarity measures for memory-based collaborative filtering algorithms. In the third chapter, the problem statement is formulated by presenting a comparative analysis of memory-based collaborative filtering algorithms performance from a *user-to-user*, respectively *item-to-item similarity* point of view. The fourth chapter outlines the conducted numerical experiments and the obtained results. Lastly, conclusions are drawn and the future work perspectives are defined, highlighting that the proposed comparative analysis is a useful tool for deciding which is the best similarity measure to apply in memory-based collaborative filtering methods.

2 Related Work

Recommendation systems have a huge impact on reducing the negative influence of overwhelming information on websites. The most widely used recommendation technique is collaborative filtering, which implies rating certain items to generate recommendations for a user, based on similar users or items.

The most popular algorithm used in collaborative filtering is the k *Nearest Neighbors* (kNN) [5]. In this comparative study, both user-to-user and item-to-item versions of the kNN algorithm are considered. The kNN's performance highly depends on the choice of similarity measure in the determination of the k most similar users (neighbors) or items. The calculated rating prediction can be improved just as much as the similarity measure provides better results.

In literature, the Pearson Correlation Coefficient (PCC) is the most widely spread similarity measure, used in a variety of collaborative filtering approaches [8,18] or [29]. The same degree of popularity is shared by the Cosine similarity measure (COS), which is included as well in numerous studies, such as [1] or [8]. However, in [25] a series of disadvantages for both PCC and COS similarity measures are presented. For example, computing the similarity using PCC may result in unbalanced values, if considering that two users are similar when one of them rated a very small number of items and another one rated a large number of items. Moreover, the COS similarity measure is negatively affected by the sparsity problem, while the performance of the PCC similarity measure is positively affected.

Other popular traditional similarity measures used in recommender systems research papers are: the Jaccard Similarity (JAC) [21], the Spearman's Rank Correlation (SRC) [27] or the Euclidean Distance (EUC) [9].

Generally, the traditional similarity measures consider in the computation only the users' ratings and ignore the context in which these were given by the users. Therefore, multiple proposed approaches are trying to improve the results of the traditional similarity measures by either optimizing an existing one or by designing a new one.

The Constrained Pearson Correlation Coefficient (CPC) similarity measure improves PCC by considering the impact of positive and negative ratings [32]. To overcome the limitations of COS, the Adjusted Cosine Similarity Measure (ACOS) was used in several papers [24,31]. COS similarity measure does not consider the case when users use different rating scales, while ACOS solves this issue by subtracting the average rating provided by the user.

In [4] a novel similarity measure for the collaborative filtering technique is presented. Taking into consideration contextual information about users, a singularity measure was designed for each item by analyzing the ratings given by a pair of users. The main idea is to classify the rating into positive and non-positive ones and to calculate the singularity values of each user and item. High values of singularity between the ratings of two users/items produce a great impact over the similarity. The singularity approach [4] is compared with traditional ones (PCC, SRC, and COS). The proposed approach significantly improves the recommendation process, on average, by 20% for recall and by 60% for precision.

The goal of the approach presented in [7] is to improve the results of the Pearson Correlation Coefficient by designing a new metric based on both the Jaccard similarity measure [22] and the Mean Square Differences (MDS) [30] metric. The new metric enhances the numerical values of the user ratings with non-numerical information based on the arrangement of ratings for each pair of users. The kNN algorithm is applied to compare the results of the newly proposed metric to the ones obtained using PCC. Results show that the proposed metric outperforms PCC when applied to MovieLens [26] and Netflix [28] data sets (using one-to-five user ratings). On the other hand, the new metric does not manage to improve PCC when applied to the FilmAffinity dataset (having one-to-ten user ratings) [7].

Having the goal of improving the recommendation system's performance in the cold-start context, a new heuristic user-based similarity measure was proposed in [2]. The so-called PIP similarity measure is based on three factors: Proximity, Impact, and Popularity. The proximity factor considers the arithmetic difference between two ratings and whether the ratings are in agreement or disagreement. If two ratings are in disagreement, a penalty is assigned to the ratings. The impact factor considers how strongly an item is liked or disliked by a user, as this means that a clear preference has been expressed for an item and, therefore, the similarity measure's results are more reliable. The popularity factor considers those ratings that are further from the average rating of a co-rated item. The conducted experiments considered several traditional similarity measures: PCC, COS, CPC, and SRC. The best overall results were obtained for the PIP similarity measure [2].

In [3], a new similarity model that combines the benefits of three measures: CPC, Jaccard, and Inverse User Frequency (IUF) similarity to determine the target user's neighborhood is presented. The user's taste is considered through the CPC and Jaccard measures by favoring the positive impact and number of rated movies for each user. Moreover, the focus is on less known items by using IUF. IUF measure determines the significance of item i in the similarity calculation. It decreases the weight on common items, as these are less beneficial in the recommendation process. A disadvantage is that the number of common ratings is not taken into account. All in all, the proposed model [3] enhances the similarity weights by considering the above-mentioned aspects. Several experiments were conducted on the MovieLens data set [26] to compare the proposed approach to a set of traditional similarity measures: PC, COS, CPC, Jaccard, and IUF. Results verify the accuracy of the suggested similarity model.

The paper presented in [14] aims to define a new similarity measure that considers all rated items and solves the problem of co-rated items in datasets, even for the extremely sparse data sets. To improve the adaptability of the similarity metric in the case of the sparse rating data, the proposed similarity model [14] consists of three impact factors. The first one determines the similarity between users. The second one was designed to punish the user pairs with a small proportion of the number of co-rated items. The third one was defined to weigh each user's rating preference. To validate the proposed similarity measure, experiments were conducted on four data sets: MovieLens 100 K [26], FilmTrust, CiaoDVD, and Epinions data sets. As evaluation metrics, MAE and RMSE were used. The experiment results show that the proposed measure achieves better performance on all four datasets compared to all other measures, especially on extremely sparse datasets. The advantages of the proposed model are more pronounced with the increasing of sparsity.

In addition to these approaches, the proposed one aims to offer a solution to one of the most urgent questions in recommendation systems research: which is the most effective similarity measure to be selected for memory-based collaborative filtering algorithms, considering the dimensionality and sparsity of the used data set? Several experiments are conducted in this study to prove that the accuracy of the generated recommendations is visibly affected by the choice of the similarity measure.

3   Problem Statement

The goal of this approach is to compare the memory-based collaborative filtering algorithms from the choice of similarity measure point of view. The ultimate purpose is to determine, for both user-based (UBCF) and item-based (IBCF) collaborative filtering algorithms, the most appropriate similarity measure to be selected. This approach seeks also to observe the algorithms' performance, equalities, and differences. Moreover, the proposed case study was designed to offer an answer to the following four research questions of interest in literature:

- RQ_1. Which is the most effective similarity measure to be selected for each collaborative filtering perspective?
- RQ_2. Which is a relevant k value for UBCF, respectively IBCF algorithms?
- RQ_3. Which are the characteristics of similarity measures influencing the recommendation process in terms of user-to-user or item-to-item collaborative filtering?
- RQ_4. How do the sparsity and dimensionality of the data set impact the choice of similarity measure?

3.1 User-Based Collaborative Filtering

The most popular algorithm, used in a variety of collaborative filtering approaches [5, 8, 18, 20, 35], is the *user-to-user version of the k Nearest Neighbors* (UBCF). Below are presented the main steps of the UBCF algorithm:

- A set of k users (called neighbors) for the target user u is determined using one of the selected similarity measures. The obtained k neighbors are the most similar users to u.
- The rating prediction of user u for item i is calculated based on the ratings of the neighbors for item i:
  $p_{u,i} = \frac{\sum_{v=1}^{k} r_{v,i} * sim(u,v)}{\sum_{v=1}^{k} sim(u,v)}$, where the meaning of the variables is the following:

- k is the size of the users neighborhood.
- $r_{v,i}$ is the rating of neighbor v for item i.
- $sim(u, v)$ is the similarity between the target user u and the neighbor v.

- Those n items most suitable for user u are selected based on the rating prediction.
- The generated top-n recommendation list is provided for target user u.

The major drawbacks of the UBCF algorithm are low scalability and data sparsity in the recommendation system databases. The data sparsity causes problems in the calculation of the similarity measures and accentuates the cold-start conditions, due to insufficient ratings to be used in users' comparisons [6]. Besides, the UBCF's performance depends on the choice of similarity measures in the determination of the k most similar users.

3.2 Item-Based Collaborative Filtering

The *item-based version of the k Nearest Neighbors* (IBCF) method [13, 23, 31] is more stable in comparison to UBCF, as the average item has a lot more ratings than the average user. Therefore, an individual rating does not have such a major impact.

In the IBCF algorithm, the first step is to select k most similar items to the target item i from the set of items the target user has rated. Based on the similarity values, the rating prediction for user-item pairs not present in the dataset is calculated by taking the weighted average of the target user's ratings on these similar items.

$p_{u,i} = \frac{\sum_{j=1}^{k} r_{u,j} * sim(i,j)}{\sum_{j=1}^{k} sim(i,j)}$, where the meaning of the variables is the following:

- k is the size of the items neighborhood.
- $r_{u,j}$ is the rating of user u for item j.
- $sim(i, j)$ is the similarity between the target item i and the neighbor item j.

Two shortcomings in the IBCF method are the *popularity bias*, as the system tends to recommend popular items and the *item cold-start problem*, due to the impossibility to recommend new items since they have not been rated yet.

3.3 Similarity-Based Scenarios

In this section, the most popular traditional and custom similarity measures suitable to be used for the memory-based collaborative filtering approaches are described. The following set of similarity measures was selected to be used both in the computation of the users' or items' neighborhood and further when determining the rating prediction of the target user u for an item i.

Pearson Correlation Coefficient Similarity (PCC): is used in numerous collaborative filtering approaches [9,17,18,30,34]. PCC has the target to determine each users' or items' deviations from their average ratings, while considering the linear adjustment between the two users/items. The result is a value in the $[-1,1]$ range, where: " -1 " represents a negative correlation, "1" a positive one and "0" (*zero order correlation*) describes no relation.

Constrained Pearson's Correlation (CPC): is a modified version of PCC that considers in the computation only the pairs of ratings that are either both being positive or both being negative [32]. CPC uses the median value of ratings, instead of the average: $median\_value = 3$ in the scale $[1 - 5]$.

Cosine Similarity (COS): considers the angle between two vectors of ratings, where a smaller angle represents greater similarity. Since the cosine of two vectors is determined, the output will always range in $[-1,1]$. The greatest drawback of COS is that null preferences are treated as negative ones [1].

Adjusted Cosine Similarity (ACOS): has been applied exclusively for the item-based collaborative filtering approach. This measure takes into account that different users could have contrasting rating schemes. For example, some users might tend to highly rate items, while others might accord lower ratings as a preference. To avoid this, the average ratings for each user are subtracted from each user's rating for the current pair of items.

Euclidean Distance (EUC): is defined as the "ordinary" straight-line distance between two points, in the recommendation systems scenario it is calculated for two users/items [15].

Spearman's Rank Correlation (SRC): computes the similarity between two vectors based on the similarity of ranks of values in the vectors. SRC performs better on small data sets, as the computation and storage of the ranks takes long time [11,16,33].

Jaccard Similarity Measure (JAC): considers the number of commonly preferred items between two users. The basic idea is that users/items are more similar if they have more common ratings. The drawback is that it does not consider the absolute rating [10].

Proximity-Impact-Popularity (PIP): is a custom similarity included in this comparative study for the user-based collaborative filtering approach, using the formulas defined in [2].

3.4   Evaluation Measures

In the evaluation step, precision and mean absolute error (MAE) evaluation measures were used. Precision is a classification accuracy metric [19] used for measuring how frequently the recommender system makes correct decisions when evaluating if an item is good for the target user.

$$precision(u) = \frac{|recommended \cap relevant|}{|recommended|},$$

where:

- u is the target user.
- *recommended* is the set of generated recommendations.
- *relevant* is the set of relevant recommendations. A recommended item is relevant if it was rated by the target user u.

The mean absolute error (MAE) is a predictive accuracy metric [19], measuring the average absolute deviation between a predicted rating and the user's true rating. The following formula was used for computing MAE, taking the sum of the difference between the user's rating ($r_{u,i}$) and the predicted rating ($p_{u,i}$) and dividing it by the number of rated items (N):

$$MAE(u) = \frac{\sum_{i=1}^{N} |p_{u,i} - r_{u,i}|}{N}$$

4   Numerical Experiments

Several numerical experiments were conducted, considering the previously presented similarity measures and memory-based collaborative filtering techniques (UBCF and IBCF).

4.1   Datasets

Two data sets, that are different in terms of dimensionality and sparsity, were chosen for the numerical experiments.

The *MovieLens 1M* [26] data set contains 1 million ratings applied to 4.000 movies by 6.000 users. The *DataFiniti - Hotel Reviews* [12] data set consists of 10 000 reviews for 1670 hotels. Both data sets consider one-to-five user ratings.

From a sparsity point of view, *MovieLens* has 95.83%, while *DataFiniti - Hotel Reviews* 99.91%.

4.2   Results

UBCF Approach. In the UBCF approach, several similarity measures have been applied to determine the k most similar users. In this context, different scenarios have been defined, considering several values for k neighbors in the $[3, 50]$ range. The choice of the k nearest neighbors for the neighborhood formation results in a compromise: a very small k leads to a small set of candidate items to be recommended, as there are not sufficient neighbors to support the predictions. In contrast, a very large k impacts precision, as the particularities of user's preferences can be softened due to the large neighborhood size. The optimal k value depends on the characteristics of the data set, such as sparsity and dimensionality. The best results were achieved for k values equal to 10 and 50 and have been included in this study.

Tables 1 and 2 reflect the performance of the recommendation system in terms of mean absolute error (MAE) and precision for the applied similarity metrics on the *MovieLens*, respectively *DataFiniti - Hotel Reviews* datasets. The number of generated recommendations was determined experimentally and the optimal value obtained was $n = 5$. Greater values have shown to decrease the quality of the recommendation list.

Table 1. MAE and Precision for UBCF on MovieLens

Similarity measure	MAE		Precision	
	k = 10	k = 50	k = 10	k = 50
Pearson correlation	0.53	0.27	0.75	0.85
Constrained Pearson correlation	0.32	0.19	0.82	0.82
Cosine similarity	0.69	0.70	0.67	0.62
Euclidean similarity	1.22	0.94	0.3	0.25
Spearman rank coefficient	0.26	0.34	0.73	0.75
Jaccard similarity	0.14	0.25	0.82	0.75
PIP similarity	**0.09**	**0.01**	**0.86**	**0.92**

Table 2. MAE and Precision for UBCF on DataFiniti - Hotel Reviews

Similarity measure	MAE		Precision	
	k = 10	k = 50	k = 10	k = 50
Pearson correlation	0.57	0.66	0.60	0.64
Constrained Pearson correlation	0.35	0.36	0.85	0.76
Cosine similarity	0.20	**0.07**	0.72	**0.93**
Euclidean similarity	1.59	1.41	0.30	0.40
Spearman rank coefficient	**0.04**	0.20	**0.90**	0.55
Jaccard similarity	0.09	0.13	0.48	0.46
PIP similarity	0.35	0.71	0.84	0.64

The presented results illustrate that *PIP* similarity measure has the best performance for UBCF (RQ_1) for both values of k, when utilized for large datasets (*MovieLens 1M*). Besides, *PIP* similarity measure is a better choice when applied on data of lower sparsity (RQ_4).

To determine those characteristics that are relevant for a user-based recommender system, the *PIP's* similarity features have been analyzed. Therefore, proximity (if the ratings of two users are in agreement [2]), impact (the strength of preference for an item) and popularity (the ratings that are further from the average of a co-rated item) are the features determining the best quality of recommendations in the UBCF scenario (RQ_3). The best results have been achieved considering $k = 50$ neighbors. A greater value for k (for large datasets) means a larger neighborhood and more rated items in comparison with a smaller value (RQ_2).

On the other hand, the *Spearman's Rank Coefficient* performs better on smaller datasets (*DataFiniti - Hotel Reviews 10K*) with greater sparsity (99.91%) (RQ_4) and considering a lower neighborhood size ($k = 10$) (RQ_2).

IBCF Approach. The IBCF approach has been designed considering the presented similarity measures, different values for the k items neighborhood (10, respectively 50) and a resulted list of $n = 5$ suggested movies. Tables 3 and 4 present MAE and precision values for IBCF approach for all similarity-based scenarios for both datasets.

Table 3. MAE and Precision for IBCF on MovieLens

Similarity measure	MAE		Precision	
	k = 10	k = 50	k = 10	k = 50
Pearson correlation	0.48	0.58	0.55	0.64
Constrained Pearson correlation	0.40	0.34	0.65	0.62
Cosine similarity	0.78	0.76	0.48	0.60
Euclidean similarity	1.37	1.02	0.575	0.577
Spearman's rank coefficient	**0.04**	**0.06**	**0.88**	**0.90**
Jaccard similarity	0.54	0.45	0.86	0.88
Adjusted cosine similarity	0.25	0.35	0.79	0.70

Ranks (absolute numerical values) are valuable features for items, highlighting the preference of a user for an item. The rating prediction computation is greatly influenced by the similarity between the k most similar movies and the target movie. Therefore, this idea validates that *Spearman's Rank Coefficient* fits best in the IBCF scenario for large datasets (*MovieLens 1M*) (RQ_1, RQ_2, and RQ_4).

Table 4. MAE and Precision for IBCF on DataFiniti - Hotel Reviews

Similarity measure	MAE		Precision	
	k = 10	k = 50	k = 10	k =50
Pearson correlation	0.40	0.12	0.50	0.66
Constrained Pearson correlation	0.16	0.22	0.70	0.62
Cosine similarity	0.16	0.18	0.46	0.42
Euclidean similarity	0.65	0.63	0.55	0.65
Spearman's rank coefficient	0.32	0.29	0.62	0.54
Jaccard similarity	**0.07**	**0.11**	**0.76**	**0.84**
Adjusted Cosine similarity	0.07	0.13	0.70	0.58

In case of smaller datasets with greater data sparsity (*DataFiniti - Hotel Reviews*) (*RQ₄*), the *Jaccard* similarity measure achieved the best results (RQ_1). This idea is sustained by the small set of users that rated the same items (RQ_3).

5   Conclusions

In the presented study, several experiments were conducted to offer an answer to a set of essential questions in memory-based collaborative filtering approaches. The main difficulty in the design of a recommender system lies upon the proper choice of the similarity measure.

The used data sets, *MovieLens* [26] and *DataFiniti - Hotel Reviews* [12], were chosen in terms of different dimensionality and sparsity features. The results of the conducted numerical experiments lead to the following conclusions. In terms of large data sets and lower data sparsity, the *PIP* similarity fits the user-based context, while the *Spearman's Rank Coefficient* could be a proper selection for the item-based context. In contrast, when having a smaller data set with high sparsity, the *Jaccard* similarity suits the item-based context. For the user-based scenario, multiple similarities can be chosen, depending on the neighborhood size. Moreover, questions like which is an appropriate k value for the size of the neighborhood or which characteristics of similarity measures positively influence the recommendation process, are discussed in this analysis.

As future work, several datasets will be used to validate and generalize the obtained results and to explore an unsupervised flavor in the user/item profile definition.

References

1. Adomavicius, G., Tuzhilin, A.: Toward the next generation of recommender systems: a survey of the state-of-the-art and possible extensions. IEEE Trans. Knowl. Data Eng. **6**, 734–749 (2005)

2. Ahn, H.J.: A new similarity measure for collaborative filtering to alleviate the new user cold-starting problem. Inf. Sci. **178**(1), 37–51 (2008)
3. AL-Bakri, N.F., Hashim, S.H.: A modified similarity measure for improving accuracy of user-based collaborative filterin. Iraqi J. Sci. **59**(2B), 934–945 (2018)
4. Bobadilla, J., Ortega, F., Hernando, A.: A collaborative filtering similarity measure based on singularities. Inf. Process. Manage. **48**(2), 204–217 (2012)
5. Bobadilla, J., Ortega, F., Hernando, A., Gutiérrez, A.: Recommender systems survey. Knowl. Based Syst. **46**, 109–132 (2013)
6. Bobadilla, J., Serradilla, F.: The effect of sparsity on collaborative filtering metrics. In: Proceedings of the Twentieth Australasian Conference on Australasian Database-Volume 92, pp. 9–18. Australian Computer Society, Inc. (2009)
7. Bobadilla, J., Serradilla, F., Bernal, J.: A new collaborative filtering metric that improves the behavior of recommender systems. Knowl. Based Syst. **23**(6), 520–528 (2010)
8. Breese, J.S., Heckerman, D., Kadie, C.: Empirical analysis of predictive algorithms for collaborative filtering. In: Proceedings of the Fourteenth Conference on Uncertainty in Artificial Intelligence, pp. 43–52. Morgan Kaufmann Publishers Inc. (1998)
9. Candillier, L., Meyer, F., Boullé, M.: Comparing state-of-the-art collaborative filtering systems. In: Perner, P. (ed.) MLDM 2007. LNCS (LNAI), vol. 4571, pp. 548–562. Springer, Heidelberg (2007). https://doi.org/10.1007/978-3-540-73499-4_41
10. Candillier, L., Meyer, F., Fessant, F.: Designing Specific weighted similarity measures to improve collaborative filtering systems. In: Perner, P. (ed.) ICDM 2008. LNCS (LNAI), vol. 5077, pp. 242–255. Springer, Heidelberg (2008). https://doi.org/10.1007/978-3-540-70720-2_19
11. Casinelli, P.: Evaluating and implementing recommender systems as web services using apache mahout. Sergio Alvarez, Advisor (2014)
12. DataFiniti: Datafiniti - hotel reviews Dataset. https://data.world/datafiniti/hotel-reviews
13. Deshpande, M., Karypis, G.: Item-based top-N recommendation algorithms. ACM Trans. Inf. Syst. (TOIS) **22**(1), 143–177 (2004)
14. Feng, J., Fengs, X., Zhang, N., Peng, J.: An improved collaborative filtering method based on similarity. PloS One **13**(9), e0204003 (2018)
15. Goldberg, K., Roeder, T., Gupta, D., Perkins, C.: Eigentaste: a constant time collaborative filtering algorithm. Inf. Retrieval **4**(2), 133–151 (2001)
16. Guo, S., et al.: Analysis and evaluation of similarity metrics in collaborative filtering recommender system (2014)
17. Herlocker, J., Konstan, J.A., Riedl, J.: An empirical analysis of design choices in neighborhood-based collaborative filtering algorithms. Inf. Retrieval **5**(4), 287–310 (2002)
18. Herlocker, J.L., Konstan, J.A., Borchers, A., Riedl, J.: An algorithmic framework for performing collaborative filtering. In: 22nd Annual International ACM SIGIR Conference on Research and Development in Information Retrieval, SIGIR 1999, pp. 230–237. Association for Computing Machinery, Inc (1999)
19. Herlocker, J.L., Konstan, J.A., Terveen, L.G., Riedl, J.T.: Evaluating collaborative filtering recommender systems. ACM Trans. Inf. Syst. (TOIS) **22**(1), 5–53 (2004)
20. Jin, R., Chai, J.Y., Si, L.: An automatic weighting scheme for collaborative filtering. In: Proceedings of the 27th Annual International ACM SIGIR Conference on Research and Development in Information Retrieval, pp. 337–344. ACM (2004)

21. Koutrika, G., Bercovitz, B., Garcia-Molina, H.F.: Expressing and combining flexible recommendations. In: Proceedings of the 35th SIGMOD International Conference on Management of Data (SIGMOD'09), Providence, RI, USA. vol. 29
22. Koutrika, G., Bercovitz, B., Garcia-Molina, H.: Flexrecs: expressing and combining flexible recommendations. In: Proceedings of the 2009 ACM SIGMOD International Conference on Management of data, pp. 745–758. ACM (2009)
23. Linden, G., Smith, B., York, J.: Amazon. com recommendations: item-to-item collaborative filtering. IEEE Internet Comput. **7**(1), 76–80 (2003)
24. Liu, F., Li, H., Ma, Z.J., Zhu, E.Z.: Collaborative filtering recommendation algorithm based on item similarity learning. In: Current Trends in Computer Science and Mechanical Automation, vol. 1, pp. 322–335. Sciendo Migration, UK (2017)
25. Liu, H., Hu, Z., Mian, A., Tian, H., Zhu, X.: A new user similarity model to improve the accuracy of collaborative filtering. Knowl. Based Syst. **56**, 156–166 (2014)
26. MovieLens: Movielens Dataset. http://www.grouplens.org/
27. Mulla, N., Girase, S.: A new approach to requirement elicitation based on stakeholder recommendation and collaborative filtering. Int. J. Softw. Eng. Appl. **3**(3), 51 (2012)
28. Netflix: Netflix Movie Dataset. http://www.grouplens.org/
29. Resnick, P., Iacovou, N., Suchak, M., Bergstrom, P., Riedl, J.: Grouplens: an open architecture for collaborative filtering of netnews. In: Proceedings of the 1994 ACM Conference on Computer Supported Cooperative work, pp. 175–186. ACM (1994)
30. Sanchez, J., Serradilla, F., Martinez, E., Bobadilla, J.: Choice of metrics used in collaborative filtering and their impact on recommender systems. In: 2008 2nd IEEE International Conference on Digital Ecosystems and Technologies, pp. 432–436. IEEE (2008)
31. Sarwar, B.M., Karypis, G., Konstan, J.A., Riedl, J., et al.: Item-based collaborative filtering recommendation algorithms. WWW **1**, 285–295 (2001)
32. Shardanand, U., Maes, P.: Social information filtering: algorithms for automating word of mouth. In: Chi. vol. 95, pp. 210–217. Citeseer (1995)
33. Shimodaira, H.: Similarity and recommender systems. School of Informatics, The University of Eidenburgh 21 (2014)
34. Weng, L.T., Xu, Y., Li, Y., Nayak, R.: An improvement to collaborative filtering for recommender systems. In: International Conference on Computational Intelligence for Modelling, Control and Automation and International Conference on Intelligent Agents, Web Technologies and Internet Commerce (CIMCA-IAWTIC 2006), vol. 1, pp. 792–795. IEEE (2005)
35. Zhao, Z.D., Shang, M.S.: User-based collaborative-filtering recommendation algorithms on Hadoop. In: 2010 Third International Conference on Knowledge Discovery and Data Mining, pp. 478–481. IEEE (2010)

Constructing Interpretable Decision Trees Using Parallel Coordinates

Vladimir Estivill-Castro[✉], Eugene Gilmore, and René Hexel

Griffith University, Brisbane, Australia
{v.estivill-castro,r.hexel}@griffith.edu.au,
eugene.gilmore@griffithuni.edu.au

Abstract. The interest in interpretable models that are not only accurate but also understandable is rapidly increasing; often resulting in the machine-learning community turning to decision tree classifiers. Many techniques of growing decision trees use oblique rules to increase the accuracy of the tree and decrease its overall size, but this severely limits understandability by a human user. We propose a new type of oblique rule for decision tree classifiers that is interpretable to human users. We use the parallel coordinates system of visualisation to display both the dataset and rule to the user in an intuitive way. We propose the use of an evolutionary algorithm to learn this new type of rule and show that it produced significantly smaller trees compared to a tree created with axis-parallel rules with minimal loss in accuracy.

1 Introduction

In recent years, interest in the ability to deliver understandable machine-learning models has increased [25]. Deep neural networks have been able to achieve an impressive level of accuracy in a variety of domains [30]. Despite this, the machine learning community recognises now the importance of eXplainable AI (XAI) [1]; that is, the priorities also include the ability of humans to understand how these models are reaching their decisions. The European Union has recently introduced regulations [2] that decisions by an automated system affecting a citizen must be explainable to the citizen. This need for understandability is of critical consequence, in particular in domains such as medicine [22], credit scoring [27], and churn prediction [35]. Moreover, insights into the phenomena, links between independent and dependent variables, and understanding of relationships is usually more important than black-box classification [22, 27, 35]. Even more relevant is the value of incorporating humans' expertise and experience. Researchers insist for techniques that building classifiers with the human-in-the-loop [15].

Interpretability [12] is the key characteristic of decision trees. Thus, the area of XAI has focused on decision trees [1, 33] and decision forests [26]. One technique has been to use a decision tree or trees as a surrogate for a black-box model where the decision tree is used for the explanation while the black-box model is used for the prediction [4]. When solely using decision trees to learn interpretable

© Springer Nature Switzerland AG 2020
L. Rutkowski et al. (Eds.): ICAISC 2020, LNAI 12416, pp. 152–164, 2020.
https://doi.org/10.1007/978-3-030-61534-5_14

models, most research has been focused on either making these trees smaller, or increasing their accuracy to better match the accuracy of black-box models [39]. However, little research has examined different forms of rule splits at each node of a decision tree. We introduce a new type of split for internal nodes of a decision tree as well as a method of growing these trees using a genetic algorithm. We argue that this provides a suitable trade-off between extremely sophisticated splits that reduce the length of branches in the tree (and thus rules, but result in unintelligible tests on attributes), versus the alternative of simple binary tests but more extended rules. In all cases, the sacrifice in accuracy should be minimised. We also argue that this new form of rule split lends itself to human in the loop learning of decision trees classifiers.

2   Supervised Learning

2.1   The Starting Point Is Greedy Hill-Climbing

The original goal of supervised learning is to learn a classifier from a supervised sequence T of vectors (of the form $(\boldsymbol{x}_i, y_i)_{i=1,...,n}$), that minimises the misclassification rate MS given by $MS = E[F(\boldsymbol{x}) \neq c(\boldsymbol{x})]$ (the expectation is with respect to the distribution of unseen cases). The vector $\boldsymbol{x}$ is the independent variable and holds d attributes. The set T is a matrix of n rows and $d+1$ columns. Thus, a classifier $F : X \rightarrow Y$ labels an un-labelled case $\boldsymbol{x}$ as belonging to a class $F(\boldsymbol{x})$ among a finite set of categories $C = \{C_1, C_2, \ldots, C_k\}$ ($y_i \in C$, $\forall i = 1, \ldots, n$). Machine learning uses T to build a predictor for the dependent variable y.

For assessing performance as accuracy, the common approach is V-fold validation [3]. We note that the understandability and generalisation capacity of the classifier is correlated to its length [24, Section 3.6.2]. Other criteria to assess the quality of the learning included such metrics as minimum-description length [31]. Therefore, aiming for short and shallow trees, (in what could be considered a variant of Occam's Razor), the construction of decision trees follows a fundamental greedy strategy that starts from a single-node tree and recursively operates on the input T with two steps.

1. If the set T is such that all y_i are equal or meet some homogeneity criteria H, we call T and its associated tree-node "pure" [5] and we stop here with the prediction given by a decision procedure D.
2. Alternatively, we select an informative criterion or question Q on some of the attributes and horizontally split the set T by the criterion Q into subsequences $T_1, \ldots, T_t$ for which we apply the method recursively.

As described in the seminal book by Breiman et al. [5, Page 22], the entire construction of the tree then revolves around three elements:

1. The selection of the splits (choice of Qs).
2. The decision procedure H to declare a node terminal.
3. The procedure D for assigning each terminal node to a class.

2.2   Higher Accuracy and Shorter (Oblique) Trees

Although basic decision trees perform tests over one attribute, tests with more than one attribute lead to so-called "oblique test" [7,14,28] or "variable combinations" [5, Section 5.2]. These tests are a linear combination of all numerical attributes [5, Section 5.2.2]. When decision trees use oblique tests, an oblique hyperplane in the feature space [14] splits T. Oblique decision trees frequently grow smaller and more accurate decision trees (standard trees are a subset of oblique trees). However, decision trees with oblique splits are generally more difficult to interpret [7]: since the splits are now represented by a hyperplane in d-dimensional feature space, the split becomes difficult to describe to a human.

2.3   Our Choice of Parallel Coordinates

We demonstrate how to use *parallel coordinates* [19] for effectively growing interpretable trees with rules testing more than one attribute. Parallel coordinates efficiently visualise high-dimensional datasets [21]. Common data visualisation techniques (such as the scatter diagram) rely on mapping data onto a Cartesian plane. This mapping is quite effective in datasets with three or fewer dimensions. Beyond this, however, it becomes difficult to obtain a complete representation of the dataset and the potential relationship between attributes [37]. But the parallel coordinates approach to the visualisation of datasets is not dependent on the number d of dimensions of that dataset [10]. A dataset of any dimensionality d is represented and projected in a two-dimensional drawing. This breakthrough in the presentation of high-dimensional datasets is achieved by drawing all axes parallel to each other rather than requiring all axis to be orthogonal to each other.

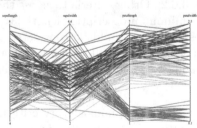

In an d-dimensional dataset, each observation is represented by a poly-line that crosses each of the parallel axes. Figure 1 shows the Iris dataset being visualised using parallel coordinates. Each instance in the dataset appears as a poly-line that intercepts each axis at the normalised value of that attribute for that instance. Despite its advantages for visualising high dimensional datasets, parallel

Fig. 1. The Iris Dataset visualised using parallel coordinates [23].

coordinates are used infrequently by the machine learning community [20].

3   Decision Trees Using Parallel Coordinates

We introduce the interactive use of parallel coordinates to, not only construct the tree fully autonomously, but also to enable human drivers to incorporate expertise in the tree. Previous efforts to involve humans in building a tree have involved the human to chose a very restricted shape (line or axis-parallel rectangle) in a Cartesian visualisation of two attributes [36]. These proposals not only have the disadvantage of a weak visualisation but they are fully manual (leaving the human without the powerful heuristic search of the computer). In sharp contrast, we propose a new algorithm Q for recursively splitting the nodes of a decision tree under construction. In our system, the split Q

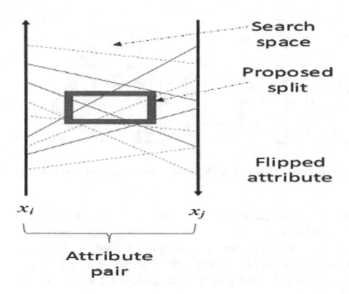

Search space

Proposed split

Flipped attribute

x_i x_j

Attribute pair

Fig. 2. Using a rectangle region in between two parallel coordinates.

will be chosen by the human but assisted with resources (information summaries and indicators). Our Q does not involve all the attributes (recall that oblique splits of d attributes are hard to understand). Our Q is visible as a rectangular region between at most two attribute axes on a parallel coordinates visualisation of the dataset (and will have an interpretation comprehensive to humans).

Figure 2 shows our proposed method of using parallel coordinates for selecting a split Q. The splits are oblique but are restricted to two attributes, so that they remain interpretable to the user. Each split Q is represented by a rectangle in parallel coordinates space between (but including) the two selected attributes (therefore, standard splits of decision trees are also included). An instance is said to match this rule if it intersects this rectangle in the parallel coordinates display. Despite only using two attributes, a dataset with d attributes will have $d(d-1) = O(d^2)$ possible ordered choices with the additional possibility to flip one of these axes for a total of $2d(d-1)$ possible axes combinations.

These rectangles are interpretable by users as follows. A vertical range $[a, b]$ over one attribute x_i (a horizontally flat rectangle $[a, b] \times [x_i, x_i]$) corresponds to selecting a range (a band) of values for attribute x_i (and thus, to the standard form of orthogonal splits in decision trees). That is, one branch of the tree is $\{x \mid a \leq x_i \leq b\}$ while the other branch is $\{x \mid (x_i < a) \vee (x_i > b)\}$. Alternatively, the range $[a, b]$ corresponds to the line L given by $x_i = (a+b)/2$ with the margin $(b-a)/2$, and those instances that fall within the margin are one branch of the binary split, while the other branch is those outside the margin (refer to Fig. 3). As the vertical range travels from left to right in the parallel-coordinate space, starting with attribute x_i to attribute x_j, the line L changes slope. That is, a horizontally flat rectangle given by $[a, b] \times [u, u]$ with $x_i \leq u \leq x_j$) represents a line with margin $(b - a)/2$ but with a slope that, in a 2D Cartesian space for x_i, x_j, is between horizontal to vertical.

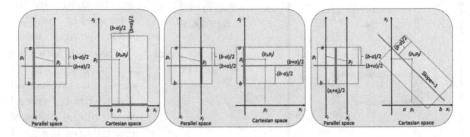

Fig. 3. Illustration of a range selection in Parallel-space versus Cartesian space.

Thus, if we consider not only a range (which is a rectangle of minimal horizontal size in parallel-coordinate space) but a progressively wider rectangle $[a, b] \times [u, v]$ (where $x_i \leq u \leq v \leq x_j$), we are enlarging the set of slopes. If we manipulate the vertical dimension of the rectangle (the values a and b), we affect the position of the line and the width of the margin. Note the connection to support vector machines.

The use of parallel coordinates allows for the easy capturing of a number of interesting relationships between attributes. We emphasise the following.

1. Due to the point-line duality in parallel coordinates [19], shrinking a rectangle into a point (in parallel-coordinates space) corresponds to a split where instances approximately follow a linear correlation between the two attributes.
2. Squeezing the rectangle to a horizontal line segment L in parallel coordinates space translates to a linear correlation of the two attributes that is rotated around a point with the amount of rotation dictated by the length L.
3. If we squeeze the rectangle so it approaches a vertical segmemt L in parallel coordinates space, it translates to a set of parallel linear correlations with the width of this set being determined by the length L.

To illustrate the power of using our suggested form of rule split for decision trees, we constructed a synthetic dataset. This dataset has three attributes ($d = 3$) and 400 instances with two classes. We generated the data with uniformly distributed random values for each individual attribute, but there is a linear correlation between the first and second attribute for one class, and also for the second class, the second and third attribute are correlated. These relationships are generated with a small amount of random noise.

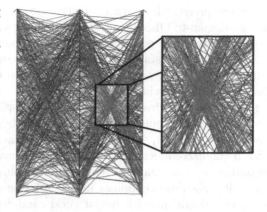

Fig. 4. The learnt rule is shown in green between the second and third attributes.

Figure 4 shows the rule that is learnt using our system with rectangular regions in parallel coordinates. Due to the linear relationship between the two attributes, the rectangle is completely slim and has taken the form of a line. Although this is a rather simplistic example we argue that it allows a human to easily understand a simple and accurate classifier where other systems would either create an inaccurate classifier or an uninterpretable tree. On this dataset, WEKA's implementation of C4.5 produces a naive one-node tree with 50% accuracy. Recent studies have looked at techniques for learning smaller trees for the sake of understandability [4]. But, these approaches do not offer effective visualisation of their oblique splits. In recent years there have been numerous techniques proposed to grow accurate and shorter oblique decision trees using evolutionary algorithms [7,33]; however, these techniques rely on finding a hyperplane that splits the data. The ability to understand this hyperplane by a human user is a problem that seems to be largely ignored in the literature.

We argue that this form of split representation has numerous benefits:

1. Logic rules derived from the decision tree for explaining classification decisions use splits on more than one attribute and remain understandable by humans due to their ease for visualisation.
2. A user can review the rule in the context of the entire dataset and the patterns exhibited by the dataset under classification.
3. Linear relationships between multiple attributes can be easily captured due to the point-line duality in parallel coordinates [19].
4. Flipping an axes is an additional operation rarely considered in OLAP.

Moreover, when combining this approach with a human-in-the-loop learning system, the user will be able to select and manage the subset of attributes visible in the construction. Therefore, the user adjusts which and how many attributes are under consideration, enabling the exploration of arbitrarily large number of dimensions. But then again, the system will offer insights into which attributes to include into the visible data set, as well as the order in which they are presented. Adding an attribute or removing an attribute from view are analogous to OLAP's operations (slicing and dicing), while OLAP's pivoting corresponds to the parallel-coordinates visualisation order [8]. OLAP has been particularly successful in business intelligence applications [9] and for successful analyses of human participation and human expertise and insights are critical for successfully driving the process.

When moving from a single attribute split to an oblique split, the search space increases exponentially with the number of dimensions in the dataset. To tackle this problem, we use the Gain Ratio as used in the traditional C4.5 algorithm [32] in conjunction with a differential evolution algorithm [34]. Differential evolution initially encodes N_P candidate solutions as real-valued vectors, starting with N_P random points in the solution space. It is possible, however, to seed the algorithm with initial good candidates. The user shall supply a cost function, as well as mutation and crossover factors, and the limit G of iterations. At each iteration, crossover and mutation operations are applied to each candidate solution. There are a number of different variants of the differential evolution algorithm, the notation DE/A/B/C is used to describe these different variants. Our experiments and discussions for the remainder of this paper focus on the classic DE/rand/1/bin variant because OC1-DE [33] uses such variant. Our algorithm works as follows.

Table 1. Datasets used.

Dataset	Attributes	Instances	Classes	Dataset	Attributes	Instances	Classes
iris		150	3	liver	6	345	2
cryotherapy	6	90	2	seeds	7	210	3
ecoli	7	336	8	car	6	1728	4
breast-cancer-wisconsin	9	699	2	glass	9	214	6
vowel	10	990	11	page-blocks	10	5473	5
wine	13	178	3	heart	13	270	2
credit	14	690	2	vehicle	18	846	4
ionosphere	34	351	2				

1. At each non-terminal node with data T, pairs of attributes are selected[1].
2. For each pair of attributes, an initial population of candidate solutions is randomly generated. Each solution consists of four values, the x_i coordinates of the left and right side of the rectangle and the x_j coordinates of the top and bottom of the rectangle.

---

[1] We use only adjacent attributes in the visualisation as pairs due to the computational cost of evaluation of every possible attribute pair and maintaining the mental map of the user. This reduces the complexity from $O(d^2)$ to $O(d)$, and the user can still permute attributes at will to create pairs.

3. The differential evolution algorithm runs for each attribute pair and the best candidate solution is recorded. The cost of candidates is defined as the inverse of the information gain of the split.
4. We take the candidate solution with the lowest cost overall attribute pairs as the split Q for this node.
5. The splitting process is repeated for each child node until all leaf nodes meet a criteria H, which for simplicity, we make the node is pure.
6. Prune the tree and avoid over-fitting. with C4.5's pruning strategy [32]

We generate a fraction of the initial solutions using C4.5 single attribute splits, increasing the accuracy of our method. Single attribute splits are calculated for both attributes under examination using C4.5's rule to chose a split. Each later candidate derives uniformly from one of the two attributes. C4.5's split on a single attribute is a range $v_1 \leq x_i \leq v_2$. But, we convert this split to our parallel-coordinates rule representation by constructing a narrow box located next to the left or right axis depending on the original attribute. The height and position of the box closely approximates C4.5's single attribute split.

4 Experiments

Although the intention of our system is to let the user guide the construction of a tree, we evaluate the effectiveness of our algorithm for finding splits in parallel coordinates space by allowing it to grow complete trees autonomously. This demonstrates the power of our system's suggestions. We test the algorithm against a number of popular datasets in the UCI repository [23]. Table 1 shows the details of these datasets.

Table 2. F-Measure scores averaged over 5 runs of 10-fold stratified cross-validation.

Dataset	C45V1	C45V2	Weka J48	PC-DE (seed C45V1)	PC-DE (seed C45V2)	OC1	OC1-DE
iris	**0.95(2)**	0.90(7)	**0.95(2)**	0.93(6)	0.94(4.5)	0.94(4.5)	**0.95(2)**
liver	**0.65(1)**	0.60(7)	0.64(2.5)	0.63(4.5)	0.64(2.5)	0.63(4.5)	0.61(6)
cryotherapy	**0.91(2)**	0.89(5)	0.90(4)	**0.91(2)**	**0.91(2)**	0.86(7)	0.88(6)
seeds	0.92(2.5)	0.88(7)	**0.94(1)**	0.90(6)	0.91(4.5)	0.92(2.5)	0.91(4.5)
ecoli	0.50(5)	0.41(7)	**0.55(1)**	0.50(5)	0.51(2.5)	0.50(5)	0.51(2.5)
car	0.88(6)	0.91(3)	0.90(4.5)	**1.00(1)**	0.99(2)	0.90(4.5)	0.85(7)
breast-cancer-wisconsin	0.94(3)	0.93(6)	0.94(3)	0.93(6)	0.93(6)	**0.95(1)**	0.94(3)
glass	**0.69(1)**	0.62(5.5)	0.62(5.5)	0.62(5.5)	0.64(2)	0.62(5.5)	0.63(3)
vowel	**0.79(2)**	0.71(7)	**0.79(2)**	0.74(6)	0.76(4)	**0.79(2)**	0.75(5)
page-blocks	0.84(2)	0.80(5.5)	**0.85(1)**	0.80(5.5)	0.81(4)	0.83(3)	0.56(7)
wine	**0.93(2)**	0.92(4)	**0.93(2)**	0.90(5.5)	0.90(5.5)	**0.93(2)**	0.89(7)
heart	0.76(2)	0.70(6)	**0.78(1)**	0.70(6)	0.70(6)	0.75(3.5)	0.75(3.5)
credit	0.84(3.5)	0.84(3.5)	0.84(3.5)	0.82(6)	0.81(7)	0.84(3.5)	**0.86(1)**
vehicle	0.72(2.5)	0.69(5.5)	**0.73(1)**	0.71(4)	0.72(2.5)	0.69(5.5)	0.58(7)
ionosphere	**0.92(1)**	0.87(5.5)	0.89(2.5)	0.88(4)	0.87(5.5)	0.89(2.5)	0.81(7)
Average Rank	2.50	5.63	2.43	4.87	4.03	3.77	4.77

Calculating the F-Measure is delicate, especially for multi-class classification problems and with cross-validation [11]. Nevertheless, when evaluating a classifier, we use the F-Measure to quantify the predictive power, since this is resilient to class imbalance in a dataset. We use 10-fold stratified cross validation and perform this for 5 repeated runs. We then average the result across all 5 runs.

In particular, to ensure consistent results across all methods, when using other machine-learning packages to train classifiers, we record the raw results and calculate the F-Measure as suggested by Forman et al. [11].

We also measure the size of the decision tree constructed and the depth of its deepest node. This size and depth is measured by training the classifier on the full dataset for five individual runs and taking the average across all runs[2].

The best possible splits of C4.5 provide some of the initial candidate solutions for our genetic algorithm. Because of this, we first evaluate the performance of our implementation in comparison to Weka's J48 implementation of C4.5. We test two different versions of our implementation of C4.5, one that looks for a split Q of the form $x_i >= S_1$. We call this version C45V1. This is the traditional implementation of C4.5 and the type of split that Weka's J48 uses. We also test a version, C45V2, looking for splits of the form $S_1 <= x_i <= S_2$.

We next evaluate our parallel-coordinates algorithm, named PC-DE. We run this algorithm in two different configurations, one seeded with initial candidates from C45V1 and one seeded with candidates from C45V2[3]. For the differential evolution algorithm, we use a population size of 50, cross-over rate of 0.4, mutation factor of 0.6, for 100 iterations with 15% of the population seeded.

We also run all 15 dataset against the OC1 algorithm [29], an algorithm for induction of oblique decision trees where the split point at each node is a hyperplane across all attributes. Finally we run the OC1-DE [33] algorithm, a version of OC1 using differential evolution to find the hyperplanes for OC1[4]. Table 2 and Table 3 respectively, show the F-Measure and tree structure results. Each row of these tables also includes in brackets the rank of each algorithm for that dataset, but the last row shows the average rank.

From the average rank we can already contrast the performance of each algorithm. Nevertheless, we perform some statistical analysis to determine differences in these algorithms. We make use of the scmamp [6] R-package for all statistical analysis of results. To compare the results of these algorithms we first use Iman Davenport's correction [18] of the Friedman test [13] to check if there exists a significant difference in the performance of at least one of these algorithms. This test computes the p-value which is used to accept or reject the null hypothesis H_0 that all algorithms perform equally. We perform this test on the F-Measure generated with each method and find a p-value of 1.449×10^{-5}. Using a significance level of 5% we can reject the null hypothesis that the predictive power of each algorithm is the same. Having rejected the null hypothesis we can

---

[2] We only run once on the full dataset when measuring the size and the depth of the deepest leaf for C4.5 and J48 since these algorithms are completely deterministic.

[3] We make available the sourcecode for our algorithm here.

[4] We thank the authors of the OC1-DE algorithm [33] for providing their source code.

Table 3. Tree size and depth for each algorithm.

Dataset	DeepestLeaf/Tree Size						
	C45V1	C45V2	Weka J48	PC-DE (seed C45V1)	PC-DE (seed C45V2)	OC1	OC1-DE
iris	6/17(7)	5/13(6)	4/9(4)	5/9(4)	5/9(4)	**4/7(1.5)**	**4/7(1.5)**
liver	13/145(7)	21/99(6)	14/85(4)	**9.8/49.8(1)**	10/52.2(2)	18.8/98.6(5)	11.6/63(3)
cryotherapy	9/21(7)	6/17(6)	2/7(3.5)	**3/5(1.5)**	**3/5(1.5)**	3/7(3.5)	4.8/10.6(5)
seeds	8/25(6.5)	8/25(6.5)	5/15(5)	5.2/10.2(2.5)	5.2/10.2(2.5)	**3/5(1)**	5.6/11.8(4)
ecoli	13/93(7)	10/75(6)	7/37(3)	7.2/39.4(4)	7.4/39.8(5)	**4/7(1)**	8/32.6(2)
car	12/205(7)	12/139(5)	11/145(6)	9.2/44.2(2)	**9.6/42.6(1)**	9.6/62.2(3)	10/91.8(4)
breast-cancer	11/83(7)	9/67(6)	7/27(3)	7.2/30.6(4)	7.6/32.2(5)	**4/7(1)**	7.4/19.8(2)
glass	11/81(7)	11/57(5.5)	11/57(5.5)	7.2/36.6(2)	7.2/37(3)	**4/11(1)**	9/41(4)
vowel	13/245(7)	13/207(5)	15/211(6)	10/128.2(2)	10.2/131(3)	**10/123(1)**	13/176.6(4)
page-blocks	16/295(7)	17/179(6)	14/117(3)	11.4/133.4(5)	11.2/129(4)	11/91(2)	**9.6/62.6(1)**
wine	5/19(7)	4/11(5)	3/9(3)	4/9(3)	4/9(3)	**3/7(1)**	5.4/14.2(6)
heart	10/71(7)	11/49(6)	7/47(5)	9.8/34.6(3)	10/35.4(4)	**4/11(1)**	7.8/32.6(2)
credit	15/165(7)	12/77(6)	15/69(5)	9.6/67.4(4)	9.8/64.2(3)	**4/7(1)**	6/18.6(2)
vehicle	19/257(7)	29/179(5)	33/205(6)	11.8/97(2)	12.6/99.4(3)	**13/67(1)**	15.2/110.6(4)
ionosphere	9/39(7)	5/11(2)	7/23(5)	6.4/16.6(4)	6.4/15.8(3)	**2/3(1)**	9.2/37(6)
Average Rank	6.97	5.47	4.47	2.93	3.13	1.67	3.37

proceed to pair-wise comparisons between individual algorithms. For these pair-wise comparisons we use the Bergmann-Hommel test [16] to check for differences in performance. Figure 5 shows a graph of the results of this test for the F-Measure results of each algorithm. The nodes in the graph represent each algorithm with their average rank, a link between two nodes shows that there is no significant difference in the performance between these two algorithms.

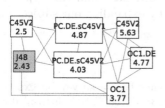

Fig. 5. Results of the Bergmann-Hommel test.

Figure 5 shows links between algorithms where no significant difference is present. Thus, for most of the algorithms, we cannot say that there exists a significant difference in predictive performance. This includes predictive performance between OC1 and OC1-DE. We attribute this to the well-known issue of reproducibility [17]. This graph also shows that PC-DE based methods as well as OC1 do not perform significantly differently to other methods in terms of predictive performance. Despite a large difference in the performance between C45V1 and C45V2, the impact of which version is used in our PC-DE algorithm is minimal. Nevertheless, seeding with C45V1 appears to have slightly advantage and as such we focus on this version of our algorithm for further analysis. In a direct comparison between PC-DE(seeded C45V1) and J48 (the best performing single attribute split algorithm) we would expect that oblique tests would lead to more accurate trees given their increased expressive power. We attribute the slight loss in predictive performance to the trees that are learnt being significantly smaller. Indeed the trees learnt with our

PC-DE(seeded C45V1) algorithm are on average 21% smaller than trees grown with J48 and in some cases are half the size or less. This difference in size comes at the cost of an average loss in F-Measure of 0.019. We perform the Wilcoxon signed-ranks test [38] between these two algorithms for both F-Measure and tree size. For 15 datasets results are statistically significant with a p-value of 0.05 the exact critical value is 25. When comparing the size of trees the minimum sum of ranks for positive and negative difference is 21 for tree size while for F-Measure it is 19. Both of these being below the critical value shows that using the Wilcoxon, both the difference in tree size and F-measure are statistically significant. Given that smaller trees are much more interpretable to users, we argue that this type of oblique split lends itself very well to application that value human understandability.

5   Conclusion

We have presented a new type of oblique split for decision tree classifiers. We have shown how parallel coordinates can be effectively used to make this type of oblique split interpretable to a human user as well as the very promising potential for the use of parallel coordinates in the machine learning community. We have also demonstrated how this new type of split can be learnt with an evolutionary algorithm to grow complete trees. We find that using this technique, we are able to grow trees that are substantially smaller with minimal impact on their accuracy. In future work, we would like to look at methods of GPU processing to speed up the learning process and with this, the ability to examine all possible combinations of attribute pairs in the dataset. We would also like to further investigate the effectiveness of using parallel coordinates and this type of rule split for a human in the loop learning systems by expanding our subject pool.

References

1. Adadi, A., Berrada, M.: Peeking inside the black-box: a survey on explainable artificial intelligence (xai). IEEE Access **6**, 52138–52160 (2018). https://doi.org/10.1109/ACCESS.2018.2870052
2. Ala-Pietilä, P., et al.: European union: general data protection regulation (EU) 2016/679. Techinal. report., European Commission, B-1049 Brussels (8th April 2016)
3. Arlot, S., Celisse, A., et al.: A survey of cross-validation procedures for model selection. Stat. Surv. **4**, 40–79 (2010)
4. Blanco-Justicia, A., Domingo-Ferrer, J.: Machine learning explainability through comprehensible decision trees. In: Holzinger, A., Kieseberg, P., Tjoa, A.M., Weippl, E. (eds.) CD-MAKE 2019. LNCS, vol. 11713, pp. 15–26. Springer, Cham (2019). https://doi.org/10.1007/978-3-030-29726-8_2
5. Breiman, L., Friedman, J., Olshen, R., Stone, C.: Classification and Regression Trees. Wadsworth and Brooks, Monterrey (1984)
6. Calvo, B., Santafé-Guzmán, R.: scmamp: Statistical comparison of multiple algorithms in multiple problems. The R J. **8**(1) August 2016

7. Cantú-Paz, E., Kamath, C.: Inducing oblique decision trees with evolutionary algorithms. IEEE Trans. Evol. Comput. **7**(1), 54–68 (2003)
8. Chaudhuri, S., Dayal, U.: An overview of data warehousing and OLAP technology. SIGMOD Rec. **26**(1), 65–74 (1997). https://doi.org/10.1145/248603.248616
9. Chaudhuri, S., Dayal, U., Narasayya, V.: An overview of business intelligence technology. Commun. ACM **54**(8), 88–98 (2011). https://doi.org/10.1145/1978542.1978562
10. Few, S.: Multivariate analysis using parallel coordinates. Perceptual Edge (September 12th 2006). www.perceptualedge.com. Accessed 5 Nov 2019
11. Forman, G., Scholz, M.: Apples-to-apples in cross-validation studies: Pitfalls in classifier performance measurement. SIGKDD Explor. Newsl. **12**(1), 49–57 (2010). https://doi.org/10.1145/1882471.1882479
12. Freitas, A.A.: Comprehensible classification models: a position paper. SIGKDD Explor. **15**(1), 1–10 (2013)
13. Friedman, M.: The use of ranks to avoid the assumption of normality implicit in the analysis of variance. J. Am. Stat. Assoc. **32**, 675–701 (1937)
14. Health, D.G., Kasif, S., Salzberg, S.: Induction of oblique decision trees. In: 13th International Joint Conference on Artificial Intelligence, pp. 1002–1007. Morgan Kaufmann (1993)
15. Holzinger, A.: Interactive machine learning for health informatics: when do we need the human-in-the-loop? Brain Inform. **3**(2), 119–131 (2016). https://doi.org/10.1007/s40708-016-0042-6
16. Hommel, G.: A stagewise rejective multiple test procedure based on a modified Bonferroni test. Biometrika **75**(2), 383–386 (1988). https://doi.org/10.1093/biomet/75.2.383
17. Hutson, M.: Artificial intelligence faces reproducibility crisis. Science **359**(6377), 725–726 (2018). https://doi.org/10.1126/science.359.6377.725
18. Iman, R., Davenport, J.: Approximations of the critical region of the friedman statistic. Commun. Stat. Theor. Meth. **99**(6), 571–595 (1980)
19. Inselberg, A.: Parallel Coordinates : Visual Multidimensional Geometry and its Applications. Springer, NY (2009)
20. Inselberg, A., Avidan, T.: Classification and visualization for high-dimensional data. In: 6th ACM SIGKDD International Conference on Knowledge Discovery and Data Mining, 20th–23rd August, pp. 370–374. ACM, Boston, MA, USA (2000)
21. Johansson, J., Forsell, C., Lind, M., Cooper, M.: Perceiving patterns in parallel coordinates: determining thresholds for identification of relationships. Inf. Vis. **7**(2), 152–162 (2008). https://doi.org/10.1057/palgrave.ivs.9500166
22. Lavrač, N.: Selected techniques for data mining in medicine. Artif. Intell. Med. **16**(1), 3–23 (1999)
23. Lichman, M.: UCI machine learning repository (2013). https://archive.ics.uci.edu/ml
24. Mitchell, T.M.: Machine Learning. McGraw-Hill, New York (1997)
25. Monroe, D.: AI, explain yourself. Commun. ACM **61**(11), 11–13 (2018). https://doi.org/10.1145/3276742
26. Moore, A., Murdock, V., Cai, Y., Jones, K.: Transparent tree ensembles. In: 41st International ACM SIGIR Confernce on Research & Development in Information Retrieval, pp. 1241–1244. SIGIR 2018. ACM, NY (2018). https://doi.org/10.1145/3209978.3210151

27. Mues, C., Huysmans, J., Vanthienen, J., Baesens, B.: Comprehensible credit-scoring knowledge visualization using decision tables and diagrams. In: Enterprise Information Systems VI, pp. 109–115. Springer (2006). https://doi.org/10.1007/1-4020-3675-2_13
28. Murthy, S.K., Kasif, S., Salzberg, S.: A system for induction of oblique decision trees. J. Artif. Int. Res. **2**(1), 1–32 (1994)
29. Murthy, S., Kasif, S., Salzberg, S., Beigel, R.: OC1: Randomized induction of oblique decision trees. In: 11th National Conference on Artificial Intelligence, AAAI Press. pp. 322–327. AAAI 1993 (1993)
30. Pouyanfar, S., et al.: A survey on deep learning: algorithms, techniques, and applications. ACM Comput. Surv. **51**(5), 1–36 (2018). https://doi.org/10.1145/3234150
31. Quinlan, J.R., Rivest, R.L.: Inferring decision trees using the minimum description length principle. Inf. Comput. **80**(3), 227–248 (1989). https://doi.org/10.1016/0890-5401(89)90010-2
32. Quinlan, J.: C4.5: Programs for Machine Learning. Morgan Kaufmann Publishers, San Mateo, CA (1993)
33. Rivera-Lopez, R., Canul-Reich, J., Gámez, J.A., Puerta, J.M.: OC1-DE: a differential evolution based approach for inducing oblique decision trees. In: Rutkowski, L., Korytkowski, M., Scherer, R., Tadeusiewicz, R., Zadeh, L.A., Zurada, J.M. (eds.) ICAISC 2017. LNCS (LNAI), vol. 10245, pp. 427–438. Springer, Cham (2017). https://doi.org/10.1007/978-3-319-59063-9_38
34. Storn, R., Price, K.: Differential evolution-a simple and efficient heuristic for global optimization over continuous spaces. J. Glob. Optim. **11**(4), 341–359 (1997)
35. Verbeke, W., Martens, D., Mues, C., Baesens, B.: Building comprehensible customer churn prediction models with advanced rule induction techniques. Expert Syst. Appl. **38**(3), 2354–2364 (2011)
36. Ware, M., Frank, E., Holmes, G., A., H.M., Witten, I.H.: Interactive machine learning: letting users build classifiers. Int. J. Hum. Comput. Stud. **55**(3), 281–292 (2001)
37. Wegman, E.J.: Hyperdimensional data analysis using parallel coordinates. J. Am. Stat. Assoc. **85**(411), 664–675 (1990)
38. Wilcoxon, F.: Individual comparisons by ranking methods. In: Breakthroughs in Statistics: Methodology and Distribution, pp. 196–202. Springer, NY (1992). https://doi.org/10.1007/978-1-4612-4380-9_16
39. Yang, Y., Morillo, I.G., Hospedales, T.M.: Deep neural decision trees. In: ICML Workshop on Human Interpretability in Machine Learning (WHI 2018) (2018)

A Framework for e-Recruitment Recommender Systems

Mauricio Noris Freire[(✉)] and Leandro Nunes de Castro

Natural Computing and Machine Learning Laboratory (LCoN),
Mackenzie Presbyterian University, São Paulo/SP, Brazil
mauricionoris@gmail.com

Abstract. e-Recruitment Recommender Systems have been attracting
attention over the last few years. It is an economically relevant field
and can potentially revolutionize how organizations execute talent search
and acquisition. This paper briefly discusses the e-Recruitment problem
and presents a framework together with three recommendation models
aiming to overcome the particular challenges presented in this field.

Keywords: e-Recruitment · Framework · Recommender system

1 Introduction

The advances of the Internet revolutionized how the information flows inside
and outside organizations. Almost all aspects of businesses were influenced by
it. The use of Internet by the world's population went from 34.6% in 2012 [15]
to 56.8% in 2019 [12], an increase of 64.2% in only seven years. There will be
a moment in history in which almost all transactions will be made digitally,
and organizations are pushed to review their processes to a cheaper, scalable
and digital version. Regardless of the size and nature of business, enterprises
have been tackling challenges regarding their human resources. "Recruitment is
on the cusp of digital disruption. Just as business has entered the age of the
consumer, arguably, recruitment is entering the age of the candidate. Websites,
like Glassdoor and LinkedIn, empower candidates with more information than
ever about potential employers, allowing them to reach out directly to people
they want to work with, regardless of whether they are hiring or not..."[16, pp.
304–305]

This paper proposes a framework which allows the integration between Recommender Systems (RS) and Application Tracking Systems (ATS). In addition, it suggests three recommendation models to be implemented using such
framework.

2 Theoretical Background

Typically, recommendation systems produce a score, known generically as utility, for items to choose from, or a list of the N most recommended or highest

L. Rutkowski et al. (Eds.): ICAISC 2020, LNAI 12416, pp. 165–175, 2020.
https://doi.org/10.1007/978-3-030-61534-5_15

score items [3]. The main approaches on recommender systems for e-recruitment are based on content (CBR); collaborative (CF); knowledge (KBR); or Hybrid [9,11,16]. The problem of matching jobs and candidates can be seen from two distinct perspectives: a) find relevant candidates to a job opening; and b) select the suitable jobs to a specific candidate. Regardless of the recommendation focus and the approach used, it is common sense that USER is the term designed to receive a set of objects recommended to it and ITEM is one of the objects recommended to a specific user. A recommender system that embraces both perspectives is known as a bidirectional recommender system [10] and treats interchangeably users and items in a single solution. Looking at candidates past job titles is not always the indication of which job titles are the candidate willing to evaluate for his next move. Several studies address career trajectories [1,2,8,17–19]. Finally, in [16], the authors summarize the recruitment process, the categories of e-recruitment platforms and present approaches to run the job-candidate recommendation, their characteristics and challenges.

3   The e-Recruitment Problem

E-recruitment is generically composed of two sub-processes, as illustrated in Figure 1. Recommendations are useful in both sub-processes.

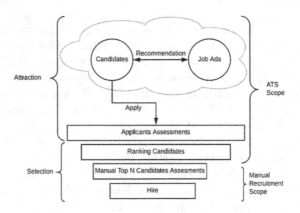

Fig. 1. e-Recruitment overview

The goal of the **Attraction** sub-process is to generate awareness to a job vacancy among active or passive job postulants. Spreading the information about the existence of the opportunity and receiving as much audience and applications as possible are the main goals of this phase. At this stage, recommendation is bidirectional, where candidates are recommended to jobs, and jobs to candidates. Also, the criteria to decide if a candidate fits a job during this stage must be more flexible but keeping a certain exclusion degree to avoid an overload of information and the attraction of unsuitable candidates. Differently from the

Selection sub-process, the goal of a recommender is to evaluate among a set of candidates which ones are best suited for a position based on a specific fitness function for that job position.

Thus, if during the Attraction phase a plethora of recommender systems approaches could be employed to approximate candidates to job vacancies, at the Selection phase a content-based approach is the main technique to filter the best suited candidates and could be leveraged by a semantic context and/or integration with social networks to enhance a candidate profile, collect endorsements and other types of information to validate and select the best suited candidates. Additionally, third-party digital assessment systems can be integrated with the solution providing data to enrich the user profile.

e-Recruitment can also occur without an ATS support, and in such situations, the recommendation itself can improve only over the attraction sub-process, where the candidates interact with job-boards. In this scenario, the selection is going to be performed offline.

The matching process in this domain is highly contextual, bidirectional and demographic sensitive. The quest for the right candidate involves assessing hard and soft skills with the right cultural alignment. Furthermore, each job vacancy carries intrinsic properties which influence the value of a recommendation: urgency, specialization level, employer brand attractiveness, compensation package and current team characteristics, among others.

Building and keeping up to date applicant profiles is a crucial condition to generate useful recommendations. The information provided by the user during a registration in an e-Recruitment platform could sometimes appear incoherent with the observed behavior. In [4], it is presented a technique to update user information based on the users' applications. It states that it is possible to identify the user's flexibility over criteria like salary, location, job title, among others.

In summary, e-recruitment recommender solutions deserve the following considerations: **1)** A single recommender does not perform well in every scenario. The characteristics and specificities of each application, the specialization level, location and culture could make the same recommender suitable for a given company, but unsuitable for a different one; **2)** Specialized approaches usually overcome generic ones; and **3)** Collaborative filter can generate good results in the attraction sub-process but cannot avoid unwanted and unskilled candidates to advance during the selection sub-process without a proper triage.

4   The Proposed Framework

The framework proposed is expansible and can be customized to allow a hybrid implementation of recommenders, by switching and/or cascading different models, aiming accommodate several algorithms working together as a single solution. By using this approach, it is possible to: **1)** Create conditions to have a comprehensive toolset of algorithms working simultaneously; **2)** Allow one recommendation method to corroborate with another by identifying specific items recommended by more than one approach; **3)** Collect implicit and explicit feedbacks from users; **4)** Parametrize ontologies to improve the match over concepts rather than only over terms; **5)** Allow candidates and recruiters to tune how to receive recommendations; **6)** Expand the solution to integrate with novel interoperable methods; **7)** Allow the choice of specific methods; **8)** Define how the final recommendation list is composed; **9)** Perform a sensitivity analysis of the tunable parameters.

Figure 2 illustrates the proposed framework. The recommendations can be performed using a single or an ensemble of recommenders. An adoption of a common interface makes it possible to expand the set of recommendation algorithms without impact. The proposed framework is composed of two parts: 1) an architecture which modularizes and encompasses all the main features of RS; and 2) the consumer part of these functionalities, the Applicant Tracking System (ATS), which parametrizes, demands and receives recommendations. The modules of the architecture are: a) Parametrization; b) Recommender; c) Ordered Items; and d) Feedback. The Parametrization module allows the definition of all hyperparameters which establish the context and the form of a desired recommendation. The Recommender module captures the setup parametrized and encapsulates the recommendation engines to generate a ranking list. The Ordered Items module transforms the generated list into a ranking in terms of attractiveness. Finally, the Feedback module records, explicitly or implicitly, all interactions between a user and a recommended item, generating a database which could be used in expanded recommended models refining the final list.

In summary, this framework proposes a common interface to generate personalized lists of recommended items for a determined context. Using a similar interface, a candidate can request a list of jobs and a recruiter can request a list of candidates for a specific job.

Once a recommendation is generated, its usefulness is assessed. From the candidate's perspective, are the jobs listed to him relevant at that moment? And from the recruiter's perspective, is the list of recommended candidates aligned with the expectations? If not in any case, why? To address such questions, the literature suggests to collect and analyze feedbacks from these actors [6,7,13,14]. The feedbacks can be either explicit, where the user is invited to inform his preferences, generally by giving some rate based on a scale; or implicit, where instead of questioning directly the user, it is observed the behavior associated with the items presented in the recommended list. It could be the time spent during navigation over items, page scrolls, etc. In other words, it relates to all events that could be captured and recorded when a user is interacting with an item which was presented to him by a recommender system. A hybrid feedback is a combination of the classical approaches by using implicit data or allowing the user to give explicit feedback only when he chooses to express his interest [5].

Another interesting feature of the proposed framework is that it performs bidirectional recommendations using the same or a specific recommender algorithm, depending exclusively on the user-defined parameters. Each recommendation algorithm, represented by the list Rec 00 to Rec N, has its own set of

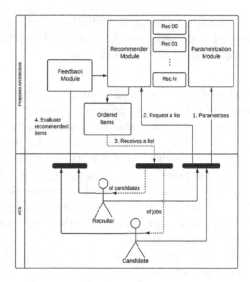

Fig. 2. Framework architecture

parameters. However, there is a special set of parameters designed to balance and integrate models like the weight between models, score threshold, ontologies, among others.

During the attraction phase, the objective of a recommendation is to popularize the existence of a opportunity and recommend suitable items (jobs or candidates), depending on the point of view, that could be relevant. Several approaches can add value to this phase: collaborative filtering and content-based algorithms can identify and select a list of relevant items to show to the user. A form of identifying the usefulness of the recommended item to a user at this stage is to observe his behavior in relation to the item. Did the user show interest? To answer this question, both explicit feedbacks, by asking the user to rate the presented item, and implicit feedbacks, by capturing navigation indicators or by getting some business-related actions, can be used.

From the candidate's point-of-view, it is only at the Attraction phase that the recommender can add value to his quest. Once the candidate decides to apply for a recommended job, the system has achieved its objective.

By contrast, from the recruiter's point-of-view, the recommender system has a role both in the Attraction and Selection phases. The candidates are presented to the recruiter for his evaluation, manual filtering, and rating. This is fine if there are only a few candidates to evaluate but, sometimes, hundreds of candidates are presented, and a manual filtering process would not be efficient. Consequently, a recommender system can, by matching job requirements with the candidates' skills, score the candidates based on their attributes and refine the list presented to the recruiter. The matching process can be leveraged by defining ontologies and capturing external information from social networks. The recruiters can establish rules to perform a different match for each job. Depending on the number of qualified candidates for a specific job, the criteria and weighs for each attribute can be increased, decreased, or even ignored. The job selection criterion can also vary depending on the field in which it lies.

An Item-to-Item Model. can be implemented in a way that establishes a similarity score among jobs (past and present) allowing to retrieve a list of well assessed candidates in previous ones to generate a recommendation list for a new job vacancy. The main objectives are: a) to provide flexibility to define scores by tuning the weights among features; b) to generate a list of candidates evaluated during past hiring processes; c) to capture a contextual preference of users which participated in similar processes and, because of that, may have a particular interest to participate in this new suggested opportunity. This recommendation technique generates potential candidates and could be useful during the attraction sub-process.

The job posts' features that are going to be included in the comparison and their respective weights to compose the final similarity score can be parametrized. For text features, it can be employed the TF-IDF (term frequency - inverse document frequency) matrix for each property during pre-processing the information.

Figure 3 illustrates this process. It is suggested to normalize the distance calculation for numerical features, and for location features it is suggested to consider the distance between the job locations. It is expected two sets as input: **1)** a list of jobs already finished; and **2)** a list of open jobs vacancies to generate recommendations. Both lists contain all necessary features. Then, the data is cleaned, and a similarity score is calculated. Finally, it is returned a list with similarity score ordered in descending order.

The final score is calculated by using the weighed sum of each feature. The input data for this module include a) the similarity value between the vacant recommendation object compared to all others for each property; and b) the weight that characterizes the importance of a given property in the score value. At the end of this process, the vacancies are sorted in descending order, that is, the vacancies with greater similarity will be the first recommended. The module outputs the set of recommended vacancies and their respective scores.

The input data for this model include: **1)** the list of vacancies similar to each recommended vacancy and their respective candidates at each stage of their selection process and their score; **2)** the threshold parameter that signals the minimum similarity that a vacancy must have with the recommend candidates; and **3)** the parameter that informs which stage in the selection process that will be considered. The return of this module is the set of candidates recommended for the vacancy recommended, or an empty set if there are not enough similar vacancies.

The limitations of this approach are associated with the existence of a large set of historical hiring processes. The cold start problem also impacts this model once candidates which did not apply cannot be recommended. However, generally candidates are added to a database by applying for a job and that fact could mitigate this problem.

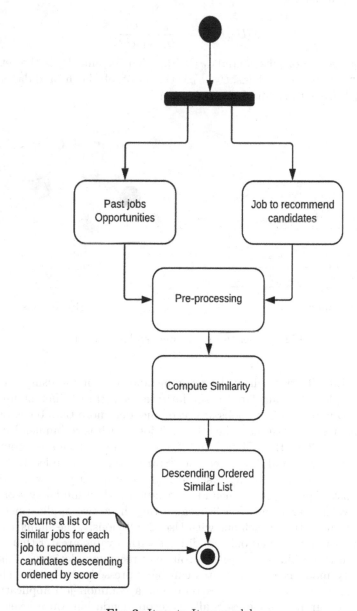

Fig. 3. Item-to-Item model

An User-to-User Model. can also be implemented computing similarities among users by several measures and, at the same time, keeping the essence of the model. However, here the comparison between users will be measured by the Jaccard's similarity, which counts the job vacancies that both candidates applied for (inner set) over all applications (union set). Equation (1) presents the similarity measure.

$$S(U_a, U_b) = \frac{U_a \cap U_b}{U_a \cup U_b} \tag{1}$$

where U_a is the set of jobs candidate "a" applied for, and U_b is the set of jobs candidate "b" applied for. Thus, $U_a \cap U_b$ is the set of jobs both candidates applied for, and $U_a \cup U_b$ is the sum of all applications.

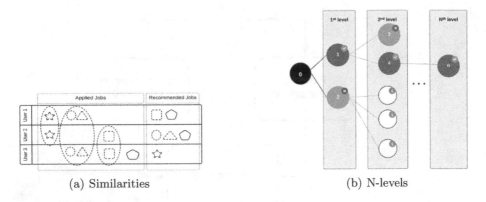

(a) Similarities   (b) N-levels

Fig. 4. User-to-User recommendation model

Figure 4(a) illustrates how the recommendation is made using this model. In this example, it is calculated a similarity among three different users. It is interesting to note that some jobs are recommended more than once, by two or more candidates. For instance, the "Square" job which is recommended to User 1 by Users 2 and 3; or the "Circle" and "Triangle" jobs which are recommended to User 2 by Users 1 and 3; or even the "Star" job recommended to User 3 by Users 1 and 2. This is a strength signal and, consequently, it will take precedence on a list of jobs to recommend to a candidate. The similarity score will be greater between User 1 and User 3 because they have two applications in common against one between each one with User 2. Obviously, the similarity score is used to rank candidates and only candidates with a value greater than a certain parametrized threshold will serve as a source of recommendations. Additionally, the similarity map among candidates can be expressed as a graph. The nodes represent candidates and the edges represent a common job application. The perception of a graph among users allows recommendations on n levels. Taking for instance a user candidature, represented by node "0" in Figure 4(b), the model can generate recommendations to candidates related to him (nodes 1 and

2). Assuming the validation of recommended users, somehow (automatically or manually) the validated recommendation can be used as a source for further recommendations. As illustrated, the candidate represented by node 1 was considered valid and the user represented by node 2 was not. Then, the users similar to Candidate 1 can also be recommended, and the process can be recurrent until the number of recommended candidates suffices.

This model captures the contextual ephemeral interest that groups of candidates could share for job opportunities disregarding their skills or backgrounds. This method can be employed to generate leads of candidates during the Attraction phase. By considering the similarity index S obtained among users, it is possible to recommend vacancies for which one of the two have not applied. This collaborative technique contextually captures the common interest of the candidates. If both candidates have applied for the same vacancy, it is inferred that they share similar interests and, therefore, can be considered similar in that context, regardless of having different skills and knowledge. However, it is not being evaluated, in this case, if one candidate has more affinity for the vacancy than another, but if they both share a common interest.

The Weighted Multidimensional Content-Based Model. computes similarity between job vacancies and potential candidates. It is a user-item content-based recommender enriched with candidate indications. The key difference over traditional approaches is the similarity calculation split by dimension. Using this method, the features are grouped in a way to distinguish candidates by: **1)** who he is, grouped as the **CPA** (Candidate Personal Attributes) and the expected professional **EPA** (Expected Personal Attributes) metrics; **2)** what he can do, grouped as the **CTS** (Candidate Technical Skills) and **RTS** (Required Technical Skills) metrics and; **3)** by the alignment of the conditions offered **JC** (Job Characteristics) with the **CI** (Candidate Interests); and **4)** any Social Endorsement **(SE)** a candidate may have and can distinguish him from other candidates.

Metric	Similarity
WHO=PAT/EPA	Personal features
WHAT=RTS/CTS	Skills
HOW=CI/JC	Conditions
SE	Social Endorsements

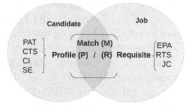

Fig. 5. Match calculation

Figure 5 illustrates the calculation. The **Match (M)** determines the fitness of a candidate over configurable thresholds and the result could be **Unqualified**, **Good fit** or **Overqualified**. Thus, the assessment of a candidate is independent of each dimension and because each job has its own particularities, so does the desired professional profile for it. For instance, some hiring processes may require great emphasis on technical skills while another may not. The proposed method allows the assignment of weights to each of the components, adapting how the match is performed accordingly. Equation (2) presents the calculation.

$$M_{(j,c)} = \sum \begin{pmatrix} WHO_{(j,c)} & W_{(who)} \\ WHAT_{(j,c)} & W_{(what)} \\ HOW_{(j,c)} & W_{(how)} \end{pmatrix} + SE_{(c)} \tag{2}$$

5   Final Discussions and Future Trends

This paper discusses the e-Recruitment problem and presents a framework together with three models. The widespread job requirements, seniority levels, and other characteristics represent a challenge in creating a "silver-bullet" algorithm that performs well in all situations. Flexibility is the key characteristic of a model for e-Recruitment Recommender System and the models proposed together with the framework tend to be a more comprehensive solution to work on a vast number of different scenarios. Employing the proposed framework encapsulates specific parts allowing the reuse of common components, thus reducing the time needed to deploy novel solutions and establishing a standard interface facilitating the interoperability among models.

As future works, the execution of experiments to validate the effectiveness of the proposed solution regarding the *Precision*, as returning only relevant candidates, and *Recall* by assessing if good candidates aren't returned as expected in a manual recruitment situation.

Acknowledgment. Process number 18/16899-6, Fundação de Amparo à Pesquisa do Estado de São Paulo/Brasil (FAPESP).

References

1. Cacho, C.: A Language Model based Job Recommender. Ph.D. thesis (2015)
2. Dave, V.S., Zhang, B., Al Hasan, M., AlJadda, K., Korayem, M.: A Combined representation learning approach for better job and skill recommendation. In: Proceedings of the 27th ACM International Conference on Information and Knowledge Management, pp. 1997–2005 (2018). https://doi.org/10.1145/3269206.3272023
3. Deshpande, M., Karypis, G.: Item-basedtop-n recommendation algorithms. ACM Trans. Inf. Syst. (TOIS) **22**(1), 1–35 (2004). papers://5e3e5e59-48a2-47c1-b6b1-a778137d3ec1/Paper/p1769
4. Hong, W., Zheng, S., Wang, H.: Dynamic user profile-based job recommender system. In: Proceedings of the 8th International Conference on Computer Science and Education, ICCSE 2013, pp. 1499–1503, no. ICCSE, IEEE (2013). https://doi.org/10.1109/ICCSE.2013.6554164, https://ieeexplore.ieee.org/abstract/document/6554164/
5. Isinkaye, F.O., Folajimi, Y.O., Ojokoh, B.A.: Recommendation systems: principles, methods and evaluation. Egypt. Inform. J. **16**(3), 261–273 (2015). https://doi.org/10.1016/j.eij.2015.06.005

6. Köster, M.: Interactive Recommender Systems For a Professional Social Network. Ph.D. thesis (2017)
7. Lerche, L.: Using Implicit Feedback for Recommender Systems: Characteristics, Applications, and Challenges. Technical report (2016). https://eldorado. tu-dortmund.de/bitstream/2003/35775/1/Dissertation_Lerche.pdfcore.ac.uk/ download/pdf/83041762.pdf
8. Li, L., Jing, H., Tong, H., Yang, J., He, Q., Chen, B.C.: NEMO. In: Proceedings of the 26th International Conference on World Wide Web Companion - WWW 2017 Companion, pp. 505–513. ACM Press, New York, USA (2017). https://doi.org/10. 1145/3041021.3054200
9. Lu, J., Wu, D., Mao, M., Wang, W., Zhang, G.: Recommender system application developments: a survey. Dec. Support Syst. **74**, 12–32 (2015). https://doi.org/10. 1016/j.dss.2015.03.008
10. Malinowski, J., Wendt, O., Keim, T., Weitzel, T.: Matching people and jobs: a bilateral recommendation approach. In: Proceedings of the Annual Hawaii International Conference on System Sciences, **6**(C), 1–9 (2006). https://doi.org/10.1109/ HICSS.2006.266
11. Mansur, F., Patel, V., Patel, M.: A review on recommender systems. In: 2017 International Conference on Innovations in Information, Embedded and Communication Systems (ICIIECS), vol. 2018-January, pp. 1–6. IEEE (March 2017). https://doi.org/10.1109/ICIIECS.2017.8276182, http://ieeexplore.ieee.org/ document/8276182/
12. Miniwatts, M.G.: World Internet Users Statistics and 2019 World Population Stats. https://www.internetworldstats.com/stats.htm
13. Peska, L.: Multimodal implicit feedback for recommender systems. CEUR Workshop Proceedings **1885**, pp. 240–245 (2017)
14. Reusens, M., Lemahieu, W., Baesens, B., Sels, L.: A note on explicit versus implicit information for job recommendation. Decision Support Systems **98**, 26–35 (2017). https://doi.org/10.1016/j.dss.2017.04.002, https://www.sciencedirect. com/science/article/pii/S0167923617300611
15. Shaqiri, A.: Impact of information technology and internet in businesses. Acad. J. Bus. Admin. Law Soc. Sci. **1**(1), 73–79 (2015). www.retailresearch
16. Shermon, G.: Digital Cultures: Age of the Intellect (2017), https://books.google. co.id/books?id=k9uQDgAAQBAJ
17. Uliana, R.M., De Castro, L.N.: Identifying Career Boundaries Using Minimum Description Length on a Graph. IEEE Access **6**, 42407–42421 (2018). https://doi. org/10.1109/ACCESS.2018.2856886
18. Xu, Y., Li, Z., Gupta, A., Bugdayci, A., Bhasin, A.: Modeling professional similarity by mining professional career trajectories. In: Proceedings of the 20th ACM SIGKDD international conference on Knowledge discovery and data mining - KDD 2014, pp. 1945–1954. KDD 2014, ACM Press, New York, USA (2014). https://doi. org/10.1145/2623330.2623368
19. Zhang, C., Wang, H.: Resumevis: a visual analytics system to discover semantic information in semi-structured resume data. ACM Trans. Intell. Syst. Technol. **10**(1), 1–25 (2018). https://doi.org/10.1145/3230707

The Influence of Feature Selection on Job Clustering for an E-recruitment Recommender System

Joel J. S. Junior, Fabricio G. Vilasbôas, and Leandro N. de Castro[✉]

Natural Computing and Machine Learning Laboratory (LCoN), Graduate Program in Electrical Engineering and Computing, Mackenzie Presbyterian University, São Paulo, Brazil
`gomesvilasboas@gmail.com`, `lnunes@mackenzie.br`

Abstract. Recommender systems aim to effectively recommend items to the user based on their profile. An online recruitment system recommends jobs for a candidate according to his profile and can also act in reverse, recommending more qualified candidates for a particular job. Defining which variables will be used impacts directly the recommendation quality so that, when using the most important variables, we have a better assertiveness in the process. The goal of this work is to select the most important features of an online recruitment database using feature selection techniques. More specifically, we used the algorithms of Mitra, SUD and ACA to perform feature selection. The datasets used were derived from the original dataset assuming three distinct scenarios: the dataset containing the attributes related with the jobs' features; the dataset containing the bag of words of the description feature of the jobs; and the dataset resulting from the union of the two previous ones. The features' subsets selected in each of the above scenarios had their performance evaluated in a clustering task. The results obtained in each scenario show a performance gain of the clustering process when feature selection is made over the original data. Also, it was observed that the jobs' features result in better performance than the other two cases.

Keywords: Recommender system · E-recruitment · Feature selection

1   Introduction

The traditional candidate recruitment process used by companies relies on announcing available job positions, analyzing resumes, calling up candidates' friends and referrals, conducting various interviews, and other steps. This whole process is very expensive and time consuming, in addition to limiting the pool of candidates to the job vacancy [1, 2]. The probability of hiring a candidate who best suits the job vacancy is very low.

With the technological development and growth of the Internet, the availability of information has grown so that today recruiters have access to diverse curricula over the internet, being able to select among them the best qualified candidate for a given job [2, 3]. As a result, online recruitment companies, called e-recruitment, have come up

© Springer Nature Switzerland AG 2020
L. Rutkowski et al. (Eds.): ICAISC 2020, LNAI 12416, pp. 176–187, 2020.
https://doi.org/10.1007/978-3-030-61534-5_16

with specialized referral systems to meet the current demand for candidates and vacancies [1, 3]. In general, the candidate submits his/her curriculum vitae to these systems in text files or through forms on the platform, and recruiters enter employment opportunities specifying the characteristics and requirements of the vacancies. The system then calculates the best combination of candidate and vacancy. The recommendation can be made in two directions: jobs are recommended to candidates, and candidates are recommended to job vacancies [3].

E-recruitment systems, however, face the problem of dealing with unstructured data from job descriptions and candidate CVs. Techniques are applied to such data, such as stemming and stopwords removal, in order to structure it [3]. However, structuring text data usually results in high dimensionality, because each token becomes a feature in the dataset, making the recommendation computationally intensive and sometimes less assertive. Therefore, feature selection becomes a necessary step to provide a more efficient and effective job-candidate match.

The dataset used in this project was obtained from a start-up in e-recruitment and, thus, corresponds to real-world data about job vacancies. It is formed by two subsets of features: structured and unstructured; and does not have a target class. The feature selection investigation proposed here uses filtering (unsupervised) approaches, since there is no information about the target class. More specifically, three feature selection methods are used: Mitra [4]; SUD [5]; and ACA [6]. These methods are compared with one another and with the well-known Principal Component Analysis (PCA). The experiments are divided in three scenarios: using only the structured data; using only the unstructured (job description) data; using both subsets of features.

This paper is organized as follows. Section 2 describes the feature selection process as well as the algorithms that will be used and compared in this work. Section 3 describes the methodology and presents the obtained results; and, finally, Sect. 4 presents the conclusion and final remarks.

2 Feature Selection

Feature selection is the process that aims to reduce the number of attributes (search space dimension) by selecting a subset of features that best meet a previously established quality criterion and can be used for different tasks, including classification and clustering [7–9].

Formally, we can define the attribute selection as follows: for the original feature set X, with cardinality $|X| = n$, there is a subset X' with cardinality $|X'| = d, X' \subseteq X$, which is selected according to the evaluation criterion adopted, denoted by the evaluation function $J(X'), J: X' \subseteq X \rightarrow \Re$. The task of selecting features consists of finding X', $X' \subseteq X$, so that $J(X')$ is maximal, assuming that a larger value of $J(X')$ corresponds to a better evaluation [8, 9].

Feature selection can be divided into four steps [8, 10]:

1. **Subset generation**: In this step a subset of candidate features is produced using a search strategy. This step is essentially a heuristic search process in which two important aspects must be defined: one or more initial points, and the search strategy.

A search algorithm is responsible for guiding the selection process according to some strategy. In this sense, search strategies that can be used to avoid the complete enumeration of all possible feature subsets include *forward selection, backward deletion*, a hybrid method (forward selection and backward deletion), and a *random method*.

2. **Subset evaluation**: in this step the feature subset is evaluated according to some criterion, comparing it with the best subset obtained so far, so that the best of the two is used in the next step. The evaluation criteria can be categorized in *dependent* (the evaluation is done based on the data mining algorithm that will be used); or *independent* (the data mining algorithm is not used to evaluate the subset).

3. **Stopping criterion**: determines when the iterative part of the process should end. If the adopted criterion is reached, then the algorithm moves to the next step, otherwise the process returns to the first step. In other words, subsets are generated iteratively until the best one meets this criterion. Some criteria adopted include the search termination; some pre-defined value, such as minimum (or maximum) number of features; a pre-defined number of iterations without improvement in the feature subset; or a sufficiently good subset is obtained.

4. **Validation**: some prior knowledge or criterion is used to evaluate the quality of the result.

A Feature Selection Algorithm (FSA) is a computational approach to solve the problem of selecting features based on a definition of relevance, or evaluation criterion. The relevance adopted is strongly linked with the final objective. Based on the evaluation criteria and the data mining algorithm adopted, the feature selection algorithms can be divided into [7, 8]:

- **Embedded**: when the data mining algorithm has an embedded FSA, explicitly or not.
- **Filter**: when the FSA is based on general data features and is independent of the mining algorithm. Its use usually occurs in an earlier stage, in the pre-processing, so that it acts as a filter of the variables that will be used.
- **Wrapper**: when the FSA has its own mining algorithm used as the evaluation criterion of the generated subset. Although this method increases the performance of the mining process, it usually causes a high computational cost.
- **Hybrid**: a way to obtain the best result using the Filter and Wrapper models at different stages of the subset generation.

3   Feature Selection Algorithms Investigated

In this paper we used unsupervised (filter) feature selection techniques. We chose three FSA to implement and evaluate: Mitra [4]; SUD [5]; and ACA [6].

3.1   Mitra

The algorithm described in Mitra et al. [4] is based on the grouping of features according to their similarities. The algorithm works in two steps: 1) divide the initial feature set into homogeneous groups; and 2) select representatives from each group. The similarity of features is calculated based on the linear dependence between them, using the Maximum Information Compression Index [4, 11]:

$$2\lambda_2(x, y) = a - \sqrt{a^2 - 4var(x)var(y)\left(1 - \rho(x, y)^2\right)} \tag{1}$$

where x and y are two features, $var(x)$ is the variance of x and $\rho(x, y)$ is the correlation coefficient between x and y, and $a = var(x) + var(y)$. The values obtained are contained in the interval $0 \leq \lambda_2(x, y) \leq 0.5 (var(x) + var(y))$, where two variables are totally similar (linearly dependent) when λ_2 is equal to zero and the more dissimilar, the greater the value of λ_2.

The algorithm works as follows [4]:

1. Calculate the n neighbors closest to each feature in the original feature set.
2. Among the subsets formed, select the subset with the shortest distance between the main feature and the farthest neighbor of the set. Discard the features belonging to the subset (n neighbors) while maintaining only the main feature.
3. In the first iteration, save the calculated value between the main feature and the farthest neighbor of the selected subset. This value will be used as an error threshold ε.
4. In the following iterations, check the λ_2 value of the subset, if it is greater than ε there is a decrease in the value of n.
5. Repeat the process with the remaining features until all features are in the same subset.
6. At the end of the algorithm we obtain as a result a list of features, each being a representative of a feature subset.

3.2 SUD

The SUD algorithm [5] is a backward sequential feature selection method. It is focused on determining the relative importance of each feature, as determined by the feature subset entropy, such that the most important features, when removed from the dataset, promote an increase in the entropy value:

$$E = -\sum_{i=1}^{N} \sum_{j=1}^{N} \left(S_{ij} \times \log S_{ij} + (1 - S_{ij}) \times \log(1 - S_{ij})\right) \tag{2}$$

where N is the number of objects being considered and S_{ij} is the similarity measure between two objects x_i and x_j.

When all variables are numeric or ordinal, S_{ij} is defined as [5]:

$$S_{ij} = e^{-\alpha \times D_{ij}} \tag{3}$$

where D_{ij} is the normalized Euclidean distance defined as: $D_{ij} = \sqrt{\sum_{k=1}^{M} \left(\frac{x_{ik} - x_{jk}}{max_k - min_k}\right)^2}$, where max_k and min_k are the largest and smallest values, respectively, of the k-th feature; and $\alpha = \frac{-\ln 0.5}{\bar{D}}$, where $\bar{D}$ is the average distance among the objects.

For nominal features, S_{ij} is defined as:

$$S_{ij} = \frac{\sum_{k=1}^{M} |x_{ik} = x_{jk}|}{M} \tag{4}$$

where $|x_{ik} = x_{jk}| = 1$ if $x_{ik} = x_{jk}$ and 0 otherwise, and M is the number of features being considered.

The algorithm works as follows [5], where M is the number of features:

```
1.  Let O be the ordered feature set, initially empty, according to
    their importance, with the first elements being the least important
    and the last being the most important.
2.  M—1 iterations are performed.
3.  For each iteration, the entropy is calculated after removing a fea-
    ture v from the set of remaining features T. Initially, T contains
    all existing features. For each v in T it is calculated:
4.  Tv = the set T without the feature v.
5.  The entropy of Tv.
6.  Feature v, which, when removed causes the Tv entropy to be the
    smallest of all Tv, is the least important feature and is added to
    the end of O.
7.  T = Tv
8.  Returns the set O.
```

To obtain a list of the most important features, simply reverse the order of the resulting set, so that the first features become the most important and the last the least important ones. To reduce the dimensionality of the base simply select the first d features of the resulting set. An apparent disadvantage is that d is dependent on the database in which the algorithm is applied and it is necessary to determine it empirically, that is, to find the minimum quantity that, if exceeded, does not lead to an improvement in the performance and final results of the algorithm [5].

3.3 ACA

The ACA algorithm was proposed in Au et al. [6]. Their strategy is to group the attributes into subsets based on their similarity. To calculate similarity, the *Interdependence Redundancy Measure* is used, capable of showing negative and positive correlations, as well as interdependence and proximity of values, whilst being robust for dealing with outliers.

The notation used to describe the algorithm and the measures associated with it will be as follows: let O be a dataset containing p attributes, let A_i, $i \in \{1, \ldots, p\}$ be each attribute of the dataset O and v_{ik}, $k \in \{1, \ldots, m\}$, $i \in \{1, \ldots, p\}$, be the value of feature A_i in object k.

The Interdependence Redundancy Measure between two attributes A_i and A_j, $i, j \in \{1, \ldots, p\}$, $i \neq j$, is defined as [6]:

$$R(A_i : A_j) = \frac{I(A_i : A_j)}{H(A_i, A_j)} \tag{5}$$

where $I(A_i : A_j)$ is the mutual information measure between A_i and A_j, defined as:

$$I(A_i : A_j) = \sum_{k=1}^{m_i} \sum_{l=1}^{m_j} \Pr(A_i = v_{ik} \wedge A_j = v_{jl}) \times \log \frac{\Pr(A_i = v_{ik} \wedge A_j = v_{jl})}{\Pr(A_i = v_{ik})\Pr(A_j = v_{jl})} \tag{6}$$

and $H(A_i, A_j)$ is the entropy measure between A_i and A_j, defined as:

$$H(A_i, A_j) = -\sum_{k=1}^{m_i} \sum_{l=1}^{m_j} \Pr(A_i = v_{ik} \wedge A_j = v_{jl}) \times \log \Pr(A_i = v_{ik} \wedge A_j = v_{jl}) \tag{7}$$

In the above equations Pr is the probability function defined as: let σ be function SELECT from relational algebra, the probability of an attribute A_i be equal to v_{ik} is given by:

$$\Pr(A_i = v_{ik}) = \frac{\left|\sigma_{A_i = v_{ik}}(R)\right|}{\left|\sigma_{A_i \neq NULL}(R)\right|} \tag{8}$$

and the joint probability of two distinct features A_i and A_j assuming values v_{ik} and v_{jl}, respectively, is given by:

$$\Pr(A_i = v_{ik} \wedge A_j = v_{jl}) = \frac{\left|\sigma_{A_i = v_{ik} \wedge A_j = v_{jl}}(R)\right|}{\left|\sigma_{A_i \neq NULL \wedge A_j \neq NULL}(R)\right|} \tag{9}$$

with $i, j \in \{1, \ldots, p\}$, $i \neq j$, e $k, l \in \{1, \ldots, m\}$.

Linked to the interdependence redundancy measure, the algorithm also used another measure to calculate the interdependence of a feature within a group (or subset) $C = \{A_j \mid j = 1, \ldots, p\}$, $C \subseteq O$, called *Multiple Interdependence Redundancy Measure* (IRM) [6], defined as:

$$MR(A_i) = \sum_{j=1}^{P} R(A_i : A_j) \tag{10}$$

The algorithm uses the concept of a mode to group the features into the corresponding subsets. The mode of a subset $C = \{A_j \mid j = 1, \ldots, p\}$, denoted by $\eta(C)$, is the feature $A_i \in C$, such that $MR(A_i) > MR(A_j)$, for all $A_j \in C$. The algorithm follows the following steps:

1. The algorithm takes as an argument the number of groups to be formed, k, which is an integer and $k \in \{2, \ldots, p\}$. From among the p features, k distinct mode candidates are selected.
2. Each feature is added to the subset whose IRM between the mode of the subset and the feature is greater.
3. Once the groups have been defined, a new mode candidate is calculated for each group. The new mode candidate will be the feature of the group that has the highest IRM value, in other words, for each C_r, with $r \in \{1, \ldots, k\}$, we assign $\eta_r = A_i$ if $MR(A_i) \geq MR(A_j)$, for all A_i, $A_j \in C_r$, $i \neq j$.
4. Steps 2 and 3 are repeated until there is no change in the modes or a pre-defined number of iterations is reached.

The result of the algorithm are groups of features, from which one can choose a feature as representative, moving from a representation of the dataset using p features, to a representation using r features.

Different from the SUD algorithm, in ACA the value of k defines the final number of groups. To find the ideal value of k, it is suggested an empirical approach, in which values are tested until one finds the value that produces more similar subsets, $k = \arg max_{k \in \{2,\ldots,p\}} \sum_{r=1}^{k} \sum_{A_i \in C_r} R(A_i : \eta_r)$.

4   Performance Evaluation

The experiments designed aim to evaluate the performance of the three feature selection algorithms (ACA, SUD and Mitra) when applied to select features in a clustering task. These methods will be compared with one another and the well-known Principal Component Analysis (PCA). The clustering algorithm that will be used is the k-means algorithm, and the *Silhouette Coefficient* will be used to evaluate the clustering. As the k-means is stochastic, each experiment will be executed 10 times and the result presented will be the mean $\pm$ standard deviation from the 10 runs.

4.1   Methodology

The original data set contains 1,933 job vacancies and consists of the following job information: job title, requested language spoken, work period, salary, area of activity, contracting model, level of education, benefits, previous experience required, location, vacancy responsible, number of vacancies, and job description. All job features are either numeric or nominal, except for the job description attribute, which corresponds to a text field used by the company to describe the job.

The attributes of the original dataset were separated into three distinct subsets, forming three test scenarios. The first feature subset (**C1**) contains only those features related to the job vacancies, disregarding the job description attribute. The second subset (**C2**) contains only the job description attribute, which is the textual part descriptive of the job vacancy. This unstructured data was structured using a bag of words method. The third subset (**C3**) is the union of the two previous ones. For each scenario the following

k-means k values will be considered: $\{2, 4, 6, 8\}$. Each subset and each value of k leads to a set of four experiments:

1. The first experiment will serve as benchmarking to compare the performance of the feature selection algorithms. In it the dataset will be evaluated containing all the attributes.
2. The second experiment will apply the Mitra algorithm to select the features. This algorithm automatically determines the number of features to be used.
3. The third experiment will apply the SUD algorithm to select the features. The value of d to be used by SUD will be the same as determined by Mitra.
4. The fourth experiment will apply the ACA algorithm to select the features. The value of d to be used by ACA will be the same as determined by Mitra.

Each experiment will be evaluated using the following procedure: apply the feature selection algorithm, execute the clustering algorithm in each scenario, and calculate the silhouette measure of the formed clusters.

The Silhouette Coefficient [12] is a metric used to assess a clustering considering its compactness and separation. The metric is based on the distance that an object is from other clusters, considering that the distance between an object and a cluster is given by the average distance between the object and each element of its cluster. Formally, for each object i the silhouette coefficient $s(i)$ of this object is defined as:

$$s(i) = \frac{b(i) - a(i)}{\max\{a(i), b(i)\}} \tag{11}$$

where $a(i)$ is the distance between the object and the other cluster objects to which it belongs, and $b(i)$ is the average Euclidean distance between the object and the nearest cluster without considering its own cluster. The possible values of the coefficient are $-1 \le s(i) \le 1$, so that values close to 1 indicate that the distance of the object to the cluster to which it belongs is smaller than the distance from it to any other cluster; values close to -1 indicate the opposite, the object is closer to another cluster; and values close to 0 indicate that the clusters are very close, overlapping one another, making it more difficult to assign the object to a specific cluster. The Silhouette Coefficient of the whole cluster is determined by the average of all objects.

4.2 Results and Discussion

The results obtained are summarized in Table 1. In the first scenario, the dataset consists only of the structured features (*job title, requested language spoken, work period, salary, area of activity, contracting model, level of education, benefits, previous experience required, location, vacancy responsible, number of vacancies*), disregarding the *job description* feature.

It is observed that for the four k-means k values to group the data ($\{2, 4, 6, 8\}$), clustering without feature selection (SF) results in a low silhouette value. The application of the feature selection methods promoted a significant increase in the k-means performance, and it should be noted that the algorithm SUD was the one that obtained

Table 1. Performance of the feature selection methods. **C1**: all features of the base with the exception of the job description; **C2**: Structured job description feature using the bag of words; **C3**: union of all features; WFS: results obtained without feature selection; D: original number of features; d: number of features after selection; k = number of k used in k-means.

	k	2	4	6	8
C1	WFS	0.40 ± 0.00	0.33 ± 0.00	0.36 ± 0.00	0.37 ± 0.00
D = 48	Mitra	0.73 ± 0.00	0.78 ± 0.00	0.84 ± 0.00	0.88 ± 0.00
d = 23	SUD	0.94 ± 0.00	0.96 ± 0.00	0.96 ± 0.00	0.98 ± 0.00
	ACA	0.45 ± 0.00	0.54 ± 0.00	0.64 ± 0.00	0.72 ± 0.00
	PCA	0.41 ± 0.00	0.34 ± 0.00	0.36 ± 0.00	0.40 ± 0.00
C2	WFS	0.81 ± 0.00	0.84 ± 0.00	0.84 ± 0.00	0.85 ± 0.00
D = 1774	Mitra	0.82 ± 0.00	0.82 ± 0.00	0.82 ± 0.00	0.82 ± 0.00
d = 886	SUD	0.82 ± 0.00	0.85 ± 0.00	0.86 ± 0.00	0.85 ± 0.00
	ACA	0.81 ± 0.00	0.81 ± 0.00	0.82 ± 0.00	0.83 ± 0.00
	PCA	0.81 ± 0.00	0.84 ± 0.00	0.84 ± 0.00	0.85 ± 0.00
C3	WFS	0.38 ± 0.00	0.30 ± 0.00	0.33 ± 0.00	0.35 ± 0.00
D = 1822	Mitra	0.39 ± 0.00	0.32 ± 0.00	0.34 ± 0.00	0.37 ± 0.00
d = 910	SUD	0.41 ± 0.00	0.36 ± 0.00	0.38 ± 0.00	0.42 ± 0.00
	ACA	0.51 ± 0.00	0.55 ± 0.00	0.60 ± 0.00	0.63 ± 0.00
	PCA	0.38 ± 0.00	0.30 ± 0.00	0.33 ± 0.00	0.35 ± 0.00

a silhouette closer to 1 in all cases. The PCA, however, did not present a significant improvement in the k-means performance in the situations analyzed in this scenario.

In the second scenario (**C2**), considering only the description attribute structured using a bag of words, it was noted that the feature selection practically did not influence the clustering result, although it reduces the number of attributes from 1,774 to 886, reducing the computational cost of the process. In addition to the similar performance of all methods, it was significantly lower than the best performance of scenario 1 (**C1**). The performance of the algorithms was affected in this scenario mainly because, among the 1,933 job records, only 272 have a job description.

In the third and last scenario (**C3**), corresponding to the union of the two feature subsets, it is observed that the database without feature selection has low silhouettes in the four situations, contained in the range of 0.30 and 0.38. The Mitra algorithm presented little improvement, so that the performance of the clustering algorithm did not show improvement with feature selection. The SUD algorithm presented a slightly better performance than the Mitra in the four situations, but it was the ACA algorithm that obtained the best performance among all the algorithms, with Silhouettes between 0.51 and 0.64. The PCA also did not result in a feature set that promotes performance improvement when compared to the absence of selection.

In summary, it is noted that the set of attributes without the job description feature selected by the SUD method obtained the best overall performance. However, the use of the structured job description attribute with the bag of words resulted in more stable k-means performance for all feature selection methods, including when compared to base usage without selection. It was observed that the use of all the combined algorithms deteriorated the performance of k-means.

4.3   Some Notes on the Running Time

To assess the running time of the feature selection methods, we tested them using two different compute nodes. The first compute node, named Skylake, is composed of two Intel® Xeon® Platinum 8160 processors @ 2.10 GHz, each one with 24 physical cores (48 logical) and 33 MB of cache memory, 190 GB of RAM, two Intel® SolidState Drive Data Center (Intel® SSD DC) S3520 SERIES with 1.2 TB e 240 GB store capacity and a CentOS* 7 operation system running kernel version 3.10.0-693.21.1.3l7.x86_64. The second compute node, named Phi, is composed of one Intel(R) Xeon Phi(TM) CPU 7250 @ 1.40 GHz, with 69 physical cores (272 logical) and 34 MB of cache memory, 115 GB of RAM, two INTEL SSDSC2BB480G7 each one with 480 GB store capacity and a CentOS 7 operation system running kernel version 3.10.0-862.3.3.el7.x86_64.

All algorithms presented in this paper were developed using Python programming language. Thus, we have used Intel Distribution for Python as the main software environment to perform all the experiments. The Intel Distribution for Python is an Intel's effort to provide optimized Python packages to its processing platforms SciKit Learn, TensorFlow, Keras, Numpy, SciPy and Pandas are some examples of optimized packages.

We performed some experiments aiming at investigating Intel's High Performance Computing (HPC) platforms. To this performance investigation we have selected the best algorithm presented in the previous section: SUD. Figure 1 presents its total running time

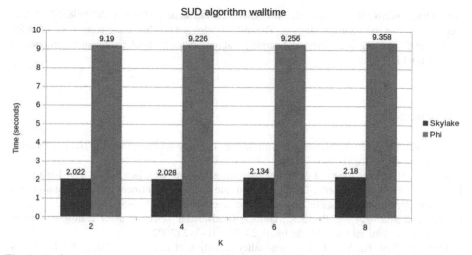

Fig. 1. Performance comparison between the Skylake and Phi nodes. Darkgray: Phi. Light gray: Skylake.

or wall time. In the x axis are the k values (number of centroids), and in the y axis we have the wall time in seconds. The dark gray bars present the wall time performed on Skylake, and the light gray bars present the wall time performed on Phi.

As expected, by observing Fig. 1, we note that the wall time increases when k increases. Another important observation is the performance. The Skylake compute node performed about $4\times$ faster than the Phi compute node.

5   Final Remarks and Future Trends

This work aimed to investigate the influence of feature selection on the task of grouping data from an e-recruitment database. The algorithms of Mitra, SUD and ACA were used for feature selection and these were analyzed and compared with each other and with the PCA. The feature selection algorithms were evaluated in three distinct scenarios: considering all features except the job description feature; considering only the job description feature; considering both subsets of features.

In none of the scenarios did the PCA prove to be superior to the feature selection algorithms tested, having, on the contrary, presented little or no improvement in most cases. Among the feature selection algorithms, it was possible to observe that the three methods presented better performance using the structured features, in contrast they presented little or no improvement in the unstructured (job description) scenario. In the mixed scenario, the performance was also affected, but slightly better than the first scenario.

In terms of computational running time, it could be observed that the use of an optimized architecture resulted is a significant improvement in performance (over $4\times$ faster) when compared with a standard architecture. For future investigation we plan to use the feature selection methods to select the features to be used in the recommender system for e-recruitment.

Acknowledgements. The authors thank CAPES, CNPq, Fapesp (Proc. n. 2016/08352-1), and Mackpesquisa for the financial support. The authors also acknowledge the support of Intel for the Natural Computing and Machine Learning Laboratory as an Intel Center of Excellence in Artificial Intelligence.

References

1. Yoon Kin Tong, D.: A study of e-recruitment technology adoption in Malaysia. Ind. Manag. Data Syst. **109**(2), 281–300 (2009)
2. Capelli, P.: Making the most of on-line recruiting. Harvard Bus. Rev. **79**(3), 139–148 (2001)
3. Faliagka, E., Tsakalidis, A., Tzimas, G.: An integrated e-recruitment system for automated personality mining and applicant ranking. Internet Res. **22**(5), 551–568 (2012)
4. Mitra, P., Murthy, C.A., Pal, S.K.: Unsupervised feature selection using feature similarity. IEEE Trans. Pattern Anal. Mach. Intell. **24**(3), 301–312 (2002)
5. Dash, M., Liu, H., Yao, J.: Dimensionality reduction of unsupervised data. In: 1997 Proceedings of Ninth IEEE International Conference on Tools with Artificial Intelligence (1997)

6. Au, W.H., Chan, K.C., Wong, A.K., Wang, Y.: Attribute clustering for grouping, selection. IEEE/ACM Trans. Comput. Biol. Bioinf. **2**(2), 83–101 (2005)
7. Liu, H., Yu, L.: Toward integrating feature selection algorithms for classification and clustering. IEEE Trans. Knowl. Data Engineering **17**(4), 491–502 (2005)
8. Molina, L., Belanche, L., Nebot, À.: Feature Selection Algorithms: A Survey and Experimental Evaluation (2002)
9. Jain, A., Zongker, D.: Feature selection: evaluation, application, and small sample performance. IEEE Trans. Pattern Anal. Mach. Intell. **19**(2), 153–158 (1997)
10. Liu, L., Kang, J., Yu, J., Wang, Z.: A comparative study on unsupervised feature selection methods for text clustering. In: Proceedings of Natural Language Processing and Knowledge Engineering (2005)
11. Bharti, K.K., Singh, P.: A survey on filter techniques for feature selection in text mining. In: Babu, B.V., et al. (eds.) Proceedings of the Second International Conference on Soft Computing for Problem Solving (SocProS 2012), December 28-30, 2012. AISC, vol. 236, pp. 1545–1559. Springer, New Delhi (2014). https://doi.org/10.1007/978-81-322-1602-5_154
12. Rousseeuw, P.J.: Silhouettes: a graphical aid to the interpretation and validation of cluster analysis. J. Comput. Appl. Math. **20**, 53–65 (1987)

n-ary Isolation Forest: An Experimental Comparative Analysis

Paweł Karczmarek[1]([✉]), Adam Kiersztyn[1], and Witold Pedrycz[2,3,4]

[1] Department of Computer Science, Lublin University of Technology,
ul. Nadbystrzycka 36B, 20-618 Lublin, Poland
pawel.karczmarek@gmail.com, adam.kiersztyn.pl@gmail.com
[2] Department of Electrical and Computer Engineering, University of Alberta,
Edmonton, AB T6R 2V4, Canada
wpedrycz@ualberta.ca
[3] Department of Electrical and Computer Engineering, Faculty of Engineering,
King Abdulaziz University, Jeddah 21589, Saudi Arabia
[4] Systems Research Institute, Polish Academy of Sciences, Warsaw, Poland

Abstract. One of the most challenging problems of modern data mining and Computational Intelligence society has been the task of anomaly detection in large datasets, particularly containing mixed data, namely categorical, spatial, or spatio-temporal. In this study, we discuss various versions of the well-known Isolation Forest method as a efficient tool for finding outliers or anomalies. The versions are based on binary, ternary, etc. search trees. Traditional Isolation Forest is based on searching binary search trees. We build and investigate n-ary search trees and analyze their efficiency in the context of anomaly detection.

Keywords: Isolation Forest · Outlier detection · Anomaly detection · Binary trees · n-ary trees

1   Introduction

The issue of detecting anomalies in data sets is one of the most important problems of data analysis and Computational Intelligence. The problem is very complex due to the fact that the data can appear in various forms, they can create complex connections, as well as relate to various aspects of life, e.g. transport, business analysis, security issues, etc. Moreover, many of the anomalies present in databases are generated by people consciously (e.g. attempting to impersonate someone) or unconsciously (simple mistakes). That is why finding an anomaly sometimes becomes a very complicated task.

Many methods of finding anomalies in databases have their roots in classic machine learning tools, e.g. k-nearest neighbor-based methods [1,12,17], support vector machines [19], deep learning (including autoencoders or long-short term memory, self- organizing maps, or generative adversarial networks) [2,3,5,7,16,18,20], Fuzzy C-means and fuzzy C-medoids-related proposals [4,8–10], or Isolation Forest [13,14] and its enhancements [11,15]. The last one is

© Springer Nature Switzerland AG 2020
L. Rutkowski et al. (Eds.): ICAISC 2020, LNAI 12416, pp. 188–198, 2020.
https://doi.org/10.1007/978-3-030-61534-5_17

based on searching binary trees and is trained on a subset of the analyzed data set. The enhancements use clustering to find divide the initial set onto two sets or build the search trees with more number of nodes.

The purpose of this work is to present an analysis of the Isolation Forest method in a situation where we have different search trees (binary, ternary and, in general, *n*-ary). We analyze an impact of n and check the effectiveness of these various approaches. In a series of experiments, we present the results dealing with artificially generated data sets. The originality of this work comes from that such attempt of building *n*-ary search trees incorporated with the Isolation Forest has not been presented in the literature. Moreover, it is interesting to quantify the performance of various modifications of this approach. Finally, an experimental evidence will show the flexibility of the method, i.e., that it is easy to match the parameter n to the data.

The rest of the work has the following structure. The Sect. 2 is devoted to the Isolation Forest method. In the third section we describe the results of experiments and carry out comparative analysis, while Sect. 4 contains conclusions and future research directions.

2   Isolation Forest

Isolation Forest [13, 14] is constructed in two main stages. The first is the training process during which we build binary search trees on a basis of random samples of the dataset. The second one is the scoring. It based on the searching binary trees for all the records in the dataset. First, let us recall the intuitive description of the approach. Let us assume that A is the whole dataset containing R records. Each of them has B attributes. One constructs t decision trees. The number of records which are randomly chosen to build the decision tree m, namely $X \subset A, X = \{x_i : i = 1, \ldots, m\}$, is used to build a decision tree. This decision tree is built in a following manner: There is randomly chosen an attribute $b \in B$ and its value v. This value is a point of division of the set into two subsets assigned to two nodes of the root. Again, for the subsets next attributes and their values are randomly selected. Obviously, the filter coming from the root still is applied. This process is going on until the consecutive subsets have zero or one element or a predefined depth of a tree is reached. Typically, it is suggested to work with a depth $l = \log_2 m$. Such tree is a part of a forest (a so-called Isolation Forest). For all elements of the dataset the anomaly scores are calculated for each of the trees of the forest. The final result is the sum of all the scores obtained during the iteration through the whole forest of binary trees. The general idea is that the deeper the tree is traced, the lower anomaly score is obtained for the dataset record. Moreover, the original version of the method assumes slightly complicated formula for normalization of the results.

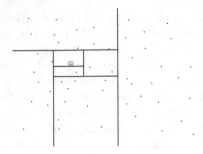

Fig. 1. Constructing a binary decision tree (Color figure online)

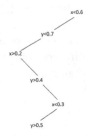

Fig. 2. Constructing a binary decision tree (a chosen path)

Figure 1 shows the above-described process of building a tree. Note that there are six divisions to stop the process of decision tree construction (the point which is a singleton is marked red). The process of finding the same point when tracing decision tree is depicted at Fig. 2. Here, we shortly discuss the modifications of binary search tree-based Isolation Forest. They are n-ary Isolation Forest. The only difference is that instead of two nodes each root has n nodes (unless a part of them is empty or it is a singleton), see Fig. 3. Note that in this case to reach the marked points one needs to check three possible ways (divisions). Figure 3 shows the above-described process of building a tree. Note that there are six divisions to stop the process of decision tree construction (the point which is called a singleton is marked red).

In the "classic" Isolation Forest method, the formula for calculating the anomaly scores for each data record is relatively complicated. Namely, it reads as

$$s(x) = 2^{-\frac{e(x)}{c(m)}}, \tag{1}$$

where

$$c(m) = \begin{cases} 2H(m-1) - 2(m-1)/m & \text{for } m > 2 \\ 1 & \text{for } m = 1 \\ 0 & \text{for } m = 0 \end{cases}, \tag{2}$$

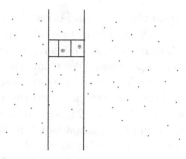

Fig. 3. The intuition behind the ternary decision tree building (Color figure online)

while
$$H(i) = \ln(i) + 0.5772156649, \tag{3}$$

and E returns the number of comparisons when searching the binary search tree increased by the value of $c(y)$ at the last node, i.e., when the trace reaches the maximal depth of the tree and y is the number of elements located at the node. Moreover, the function $c(\cdot)$ is used to normalize the results. It is difficult to generalize these formulae to the case with more divisions of the tree. Our novel modification is based on the introduction of an arbitrary number of nodes at each tree. Such trees can be more elastic and during their searching the trace can be shorted because of their width. However, it is difficult to find a proper normalizing function estimating the number of unsuccessful searches in the case of *n*-ary search tree would appear as the function $c(\cdot)$ in the formulae above. Therefore, we apply the following function instead of $c(\cdot)$ [6]

$$d(n) = \sqrt{2\pi m n (n-1)}. \tag{4}$$

Next, we modify the original algorithm as follows. The maximal depth (or height) of *n*-ary search tree is assumed to be

$$l = \lceil \log_n m \rceil, \tag{5}$$

where n is a number of nodes at one root and m is a number of elements used to build the sample training tree. In this way the length of a search trace is limited. The strength of this approach is that the trace of the *n*-ary search tree is shorter. However, at each node we need more comparisons, namely $n-1$, but this may make the method more flexible and more matched to the data.

3   Experimental Results

Our experiments have been conducted using the set of two-dimensional tables of records (x, y-coordinates) containing 100200 records. These points are randomly generated. Locations of 200 points are chosen from the whole area of interest. The rest of the points are clustered in the geometrical figures. Since in the works

[13,14] it its suggested to train the Isolation Forest using the subsets of samples containing $m = 256$ or $m = 128$ records in practical applications, here, for our experiments we use $m = 250$ records as the sample size and build the forest containing 100 trees in each experiment. We think that this is sufficiently big number for all tested n-ary search trees. Moreover, instead of classic anomaly score used in the isolation fores, we just calculate the depth of the tree when tracing the binary (or n-ary, $n = 2, 3, \ldots, 21$) search tree. This approach seems to be intuitive because if any point is somehow isolated then there is more chance to isolate it earlier (it is not near any other group of points).

The obtained results are depicted at the Figs. 4, 5, 6, 7, 8, and 9 for 2, 3, 4, 5, 6, and 8-ary Isolation Forest versions, respectively. The red color means that the point is suspected to by the isolated one. The green corresponds to normal rather than isolated points. It is easy to see that there are no evident similarities between them. However, ternary and 4-ary versions seem to be more precise when considered are the points laying *far* from the figures. But these cases are also relatively oversensitive and give relatively high anomaly scores for the *inner* points. 5-ary and 6-ary Isolation Forests work quite similarly. Particularly, 6-ary Isolation Forest gives very accurate results when observing the figures (it marks both *inner* and *outer* points). Our next observation is that the more nodes, the more points are suspected to be isolated. This situation takes place at the 8-ary version and higher, see Fig. 10. An interesting fact is noticeable from the heat map of correlation between the results of all methods. Namely, it is hard to say, that the n-ary Isolation Forest versions for lower values of n give, even approximately, correlated results. Only higher values of n gives quite correlated results. The source of this fact may be that there are different values of maximal depth of a search trees for the lowest values of n, see Eq. (5).

The next figure (Fig. 11) shows that the anomaly scores obtained by all the methods are rather stable because of low standard deviation. However, the span of the values understood as the difference between maximal and minimal value is getting higher for higher n. This shows that it is easier to distinguish points and classify their degree of isolation. However, this can also be a sign of considerable randomness in the results returned by these methods.

The collection has 196 outliers (identified with noise, i.e. elements not belonging to clusters), which is close to 0.2% of all cases considered. In the case of using as a measure of classification as outlier the distance to the maximum value in the set, it turns out that for 5-ary Isolation Forest all classified as outliers (regardless of the level of distance from the maximum value) belong to the set of noise. The distance from the maximum value is understood here as the value determined by the formula

$$\text{threshold}\,(\alpha) = \{x \in A : s\,(x) - \max s\,(x) < \alpha\} \tag{6}$$

Accumulated interest for the correct classification is presented in the figure. Figure 12 indicates the percentage of the number of elements belonging to the noise among all elements belonging to the cut-off at a given level.

When using the classifier of the percentage of noise elements belonging to a given quantile of a set of function values as a measure of effectiveness, we obtain the summary presented in the Fig. 13. As can be seen in the case of 6-ary Isolation Forest, the largest percentage of noise elements was classified into a given quantile of the set of values. This means that, for example, nearly half of the elements with the highest isolation values belong to the 0.999 quantile. In other words, out of 100 elements with the highest level of isolation, 47 are elements of noise. Finally, an interesting observation of Fig. 13 is that there is a slight dependency between the value of function (5) and the number of correct outlier detections.

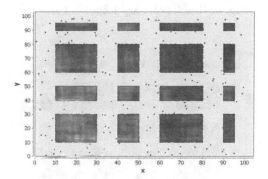

Fig. 4. Results of Binary Isolation Forest

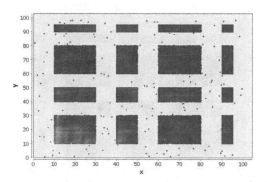

Fig. 5. Results of Ternary Isolation Forest

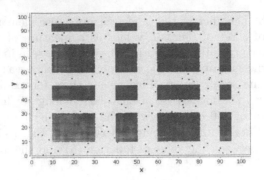

Fig. 6. Results of 4-ary Isolation Forest

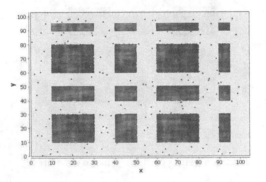

Fig. 7. Results of 5-ary Isolation Forest

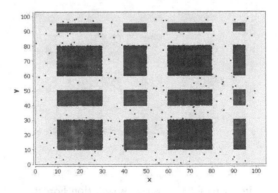

Fig. 8. Results of 6-ary Isolation Forest

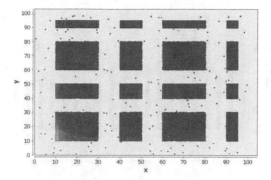

Fig. 9. Results of 8-ary Isolation Forest

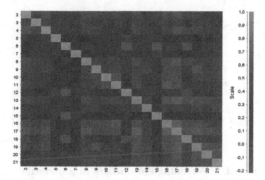

Fig. 10. Correlation heat map of the results obtained by various methods

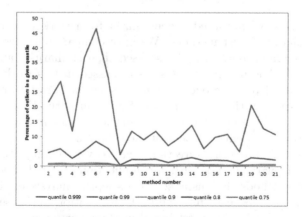

Fig. 11. A summary of the statistics of the methods

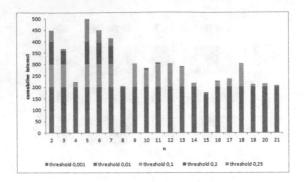

Fig. 12. Percentage of properly classified outliers

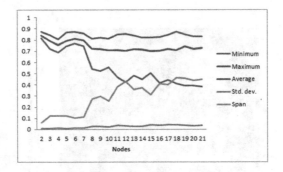

Fig. 13. Percentage of outliers in a quantile

4   Conclusions and Future Work

In this study, we have proposed a generalized framework to construct a so-called n-ary Isolation Forest methods. We have compared the results obtained for artificialy generated dataset and discussed their similarities and differences for 20 values of n. The preliminary results discussed in this work suggest that it is hard to a priori propose one version of Isolation Forest to apply for any dataset as for various n the results may differ significantly. However, there are a few regularities, e.g., a correlation of results for higher n values, which may suggest the directions of enhancement of the proposal.

Therefore, the future work directions may cover, among others, a development of a framework to establish an application-oriented modifications of Isolation Forest methods, for instance, an in-depth analysis of time series or spatio-temporal datasets, e.g., intermodal transporation databases. Moreover, we are going to work with fuzzy set-based methods, or more generally, Granular Computing-based enhancement of this approach. Finally, an interesting approach may be to built a similar to K-Means-Based Isolation Forest [11] technique related to Fuzzy C-Means Isolation Forest.

Acknowledgements. Funded by the National Science Centre, Poland under CHIST-ERA programme (Grant no. 2018/28/Z/ST6/00563).

References

1. Angiulli, F., Pizzuti, C.: Fast outlier detection in high dimensional spaces. In: Elomaa, T., Mannila, H., Toivonen, H. (eds.) PKDD 2002. LNCS, vol. 2431, pp. 15–27. Springer, Heidelberg (2002). https://doi.org/10.1007/3-540-45681-3_2
2. Chalapathy, R., Chawla, S.: Deep learning for anomaly detection: a survey. arXiv:1901.03407
3. de la Hoz, E., de la Hoz, E., Ortiz, A., Ortega, J., Martínez-Álvarez, A.: Feature selection by multi-objective optimisation: application to network anomaly detection by hierarchical self-organising maps. Knowl.-Based Syst. **71**, 322–338 (2014)
4. D'Urso, P., Massari, R.: Fuzzy clustering of mixed data. Inf. Sci. **505**, 513–534 (2019)
5. Erfani, S.M., Rajasegarar, S., Karunasekera, S., Leckie, C.: High-dimensional and large-scale anomaly detection using a linearone-class SVM with deep learning. Pattern Recogn. **58**, 121–134 (2016)
6. Flajolet, P., Odlyzko, A.: The average height of binary trees and other simple trees. J. Comput. Syst. Sci. **25**(2), 171–213 (1982)
7. Habeeb, R.A.A., Nasaruddin, F., Gani, A., Hashem, I.A.T., Ahmed, E., Imran, M.: Real-time big data processing for anomaly detection: a survey. Int. J. Inf. Manag. **45**, 289–307 (2019)
8. Izakian, H., Pedrycz, W.: Anomaly detection in time series data using a fuzzy c-means clustering. In: 2013 Joint IFSA World Congress and NAFIPS Annual Meeting (IFSA/NAFIPS), Edmonton, AB, pp. 1513–1518 (2013)
9. Izakian, H., Pedrycz, W., Jamal, I.: Clustering spatiotemporal data: an augmented fuzzy c-means. IEEE Trans. Fuzzy Syst. **21**(5), 855–868 (2013)
10. Izakian, H., Pedrycz, W.: Anomaly detection and characterization in spatial time series data: a cluster-centric approach. IEEE Trans. Fuzzy Syst. **22**(6), 1612–1624 (2014)
11. Karczmarek, P., Kiersztyn, A., Pedrycz, W., Al, E.: K-means-based isolation forest. Knowl.-Based Syst. **195**, 105659 (2020)
12. Knorr, E.B., Ng, R.T., Tucakov, V., et al.: Distance-based outliers: algorithms and applications. VLDB Int. J. Very Large Data Bases **8**(3–4), 237–253 (2000)
13. Liu, F.T., Ting, K.M., Zhou, Z.-H.: Isolation forest. In: 2008 Eighth IEEE International Conference on Data Mining, pp. 413–422 (2008)
14. Liu, F.T., Ting, K.M., Zhou, Z.-H.: Isolation-based anomaly detection. ACM Trans. Knowl. Discov. Data (TKDD) **6**(1) (2012). article no. 3
15. Liu, J., Tian, J., Cai, Z., Zhou, Y., Luo, R., Wang, R.: A hybrid semi-supervised approach for financial fraud detection. In: 2017 International Conference on Machine Learning and Cybernetics (ICMLC), Ningbo, pp. 217–222 (2017)
16. Malhotra, P., Vig, L., Shroff, G., Agarwal, P.: Long short term memory networks for anomaly detection in time series. In: European Symposium on Artificial Neural Networks, Computational Intelligence and Machine Learning, pp. 89–94 (2015)
17. Ramaswamy, S., Rastogi, R., Shim, K.: Efficient algorithms for mining outliers from large data sets. In: Proceedings of the 2000 ACM SIGMOD International Conference on Management of Data, pp. 427–438 (2000)

18. Schlegl, T., Seebock, P., Waldstein, S.M., Schmidt-Erfurth, U., Langs, G.: Unsupervised anomaly detection with generative adversarial networks to guide marker discovery. In: IPMI 2017: Information Processing in Medical Imaging, pp. 146–157 (2017)
19. Schölkopf, B., Platt, J.C., Shawe-Taylor, J., Smola, A.J., Williamson, R.C.: Estimating the support of a high-dimensional distribution. Neural Comput. **13**(7), 1443–1471 (2001)
20. Zhou, C., Paffenroth, R.C.: Anomaly detection with robust deep autoencoders. In: KDD 2017 Proceedings of the 23rd ACM SIGKDD International Conference on Knowledge Discovery and Data Mining, Halifax, pp. 665–674 (2017)

In-The-Limit Clustering Axioms

Mieczysław A. Kłopotek[1]([✉]) [iD] and Robert A. Kłopotek[2] [iD]

[1] Institute of Computer Science, Polish Academy of Sciences, Warsaw, Poland
`mieczyslaw.klopotek@ipipan.waw.pl`
[2] Faculty of Mathematics and Natural Sciences. School of Exact Sciences, Cardinal
Stefan Wyszyński University in Warsaw, Warsaw, Poland
`r.klopotek@uksw.edu.pl`

Abstract. The paper studies the major reason for the contradictions in the Kleinberg's axiomatic system for clustering [9]. We found that the so-called consistency axiom is the single source of problems because it creates new clusters instead of preserving the existent ones. Furthermore, this axiom contradicts the practice that data to be clustered is a sample of the actual population to be clustered. We correct this axiom to fit this requirement. It turns out, however, that the axiom is then too strong and implies isomorphism. Therefore we propose to relax it by allowing for centric consistency and demonstrate that under centric consistency, the axiomatic framework is not contradictory anymore. The practical gain is the availability of true cluster preserving operators.

Keywords: Cluster analysis · Clustering axioms · k-means algorithm

1 Introduction

As the number of clustering algorithms is growing rapidly, a research effort is going on to formalize the concepts of clusters, clustering, and clustering algorithms. Various axiomatic frameworks have been proposed, e.g., for unsharp partitioning by [14], for graph clustering by [10], for cost function driven algorithms by [4], for linkage algorithms by [2], for hierarchical algorithms by [6,7,13], for multiscale clustering by [5], for settings with increasing sample sizes by [8], for community detection by [16], for pattern clustering by [12], and for distance based clustering [9]. The latter work by Kleinberg is heavily cited (over 600 times, according to Google Scholar). However, nobody seems to draw attention to the major drawback of that axiomatic system that is the inadequacy for Euclidean embedding based distances and the fact that algorithms cluster samples and not entire populations. Last but not least, Kleinberg's axiomatic system is contradictory.

In this paper, we aim at eliminating these deficiencies. In particular, we show that the so-called consistency axiom is the single source of problems because it creates new clusters instead of preserving the existent ones (Sect. 3). Furthermore, this axiom contradicts the practice that data to be clustered is a sample of the actual population to be clustered. We correct this axiom to fit this

© Springer Nature Switzerland AG 2020
L. Rutkowski et al. (Eds.): ICAISC 2020, LNAI 12416, pp. 199–209, 2020.
https://doi.org/10.1007/978-3-030-61534-5_18

requirement (Sect. 4). It turns out, however, that the axiom is then too strong and implies isomorphism. Therefore we propose to relax it by allowing for centric consistency (Sect. 5) and demonstrate that under centric consistency, the axiomatic framework is not contradictory any more (Sect. 6). The practical gain is the availability of true cluster preserving operators.

2   Preliminaries

Kleinberg [9, Section 2] defines clustering function as:

Definition 1. *A* clustering function *is a function f that takes a distance function d on [set] S [of size n ≥ 2] and returns a partition Γ of S. The sets in Γ will be called its* clusters.

Definition 2. *With the set $S = \{1, 2, \ldots, n\}$ [...] we define a distance function to be any function $d : S \times S \to \mathbb{R}$ such that for distinct $i, j \in S$ we have $d(i, j) \geq 0, d(i, j) = 0$ if and only if $i = j$, and $d(i, j) = d(j, i)$.*

Given that, Kleinberg [9] formulated axioms for distance-based cluster analysis, which are rather termed properties by others, e.g., [3].

Property 1. *Let Range(f) denote the set of all partitions Γ such that $f(d) = Γ$ for some distance function d. A function f has the* richness *property if Range(f) is equal to the set of all partitions of S.*

Property 2. *A function f has the* scale-invariance *property if for any distance function d and any $\alpha > 0$, we have $f(d) = f(\alpha \cdot d)$.*

Property 3. *Let Γ be a partition of S, and d and d′ two distance functions on S. We say that d′ is a Γ-transformation of d if (a) for all $i, j \in S$ belonging to the same cluster of Γ, we have $d'(i, j) \leq d(i, j)$ and (b) for all $i, j \in S$ belonging to different clusters of Γ, we have $d'(i, j) \geq d(i, j)$. The clustering function f has the* consistency *property if for each distance function d and its Γ-transformation d′ the following holds: if $f(d) = Γ$, then $f(d') = Γ$*

Kleinberg demonstrated that his three *axioms* (Properties 1, 2, 3) cannot be met all at once (but only pair-wise), see his Impossibility Theorem [9, Theorem 2.1]. In order to resolve the conflict, there was proposed a replacement of consistency axiom with order-consistency axiom [15], refinement-consistency ([9]), inner/outer consistency [3], order-invariance and so on (see [1]).

However, none of these approaches seems to address the root of the problem. Many clustering algorithms, including k-means, kernel-k-means, and their variants rely explicitly on the embedding into Euclidean space, which Kleinberg ignores. Therefore we discuss embedding of the data points in a fixed-dimensional Euclidean space, with distance between data points implied by the embedding[1]

---

[1]   An *embedding* of a data set S into the m-dimensional space $\mathbb{R}^m$ is a function $\mathcal{E} : S \to \mathbb{R}^m$ inducing a distance function $d_{\mathcal{E}}(i, j)$ between these data points being the Euclidean distance between $\mathcal{E}(i)$ and $\mathcal{E}(j)$.

Subsequently, whenever we talk about distance, we mean Euclidean distance.

Furthermore, the Kleinberg's axioms seem to be different in nature. While Property 1 addresses the value range of the clustering function, the other two address the transformations of the function domain, which are intended to be clustering preserving. However, the Γ-transform described in Property 3 allows for cluster formation, which is an internal contradiction to its intention. We will address this in the next section (Sect. 3).

3 Convergent Consistency as a Way to Resolve Kleinberg's Impossibility

Let us diverge for a moment from the assumption of embedding in the fixed dimensional space and resume Kleinberg's distance definition.

The paper [9] showed that invariance and consistency imply antichain property (his Theorem 3.1). The proof of that Theorem reveals, however, the mechanism behind creating the contradiction in his axiomatic system: the consistency operator creates new structures (hence new clusters) in the data. His proof goes as follows: He introduces the concept of a distance function d" (a, b)-conforming" to a partition Γ of the data if for all pairs of data points i, j $d(i, j) \leq a$, if both belong to the sane cluster and $d(i, j) \geq b$ if they don't. With respect to a given clustering function f, we say that a pair of positive real numbers (a, b) is Γ-forcing if, for all distance functions d that (a, b)-conform to Γ we have $f(d) = \Gamma$.

Let f be a clustering function that satisfies Kleinerg's consistency property. He claims that for any partition $\Gamma \in Range(f)$, there exist positive real numbers $a < b$ such that the pair (a, b) is Γ-forcing. By definition of Kleingerg's Range functional, as $\Gamma \in Range(f)$, there must exist a distance function d such that $f(d) = \Gamma$. Let a_0 be the minimum distance among pairs of points in the same cluster of Γ and let b_0 be the maximum distance among pairs of points that do not belong to the same cluster of Γ. Choose numbers $a < b$ so that $a \leq a_0$ and $b \geq b_0$. Then any distance function d_0 that (a, b)-conforms to Γ must be a Kleinberg's consistency transformation of d, and so by the consistency property, $f(d_0) = \Gamma$. It follows that the pair (a, b) is Γ-forcing. Now suppose further that the clustering function f satisfies Scale-Invariance, and that there exist distinct partitions $\Gamma_0, \Gamma_1 \in Range(f)$ such that Γ_0 is a refinement of Γ_1, that is each cluster of Γ_0 is a subset of a cluster in Γ_1. Then Kleinberg shows that this leads to a contradiction: Let (a_0, b_0) be a Γ_0-forcing pair, and let (a_1, b_1) be a Γ_1-forcing pair, with $a_0 < b_0$ and $a_1 < b_1$. As already shown, such a_0, b_0, a_1, b_1 exist. Let a_2 be any number $a_2 \leq a_1$, and let ϵ such that $0 < \epsilon < a_0 a_2 b_0^{-1}$. It is now straightforward to construct a distance function d with the following properties: For pairs of points i, j that belong to the same cluster of Γ_0, we have $d(ij) \leq \epsilon$. For pairs i, j that belong to the same cluster of Γ_1, but not to the same cluster of Γ_0 we have $a_2 \leq d(i, j) \leq a_1$. For pairs i, j not in he same cluster of Γ_1 we have $d(i, j) \geq b_1$. The construction may proceed as follows: Let d_1 be a function (a_1, b_1)-conforming to a partition Γ_1. Let us obtain d_2 from d_1 by scaling up the minimum distance d_1 within a cluster of Γ_1 so that it exceeds a_2.

Then obtain from d_2 the d_3 by consistency transformation for Γ_1, changing distances only within clusters of Γ_1 so that they are bigger than a_2, but smaller than a_1. From this, obtain a d_4 by consistency transform over Γ_0 by reducing the distances below ϵ if the data points are in the same Γ_0 cluster, and retaining the remaining distances. The d_4 is our d.

The distance function d (a_1, b_1)-conforms to Γ_1 and so we have $f(d) = \Gamma_1$. Now set $\alpha = b_0 a_{21}^{-1}$, and define $d' = \alpha d$. By Scale-Invariance, we must have $f(d') = f(d) = \Gamma_1$. But for points i, j in the same cluster of Γ_0 we have $d'(i; j) \leq \epsilon b_0 a_2^{-1} < a_0$, while for points i, j that do not belong to the same cluster of Γ_0 we have $d'(i, j) \geq a_2 b_0 a_2^{-1} \geq b_0$. Thus d' (a_0, b_0)-conforms to Γ_0 and so we must have $f(d') = \Gamma_0$. As $\Gamma_0 \neq \Gamma_1$, this is a contradiction.

So far, the proof of Kleinberg. Now let us point to suspicious steps of the proof. d_1 was a legitimate distance function generating Γ_1 under f. Then there was a sequence of transforms changing $d_1 \rightarrow d_2 \rightarrow d_3 \rightarrow d_4$. The step that we question here is the transformation $d_3 \rightarrow d_4$. This was a structure generating step, and no wonder that Γ_0 was obtained out of Γ. By the way, this step could be applied not only to creating new clusters from a single existent one but also to invert this operation, which is to create a combined cluster from several clusters. So the Γ-transformation is a full-fledged cluster creation operation instead of cluster preserving one, as was intended.

This behavior should be prohibited if the transformation shall produce the same clustering of data, as consistency property assumes. We insist that if $d(i, j) \leq d(k, l)$, then also $d'(i, j) \leq d'(k, l)$ and $d(i, j)/d(k, l) \leq d'(i, j)/d'(k, l)$ for any data points i, j within the same cluster and k, l within the same cluster (that is the longer distances decrease faster). This would prohibit the step $d_3 \rightarrow d_4$ and hence remove Kleinberg's contradiction. To prohibit the creation of new structures outside of clusters, one should also consider the same condition when i, j stem from different clusters, and l, k stem from different clusters shorter distances grow more rapidly). So define:

Property 4. *Define the convergent-Γ-transform as Γ-transform from Property 3 in which if $d(i, j) \leq d(k, l)$, then also $d'(i, j) \lesssim d'(k, l)$ and $d(i, j)/d(k, l) \leq d'(i, j)/d'(k, l)$. The clustering function f has the convergent consistency property if for each distance function d and its convergent Γ-transformation d' the following holds: if $f(d) = \Gamma$, then $f(d') = \Gamma$*

Under these circumstances one can define a new brand of single linkage algorithm, the quotient single link algorithm. First of all, the order preserving requirement ensures that the edges are considered in the same order whatever termination condition is imposed. Let us now look for a termination condition that will not be violated by the transformation definition. An edge is added only if the quotient of the longest to the shortest edge in the emerging cluster does not exceed a predefined threshold. This single link algorithms with this stopping criterion fits the Kleinberg's axiomatic framework given that the consistency is updated as indicated above.

Theorem 1. *The axioms of richness, scale-invariance and convergent-consistency are not contradictory.*

Proof. Just consider the quotient single link algorithm as an easy to verify example for which all three axioms hold.

4   Subsampling Consistency

The Kleinberg's consistency axiom suffers from a further practical weakness. The typical clustering function applications consist of using the clustering function to cluster a sample from the population with the hope that it will reflect the true structure of the population. We would expect from the clustering preserving operation the following: If $\Gamma = f(S_n, d)$ and $\Gamma' = f(S_{n'}, d)$ where $S \subset S_{n'}$ are two samples from the same population and of different sizes n, n', and if Γ agrees with Γ' that is objects in the same cluster of Γ are in the same cluster of Γ', then for any permissible Γ-transformation yielding distance function d'_{S_n} there should exist a Γ'-transformation yielding distance function $d'_{S_{n'}}$ agreeing on elements from S_n. Furthermore, if $S_{n'}$ consists of points from the "vicinity" of elements S_n of some small radius, then Γ and Γ' should agree (so-called perturbation robustness [11]).

Let us now consider an infinite population in a fixed dimensional Euclidean space $\mathbb{R}^m$ described by a probability density function over this space such that for any point of density bigger than 0 there exists a ball of positive radius containing it and only points of positive density.

Now consider a sample S_n and its clustering Γ. Take a cluster C from it and a sample point P. In its vicinity $\epsilon_P > 0$ of non-zero density, we can choose an m-simplex (m+1 points) with edge length say ϵ_P. Distinguish one of its corners A_1 and the height from this point and two points on this height: A_2 on the opposite face and A_3 at 2/3 of the height $(2|A_1 A_3| = |A_3 A_2|$. By increasing the sample size in this vicinity, we can find m+1 points in the ϵ vicinity of the corner points of the simplex and of A_2, A_3, with $\epsilon << \epsilon_P$. Let the points B_1, B_2, B_3 be in the vicinity of A_1, A_2, A_3. Let the images of B_1, B_2, B_3 under convergent Γ-transform be B'_1, B'_2, B'_3. Let line segments $B_1 B_2, B_2 B_3, B_1 B_3$ be shortened (multiplied) by factors $\gamma_{13}, \gamma_{32}, \gamma_{12}$ resp. upon transformation. Necessarily $\gamma_{13} \geq \gamma_{32} \geq \gamma_{12}$. Consider one-dimensional space $m = 1$.

Obviously $|B'_1 B'_2| = |B'_1 B'_3| + |B'_3 B'_2| = \gamma_{13}|B_1 B_3| + \gamma_{32}|B_3 B_2| \geq \gamma_{12}|B_1 B_3| + \gamma_{12}|B_3 B_2| = |B'_1 B'_2|$ which implies $\gamma_{13} = \gamma_{32} = \gamma_{12}$ that is a proportional decrease of length. In $m > 1$ dimensional space we get the same conclusion in the limit, by decreasing the ϵ vicinity (in m dimensions we have no guarantee that $B'_1 B'_2, B3'$ lie on the same line but by decreasing ϵ we can approximate linearity with any degree). By rotating the simplex and taking A_2, A_3 from vicinities of other cluster points, we come to the conclusion that each whole cluster distances can only be decreased proportionally. By selecting more points A from different clusters we conclude that the entire convergent Γ - transform must be an identity transform if the same clustering must hold in the limit. So we have just proven (in an outline) that:

Theorem 2. *If the in-the-limit condition has to hold then the convergent-Γ=-transform must be an isomorphism.*

5   Centric Consistency

The Kleinberg's consistency property, after correction for not creating new structures and being consistent in the limit, turns out to be too rigid.

So let us look for ways of weakening this rigidness. From the informal point of view, a clustering preserving operation should care only about cluster points close to other clusters so that the gap does not decrease, while it is not so important about other cluster points. This idea can be formalized in one of possible incarnations that we will call here "centric consistency".

Definition 3. *Let Γ be a partition embedded in $\mathbb{R}^m$. Let $C \in \Gamma$ and let μ_c be the center of the cluster C. We say that we execute the Γ^* transform (or a centric consistency transformation) if for some $0 < \lambda \leq 1$ we create a set C' with cardinality identical with C such that for each element $x \in C$ there exists $x' \in C'$ such that $x' = \mu_c + \lambda(x - \mu_c)$, and then substitute C in Γ with C'.*

Note that the set of possible centric consistency transformations for a given partition is neither a subset nor superset of the set of possible Kleinberg's consistency transformations. Instead it is a k-means clustering model-specific adaptation of the general idea of shrinking the cluster. The first differentiating feature of the centric consistency is that no new structures are introduced in the cluster at any scale. The second important feature is that the requirement of keeping the minimum distance to elements of other clusters is dropped, and only cluster centers do not get closer to one another.

Note also that the centric consistency does not suffer from the impossibility of transformation for clusters that turn out to be internal.

Property 5. *A clustering method matches the condition of centric consistency if, after a Γ^* transform, it returns the same partition.*

Let us now demonstrate theoretically, that k-means algorithm really fits at least in the simplest case of $k = 2$.

Theorem 3. *k-means algorithm satisfies centric consistency in the following way: if the partition Γ is a global minimum of k-means, and $k = 2$, and the partition Γ has been subject to centric consistency yielding Γ', then Γ' is also a global minimum of k-means.*

Proof. Let the optimal clustering for a given set of objects X consists of two clusters: T and Z. The subset T shall have its gravity center $\mu(T)$ at the origin of the coordinate system. The quality of this partition $Q(\{T, Z\}) = n_T Var(T) + n_Z Var(Z)$ where n_T, n_Z denote the cardinalities of T, Z and $Var(T), Var(Z)$ their variances (averaged squared distances to gravity center). We will prove by contradiction that by applying our Γ transform, we get partition that will still be optimal for the transformed data points. We shall assume the contrary that is that we can transform the set T by some $1 > \lambda > 0$ to T' in such a way that optimum of 2-means clustering is not the partition $\{T', Z\}$ but another one, say

$\{A' \cup D, B' \cup C\}$ where $Z = C \cup D$, A' and B' are transforms of sets A, B for which in turn $A \cup B = T$. It may be easily verified that

$$Q(\{A \cup B, C \cup D\}) = n_A Var(A) + n_A \mathbf{v}_A^2 + n_B Var(B) + n_B \mathbf{v}_B^2$$

$$+ n_C Var(C) + n_D Var(D) + \frac{n_C n_D}{n_C + n_D}(\mathbf{v}_C - \mathbf{v}_D)^2$$

while

$$Q(\{A \cup C, B \cup D\}) = n_A Var(A) + n_D Var(D) + + \frac{n_A n_D}{n_A + n_D}(\mathbf{v}_A - \mathbf{v}_D)^2$$

$$+ n_B Var(B) + n_C Var(C) + + \frac{n_B n_C}{n_B + n_C}(\mathbf{v}_B - \mathbf{v}_C)^2$$

and

$$Q(\{A' \cup B', C \cup D\}) = n_A \lambda^2 Var(A) + n_A \lambda^2 \mathbf{v}_A^2 + n_B \lambda^2 Var(B) + n_B \lambda^2 \mathbf{v}_B^2$$

$$+ n_C Var(C) + n_D Var(D) + \frac{n_C n_D}{n_C + n_D}(\mathbf{v}_C - \mathbf{v}_D)^2$$

while

$$Q(\{A' \cup C, B' \cup D\}) = n_A \lambda^2 Var(A) + n_D Var(D) + + \frac{n_A n_D}{n_A + n_D}(\lambda \mathbf{v}_A - \mathbf{v}_D)^2$$

$$+ n_B \lambda^2 Var(B) + n_C Var(C) + + \frac{n_B n_C}{n_B + n_C}(\lambda \mathbf{v}_B - \mathbf{v}_C)^2$$

The following must hold:

$$Q(\{A' \cup B', C \cup D\}) > Q(\{A' \cup D, B' \cup C\}) \tag{1}$$

$$Q(\{A \cup B, C \cup D\}) < Q(\{A \cup D, B \cup C\}) \tag{2}$$

Additionally also

$$Q(\{A \cup B, C \cup D\}) < Q(\{A \cup B \cup C, D\}) \tag{3}$$

$$Q(\{A \cup B, C \cup D\}) < Q(\{A \cup B \cup D, C\}) \tag{4}$$

These two latter inequalities imply:

$$\frac{n_C n_D}{n_C + n_D}(\mathbf{v}_C - \mathbf{v}_D)^2 < \frac{(n_A + n_B)n_C}{(n_A + n_B) + n_C}\mathbf{v}_C^2$$

and

$$\frac{n_C n_D}{n_C + n_D}(\mathbf{v}_C - \mathbf{v}_D)^2 < \frac{(n_A + n_B)n_D}{(n_A + n_B) + n_D}\mathbf{v}_D^2$$

We get for an extreme contraction ($\lambda = 0$) yielding sets $A", B"$ out of A, B:

$$Q(\{A" \cup B", C \cup D\}) - Q(\{A" \cup C, B" \cup D\})$$

$$= \frac{n_C n_D}{n_C + n_D}(\mathbf{v}_C - \mathbf{v}_D)^2 - \frac{n_A n_D}{n_A + n_D}\mathbf{v}_D^2 - \frac{n_B n_C}{n_B + n_C}\mathbf{v}_C^2$$

$$= \frac{n_C n_D}{n_C + n_D}(\mathbf{v}_C - \mathbf{v}_D)^2$$

$$- \frac{n_A n_D}{n_A + n_D}\frac{(n_A + n_B) + n_D}{(n_A + n_B)n_D}\frac{(n_A + n_B)n_D}{(n_A + n_B) + n_D}\mathbf{v}_D^2$$

$$- \frac{n_B n_C}{n_B + n_C}\frac{(n_A + n_B) + n_C}{(n_A + n_B)n_C}\frac{(n_A + n_B)n_C}{(n_A + n_B) + n_C}\mathbf{v}_C^2$$

$$= \frac{n_C n_D}{n_C + n_D}(\mathbf{v}_C - \mathbf{v}_D)^2$$

$$- \frac{n_A}{n_A + n_B}\left(1 + \frac{n_B}{n_A + n_D}\right)\frac{(n_A + n_B)n_D}{(n_A + n_B) + n_D}\mathbf{v}_D^2$$

$$- \frac{n_B}{n_A + n_B}\left(1 + \frac{n_A}{n_B + n_C}\right)\frac{(n_A + n_B)n_C}{(n_A + n_B) + n_C}\mathbf{v}_C^2$$

$$< \frac{n_C n_D}{n_C + n_D}(\mathbf{v}_C - \mathbf{v}_D)^2$$

$$- \frac{n_A}{n_A + n_B}\frac{(n_A + n_B)n_D}{(n_A + n_B) + n_D}\mathbf{v}_D^2$$

$$- \frac{n_B}{n_A + n_B}\frac{(n_A + n_B)n_C}{(n_A + n_B) + n_C}\mathbf{v}_C^2 < 0$$

because the linear combination of two numbers that are bigger than a third yields another number bigger than this. Let us define a function

$$h(x) = +n_A x^2 \mathbf{v}_A^2 + n_B x^2 \mathbf{v}_B^2 + \frac{n_C n_D}{n_C + n_D}(\mathbf{v}_C - \mathbf{v}_D)^2$$

$$- \frac{n_A n_D}{n_A + n_D}(x\mathbf{v}_A - \mathbf{v}_D)^2 - \frac{n_B n_C}{n_B + n_C}(x\mathbf{v}_B - \mathbf{v}_C)^2$$

It can be easily verified that $h(x)$ is a quadratic polynomial with a positive coefficient at x^2. Furthermore $h(1) = Q(\{A \cup B, C \cup D\}) - Q(\{A \cup C, B \cup D\}) < 0$, $h(\lambda) = Q(\{A' \cup B', C \cup D\}) - Q(\{A' \cup C, B' \cup D\}) > 0$, $h(0) = Q(\{A" \cup B", C \cup D\}) - Q(\{A" \cup C, B" \cup D\}) < 0$. However, no quadratic polynomial with a positive coefficient at x^2 can be negative at the ends of an interval and positive in the middle. So we have the contradiction. This proves the thesis that the (globally) optimal 2-means clustering remains (globally) optimal after transformation.

6   *Auto*-means Algorithm

After reducing the restrictions imposed by Kleinberg's consistency axiom, we have to verify if we did not introduce another contradiction ion the axiomatic framework. So we have to find a clustering algorithm for which the properties of richness (or near richness), scale-invariance, and centric consistency hold. Note that k-means has only the property of k-richness because it can produce only a fixed number of clusters. To approximate the true richness, an algorithm has to be found that operates like k-means but automatically selects the k, and the range of k is at least broad. We will use here a brand of hierarchical k-means, embedded in $\mathbb{R}^m$. Note that hierarchical $k$means does not produce the same clustering as k-means hence special care is needed.

Let us introduce the *Auto*-means Algorithm. This algorithm can be considered as a hierarchical application of k-means with $k = 2$ with a special stopping criterion. The algorithm is continued if at the step dividing the data set into two,

- both created clusters A, B clusters have cardinalities such that $p \leq |A|/|B| \leq 1/p$ for some parameter $0 < p < 1$, and $|A| \geq m + 1, |B| \geq m + 1$, where m is the dimensionality of the data set, and
- both A and B can be enclosed in a ball centered at each gravity center with a common radius R such that the distance between gravity centers is not smaller than $(2 + g)R$, where $g > 0$ is a relative gap parameter.

We shall prove that

Theorem 4. *For appropriate p and g, the auto-means algorithm has the property of (near) richness, scale invariance and centric consistency.*

Proof (An outline). Assume a $g = 6, p = 2$. Assume the algorithm 2-means created clusters A,B, each enclosed in a ball of radius R, subject to further clustering. Assume that in cluster A, a lower level cluster was subjected to centric Γ transformation, so that A' cluster emerged. The outcome should be so, contrary to the claim of the theorem, that now the 2-means would have divided the set $A' \cup B$ into C, D. Let $C = A'_1 \cup B_1$ and $D = A_2{}' \cup B_2$ where $A' = A'_1 \cup A'_2, B = B_1 \cup B_2$. Denote the gravity center of a set A with $\mu(A)$. Assume now that $\|\mu(A'_1) - \mu(C)\| > 2R, \|\mu(B_1) - \mu(C)\| > 2R, \|\mu(A'_2) - \mu(D)\| > 2R, \|\mu(B_2) - \mu(D)\| > 2R$. Then A', B would be a clustering with lower k-means cost than C, D. Assume now that $\|\mu(A'_1) - \mu(C)\| \leq 2R, \|\mu(A'_2) - \mu(D)\| \leq 2R$. This would be contrary to the assumption of $p = 2$. The symmetric situation is also excluded. So assume that $\|\mu(A'_1) - \mu(C)\| \leq 2R, \|\mu(B_2) - \mu(D)\| \leq 2R$. Hence $\|\mu(B_1) - \mu(D)\| \leq 4R$, so clustering $A'_1, B_1 \cup D$ would be a better one than C, D. So assume that $\|\mu(A'_1) - \mu(C)\| \leq 2R$, whereas $2R < \|\mu(A'_2) - \mu(D)\| \leq 4R$. Switching from C, D to A', B would decrease the distance of A'_2, B_2 to the balls around centers of A'_1, B_1 with radii equal to their distances to centres of C, D so that the cost function of k-means is lower for A', B partition. The above considerations are also valid in case of empty subsets. This means that if any subcluster of A is subject to centric Γ transform, no impact occurs for A, B partition by 2-means. This is valid recursively, till we are to partition the cluster subject to centric consistency. As scaling does not affect k-means, the hierarchical clustering will proceed as before the centric transform. Hence the clustering remains the same under centric consistency of a cluster in the hierarchy. As k-means is invariant under scaling, scaling invariance is granted. As by appropriate choice of distances, we can achieve any nesting of clusters. Near richness is achieved with the constraint that there are minimal sizes of clusters. The maximum auto-selected k as a function of sample size and dimensionality can be easily computed.

7 Conclusions

We have shown in this paper that the contradiction in Kleinberg's axiomatic system may be annihilated if the condition of convergent consistency is introduced. We demonstrate that this property leads to a too strong rigidness in cluster preserving transformations if we study the clustering of samples taken from a continuous population. As a remedy, we propose centric consistency axiom that proved to be less rigid, and not producing contradictions. The practical gain is the availability of true cluster preserving operators.

References

1. Ackerman, M.: Towards theoretical foundations of clustering. university of Waterloo, PhD Thesis (2012)
2. Ackerman, M., Ben-David, S., Loker, D.: Characterization of linkage-based clustering. COLT **2010**, 270–281 (2010)
3. Ackerman, M., Ben-David, S., Loker, D.: Towards property-based classification of clustering paradigms. In: Advances in Neural Information Processing Systems, vol. 23, pp. 10–18. Curran Associates, Inc. (2010)
4. Ben-David, S., Ackerman, M.: Measures of clustering quality: a working set of axioms for clustering. In: Koller, D., Schuurmans, D., Bengio, Y., Bottou, L. (eds.) Advances in Neural Information Processing Systems, vol. 21, pp. 121–128. Curran Associates, Inc. (2009)
5. Carlsson, G., Mémoli, F.: Persistent clustering and a theorem of j. kleinberg. arXiv preprint arXiv:0808.2241 (2008)
6. Carlsson, G., Mémoli, F.: Characterization, stability and convergence of hierarchical clustering methods. J. Mach. Learn. Res. **11**, 1425–1470 (2010)
7. Gower, J.C.: Clustering axioms. Classification Society of North America Newsletter, pp. 2–3, July 1990
8. Hopcroft, J., Kannan, R.: Computer science theory for the information age, chapter 8.13.2. A Satisfiable Set of Axioms (2012). p. 272ff
9. Kleinberg, J.: An impossibility theorem for clustering. In: Proceedings NIPS 2002, pp. 446–453 (2002). http://books.nips.cc/papers/files/nips15/LT17.pdf
10. van Laarhoven, T., Marchiori, E.: Axioms for graph clustering quality functions. J. Mach. Learn. Res. **15**, 193–215 (2014)

11. Moore, J., Ackerman, M.: Foundations of perturbation robust clustering. In: IEEE ICDM, vol. 2016, pp. 1089–1094 (2016). https://doi.org/10.1109/ICDM.2016.0141
12. Shekar, B.: A knowledge-based approach to pattern clustering. Ph.D. thesis, Indian Institute of Science (1988)
13. Thomann, P., Steinwart, I., Schmid, N.: Towards an axiomatic approach to hierarchical clustering of measures (2015)
14. Wright, W.: A formalization of cluster analysis. Pattern Rec. **5**(3), 273–282 (1973)
15. Zadeh, R.B., Ben-David, S.: A uniqueness theorem for clustering. In: Proceedings of the Twenty-Fifth Conference on Uncertainty in Artificial Intelligence, pp. 639–646. UAI 2009, AUAI Press, Arlington, Virginia, United States (2009)
16. Zeng, G., Wang, Y., Pu, J., Liu, X., Sun, X., Zhang, J.: Communities in preference networks: refined axioms and beyond. In: ICDM 2016, pp. 599–608 (2016)

Hybrid Features for Twitter Sentiment Analysis

Sergiu Limboi[✉] and Laura Dioşan

Faculty of Mathematics and Computer Science, Babeş-Bolyai University,
Cluj-Napoca, Romania
{sergiu,lauras}@cs.ubbcluj.ro

Abstract. The Twitter platform is one of the most popular social media environments that gathers concise messages regarding the topics of the moment expressed by its users. Processing sentiments from tweets is a challenging task due to the natural language complexity, misspelling and short forms of words. The goal of this article is to present a hybrid feature for Twitter Sentiment Analysis, focused on information gathered from this social media. The baseline perspective is presented based on different scenarios that take into consideration preprocessing techniques, data representations, methods and evaluation measures. Also, several interesting features are detailed described: the hashtag-based, the fused one, and the raw text feature. All these perspectives are highlighted for proving the high importance and impact that the analysis of tweets has on social studies and society in general. We conducted several experiments that include all these features, with two granularity tweets (word and bigram) on Sanders dataset. The results reveal the idea that best polarity classification performances are produced by the fused feature, but overall the raw feature is better than other approaches. Therefore, the domain-specific features (in this case Twitter hashtags) represent information that can be an important factor for the polarity classification task, not exploited enough.

Keywords: Sentiment analysis · Twitter · Hashtags

1 Introduction

Nowadays there is an increased interest from various areas like politics, business, economy or marketing to find answers to questions regarding people's opinions and feelings. Some of the questions can be "What do they hate about iPhone 6?", "Does it worth watching this movie?". This interest leads to the analysis of social media content which is very useful in activities like opinion mining from product reviews, emotion detection or sentiment classification. Twitter is considered "a valuable online source for opinions" [18] and shows a way to catch the public's ideas and interests for social studies.

Bearing in mind all these questions, it arrives at the point when it needs a methodology or area that can solve these issues and can help people to analyze

© Springer Nature Switzerland AG 2020
L. Rutkowski et al. (Eds.): ICAISC 2020, LNAI 12416, pp. 210–219, 2020.
https://doi.org/10.1007/978-3-030-61534-5_19

the context in order to understand it. Therefore, the emotional polarity problem can be expressed as a classification one by identifying if textual items reveal a positive or negative emotion/opinion. The analysis of Twitter is a research area with high and growing interest where the main concept is a tweet. It is composed of two main parts: a short and simple text message (maximum 140 characters) which is posted on the social media and hash-tags and hypertext-based elements: related media (maps, photos, videos) and websites. Hash-tags [13] are keywords prefixed with the "#" symbol that can appear in a tweet. Twitter users use this notation to categorize their messages and enable or mark them to be more easily found in search. Based on tweets messages that are provided as input for the emotional polarity problem, we can define the output which is represented as a binary opinion (categorical two-point scale: positive, negative). The main contributions of the current paper are at the level of feature extraction and representation derived from tweets. Features can be handcrafted (keywords, list of words, n-grams, frequencies) or can be automatically extracted from data (features learned by a Machine Learning algorithm, also known as embeddings). We decided to use the handcrafted feature because the automatic features require either an external lexicon or a pre-trained word embedding. Behinds, in the case of short-texts, the automatically extracted features have not improved the classification process (in terms of classification quality and required resources), yet. Considering these aspects, we propose to combine the features extracted from both parts of a twitter message (text and hash-tags) in order to test if the fusion of them brings relevant information in the classification process.

The remaining of the proposed paper is structured as follows: section two presents a literature overview of exploring features for Twitter Sentiment Analysis. Section three describes in detail our approach focusing on the Sentiment Analysis process and several extracted features from tweets. Then, in the fourth section, the dataset, numerical experiments, and relevant findings are highlighted. In section five, conclusions are outlined and the future work perspectives are defined, pointing out that this approach improves the Twitter Sentiment Analysis by considering domain-specific features.

2 Related Work

In literature, there are various approaches that explore the Twitter polarity classification problem considering a set of relevant features that can be used for the sentiment analysis process.

Baseline features like bag-of-words, unigrams, bigrams and part-of-speech are used in [2,3,5–7,10]. Other approaches used lexicon or semantic features, when the words are enhanced with polarity based on an external knowledge base [6,7, 11]. An interesting point is represented by the micro-blogging features indicating the presence of positive, negative or neutral emoticons, abbreviations or URLs [6,7]. Word embedding features are quite used in sentiment analysis [8,14–17]. In comparison with these approaches, ours present a mixed feature perspective that is based on the message's text and the Twitter-specific information that is represented by hash-tags. Several scenarios are combined in order to prove the valuable information that is brought by these keywords to the short messages posted on the Twitter environment.

3 Proposed Approach

Twitter Sentiment Analysis is a challenging task due to the short length of messages and a variety of domain-specific elements: hash-tags, re-tweets, emoticons, abbreviations or colloquial style specific for an online platform. Our approach presents a process applied to the Twitter data, focusing on feature extraction and data representation steps.

3.1 Sentiment Analysis

The features of sentiment analysis can be the following: scalability, real-time analysis, adaptability. The sentiment analysis area defines multiple concepts like opinion, polarity, subject or opinion holder. An *opinion* is an expression that reflects people's feelings about a specific topic. This expression can take various forms: written or text-based, spoken or voice-based and behavior or gesture-based. Sentiment analysis can be modeled as a classification problem that implies *subjectivity* (classify opinions into subjective and objective ones) and *polarity* (classify expressions into negative, positive and neutral), based on input represented as textual information (documents, messages, etc). In this paper, we focus on the polarity classification task.

Phases. Sentiment Analysis, visualized as a polarity classification task (detecting opinions and classifying them into positive, negative or neutral), implies the next phases. The initialization step prepares the data for the classification algorithm. Data collection means to retrieve data and analyze the content of it (How many messages are positive, negative, neutral? Is the data balanced?). If the data is not already labeled, manual annotation is required to validate the approach. The preprocessing phase means to transform the unstructured information into a clear one without misspellings, abbreviations or slang words. Then, a feature extraction stage determines how data is represented in terms of relevant features. The next step is represented by the learning phase when a training model is passed to a Machine Learning algorithm. The last stage is the evaluation when performance measures are computed to reflect how good is the methodology.

Preprocessing Techniques. The preprocessing step is very important for the polarity classification task by providing clean and relevant information for the next phases.

   Cleaning operations are those that involve only to normalize words from textual information and to remove the disadvantages given by the freeway of writing opinions. Therefore, can be applied the following methods that are used to define a uniform text [1]: remove the URLs, hashtags from messages, remove the numbers and special characters, replace repeated sequences with only one, remove blank spaces, lowercasing.

Negation is an essential operation because negative words influence a lot the polarity of a message. Ignoring negation is one of the causes of misclassification. So, all negative words (can't, don't, never) are replaced with *not*. **Dictionary** approach means to convert slang words or abbreviations with their formal forms. Then, a word like "l8" will be converted to "late" [1] or "approx." to "approximately". **Removing stop words** is very important and it can improve the performance of the classifier. Stop words can be pronouns or articles (e.g. our, me, myself, that, because, etc).

Stemming means to reduce the inflective or derivation form to a common radix of it (e.g. cars become car). Stemming implies cutting off the prefixes or suffixes of a word. A flavor of stemming is **lemmatization** that works with morphological context based on dictionaries (e.g. studies becomes study).

Feature Extraction. In this phase, the relevant features from the text are extracted and used as inputs for the classification algorithms. Text mining deals with several attributes, but only some of them are frequently used in the context of tweets (e.g. hash-tags).

We have experimented with several text representations. First, we investigate the classic approach Bag-of-words, when a message is represented as the bag of its words. The set of all the words from all the messages forms the vocabulary (of size VS), which is used for mapping each message into a vector of length VS, in which the ith entry contains the number of occurrences of the word i in the message. Such an approach is very easy to be computed and very intuitive, but it is not able to emphasize the spatial characteristics of the text, losing grammar and ordering information. A flavor of the previous method is Bag-of-n-grams that tries somehow to gain back some of the word order information lost by the bag-of-words approach: the frequency of short char sequences (of length two, three, etc.) can be used to construct word vectors. One major downside of the bag-based approaches is the non-linear dependence of the vocabulary size on the number of unique words/n-grams, which can be very large for large corpora. Filtering techniques are commonly used to reduce the vocabulary size. But in the twitter case, the vocabulary is not so large.

Document-term matrix representation reflects the frequency of extracted words from a collection of documents (texts, sentences). In this paper, the two mentioned granularities for the document-term matrix representation are used: word and bi-gram granularity. In other words, each row from the matrix corresponds to a message and columns represent the granularity level (word/bi-gram). **Bi-gram** granularity means a list of unordered words of size 2.

For both bag-based approaches, two weighting schemes were investigated. In fact, two scenarios are defined for determining the values from the matrix which represent the frequencies determined at granularity level (word or bi-grams).

The value from each cell can be integer or real. In the case of integer values, it describes how many times a word or bigram appears into a tweet (message). The real values are computed considering **TF** (term frequency) and **IDF** (inverse document frequency) formula:

$TF(t) = \frac{m}{M}$ and $IDF(t) = log(\frac{N}{n})$, where m is the number of times term t appears in the message, M is the number of terms in the message, N is the number of messages and n is the number of messages where term t appears [12]. This method re-weights the above word (or n-gram) frequency vectors with the inverse document frequency (IDF) of each word. The TF term grows as the word appears more often, while the IDF term increases with the word's rarity. This is meant to adjust the frequency scores for the fact that some words appear more (or less) frequently in general.

Feature-Based Approaches. Hashtags are valuable indicators for a tweet representing the keywords of the message preceded by the hash sign (#). Even though a tweet has text, hashtags, and hypertext elements, we took into consideration only the first two because hypertexts offer diverse information, from type perspective (links, videos, etc) and also from semantic one (meaning). Besides this, the multimedia concepts are not present in each tweet, so the dataset would be decreased considerably for our analysis. Based on these reasons, we outlined four perspectives that are applied to the Twitter polarity classification task. **Baseline Sentiment Analysis (BSA)** is the perspective where we extract the text from a tweet, removing the hashtags. For this feature, we take into consideration only the classic words belonging to a message. **Hashtag-Based Sentiment Analysis (HSA)** implies the fact that we extract the hashtags from a tweet, maintaining for each message a list of hashtags (indicators). The **Fused Sentiment Analysis approach (FSA)** combines BSA with HSA, providing as input for the sentiment classifier, the classic text of the message concatenated with the list of hashtags. Last but not least, we depicted a **Raw text feature Sentiment Analysis (RSA)**, where hashtags are considered common words: we remove the special sign # and we pass to the classifier the text in its initial form.

Machine Learning Algorithms and Performance Measures. Various techniques like lexicon-based, machine learning methods or hybrid approaches can be applied for the classification task. For this paper, the focus is on machine learning algorithms. In our approaches, three classification methods [9] are involved: Naïve Bayes (a probabilistic algorithm based on Bayes theorem), Support Vector Machine (SVM) (a deterministic algorithm used for finding a hyperplane that separates the data input in two classes, each of one side of it) and Logistic regression (a statistical classifier based on a logistic function). In terms of performance measures, accuracy, precision, recall, and f-score can be computed to indicate which algorithm fits the best.

4   Numerical Experiments

Several experiments were conducted focusing on preprocessing techniques, data representation in terms of relevant extracted features (BSA, HSA, FSA, and RSA) and Machine Learning algorithms involved in the classification process.

4.1   Methodology

Dataset. For the following experiments, Sanders dataset [4] is used. It consists of 5113 annotated tweets: 519 marked as positive, 572 negative, 2333 neutral and 1689 irrelevant. These tweets are messages related to four main topics, important companies from the world, and they are Twitter, Apple, Google, and Microsoft. The focus is to classify messages into positive and negative ones. Therefore, irrelevant and neutral messages are removed and 1091 tweets are considered. Due to the fact that our approach designs four feature extraction processes, we considered only tweets that contain hashtags. Therefore, 786 messages were used for our experiments, 415 tweets being positive and 371 negative. 20 were used as testing dataset and the rest of them for training.

Data Preprocessing. Data preprocessing is an essential step in the Sentiment Analysis domain because it can improve the whole process by removing the disadvantages or problems reflected by the free writing style of microblogs (e.g. misspellings, use of slang words, abbreviations). The following techniques were applied to Sanders dataset due to the fact that it is desired to have a fast and simple procedure: cleaning operations: removal of punctuation, lowercasing; removal of stop words; stemming.

Data Representation. After the preprocessing phase, the focus is to represent the tweets for the classification algorithms. Consequently, the document-term matrix is built considering the granularity levels (word and bi-gram) and the weighting schema: determining the frequency of words/bi-grams (integer values) and the TF.IDF computation explained in the previous section.

Classification Algorithms and Evaluation Measures. As classification algorithms, Naïve Bayes (NB), Support Vector Machine (SVM) and Logistic regression (LR) are used for the Twitter Sentiment Analysis approach. For the evaluation phase, accuracy and average precision are computed (precision values for all experiments can be found here). The last metric is chosen because both classes (positive and negative) represent our focus for the polarity classification task. As parameters, for the classification task, for logistic regression, the inverse of the regularization strength parameter is considered having the value *1.5*. The *SVM* classifier with linear kernel and regularization parameter (set to value *1.0*) is also applied for the proposed approach. Last but not least, the Multinomial version of Naïve Bayes is used for the classification task.

4.2 Results

We design our case study to answer the following four research questions:

- RQ_1 Do the tweets' preprocessing bring useful knowledge for the polarity classification process?
- RQ_2 Does the weighting schema influence the sentiment analysis?
- RQ_3 How do the hashtag-based features reflect the opinion embedded in the messages?
- RQ_4 Polarity classification is sensitive to the extracted text features or the involved classifier?

BSA Feature. Based on the BSA feature, we conducted several experiments considering word and bigram granularity and two different ways of computing the values from the document-term matrix: integer values and tf.idf values. Tables 1, 2, 6 and 7 (last two tables can be found here) present the performance measures, in terms of accuracy and precision, for these scenarios. Also, we applied different preprocessing techniques to find the best procedure that can be used for considered Twitter data.

Table 1. Accuracy for BSA with word granularity (integer and tf.idf weightings)

Preprocessing technique	NB		LR		SVM	
	Integer	tfidf	Integer	tfidf	Integer	tfidf
Without preprocessing	59.49	61.39	57.59	60.13	60.13	65.19
Removal of punctuation	**77.85**	**74.68**	**73.42**	**73.42**	**70.89**	**73.42**
Removal of stop words	58.23	61.39	58.86	61.39	55.7	65.19
Lowercasing	65.19	59.49	58.23	57.59	57.59	63.29
Stemming	59.49	61.39	57.59	60.13	60.13	65.19
All	55.06	51.27	56.96	53.80	56.96	53.80

Due to the short length of messages (maximum 140 characters), applying all preprocessing techniques seems to not bring useful knowledge about data to be classified (RQ_1). Best polarity classification performances are achieved when removal of punctuation is applied. Thus, in the following experiments this preprocessing step is performed, only. If we consider the weighting scheme, tf.idf achieves better results in terms of both metrics (accuracy and precision).

HSA Feature. The second approach is based on the hashtag feature, by keeping from the initial tweet only the list of hashtags. The conducted experiments were done based on both granularity levels and both weighing mechanisms. Table 3, 8 and 9 (last two tables can be found here) present the results achieved for accuracy and precision. Considering the results from the BSA feature, we used

Table 2. Accuracy for BSA with bi-gram granularity (integer and tf.idf weightings)

Preprocessing technique	NB		LR		SVM	
	Integer	tfidf	Integer	tfidf	Integer	tfidf
Without preprocessing	59.49	59.49	58.86	62.66	59.49	60.76
Removal of punctuation	**76.58**	**74.05**	**75.32**	**73.42**	**75.95**	**72.78**
Removal of stop words	60.13	61.39	60.13	62.03	63.29	60.13
Lowercasing	61.39	56.96	63.29	62.66	62.66	61.39
Stemming	58.86	59.49	58.23	61.39	61.39	60.13
All	47.57	45.57	56.33	55.06	57.59	55.06

Table 3. Accuracy for HSA with word and bi-gram granularity (integer and tf.idf weightings)

Preprocessing technique	NB		LR		SVM		
	Integer	tfidf	Integer	tfidf	Integer	tfidf	
Without preprocessing	**66.46**	**64.65**	65.19	63.29	65.82	66.46	word
Removal of punctuation	65.19	64.56	**69.62**	**68.35**	**66.46**	**67.09**	
Without preprocessing	**64.56**	**66.46**	**67.09**	**66.46**	**65.82**	**65.19**	bi-gram
Removal of punctuation	63.29	65.19	63.29	63.92	65.19	62.03	

only the removal of punctuation as a preprocessing technique. Also, the case when no preprocessing is used is performed.

Considering the presented results, HSA-word on raw data (without preprocessing) performs better than BSA-word without preprocessing, but BSA-word achieved larger accuracy then HSA-word when preprocessing is applied (removal of punctuation). Also, for BSA-bigram best values are achieved when no preprocessing is implied, but for HSA-bigram, accuracy is better than the other feature when preprocessing is implied.

Fused Features. The third perspective is a hybrid one, implying the fusion between BSA and HSA. The text is concatenated with the list of hashtags. Same scenarios (different granularities, different types of computation values) are presented for accuracy and precision (see Tables 4, 10 and 11 (last two tables can be found here)).

Considering the previously mentioned tables, it can be observed that FSA over performs in 11 from 12 cases in comparison with BSA. BSA achieves better results than FSA for bigram granularity, with preprocessing, for SVM technique and integer values. HSA has better results than HSA in 3 cases when no preprocessing is used. In the rest scenarios, FSA reached good values.

Raw Text Feature. The last perspective implies the use of raw text when hashtags are treated as simple words. Specifically, the initial text is provided as

Table 4. Accuracy for FSA with word and bi-gram granularity (integer and tf.idf weightings)

Preprocessing technique	NB		LR		SVM		
	Integer	tfidf	Integer	tfidf	Integer	tfidf	
Without preprocessing	63.29	63.29	67.09	65.82	65.19	68.35	word
Removal of punctuation	**79.75**	**80.38**	**75.32**	**76.58**	**71.52**	**77.22**	
Without preprocessing	65.19	63.29	65.82	65.82	65.19	68.35	bi-gram
Removal of punctuation	**79.75**	**80.83**	**77.22**	**76.58**	**70.89**	**77.22**	

input for a sentiment classifier, but removing the # sign. Tables 5, 12 and 13 (last two tables can be found here) show the values reached by the RSA feature.

Table 5. Accuracy for RSA with word and bi-gram granularity (integer and tf.idf weightings)

Preprocessing technique	NB		LR		SVM		
	Integer	tfidf	Integer	tfidf	Integer	tfidf	
Without preprocessing	65.19	64.56	67.09	65.82	63.92	69.62	word
Removal of punctuation	**79.75**	**79.75**	**79.75**	**79.75**	**77.85**	**77.85**	
Without preprocessing	67.09	64.56	65.82	66.46	63.92	63.29	bigram
Removal of punctuation	**78.48**	**77.22**	**74.68**	**77.22**	**77.85**	**77.85**	

RSA feature achieves the best accuracy in all 12 cases in comparison with BSA (word and bigram granularities). RSA outperforms in 8 from 12 cases when we consider the FSA. Also, FSA produces good results for word granularity when applying NB and SVM. Overall, RSA has better results than the ones produced by HSA.

Based on the previously presented experiments we can conclude the following. Both fused and raw features are better than BSA in 11 cases from 12, due to the fact that hash-tags contains important information (RQ_3). HSA approach does not produce good values in comparison with others, considering the short length of messages. Hashtags are important keywords of tweets, but only in combination with the text. Hashtags bring important information in context (RQ_3). The best preprocessing technique is the removal of punctuation and a lot of combinations between methods decrease the performance of the process (RQ_1). Best polarity classification results are achieved for the fused feature (accuracy 80.38% for word and bigram granularity with tf.idf values and 79.75% for integer values for NB classifier) (RQ_4). Overall, the raw feature is better than the fused one in 8 cases from 12, due to the fact, that the initial text is passed as input for the classifier (RQ_3).

5   Conclusions

In the presented approach we designed several perspectives that exploit the features of the Twitter environment. Bearing in mind the fact that hashtags are important features of a tweet, a hashtag-based sentiment analysis (HSA) scenario is defined considering only the extracted hashtags from a message. Also, a combination of HSA and BSA (baseline sentiment analysis) is reflected in a fused and raw text feature. The experimental results prove the notable improvement of our representations. As future work, we want to explore the word embeddings part and also to perform a context-based analysis, by considering the order of hashtags into tweets.

References

1. Angiani, G., et al.: A comparison between preprocessing techniques for sentiment analysis in twitter. In: KDWeb, pp. 1–6 (2016)
2. Anjaria, M., Guddeti, R.M.R.: Influence factor based opinion mining of twitter data using supervised learning. In: 2014 Sixth COMSNETS, pp. 1–8. IEEE (2014)
3. Barhan, A., Shakhomirov, A.: Methods for sentiment analysis of twitter messages. In: 12th Conference of FRUCT Association, pp. 215–222 (2012)
4. Deshmukh, R., Pawar, K.: Twitter sentiment classification on Sanders data using hybrid approach. IOSR J. Comput. Eng. **17**, 118–123 (2015)
5. Go, A., Bhayani, R., Huang, L.: Twitter sentiment classification using distant supervision. CS224N Project Report, Stanford 1(12), 2009 (2009)
6. Hamdan, H., Béchet, F., Bellot, P.: Experiments with DBpedia, wordnet and sentiwordnet as resources for sentiment analysis in micro-blogging. In: Proceedings of the 7th SemEval 2013, pp. 455–459 (2013)
7. Kouloumpis, E., Wilson, T., Moore, J.: Twitter sentiment analysis: the good the bad and the omg! In: Fifth International AAAI conference on weblogs and social media, pp. 538–541 (2011)
8. Martınez-Cámara, E., et. al: Ensemble classifier for twitter sentiment analysis. In: NLP Applications: completing the puzzle, pp. 1–12 (2015)
9. Mitchell, R., Michalski, J., Carbonell, T.: An artificial intelligence approach. Springer, Heidelberg (2013). https://doi.org/10.1007/978-3-662-12405-5
10. Pak, A., Paroubek, P.: Twitter as a corpus for sentiment analysis and opinion mining. LREc, **10**, 1320–1326 (2010)
11. Saif, H., He, Y., Alani, H.: Semantic sentiment analysis of twitter. In: Cudré-Mauroux, P., et al. (eds.) ISWC 2012. LNCS, vol. 7649, pp. 508–524. Springer, Heidelberg (2012). https://doi.org/10.1007/978-3-642-35176-1_32
12. Salton, G., Buckley, C.: Term-weighting approaches in automatic text retrieval. Inf. Process. Manag. **24**(5), 513–523 (1988)
13. Sankaranarayanan, J., et al.: Twitterstand: News in tweets. In: Proceedings of the 17th ACM SIGSPATIAL, pp. 42–51. GIS 2009, ACM (2009)
14. Severyn, A., Moschitti, A.: UNITN: training deep CNN for twitter sentiment classification. In: Proceedings of the 9th SemEval 2015, pp. 464–469 (2015)
15. Tang, D., et al.: Coooolll: a deep learning system for twitter sentiment classification. In: Proceedings of the 8th SemEval 2014, pp. 208–212 (2014)
16. Wang, P., et al.: Semantic expansion using word embedding clustering and CNN for improving short text classification. Neurocomputing **174**, 806–814 (2016)
17. Yan, L., Zheng, Y., Cao, J.: Few-shot learning for short text classification. Multimedia Tools Appl. **77**(22), 29799–29810 (2018). https://doi.org/10.1007/s11042-018-5772-4
18. Zhang, L., et al.: Combining lexicon-based and learning-based methods for twitter sentiment analysis. HP Laboratories, Technical Report HPL-2011 (2011)

Computer Based Stylometric Analysis of Texts in Ukrainian Language

Anton Mazurko and Tomasz Walkowiak$^{(\boxtimes)}$ (iD)

Faculty of Electronics, Wroclaw University of Science and Technology,
Wybrzeze Wyspianskiego 27, 50-370 Wroclaw, Poland
`tomasz.walkowiak@pwr.edu.pl`

Abstract. Stylometry analysis of Slavic-language texts is less explored challenging issue in direction of computational study. The aim of the paper is to develop and verify stylometric methods in a task of authorship, age, and gender of author recognition for literary texts in Ukrainian that could give a usable accuracy. Were prepared common stylistic features using the self-designed corpus. Different feature selection and classification methods were analyzed. Also, the objective of this examination is to analyze several stylometric variables to test its statistical importance with χ^2 selection.

Keywords: Stylometric · Ukrainian · Text analysis · Classification · Machine learning

1   Introduction

Stylometry is a research field that has been extensively investigated in the last century. Moreover, it based on the assumption that there is a similarity of styles between the texts in the same group. It relies mostly on machine analysis of some features generated from texts and attempts to define unique characteristics that can identify the uncovered class of the text [12]. However, most of the stylometric analysis concerns texts in English and the authorship attribution [7]. This study aims to compare stylometric methods for texts in the Ukrainian language. Achieving the aim of the work required: applying natural language processing, reviewing existing solutions in stylometry assignments, developing a corpus for testing, implementing the algorithm, testing the validity of features, and comparing the accuracy of classifiers. The potential of experiments in such a field is addressed to exploit new dependencies through the prepared corpus of selected documents. The paper is structured as follows. It starts with some information on the Ukrainian language. Afterward, stylometry is briefly over-viewed. A short review of the types of features used in stylometry depicted subsequently. It is followed by a description of used data sets, performed for classification tasks, feature generation methods and used classifiers. The summary is the last section of the current study.

© Springer Nature Switzerland AG 2020
L. Rutkowski et al. (Eds.): ICAISC 2020, LNAI 12416, pp. 220–230, 2020.
https://doi.org/10.1007/978-3-030-61534-5_20

2 Ukrainian Language

The Ukrainian language like other Slavic languages belongs to the group of Indo-European languages [16]. It is used by around 40 million people[1]. The most similar to the Ukrainian language are Belarusian - 84% of the common vocabulary, then Polish and Serbian (70% and 68% respectively), Russian - just 62%. Found on comparative studies of Slavic languages concerning phonetics and grammar Ukrainian language has from 22 to 29 features in common with the Belarusian, Czech, Slovak and Polish languages. However, with Russian only 11 [3]. Ukrainian alphabet contains letters based on Cyrillic [16]. It includes 33 letters. Also, special characters are used, such as an apostrophe('), a soft sign ь and the accent used above letters. The Ukrainian language is divided into parts of speech such as open classes (6), closed classes (3), exclamation (1). The following study [1] presents important information related to the frequency use of letters in Ukrainian. Can be seen the most used vowels: о, а, и, і, and e. The consonants are a bit more and they form several groups. The first one constructed from such letters as н, в, т, р, с. In one of relevant studies [2] related to cryptography, information about the average frequencies of letter bigrams were found. Generally can be distinguished such most common types of letter bigrams: consonant-consonant (ст, пр, нн), vowel-consonant (ов, ер, ан, ен, ом), consonant-vowel (на, но, ко), vowel-vowel (ія). Important features of any language are the frequencies of separate words. The top 10 most-used words are і, не, на, що, я, в, з, а, у, цей.

3 Stylometry

Stylometry is a collection of methods for statistical analysis of the similarity of the literary style between works, in terms of authorship, genre or others [8]. The second part of the name "metry" refers to the conversion, measuring the occurrence of individual letters, sets of them, sentence length, etc. The data is used to present the so-called individual style text units assigned to selected classes. You can not explain why the sentence was written in a particular way, for different thinking of each other for following simple reason: the techniques and rules used when writing is used at the level of the subconscious [8]. In stylometric studies and literature, the above phenomenon is referred to as "fingerprint". Over time, writing habits can change, a phenomenon known as "evolution of style". Style is likely an auxiliary element in the detection of that or other similarities between sets of texts, which can also be represented graphically, eg. with the help of Burrows Delta [10] or Principal Component Analysis (PCA) [9]. Using stylometry, also the problem of estimating the time interval in which the certain work has been published can be resolved. Such methods are based on changes in the use of words in texts over the centuries.

One of the most important studies associated with stylometry found in Ukrainian carried out by scientists contains developed methods for recognizing

---

[1] https://www.mustgo.com/worldlanguages/ukrainian/.

the style of the author based on linguometry, stylometry, glottochronology [4]. The main idea was to use an algorithm to compare two text fragments prepared earlier. Only significant words from the list were left out of each part: prepositions, conjunctions, particles whose total number was 71, while the remaining ones were cut out. Then, a table was created with the values of AF (absolute frequency), RF (relative frequency), RF in the reference table. Based on this data, correlation coefficients were obtained and the most similar fragments were uncovered.

Another article related to the analysis in Ukrainian presents a comparison of two texts written by Ivan Franko from 1884 and 1907 years [6]. The authors showed the evolution in the style of the author based on part of speech statistics.

4   Performed Stylometric Analysis

4.1   Data Sets and Classes

During the work with textual data, attention should be paid to coding Cyrillic characters - letters used in east Slavic languages, which was used to represent the Ukrainian language [16]. Coding is becoming less frequent other than Unicode (UTF-8), but some of the files found in CP1251 prepared to work with Cyrillic characters. Finally, a Ukrainian language corpus was built. An example of one of the filename is FRAN_31. Analyzing the length of all texts the shortest one contains less than 6200 characters. Then each text was divided by size: short (6,000 characters), medium-length (10,000 characters), long (20,000 characters) (Table 1).

Table 1. Statistical values of texts.

function	size (in characters)
Min	6189
Average	205344
Max	1317446

The next step is to divide each unit into smaller equal parts. The assumption was used to extract N parts from each text, where $1 \leq N \leq 5$. Additionally were used certain filters to clean unnecessary data from documents: a filter that removes stop words and filter blocked non-exception words.

Corpus of data often has a big impact on stylometric analysis, because training data is the main limitation. The study was conducted on a collection of Ukrainian author's novels. The data used for experiments are sourced from the 'УкрЛіб' digital library at ukrlib.com.ua. The originally prepared corpus consists of 90 texts written most in Ukrainian. Few of those novels were translated into the Ukrainian language. Consequently, the new three sets were obtained by dividing texts from the first set into parts of equal size. Set differs than with the number of texts and the size of each of them (see Table 2).

Table 2. Number of input texts and parts after dividing

Name	Number
# short fragments	403
# middle fragments	345
# long fragments	308

4.2 Features Used in Stylometry

Features are the numerical values that represent the properties of the analyzed textual unit. Researchers from the United States, precisely from Pace University [5] presented a big set that contains 228 features in their study of stylometry. Most of them (166) were syntax-based. Fewer numbers belong to the character category (49), remaining based on words.

Finally, a set of features has been prepared specially for Ukrainian. Some values that couldn't be just converted from English required additional work (Table 3).

Table 3. Examples of generated features based on last reminded study after preparation:

Name of group	Example
Character-based	Number of alphabetic characters
	Number of vowels
	Number of most frequent consonants (н,в,т,р,с)
Word-based	Number of 5-char words
	Dictionary richness (number of different words)
	Number of words with single occurrence
Syntax-based	Number of commas
	Number of verbs
	Number of noun-verb bigrams (NV)

Character-Based. Current group contains easiest-to-obtain values. But for start was required to find some statistical facts especially for the selected language. Without such information, it is impossible to know which are the most frequent vowels in usage. Also to know how to sort consonants from higher to lower in usage scale. Obtaining them doesn't require any complicate calculations except simple counting with regular expression.

Word-Based. Features related to full-words, contain the smallest part of total items. Only 13 values that are most related to the size of the word. Taken attention to the length of words from 1 to 7 characters. There is also a marker that responds to vocabulary richness, i.e. to count of unique tokens. Values in this category obtained only from counting.

Features Based on Syntax. Current is the bigger group of features in comparing to others. It contains markers that could be acquired with the usage of the special technique of NLP only. After mapping each word to certain part-of-speech, it was possible to count those items separately. Other values have been gotten thanks such preparation also. The bigger part of attributes requires to make research and found a set of most common words. It was an important factor because after that be able to approve the importance of certain markers in studied language.

4.3   Classification

Targets. Usually, after the counting process, the obtained numbers need to be assigned to some target value in the other words to a certain class or label. After prepared the relation of feature numbers to the label like examples with answers, the machine learning algorithm could be trained. Type of learning with answers is defined as supervised learning.

In the current study, three different classification tasks were analyzed gender, age-range and authorship. Selected elements are most common in the stylometry area. Gender divides into 2 parts. Age ranges of authors were customized to make parts more or less on the same level. Final set of ranges: 0–29, 30–35, 36–45, 46–55, 55–x. Authorship has no constant size of labels. This is caused by dividing text documents into different lengths. Labels proportion of short, middle and long fragments as 39/34/31. Despite different values experiments based on authorship were not skipped in this work (Table 4).

Table 4. Number of text units in each class

Category name	Size	Number of elements				
Gender	L	181	122	–	–	–
	M	216	145	–	–	–
	S	241	162	–	–	–
Age	L	55	41	68	72	67
	M	70	59	79	82	71
	S	80	77	85	89	72

Preprocessing. Before classification input data must be pre-processed. Usually, this is values which placed in columns of the array with data rows. It need to be done for the confidence of data integrity. Techniques that were used became widely-used Min-Max and Z-Score [14]. With their help, all values were in some ways modified.

In the case of Min-Max data are subject to change where output values belong to the closed range [0, 1]. Second function Z-Score used for place raw data around the origin of a coordinate system.

Dimension Reduction. As each feature in the sequence is a separate dimension scale of calculations could be increased. Then next step after normalization is decrease count of attributes with the usage of certain methods. There are multiple examples of that but selected were only χ^2 [13] and PCA [7].

χ^2 belongs to the statistical test group. This is a one-dimension selection based on finding the biggest impact of style-marker on the result. Then n elements with highest with best Chi-square scores are filtered from the rest an treated a new feature vector.

PCA is a linear transformation that projects data onto a set of orthogonal axes. Columns of the projection matrix are taken as eigenvectors of the covariance matrix of the features, where the eigenvectors are ordered by descending value of the corresponding eigenvalues. Then n elements co-responding to the highest eigenvalues are selected as a new (reduced) feature vector.

ML Algorithms. Results were acquired by following algorithms: Support Vector Machines(SVM), Neural Network (MLP), Decision Tree (DT), Naive Bayes (NB) [11]. SVM uses the concept of hyperplane and kernels to assign input elements to unknown classes. DT is the simplest classifier based on rules. CART is the most common decision tree variation, which is based on growing and cutting their nodes during the learning process. Third one algorithm based on counting and probabilities. Naive Bayes is a type of classic Bayes classifier, with the assumption that input data is not correlated. In fact, in reality, it could be false, but after all, it has high accuracy in distinguishing labels. NB is also faster in calculations if compare to the initial approach. Neural Network is the last used in the recognition algorithm, exactly the multilayer perceptron was used.

Results Estimation. After calculating results must be chosen way to estimate output values. Confusion matrix, k-fold cross-validation are examples of them. Selected was the last one. It based on a random separation of sets by training and testing in some proportions, where also training randomly divides into 50/50 internal training and validation sets. Learning and verification take place with these two parts. When the calculated accuracy error rate is acceptable then proceed to check the intelligent algorithm with the usage of the testing set. In the current iteration, the error rate is obtained one more time. Final accuracy is an average of intermediate results after k iterations. In all experiments a stratified variation of validation [18] with the number of splits k = 5 was used. In comparison to standard approach, it will take similar label distribution into consideration across each fold.

Tools. The most common founded NLP tool called NLTK doesn't support Ukrainian, therefore for POS tagging was selected UDPipe [17]. It is a generic powerful linguistic tool that is associated with UD (Universal Dependencies) framework that supports more then 70 languages, including Ukrainian. Moreover scikit-learn [15] was used for machine learning algorithms.

5 Results

5.1 Gender Classification

Among all tested classification algorithms the highest accuracy had MLP and SVM as 65.66% and 70.97% respectively. The used configuration was: Z-Score for normalization, kernel=rbf, and C=1.0 for SVM, and solver=sgd for MLP. After applying χ^2 dimension reduction the maximum accuracy obtained was enlarged to 83.75% (MLP) and 82.52% (SVM) with a number of features equal to 108 and 111 accordingly.

A list of the 10 most important attributes using χ^2 are presented in Table 5. It could be noticed that it consists of punctuation parameters and the most common consonants.

Table 5. 10 most important features obtained by χ^2 in gender task

Ranking	Feature index	Description
1	68	Number of quotes and double quotes (') and (")
2	65	Number of commas (,)
3	63	Number of eight punctuation symbols (.,?!;:'")
4	198	Number of sentences with count of words 1–10
5	67	Number of colons (:) and semicolons (;)
6	23	number of 3rd most common consonants (з,б,г,ч,х)
7	69	number of non-alphabetic non-punctuation and non-space characters
8	71	number of personal pronouns of 1st person
9	100	number of 5th most common word (я)
10	79	Number of conjunctions

5.2 Impact of Dimension Reduction Methods

Figure 1 shows the impact of the number of selected features on the classification accuracy for SVM classifier. In the category of gender recognition, the highest accuracy was 82.52% with χ^2 method and vector of 111 elements. A smaller

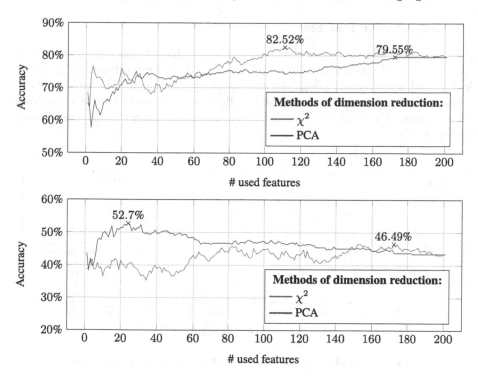

Fig. 1. Comparison of χ^2 and PCA in gender (a) and age (b) tasks.

improvement was reached by the PCA method, even with a bigger size of features. In case of age, the better results are for PCA. Interesting is the fact that with only 24 items with principal components with a difference more than 6%, accuracy is higher than 172 features from χ^2.

Authorship required a lot more features for both analyzed approaches. χ^2 was received the highest result from all experiments - 96.67%. Details are shown in Table 6.

Table 6. Accuracies archived with SVM classifier with longest text units, without any word-filter, using Z-Score

Category name	Reduction method	# features	Accuracy
Gender	χ^2	111	82.52%
	PCA	172	79.55%
Age	χ^2	172	46.49%
	PCA	24	52.70%
Authorship	χ^2	155	96.67%
	PCA	179	93.75%

5.3 Impact of a Text Size

Text size is an additional parameter that was studied. Results are presented in Fig. 2. The used configuration was: SVM, without stop-word filter, χ^2, Z-Score. As it could be expected, longer documents give better results. However, we can notice that two lines related to the middle and long sizes of texts sometimes are trimmed. The biggest difference in accuracy is between short and middle fragments sizes.

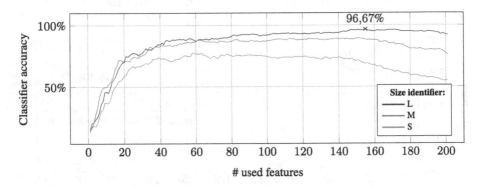

Fig. 2. Impact of fragments size on authorship recognition accuracy

5.4 Impact of Stop-Words Filter

In the next set of experiments, different stop-word filters were analyzed: T (all words together, i.e. no filtering), N (only non stop-words present), O (only stop-words present). The highest impact was detected in the authorship task, see Fig. 3. We can notice that filtering is decreasing the results.

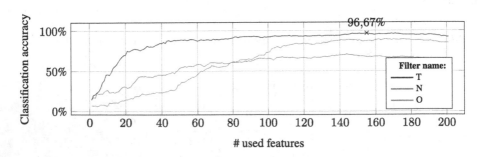

Fig. 3. Impact of stop-words filter on authorship recognition accuracy

5.5   Classification Tasks

Table 7 presents the best parameters for different classifiers in analysed recognition tasks. The best results were obtained by support vector machines, only in the category of age first place was taken by MLP, but second by SVM. An interesting fact that during distinguishing authorship Naive Bayes classifier had a second place, but in the other cases had one of the last positions.

Table 7. Best set of parameters in various classification tasks for selected approaches

Task	Size	Filter	Reduction	# features	Normalis.	Classifier	Accuracy
Gender	L	–	χ^2	111	Z-Score	SVM	82.52%
	L	–	PCA	18	Min-Max	DT	70.18%
	M	O	χ^2	51	–	NB	73.14%
	L	–	χ^2	108	Z-Score	MLP	83.75%
Age	L	–	PCA	24	Z-Score	SVM	52.70%
	L	O	χ^2	91	Z-Score	DT	43.11%
	L	–	χ^2	4	–	NB	41.50%
	L	O	χ^2	157	Z-Score	MLP	46.57%
Authorship	L	–	χ^2	155	Z-Score	SVM	96.67%
	L	–	χ^2	41	Z-Score	DT	57.92%
	M	O	χ^2	194	–	NB	90.80%
	L	–	PCA	27	Z-Score	MLP	79.58%

6   Summary

A large number of experiments were performed. The set of the most important style-markers was found and the impact of parameters like text length and present of stop-word filter was analysed. Selected classifiers and different tasks were compared among themselves. The best achieved accuracy in the authorship attribution task was 96.67% with Z-Score normalisation and SVM classifier.

References

1. Архипова, О.О. and Журавльов, В.М.: Частотний аналіз використання букв української мови. Радіоелектроніка. Інформатика. Управління. 2 (2009)
2. Барсуков, Є.С. and Сушко, С.О. and Фомичова, Л.Я.: Частоти повторюваності букв і біграм у відкритих текстах українською мовою. Науково-технічний журнал "Захист інформації" 12(3) (2010)
3. Клименко, Н.: День української мови: 10 фактів про мову, якою ми спілкуємось. https://inspired.com.ua/stream/10-facts-ukrainian-language (2015)
4. Bobyk, I., Lytvyn, V., Pukach, P., Uhryn, D., Vysotska, V.: Development of a method for the recognition of author's style in the Ukrainian language texts based on linguometry, stylemetry and glottochronology. Eastern Eur. J. Enterp. Technol. 4(2), 88 (2017)

5. Boga, M., et al.: Evaluation of a stylometry system on various length portions of books. In: Proceedings of Student-Faculty Research Day (2012)
6. Buk, S.: Quantitative comparison of texts (on the material of the 1884 and 1907 editions of the novel "Boa Constrictor" by ivan franko). Ukrainian Literary Studies, pp. 179–192 (2012)
7. Can, M.: Authorship attribution using principal component analysis and competitive neural networks. Math. Comput. Appl. **19**(1), 21–36 (2014)
8. Eder, M., Piasecki, M., Walkowiak, T.: Open stylometric system based on multi-level text analysis. Cogn. Stud.— Études Cognitives, 17 (2017)
9. Eder, M., Rybicki, J., Kestemont, M.: Stylometry with R: a package for computational text analysis. R J. **8**(1), 107–121 (2016)
10. Evert, S., Annidis, F., Pielström, S., Schöch, C.: Towards a better understanding of burrows's delta in literary authorship attribution. In: Proceedings of NAACL-HLT Fourth Workshop on Computational Linguistics for Literature, pp. 79–88 (2015)
11. Hastie, T.J., Tibshirani, R.J., Friedman, J.H.: The elements of statistical learning: data mining, inference, and prediction. Springer series in statistics, Springer, New York (2009), autres impressions : 2011 (corr.), 2013 (7e corr.)
12. Koppel, M., Schler, J., Argamon, S.: Computational methods in authorship attribution. J. Am. Soc. Inform. Sci. Technol. **60**(1), 9–26 (2009)
13. Liu H., Setiono R.: Chi2: feature selection and discretization of numeric attributes. In: Proceedings of 7th IEEE International Conference on Tools with Artificial Intelligence, Herndon, VA, USA, pp. 388–391 (1995)
14. Mohd Nawi, N., Atomi, W., Gillani, R., Muhammad, S.: The effect of data preprocessing on optimized training of artificial neural networks, vol. 11, June 2013
15. Pedregosa, F., et al.: Scikit-learn: machine learning in Python. J. Mach. Learn. Res. **12**, 2825–2830 (2011)
16. Aleksandra, S.: Zasady latynizacji języka ukraińskiego. http://ksng.gugik.gov.pl/pliki/latynizacja/ukrainski.pdf (2018)
17. Straka, M., Straková, J.: Tokenizing, pos tagging, lemmatizing and parsing UD 2.0 with UDpipe. In: Proceedings of the CoNLL 2017 Shared Task: Multilingual Parsing from Raw Text to Universal Dependencies, pp. 88–99. Association for Computational Linguistics, Vancouver, Canada (2017)
18. Zeng, X., Martinez, T.R.: Distribution-balanced stratified cross-validation for accuracy estimation. J. Exp. Theoret. Artif. Intell. **12**(1), 1–12 (2000). https://doi.org/10.1080/095281300146272

Newsminer: Enriched Multidimensional Corpus for Text-Based Applications

Sahudy Montenegro González[1]([⊠]), Tiemi C. Sakata[1], and Rodrigo Ramos Nogueira[2]

[1] Federal University of São Carlos, Sorocaba 18052-780, Brazil
sahudy@ufscar.br
[2] University of Coimbra, Coimbra, Portugal

Abstract. News websites are rich sources of terms that can compose a linguistic corpus. By introducing a corpus into a Data Warehousing environment, applications can take advantage of the flexibility that a multidimensional model and OLAP operations provide. This paper presents *Newsminer*, an exploratory OLAP framework, which offers a consistent and clean set of texts as a multidimensional corpus for consumption by external applications. The proposal integrates real-time gathering of news and semantic enrichment, which adds automatic annotations to the corpus. The multidimensional facet allows users and applications to obtain different corpora by selecting news categories, time slice, and term selection. We performed two experiments to evaluate the semantics enrichment and the feasibility of real-time during *Newsminer's* ETL.

Keywords: News websites · Multidimensional database · Text corpus · Semantic enrichment · News categorization · Exploratory OLAP

1 Introduction

The integration of Online Analytical Processing (OLAP) and Data Mining (DM) is a widely discussed topic of research. Proposals such as [1] provided architectural solutions for this integration. One of the advantages of the integration is to provide clean data for data mining applications to explore data cubes. As exposed by [2], the integration of OLAP and DM is not just for DM applications to take advantage of OLAP, Data Warehouse (DW), and Extract-Transform-Load (ETL) processes. DM techniques can be used to capture the semantics of data sources, such as discovering Data Warehouse elements and data hidden in the data sources. Hence, the process works both ways. These discoveries can be used later by DM applications to be explored as part of OLAP data cubes.

Exploratory OLAP is a concept presented in [3], where new data sources and new ways of structuring, integrating and querying data are explored. The exploration of new external data sources allows enhancing OLAP results for users' queries dynamically. In the case of web data sources, Data Warehouse environments have the challenge of working with unstructured data written in natural language. Data Warehouse technology has evolved to process, store, and retrieve such data [4–6]. In particular, news websites

© Springer Nature Switzerland AG 2020
L. Rutkowski et al. (Eds.): ICAISC 2020, LNAI 12416, pp. 231–242, 2020.
https://doi.org/10.1007/978-3-030-61534-5_21

are rich sources of texts, which can compose a linguistic corpus. A text corpus is a large, structured set of terms that can serve as a basis for data and text mining applications. If a Data Warehouse environment stores a corpus, applications can take advantage of the flexibility that a multidimensional model and OLAP operations provide [1]. These benefits are the navigation through the data, the selection of relevant data cubes, and data analysis at different levels of abstraction. OLAP operators enable aggregation, disaggregation, rotation, and filtering over any set of data.

However, there are challenges related to deal with web data. One is the exploitation of news sources in real-time or near real-time, since working on an up-to-date corpus may be necessary for some applications, such as E-business applications and stockbroking. A second challenge is the lack of completeness of the data. For example, by December 2016, of about 200.000 news stories collected by us, 27.5% has no defined category by the source. Moreover, automatic annotations are relevant elements for a set of texts [7]. Annotations make the corpus useful for linguistics and add semantics to the corpus. An example of an annotation is to label the speech part of each word (noun, adjective, verb, etc.). Another example is storing the category of each text in the set.

In this context, this paper presents *Newsminer*. This exploratory OLAP framework provides a consistent and clean set of data in the form of a multidimensional corpus for consumption by external applications and users. The corpus is a set of terms stored according to a multidimensional model. Multidimensionality allows exploring data sets at different levels of abstraction. The multidimensional feature enables users and applications to obtain diverse text corpus for a category depending on the time slice. When a dataset holds the temporal aspect, it makes sense to use a corpus of that same period to conduct data analytics because its terms are more likely the terms of the corpus.

Usually, researches have collected data to build a corpus from social media, news websites, etc. with a specific purpose. For example, the work described in [8] used Twitter to detect emerging drug terms. A corpus based on opinion articles and the comments posted in response to the articles in a Canadian newspaper was created by [9] for the analysis of online news comments. The authors of [10] created a corpus of news articles manually annotated for analyzing propaganda.

Therefore, we believe that not just DM applications could take advantage of our approach. Any application that captures analyzes and explores the semantics of text documents can benefit from *Newsminer*, such as those based on natural language processing and information extraction and retrieval. For example, our tool offers words association that can be useful to automatic semantic-aware multidimensional design, semantic disambiguation, redundancy reduction, among others.

This paper is organized into sections. Section 2 describes the *Newsminer's* architecture. Section 3 answers the research questions from experiments and discusses the results. The last section presents the final remarks about our proposal.

2   *Newsminer*: Architecture

The primary goal of *Newsminer* is to serve as a clean and organized, multidimensional data source for text analytics applications. The specific objectives are:

- to propose a multidimensional model that can store the set of texts and capture the temporal property of the news;
- to collect news articles in real-time;
- to add automatic semantic annotations, linguistic or otherwise, dynamically to the corpus;
- to make data available for multidimensional user and application queries;
- and finally, to propose an architecture that achieves the integration of previous objectives.

Figure 1 illustrates the proposed architecture for *Newsminer*. The architecture is organized into five layers: Data sources, ETL+, Corpus, OLAP, and Consumer/Requester. We can notice that the framework supports interactions and iterations because applications (in the layer Consumer/Requester) not only consume data cubes, they can request data that better fit their needs. Data sources are dynamic since they are news collected from websites. At first, we provide a corpus of English texts. As part of the ETL+, the crawler extracts data from digital newspapers to obtain the corpus online. The web crawler collects news in the English language from The Guardian, CNN, BBC, Fox News, NyPost, China Daily, and CNBC websites.

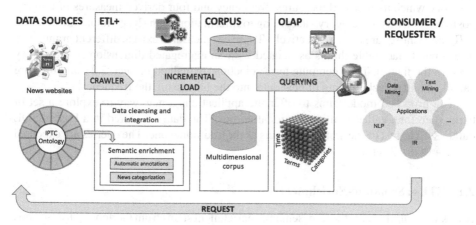

Fig. 1. Architecture of *Newsminer.*

Additionally, when possible, it extracts the news' category. Furthermore, if users or applications demand data not found in the database, the crawler is activated online to search for them. Once the data are locally stored, the texts are cleaned and transformed, removing special characters and stopwords. Next, the semantics-enrichment module discovers semantics from data relations and metadata. All data and new elements are loaded into the DW and available for querying by users and applications.

Newsminer's multidimensional database consolidates and stores news texts that have been collected and transformed. It provides the resources to explore and analyze the news from different perspectives and to carry out multidimensional queries. Figure 2 illustrates two data cubes in the x-DFM (Extended Dimensional Fact Model) graphical notation [11], which represent fact tables at different levels of granularity.

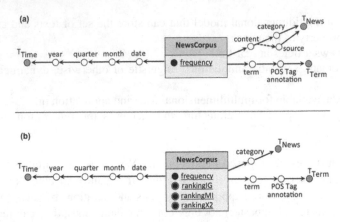

Fig. 2. *Newsminer's* multidimensional model.

The first diagram in Fig. 2(a) shows the structure of the cube at the most granular level. Each node represents a level in the hierarchy (from the most granular level to the most aggregate level (all). The second diagram, Fig. 2(b), depicts the cube of relevant terms by category which includes all measures: frequency and four derived measures of ranking positions of terms by category - according to Information Gain (IG), Mutual Information (MI), and Chi-square (X^2), respectively. These last measures exist at different granularity in a separate fact table that is associated with an aggregated dimension (see category node in the figure). They compute term selection (explained in Sect. 2.2), and they are calculated after each loading of new data into the base using the frequency.

The proposed model aims to offer the applications a new way to explore a set of texts, therefore, called multidimensional corpus. The data are stored in a PostgreSQL database. The rest of the architecture acts as the traditional one. The queries are executed using a ROLAP server.

2.1 ETL+: Semantic-Enrichment

In this work, the basis of the term semantic enrichment stems from the approach described in [2] and [12]. The authors introduced a data enrichment layer responsible for detecting new structural elements using data mining and other techniques. In this case, the discovered elements can be metrics, dimensions, or hierarchical levels and can represent static or dynamic properties of the data.

Our proposal for a semantic enrichment module adds semantic properties to the data collected. Initially, two types were defined: the news category and the POS-Tagging annotation for each term of the texts. The POS-Tagging annotation recognizes the morphological class of each term.

As already mentioned, about 27.5% of the news has no defined category by the source. For this reason, the categorization becomes a target of semantic enrichment. The 17 categories of the IPTC (International Press Telecommunications Council) ontology (https://iptc.org/) defined the classes for the news. To discover the news category, five classification methods, generally used in the literature, were evaluated. The best method is used at the ETL stage, offering categorized texts for applications and users.

2.2 How Can Applications Use *Newsminer?*

Multidimensional queries can be performed using the web prototype available at http://lasid.sor.ufscar.br/newsminer/ or via programming, through an API. The purpose is to explore and navigate the data contained in the Data Warehouse, allowing flexible selection of some or all of the data and analysis of the data at different levels of abstraction. Some types of multidimensional queries have been predefined. The types of queries are:

- *Ranking of terms*: returns the terms that occur the most throughout the bank or in a specific category. For example, in the Politics category, in the period between January 2015 and December 2016, the two highest occurrence terms were "Clinton" and "Trump", the surnames of the candidates for the presidency of the United States in the selected period.
- *Association between terms*: given a term, returns the words that occurred the most throughout the database or in a particular category. For example, in the Economy, Business and Finance category, the three terms that are most associated with "dollar" are "economy", "market", and "investors".
- *Categorization of texts*: given an input text, this query returns its category. For example, given the text "Brazilian President Michel Temer is struggling with a loss in the political and in the economy", the query returns that the phrase belongs to the Politics category.
- *Textual search*: this query has as input a set of terms and returns the Top-K texts where these terms appear together.
- *Data cube*: to turn flexible user and application queries, *Newsminer* offers an exploratory query, which contains all attributes in the multidimensional model. With this query, the user easily retrieves all data, explores the multidimensionality, and applies filters, generating any cube from the database.

We developed a RESTful API that allows applications requesting and consuming data using the same queries above. *Newsminer's* API is available at http://lasid.sor.ufscar.br/newsminer/api.

Text analytics applications and machine learning algorithms need to perform dimensionality reduction. One of the techniques for achieving dimension reduction is term selection based on term frequency [13]. Thus, applications can obtain the corpus through terms that reflect their importance for each category. Applications can choose which measure to use to request the data via interface or API. Table 1 shows the Top-5 terms in the Sports category without and with term selection. The data cube illustrated in Fig. 2(b) provides this case scenario.

Table 1. Case scenario for the Sports category.

Ranking	Frequency	Information gain	X2	Mutual information
1	team	smartphones	championship	hippy
2	game	bitcoin	score	copied
3	season	cells	squad	heist
4	league	laptop	injury	store
5	time	cia	clubs	branson

3 Experiments

We performed some experiments to answer two research questions: (1) *is the semantics enrichment during the ETL+ process, in particular, the automatic categorization of news, indeed enriching the dataset?* (2) *is Newsminer's ETL+ process possible in real-time?* To perform the experiments, we used an X3430 Tower Server with Intel Xeon X3430 processor (four cores - 2.4 GHz) and 8 GB of RAM.

3.1 Datasets

We use two datasets to validate the first experiment: (1) the *NewsMinerCollection* [14], a dataset of news collected and cleaned; (2) the 20 Newsgroups dataset, a collection of public data, commonly used in scientific work for text classification [15].

The *NewsMinerCollection* was built by collecting news from 1990 until 2016 by the web crawler. This dataset contains 7000 news items equally distributed among the seven categories: Art, Culture and Entertainment, Sport, Lifestyle and Leisure, Politics, Economy, Business and Finance, Environmental Issues and Science and Technology. The *NewsMinerCollection* is ready to be used by other applications, and it is one of the contributions of this paper.

The 20 NewsGroups dataset contains approximately 20,000 news documents, partitioned (nearly) across 20 different categories. We use this dataset to test the classification methods since it is not balanced; it has other categories and also contains news. The 20 NewsGroups dataset is available at http://qwone.com/~jason/20Newsgroups/.

3.2 Experiment 1: Categorization of News

This experiment is focused on answering the first research question. We are concerned about finding the best transformation to be applied to the news with the best classification method to categorize the news according to the IPTC ontology.

We applied four transformation settings to the original dataset to evaluate which one obtains the best result with the classification methods:

1. full text (FT) – no transformation (all words in the news);
2. stopwords cleansing (SW) – all words except stopwords;

3. substantive (NN) – only nouns; and
4. keyphrases (KP) – nouns and keyphrases.

The four datasets are available as part of the *NewsMinerCollection* at http://lasid. sor.ufscar.br/newsminer/datasets/. We used the baseline methods for text classification because they perform online and incremental learning: Perceptron Neural Network, Naïve Bayes Multinominal (NBM), Bernoulli (NBB), Stochastic Gradient Descent (SGD) and Rocchio. Although the Support Vector Machine (SVM) classifier achieves the best performance for various text classification tasks, it is not suitable for real-time systems. A grid search technique adjusted the parameter values of each classification method. We use the implementations of these algorithms from the Scikit-learn library [16] to obtain the results.

3.2.1 Results

We carried out this study using the following experiment protocol. Our experiments were diligently designed to ensure statistically sound results. In this way, we performed 10-fold cross-validation for each method and dataset. The performance is evaluated based on the well-known machine learning evaluation metric F-Measure. We present the average F-measure obtained by each classifier for each dataset in 10 runs. Table 2 shows the results achieved by each classifier for the *NewsMinerCollection*.

Table 2. Results achieved by the classifiers for the *NewsMinerCollection* for each transformation setting.

	Perceptron	NBM	NBB	SGD	Rocchio
FT	0.91±0.0021	0.89±0.0011	0.89±0.0013	0.85±0.0052	0.85±0.0009
SW	0.92±0.0019	0.91±0,0006	0.92±0.0015	0.88±0.0037	0.86±0.0004
NN	0.91±0.0017	0.91±0.0010	0.9±0.0010	0.87±0.0030	0.85±0.0007
KP	0.91±0.0016	0.90±0.0010	0.88±0.0010	0.86±0.0046	0.87±0.0004

The results indicate that, among all evaluated approaches, Perceptron attained the best performance for the *NewsMinerCollection*. Also, NBM and NBB showed a good performance similar to Perceptron. To support our claims, we also performed a statistical analysis of the results. For that, we used the Friedman test [17] and 95% confidence interval. The null hypothesis, in this case, states that all methods have similar performances. The analysis suggests that there is no difference between Perceptron, NBM, and NBB methods. It also indicates that there is a significant statistical difference between these methods and the SGD and Rocchio. Thus, the null hypothesis is rejected.

We also investigated the best transformation setting on the *NewsMinerCollection,* analyzing all ten runs for each transformation and method. For reasons of space and clarity, we show in Table 3, the results of the best classification methods (Perceptron, NBM, and NBB). Note that the bold values indicate the best scores.

We performed a statistical analysis based on the average ranking of each classification method illustrated in Table 3. For that, we used the paired T-test [18], with a

Table 3. F-measure achieved by each run (1 to 10) of each transformation setting (FT, SW, NN, KP) using the best classification methods (Perceptron, NBM, and NBB) for the *NewsMinerCollection*.

Perceptron				NBM				NBB			
FT	SW	NN	KP	FT	SW	NN	KP	FT	SW	NN	KP
0.92	**0.92**	0.91	0.91	0.89	0.91	0.91	0.90	0.89	0.92	0.89	0.88
0.92	**0.92**	0.91	0.91	0.89	0.91	0.91	0.90	0.89	0.92	0.90	0.88
0.91	**0.92**	0.91	0.91	0.89	0.91	0.91	0.90	0.89	0.92	0.90	0.88
0.91	**0.93**	0.91	0.91	0.89	0.91	0.91	0.90	0.89	0.92	0.90	0.88
0.91	**0.92**	0.91	0.91	0.90	0.91	0.91	0.90	0.89	0.91	0.89	0.88
0.91	**0.92**	0.91	0.91	0.89	0.91	0.91	0.90	0.89	0.91	0.90	0.88
0.91	**0.92**	0.91	0.91	0.89	0.91	0.91	0.90	0.89	0.92	0.90	0.88
0.92	**0.92**	0.91	0.91	0.89	0.91	0.91	0.90	0.89	0.92	0.89	0.88
0.91	**0.92**	0.91	0.91	0.89	0.91	0.91	0.90	0.89	0.92	0.89	0.88
0.91	**0.92**	0.91	0.91	0.89	0.91	0.91	0.90	0.89	0.92	0.89	0.88

confidence interval $= 95\%$. The analysis suggests that there is a significant statistical difference between Perceptron with the SW transformation setting and the other evaluated approaches.

We run the same experiment to the 20 NewsGroups dataset. Table 4 shows the results achieved by each classifier. Note that we highlighted in bold the best outcome for each method. The best result was also performed by the Perceptron method with the SW transformation setting.

Table 4. Results achieved by the evaluated classification methods for the 20 NewsGroups dataset.

	Perceptron	NBB	NBM	SGD	Rocchio
FT	0.83±0.0021	0.73±0.0011	**0.77**±0.0011	0.77±0.0052	0.75±0.0009
SW	**0.844**±0.0019	0.737±0.0006	0.76±0.0006	**0.80**±0.0037	**0.79**±0.0004
NN	0.81±0.0017	**0.74**±0.0009	0.76±0.0010	0.77±0.0030	0.77±0.0007
KP	0.836±0.0016	0.73±0.0010	0.76±0.0010	0.77±0.0046	0.78±0.0004

The statistical results are consistent with the individual best results. So, we conclude that it is possible to enrich the dataset during the ETL process using the Perceptron classifier method with SW transformation.

Furthermore, we collected the medians of the execution times for the classifier after ten runs. The processing time was computed from the runtime of the training phase plus the execution time of the testing phase, for all 7.000 news. Perceptron classifier obtained a good execution time of 13 min. It also performs online learning, updating the prediction model incrementally. This property is of great importance for categorizing news in real-time.

The categorization of news is a task already accomplished by several works of the literature. The experiments described in [19] used SVM over several news structures for online news. The best score for the F-measure reaches to 81.7%. In [20] is presented experiments using Naïve Bayes, SVM, and artificial neural networks classifiers in conjunction with feature extraction and selection for Azerbaijani news articles, reaching almost 89% of accuracy.

3.3   Experiment 2: Is ETL in Real-Time Possible?

According to [21, 22], the data acquisition process introduces the highest data latency. Therefore, this experiment aims to verify if it is possible to execute the ETL + process in real-time (or close to real-time). Therefore, applications can collect new news articles, via API, and obtain a set of current and up-to-date texts.

Knowledge discovery techniques have been employed to semantically enrich data and metadata in Data Warehouse environments during the ETL process. Some papers that use this approach are described in [2, 12, 23, 24].

For this experiment, we used the 7,000 URLs of the news articles used in Experiment 1 (*NewsMinerCollection*). We collect three execution times: web crawler runtime, preprocessing time, and loading time. The preprocessing time consists of the execution time of the cleansing and transformation steps, removing stopwords, and calculating the frequency of terms. For each URL, we computed the median time of 10 runs.

3.3.1   Results

Table 5 illustrates the results obtained during the ETL+ process. The first column indicates the number of news articles collected ($|D|$), and the others are web crawler's collection time (WC), preprocessing time (PT), and loading time (LT).

Table 5. Median time (*milliseconds*) of *Newsminer's* extraction, transformation, and loading per news article.

$|D|$	WC (ms)	PT (ms)	LT (ms)	Total (ms)
100	1926	092	110	2128
200	1953	115	103	2170
300	2007	127	111	2245
400	1984	111	111	2206
500	2015	129	111	2255
600	1964	126	113	2203
700	1961	111	111	2184
800	1954	115	110	2179
900	1954	112	110	2176
1000	2006	113	113	2231
2000	1986	113	110	2209
3000	1976	098	110	2184
4000	1965	118	116	2199
5000	1967	106	106	2179
6000	1917	107	108	2131
7000	1810	111	109	2030

The execution times were collected for different subsets of news articles, whose size increase gradually, first in intervals of 100 and then in intervals of 1.000 news articles. The average runtime, regardless of the volume collected, is 2 s per article for our hardware.

The average number of articles (between stories and videos) that an American newspaper publishes per day is 500 [25]. *Newsminer* currently works over seven sources. This roughly means that daily we could process 3.500 news reports. The processing time is 117 min (3.500 news in almost 2 h or 17 min to process 500 news articles).

If we considered that the processing time of the categorization for all the articles in the dataset is 13 min, we could say that the overall execution time of the ETL+ is at most 246 min (4 h and 10 min). As the Perceptron classifier supports online learning, news articles are incorporated into the prediction model incrementally, and they don't have to be processed every time, so it is possible that the execution time does not exceed 13 min.

These results need to be improved but are compatible with some of the applications presented in [21, 22]. However, applications can collect daily news in real-time, and thus obtain a set of current and up-to-date texts. To improve this time, we can deal with techniques of distributed data processing or parallelism.

4 Conclusions and Future Work

Online news is a significant data source for text analytics applications. In this study, we have described a general framework for building a multidimensional text corpus. We can automatically collect online news by activating the crawler. Our experimental study answered the research questions.

This study has made several contributions. First, we proposed a general framework for building a multidimensional corpus from news websites. With such a framework, we can automatically gather news from the web and organize it into different categories, thus providing authentic and up-to-date information to applications and users. Therefore, we believe such a unique framework is relevant and advantageous to researchers from these fields. Second, we provided a new consistent and clean dataset of 7000 news in English, the *NewsMinerCollection*, categorized for future research. Third, we examined five high-performance algorithms for four dataset variations to identify which machine learning algorithm yields better classification results upon what kind of transformation works best for classifying online news articles. Also, we confirmed the viability of enriching the corpus by classifying online news automatically. Thus, semantic enrichment in the ETL process fulfills the news category based on the IPTC ontology. The category of the news reflects directly on relationships between terms. For last, in addition to category discovery, we provided to applications with the automatic extraction of semantic annotations such as the part of speech - POS-tagging - to each term. Besides, we integrated Information Theory measures that are commonly used in conjunction with text mining research to reduce dimensionality using term selection. Initially, we implemented Information Gain, Mutual Information, and Chi-square measures.

The multidimensional corpus based on the news allows being querying by time, categories, and terms. It is available as cubes of data via web and API for consumption by the applications and users. We only focus on English news sources. However, future research could easily extend to incorporate multilingual processing to deal with news sources in other languages. Also, we intend to enhance news categorization to add classification based on IPTC's subcategories and multi-classes (more than one category or subcategory label per news article). To improve the ETL's runtime, we envision techniques of distributed data processing or parallelism.

Acknowledgments. This work is a result of the financial support provided by FAPESP (São Paulo Research Foundation, Brazil), grant number 2011/12115-1. The authors acknowledge the CAPES' graduate program.

References

1. Han, J., Kamber, M., Pei, J.: Data Mining: Concepts and Techniques, San Francisco. Morgan Kaufmann Publishers Inc., California (2011)
2. Mansmann, S., Rehman, N.U., Weiler, A., Scholl, M.H.: Discovering OLAP dimensions in semi-structured data. Inf. Syst. **44**, 120–133 (2014)
3. Abello, A.: Using semantic web technologies for exploratory OLAP: a survey. IEEE Trans. Knowl. Data Eng. **27**(2), 571–588 (2015)
4. Berbel, T.R.L., González, S.M.: How to help end users to get better decisions? Personalizing OLAP aggregation queries through semantic recommendation of text documents. Int. J. Bus. Intell. Data Min. **10**(1), 1–18 (2015)
5. Mendoza, M., Alegría, E., Maca, M., Cobos, C., León, E.: Multidimensional analysis model for a document warehouse that includes textual measures. Decis. Support Syst. **72**(1), 44–59 (2015)
6. Gallinucci, E., Golfarelli, M., Rizzi, S., Abelló, A., Romero, O.: Interactive multidimensional modeling of linked data for exploratory OLAP. Inf. Syst. **77**, 86–104 (2018)
7. Hovy, E., Lavid, J.: Towards a 'science' of corpus annotation: a new methodological challenge for corpus linguistics. Int. J. Transl. **22**(1), 13–36 (2010)
8. Simpson, S.S., Adams, N., Brugman, C.M., Conners, T.J.: Detecting novel and emerging drug terms using natural language processing: a social media corpus study. JMIR Public Health Surveill. **4**(1), e2 (2018)
9. Kolhatkar, V., Wu, H., Cavasso, L., Francis, E., Shukla, K., Taboada, M.: The SFU opinion and comments corpus: a corpus for the analysis of online news comments. Corpus Pragmatics **4**(2), 155–190 (2019). https://doi.org/10.1007/s41701-019-00065-w
10. Da San Martino, G., Yu, S., Barrón-cedeño, A., Petrov, R., Nakov, P.: Fine-grained analysis of propaganda in news article. In: Proceedings of the 2019 Conference on Empirical Methods in Natural Language Processing and the 9th International Joint Conference on Natural Language Processing (EMNLP-IJCNLP), Hong Kong, China, pp. 5636–5646 (2019)
11. Mansmann, S.: Extending the multidimensional data model to handle complex data. J. Comput. Sci. Eng. **1**(2), 125–160 (2007)
12. Rehman, N.U., Mansmann, S., Weiler, A., Scholl, M.H.: Building a data warehouse for Twitter stream exploration. In: IEEE/ACM International Conference on Advances in Social Networks Analysis and Mining, Istanbul, pp. 1341–1348 (2012)
13. Sebastiani, F.: Machine learning in automated text categorization. ACM Comput. Surv. **34**(1), 1–47 (2002)
14. Sakata, T.C., Nogueira, R., González, S.M.: NewsMinerCollection (2017). http://dx.doi.org/10.17632/9j47dhd4kx.2

15. Lang, K.: Newsweeder: Learning to Filter Netnews. In: Proceedings of the 12th International Conference on Machine Learning, Tahoe City, California, pp. 331–339 (1995)
16. Pedregosa, F.: Scikit-learn: machine learning in Python. J. Mach. Learn. Res. **12**, 2825–2830 (2011)
17. Demsar, J.: Statistical comparisons of classifiers over multiple data sets. J. Mach. Learn. Res. **7**, 1–30 (2006)
18. Nadeau, C., Bengio, Y.: Inference for the generalization error. Mach. Learn. **52**, 239–281 (2003)
19. Dai, Z., Taneja, H., Huang, R.: Fine-grained structure-based news genre categorization. In: Proceedings of the Workshop on Events and Stories in the News, Santa Fe, USA, pp. 61–67 (2018)
20. Suleymano, U., Rustamov, S.: Automated news categorization using machine learning methods. In: IOP Conference Series: Materials Science and Engineering, vol. 459, Aegean International Textile and Advanced Engineering Conference (AITAE 2018), Lesvos, Greece (2018)
21. Vaisman, A., Zimányi, E.: Data warehouses: Next challenges, Business Intelligence, Vols. First European Business Intelligence Summer School, pp. 1–26 (2012)
22. Bouaziz, S., Nabli, A., Gargouri, F.: From traditional data warehouse to real time data warehouse. In: Madureira, A.M., Abraham, A., Gamboa, D., Novais, P. (eds.) ISDA 2016. AISC, vol. 557, pp. 467–477. Springer, Cham (2017). https://doi.org/10.1007/978-3-319-53480-0_46
23. Wagner, R., de Macedo, J.A.F., Raffaetà, A., Renso, C., Roncato, A., Trasarti, R.: Mob-warehouse: a semantic approach for mobility analysis with a trajectory data warehouse. In: Parsons, J., Chiu, D. (eds.) ER 2013. LNCS, vol. 8697, pp. 127–136. Springer, Cham (2014). https://doi.org/10.1007/978-3-319-14139-8_15
24. Victor, S., Rex, M.M.X.: Analytical implementation of web structure mining using data analysis in educational domain. Int. J. Appl. Eng. Res. **11**(4), 2552–2556 (2016)
25. Meyer, R.: How many stories of newspapers publish per day?, 26 May 2016. https://www.theatlantic.com/technology/archive/2016/05/how-many-stories-do-newspapers-publish-per-day/483845/. Accessed 23 Oct 2019

Detecting Causalities in Production Environments Using Time Lag Identification with Cross-Correlation in Production State Time Series

Dirk Saller[1], Bora I. Kumova[1($\boxtimes$)], and Christoph Hennebold[2]

[1] Baden-Württemberg Cooperative State University, Mosbach, Germany
{dirk.saller,bora.kumova}@mosbach.dhbw.de
[2] Fraunhofer Institute for Manufacturing Engineering and Automation IPA, Stuttgart, Germany
christoph.hennebold@ipa.fraunhofer.de

Abstract. One objective of smart manufacturing is to resolve complex causalities of production processes, in order to minimize machine idle times. We introduce a methodology for mining from raw state time series of machines, possible causal relations between the machines of a given production environment. By applying the similarity measure cross-correlation on binary production state time series of two machines pairwise, we obtain a probability distribution, whose characteristic properties imply possible causal orderings of the two machines. In case of complex causalities, the measure may be applied to all possible machines pairwise, in order to extract a complete web of statistically significant causalities, without any prior context information of the environment. In this paper, we analyze the characteristic properties of such probability distributions and postulate four hypotheses, which constitute the steps of our methodology. Furthermore, we discuss the stochastic and temporal conditions that are necessary for the transitive propagation of causal states.

Keywords: Production process optimization · Time lag identification · Nominal-valued time series · Cross-correlation · Knowledge mining

1 Introduction

In industrial production, almost all automated or semi-automated production processes produce a variety of digital data that are stored in some kind of database. In particular, if a production process contains several steps performed by independent machines, the current state of each machine can be measured at any time. Measured machine data have often common economic constraints, coming from standard management and controlling needs, such as cost control or operating accounting, and are handled quite differently by varying companies. Although learning from data is a core feature of industrial internet

C. Hennebold—This work was partially supported by the Ministry of Economic Affairs of the state Baden-Württemberg (Center for Cyber Cognitive Intelligence (CCI) – Grant No. 017-192996).

© Springer Nature Switzerland AG 2020
L. Rutkowski et al. (Eds.): ICAISC 2020, LNAI 12416, pp. 243–252, 2020.
https://doi.org/10.1007/978-3-030-61534-5_22

of things (IIoT), particularly in subsystems like smart Manufacturing Execution Systems (MES) [1, 3, 6, 7], applications that efficiently minimize idle times in production processes have not yet been explored sufficiently in the literature.

Smart manufacturing utilizes data analytics to refine complicated production processes and minimize machine idle times [9]. Manufacturing machines can be highly interconnected und continuously report operation states in various numbers of state type messages. The idle state or any partial operation state of a machine of a production line can propagate through the line and cause further disturbance. Predicting such machine operations within complex production environments, out of a series of various state type messages, is a challenging task that can be tackled efficiently only with statistical approaches. The problem for two machines can be decomposed into a correlation analysis of two time series, with the objective to learn time lags, in order to predict such lags afterwards in similar series.

For instance in IT system management, estimation algorithms were proposed with iterative expectation maximization on interleaved binarized series of vital IT system signals that are fluctuating and noisy [12]. For detecting irregularities in psychophysiological time series, windowed cross-correlation [8] was combined with peak picking, where cross-correlation was normalized, i.e. transformed into a time-dependent Pearson correlation [13]. We have adopted this approach for time series in manufacturing processes, however without normalization. For predicting time lags in series of database alerts with disk capacity alerts, a non-stochastic algorithm with sorted time lag lists is proposed, in order to resolve interleaved temporal lag dependencies [14]. Linear programming approximation is proposed with average best time lag identification performance in terms of mean deviation and squared deviation and tested for virus scanning [15, 16].

Different objectives for improving similarity measures are persuit in the literature. For instance performance, such that linear time and space complexities can be approximated [4], or revealing misleading measurements for some cases of the data series [2], or measuring the accuracy of cross-correlation [5].

In this paper we consider datasets provided by two industrial companies of different production branches. We derive hypotheses only from the given data, without any additional expert or domain knowledge. In general, the raw production state time series (PSTS) contains following two types of information: (i) the time series of state values of all machines of several weeks up to several years, and (ii) the context meaning of state values within the respective company.

Our methodology is inspired by Cross-Industry Standard Process for Data Mining (CRISP-DM) [10, 11]. The paper is a proof of concept in terms of applying a standard correlation algorithm to stochastic processes of given PSTS, in order to compute causal relationships between the machines. We elaborate several hypotheses that support our methodology.

The originality of our work is due to the combination of following steps:

(i)   Visual analysis of PSTS on possible causal relations in time.
(ii) Binarization of the multivariate series and application of cross-correlation.
(iii) Formulation of hypotheses on structural and algebraic properties of the cross-correlated results.

The remainder of the paper is structured as follows: In Sect. 2 we analyze nominal valued time series as 2-dimensional graphs and discuss their meaning, as well as define a possible way of visualization. By doing so, we get a first idea on hypotheses of machine state change patterns and their possible meaning. Additionally, we discuss automated methods for clustering or categorizing these graphs.

In Sect. 2 we simplify the problem in order to apply a simple computational method for pattern recognition and categorization of machines. We transform the company-dependent multivariate PSTS into a binarized form with the states 0 = 'regular operation' and 1 = 'any other state'. This binarization is applied to both company-specific PSTS under investigation, in order to make them comparable with each other. We further transform the PSTS to an equal time resolution and equal time steps for all machines, prior calculating cross-correlations.

In Sect. 3 we evaluate the results of pairwise cross-correlated machines of a production environment, as well as discuss and define the features of the resulting diagrams. This leads us to the notion of peak-correlated machines. After performing tests concerning the robustness and reproducibility of the characteristic diagrams, we discuss their algebraic properties, which result from the cross-correlations. Finally, we summarize and discuss our results and point to open questions.

2   Visual Analysis of PSTS

2.1   Raw PSTS and Data Preprocessing

Modern production machines report state data that is utilized for production optimization. Usually, such state data is collected in form of time series and often stored together with additional information in databases or structured files. Enterprise Resource Planning (ERP) and Manufacturing Execution Systems (MES) post-process such data, in order to extract relevant information for controlling or production planning. However the original unprocessed PSTS may encode technical as well as process information throughout their historic recording, which we pre-process as follows.

For further investigation, we filter three types of data items from the raw PSTS, namely: A machine identifier (machine_id), an absolute time (time_stamp) and a state category (state_nr). We convert the time_stamp into a standardized form. The values of machine_id and state_nr depend on the specific company and solely have nominal meaning. Out of the unordered raw PSTS, we collect all time_stamps and state_nr for each machine. Hence, we get a multivariate time series for each machine. Any further data, such as affiliation of a machine to a production line is discarded. For visual analysis we use initially a time window of 24 h. If a finer resolution is required, then we may zoom in to window sizes as small as 30 min.

In our third step of preprocessing, we binarize the state categories. This is a crucial step for the methodology to be applicable to different companies and state category models. It is both, a generalization and a simplification. We binarize the multivariate state_nr, such that states are categorized into either 0 = 'on' or 1 = 'of'.

Obviously, reducing all states other than 0 to 1, leads to loss of information. But, we will demonstrate below that this information will be sufficient for detecting possible causalities. As long as a binarization can be found for a multivariate state category, our approach can be applied to any binarized state analysis. By binarizing the data, we get rid of multivariate states. That facilitates the algorithms and the methodology.

In Sect. 2.2, we visualize the preprocessed time series in a form that leads us to some hypotheses, which we investigate more deeply below. The intermediate visualizations are a touchstone for the discovery of similar patterns within the used PSTS. For instance, we evaluate the results from steps 1 and 2, where we have filtered the data in order to obtain for each machine, a multivariate nominal time series.

2.2 Visualization of PSTS

In our examples, the integer numbers that denote the state categories do not occur in successive order. For example, in case of company A, we have successive values in the interval [1, 13], others in the range of [100, 113] or even values like 20000 or 30000. In the ranges [13, 100], [113, 9000] or [10021, 20000] no values occur at all. In order to facilitate the visual analysis, we plot the intervals separately on the ordinate. To such a plot in Fig. 1 we will refer to as compact plot. All our initial analyses begins with the window size of 24 h on the abscissa.

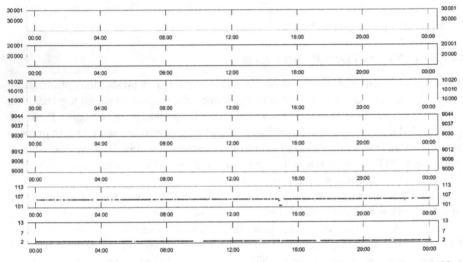

Fig. 1. Compact plot of PSTS with 7 state value ranges on ordinate. On abscissa 1 day (86400 s) of machine 3 of production environment P1 of company A on date 2015/05/19.

Figure 2 depicts the PSTS of 3 out of 20 machines of a production environment. Here the lowest line of each machine represents the 'regular operation' state with value '2' and looks like an almost continuous series that is interrupted by a few gaps. We denominate this line as *zero-line*. It is interrupted many more times by various non-regular states, which are found mostly inside the first and second vertical state ranges and particularly clustered right above the gaps of the zero-line. The fact that not all interruption states can be seen in the zero-line, is due to the print resolution. Note that the machine state is

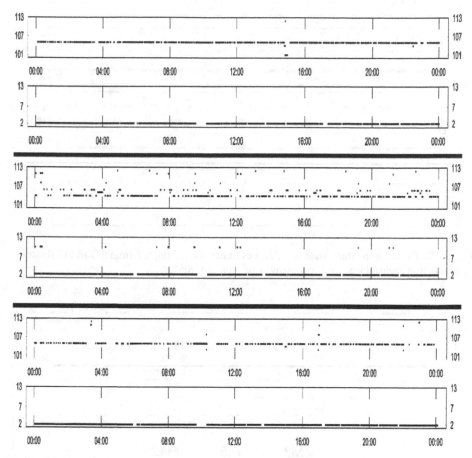

Fig. 2. PSTS with non-empty state value ranges of machines 3 (top), 5 (middle) and 12 (bottom) of production environment P1 of company A on date 2015/05/19.

plotted for a 24 h time window. Depending on the resolutions it is possible to identify similarities and dissimilarities, which leads us to a first hypothesis.

Hypothesis 1
If a PSTS of a production environment is clustered by similar interruption patterns on the zero-line, then the clusters may indicate causalities.

In order to support hypothesis 1, we inspect the PSTS of the same machine group on the preceding day. Although similar patterns are not directly recognizable in Fig. 3, we do observe certain patterns by zooming in with smaller time windows in Fig. 4[1].

In Fig. 4 we assume that in each time window (left and right columns), gaps on the zero-line of machine 3 propagate after some delay on the zero-line of machine 5, and

---
[1] We assume that the production environment does not change between different time windows. Otherwise possible causal relations in production processes and material flows cannot be verified throughout successive time windows.

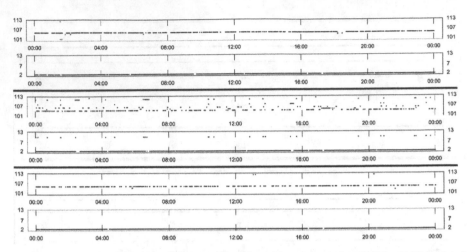

Fig. 3. PSTS with non-empty state value ranges of machines 3 (top), 5 (middle) and 12 (bottom) of production environment P1 of company A on date 2015/05/18.

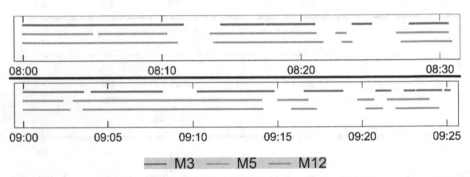

Fig. 4. Zero-lines in two different time windows of approximately 30 min each of production environment P1 of company A on date 2015/05/18.

with further delay on to machine 12. Note that the visual analysis of these two cases of 30 min windows, does not reveal a clear gap propagations, but provides strong visual indications. Additionally, the similarities from machine 5 and 12 seem to overlap with some ad-hoc interruptions of each machine[2]. Nevertheless, we will demonstrate below that cross-correlation within the 24 h windows delivers statistical significance for gap propagation and even for transitive gap propagation.

Hypothesis 2
The clustering of the zero-line by similar interruption patterns is almost independent of the time window.

---

[2] Note that our hypotheses do not claim exact laws, but should be understood as stochastic in nature. We do not provide proves for our hypotheses, but support them with obviously 'good' cases that can decompose causal correlations from machine individual stochastic effects.

Figure 4 indicates further aspects that contribute to our hypothesis:

(i)   Similar interruption patterns can be visualized by zooming in.
(ii) Similar interruption patterns may overlap.
(iii) Similar interruption patterns may be time-shifted.
(iv) Similar interruption patterns may be deformed between machines, on their width and distance of interruptions.

This deformation is an indicator for stochastic causalities and motivates the stochastic nature of our hypotheses.

3 Cross-Correlations of Binarized Time Series

We apply cross-correlations on pairs of binarized PSTS (BPSTS), in order to calculate the relationship between time series, which serve as basic indicators for possible causal correlations between machines.

Figure 5 shows the functions after cross-correlating BPSTS of the machines in Fig. 2.

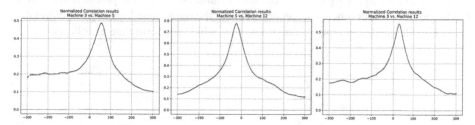

Fig. 5. Peak-correlations after cross-correlating BPSTS of machine pairs 3/5, 5/12, 3/12 that belong to production environment P1 of company A on day 2015/05/19.

The cross-correlation function uses a time-shift parameter, for combining the values of two given time series within the given window size. In cross-correlation function, the maximum size of the time shift can be set to half of the window size. Since the result of cross-correlation is a function of similarity based on the given time window and shift, one has to set them heuristically, such that the best possible similarity is calculated. In general, we do not set the shift to maximum, i.e. half width of our window of 24 h, but to a value that depend on domain knowledge, and is related to the maximum duration of material flow through the complete production line. In our example, this heuristic value was set to 300 s.

Figure 6 shows the respective results of the same machines on the preceding day Fig. 3. In the visual analysis of Fig. 3 with 24 h time window size, we were unable to recognize similar interruption pattern on the first sight, but only reproduced the assumed similarities in Fig. 4 with the higher window resolution of 30 min. Nevertheless, the computed cross-correlation values provide almost identical similarity results.

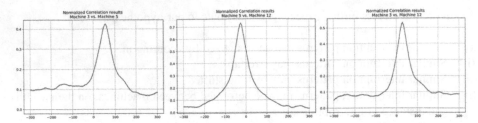

Fig. 6. Peak-correlations after cross-correlating BPSTS of machine pairs 3/5, 5/12, 3/12 that belong to production environment P1 of company A on day 2015/05/18.

Hypothesis 3

A possible causal relation is the more significant, the more the two BPSTSs cross-correlate with eachother. That is indicated by the peak of the probability distribution, which we denominate it as 'peak-correlated'.

Moreover, by observing the shapes of the graphs in Fig. 5, Fig. 6 and Fig. 7, one can identify similar features, like peak and covariance. The distance of the peak from 0 implies a mean time lag for a possible causal relation of the state changes between machine pairs. By applying this idea on other examples in different production environments and at different times, we can observe that the mean time lags of peak-correlated functions often follow a kind of transitivity law, which we formulate as follows:

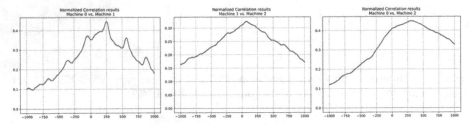

Fig. 7. Peak-correlation of machines 102/104, 104/107, 102/107 that belong to production environment P2 of company B on day 2014/09/01 with maximum shift of 720 s.

Hypothesis 4

The mean time lag of peak-correlated machines is transitive, if machines M1 and M2 peak-correlate with mean time lag T12, and machines M2 and M3 peak-correlate with mean time lag T23, then machines M1 and M3 peak-correlate with a mean time lag T13 = T12 + T23.

In order to underline the value of our approach, in Fig. 7. we compare three pairwise peak-correlated machines of another company B of a different branch[3]. We can observe that apart from a distribution-like peak-shape we see a periodical pattern. This feature is beyond the scope of the paper and is left for future work. However, note that this is another hint of domain-relevant information that is encoded in the data.

---

[3] The production environment P2 of company B comprises approximately 100 machines.

Our attention is on detecting correlations between machines, but not all cross-correlation results have a peak correlation. Figure 8 Depicts plots that are not peak-correlated or close to peak correlation[4].

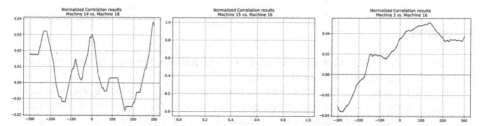

Fig. 8. Sample cross-correlation plots for non-peak-correlated machines. The left and right graphs show no significant peak correlation values, thus are not peak-correlated. The graph in the middle contains no values, as no state changes were found in the time window of BPSTS.

4 Conclusion and Outlook

We have introduced a methodology for detecting possible causalities between machines in production environments that are based solely on the raw PSTS. Our hypotheses were derived from visual features of multivariate PSTS of different production lines from two different companies. The first hypothesis explains structure, similarities and dissimilarities of different PSTS and helps identifying similar patterns.

In order to automate the investigation of such PSTS, we have binarized the multivariate PSTS by focusing on two categories, namely on the regular production state of each machine and its complement. We then have applied a cross-correlation-algorithm to the BPSTS, in order to compare pairwise machine states of different machines of a production environment in a given standardized time window size. The results strengthen our hypotheses, such that causal correlations of machines within a production environment can be discovered from raw PSTS. In this paper, we have assumed that production processes or material flows remain unchanged in the raw PSTS. The application of our methodology to topologically dynamic production environments is subject for future work.

Any found peak-correlation suggests a causal relation between the state changes of two machines. The shape of a peak-correlation depends on the semantics of the production environment and is subject to future work. We further have introduced a hypothesis for the transitivity rule for peak-correlations. In subsequent work we will elaborate algebraic structures for peak-correlations, with the objective to further support the validity of our hypotheses.

Another issue is to distinguish between different types of interruption states, which can be utilized for designing more specific causal reactions between machines. For this purpose we will analyze other categorizations, by categorizing the 'any other state'.

---

[4] As mentioned above, these categorizations are not exact, but stochastic in nature. The notion of peak-correlation depends on the maximum value and cross co-variance.

Acknowledgement. Thanks are due to the students André Berberich, Tobias Bloch and Jarno Wagner for implementing supporting software applications. Thanks also to MPDV Microlab GmbH and MAHLE Behr GmbH & Co. KG for providing real world production data and domain knowledge.

References

1. Kletti, J.: MES - Manufacturing Execution System, 2nd edn. Springer, Heidelberg (2015). https://doi.org/10.1007/978-3-540-49744-8
2. Dean, R.T., Dunsmuir, W.T.M.: Dangers and uses of cross-correlation in analyzing time series in perception, performance, movement, and neuroscience: The importance of constructing transfer function autoregressive models. Behav. Res. Methods **48**, 783–802 (2016). https://doi.org/10.3758/s13428-015-0611-2
3. Witsch, M., Vogel-Heuser, B.: Towards a formal specification framework for manufacturing execution systems. IEEE Trans. Industr. Inf. **8**(2), 311–320 (2012)
4. Salvador, S., Chan, P.: Toward accurate dynamic time warping in linear time and space. Intell. Data Anal. **11**(5), 70–80 (2007)
5. Sornette, D., Zhou, W.X.: Non-parametric determination of real-time lag structure between two time series: the 'optimal thermal causal path' method. J. Macroecon. **28**(1), 195–224 (2006)
6. Brauckmann, O.: Digitale Revolution in der industriellen Fertigung - Denkansätze. Springer, Berlin (2019). https://doi.org/10.1007/978-3-662-58037-0
7. Larreina, J., Gontarz, A., Giannoulis, C., Nguyen, V.K., Stavropoulos, P., Sinceri, B.: Smart manufacturing execution system (SMES) - the possibilities of evaluating the sustainability of a production process. In: Global Conference on Sustainable Manufacturing (GCSM), ETH Zürich (2013)
8. Hale, D.: An efficient method for computing localcross-correlations of multi-dimensional signals (2006)
9. Bi, Z., Xu, L.D., Wang, C.: Internet of Things for enterprise systems of modern manufacturing. IEEE Trans. Industr. Inf. **10**(2), 1537–1546 (2014)
10. Berthold, Michael R., Borgelt, C., Höppner, F., Klawonn, F.: Guide to Intelligent Data Analysis. TCS. Springer, London (2010). https://doi.org/10.1007/978-1-84882-260-3
11. Göpfert, T., Breiter, A.: Knowledge Discovery in Big Data: Herausforderungen durch Big Data im Prozess der Wissensgewinnung am Beispiel des CRISP-DM. In: Cunningham, D., Hofstedt, P., Schmitt, I. (eds.) Lecture Notes in Informatics, Bonn, pp. 1219–1230 (2015)
12. Zeng, C., Tang, L., Li, T., Shwartz, L., Grabarnik, G.Y.: Mining temporal lag from fluctuating events for correlation and root cause analysis. In: 10th International Conference on Network and Service Management, CNSM 2014, pp 19–27 (2014)
13. Boker, S.M., Xu, M., Rotondo, J.L., Fing, K.: Windowed cross-correlation and peak picking for the analysis of variability in the association between behavioral time series. Psychol. Methods **7**(3), 338–355 (2002)
14. Zeng, C., Tang, L., Li, T., Shwartz, L.: Discovering lag intervals for temporal dependencies. In: 18th ACM SIGKDD International Conference on Knowledge Discovery and Data Mining, pp. 633–641. ACM (2012)
15. Huber, M.F., Zöller, M.A., Baum, M.: Linear programming based time lag identification in event sequences. Automatica **98**, 14–19 (2018)
16. Zöller, M.A., Baum, M., Huber, M.F.: Framework for mining event correlations and time lags in large event sequences. In: IEEE 15th International Conference on Industrial Informatics, pp. 805–810 (2017)

Identification of Delays in AMUSE Algorithm for Blind Signal Separation of Financial Data

Ryszard Szupiluk(iD) and Paweł Rubach$^{(\boxtimes)}$ (iD)

Warsaw School of Economics, Al. Niepodleglosci 162, 02-554 Warsaw, Poland
{ryszard.szupiluk,pawel.rubach}@sgh.waw.pl

Abstract. In this article, we present a method of selecting the number of delays in the AMUSE blind signal separation (BSS) algorithm. This enhancement of the AMUSE algorithm enables the separation of signals in case of generating models that include additive noise. The choice of the set of delays is based on a new measure of the collective signal variability. The presented solution is tested both on benchmark signals as well as on real financial time series.

Keywords: Blind signal separation · AMUSE · Financial signals

1 Introduction

The goal of blind signal separation (BSS) is to reproduce unknown source signals mixed in an unknown mixing system. The currently applied BSS solutions are based on various criteria such as independence, non-negativity, variability, sparseness or smoothness of signals [1]. One of the basic methods is the AMUSE algorithm that uses second order statistics [2, 3]. This is one of the most effective separation algorithms for data for which the linear assumption of the mixing model is adequate. Thanks to its computational simplicity, it allows for a fast and simultaneous separation of many signals by performing the whole process in two iterations of time delay decorrelation. However, it has a significant limitation in that it rigorously links the separation quality and the assumed generative model.

The linear way of mixing signals is the standard adopted model in most mature solutions of BSS. In the absence of the real knowledge about the form of the mixing system, it plays the role of a working model that does not determine the real phenomenon. In practice, most separation methods constructed on the basis of this model have, however, some tolerance for different mixing models. One of the typical cases is the matter of taking into account the additive noise which additionally interferes with the already mixed data.

In the case of a standard two step AMUSE algorithm, even a relatively low level of additive noise usually results in the lack of effective separation. A possible solution to this problem is to extend the double decorrelation to a larger number of delays. However, consequently there is the question of how many delays should be taken into account and what should be their values. For physical signals such as speech signals or

© Springer Nature Switzerland AG 2020
L. Rutkowski et al. (Eds.): ICAISC 2020, LNAI 12416, pp. 253–261, 2020.
https://doi.org/10.1007/978-3-030-61534-5_23

video signals, combinations of different sets of delays can be tested by observing the effects obtained after separation and selecting the best set. However, this assessment is in principle impossible in the case of financial time series. Therefore the goal of this research is to develop a separation method that will be applicable to financial analytical signals (with no direct physical interpretation) such as trends or technical indicators and that will fulfill a certain objective quality criterion [5].

As a solution to the problem of selecting delays in the AMUSE algorithm, we propose a measure of variability, which can also be treated as a measure of smoothness or volatility. This measure enables the measuring of both individual as well as collective variability of a set of signals. The collective variability is not understood here as a simple sum of variability but is treated as a separate concept with its own interpretation.

2 Blind Separation of Signals and Problem of Additive Noise

The problem addressed by blind signal separation (BSS) is the reproduction of source signals mixed in a certain system [1, 4]. Both the system and the source signals are unknown and the identification is made only on the basis of the mixed data. To solve the BSS problem we need to make assumptions about the generating model. The most popular is the static linear model for which there are many effective solutions. In this research we focus on its extended version that takes into account the additive noise. This model can be formulated in the following way:

$$x(t) = As(t) + v(t), \tag{1}$$

where $A \in R^{(m \times n)}$ is the full column rank mixing matrix $x(t) = [x_1(t), x_2(t), \ldots, x_m(t)]^T$ is the vector of observed mixed signals, $s(t) = [s_1(t), s_2(t), \ldots, s_n(t)]^T$ is the vector of source signals and $v(t) = [v_1(t), v_2(t), \ldots, v_m(t)]^T$ is the additive mutually uncorrelated noise.

The goal of BSS is to reproduce the source signals s. This is usually achieved by adopting a linear separating system defined by the matrix W in the form of:

$$y = Wx = WAs(t) + Wv(t), \tag{2}$$

where $W = A^+$ is a pseudoinverse matrix to A. The adoption of $v = 0$ leads to a standard static linear model for which the satisfactory solution can be expressed as:

$$y = WAs = PDs, \tag{3}$$

where: P – is a permutation matrix defining the order of estimated signals, D – is a diagonal scaling matrix. This means that the estimated source signals can be scaled and ordered in a different way than the original source signals s. We also assume that $m = n$. The inclusion of additive noise considerably complicates possible solutions, because in general there is no linear transformation that could lead to the reproduction of pure source signals. However, we can still look for a system that will enable the separation of mixed signals and expect that additive noise can be removed by using classic filtration techniques. As a result, the whole problem of separation for the model (1) can be reduced to the searching for such a matrix W that satisfies:

$$WA = PD = G, \qquad (4)$$

where G is the global permutation matrix. From the point of view of existing separation techniques, the fulfillment (4) in the case of (1) is an open research task, while the existing solutions usually rely on the modification or extension of methods developed for the $x = As$ model. We present such a proposal for the AMUSE algorithm.

3 The AMUSE Algorithm

The AMUSE algorithm is a standard separation method for data with a time structure. It is based on second-order statistics using time delay decorrelation. Its main advantage is the computational simplicity and consequently high efficiency of operation even on a large number of signals.

Its basic form can be formulated as follows:

1. Let $z(t) = x(t)$, $q = 0$, $W = I$
2. Estimate the time delay correlation matrix

$$R = E\left\{z(t)z^T(t - q)\right\} \qquad (5)$$

3. Find an orthogonal matrix W_q (i.e. from SVD) which diagonalizes the matrix R
4. Perform decorrelation for given delay

$$y(t) = W_q z(t), \qquad (6)$$

5. Let $W \leftarrow W_q W$, $z(t) \leftarrow y(t)$, $q \leftarrow q + 1$ and go to step 2 until the chosen stop criterion is fulfilled
6. The separation matrix is W.

In the absence of additive noise, the high quality of separation is achieved with two iterations for the delays $q = 0$ and $q = 1$. This means that in the algorithm there are basically no arbitrarily selected parameters, what may be considered as an additional advantage.

Unfortunately, the aforementioned advantages come at a cost of a rigorous assumption that there is no additive noise. Even a relatively small amount of noise, i.e. SNR level $= 20$ dB, causes a drastic decrease in the quality of separation. To solve this problem we propose to perform a larger number of decorrelations with different delays. However, in that case there remains the question of how many delays and what values of those delays should be used.

One of the methods of choosing a set of delays may be the adoption of specific measures that could characterize the changes of separated signals. Such characteristics may be interpreted as volatility, variability or smoothness of signals. As an assessment tool this measure should be different than the variance and correlation characteristics that are directly explored in AMUSE. Additionally, it should also take into account the nature of a multivariate time series, that is, we treat variability as signal movement in a multivariate space.

4 Measure of Variability and Modified AMUSE Algorithm

In this paragraph, we develop the measure for the assessment of the variability of signals. The starting point is the measure of variability of one-dimensional signals in the form:

$$V(y) = \frac{\frac{1}{K}\sum_{k=2}^{K}|y(k) - y(k-1)|}{\delta(\max(y) - \min(y))}, \tag{7}$$

where symbol δ is the indicator of 1 that is $\delta(0) = 1$ and $\delta(y) = y$ for $y \neq 0$.

The measure $V(y)$ has a simple and intuitive interpretation. It achieves its maximum value if the changes in each step are equal to the maximum fluctuations and the value of zero if the signal is constant. The indicator $\delta(\cdot)$ prevents the division by zero. A generalization of this measure for a multidimensional case $y = [y_1, y_2, \ldots, y_n]^T$ with delay q will be a measure in the following form:

$$V_p(y) = \frac{1}{K}\frac{\sum_{k=2}^{K}||y(k) - y(k-q)||_p}{\delta(||\max(y) - \min(y)||_p)}, \tag{8}$$

where $\max(y) = [\max(y_1), \max(y_2), \ldots, \max(y_n)]^T$ and $\min(y) = [\min(y_1), \ldots, \min(y_n)]^T$ and $\|.\|_p$ is p - norm. The measure expressed by (8) we will call the collective variability. By normalizing signals to the interval $(-1, 1)$ this measure may be simplified to:

$$V_p(y) = \frac{1}{K}\frac{1}{\sqrt{n}}\sum_{k=2}^{K}||y(k) - y(k-q)||_p, \tag{9}$$

The use of the measure $V_p(y)$ to evaluate the separated signals is motivated by the expectation that individual signals are less variable than mixed ones. Such understanding may be attributed to the Central Limit Theorem, which states that under certain general conditions the distribution of the sum of two signals approaches the Gaussian distribution closer than the distribution of each individual signal. In our solution, we associate randomness and the closeness to the Gaussian distribution with variability which is typical for the approach used in the analysis of financial time series. As a result, we will get the following algorithm.

1. Let $z(t) = x(t)$, $W = I$, $i = 1$, draw time delay vector $q = [q_1, q_2, \ldots, q_K]$, with integer values and K less than observation number,
2. Estimate the time delay correlation matrix for delay $p = q_i$

$$R_{zz}(p) = E\left\{z(t)z(t-p)^T\right\}, \tag{10}$$

3. Find an orthogonal matrix W (i.e. from SVD) which diagonalizes the matrix R_{zz}
4. Perform decorrelation for given delay

$$y(t) = Wz(t) \tag{11}$$

Calculate $V_i = V(y)$

5. Let $W_i \leftarrow WW_i, z(t) \leftarrow y(t), i \leftarrow i+1$, save W_i and go to step 2 until the stopping criterion $i = n$ is fulfilled.
6. Find such i, that $\min_i V_i$.
7. The separation matrix is $W = W_i$.

It is worth noting that the above-mentioned methodology can be applied to the extended version of the AMUSE algorithm where higher order statistics are explored.

5 Practical Experiments

In this part, we examine the application of the aforementioned concept on two data sets. The first set includes simple mathematical signals that are easy to quantitatively and visually assess in terms of separation. We present the quality of separation with different levels of additive noise. We also point out that the proposed measure of variability $V_2(y)$ is in practice a good indicator of the quality of separation and can be used to select a set of delays. The second set of data includes real financial time series.

For simulated data the effectiveness of the algorithm can be evaluated using the performance index in the following form:

$$\text{PI} = \frac{1}{n(n-1)} \sum_{i=1}^{n} \left\{ \left(\sum_{k=1}^{n} \frac{|g_{ik}|}{\max_j |g_{ij}|} - 1 \right) + \left(\sum_{k=1}^{n} \frac{|g_{ki}|}{\max_j |g_{ji}|} - 1 \right) \right\} \tag{12}$$

where g_{ij} is an element of the global permutation matrix $G = WA = PD$. The PI value can be interpreted as the assessment of similarity of the estimated signals to the source with acceptable scale differences and their order.

For benchmark data shown in Fig. 1 a) that are mixed in the system represented by the matrix A with the condition number $cond(A) = 22.3$ without additive noise in the standard version of the algorithm with delays $\{0, 1\}$ we get PI $= 0.12$.

For comparison, in the case of a simple decorrelation, we obtain PI $= 0.97$ and the separation presented in Fig. 2 a).

In the case of the presence of additive noise, even with a relatively small level SNR $= 20$ dB, the basic version of the AMUSE algorithm loses the capability of effective separation achieving PI $= 0.69$, $V_2(y) = 0.0153$ (shown in Fig. 2 b)). The utilization of a larger number of delays enables one to achieve the separation quality visible in PI $= 0.07$ and $V_2(y) = 0.0138$ and depicted in Fig. 2 c).

a)   b)   c)

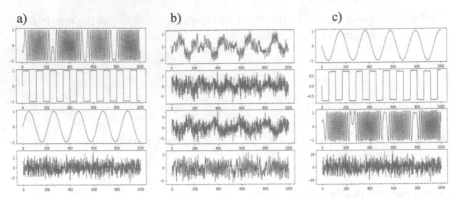

Fig. 1. Source signals a), mixed b), separated c) - using basic AMUSE without additive noise.

a)   b)   c)

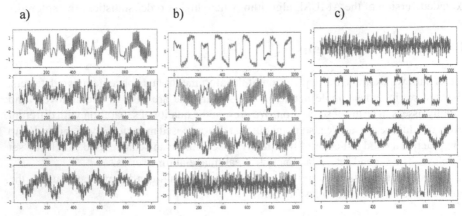

Fig. 2. a) Signals without additive noise separated using simple decorrelation, b) Signals with additive noise separated using basic AMUSE algorithm, c) Signals with additive noise separated using AMUSE with 6 delays {0, 7, 2, 7, 4, 0}.

Please note that the evaluation of the blind separation is related to the quality of the estimation of the mixing system and not to the fidelity of the reproduction of the source signals. This results from the fact that they can be "covered with noise". It is assumed, however, that the removal of noise from correctly separated signals can be achieved using classical filtration methods and is not the main task of the blind separation algorithm. As a result, the visual image and PI assessment may differ significantly.

The performance of the extended AMUSE algorithm with multiple delays is demonstrated in Table 1 which shows examples of sets of delays and the achieved PI values. These results as well as the best and average PI computed for all 2 to 7 delay combinations demonstrate that a larger number of delays leads to a lower PI and thus a better quality of separation.

Table 1. Examples of delay sets that result in a given PI level for benchmark sources with additive noise level SNR = 20 dB.

PI	Sets of delays
0.05	$\{2, 5, 3\}$, $\{5, 2, 3, 2\}$, $\{10, 2, 5, 3\}$, $\{8, 9, 5, 8, 9\}$, $\{3, 4, 4, 5, 4, 4\}$, $\{6, 5, 6, 3, 4, 5, 4\}$, $\{5, 9, 3, 4, 5, 5, 4\}$
0.1	$\{0, 5, 3\}$, $\{7, 0, 5, 3\}$, $\{5, 6, 3, 4\}$, $\{2, 10, 3, 5, 4\}$, $\{2, 1, 2, 10, 4, 2\}$, $\{10, 8, 6, 4, 2, 3, 1\}$, $\{5, 9, 10, 8, 2, 3, 1\}$
0.25	$\{10, 4\}$, $\{5, 10, 4\}$, $\{2, 10, 4, 4\}$, $\{7, 0, 9, 10, 4\}$, $\{0, 7, 0, 9, 10, 4\}$, $\{0, 3, 8, 5, 1, 7, 5\}$, $\{10, 9, 11, 3, 1, 7, 5\}$
0.5	$\{6, 2\}$, $\{7, 6, 2\}$, $\{6, 6, 8, 10\}$, $\{0, 2, 8, 3, 11\}$, $\{7, 7, 7, 9, 8, 1\}$, $\{10, 10, 8, 6, 5, 4, 10\}$, $\{4, 4, 5, 7, 4, 7, 8\}$

The Fig. 3 below demonstrates how the enhanced AMUSE algorithm performs on real stock market data. It illustrates the mixing and separation of logarithmic rates of return of two indexes (S&P 500 and WIG 20) without additive noise observed in the period of 01.01.2011 to 31.12.2018. The separation with 7 delays $\{1, 11, 10, 7, 2, 1, 6\}$ achieved PI $= 0.009$ and $V_2(y) = 0.0069$.

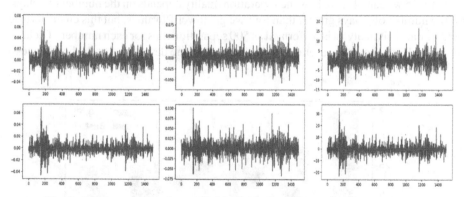

Fig. 3. Source, mixed and separated logarithmic return rates of stock indexes.

The above tests confirm that there is a link between PI and $V_2(y)$ assessments. This aspect is depicted widely in Fig. 4 which presents the relation between PI and $V_2(y)$ observed in 500 runs of separation with randomly chosen delays. The R-square for the linear regression model achieved 0.6 enabling us to draw a conclusion that PI and $V_2(y)$ measures are linearly correlated.

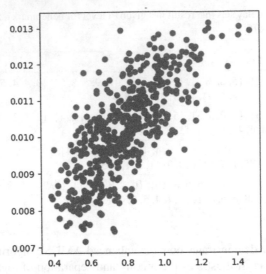

Fig. 4. PI vs. $V_2(\mathbf{y})$ observed in 500 runs of separation using AMUSE with multiple delays where $R^2 = 0.6$ for linear regression model.

In Fig. 5 we can observe how the separation quality depends on the number of delays. For the number of delays greater than four we get lower PI values, but this characteristic is rather flat. This analysis is performed as 500 separation runs for each number of delays. The red column shows the average PI while the blue one demonstrates the best (lowest) achieved PI.

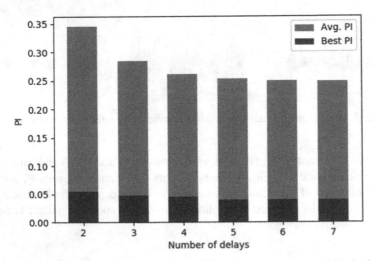

Fig. 5. The influence of the number of delays on the PI measured on benchmark signals with additive noise. (Color figure online)

6   Conclusions

The two step basis AMUSE algorithm is highly sensitive to the presence of additive noise. A solution to this problem may be the increase of the number of delays. The conducted research confirms the significant positive impact of the increase in the number of delays and their order on the quality of separation. However, at the same time it demonstrates the lack of an unambiguous rule for their selection. Depending on the form of the separated signals, the values of the mixing matrix and the level and characteristic of additive noise, the set of effective delays can be significantly different. The optimal delay values may occur in any order, not necessarily monotonic, and may also be repeated. As a result, it is not possible *a priori* to determine the optimal set in the given case. Random searching of different variants seems to be the only solution. However, this may mean difficulties in assessing the quality of separation. While in the case of benchmark signals or easily interpreted physical signals the quality of separation can be assessed based on the results themselves, however, in the case of financial signals, it may no longer be possible. For this reason we propose the collective variability measure as means to assess the quality of separation. Empirical studies prove its overall compliance with the collective variability and the performance indicator used in tested data.

References

1. Comon, P., Jutten, C.: Handbook of Blind Source Separation: Independent Component Analysis and Applications. Academic Press, Boston (2010)
2. Szupiluk R., Cichocki A.: In Polish: Ślepa separacji sygnałów przy wykorzystaniu statystyk drugiego rzędu, pp. 485–488. XXIV IC-SPETO, Ustroń, Poland (2001)
3. Tong, L., Soon, V., Huang, Y.F., Liu, R.: Indeterminacy and identifiability of blind identification. IEEE Trans. CAS **38**, 499–509 (1991)
4. Cichocki, A., Amari, S.: Adaptive Blind Signal and Image Processing. Learning Algorithms and Applications, Wiley, Chichester (2003)
5. Szupiluk, R., Ząbkowski, T., Soboń, T.: Analysis of financial time series morphology with amuse algorithm and its extensions. Acta Physica A **129**(5), 1018–1022 (2016)

6. Conclusion

References

Various Problems of Artificial Intelligence

MOEA-RS: A Content-Based Recommendation System Supported by a Multi-objective Evolutionary Algorithm

Matheus Santos Almeida and André Britto(✉) (iD)

Computation Department, Federal University of Sergipe, Aracaju, Brazil
{matheussa,rene,andre}@dcomp.ufs.br

Abstract. Most recommendation systems use only one recommendation criterion at the time, often the accuracy. However, this approach is limited and can generate biased recommendations. In this work, a content-based recommendation system for movie recommendation supported by a Multi-objective Evolutionary Algorithm is proposed. The proposed system takes advantage of Multi-objective optimization and uses three criteria: accuracy, diversity, and novelty of the recommendation. The system uses a multi-objective algorithm to solve the recommendation problem. It will be evaluated using Movielens and IMDB movie datasets and its results will be compared with the state of the art recommendation systems.

Keywords: Recommender-systems · Multi-objective-optimization · Machine-learning

1 Introduction

Recommendation systems are techniques that provide item suggestions to a user [19]. These techniques are widely used in applications that deal with a large amount of information and that need to filter a part of this information to improve the user's navigation. Some applications that use these tools are YouTube, Netflix, Amazon, among others. One of the most recurrent areas for recommendation systems is the area of movie recommendations. This area gained a lot of prominence due to the Netflix Prize, which was a competition created by the movie streaming company, Netflix, to find a recommendation system that presents better results with the system used by the company [14].

In the literature, four types of recommendation systems are recurrent: content-based, collaborative filtering, knowledge-based, and demographic. The type of system that will be presented in this work is content-based. In this system, three components are used in the recommendation process: content analysis, profile learning, and filtering. The content analysis seeks to transform a set of information from an item into a vector representation, profile learning aims

© Springer Nature Switzerland AG 2020
L. Rutkowski et al. (Eds.): ICAISC 2020, LNAI 12416, pp. 265–276, 2020.
https://doi.org/10.1007/978-3-030-61534-5_24

to create models that represent the user's preference and filtering seeks to find items that satisfy criteria related to the quality of the recommendation for the user [12].

Traditional recommendation systems take into account only one criterion at the time of recommendation, often accuracy, that is, the user's chance to like the item. However, this methodology is limited, since it does not consider that the user can use more than one criterion when making a choice [1]. Many studies already aim to make recommendations using more than one criteria, but most seek to aggregate the criteria in a single criterion [22], [9]. This type of approach has limitations, as the composition can cause loss of information.

In this work, a new approach to a content-based movie recommendation system is proposed, taking advantage of Multi-objective optimization. In our approach filtering is modeled as a multi-objective problem, and a Multi-objective Evolutionary Algorithm, called MOEA-RS, is proposed to solve the problem. In this modeling, three criteria are considered accuracy, diversity and novelty of the recommendation. Diversity is related to how much the items on the recommendation lists differ from each other, the purpose of using this criterion is to make the recommendations not be mono-thematic [8]. The novelty is how much the recommended items are different from what the user knows [8].

The problem was modeled taking into account one type of item, which are the movies, thus, the solution is a vector that corresponds to the numerical representations of a movie. As the objectives of the problem are conflicting, Since the objectives of the problem are conflicting, there will be not only an optimal solution to the problem, but a set of solutions. To find this set of solutions, a multi-objective evolutionary algorithm (MOEA) will be used. The result of the MOEA will be used by the MOEA-RS for recommendation.

Some studies model recommendation systems as multi-objective problems [15,20,21], but, unlike MOEA-RS, in these works the solution of the problem is a list of items, and the objectives are calculated from the average of the values of the items in the list, this approach can be limited because there may be information, causing MOEA-RS has advantages, since it exploits the power of a MOEA to find diversified solutions.

To evaluate the performance of MOEA-RS in movie recommendation, experiments will be carried out using traditional datasets for recommending movies and its results will be compared with the state of the art recommendation systems.

This article was organized as follows: in Sect. 2, the theoretical background used for the development of MOEA-RS; in Sect. 3, works with proposals related to the approach proposed in this article are described; in Sect. 4, MOEA-RS is presented; in Sect. 4 you will describe the experiments to evaluate the method; in Sect. 5 the experiments will be presented and in Sect. 6 the conclusions of the work will be presented.

2   Background

2.1   Recommender Systems (RS)

Recommendation systems are software tools and techniques that provide suggested items for use by a user [19]. Some examples of this tool are the recommendation systems for videos, music, and books that are widely used in streaming and e-commerce.

There are four types of recommendation systems: Collaborative Filter, Knowledge-Based, Demographic and Content-Based. In recommendation systems with Collaborative Filter, items are recommended based on the taste of a group of people who have made good evaluations of similar items previously future [2].

In Knowledge-Based Systems, user's ratings of items are not the main sources of information for the recommendation but based on similarity measures that are obtained from the user's requirements and item descriptions [2]. In Demographic RS, in addition to item evaluation, users' demographic information is used to identify similar users to assist in the recommendation process [2]. Content-based systems seek to use information about items to recommend. In this work, the system corresponds to a content-based system, this type of system will be described in the section below.

Content Based. This technique seeks to analyze a set of documents or/and item descriptions previously evaluated by a user, and build a model of the user's interests, based on the characteristics of the objects evaluated by the user [12]. Content-based recommendation systems are typically designed to explore scenarios where items can be described as a set of attributes [2].

The recommendation process in this technique has three components: content analysis, profile learning, and filtering [12].

The recommendation process is started with the content analysis component, which will receive as input the data set containing the descriptions of the items that will be used in the recommendation. In this component, items are analyzed using feature extraction, generating a new representation of this item. This new representation will be used as input for the other two components.

The content analyzer will process the movie's data and, with the feature extraction techniques, will generate a new data set that will contain the new representations of the items. After the creation of the data set containing the new representations of the items, the process of collecting data on the evaluations made by the users about the items begins. Ratings can be obtained in some ways, such as numerical ratings, implicit feedback (e.g. user actions), textual opinions. These ratings are converted into ratings in numerical format [2].

With this, data sets are built for each user containing the representations of the items evaluated by these users, each item will be labeled by the user's item evaluation. The profile learning component will receive these data sets as input and will create a profile for each user, that profile will represent the user's preferences.

Profile learning collects data that represents the user's preferences. With this data, the component tries to generalize this data using machine learning for regression, because the value that the model should estimate is real. Given the profiles generated by the Profile Learning component, the Filtering component tries to predict which items each user may be interested in. This component usually generates an ordered list of the most relevant items for the user [12].

2.2 Multi-objective Optimization

A multi-objective optimization problem (MOP) is a problem in which two or more objective functions can be optimizes [4]. A MOP solution minimizes (or maximizes) the components of a vector $f(x)$ where x is a vector of n-dimensional decision variables, $x = (x_1, ..., x_n)$, from a universe Ω. The universe Ω contains all possible x that can be used to satisfy an assessment of $f(x)$. Λ is the vector space of the objective functions for the problem.

In this type of problem, the objective functions are conflicting, so there is no better solution, but a set of the best solutions. To obtain this set of solutions, the Pareto Optimality Theory is used [4].

MOPs are solved by different research areas, among which are the Multi-objective Evolutionary Algorithms (MOEA). In general, evolutionary algorithms use a population of solutions in the search and thus allow the generation of several elements of the Pareto front in a single execution. The Multi-objective Evolutionary Optimization area aims at the application of MOEAs for the solution of MOPs [3].

MOEAs modify evolutionary algorithms in two ways: they incorporate a selection mechanism, usually based on Pareto's Optimality concepts, and they adopt mechanisms for the preservation of diversity, to avoid convergence to a single solution. Since most MOPs are complex problems, MOEAs focus on determining a set of solutions as close as possible to the Pareto Optimal Set called the approximation set.

Due to the ability of a MOEA to find diversified solutions close to the Pareto Optimal Set, this method will be used in MOEA-RS to find items that optimize the criteria defined for the recommendation.

3   Related Work

In [21], a multi-objective algorithm based on decomposition is proposed for recommendation. This algorithm seeks to solve a problem where the solution corresponds to a list of items and the objectives are the user's chance to like the items and the popularity of those items. The algorithm was evaluated using benchmark data sets and compared to traditional recommendation algorithms. The authors concluded that the algorithm provides several good alternative recommendations for a user and that the algorithm is effective in recommending new and/or unpopular items.

In [15], a recommendation system with a collaborative filter based on multi-objective optimization is proposed. In this work, a SPEA2 based algorithm is used to find a list of items that optimize three objectives: diversity, accuracy, and novelty. The method was evaluated using three datasets: Movielens, Jester, and Filmtrust. Their results have been compared with other state-of-the-art systems. The authors concluded that the system was able to generate recommendations that balanced the three objectives.

In [20], a hybrid recommendation system is proposed, which combines collaborative filtering based on user and item-based approaches with a matrix factoring approach. The system recommends a list of items based on two characteristics, the diversity of the list and the accuracy. For this, the authors propose a method, where first several recommendation lists are generated. Those lists are generated by three recommendation methods, and then a multi-objective algorithm is used to find a set of item lists that optimize these objectives. The algorithm used in this work was the NSGA-II. The system was evaluated using the Movielens dataset, which is a very common dataset in the area of recommendation systems. From the experiments, the authors concluded that the proposed method obtained better results than the other compared methods, concerning the diversity and accuracy of the recommendation.

As can be seen, all the works found had as a common characteristic, the definition of the solution to the recommendation problem as a list of items. This point is where MOEA-RS differs from the related works, because, in this work, the purpose is to define the solution as an item to be recommended and, with this, to explore the power of MOEAs in generating a population of diversified solutions.

4   MOEA-RS

The method proposed in this work consists of a multi-objective content-based movie recommendation system. The system has the same components as a recommendation system based on traditional content, the flow diagram of MOEA-RS can be seen in Fig. 1. The main difference is in the filtering stage. Unlike traditional systems that use common filtering approaches, MOEA-RS treats this component as an optimization problem multi-objective. Therefore, the system uses an MOEA to search for items (which in this work will be movies) that optimize the defined criteria.

4.1   Content Analysis

The content analysis approach used in this work will use 3 characteristics of the movies: average rating of users, year of releases, and synopsis. The average rating and the year of release are numerical characteristics, so the only treatment made by the component will be the normalization of the values to be in the range between 0 and 1. The synopsis is a textual feature and to transform it into a numerical representation, the Word2Vec [13] method will be used. That

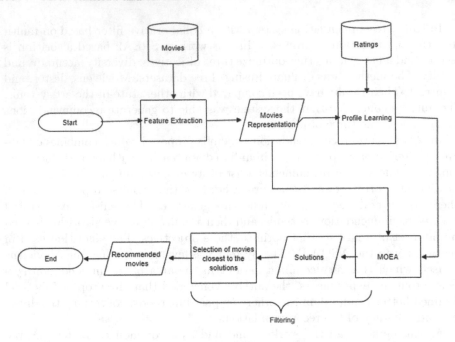

Fig. 1. Flow diagram of MOEA-RS

technique seeks to learn vector representations of words from a large number of textual data. Thus, this method cannot be used directly to generate a vector from a text, for that, it may be using vector aggregation techniques, such as the sum of vectors.

4.2   Profile Learning

This component receives as input a set of data sets, where each data set corresponds to a user's evaluations of several movies, in addition to the resulting content analysis dataset. As a result, the component will build a regression model $R_u(i)$ for each user u, which will represent a user's chance to like a movie i. These models will be used in the filtering component. Several machine learning models can be used in this component, in this work, the model used will be Ridge [7]. This model seeks to learn a relationship between the input and output variables. Unlike the standard linear model, the Ridge model uses the L2 standard as regularization of the parameters.

4.3   Filtering

To perform the filtering, the component responsible for recommending the movies, the recommendation will be modeled as a multi-objective problem, with the recommended movies being those that optimize the defined criteria.

Recommendation Problem. The recommendation system proposed in this paper seeks to recommend movies with three objectives: estimating the user's evaluation of the movie (also called accuracy), novelty, and diversity.

The estimate of the user's evaluation is obtained from the model generated in the profile learning component, thus, the objective is given by the function:

$$F1(i) = R^*(u, i), \tag{1}$$

where $R*$ is the user rating estimate u for the movie i. The novelty of an item is given by the following equation:

$$F2(i) = \min_{j \in A_u} (1 - sim(i, j)), \tag{2}$$

being A_u the set of items that have been evaluated by the user u, therefore, this objective function can be interpreted as the similarity between the recommended item and the items that have already been evaluated by the user and $sim(i, j)$ is a measure to calculate the similarity between vectors, in this work the measure used was the cosine similarity.

The third function - diversity - corresponds to a function that seeks to relate a recommended item to other items on the recommendation list, this function calculates how different the item is compared to the items on the list. The purpose of this measure is to ensure that the recommendation list is more heterogeneous. The diversity of an item compared to other items on the list can be calculated as follows:

$$F3(i) = \frac{1}{|P - i|} \sum_{j \in P - i} (1 - sim(i, j)), \tag{3}$$

where P is the set of items to be recommended, which in this method will be the population generated by MOEA.

Therefore, the recommendation can be modeled as a multi-objective optimization problem (minimization), where, given a user u, the solution corresponds to the vector representation of a movie i and the purpose of the problem is to find a solution that optimizes the previously defined functions. For this, the solution to the problem was defined as a vector that will represent the movie, where each element of this vector corresponds to a feature of the movie.

Recommendation Process. The recommendation is made from the execution of an MOEA to solve the problem described in the previous section. It is worth mentioning that MOEA will not perform a search within the set of movies, the search will be made in a set S where, being $s = [s_1, s_2, ..., s_m]$, if $s \in S$, then $l_i < s_i < u_i$, where l_i and u_i is the smallest and largest possible value of the variable i of the vector representation of the movies dataset, respectively, and m is the number of variables. In other words, the MOEA search space contains the movie space, but, unlike the movie space, this search space is continuous.

As the search is made in a space larger than the space of movies, there is no guarantee that the solutions belonging to the population resulting from

MOEA are movies from the dataset. Thus, the recommended movies will not be the individuals of the resulting population, but the items in the dataset with greater similarity to these individuals. Therefore, with $P = [p_1, p_2, ..., p_k]$ the population resulting from MOEA and D being the set of items in the dataset, the recommendation list was defined as $Q = [q_1, q_2, ..., q_k]$, where q_i is the movie closest to the solution i. If the movie most similar to the solution has already been added to the recommendation list, the next most similar movie is the chosen one.

In this work, the MOEA used to solve the problem is the NSGA-III [5]. The main contribution of NSGA-III lies on the selection procedure based on a hyperplane. This algorithm emphasizes population members that are close to a supplied set of reference points placed on this hyperplane by eliminating solutions that are far from the proposed set of reference points or that are too agglutinated to ensure either diversity and convergence.

Therefore, MOEA-RS will receive a dataset of films and user ratings as input and, with the content analysis component, a vector representation of the films will be extracted. With this representation, a profile will be created for users and, from that profile, MOEA will be used to find the best solutions, and from these solutions, the list of recommendations will be built.

5 Experiments

To evaluate the method proposed in this work, the method will be compared to other traditional techniques for movie recommendations.

For this, this section is organized as follows: in Subsect. 5.1, the dataset used in the experiments will be described; in Subsect. 5.2, the evaluation measures will be presented; in Subsect. 5.3, the parameters used for the experiments will be presented; in Subsect. 5.4 the state-of-the-art algorithms used for comparison and in Sect. 6 the results will be presented.

5.1 Dataset

To evaluate the method, two datasets will be used. The first will contain the information of the movies, this dataset was obtained from the IMDB database, this dataset has information about 3706 movies, however, only the synopsis of the movie, the opening year and the average rating of the movie on IMDB will be used. The second dataset used in these experiments was the MovieLens 1M dataset, this dataset contains 1000209 ratings from 6040 users about movies. To perform the experiments, only users who rated at least 100 movies were considered.

5.2 Evaluation Metrics

To evaluate the results obtained, 4 measures will be used: Precision, Recall, Novelty, and Diversity. The first two measures are used in binary classification problems, so to use these measures, it was defined that if the user gave a score above 3 (on a scale of 1 to 5), the movie is relevant to the user. These measures were chosen because the purpose of these experiments is to evaluate the lists of recommendations generated by the recommendation system. The Recall and Novelty measures will be used because they are measures used by MOEA-RS. Accuracy is a measure that seeks to determine the percentage of items recommended correctly and Recall is a measure that represents the fraction of relevant items that have been recommended [16]. It is worth mentioning that all recommendation systems used in the experiments should provide a list of 15 films as a result.

5.3 Parameters

To perform the experiments, the parameters were chosen from some executions of MOEA-RS with different configurations and using reduced datasets.

Thus, for content analysis, Word2Vec was implemented using the Gensin library [18]. It was experimentally defined with the window for choosing terms with size 3 and the resulting representation with size 150, the other method parameters were defined according to library standards. For profile construction, the Ridge model was implemented using the Scikit Learn library [17] and its parameters were defined using the General Cross-Validation technique, which seeks to find the best combination of parameters for a machine learning model, from the model evaluation for different divisions of the dataset [10].

For filtering, the NSGA-III, except the maximum number of iterations, was parameterized in the same way, with a population of size 16, as the list must have a maximum of 15 items, so the last solution in the resulting set will be removed, the crossover being calculated using the SBX method with a crossover probability of 0.9, the mutation being calculated with the Polynomial Mutation technique with a rate of $1/n$, where n is the size of the individual, which is the number of variables of the representation generated in profile learning.

5.4 Comparison Algorithms

The results obtained by the proposed method will be compared to the results of three other recommendation systems: traditional content-based, traditional collaborative filter, and collaborative filter with objective optimization.

The content-based recommendation system used was the Content-Based System aided by K-means(CB K-Means) [6], the collaborative filter method used was the item-based recommendation system (CF) [11] and the technique based on the collaborative filter with multi-objective optimization used was the MOEA/D-RS [21].

6 Results

In this section, the results of the experiments that seek to evaluate the MOEA-RS for the recommendation of movies, compared to related work and traditional

Table 1. Experiments results

Method	Measure	Precision	Recall	Diversity	Novelty
MOEA-RS	Mean	**0.949282**	0.141767	**0.201282**	**6.2386e−02**
	Std	0.105653	0.097391	0.156934	6.3856e−02
CF	Mean	0.941084	**0.274845**	0.072433	6.2384e−02
	Std	0.081718	0.138983	0.004091	6.3928e−02
CB K-Means	Mean	0.896302	0.234154	0.111522	6.1519e−02
	Std	0.143168	0.147292	0.161155	6.1829e−02
MOEA-D/RS	Mean	0.828279	0.194398	0.072255	6.2214e−02
	Std	0.167902	0.093568	0.003956	6.3908e−02

Table 2. Relationship between the number of films used in the recommendation process and the accuracy of the recommendation.

Number of movies	Number of users	MOEA-RS	CF-item
70–100	719	0.942672	0.925359
100–150	725	0.946123	0.938851
150–200	417	0.949416	0.941966
200–300	504	0.959696	0.953704
300–400	236	0.949976	0.951130
400–800	256	0.950488	0.954167
800–1613	26	0.994505	0.969231

recommendation systems, will be presented. The results can be seen in Table 1, in the Table, for each evaluation measure, the average and standard deviation values of all recommendations made by each method are presented.

As can be seen in the Table, MOEA-RS surpassed the method with related proposal (MOEA-D/RS) in all aspects, with emphasis on the measures of precision and diversity, where MOEA-RS showed an improvement of 14%, for the precision measure, and 178% for the diversity measure.

Concerning traditional methods (item-based CF and CB-Kmeans), MOEA-RS obtained better results for the measures of precision, diversity and novelty, with emphasis on the precision measure, in which the MOEA-RS showed an improvement of 0.8% for the CF item-based, and for the diversity measure, the MOEA-RS showed an improvement of 80% to the CB K-Means.

Another factor that can be analyzed in the results is the relationship between the number of films used in the recommendation process and the accuracy of the recommendation, this factor is important to identify if the MOEA-RS presents a difficulty that is common in recommendation systems, which is the low accuracy of item recommendations for users with few reviews. In Table 2, can be seen the relationship between the number of movies and precision, compared to item-based CF (which was the method that obtained the best precision results, after MOEA-RS).

As can be seen in the Table above, the number of movies that users influence on the accuracy of MOEA-RS, but the accuracy for users with little chance is greater than the CF based on items.

7 Conclusion

In this work, MOEA-RS was presented, which is a movie recommender systems content based supported by a multi-objective optimization algorithm that aims to find movies that optimize three measures: accuracy, diversity, and novelty. The method was evaluated on the MovieLens dataset, with more than 1 million user reviews of movies. The results of the MOEA-RS were compared to the results of other techniques in the literature.

To measure the results, four measures were used: precision, recall, diversity, and novelty. As it was presented in the experiments, MOEA-RS obtained better results than the other methods in relation to the measures of precision, diversity, and novelty, and it just did not obtain a better result, for the recall measure, than one of the methods.

Therefore, it can be concluded that MOEA-RS is a qualified method for recommending movies, as it has succeeded in surpassing methods in the literature in traditional quality measures, such as precision, and in quality measures that have added much value in a recommendation, such as diversity and novelty. However, the method can still be improved, mainly from the use of different techniques for extracting characteristics and machine learning. Other multi-objective optimization algorithms can be used and evaluated and other evolutionary operators can also be applied.

References

1. Adomavicius, G., Manouselis, N., Kwon, Y.O.: Multi-criteria recommender systems. In: Ricci, F., Rokach, L., Shapira, B., Kantor, P.B. (eds.) Recommender Systems Handbook, pp. 769–803. Springer, Boston, MA (2011). https://doi.org/10.1007/978-0-387-85820-3_24
2. Aggarwal, C.C., et al.: Recommender systems. Springer, Cham (2016). https://doi.org/10.1007/978-3-319-29659-3
3. Carvalho, A.B.d.: Novas estratégias para otimização por nuvem de partículas aplicadas a problemas com muitos objetivos (2013)
4. Coello, C.A.C., Lamont, G.B., Van Veldhuizen, D.A., et al.: Evolutionary Algorithms for Solving Multi-objective Problems, vol. 5. Springer, New York (2007). https://doi.org/10.1007/978-0-387-36797-2
5. Deb, K., Jain, H.: An evolutionary many-objective optimization algorithm using reference-point-based nondominated sorting approach, part I: solving problems with box constraints. IEEE Trans. Evol. Comput. 18(4), 577–601 (2013)
6. Himel, M.T., Uddin, M.N., Hossain, M.A., Jang, Y.M.: Weight based movie recommendation system using k-means algorithm. In: 2017 International Conference on Information and Communication Technology Convergence (ICTC), pp. 1302–1306 (2017)

7. Hoerl, A.E., Kennard, R.W.: Ridge regression: biased estimation for nonorthogonal problems. Technometrics **12**(1), 55–67 (1970)
8. Hurley, N., Zhang, M.: Novelty and diversity in top-n recommendation-analysis and evaluation. ACM Trans. Internet Technol. (TOIT) **10**(4), 14 (2011)
9. Kaymak, U., van Nauta Lemke, H.: Selecting an aggregation operator for fuzzy decision making. In: Proceedings of 1994 IEEE 3rd International Fuzzy Systems Conference, pp. 1418–1422. IEEE (1994)
10. Kohavi, R., et al.: A study of cross-validation and bootstrap for accuracy estimation and model selection. In: IJCAI, Montreal, Canada, vol. 14, pp. 1137–1145 (1995)
11. Koren, Y., Bell, R., Volinsky, C.: Matrix factorization techniques for recommender systems. Computer **42**(8), 30–37 (2009)
12. Lops, P., de Gemmis, M., Semeraro, G.: Content-based recommender systems: state of the art and trends. In: Ricci, F., Rokach, L., Shapira, B., Kantor, P.B. (eds.) Recommender Systems Handbook, pp. 73–105. Springer, Boston, MA (2011). https://doi.org/10.1007/978-0-387-85820-3_3
13. Mikolov, T., Sutskever, I., Chen, K., Corrado, G.S., Dean, J.: Distributed representations of words and phrases and their compositionality. In: Advances in Neural Information Processing Systems, pp. 3111–3119 (2013)
14. Netflix: Netflix prize (2009). http://www.netflixprize.com/community/viewtopic.php?id=1537
15. Oliveira, S., Diniz, V., Lacerda, A., Pappa, G.L.: Multi-objective evolutionary rank aggregation for recommender systems. In: 2018 IEEE Congress on Evolutionary Computation (CEC), pp. 1–8. IEEE (2018)
16. Olson, D.L., Delen, D.: Advanced Data Mining Techniques. Springer, Heidelberg (2008). https://doi.org/10.1007/978-3-540-76917-0
17. Pedregosa, F., et al.: Scikit-learn: machine learning in Python. J. Mach. Learn. Res. **12**, 2825–2830 (2011)
18. Řehůřek, R., Sojka, P.: Software framework for topic modelling with large corpora. In: Proceedings of the LREC 2010 Workshop on New Challenges for NLP Frameworks, Valletta, Malta, pp. 45–50. ELRA, May 2010. http://is.muni.cz/publication/884893/en
19. Ricci, F., Rokach, L., Shapira, B.: Introduction to recommender systems handbook. In: Ricci, F., Rokach, L., Shapira, B., Kantor, P.B. (eds.) Recommender Systems Handbook, pp. 1–35. Springer, Boston, MA (2011). https://doi.org/10.1007/978-0-387-85820-3_1
20. Wang, P., Zuo, X., Guo, C., Li, R., Zhao, X., Luo, C.: A multi objective genetic algorithm based hybrid recommendation approach. In: 2017 IEEE Symposium Series on Computational Intelligence (SSCI), pp. 1–6. IEEE (2017)
21. Wang, S., Gong, M., Ma, L., Cai, Q., Jiao, L.: Decomposition based multi objective evolutionary algorithm for collaborative filtering recommender systems. In: 2014 IEEE Congress on Evolutionary Computation (CEC), pp. 672–679. IEEE (2014)
22. Yager, R.R.: On ordered weighted averaging aggregation operators in multicriteria decision making. IEEE Trans. Syst. Man Cybern. **18**(1), 183–190 (1988)

A Study of Bi-space Search for Solving the One-Dimensional Bin Packing Problem

Derrick Beckedahl$^{(\boxtimes)}$ ⓘ and Nelishia Pillay ⓘ

University of Pretoria, Pretoria, South Africa
d.beckedahl@gmail.com, npillay@cs.up.ac.za

Abstract. Traditionally search techniques explore a single space to solve the problem at hand. This paper investigates performing search across more than one space which we refer to as bi-space search. As a proof of concept we illustrate this using the solution and heuristic spaces. In previous work two approaches for combining search across the heuristic and solution spaces have been studied. The first approach, the *sequential* approach, firstly explores the heuristic space to obtain complete solutions and then applies local search to explore the solution space created by these solutions. The second approach, the *interleaving* approach, alternates search in the heuristic and solution space on partial solutions until complete solutions are produced. This paper provides an alternative to these two approaches, namely, the *concurrent* approach, which searches the heuristic and solution spaces simultaneously. This is achieved by implementing a genetic algorithm selection hyper-heuristic that evolves a combination of low-level construction heuristics and local search move operators that explore the space of solutions (both partial and complete). The performance of the three approaches are compared, to one another as well as with a standard selection construction hyper-heuristic, using the one dimensional bin packing problem. The study revealed that the concurrent approach is more effective than the other two approaches, with the interleaving approach outperforming the sequential approach. All 3 approaches outperformed the standard hyper-heuristic. Given the potential of searching more than one space and the effectiveness of the concurrent approach, future work will examine additional spaces such as the design space and the program space, as well as extending the bi-space search to a multi-space search.

Keywords: Bi-space search · Heuristic space · Solution space · Genetic algorithms

1 Introduction

The vast majority of search algorithms employed when solving combinatorial optimization problems (COPs) restrict their search to only a single search space. For example a genetic algorithm generally searches within the solution space,

© Springer Nature Switzerland AG 2020
L. Rutkowski et al. (Eds.): ICAISC 2020, LNAI 12416, pp. 277–289, 2020.
https://doi.org/10.1007/978-3-030-61534-5_25

while genetic programming searches within the program space. The potential benefit of searching across two spaces can be seen in [11] where the performance of the graph-based hyper-heuristic (GHH) improves when introducing a solution space search. In this work we present an alternative approach to those presented in [11], namely a simultaneous approach, in which the search across the heuristic and solution spaces is optimised using a hybridised selection hyper-heuristic. A comprehensive coverage of the field of hyper-heuristics can be found in [10].

Hence, we investigate three different methods of combining search in the heuristic and solution spaces, two of which are taken from [11]. The first method performs a greedy local search on complete solutions created by a sequence of construction heuristics [11]. That is to say that a series of construction heuristics is consecutively applied until a complete solution is obtained, after which the greedy local search is applied. This method will be referred to as the sequential search approach (SSA) in this paper.

The second method is to interleave the local search with the application of the construction heuristics [11]. In other words, after the application of a single construction heuristic a partial solution is obtained, on which local search is performed until there is no improvement. The next construction heuristic in the sequence is applied to the resulting partial solution, with the process being repeated until a complete solution is obtained. For the remainder of this paper, we will refer to this method as the interleaving search approach (ISA).

In [11], it was found that the ISA method performed better than the SSA method. We hypothesize that this is due to the ISA method working on partial solutions as opposed to on complete solutions. This study uses a hybridisation of selection constructive and selection perturbative hyper-heuristics to optimise the search between the heuristic and solution spaces. We hypothesize that this approach will be an improvement on the ISA approach because, rather than forcing search in the solution space at periodic intervals, the proposed method will optimise when each space is searched. This is achieved by employing a selection hyper-heuristic which explores the space of heuristic combinations comprising low-level construction heuristics as well as local search operators. When a local search operator is encountered, the search switches to the solution space by applying said operator within the solution space. We will refer to this method as the concurrent search approach (CSA).

The work presented here differs from previous work in that a multi-point search technique has been used when searching the two spaces (as opposed to the single-point search techniques employed in [11]), as well as using a different problem domain, namely the one-dimensional bin packing problem (1BPP) from the cutting and packing class of problems. This domain was chosen as it is a well-researched problem domain, with numerous variations, that are directly applicable to industry [8,13]. The results show that the CSA method performs the best across the benchmark problem instances, with the second best performing being the ISA method.

The main contribution of the research presented in this paper is an alternative approach for search across the heuristic and solution spaces, which performs better than previous approaches applied for this purpose. This study also further emphasizes the potential of bi-space search as opposed to restricting the search to a single search space. The remainder of this paper is organized as follows. Section 2 details the different approaches, followed by the experimental setup in Sect. 3. Experimental results and analyses are provided in Sect. 4. Finally conclusions and future work are given in Sect. 5.

2 Bi-space Search Algorithms

The hyper-heuristic was implemented using a Genetic Algorithm (GA) for the high level heuristic, with the GA employing the generational control model and tournament selection. Algorithm 1 details the pseudocode for the GA, which was implemented using the *EvoHyp* [9] toolkit.

Algorithm 1. Genetic Algorithm Pseudocode

1: Create initial population
2: **for** $i \leftarrow 1, N$ **do** $\triangleright N =$ number of generations
3:      Evaluate the population
4:      Select parents of the next generation
5:      Apply the genetic operators (mutation and crossover)
6: **end for**

The following subsections describe each of the three approaches that were implemented, namely the SSA (Sect. 2.1), ISA (Sect. 2.2) and CSA (Sect. 2.3) approaches.

2.1 Sequential Search Approach (SSA)

The SSA approach is implemented by using a selection hyper-heuristic to search through combinations of low-level construction heuristics. The construction heuristics are used to build a complete solution, which is used as a starting point for a search in the solution space (local search). Each combination of low-level heuristics is evaluated by firstly applying it to create a solution. Local search is then applied to that solution, and the objective value of the resulting solution is used as the fitness of the combination. This fitness value is used to guide the hyper-heuristic search toward finding an optimal solution to the problem at hand. Algorithm 2 provides pseudocode for evaluating an individual in the SSA approach.

2.2 Interleaving Search Approach (ISA)

The ISA approach is implemented by using a selection hyper-heuristic to search through a space consisting of sequences of low-level construction heuristics (the

---

Algorithm 2. SSA Evaluate

1: **for** $i \leftarrow 1, n$ **do**   ▷ $n =$ length of heuristic sequence
2:     Apply i^{th} construction heuristic in the sequence
3: **end for**
4: **repeat**
5:     Apply perturbative heuristic
6: **until** no improvement in solution quality

---

heuristic space). The fitness of a particular heuristic sequence is determined as follows. After the application of a single heuristic within the sequence, the resulting partial solution is used as a starting point for local search (search in the solution space). As previously mentioned, an exhaustive local search, i.e. until there is no improvement, is performed on this partial solution [11]. After the local search has been conducted on the partial solution, the next construction heuristic in the sequence is applied. This procedure is repeated until a complete solution is obtained, with a final exhaustive local search being performed on the complete solution. The fitness of the solution resulting from this procedure is used as the fitness value for the heuristic sequence being evaluated. The pseudocode for this evaluation process is detailed in Algorithm 3.

Algorithm 3. ISA Evaluate

1: **for** $i \leftarrow 1, n$ **do**   ▷ $n =$ length of heuristic sequence
2:     Apply i^{th} construction heuristic in the sequence
3:     **repeat**
4:         Apply perturbative heuristic
5:     **until** no improvement in (partial) solution quality
6: **end for**

2.3   Concurrent Search Approach (CSA)

The CSA approach is implemented as a hybrid selection hyper-heuristic which searches through both constructive and perturbative low-level heuristics, i.e. a hybridisation of a selection constructive and a selection perturbative hyper-heuristic. The fitness of a heuristic sequence is determined by consecutively applying each heuristic within the sequence. When the perturbative heuristic is encountered within the sequence, then a single step of the local search procedure is performed, on the solution obtained from the application of all previous heuristics in the current sequence. This can be either a partial or complete solution. The fitness of the resulting solution is used as the fitness for the heuristic sequence. The reason for only performing a single step of the local search procedure is that the higher level search is meant to determine when each space is searched, as well as for how long the space is searched. Hence if multiple steps of the local search procedure are required, then the perturbative heuristic will appear multiple times within the sequence. Algorithm 4 details how an individual is evaluated in the CSA approach, where the heuristic in Line 2 can be either constructive or perturbative.

Algorithm 4. CSA Evaluate

1: **for** $i \leftarrow 1, n$ **do**   ▷ n = length of heuristic sequence
2:     Apply i^{th} heuristic in the sequence
3: **end for**

---

3 Experimental Setup

As previously stated, each of the bi-space search approaches were implemented for the one-dimensional bin packing problem (1BPP) domain, using the Scholl [13] benchmark data sets. These data sets are grouped into three broad categories, namely easy, medium and hard[1]. The complete benchmark consists of a total of 1210 problem instances, separated into groups of 720, 480 and 10 for easy, medium and hard respectively.

The heuristic space consists of sequences of construction heuristics for the 1BPP. In our implementation, each sequence of heuristics is represented by a string of characters, where each character corresponds to a low-level heuristic (or a local search operator in the case of the CSA approach). Each sequence is used to construct a solution in the solution space, the fitness of which is used as a measure of the quality of the heuristic sequence. The fitness of the solutions was calculated using the function proposed by Falkenauer [4], which is to minimize:

$$
f_{BPP} = 1 - \frac{\sum_{i=1}^{N}(F_i/C)^2}{N} \tag{1}
$$

where N is the number of bins, F_i the sum of the item sizes in the ith bin and C the capacity of each bin. The following low-level construction heuristics were used [10]:

- **First-Fit Decreasing**: The items to be packed are sorted in descending order, the first item in the list is placed in the first bin in which it fits. If the item does not fit into an existing bin, a new bin is created and the item placed inside.
- **Best-Fit Decreasing**: The items to be packed are sorted in descending order, the first item in the list is placed in the bin with the least residual capacity after the item has been packed. If the item does not fit into an existing bin, a new bin is created and the item placed inside.

---

[1] A full explanation of the datasets and their respective classes can be found at https://www2.wiwi.uni-jena.de/Entscheidung/binpp/index.htm.

- **Next-Fit Decreasing**: The items to be packed are sorted in descending order, the first item in the list is placed in the current bin if possible, else the item is placed in a new bin.
- **Worst-Fit Decreasing**: The items to be packed are sorted in descending order, the first item in the list is placed in the bin with the most residual capacity after the item has been packed. If the item does not fit into an existing bin, a new bin is created and the item placed inside.

The parameter values were tuned such that the performance of the GA would be as general as possible, in order to ensure that no approach had an advantage over any other. It was found that there were no changes when using larger values for the population size. A lower number of generations was found not to converge, whilst convergence occurred before reaching the generation limit when using higher values. Similar observations were made for changes in the application rates. It was found that convergence took longer to occur when a limit was imposed for the maximum depth of the offspring. Likewise for higher limits on the mutation depth. All approaches used the parameter values reported in Table 1.

Table 1. Table showing the parameter values used for the GA for all three approaches.

Parameter	Value
Population size	500
Tournament size	5
No. of generations	75
Mutation rate	0.15
Crossover rate	0.85
Max. depth of init. pop	10
Max. depth of offspring	No limit
Max. mutation depth	5

Search within the solution space was conducted through the use of a local search operator, which was adapted from [7]. This operator was chosen due to its popularity within the literature [1,7]. Algorithm 5 details the implementation of this operator. In cases where there are multiple swaps which would lead to a reduced residual capacity (free space) for a bin, the swap which leads to the greatest reduction is made. Similarly, for bins where no swaps are possible there is no action taken. When applying the local search operator on partial solutions, only the items which had been packed, i.e. only those items in the bins within the partial solution, were considered when attempting to make improvements. In addition to this, the operator was only applied in cases where two or more bins were present (no action was taken otherwise). The reasoning behind this is that in cases of only a single bin, the effect of Algorithm 5 would be the equivalent of unpacking the items in the bin and repacking them using the First Fit Descending construction heuristic. We felt that in such cases this would have negatively impacted on the performance of the hyper-heuristic search, particularly in the case of the ISA approach.

Algorithm 5. Local Search Operator
___
1: *free* ← items from least filled bin

2: **for** $i \leftarrow 1, n$ **do**   ▷ n = number of remaining bins
3:     Swap two items packed in the ith bin with two items in *free* if the residual capacity of the bin is reduced after the swap
4: **end for**

5: **for** $i \leftarrow 1, n$ **do**   ▷ n = number of remaining bins
6:     Swap two items packed in the ith bin with one item in *free* if the residual capacity of the bin is reduced after the swap
7: **end for**

8: **for** $i \leftarrow 1, n$ **do**   ▷ n = number of remaining bins
9:     Swap one item packed in the ith bin with one item in *free* if the residual capacity of the bin is reduced after the swap
10: **end for**

11: **while** *free* contains items **do**
12:     remove the first item from *free* and pack it using the First Fit Descending construction heuristic
13: **end while**

The performance of each of the three approaches was compared to one another, as well as with a standard GA searching only the heuristic space (GAHH), using the non-parametric Friedman test with the Nemenyi post-hoc test, as proposed by [2].

3.1 Technical Specifications

The simulations were performed using the Centre for High Performance Computing's (CHPC) Lengau cluster[2]. A total of 30 runs were performed for each problem instance, per approach, using an average of 12 compute threads/ cores (at a clock speed of 2.6 GHz) per run. The simulations were set up such that there were no restrictions on the memory.

4 Results and Analysis

In this section, the results obtained from each of the three approaches outlined previously are compared with each other as well as with those from a standard

---

[2] https://www.chpc.ac.za/index.php/resources/lengau-cluster.

GAHH (searching only the heuristic space). For each of the four approaches, the number of problem instances which were solved to optimality, the number of problem instances which were solved to near-optimality (one bin more than the optimum), and the number of problem instances that were more than one bin from the optimum are all reported in Table 2. The results are grouped according to the data set categories (easy, medium and hard), with the best performing approach in bold.

Table 2. Table showing the number of problem instances, for each of the data set categories, which were solved to optimality or near-optimality (one bin from the optimum), for each of the methods tested. The results in bold are for the best performing algorithm.

Prob. Set	Algorithm	No. opt	% at Opt	No. (Opt-1)	Sum	No. rem
Easy (720)	GAHH	590	81.9 %	82	672	48
	SSA	626	86.9%	63	689	31
	ISA	632	87.8%	79	711	9
	CSA	**673**	**93.5%**	**44**	**717**	**3**
Medium (480)	GAHH	242	50.4 %	121	363	117
	SSA	281	58.5%	94	375	105
	ISA	371	77.3%	67	438	42
	CSA	**428**	**89.2%**	**40**	**468**	**12**
Hard (10)	GAHH	0	00.0 %	0	0	10
	SSA	0	00.0%	0	0	10
	ISA	2	20.0%	6	8	2
	CSA	**6**	**60.0%**	**4**	**10**	**0**
Total (1210)	GAHH	832	68.8%	203	1035	175
	SSA	907	75.0%	157	1064	146
	ISA	1005	83.1%	152	1157	53
	CSA	**1107**	**91.5%**	**88**	**1195**	**15**

The performance of the approaches was ranked for each problem instance, where the performance was assessed based on the number of bins in the found solution relative to the known optimum. Solutions that were closest to the known optimum were assigned the highest rank (a value of 1, indicating the best performing approach), with solutions furthest from the optimum receiving the lowest rank (a value of 4). In the cases of ties, the average rank was assigned. Table 3 shows an example of the rank assignments for some of the problem instances.

As proposed by [2], the non-parametric Friedman test was used to determine if there is a statistically significant difference in the average ranks of each algorithm. Using the values provided in Table 4, the F-statistic evaluates to $F_F = 61.10934$. Using 4 algorithms across 1210 problem instances,

Table 3. Table showing example rank assignments for each algorithms' performance.

Prob. instance	Algorithm	Bins to Opt	Rank
N4C3W4_R	GAHH	5	4
	SSA	2	3
	ISA	1	2
	CSA	0	1
N3C3W4_Q	GAHH	2	3.5
	SSA	2	3.5
	ISA	1	2
	CSA	0	1

the value of F_F is distributed according to the F-distribution with $4 - 1 = 3$ and $(4 - 1) \times (1210 - 1) = 3627$ degrees of freedom. For an α-level of 5%, this leads to a critical value of $F_{0.05}(3, 3627) = 2.60736$, and we can therefore reject the null hypothesis which states that the algorithms are equivalent (since $F_F > F_{0.05}(3, 3627)$).

Table 4. Table showing the average rank and its square for each method implemented. Averages were calculated across all problem instances.

Algorithm	Avg. rank	$(\text{Avg. rank})^2$
GAHH	2.82397	7.97479
SSA	2.63719	6.95477
ISA	2.34174	5.48373
CSA	2.19711	4.82728

.

Proceeding with the Nemenyi post-hoc test, for an α-level of 5% the critical difference evaluates to $CD = 0.13484$. Therefore any two algorithms are significantly different if their corresponding average ranks differ by at least 0.13484. The differences in the average ranks between each of the methods are presented in Table 5. From Table 5 one can see that the performance of each of the approaches are significantly different from one another, as all the values are greater than the critical difference.

The average runtimes per problem instance for each of the approaches implemented are reported in Table 6, from which one can see that there is a considerable increase in the runtimes when incorporating local search into the algorithm. From Table 6 one can see that the SSA has, on average, more than double the runtime of the GAHH, with the ISA and CSA taking considerably longer than the SSA.

However, as previously mentioned, the CSA approach significantly outperforms the three other approaches and, as can be seen from Table 6, has over half

Table 5. Table showing the differences in average ranks between each of the methods implemented.

	GAHH	SSA	ISA	CSA
GAHH	–	0.18678	0.48223	0.62686
SSA	0.18678	–	0.29545	0.44008
ISA	0.48223	0.29545	–	0.14463
CSA	0.62686	0.44008	0.14463	–

Table 6. Table showing the average runtime per problem instance, for each of the four approaches implemented. The averages across each of the problem difficulty categories are reported, as well as the average across all problem instances.

Problem category	Average runtime per problem instance			
	GAHH	SSA	ISA	CSA
Easy	13.5 s	21.6 s	53 min 05.5 s	13 min 37.5 s
Medium	06.0 s	30.6 s	41 min 47.3 s	26 min 29.8 s
Hard	12.7 s	34.4 s	16 min 37.4 s	29 min 21.1 s
Total	10.5 s	25.3 s	48 min 18.4 s	18 min 51.6 s

the runtime of the next best performing approach. Although the CSA produces the best quality solutions, it cannot be ignored that the runtime is considerably longer than either the SSA or GAHH approaches (over 40 and 100 times longer respectively). Therefore, it is necessary to consider the required quality of solutions, as well as any time constraints that may be present for obtaining said solution (i.e.: obtaining "good enough" solutions relatively quickly versus long runtimes to obtain optimal solutions).

4.1 Comparison with the State of the Art

As the main aim of this research is not to compete with state of the art approaches at this stage, but rather to provide an alternative approach for bi-space search, a very simple local search operator has been used to explore the solution space. Hence, we do not expect the approaches presented in the paper to outperform state of the art approaches. However, for the sake of completeness we present a comparison of the performance of our approach against those taken from the literature. These include:

- HI-BP [1]: uses complex heuristics that both construct and improve solutions
- PERT-SAWMBS [5]: uses complex heuristics that both construct and improve solutions
- EXON-MBS-BFD [3]: uses a grouping genetic algorithm together with complex construction heuristics

- GGA-CGT [12]: uses a grouping genetic algorithm to explore the solution space
- IPGGA [6]: uses a grouping genetic algorithm to explore the solution space

The number of problem instances that were solved to optimality are presented in Table 7 for each of these methods.

Table 7. Table showing the number of instances solved to optimality for the CSA approach compared with those taken from the literature.

Method	Easy (/720)	Medium (/480)	Hard (/10)
HI-BP	720	480	10
PERT-SAWMBS	720	480	10
EXON-MBS-BFD	667	412	8
GGA-CGT	720	480	10
IPGGA	720	480	10
CSA	673	428	6

From Table 7 one can see that the proposed CSA approach does not compare well with the state of the art. Only the EXON-MBS-BFD is outperformed by the CSA, and only for the easier categories. This is to be expected because the GGA-CGT, EXON-MBS-BFD and IPGGA all implement a grouping genetic algorithm [3, 6, 12], which is a modification of the canonical GA for the express purpose of solving grouping problems [6], such as the 1BPP. In addition to this, the majority of the optimisation for the CSA occurs in the heuristic space. The CSA only implements very simple heuristics and move operator as opposed to the more complex heuristics used by HI-BP and PERT-SAWMBS. Hence it is understandable that the CSA performs poorly when compared with the state of the art. Future work will look at incorporating more robust search techniques, such as those used in the state of the art approaches, for exploring the search space, in the bi-space search.

Furthermore, from the *no free lunch* theorem it is known that the performance of methods differs according to the problem domain and search space. With this in mind, future work will investigate the effectiveness of selecting a search technique according to the search space and problem domain at hand, as well as including additional spaces such as the design space (ie: a multi-space search).

5 Conclusions and Future Work

A new alternative approach to bi-space search was proposed, namely the concurrent search approach (CSA). This approach was investigated using the heuristic and solution spaces, and its performance was compared with two other approaches taken from the literature (termed the sequential search approach (SSA) and interleaving search approach (ISA)), as well as with a purely heuristic space search (implemented using a GA). The Scholl benchmark datasets for the one dimensional bin packing problem were used.

Experimental results showed each of the approaches' performance were significantly (within the 95% confidence interval) different from one another, with the newly proposed approach being the best performing. All the bi-space search approaches outperformed the single-space search, thus highlighting the potential benefits of bi-space search.

Although there is a significant improvement in the quality of the solutions obtained, there is also a considerable increase in the runtimes, particularly when performing local search during the solution construction process (the ISA and CSA approaches). It is to be noted that although these approaches have longer runtimes, the proposed CSA runs over 2.5 times faster than the ISA taken from the literature. Hence, careful consideration needs to be taken with respect to both the desired quality of solutions ("good enough" versus optimal solutions) and the time available in which to find said solutions (upper bounds on the runtime).

Results from the CSA approach were also compared with state of the art approaches for the one-dimensional bin packing problem (1BPP). The intent when implementing the CSA approach was not to solve the 1BPP, thus the CSA did not perform as well as the state of the art, as was expected. Future work will investigate adapting/selecting the search technique according to the current search space at hand, as well as the use of techniques such as neighbourhood landscape analysis to better decide when to search a given space. Search across more than two spaces (ie: a multi-space search) will also be investigated.

Acknowledgements. This work was funded as part of the Multichoice Research Chair in Machine Learning at the University of Pretoria, South Africa. The authors acknowledge the Centre for High Performance Computing (CHPC), South Africa, for providing computational resources toward this research.

References

1. Alvim, A.C., Ribeiro, C.C., Glover, F., Aloise, D.J.: A hybrid improvement heuristic for the one-dimensional bin packing problem. J. Heuristics **10**(2), 205–229 (2004). https://doi.org/10.1023/b:heur.0000026267.44673.ed
2. Demšar, J.: Statistical comparisons of classifiers over multiple data sets. J. Mach. Learn. Res. **7**, 1–30 (2006)
3. Dokeroglu, T., Cosar, A.: Optimization of one-dimensional bin packing problem with island parallel grouping genetic algorithms. Comput. Ind. Eng. **75**, 176–186 (2014). https://doi.org/10.1016/j.cie.2014.06.002
4. Falkenauer, E.: A hybrid grouping genetic algorithm for bin packing. J. Heuristics **2**(1), 5–30 (1996). https://doi.org/10.1007/bf00226291
5. Fleszar, K., Charalambous, C.: Average-weight-controlled bin-oriented heuristics for the one-dimensional bin-packing problem. Eur. J. Oper. Res. **210**(2), 176–184 (2011). https://doi.org/10.1016/j.ejor.2010.11.004

6. Kucukyilmaz, T., Kiziloz, H.E.: Cooperative parallel grouping genetic algorithm for the one-dimensional bin packing problem. Comput. Ind. Eng. **125**, 157–170 (2018). https://doi.org/10.1016/j.cie.2018.08.021
7. Levine, J., Ducatelle, F.: Ant colony optimization and local search for bin packing and cutting stock problems. J. Oper. Res. Soc. **55**(7), 705–716 (2004). https://doi.org/10.1057/palgrave.jors.2601771
8. López-Camacho, E., Terashima-Marin, H., Ross, P., Ochoa, G.: A unified hyperheuristic framework for solving bin packing problems. Expert Syst. Appl. **41**(15), 6876–6889 (2014). https://doi.org/10.1016/j.eswa.2014.04.043
9. Pillay, N., Beckedahl, D.: EvoHyp - a Java toolkit for evolutionary algorithm hyperheuristics. In: 2017 IEEE Congress on Evolutionary Computation (CEC), pp. 2706–2713, June 2017. https://doi.org/10.1109/CEC.2017.7969636
10. Pillay, N., Qu, R.: Hyper-Heuristics: Theory and Applications. Natural Computing Series. Springer, Cham (2018). https://doi.org/10.1007/978-3-319-96514-7
11. Qu, R., Burke, E.K.: Hybridizations within a graph-based hyper-heuristic framework for university timetabling problems. J. Oper. Res. Soc. **60**(9), 1273–1285 (2009). https://doi.org/10.1057/jors.2008.102
12. Quiroz-Castellanos, M., Cruz-Reyes, L., Torres-Jimenez, J.S., Gomez, C.G., Huacuja, H.J.F., Alvim, A.C.: A grouping genetic algorithm with controlled gene transmission for the bin packing problem. Comput. Oper. Res. **55**, 52–64 (2015). https://doi.org/10.1016/j.cor.2014.10.010
13. Scholl, A., Klein, R., Jürgens, C.: Bison: a fast hybrid procedure for exactly solving the one-dimensional bin packing problem. Comput. Oper. Res. **24**(7), 627–645 (1997). https://doi.org/10.1016/s0305-0548(96)00082-2

Explaining Machine Learning Models of Emotion Using the BIRAFFE Dataset

Szymon Bobek[1], Magdalena M. Tragarz[2], Maciej Szelążek[2],
and Grzegorz J. Nalepa[1(✉)]

[1] Jagiellonian University, ul. Gołębia 24, 30-059 Krakow, Poland
szymon.bobek@uj.edu.pl, gjn@gjn.re
[2] AGH University of Science and Technology, Al. Mickiewicza 30,
30-059 Krakow, Poland
maciej.szelazek@agh.edu.pl

Abstract. Development of models for emotion detection is often based
on the use of machine learning. However, it poses practical challenges,
due to the limited understanding of modeling of emotions, as well as
the problems regarding measurements of bodily signals. In this paper
we report on our recent work on improving such models, by the use of
explainable AI methods. We are using the BIRAFFE data set we created
previously during our own experiment in affective computing.

1 Introduction

Affective Computing (AfC) is an interdisciplinary area devoted to computational
analysis of human emotions. An important aspect of AfC is emotion recognition,
which needs proper modeling of the phenomena [5]. In our work we assume the
James-Lange approach to emotion modeling, which postulates that the measurement of bodily reactions to the experimental stimuli can lead to emotion recognition. We use the common representation of affective data, the two dimensional
Valence/Arousal space. Furthermore, we assume the use of sensors which are
possibly non-intrusive to the subjects, e.g. wearable devices.

Practical development of models for emotion detection with the use of
machine learning (ML) methods poses many practical challenges. This is due
to the limited understanding of modeling of emotions, as well to the problems
regarding measurements of bodily signals, which still are only a subset of the
needed data. In this paper we report on our recent work to tackle the above
mentioned challenges and pave the way to improving such models, by the use of
explainable AI methods (XAI). We are using the data set we created previously
during our own experiment, we conducted in early 2019. We named it BIRAFFE:
Bio-Reactions **and F**aces **f**or **E**motion-based Personalization [8].

The rest of the paper is composed as follows. In Sect. 2 we briefly report
on our work in the area of AfC regarding the BIRAFFE experiment. In Sect. 3
we discuss selected attempts to build emotion detection models for BIRAFFE.
Section 4 provides an introduction to recent methods of XAI. Then, in Sect. 5 we

© Springer Nature Switzerland AG 2020
L. Rutkowski et al. (Eds.): ICAISC 2020, LNAI 12416, pp. 290–300, 2020.
https://doi.org/10.1007/978-3-030-61534-5_26

specify experimental procedure and results. The paper ends with Sect. 6, where we summarize our work and outline our future plans.

2   Towards Emotion Modeling with Physiological Signals with BIRAFFE

In the BIRAFFE experiment we assumed data fusion from both visual and audio stimuli, taken from standard public data bases. We combined two paradigms: in the first where subjects are exposed to stimuli, while their bodily reactions (ECG, GSR (Galvanic Skin Response)), as well as face expression) are recorded; in the second one the subjects played basic computer games.

We investigated 206 (183 provided full data) participants (31% female) between 19 and 33 ($M = 22.02$, $SD = 1.96$) took part in the study. The whole experiment lasts up to 90 min and consists of several phases. The main ones included: 1) the paper-and-pen Polish adaptation [18] of the NEO-FFI inventory [6], used to measure the Big Five personality traits. 2) Baseline signals recording. 3) Stimuli presentation and rating with the first widget for the evaluation of the emotional responses. 4) *Affective SpaceShooter 2* game. 5) Stimuli presentation and rating with the second widget. *Freud me out 2* game.

The experimental hardware included a PC, LCD screen, headphones, external web camera Sony PS4 gamepad, heyboard and mouse, as well as the BITalino (r)evolution kit platform used to obtain the ECG and GSR signals. The whole protocol was running under Python 3.6 and was written with the PsychoPy 3.0.6 library [12]. Both games were developed in Unity. Participants were instructed to navigate the whole protocol via gamepad. ECG and GSR signal are collected continuously during the whole experiment. Facial photos are taken every 333 ms (every 20 frames of the stimuli presentation, at the 60 fps rate) while the stimulus is displayed, and every 1 s during the games. Standardized emotionally-evocative images and sounds from IAPS [9] and IADS [3] datasets were used as stimuli. The same set of 120 stimuli pairs was used for all participants. Consistent stimuli pairs were mixed with inconsistent ones.

The only thing that distinguishes both stimuli sessions is the widget used for affective rating. Two widgets were prepared: 1) Valence-arousal faces widget (`emospace` gives user the possibility to rate emotions in 2D Valence-Arousal space (see [15] for original widget). As a hint we also placed 8 emoticons from the AffectButton [4] (specifically, we used the EmojiButton, which is less complicated graphically). Ratings are transformed into continuous values in the range $[-1, 1]$ on both axes. 2) 5-faces widget (`emoscale` consists of 5 emoticons and was introduced to provide simple and intuitive method of emotion assessment. Ratings are saved as numbers in the set $\{1, 2, 3, 4, 5\}$. They were randomly assigned to stimuli sessions for each participant.

The modified versions of two prototype affective games designed and developed by our team were used during the study (for comprehensive overview of the previous versions see [7]): 1) Affective SpaceShooter 2: the player controls a spaceship in order to bring down as many asteroids as possible. 2) Freud me out 2: the player has to fight different enemies (worth 10–26 points) on three levels in order to face the boss at fourth level. The resulting BIRAFFE dataset is available to download at Zenodo at https://dx.doi.org/10.5281/zenodo.3442143.

3   Emotion Classification with BIRAFFE

3.1   Data Preprocessing

Participants of the experiment were exposed to each stimulus for 15 s. According to [19], the effect of a stimulus on the ECG signal is visible in 5 s after the exposure. For EDA, the reaction occurs almost immediately. Due to, it was decided that a sample would contain: a) a record of EDA reaction that starts when the stimulus appears and lasts 15 s, and b) an ECG recording that starts 5 s after the stimulus appears and lasts 15 s, The effect of completing this stage were 9432 recordings of EDA and ECG lasting 15 s. Each entry was associated with a stimulus and an indication of the emotion chosen by the subject.

Next step was filtration of records, proper especially for the EDA data. The signal was processed using the Butterworth low-pass filter. The implementation available in the *biospPy* library was used. Then the signal was smoothed using moving average of 750 samples. The ECG signal filtration was performed using a medium-pass filter to remove baseline wander. The implementation available in the *heartPy* library was used.

Due to the use of low quality measurement equipment, part of the signals was noisy. Some records were rejected based on the following criteria: 1) ECG samples were rejected by analyzing the pulse, samples of less than 12 or more than 29 beats within 15 s were dropped. Therefore, an acceptable heart rate range was set from 48 bpm to 116 bpm. 2) EDA, signals that contained permanent fragments at 1020 level were eliminated. 1020 was the maximum size supported by the device, therefore these signals were treated as incorrect. The rejection of noisy samples resulted in a reduction in the number of available signals to 7321.

For the emospace scale a three stage approach was considered: The first approach was to predict only valence – whether the feeling was positive or negative. The second approach was to predict only arousal part of emotion. In the third approach we used the information about both valence and arousal. According to the quadrants of the coordinate system an emotion class has been assigned (Fig. 1).

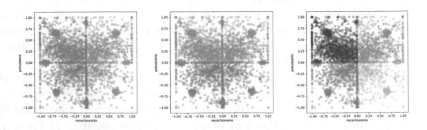

Fig. 1. Distribution of the emospace samples

In the case of a set of signals corresponding to the emoscale as a variable, we used emotion markings selected by the participants without any changes. The distribution of answers is presented in Fig. 2.

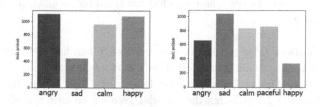

Fig. 2. Emospace and emoscale distribution of answers

3.2   Extraction of Signals

The ECG and galvanic-skin response signals in the original form are time series. To use that data for supervised learning, it was necessary to transform the time series into appropriate form. For this reason, we were separated features from ECG [17] and EDA [2] signals, presented in Table 1. The features used in the model were selected using the LASSO (*Least Absolute Shrinkage and Selection Operator*) mechanism [16]. The implementation available in the *scikit* package have been used. As a result all parameters were considered significant.

Table 1. Features extracted from EDA and ECG signals

	Feature	Description
ECG	BPM	Heart rate
	SDNN	Standard deviation for the intervals btw heartbeats
	IBI	Heartbeat interval
	SDSD	Standard deviation of differences btw heartbeat intervals
	RMSSD	Quadratic mean of differences btw heartbeat intervals
	PNN20	Percentage of differences btw intervals $>20\,$ms
EDA	Phase activity	Rapid changes in skin conductance
	Tonic activity	Slow changes in skin conductance
	Number of peaks	Number of peaks in the signal
	Maximum amplitude	Maximum magnitude of the differences
	Average amplitude	Average size of skin conduction changes

3.3   Construction of the Machine Learning Models

Four ML models were created for the purposes of the experiment: 1) *Decision-TreeClassifier* – a classifier based on a decision tree, 2) *RandomForestClassifier* – a classifier consisting of many decision trees. The score is determined by the "voting" of trees, making this classifier more stable than a single decision tree. 3) *XGBClassifier* (gradient boosted decision trees) – classifier based on adaptive gain. 4) *A neural network* implemented using the *Keras* library. The parameters were identified depending on the number of input features and the predicted variable. 67% of the data set was intended for training models, 33% for testing their performance.

Emoscale Evaluation. The results we obtained were similar, between of random model and the below average model. The worst results were achieved for the *angry* class, where the set contains the least data and is the most probable explanation. For the XGBC-classifier model *recall* measure was slightly higher than in other cases. Combined with minor *precision* factor, it is likely that the model favored *calm* and *sad* classes too much. This may be caused by the fact that these classes contained the most measurements.

Emospace Evaluation. The emospace scores vary considerably depending on the used prediction target. The use of fewer classes was intended to increase effectiveness of models. However, the effect was opposite – the models were random. The result for four classes of emotions was similar to the result for the emoscale scale – the model scores were between of random and below average.

Four Classes of Emotion. For the emospace scale, the worst results were obtained for *sad* emotion prediction. The F1 factor is close to zero for all models, which is a sign that the model very rarely claimed that *sad* was appropriate class for a sample. If it already made such a decision, then it was correct only in 20% of cases. The best results were obtained recognizing *happy* class, but these are still average results - of all the situations in which the model decided that *happy* is the right class, only 36% was correct. It recognized 57% of processed data samples corresponding to *happy* emotions (results for DecisionTreeClassifier).

Two Classes of Valence. A much better result was obtained when recognizing positive valence. However, the results show that the model favored this class. The model, created with the help of the *Keras* library, recognized as much as 94% of all samples associated with positive valence. On the other side, only in 47% of all cases, decisions about positive valence were correct. It can be concluded that the model assigned almost all samples to the most represented class in the training set. For models that are based on Trees methods (DecisionTreeClassifier and RandomForestClassifier) the results were more balanced.

Two Classes of Arousal. In this case, the models obtained much better results when recognizing high arousal. As in the case of two classes of valence, the results of models based on Trees methods were more stable, however, the impact of training data disproportion was still present.

4   Selected Methods of Explanation

Explainable AI (XAI) mechanisms can be divided into two groups [11]. The first of these analyzes the internal structure of the model. Such models are called interpretable models, and the methods used to explain their decisions model-specific mechanisms. The second group consists of mechanisms analyzing the results of the model after training it, without information about its internal architecture. Such methods are called model-agnostic methods. Here we describe three model-agnostic methods for translating decisions. These solutions could be applied to any previously trained model of any degree of complexity. They also make it possible to compare two models using the same type of explanation. The following sections detail the model-agnostic approaches to explanations of decisions of ML models. These methods work locally, they are used to translate individual decisions – not to explain the behavior of the model as whole.

4.1   Shapley Values

A set of combinations was constructed for the point by assigning the features as present or absent. Then, for each combination, prediction was calculated with and without the feature for which the analysis was performed. The difference between these values is called the *marginal contribution*. The weighted average of the marginal contributions from all combinations is the Shapley value of a feature for performed prediction. The result of repeating the procedure for each feature is complete distribution of the features for prediction.

LIME (*Local Interpretable Model-agnostic Explanations*) [10] is based on the local approximation of the model using a *local surrogate* model. An example of explanation is shown in Fig. 4. The SHAP (*SHapley Additive exPlanation*) method [11] uses theoretical optimal Shapley values that describe impact of features on the mean deviation of the model result. This method can be applied to tabular data and images. Figure 3 shows an example of how SHAP works. The developers of SHAP proposed other methods using Shapley values such as *KernelSHAP* and a highly optimized *TreeSHAP* for tree models. *KernelSHAP* [10] is a combination of the LIME method [13] and the Shapley values [11].

Fig. 3. Explanation example using SHAP [11]

The difference between LIME and KernelSHAP is the method of assigning weights to instances. In the case of LIME it is determined based on the distance from translated point, that practice could cause an effect of assigning high weight to potentially unlikely instances. As a result, the weight values determined using the KernelSHAP method, for tabular data can be unreliable. *TreeSHAP* is a version of the SHAP algorithm dedicated to models based on Decision Trees and Decision Forests. TreeSHAP is fast - compared to KernelSHAP there was a reduction of the complexity from exponential to square.

Anchor (*High-Precision Model-Agnostic Explanations*) [14] is a system that explains the operation of models through logical formulas called *anchors*. LIME system approximates the model locally and it is not clear what area covers prediction calculated by linear approximation. This can lead to a situation where close proximity LIME instances returns different translations. The Anchor system is not sensitive to this effect – by clearly defining the scope it covers, it guarantees that the translation of the decisions of each instance will always be the same and it is quite likely that approximation is accurate.

Fig. 4. Explanation example using LIME [11]

5   Evaluation of Models with Explanations

Below we describe the tests of explaining decisions of previously constructed models. Due to the randomness of models that predict only valence and arousal, we considered full emotion predictive models. The mechanisms were compared with each other in terms of weight, which was assigned to each of the features. To test the fidelity of the translation, the `examine_local_fidelity` method was used [1]. It was proceed for all classifiers except of the model created using *Keras* library, because the method uses `shap.TreeExplainer` which does not support sequential models. To check the stability the points selected for testing were close to each other and belong to the same classes of emotions.

5.1   Emoscale

In the case of first sample, none of the models made the correct decision at both points. However these points are very closely together in the space of the characteristics. Therefore, it can be assumed that the translation of the model decision for these points could indicate on the basis of which characteristics (or set of characteristics) models distinguish emotion *calm* from *sad*. For confirmation, explanation of the XGBoostClassifier model was tested using the Anchor.

Model made an incorrect decision for point A – it classified the features as *calm*. The translation is compatible with the exception of the part related to `amplitude_avg` feature. Therefore, it can be concluded that this difference could have influenced other model decisions. However, this relationship is not visible in SHAP and Lime translations.

For sample number two, the only classifier that matched the result is XGBoostClassifier. Translations of this model decisions in points A and B are mostly consistent. LIME translations contain `max_amplitude` with negative weight and `rmssd` and `bpm` with positive weight. The SHAP translation matches the relevance of `bpm` feature. However, in the case of LIME, there is the difference, as feature `phasic_avg`, which in the translation of point A received a positive weight, in the translation of point B received a negative one. Translations of the XGBoostClassifier model decision for A and B points by the Anchor mechanism were consistent. In the case of point A, only model that not recognized emotion correctly was the RandomForestClassifier (Table 2).

Table 2. Prediction results no. 1 and no. 2

	real emotion	**sad**
A	DecisionTree	calm
	RandomForest	**sad**
	XGB	calm
	Keras	calm
B	DecisionTree	**sad**
	RandomForest	angry
	XGB	**sad**
	Keras	**sad**

	real emotion	**calm**
A	DecisionTree	**calm**
	RandomForest	sad
	XGB	**calm**
	Keras	**calm**
B	DecisionTree	sad
	RandomForest	angry
	XGB	**calm**
	Keras	sad

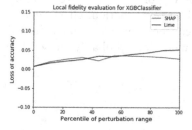
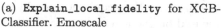

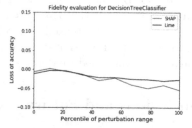

(a) `Explain_local_fidelity` for XGB-Classifier. Emoscale

(b) `Explain_local_fidelity` for DecisionTreeClassifier. Emoscale

Fig. 5. .

Fidelity is a measure that describes how precisely translation approximates the original model, so it is one of the most important metrics. In this work, fidelity is tested using the `examine_local_fidelity`[1] method. The expected result is represented by loss of accuracy during increasing data perturbation. Results of emoscale evaluation through `examine_local_fidelity` of SHAP and LIME frameworks were similar to emospace scale. Based on the graphs however, is visible that LIME translation for the XGBoostClassifier model best reflected tested model. Unlike the rest, *accuracy* was decreasing after applying perturbations. The differences between the results are shown in Fig. 5 and Fig. 5b.

5.2   Emospace Scale

In the case of the 1st sample, in terms of consistency, the translations of the DecisionTreeClassifier model were thebest. Both, for LIME and SHAP, three of the four features had similar importance in both points. Translations of this model also stand out in the case of Anchor, as it was short, had high precision and coverage ratio. Both for A and B points coverage was equal to 0.38 which means that the translation was appropriate for 38% of points from the perturbation space. Predictions made by the Anchor mechanism for others models contain multiple features, which is a suggestion that points could be close to borders between anchors. The results for points A and B are consistent in `amplitude_avg` feature. Both rules have high precision ratio (for A – 0.97, for B – 0.95). It means that these features are almost exclusively responsible for making decision.

In the case of the 2nd sample, the RandomForestClassififier (correct prediction in both cases) and Keras model (incorrect prediction in both cases) were compared to verify translation stability. RandomForestClassifier despite a good result was not consistent – the decision has been taken on the basis of different features despite proximity of points A and B. In the case of the Keras model, classifications were more consistent - similar features determined decision in both A and B points translations, however, with different weights.

The Keras model was also tested by Anchor. Results had high efficiency ratio (>97% in both points), coverage ratio indicated that the translation was appropriate for around 8% perturbed scale. Translation of point B was more precise, as the ranges were smaller. With increasing of data perturbation, effectiveness of translations was not decreased. Therefore, it can be concluded that translations were not precise representation of models, which was probably caused by randomness of the analyzed models.

6   Conclusions and Future Work

In the paper we reported on a practical experiment in the acquisition of physiological data for affective computing. We focused on the attempts to build and evaluate machine learning models for emotion detection. The development of such models is difficult, and their accuracy is often questionable. This is due to the fact that there is no consensus regarding proper conceptual modeling of emotions. Usually only a small subset of physiological signals is available. To approach this challenge, we used state-of-the art models for explanations in ML. They proved to be useful in understanding the performance of the resulting models, and support us in the future selection of features.

As the future work, we are planning to use the explanations to improve feature selection for our models. In fact, we are interested in context-dependent models, that would produce useful results even with limited selection to physiological signals. This is why, explaining the impact of specific features on the model accuracy is important. Finally, our focus is on personalization of emotion detection which also can be improved thanks to explanations.

References

1. ml_models_explainability. https://github.com/greghvk/ml_models_explainability (2019). Accessed 12 Dec 2019
2. Bazarnik, A.: Aktywnosc elektrodermalna w metodzie biofeedback - zastosowanie kliniczne na przykladzie padaczki. Zeszyty Naukowe Towarzystwa Doktorantów Uniwersytetu Jagiellonskiego. Nauki Scisle, 157–175 (2016)
3. Bradley, M.M., Lang, P.J.: The international affective digitized sounds (2nd edition; iads-2): Affective ratings of sounds and instruction manual. technical report B-3. Technical report, University of Florida, Gainsville, FL (2007)
4. Broekens, J., Brinkman, W.P.: AffectButton: a method for reliable and valid affective self-report. Int. J. Hum Comput Stud. **71**(6), 641–667 (2013)
5. Calvo, R.A., D'Mello, S.K., Gratch, J., Kappas, A. (eds.): The Oxford Handbook of Affective Computing. Oxford Library of Psychology. Oxford University Press, Oxford (2015)
6. Costa, P., McCrae, R.: Revised NEO Personality Inventory (NEO-PI-R) and NEO Five Factor Inventory (NEO-FFI). Professional manual. Psychological Assessment Resources, Odessa, FL (1992)
7. Jemioło, P., Giżycka, B., Nalepa, G.J.: Prototypes of arcade games enabling affective interaction. In: Rutkowski, L., Scherer, R., Korytkowski, M., Pedrycz, W., Tadeusiewicz, R., Zurada, J.M. (eds.) ICAISC 2019. LNCS (LNAI), vol. 11509, pp. 553–563. Springer, Cham (2019). https://doi.org/10.1007/978-3-030-20915-5_49
8. Kutt, K., et al.: BIRAFFE: Bio-reactions and faces for emotion-based personalization. In: AfCAI 2019: Workshop on Affective Computing and Context Awareness in Ambient Intelligence. CEUR Workshop Proceedings, CEUR-WS.org (2020)
9. Lang, P.J., Bradley, M.M., Cuthbert, B.N.: International affective picture system (IAPS): affective ratings of pictures and instruction manual. technical report B-3. Technical report, The Center for Research in Psychophysiology, University of Florida, Gainsville, FL (2008)
10. Lundberg, S., Lee, S.: A unified approach to interpreting model predictions. CoRR abs/1705.07874 (2017). http://arxiv.org/abs/1705.07874
11. Molnar, C.: Interpretable Machine Learning (2019). https://christophm.github.io/interpretable-ml-book/
12. Peirce, J., et al.: Psychopy2: experiments in behavior made easy. Behav. Res. Methods **51**(1), 195–203 (2019). https://doi.org/10.3758/s13428-018-01193-y
13. Ribeiro, M., Singh, S., Guestrin, C.: Model-agnostic interpretability of machine learning, June 2016

14. Ribeiro, M.T., Singh, S., Guestrin, C.: Anchors: high-precision model-agnostic explanations. In: AAAI (2018)
15. Russell, J., Weiss, A., Mendelsohn, G.: Affect grid: a single-item scale of pleasure and arousal. J. Pers. Soc. Psychol. **57**(3), 493–502 (1989). https://doi.org/10.1037/0022-3514.57.3.493
16. Saeys, Y., Inza, I.n., Larrañaga, P.: A review of feature selection techniques in bioinformatics. Bioinformatics **23**(19), 2507–2517 (2007). https://doi.org/10.1093/bioinformatics/btm344
17. Shaffer, F., Ginsberg, J.: An overview of heart rate variability metrics and norms. Front. Public Health **5**, 258 (2017)
18. Zawadzki, B., Strelau, J., Szczepaniak, P., Śliwińska, M.: Inwentarz osobowości NEO-FFI Costy i McCrae. Polska adaptacja. Pracowania Testów Psychologicznych PTP, Warszawa (1998)
19. Zhu, J., Ji, L., Liu, C.: Heart rate variability monitoring for emotion and disorders of emotion. Physiol. Meas. **40**(6), 064004 (2019). https://doi.org/10.1088/1361-6579/ab1887

Pre-training Polish Transformer-Based Language Models at Scale

Sławomir Dadas[⊠], Michał Perełkiewicz, and Rafał Poświata

National Information Processing Institute, Warsaw, Poland
{sdadas,mperelkiewicz,rposwiata}@opi.org.pl

Abstract. Transformer-based language models are now widely used in Natural Language Processing (NLP). This statement is especially true for English language, in which many pre-trained models utilizing transformer-based architecture have been published in recent years. This has driven forward the state of the art for a variety of standard NLP tasks such as classification, regression, and sequence labeling, as well as text-to-text tasks, such as machine translation, question answering, or summarization. The situation have been different for low-resource languages, such as Polish, however. Although some transformer-based language models for Polish are available, none of them have come close to the scale, in terms of corpus size and the number of parameters, of the largest English-language models. In this study, we present two language models for Polish based on the popular BERT architecture. The larger model was trained on a dataset consisting of over 1 billion polish sentences, or 135 GB of raw text. We describe our methodology for collecting the data, preparing the corpus, and pre-training the model. We then evaluate our models on thirteen Polish linguistic tasks, and demonstrate improvements over previous approaches in eleven of them.

Keywords: Language modeling · Natural Language Processing

1 Introduction

Unsupervised pre-training for Natural Language Processing (NLP) has gained popularity in recent years. The goal of this approach is to train a model on a large corpus of unlabeled text, and then use the representations the model generates as an input for downstream linguistic tasks. The initial popularization of these methods was related to the successful applications of pre-trained word vectors (embeddings), the most notable of which include Word2Vec [30], GloVe [34], and FastText [5]. These representations have contributed greatly to the development of NLP. However, one of the main drawbacks of such tools was that the static word vectors did not encode contextual information. The problem was addressed in later studies by proposing context-dependent representations of words based on pre-trained neural language models. For this purpose, several language model architectures which utilize bidirectional long short-term memory (LSTM) layers

© Springer Nature Switzerland AG 2020
L. Rutkowski et al. (Eds.): ICAISC 2020, LNAI 12416, pp. 301–314, 2020.
https://doi.org/10.1007/978-3-030-61534-5_27

have been introduced. The popular models such as ELMo [35], ULMFiT [17], and Flair [1], have led to significant improvements in a wide variety of linguistic tasks. Shortly after, Devlin et al. [15] introduced BERT - a different type of language model based on transformer [42] architecture. Instead of predicting the next word in a sequence, BERT is trained to reconstruct the original sentence from one in which some tokens have been replaced by a special *mask token*. Since the text representations generated by BERT have proved to be effective for NLP problems - even those which were previously considered challenging, such as question answering or common sense reasoning - more focus has been put on transformer-based language models. As a result, in the last two years we have seen a number of new methods based on that idea, with some modifications in the architecture or the training objectives. The approaches that have gained wide recognition include RoBERTa [26], Transformer-XL [13], XLNet [47], Albert [24], and Reformer [19].

The vast majority of research on both transformer-based language models and transfer learning for NLP is targeted toward the English language. This progress does not translate easily to other languages. In order to benefit from recent advancements, language-specific research communities must adapt and replicate studies conducted in English to their native languages. Unfortunately, the cost of training state-of-the-art language models is growing rapidly [33], which makes not only individual scientists, but also some research institutions unable to reproduce experiments in their own languages. Therefore, we believe that it is particularly important to share the results of research - especially pre-trained models, datasets, and source code of the experiments - for the benefit of the whole scientific community. In this article, we describe our methodology for training two language models for Polish language based on BERT architecture. The smaller model follows the hyperparameters of an English-language BERT-base model, and the larger version follows the BERT-large model. To the best of our knowledge, the latter is the largest language model for Polish available to date, both in terms of the number of parameters (355M) and the size of the training corpus (135 GB). We have released both pre-trained models publicly[1]. We evaluate our models on several linguistic tasks in Polish, including nine from the KLEJ benchmark [38], and four additional tasks. The evaluation covers a set of typical NLP problems, such as binary and multi-class classification, textual entailment, semantic relatedness, ranking, and Named Entity Recognition (NER).

1.1 Language-Specific and Multilingual Transformer-Based Models

In this section we provide an overview of models based on the transformer architecture for languages other than English. Apart from English, the language on which NLP research is most focused currently is Chinese. This is reflected in the number of pre-trained models available [9,15,41,46]. Other languages for which we found publicly available pre-trained models included: Arabic [3], Dutch

---

[1] https://github.com/sdadas/polish-roberta.

[14, 44], Finnish [43], French [25, 29], German, Greek, Italian, Japanese, Korean, Malaysian, Polish, Portuguese [40], Russian [23], Spanish [6], Swedish, Turkish, and Vietnamese [31]. Models covering a few languages of the same family are also available, such as SlavicBERT (Bulgarian, Czech, Polish, and Russian) [4] and NordicBERT[2] (Danish, Norwegian, Swedish, and Finnish). The topic of massive multilingual models covering tens, or in some cases more than a hundred languages, has attracted more attention in recent years. The original BERT model [15] was released along with a multilingual version covering 104 languages. XLM [8] (15, 17 and 100 languages) and XLM-R [7] (100 languages) were released in 2019. Although it was possible to use these models for languages in which no monolingual models were available, language-specific pre-training usually leads to better performance. To date, two BERT-base models have been made available for Polish: HerBERT [38] and Polbert[3], both of which utilize BERT-base architecture.

1.2 Contributions

Our contributions are as follows: 1) We trained two transformer-based language models for Polish, consistent with the BERT-base and BERT-large architectures. To the best of our knowledge, the second model is the largest language model trained for Polish to date, both in terms of the number of parameters and the size of the training corpus. 2) We proposed a method for collecting and pre-processing the data from the Common Crawl database to obtain clean, high-quality text corpora. 3) We conducted a comprehensive evaluation of our models on thirteen Polish linguistic tasks, comparing them to other available transformer-based models, as well as recent state-of-the-art approaches. 4) We made the source code of our experiments available to the public, along with the pre-trained models.

2 Language Model Pre-training

In this section, we describe our methodology for collecting and pre-processing the data used for training BERT-base language models. We then present the details of the training, explaining our procedure and the selection of hyperparameters used in both models.

2.1 Training Corpus

Transformer-based models are known for their high capacity [18, 21], which means that they can benefit from large quantities of text. An important step in the process of creating a language model, therefore, is to collect a sufficiently large text corpus. We have taken into account that the quality of the text used

---

[2] https://github.com/botxo/nordic_bert.
[3] https://github.com/kldarek/polbert.

for training will also affect the final performance of the model. The easiest way to collect a large language-specific corpus is to extract it from Common Crawl - a public web archive containing petabytes of data crawled from web pages. The difficulty with this approach is that web-based data is often noisy and unrepresentative of typical language use, which could eventually have a negative impact on the quality of the model. In response to this, we have developed a procedure for filtering and cleaning the Common Crawl data to obtain a high-quality web corpus. The procedure is as follows:

1. We download full HTML pages (WARC files in Common Crawl), and use the resulting metadata to filter the documents written in Polish language.
2. We use *Newspaper3k*[4] - a tool which implements a number of heuristics for extracting the *main content* of the page, discarding any other text such as headers, footers, advertisements, menus, or user comments.
3. We then remove all texts shorter than 100 characters. Additionally, we identify documents containing the words: 'przeglądarka', 'ciasteczka', 'cookies', or 'javascript'. The presence of these words may indicate that the extracted content is a description of a cookie policy, or default content for browsers without JavaScript enabled. We discard all such texts if they are shorter than 500 characters.
4. In the next step, we use a simple statistical language model (KenLM [16]), trained on a small Polish language corpus to assess the quality of each extracted document. For each text, we compute the perplexity value and discard all texts with perplexity higher than 1000.
5. Finally, we remove all duplicated texts.

The full training corpus we collected is approximately 135 GB in size, and is composed of two components: the web part and the base part. For the web part, which amounts to 115 GB of the corpus, we downloaded three monthly dumps of Common Crawl data, from November 2019 to January 2020, and followed the pre-processing steps described above. The base part, which comprises the remaining 20 GB, is composed of publicly available Polish text corpora: the Polish language version of Wikipedia (1.5 GB), the Polish Parliamentary Corpus (5 GB), and a number of smaller corpora from the CLARIN (http://clarin-pl.eu) and OPUS (http://opus.nlpl.eu) projects, as well as Polish books and articles.

2.2   Training Procedure

The authors of the original BERT paper [15] proposed two versions of their transformer-based language model: BERT-large (more parameters and higher computational cost), and BERT-base (fewer parameters, more computationally efficient). To train the models for Polish language, we adapted the same architectures. Let L denote the number of encoder blocks, H denote the hidden size of the token representation, and A denote the number of attention heads. Specifically, we used $L = 12, H = 768, A = 12$ for the base model, and

---

[4] https://newspaper.readthedocs.io/en/latest/.

$L = 24, H = 1024, A = 16$ for the large model. The large model was trained on the full 135 GB text corpus, and the base model on only the 20 GB base part. The training procedure we employed is similar to the one suggested in the RoBERTa pre-training approach [26]. Originally, BERT utilized two training objectives - Masked Language Modeling (MLM), and Next Sentence Prediction (NSP). We trained our models with the MLM objective, since it has been shown that NSP fails to improve the performance of the pre-trained models on downstream tasks [26]. We also used dynamic token masking, and trained the model with a larger batch size than the original BERT. The base model was trained with a batch size of 8000 sequences for 125 000 training steps: the large model was trained with a batch size of 30 000 sequences for 50 000 steps. The reason for using such a large batch size for the bigger model is to stabilize the training process. During our experiments, we observed significant variations in training loss for smaller batch sizes, indicating that the initial combination of learning rate and batch size had caused an exploding gradient problem. To address the issue, we increased the batch size until the loss stabilized.

Both models were pre-trained with the Adam optimizer using the following optimization hyperparameters: $\epsilon = 1e{-}6, \beta_1 = 0.9, \beta_2 = 0.98$. We utilized a learning rate scheduler with linear decay. The learning rate is first increased for a warm-up phase of 10 000 update steps to reach a peak of $7e{-}4$, and then linearly decreased for the remainder of the training. We also mimicked the dropout approach of the original BERT model: a dropout of 0.1 is applied on all layers and attention weights. The maximum length of a sequence was set to 512 tokens. We do not combine sentences from the training corpus: each is treated as a separate training sample. To encode input sequences into tokens, we employed SentencePiece [22] Byte Pair Encoding (BPE) algorithm, and set the maximum vocabulary size to 50 000 tokens.

3 Evaluation

In this section, we discuss the process and results of evaluating our language models on thirteen Polish downstream tasks. Nine of these tasks constitute the recently developed KLEJ benchmark [38]; three of them have already been introduced in Dadas et al. [12]; and the last, named entity recognition, was a part of the PolEval[5] evaluation challenge. First, we compare the performance of our models with other Polish and multilingual language models evaluated on the KLEJ benchmark. Next, we present detailed per-task results, comparing our models with the previous state-of-the-art solutions for each of the tasks.

3.1 Task Descriptions

NKJP (The National Corpus of Polish (Narodowy Korpus Języka Polskiego)) [36] is one of the largest text corpora of the Polish language, consisting of texts

---

[5] http://2018.poleval.pl/index.php/tasks.

from Polish books, news articles, web content, and transcriptions of spoken conversations. A part of the corpus, known as the 'one million subcorpus', contains annotations of named entities from six categories: 'persName', 'orgName', 'geogName', 'placeName', 'date', and 'time'. The authors of the KLEJ benchmark used this subset to create a named entity classification task [38]. The resulting dataset consisted of 20 000 sentences belonging to six classes. The task is to predict the presence and type of each named entity. Classification accuracy is also reported.

8TAGS is a corpus created by Dadas et al. [12] for their study on the subject of sentence representations in Polish language. This dataset was created automatically by extracting sentences from headlines and short descriptions of articles posted on the Polish social network, wykop.pl. It contains approximately 50 000 sentences, all longer than thirty characters, from eight popular categories: film, history, food, medicine, automotive, work, sport, and technology. The task is to assign a sentence to one of these classes in which classification accuracy is the measure.

CBD (Cyberbullying Detection) [37] is a binary classification task, the goal of which is to determine whether a Twitter message constitutes a case of cyberbullying or not. This was a sub-task of task 6 in the PolEval 2019 competition. The dataset prepared by the competition's organizers contains 11 041 tweets, extracted from nineteen of the most popular Polish Twitter accounts in 2017. The F1-score was used to measure the performance of the models.

DYK 'Did you know?' (*'Czy wiesz?'*) [27] is a dataset used for the evaluation and development of Polish language question answering systems. It consists of 4721 question-answer pairs obtained from the *Czy wiesz...* Polish Wikipedia project. The answer to each question was found in the linked Wikipedia article. Rybak et al. [38] used this dataset to devise a binary classification task, the goal of which is to predict whether the answer to the given question is correct or not [38]. The F1-score was also reported for this task.

PSC The Polish Summaries Corpus [32] is a corpus of manually created summaries of Polish language news articles. The dataset contains both abstract free-word summaries and extraction-based summaries created by selecting text spans from the original documents. Based on PSC, [38] formulated a text-similarity task [38]. They generate positive pairs by matching each extractive summary with the two least similar abstractive ones in the same article. Negative pairs were obtained by finding the two most similar abstractive summaries for each extractive summary, but from different articles. To calculate the similarity between summaries, they used the BPE token overlap. The F1-score was used for evaluation.

PolEmo2.0 [20] is a corpus of consumer reviews obtained from four domains: medicine, hotels, products, and school. Each of the reviews is annotated with one of four labels: positive, negative, neutral, or ambiguous. In general, the task is to choose the correct label, although here two special versions of the task are distinguished: PolEmo2.0-IN and PolEmo2.0-OUT. In PolEmo2.0-IN, both the training and test sets come from the same domains, namely medicine and hotels. In PolEmo2.0-OUT, however, the test set comes from the product and school domains. In both cases, accuracy was used for evaluation.

Allegro Reviews (AR) [38] is a sentiment analysis dataset of product reviews from the e-commerce marketplace, allegro.pl. Each review has a rating on a five-point scale, in which one is negative, and five is positive. The task is to predict the rating of a given review. The macro-average of the mean absolute error per class (wMAE) is applied for evaluation.

CDSC (The Compositional Distributional Semantics Corpus) [45] is a corpus of 10 000 human-annotated sentence pairs for semantic relatedness and entailment, in which image captions from forty-six thematic groups were used as sentences. Two tasks are proposed based on this dataset. The CDSC-R problem involves predicting the relatedness between a pair of sentences, on a scale of zero to five. In this task, the Spearman correlation is used as an evaluation measure. CDSC-E's task is to classify whether the premise entails the hypothesis (entailment), negates the hypothesis (contradiction), or is unrelated (neutral). For this task, accuracy is reported.

SICK [12] is a manually translated Polish language version of the English Natural Language Inference (NLI) corpus, SICK (Sentences Involving Compositional Knowledge) [28], and consists of 10 000 sentence pairs. As with the CDSC dataset, two tasks can also be distinguished here. SICK-R is the task of predicting the probability distribution of relatedness scores (ranging from 1 to 5) for the sentence pair, in which the Spearman correlation is used for evaluation. SICK-E is a multiclass classification problem in which the relationship between two sentences is classified as entailment, contradiction, or neutral. Accuracy is used once again to measure performance.

PolEval-NER 2018 [2] was task 2 in the PolEval 2018 competition, the goal of which was to detect and assign the correct category and subcategory (if applicable) to a found named entity. In this study the task was simplified, as only the main categories had to be found. The effectiveness of the models is verified by the F1-score measure. This task was prepared on the basis of the NKJP dataset previously presented.

3.2 Task-Specific Fine-Tuning

To evaluate our language models on downstream tasks, we fine-tuned them separately for each task. In our experiments, we encounter three types of problem: classification, regression, and Named Entity Recognition (NER). In classification tasks, the model is expected to predict a label from a set of two or more classes. Regression concerns the prediction of a continuous numerical value. NER is a special case of sequence tagging, i.e. predicting a label for each element in a sequence. The dataset for each problem consists of training and test parts, and in most cases also includes a validation part. The general fine-tuning procedure is as follows: we train our model on the training part of the dataset for a specific number of epochs. If the validation set is available, we compute the validation loss after each epoch, and select the model checkpoint with the best validation loss. For datasets without a validation set, we select the last epoch checkpoint. Then, we perform an evaluation on the test set using the selected checkpoint.

In the case of classification and regression tasks, we attach an additional fully-connected layer to the output of the *[CLS]* token, which always remains in the first position of a sequence. For classification, the number of outputs for this layer is equal to the number of classes, and the softmax activation function is used. For regression, it is a linear layer with a single output. The models are fine-tuned with the Adam optimizer using the following hyperparameters: $\epsilon = 1e-6, \beta_1 = 0.9, \beta_2 = 0.98$. A learning rate scheduler with polynomial decay is utilized. The first 6% of the training steps are reserved for the warm-up phase, in which the learning rate is gradually increased to reach a peak of $1e-5$. By default, we train for ten epochs with a batch size of sixteen sequences. The specific fine-tuning steps and exceptions to the procedure are discussed below:

Classification on imbalanced datasets - Some of the binary classification datasets considered in the evaluation, such as CBD, DYK, and PSC, are imbalanced, which means that they contain significantly fewer samples of the first class than of the second class. To counter this imbalance, we utilize a simple resampling technique: samples for the minority class in the training set are duplicated, and some samples for the majority class are randomly discarded. We set the resampling factor to 3 for the minority class, and 1 (DYK, PSC) or 0.75 (CBD) respectively for the majority class. Additionally, we increase the batch size for those tasks to thirty-two.

Regression - In many cases, a regression task is restricted to a specific range of values for which the prediction is valid. For example, Allegro Reviews contains user reviews with ratings between one and five stars. For fine-tuning, we scale all the outputs of regression models to be within the range of $[0, 1]$, and then rescale them to their original range during evaluation. Before rescaling, any negative prediction is set to 0, and any prediction greater that 1 is limited to 1.

Named entity recognition - Since sequence tagging, in which the model is expected to generate per-token predictions, is different from simple classification or regression tasks, we decided to adapt an existing named entity recognition approach for fine-tuning using our language models. For this purpose, we employed a method from Shibuya and Hovy [39], who proposed a transformer-based named entity recognition model with a Conditional Random Fields (CRF) inference layer, and multiple Viterbi-decoding steps to handle nested entities. In our experiments, we used the same hyperparameters as the authors.

3.3   Results and Discussion

In this section, we demonstrate the results of evaluating our language models on downstream tasks. We repeated the fine-tuning of the models for each

Table 1. Results on the KLEJ benchmark.

Model	Average	NKJP	CDSC-E	CDSC-R	CBD	PE2-I	PE2-O	DYK	PSC	AR
Base models										
mBERT	79.5	91.4	93.8	92.9	40.0	85.0	66.6	64.2	97.9	83.3
SlavicBERT	79.8	93.3	93.7	93.3	43.1	87.1	67.6	57.4	98.3	84.3
XLM-100	79.9	91.6	93.7	91.8	42.5	85.6	69.8	63.0	96.8	84.2
XLM-17	80.2	91.9	93.7	92.0	44.8	86.3	70.6	61.8	96.3	84.5
HerBERT	80.5	92.7	92.5	91.9	50.3	89.2	76.3	52.1	95.3	84.5
XLM-R base	81.5	92.1	94.1	93.3	51.0	89.5	74.7	55.8	98.2	85.2
Polbert	81.7	93.6	93.4	93.8	52.7	87.4	71.1	59.1	98.6	85.2
Our model	**85.3**	**93.9**	**94.2**	**94.0**	**66.7**	**90.6**	**76.3**	**65.9**	**98.8**	**87.8**
Large models										
XLM-R large	87.5	94.1	**94.4**	94.7	70.6	92.4	81.0	72.8	**98.9**	88.4
Our model	**87.8**	**94.5**	93.3	**94.9**	**71.1**	**92.8**	**82.4**	**73.4**	98.8	**88.8**

task five times. The scores reported are the median values of those five runs. Table 1 demonstrates the evaluation results on the KLEJ benchmark, in comparison with other available Polish and multilingual transformer-based models. The results of other approaches are taken from the KLEJ leaderboard. We split the table into two sections, comparing the BERT-base and BERT-large architectures separately. We can observe that there is a wider selection of base models, and most of them are multilingual, such as the original multilingual BERT (mBERT) [15], SlavicBERT [4], XLM [8], and XLM-R [7]. The only models pre-trained specifically for Polish language are HerBERT [38] and Polbert. Among the base models, our approach outperforms others by a significant margin. In the case of large models, only the XLM-RoBERTa (XLM-R) pre-trained model has been available until now. XLM-RoBERTa is a recently published multilingual transformer trained on 2.5 TB of data in 100 languages. It has been shown to be highly competitive against monolingual models. A direct comparison with our Polish language model demonstrates a consistent advantage of our model - it has achieved better results in seven of the nine tasks included in the KLEJ benchmark.

Table 2 shows a more detailed breakdown of the evaluation results, and includes all the tasks from the KLEJ benchmark, and four additional tasks: SICK-R, SICK-R, 8TAGS, and PolEval-NER 2018. For each task, we define the task type (classification, regression, or sequence tagging), the metric used for evaluation, the previous state-of-the-art, and our results including the absolute difference to the SOTA. The competition between XLM-R and our large model dominates the results, since both models have led to significant improvements in linguistic tasks for Polish language. In some cases, the improvement over previous approaches is greater than 10%. For example, the CDB task was a part of the PolEval 2019 competition, in which the winning solution by Czapla et al. [10] achieved an F1-score of 58.6. Both our model and the XLM-R large model outperform that by at least twelve points, achieving an F1-score of over 70. The comparison for the named entity recognition task is also interesting.

Table 2. Detailed results for Polish language downstream tasks. In some cases, we used the datasets and task definitions from the KLEJ benchmark, which are different from the original tasks they were based on (they have been reformulated or otherwise modified by the benchmark authors). We denote such tasks with (KLEJ). The abbreviated task types are: C - classification, R - regression, and ST - sequence tagging.

Task		Metric	Previous SOTA		Base model	Large model
Multi-class classification						
NKJP (KLEJ)	C	Accuracy	XLM-R large [7]	94.1	93.9 (−0.2)	**94.5** (+0.4)
8TAGS	C	Accuracy	ELMo [12]	71.4	77.2 (+5.8)	**80.8** (+9.4)
Binary classification						
CBD	C	F1-score	XLM-R large [7]	70.6	66.7 (−2.9)	**71.1** (+0.5)
DYK (KLEJ)	C	F1-score	XLM-R large [7]	72.8	65.9 (−6.9)	**73.4** (+0.6)
PSC (KLEJ)	C	F1-score	XLM-R large [7]	**98.9**	98.8 (−0.1)	98.8 (−0.1)
Sentiment analysis						
PolEmo2.0-IN	C	Accuracy	XLM-R large [7]	92.4	90.6 (−1.8)	**92.8** (+0.4)
PolEmo2.0-OUT	C	Accuracy	XLM-R large [7]	81.0	76.3 (−4.7)	**82.4** (+1.4)
Allegro Reviews	R	1-wMAE	XLM-R large [7]	88.4	87.8 (−1.0)	**88.8** (+0.4)
Textual entailment						
CDSC-E	C	Accuracy	XLM-R large [7]	**94.4**	94.2 (−0.2)	93.3 (−1.1)
SICK-E	C	Accuracy	LASER [12]	82.2	86.1 (+3.9)	**87.7** (+5.5)
Semantic relatedness						
CDSC-R	R	Spearman	XLM-R large [7]	94.7	94.0 (−0.7)	**94.9** (+0.2)
SICK-R	R	Spearman	USE [12]	75.8	82.3 (+6.5)	**85.6** (+9.8)
Named entity recognition						
Poleval-NER 2018	ST	F1-score	Dadas [11]	86.2	87.9 (+1.7)	**90.0** (+3.8)

The previous state-of-the-art solution by Dadas [11] is a model that combined neural architecture with external knowledge sources, such as entity lexicons or a specialized entity linking module based on data from Wikipedia. Our language model managed to outperform this method by 3.8 points without using any structured external knowledge. In summary, our model has demonstrated an improvement over existing methods in eleven of the thirteen tasks.

4   Conclusions

We have presented two transformer-based language models for Polish, pre-trained using a combination of publicly available text corpora and a large collection of methodically pre-processed web data. We have shown the effectiveness of our models by comparing them with other transformer-based approaches and recent state-of-the-art approaches. We conducted a comprehensive evaluation on a wide set of Polish linguistic tasks, including binary and multi-class classification, regression, and sequence labeling. In our experiments, the larger model performed better than other methods in eleven of the thirteen cases. To accelerate research on NLP for Polish language, we have released the pre-trained models publicly.

References

1. Akbik, A., Blythe, D., Vollgraf, R.: Contextual string embeddings for sequence labeling. In: Proceedings of the 27th International Conference on Computational Linguistics, pp. 1638–1649 (2018)
2. Aleksander Wawer, E.M.: Results of the PolEval 2018 shared task 2: named entity recognition. In: Proceedings of the PolEval 2018 Workshop, pp. 53–62 (2018)
3. Antoun, W., Baly, F., Hajj, H.: AraBERT: transformer-based model for Arabic language understanding. arXiv preprint arXiv:2003.00104 (2020)
4. Arkhipov, M., Trofimova, M., Kuratov, Y., Sorokin, A.: Tuning multilingual transformers for language-specific named entity recognition. In: Proceedings of the 7th Workshop on Balto-Slavic Natural Language Processing, Florence, Italy, pp. 89–93. Association for Computational Linguistics, August 2019. https://www.aclweb.org/anthology/W19-3712
5. Bojanowski, P., Grave, E., Joulin, A., Mikolov, T.: Enriching word vectors with subword information. Trans. Assoc. Comput. Linguist. **5**, 135–146 (2017)
6. Cañete, J., Chaperon, G., Fuentes, R., Pérez, J.: Spanish pre-trained Bert model and evaluation data. In: Practical ML for Developing Countries Workshop @ ICLR 2020 (2020)
7. Conneau, A., et al.: Unsupervised cross-lingual representation learning at scale. arXiv preprint arXiv:1911.02116 (2019)
8. Conneau, A., Lample, G.: Cross-lingual language model pretraining. In: Wallach, II., Larochelle, H., Beygelzimer, A., d' Alché-Buc, F., Fox, E., Garnett, R. (eds.) Advances in Neural Information Processing Systems, vol. 32, pp. 7059–7069. Curran Associates, Inc. (2019). http://papers.nips.cc/paper/8928-cross-lingual-language-model-pretraining.pdf
9. Cui, Y., Che, W., Liu, T., Qin, B., Yang, Z., Wang, S., Hu, G.: Pre-training with whole word masking for Chinese BERT. arXiv preprint arXiv:1906.08101 (2019)
10. Czapla, P., Gugger, S., Howard, J., Kardas, M.: Universal language model fine-tuning for polish hate speech detection. In: Proceedings of the PolEval 2019 Workshop, p. 149 (2019)
11. Dadas, S.: Combining neural and knowledge-based approaches to named entity recognition in polish. In: Rutkowski, L., Scherer, R., Korytkowski, M., Pedrycz, W., Tadeusiewicz, R., Zurada, J.M. (eds.) ICAISC 2019. LNCS (LNAI), vol. 11508, pp. 39–50. Springer, Cham (2019). https://doi.org/10.1007/978-3-030-20912-4_4
12. Dadas, S., Perełkiewicz, M., Poświata, R.: Evaluation of sentence representations in polish. In: Proceedings of The 12th Language Resources and Evaluation Conference, Marseille, France, pp. 1674–1680. European Language Resources Association, May 2020. https://www.aclweb.org/anthology/2020.lrec-1.207
13. Dai, Z., Yang, Z., Yang, Y., Carbonell, J., Le, Q., Salakhutdinov, R.: Transformer-XL: attentive language models beyond a fixed-length context. In: Proceedings of the 57th Annual Meeting of the Association for Computational Linguistics, , Florence, Italy, pp. 2978–2988. Association for Computational Linguistics, July 2019. https://www.aclweb.org/anthology/P19-1285
14. Delobelle, P., Winters, T., Berendt, B.: Robbert: a Dutch roberta-based language model. arXiv preprint arXiv:2001.06286 (2020)

15. Devlin, J., Chang, M.W., Lee, K., Toutanova, K.: BERT: pre-training of deep bidirectional transformers for language understanding. In: Proceedings of the 2019 Conference of the North American Chapter of the Association for Computational Linguistics: Human Language Technologies, Volume 1 (Long and Short Papers), Minneapolis, Minnesota, pp. 4171–4186. Association for Computational Linguistics, June 2019. https://www.aclweb.org/anthology/N19-1423

16. Heafield, K.: KenLM: faster and smaller language model queries. In: Proceedings of the Sixth Workshop on Statistical Machine Translation, pp. 187–197 (2011)

17. Howard, J., Ruder, S.: Universal language model fine-tuning for text classification. In: Proceedings of the 56th Annual Meeting of the Association for Computational Linguistics (Volume 1: Long Papers), pp. 328–339 (2018)

18. Jawahar, G., Sagot, B., Seddah, D.: What does BERT learn about the structure of language? In: ACL 2019–57th Annual Meeting of the Association for Computational Linguistics. Florence, Italy, July 2019. https://hal.inria.fr/hal-02131630

19. Kitaev, N., Kaiser, L., Levskaya, A.: Reformer: the efficient transformer. In: International Conference on Learning Representations (2020)

20. Kocoń, J., Miłkowski, P., Zaśko-Zielińska, M.: Multi-level sentiment analysis of PolEmo 2.0: extended corpus of multi-domain consumer reviews. In: Proceedings of the 23rd Conference on Computational Natural Language Learning (CoNLL), Hong Kong, China, pp. 980–991. Association for Computational Linguistics, November 2019. https://www.aclweb.org/anthology/K19-1092

21. Kovaleva, O., Romanov, A., Rogers, A., Rumshisky, A.: Revealing the dark secrets of BERT. In: Proceedings of the 2019 Conference on Empirical Methods in Natural Language Processing and the 9th International Joint Conference on Natural Language Processing (EMNLP-IJCNLP), Hong Kong, China, pp. 4365–4374. Association for Computational Linguistics, November 2019. https://www.aclweb.org/anthology/D19-1445

22. Kudo, T., Richardson, J.: SentencePiece: a simple and language independent subword tokenizer and detokenizer for neural text processing. In: Proceedings of the 2018 Conference on Empirical Methods in Natural Language Processing: System Demonstrations, Brussels, Belgium, pp. 66–71. Association for Computational Linguistics, November 2018. https://www.aclweb.org/anthology/D18-2012

23. Kuratov, Y., Arkhipov, M.: Adaptation of deep bidirectional multilingual transformers for Russian language. arXiv preprint arXiv:1905.07213 (2019)

24. Lan, Z., Chen, M., Goodman, S., Gimpel, K., Sharma, P., Soricut, R.: Albert: a lite BERT for self-supervised learning of language representations. In: International Conference on Learning Representations (2020)

25. Le, H., et al.: Flaubert: unsupervised language model pre-training for French. arXiv preprint arXiv:1912.05372 (2019)

26. Liu, Y., et al.: Roberta: a robustly optimized BERT pretraining approach. arXiv preprint arXiv:1907.11692 (2019)

27. Marcińczuk, M., Ptak, M., Radziszewski, A., Piasecki, M.: Open dataset for development of polish question answering systems. In: Vetulani, Z., Uszkoreit, H. (eds.) Proceedings of Human Language Technologies as a Challenge for Computer Science and Linguistics 2013, pp. 479–483. Fundacja UAM, Poznań (2013)

28. Marelli, M., Menini, S., Baroni, M., Bentivogli, L., Bernardi, R., Zamparelli, R.: A SICK cure for the evaluation of compositional distributional semantic models. In: Proceedings of the Ninth International Conference on Language Resources and Evaluation (LREC 2014), Reykjavik, Iceland, pp. 216–223. European Language Resources Association (ELRA), May 2014. http://www.lrec-conf.org/proceedings/lrec2014/pdf/363_Paper.pdf

29. Martin, L., et al.: CamemBERT: a tasty French language model. arXiv preprint arXiv:1911.03894 (2019)
30. Mikolov, T., Sutskever, I., Chen, K., Corrado, G.S., Dean, J.: Distributed representations of words and phrases and their compositionality. In: Advances in Neural Information Processing Systems, pp. 3111–3119 (2013)
31. Nguyen, D.Q., Nguyen, A.T.: Phobert: pre-trained language models for Vietnamese. arXiv preprint arXiv:2003.00744 (2020)
32. Ogrodniczuk, M., Kopeć, M.: The polish summaries corpus. In: Chair), N.C.C., Choukri, K., Declerck, T., Loftsson, H., Maegaard, B., Mariani, J., Moreno, A., Odijk, J., Piperidis, S. (eds.) Proceedings of the Ninth International Conference on Language Resources and Evaluation (LREC 2014), Reykjavik, Iceland. European Language Resources Association (ELRA), May 2014
33. Peng, T.: The staggering cost of training SOTA AI models, June 2019. https://syncedreview.com/2019/06/27/the-staggering-cost-of-training-sota-ai-models/
34. Pennington, J., Socher, R., Manning, C.: Glove: global vectors for word representation. In: Proceedings of the 2014 conference on empirical methods in natural language processing (EMNLP), pp. 1532–1543 (2014)
35. Peters, M., Neumann, M., Iyyer, M., Gardner, M., Clark, C., Lee, K., Zettlemoyer, L.: Deep contextualized word representations. In: Proceedings of the 2018 Conference of the North American Chapter of the Association for Computational Linguistics: Human Language Technologies, Volume 1 (Long Papers), vol. 1, pp. 2227–2237 (2018)
36. Przepiórkowski, A., Banko, M., Górski, R.L., Lewandowska-Tomaszczyk, B.: Narodowy Korpus Jezyka Polskiego [Eng.: National Corpus of Polish]. Wydawnictwo Naukowe PWN, Warsaw (2012)
37. Ptaszynski, M., Pieciukiewicz, A., Dybała, P.: Results of the PolEval 2019 shared task 6: first dataset and open shared task for automatic cyberbullying detection in polish Twitter. In: Proceedings of the PolEval 2019 Workshop, p. 89 (2019)
38. Rybak, P., Mroczkowski, R., Tracz, J., Gawlik, I.: KLEJ: comprehensive benchmark for polish language understanding. arXiv preprint arXiv:2005.00630 (2020)
39. Shibuya, T., Hovy, E.: Nested named entity recognition via second-best sequence learning and decoding. arXiv preprint arXiv:1909.02250 (2019)
40. Souza, F., Nogueira, R., Lotufo, R.: Portuguese named entity recognition using BERT-CRF. arXiv preprint arXiv:1909.10649 (2019). http://arxiv.org/abs/1909.10649
41. Sun, Y., et al.: Ernie 2.0: a continual pre-training framework for language understanding. arXiv preprint arXiv:1907.12412 (2019)
42. Vaswani, A., et al.: Attention is all you need. In: Advances in Neural Information Processing Systems, pp. 5998–6008 (2017)
43. Virtanen, A., et al.: Multilingual is not enough: Bert for finnish. arXiv preprint arXiv:1912.07076 (2019)
44. de Vries, W., van Cranenburgh, A., Bisazza, A., Caselli, T., van Noord, G., Nissim, M.: Bertje: a Dutch BERT model. arXiv preprint arXiv:1912.09582 (2019)
45. Wróblewska, A., Krasnowska-Kieraś, K.: Polish evaluation dataset for compositional distributional semantics models. In: Proceedings of the 55th Annual Meeting of the Association for Computational Linguistics (Volume 1: Long Papers), Vancouver, Canada, pp. 784–792. Association for Computational Linguistics, July 2017. https://www.aclweb.org/anthology/P17-1073

46. Xu, L., Zhang, X., Dong, Q.: CLUECorpus2020: a large-scale Chinese corpus for pre-training language model. arXiv preprint arXiv:2003.01355 (2020)
47. Yang, Z., Dai, Z., Yang, Y., Carbonell, J., Salakhutdinov, R.R., Le, Q.V.: XLNet: generalized autoregressive pretraining for language understanding. In: Advances in Neural Information Processing Systems, pp. 5754–5764 (2019)

On a Streaming Approach for Training Denoising Auto-encoders

Piotr Duda[1](✉) and Lipo Wang[2]

[1] Czestochowa University of Technology, Czestochowa, Poland
piotr.duda@pcz.pl
[2] Nanyang Technological University, Singapore, Singapore

Abstract. Learning deep neural networks requires huge hardware resources and takes a long time. This is due to the need to process huge data sets multiple times. One type of neural networks that are particularly useful in practice are denoising autoencoders. It is, therefore, necessary to create new algorithms that reduce the training time for this type of networks. In this work, we propose a method that, in contrast to the classical approach, where each data element is repeatedly processed by the network, is focused on processing only the most difficult to analyze elements. In the learning process, subsequent data may lose their significance and others may become important. Therefore, an additional algorithm has been used to detect such changes. The method draws inspiration from boosting algorithms and drift detectors.

Keywords: Denoising autoencoders · Artificial neural networks · Drift detectors.

1 Introduction

In recent years, we can easily observe the rapid development of deep learning techniques. This mainly applies to various types of neural networks. Among the most popular techniques are convolutional neural networks [26], which are often used to images analysis; recursive neural networks, commonly used, among others, to natural language processing [40]; or restricted Boltzman machines used for density estimation or detection of changes in incoming data [21]. Less popular techniques, like spiking neural networks, are also developing significantly [28].

Much attention should be paid to autoencoders, which are a special type of neural networks. Their task is to recreate at the output the information given at the input. Depending on the application, several types of autoencoders are distinguished, such as sparse, contrastive, variational, and denoising autoencoders. In this work, we will focus on denoising encoders. This means that noisy data elements are fed to the autoencoder input, and at the output, we expect to

This work was supported by the Polish National Science Centre under grant no. 2017/27/B/ST6/02852.

receive noise-free information. This approach is particularly useful in working with missing and uncertain data.

A spectacular performance deep neural networks in solving speech and image processing problems, have made both researchers and companies pay special attention to them. However, training such models require the collection of huge amounts of data, and the learning process, epoch after epoch, makes that data are processed many times. As a result, training deep models requires both a lot of time and computers with sufficient computing power [1,18,24,27].

On the other hand, the problem of analysis of the huge amounts of data, so-called Big Data analysis (BDA), has become a separate research field [25]. Among the various approaches, one of the most promising is data stream mining (DSM). This approach requires that the data are not stored in the system but are processed as soon as arrive from the stream, and next, forgotten as soon as possible. Another important condition is to ensure that the algorithm can respond immediately, regardless of the rate at which data elements arrive. Therefore, it is not recommended to use long-term learning processes, such as epoch learning of neural networks. The last but not least feature of DSM is the ability of algorithms to detect and react to changes in the environment. This phenomenon is called concept-drift. Data stream mining can be applied in many fields, i.e. iterative learning control [35,36].

DSM algorithms can be divided by the way they process data. The on-line algorithms process single data elements immediately after arrival. This group includes, among others, the classification [20,32,33,39], regression [10,11,19,31] and density estimation algorithms [13]. This approach is also used in other, more complex systems [43]. Another approach is to process data chunks. This method is often combined with ensembles of classifiers [9,12]. There are also solutions based on storing in memory only a constant number of recently arrived data elements. This approach is called sliding windows [3].

We can also divide these algorithms by the way they react to concept drift. We distinguish a passive and active approach here. The passive approach is based on the self-adaptation of the model to changes in the environment through its continuous learning. In an active approach, the algorithm indicates the moment when the concept changed and then tries to create a new model that will be better adapted to the new environment. The change detection mechanism is called the drift detector (DD). The other approach to detecting changes is proposed in [34,37].

In the classic approach of neural network training, data from the training set are divided into batches and given into the network's input. After forward propagation, the network error is calculated and propagated backward, to change the values of the weights. Such a process is sometimes unfavorable, as the processing of data elements that do not tune the network takes the same amount of time as the processing of important data (i.e. those that have the greatest impact on the learning process). Work [8] shows how we can select subsets of training data so that the network can learn from the most important data. In contrast to this work, which focuses only on the classification task, we concentrate now on applying this method to learning the denoising autoencoders.

The rest of the paper is divided into the following sections. In Sect. 2 recent works on autoencoders and drift detectors are presented. Section 3 describes the proposed algorithm. The simulation results are presented in Sect. 4. Finally, the conclusions are given in Sect. 5.

2   Related Works

One of the most interesting structures applicable to unsupervised learning are autoencoders [2], which learn how to reconstruct original data. In [7] the authors presented a denoising autoencoder that extracts features from data with noise. In [16] the authors proposed a convolutional denoising autoencoder to process medical images. In [42] an application of denoising autoencoders to the recommender system is presented. Solving the problem of single-channel audio signal separation is considered [17]. In [41] the authors apply autoencoders to improve electricity price forecasting.

One of the most important tools developed within SDM is the drift detector. Several approaches are proposed in the literature. The Drift Detection Method (DDM) [14] monitors the correctness of classification by the current model. Treating observations as a result of Bernoulli trials, the authors propose a statistical test to inform about warning or alarm state. In paper [15] the authors propose the Adaptive Random Forests algorithm, which combines classical random forest procedure with Hoeffding's decision trees. To react to changes in data stream, a procedure based on the ADWIN algorithm [3] and the Page-Hinkley test [30] can be applied. In [5], the authors proposed the WSTD algorithm, which applied the Wilcoxon rank-sum statistical test to improve false positive detection. In [6], the authors proposed computing multiple models explanations over time and observing the magnitudes of their changes.

It should also be noted that several authors tried to merge the fields of deep learning and data stream mining. In [4] the authors combined the evolving deep neural network with the Least Squares Support Vector Machine. Deep neural networks were also successfully applied in semi-supervised learning tasks in the context of streaming data. It was demonstrated how such structures can be used for online learning from data streams. In [29] the Deep Hybrid Boltzmann Machines and Denoising Autoencoders were proposed. In [38] the idea was to train the Deep Belief Network in an unsupervised manner based on the unlabeled data from the stream. Then, few available labeled elements were used to occasionally fine-tune the model to the current data concept. In [21] and [22] the authors proposed to apply the RBM as a concept drift detector. It was demonstrated that the properly learned RBM can be used to monitor possible changes in the underlying data distribution. This method was further analyzed from the resource-awareness perspective in [23].

3   The BBTADD Algorithm for Denoising Autoencoders

The approach presented in this paper is mainly based on the BBTA algorithm proposed in [8].

Let T be a training set consisting of N elements, where each of them is d-dimensional feature vector X_i for $i = 1, \ldots, N$, i.e.

$$T = \{X_i | i = 1, \ldots, N, X_i \in \mathbf{A}\}, \tag{1}$$

where $\mathbf{A}$ is a d-dimensional feature space. Moreover, a new factor has been added to each element describing a probability of drawing (*pod*) from the stream.

$$T^S = \{(X_i, v_i) | X_i \in T, v_i \in (0, 1)\}. \tag{2}$$

Through subsequent, independent draws of elements from the set T^S, we can create a data stream S_t as follows

$$S_t = (Y_1, \ldots, Y_t | Y_i = (X_{j_i}, c_{j_i}), 1 \leq i \leq t, 1 \leq j_i \leq N), \tag{3}$$

where t is an index of the last element coming from the stream.

The denoising autoencoder is a function mapping from set $\mathbf{A}$ to itself, $f : \mathbf{A} \to \mathbf{A}$. Without loss of generality, we can assume that the autoencoder consists of l layers. Then the function f can be expressed in the following way

$$f(X) = \phi_l \circ \phi_{l-1} \circ \cdots \circ \phi_1(X), \tag{4}$$

where X is the input vector. A single layer $\phi_j : \mathbf{Z_{j-1}} \to \mathbf{Z_j}$, where $j = 1, \ldots, l$, $\mathbf{Z_j}$ is an N_j dimensional space of $(j-1)$-th layer output values, $\mathbf{Z_0} = \mathbf{Z_l} = \mathbf{A}$, can be defined as follows

$$\phi_j(z) = [\rho_j^1(\textstyle\sum_{i=1}^{N_{j-1}} w_{i,1} z_i + b_1), \ldots, \rho_j^{N_j}(\textstyle\sum_{i=1}^{N_{j-1}} w_{i,N_j} z_i + b_{N_j})] \tag{5}$$

where $z = [z_1, \ldots, z_{N_j}] \in \mathbf{Z_{j-1}}$, $w_{i,m}$ is a weight between the i-th neuron of the $(j-1)$-th layer and the m-th neuron of the j-th layer, ρ_j^m is an activation function for the m-th neuron on the j-th layer and b_m is the bias for the m-th neuron.

The classic approach to learning multidimensional neural networks involves updating weights according to the following formula

$$w_{i,m} := w_{i,m} - \eta \frac{\partial L}{\partial w_{i,m}}, \tag{6}$$

where $\eta > 0$ is the learning rate and L is a loss function.

In [8], three methods of determining v_i value were proposed. In our work we will use the NLB approach. First, the temporary values v_i are determined according to the following formula

$$v_i' = tanh(L(X_i))/M_i, \tag{7}$$

where M_i indicates the number of times the i-th data element was drawn in the past. In consequence, big values of loss function give high index of drawing this element, close to 1, and the small ones close to 0.

Next, as values v_i' are not probability mass function (since they do not have to sum up to 1), they are normalized after processing the whole mini-batch in the following way

$$v_i = \begin{cases} v_i'/Z, & \text{for } x_i \in B \\ v_i/Z, & \text{for } x_i \in T \backslash B \end{cases} \tag{8}$$

where Z is a normalization factor, given as

$$Z = \sum_{\{v_i'|X_i \in T\}} v_i'. \tag{9}$$

After processing one mini-batch of data, another one is generated and the procedure is repeated until the stopping condition is fulfilled.

Changing the weights of the network only according to elements that are not well classified can lead to network untune, which means to misclassifying elements that previously processed correctly. Another threat is the fact that constantly analyzing the same data can lead to network overfitting. Consequently, an important element of the algorithm is the drift detector, which allows indicating a moment since when elements draw according to the current *pod* values do not affect the learning process well.

As in [8], we used the CuSum algorithm as a drift detector, given by the following formula

$$Cus_0 = 0, \tag{10}$$
$$Cus_i = max(0, Cus_{i-1} + L(B_{i-1}) - L(B_i) - \alpha), \tag{11}$$

for $i = 1, 2, \ldots$, where $L(B_i)$ is a value of the loss function in the i-th mini-bath and α is a fixed parameter. The drift is detected when Cus_i exceeds the value of the threshold λ_C.

The summary of the BBTADD algorithm is presented in Algorithm 1.

4   Experimental Results

In this chapter, the application of the algorithm described in Sect. 3 is tested for autoencoders training. To this end, the MNIST data set is used. The training set consists of 60 000 elements representing hand-drawn numbers. The test set has 10 000 elements. The performance of the proposed method will be compared with the performance of the autoencoder trained by the classical approach.

To perform the simulations, a convolution neural network consists of 9 layers was used. The first 5 layers are convolution and max-pooling layers, alternately placed. The convolution layers consist of 16, 8, and 8 filters, respectively. Next, the two alternately arranged deconvolution and upsampling layers are placed.

Input: S - data stream, M - batch size, α, λ_C
1 CuSum = 0 ;
2 Collect a new batch B from the stream S;
3 **for** *every data element in B* **do**
4 │   Increase counter of drawn of the current element;
5 │   Train the network on current element;
6 │   Compute loss function for a current element;
7 │   Update v_i according to (7)
8 **for** *every data element in T* **do**
9 │   Update *pods* according to (8)
10 Compute loss function on a validation set;
11 Update CuSum according to (10);
12 **if** *CuSum* > λ_C **then**
13 │   Reinitialize *pod's* values;
14 │   *Return to line 1*;
15 **else**
16 │   *Return to line 2*;

Algorithm 1: The BBATDD algorithm.

The deconvolution layers consist of 8 and 1 filters, respectively. The sizes of the filters in all convolution and deconvolution layers was set to 3 on 3, and in pooling and upsampling to 2 on 2. The relu activation function was used. The diagram of the network is presented in Fig. 1.

```
Layer (type)                    Output Shape          Param #
=================================================================
input_1 (InputLayer)            [(None, 28, 28, 1)]    0

conv2d (Conv2D)                 (None, 28, 28, 16)     160

max_pooling2d (MaxPooling2D)    (None, 14, 14, 16)     0

conv2d_1 (Conv2D)               (None, 14, 14, 8)      1160

max_pooling2d_1 (MaxPooling2     (None, 7, 7, 8)        0

conv2d_2 (Conv2D)               (None, 7, 7, 8)        584

up_sampling2d (UpSampling2D)    (None, 14, 14, 8)      0

conv2d_3 (Conv2D)               (None, 14, 14, 8)      584

up_sampling2d_1 (UpSampling2    (None, 28, 28, 8)      0

conv2d_transpose (Conv2DTran    (None, 28, 28, 1)      73
=================================================================
```

Fig. 1. Convolutional autoencoder

The first experiment presents a comparison of the network training in a classic way and using the BBTADD algorithm. The size of the batches used during training was set to 128 elements. The classical network has been trained by 100 epochs, which is equivalent to 46,875 batches used for learning the BBTADD algorithm. Figure 2 shows the loss function obtained for both approaches on the test set. The loss function used during training is binary cross-entropy. It can be easily seen that the value of the loss function for the proposed algorithm decreases faster compared to the classical approach.

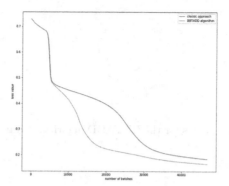

Fig. 2. The loss function computed on the test set for subsequent batches

An example of denoising images obtained by using the classic approach and the BBTADD algorithm is shown in the Figs. 3 and 4, respectively.

Fig. 3. The original and denoised images by the classic autoencoder

Fig. 4. The original and denoised images by the BBTADD algorithm

The next experiment was a comparison of the performance of the proposed algorithm trained on different batch sizes. For this purpose, the number of elements in a batch was set to 128, 256, 512, and 1024. The values of the loss function for these simulations are presented in Fig. 5. It shows that smaller batch sizes allow for greater accuracy. On the other hand, it is also important to compare the training time for different batch sizes. Calculations on larger batches are faster. For batches from 128 to 1024, they take 2555, 1311, 719, and 1024 s, respectively.

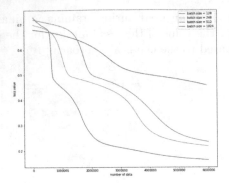

Fig. 5. The loss function values for the BBTADD algorithm trained with different sizes of batches

5   Conclusions

This paper explores the possibility of training autoencoders by selecting certain subsets of data from the training set. The carried out simulations showed the usefulness of the proposed method. The values of the loss function decreased faster than in the case of autoencoders trained classically. The effects of noise reduction on the image data were satisfactory. In the future, the proposed method will be used to train deeper models as well as it will be applied to other types of data.

References

1. Akdeniz, E., Egrioglu, E., Bas, E., Yolcu, U.: An ARMA type pi-sigma artificial neural network for nonlinear time series forecasting. J. Artif. Intell. Soft Comput. Res. **8**(2), 121–132 (2018)
2. Bengio, Y.: Learning deep architectures for AI. Found. Trends Mach. Learn. **2**(1), 1–127 (2009)
3. Bifet, A., Gavaldà, R.: Adaptive learning from evolving data streams. In: Adams, N.M., Robardet, C., Siebes, A., Boulicaut, J.-F. (eds.) IDA 2009. LNCS, vol. 5772, pp. 249–260. Springer, Heidelberg (2009). https://doi.org/10.1007/978-3-642-03915-7_22
4. Bodyanskiy, Y., Vynokurova, O., Pliss, I., Setlak, G, Mulesa, P.: Fast learning algorithm for deep evolving GMDH-SVM neural network in data stream mining tasks. In: 2016 IEEE First International Conference on Data Stream Mining Processing (DSMP), pp. 257–262, August 2016
5. deBarros, R.S.M., Hidalgo, J.I.G., de Lima Cabral, D.R.: Wilcoxon rank sum test drift detector. Neurocomputing **275**, 1954–1963 (2018)
6. Demsar, J., Bosnic, Z.: Detecting concept drift in data streams using model explanation. Expert Syst. Appl. **92**, 546–559 (2018)
7. Du, B., Xiong, W., Wu, J., Zhang, L., Zhang, L., Tao, D.: Stacked convolutional denoising auto-encoders for feature representation. IEEE Trans. Cybern. **47**(4), 1017–1027 (2016)

8. Duda, P., Jaworski, M., Cader, A., Wang, L.: On training deep neural networks using a streaming approach. J. Artif. Intell. Soft Comput. Res. **10**(1), 15–26 (2020)
9. Duda, P., Jaworski, M., Rutkowski, L.: On ensemble components selection in data streams scenario with reoccurring concept-drift. In: 2017 IEEE Symposium Series on Computational Intelligence (SSCI), pp. 1–7. IEEE (2017)
10. Duda, P., Jaworski, M., Rutkowski, L.: Convergent time-varying regression models for data streams: tracking concept drift by the recursive Parzen-based generalized regression neural networks. Int. J. Neural Syst. **28**(02), 1750048 (2018)
11. Duda, P., Jaworski, M., Rutkowski, L.: Knowledge discovery in data streams with the orthogonal series-based generalized regression neural networks. Inf. Sci. **460**, 497–518 (2018)
12. Duda, P., Jaworski, M., Rutkowski, L.: Online GRNN-based ensembles for regression on evolving data streams. In: Huang, T., Lv, J., Sun, C., Tuzikov, A.V. (eds.) ISNN 2018. LNCS, vol. 10878, pp. 221–228. Springer, Cham (2018). https://doi.org/10.1007/978-3-319-92537-0_26
13. Duda, P., Rutkowski, L., Jaworski, M., Rutkowska, D.: On the Parzen kernel-based probability density function learning procedures over time-varying streaming data with applications to pattern classification. IEEE Trans. Cybern. **50**(4), 1683–1696 (2020)
14. Gama, J., Medas, P., Castillo, G., Rodrigues, P.: Learning with drift detection. In: Bazzan, A.L.C., Labidi, S. (eds.) SBIA 2004. LNCS (LNAI), vol. 3171, pp. 286–295. Springer, Heidelberg (2004). https://doi.org/10.1007/978-3-540-28645-5_29
15. Gomes, H.M., et al.: Adaptive random forests for evolving data stream classification. Mach. Learn. 1469–1495 (2017). https://doi.org/10.1007/s10994-017-5642-8
16. Gondara, L.: Medical image denoising using convolutional denoising autoencoders. In: 2016 IEEE 16th International Conference on Data Mining Workshops (ICDMW), pp. 241–246. IEEE (2016)
17. Grais, E.M., Plumbley, M.D.: Single channel audio source separation using convolutional denoising autoencoders. In: 2017 IEEE Global Conference on Signal and Information Processing (GlobalSIP), pp. 1265–1269. IEEE (2017)
18. Hou, Y., Holder, L.B.: On graph mining with deep learning: introducing model r for link weight prediction. J. Artif. Intell. Soft Comput. Res. **9**(1), 21–40 (2019)
19. Jaworski, M.: Regression function and noise variance tracking methods for data streams with concept drift. Int. J. Appl. Math. Comput. Sci. **28**(3), 559–567 (2018)
20. Jaworski, M., Duda, P., Rutkowski, L.: New splitting criteria for decision trees in stationary data streams. IEEE Trans. Neural Netw. Learn. Syst. **29**(6), 2516–2529 (2017)
21. Jaworski, M., Duda, P., Rutkowski, L.: On applying the restricted Boltzmann machine to active concept drift detection. In: 2017 IEEE Symposium Series on Computational Intelligence (SSCI), pp. 1–8. IEEE (2017)
22. Jaworski, M., Duda, P., Rutkowski, L.: Concept drift detection in streams of labelled data using the restricted Boltzmann machine. In: 2018 International Joint Conference on Neural Networks (IJCNN), pp. 1–7. IEEE (2018)
23. Jaworski, M., Rutkowski, L., Duda, P., Cader, A.: Resource-aware data stream mining using the restricted Boltzmann machine. In: Rutkowski, L., Scherer, R., Korytkowski, M., Pedrycz, W., Tadeusiewicz, R., Zurada, J.M. (eds.) ICAISC 2019. LNCS (LNAI), vol. 11509, pp. 384–396. Springer, Cham (2019). https://doi.org/10.1007/978-3-030-20915-5_35
24. Kamimura, R.: Supposed maximum mutual information for improving generalization and interpretation of multi-layered neural networks. J. Artif. Intell. Soft Comput. Res. **9**(2), 123–147 (2019)

25. Koren, O., Hallin, C.A., Perel, N., Bendet, D.: Decision-making enhancement in a big data environment: application of the k-means algorithm to mixed data. J. Artif. Intell. Soft Comput. Res. **9**(4), 293–302 (2019)
26. Kumarratneshk, R., Weilleweill, E., Aghdasi, F., Sriram, P.: A strong and efficient baseline for vehicle re-identification using deep triplet embedding. J. Artif. Intell. Soft Comput. Res. **10**(1), 27–45 (2020)
27. Ludwig, S.A.: Applying a neural network ensemble to intrusion detection. J. Artif. Intell. Soft Comput. Res. **9**(3), 177–188 (2019)
28. Nobukawa, S., Nishimura, H., Yamanishi, T.: Pattern classification by spiking neural networks combining self-organized and reward-related spike-timing-dependent plasticity. J. Artif. Intell. Soft Comput. Res. **9**(4), 283–291 (2019)
29. Ororbia, A.G.I., Giles, C.L., Reitter, D.: Online semi-supervised learning with deep hybrid Boltzmann machines and denoising autoencoders. CoRR, abs/1511.06964 (2015)
30. Page, E.S.: Continuous inspection schemes. Biometrika **41**(1/2), 100–115 (1954)
31. Pietruczuk, L., Rutkowski, L., Jaworski, M., Duda, P.: The Parzen kernel approach to learning in non-stationary environment. In: 2014 International Joint Conference on Neural Networks (IJCNN), pp. 3319–3323. IEEE (2014)
32. Pietruczuk, L., Rutkowski, L., Jaworski, M., Duda, P.: A method for automatic adjustment of ensemble size in stream data mining. In: 2016 International Joint Conference on Neural Networks (IJCNN), pp. 9–15. IEEE (2016)
33. Pietruczuk, L., Rutkowski, L., Jaworski, M., Duda, P.: How to adjust an ensemble size in stream data mining? Inf. Sci. **381**, 46–54 (2017)
34. Rafajłowicz, E., Rafajłowicz, W.: Testing (non-) linearity of distributed-parameter systems from a video sequence. Asian J. Control **12**(2), 146–158 (2010)
35. Rafajłowicz, E., Rafajłowicz, W.: Iterative learning in repetitive optimal control of linear dynamic processes. In: Rutkowski, L., Korytkowski, M., Scherer, R., Tadeusiewicz, R., Zadeh, L.A., Zurada, J.M. (eds.) ICAISC 2016. LNCS (LNAI), vol. 9692, pp. 705–717. Springer, Cham (2016). https://doi.org/10.1007/978-3-319-39378-0_60
36. Rafajłowicz, E., Rafajłowicz, W.: Iterative learning in optimal control of linear dynamic processes. Int. J. Control **91**(7), 1522–1540 (2018)
37. Rafajłowicz, E., Wnuk, M., Rafajłowicz, W.: Local detection of defects from image sequences. Int. J. Appl. Math. Comput. Sci. **18**(4), 581–592 (2008)
38. Read, J., Perez-Cruz, F., Bifet, A.: Deep learning in partially-labeled data streams. In: Proceedings of the 30th Annual ACM Symposium on Applied Computing, SAC 2015, New York, NY, USA, pp. 954–959. ACM (2015)
39. Rutkowski, L., Pietruczuk, L., Duda, P., Jaworski, M.: Decision trees for mining data streams based on the McDiarmid's bound. IEEE Trans. Knowl. Data Eng. **25**(6), 1272–1279 (2013)
40. Shewalkar, A., Nyavanandi, D., Ludwig, S.A.: Performance evaluation of deep neural networks applied to speech recognition: RNN, LSTM and GRU. J. Artif. Intell. Soft Comput. Res. **9**(4), 235–245 (2019)
41. Wang, L., Zhang, Z., Chen, J.: Short-term electricity price forecasting with stacked denoising autoencoders. IEEE Trans. Power Syst. **32**(4), 2673–2681 (2016)
42. Wu, Y., DuBois, C., Zheng, A.X., Ester, M.: Collaborative denoising auto-encoders for top-n recommender systems. In: Proceedings of the Ninth ACM International Conference on Web Search and Data Mining, pp. 153–162 (2016)
43. Zalasinski, M., Lapa, K., Cpalka, K., Przybyszewski, K., Yen, G.G.: On-line signature partitioning using a population based algorithm. J. Artif. Intell. Soft Comput. Res. **10**(1), 5–13 (2020)

Methods of Searching for Similar Device Fingerprints Using Changes in Unstable Parameters

Marcin Gabryel[1]([✉]) and Krzysztof Przybyszewski[2,3]

[1] Institute of Computational Intelligence, Czestochowa University of Technology,
Al. Armii Krajowej 36, 42-200 Częstochowa, Poland
`marcin.gabryel@iisi.pcz.pl`
[2] Information Technology Institute, University of Social Sciences, 90-113 Łodz, Poland
[3] Clark University Worcester, Worcester 01610, MA, USA

Abstract. Web-based device fingerprints (also known as browser fingerprints) are designed to identify the user without leaving a trace in the form of cookies. Some institutions believe that this technique violates the privacy of Internet users; however, it allows for an effective fight against fraudsters generating abusive traffic, which brings losses in Internet advertising. Acquiring the parameters that make up a device fingerprint is rather easy as it is done using JavaScript. Most available parameters, however, do not allow for a clear distinction between users or change quite often over time and are therefore considered unstable. This paper presents an algorithm for searching similar web-based device fingerprints, taking into account changing, unstable parameters obtained from the browser and HTTP headers. The presented algorithm is based on the LSH (Locality-Sensitive Hashing) algorithm, which is commonly used to quickly search for similar documents. The effectiveness of the algorithm performance has been checked by using a database of several thousand visits to various websites.

Keywords: Web-based device fingerprint · Browser fingerprint ·
Locality-Sensitive Hashing

1 Introduction

By using the HTTP mechanism - the so-called cookies, i.e. the ability to store certain information on the client's computer – it is rather easy to identify the user by giving them a unique identifier. Many websites tracking their users use this technique, among other things, to keep track of their current interests and to adjust relevant advertising themes. Nowadays, there is a growing emphasis on privacy, and users are increasingly aware of the possibility of being tracked. This information is provided by the websites themselves, which have been forced to provide information about the use of cookies. There are a number of tools that block user tracking. However, apart from obvious privacy issues, user identification has positive applications. Internet advertising is repeatedly abused in connection with the generation of Internet abusive traffic. This most often manifests itself

L. Rutkowski et al. (Eds.): ICAISC 2020, LNAI 12416, pp. 325–335, 2020.
https://doi.org/10.1007/978-3-030-61534-5_29

in the generation of unnatural clicks, advertisement displays or an automatic entering of personal data into contact forms. Cookies are the easiest method of tracking a user on the Internet and at the same time the easiest one to avoid. Therefore, other methods are used to identify the user online. One method is to generate a so-called web-based device fingerprint (or browser fingerprint), which attempts to identify the user's device and browser on the basis of the unique properties and parameters of the browser. Among the parameters that are obtained are the name and version of the browser and of the operating system, screen information, system font set, canvas fingerprint, HTTP headers, WebGL fingerprint, AudioContext fingerprint, timezone, languages set in the browser, information about installed plug-ins and many others.

The challenge of generating a device fingerprint is to balance fingerprint features with regard to their diversity and stability. The more features are used to create a fingerprint, the more likely it is that all data records will be different. The more traits are used, the more likely it is that individual parameter values will change, thus affecting the stability of a fingerprint. In practice, the values of some features naturally tend to change over time. This is due to browser or operating system updates, installation of new fonts or plugins. Therefore, in most cases, a high level of feature variation reduces the stability. A high level of stability can often only be achieved by including as few features as possible. As far as fingerprint extraction is concerned, it is necessary to find a compromise between diversity and stability.

There are many studies in the literature which describe new methods of obtaining parameters improving the determination of the uniqueness of a given device. At the same time, many organizations (including browser manufacturers) are announcing that the possibility of user identification through fingerprinting mechanisms will be limited. There are also tools available that hinder the process of acquiring parameter values that make up the device fingerprint [8]. One of the first descriptions of the browser fingerprint identification technique appeared in 2011 [3]. The authors proved that by using only a few parameters, such as part of the IP address, font list, time zone, and screen resolution, they were able to discern most users of popular browsers. A major breakthrough was the introduction of canvas fingerprint [4], which based its operation on generating images using the possibilities offered by HTML5. It turns out that graphic processing units generate images in different ways. This allows for a relatively good identification of the user's browser. A similar principle is used to gen-erate AudioContext fingerpint, where it is a property of machine's audio stack itself. This is conceptually similar to canvas fingerprinting: audio signals processed on dif-ferent machines or browsers can vary slightly due to hardware or programming dif-ferences between machines, while the same combination of a machine and browser will still give the same output.

There are a number of studies and compilations providing information concerning the analysis of parameters constituting device fingerprints [5, 6]. One of the most recent studies [1] describes in quite a detailed way the capabilities of the acquired data and the usefulness of creating unique identifiers for browsers. It also contains information about the stability of particular parameters during the tests carried out on working websites. A quite interesting observation from the conducted research is the fact that the stability of collected parameters is maintained for an average of 6 days. However, individual parameters may change earlier.

Another problem is storing such a large and diverse amount of data. For the purpose of a quick search for similar fingerprints, their values are stored in a database in the form of hashes (generated, for example, by the SHA1 algorithm). A pair of fingerprints is considered identical when their hashes are the same. Unfortunately, a change of at least one parameter forming a fingerprint causes the whole hash to change.

The conclusions from the studies described above and the access to several thousand data collected from different types of websites have prompted the author to develop an algorithm that could allow for a comparison of device fingerprints, taking into account parameter changes occurring in particular parameters. The algorithm is based on the popular and fast Locality-Sensitive Hashing (LSH) similar documents search algorithm. The parameters were divided in terms of stability into two groups: one with low or no variability at all and the other with high variability. The algorithm consists of two parts:

- Search for fingerprints potentially similar to the tested fingerprint by using the first group of stable parameters.
- The fingerprints obtained in the search described in the previous point are then searched for target fingerprints using the values of the unstable group parameters. This is done with a much greater degree of probability that the two fingerprint pairs are similar to each other.

The paper presents experimental studies showing the influence of the values of different parameters of the LSH algorithm on the search results, the selection of their optimal values and a comparison with the results obtained from the search conducted using hashing.

The article is divided into the following sections where Sect. 2 describes the LSH algorithm and details of device fingerprinting. Section 3 presents the algorithm for generating and searching for fingerprints. The next section presents the results of the algorithm's performance. The paper ends with conclusions.

2 Algorithms Used in the Research

2.1 Locality-Sensitive Hashing

The main task of the Locality-Sensitive Hashing (LSH) algorithm is to quickly compare documents in terms of their contents. The LSH algorithm consists of three steps:

- transforming the document into a set of characters of length k (the shingling method, also known as k-shingles or k-grams method),
- compressing the shingles set using the "minhashing" method, so that the similarity of the base sets of documents in their compressed versions can still be checked.
- the LSH algorithm, which allows us to find the most similar pairs of documents or all pairs that are above some lower bound in similarity.

Shingling is an effective method of representing a document as a set. To generate the set, we need to select short phrases or sentences from the document, the so-called shingles. This causes documents to have many common elements in their sets even if the sentences appear in documents in a different order.

The next step consists in creating the so-called characteristic matrix, where the columns contain sets of shingles of individual documents, and the consecutive lines correspond to individual shingles. In the matrix cells at the intersection of row i and column j there is value 1 in the case of the i-th shingle in the j-th document.

The idea of hashing is to convert each document to a small signature using hashing function H. If d stands for a document, then $H(d)$ stands for the signature. The H function should be selected so that if the similarity of $sim(d_1, d_2)$ is high, then the probability that $H(d_1) = H(d_2)$ would also be high. If the similarity of $sim(d_1, d_2)$ is small, then the probability that $H(d_1) = H(d_2)$ would be low. In the case when the well-known Jaccard similarity index is used, then MinHash is an appropriate hash function.

In the MinHash algorithm a so-called SIG signature matrix is created with the dimensions $m \times n$, where each of the m documents corresponds to n signatures. The matrix is calculated by performing random and independent n permutations of m rows of the characteristic matrix. The MinHash value for the column of the j-th document is the number of the first row (in the order resulting from the permutations), for which this column has value 1. These calculations are time-consuming, therefore instead of selecting random n row permutations, random n hash functions $h_1, h_2, \ldots, h_n$ are selected. The signature matrix is built taking into account each row in the given order. Let $SIG_{k,j}$ be an element of the signature matrix for the k-th hash function and column j of document d_j. Initially, set $SIG_{k,j}$ to ∞ for all values of k and j. For each row i from the signature matrix, follow these steps:

1. Calculate $h_1(j), h_2(j), \ldots, h_n(j)$.
2. For each column j, check if there is 1 in row i. If yes, then for each $k = 1, 2, \ldots, n$, set $SIG_{k,j} = \min(SIG_{k,j}, h_k(j))$.

The idea of the LSH algorithm allows to check similarity of two elements. As a result of its operation, information is returned whether the pair forms a so-called "candidate pair", i.e. whether their similarity is greater than a specified threshold t (similarity threshold). Any pair that hashed to the same bucket is considered as a "candidate pair". Dissimilar pairs that do hash to the same bucket are false positives. On the other hand, those pairs, which despite being similar do not hash to the same bucket under at least one of the hash functions, are false negatives.

A possible approach to the LSH algorithm is to generate hashes for elements several times. For this purpose a suitable signature matrix can be generated:

1. The signature matrix is divided into b bands, and each band is divided into r rows.
2. For each band, pairs of columns that have the same values are checked. If there is such a pair in one band, it becomes a candidate pair and is thrown into the bucket.
3. Parameters b and r should be selected so as to find as many similar pairs as possible, but at the same time as few *false positives* and *false negatives* as possible.

If s is the Jaccard similarity index between a pair of documents, the probability that they are a one-candidate pair equals:

$$p_c = 1 - \left(1 - s^r\right)^b, \tag{1}$$

where s is the Jaccard similarity coefficient defined by the following formula:

$$s = \frac{|d_1 \cap d_2|}{|d_1 \cup d_2|} \tag{2}$$

for two documents d_1 and d_2. A detailed description of particular parts of the LSH algorithm can be found in a number of works including [2].

2.2 Device Fingerprint

Fingerprint is generated on the basis of the parameters provided by a browser and on the basis of hardware capabilities of the device. This operation requires analysis of the JavaScript language of many web browsers, including those running on mobile devices. The algorithm for generating a unique fingerprint identifier given to identify the browser and the device on which the browser is operating consists in collecting as many parameters as possible the browser's API and performing the hash function on them. It is assumed that the generated hash should be unique enough to distinguish between the devices used.

To quantify the level of identifying information in a fingerprint is used the entropy. The higher the entropy is, the more unique and identifiable a fingerprint will be. Let H be the entropy, X – a discrete random variable with possible values $\{x_1, \ldots, x_n\}$ and $P(X)$ - a probability mass function. The entropy follows this formula:

$$H(X) = -\sum_i P(x_i) log_b P(x_i). \tag{3}$$

For $b = 2$ it is the Shannon entropy and the result is in bits. One bit of entropy reduces by half the probability of an event occurring.

A device fingerprint is created from many different parameters with a varied number of bits of the entropy. For the tests carried out in this work, the set presented in Table 1 was downloaded from the browser. The data was obtained from 80,000 different devices from which the users accessed different websites. The table does not include parameters with entropy below 0.1. Some parameters, such as *screen_id* and User-agent were broken down into individual elements. For *screen_id* it is *width, height, available_width* and *available height*. In the case of User-agent the whole sequence was divided into elements starting with prefix *ua*. The parameters were divided into two groups: group 1 – stable parameters, which do not get changed naturally and group 2 – parameters which get changed naturally (unstable).

Table 1. Device fingerprint obtainable features

Feature	No. of bits of entropy	Group	Feature	No. of bits of entropy	Group
device_memory	1.84	1	browser_plugins_hash	1.59	2
do_not_track_val_id	0.39	1	user-agent	9.80	–
fonts	3.15	1	br_version	3.08	2
audio_params_id	0.98	1	os_version	3.59	2
webgl_vendor_id	1.84	1	app_version	9.79	2
webgl_renderer_id	6.99	1	platform	1.74	1
logic_cores	1.64	1	ua_device_brand_name	2.52	1
platform_id	1.74	1	ua_device_model	4.88	1
timezone	0.43	1	ua_client_name	2.17	1
app_version_id	9.79	1	ua_client_version	4.03	2
touch_enabled	1.00	1	ua_client_type	0.41	1
max_touch_points	1.28	1	ua_device_type	1.34	1
screen_id	5.87	–	ua_device_brand	2.52	1
width	3.83	2	ua_device_code	5.07	1
height	4.50	2	ua_os_name	1.21	1
av_width	3.96	2	ua_os_version	3.42	1
av_height	5.33	2	ua_preferred_client_name	2.56	1
adblock_enabled	0.59	1	ua_preferred_client_version	4.31	2
canvas_2d_fingerprint	6.34	1	ua_preferred_client_type	0.25	1

3 Proposed Algorithm

Commonly used algorithms used for generating device fingerprint [6, 7] generate a unique fingerprint identifier in the form of a hash, which is an alphanumeric sequence of a fixed length. To this end is used a hash function which generates a short hash as an identifier of a large set of data. Two identical sets of data always generate the same hash value. The prerequisite for selecting a new hash function is to check whether the same hash value exists for different datasets. The identifiers created in this way make it impossible to quickly compare them with each other instead of comparing the data set values. However, commonly used hash functions have one disadvantage, i.e. even a small change of one parameter generates a completely different hash value. In the case of a device fingerprint, many of the values that make up a fingerprint are variable over the length of time during which a given device or browser is used, and they, for instance, include screen sizes or software versions. The purpose of this paper is to try to find such a method of fingerprint encoding so that it would be possible to efficiently determine the similarity of two fingerprints despite minor parameter changes. This in turn will make it possible to identify the browser as the same even if there are changes in the parameters during subsequent visits to the website.

The algorithm is based on the LSH and uses the possibility of adjusting the similarity probability value of two documents. This algorithm needs to have the following operating parameters adjusted – the number of bands b and the resulting number of rows r. The adjustment of these values results from the adopted number of MinHash signatures n encoding the documents and similarity threshold t.

For a given number of signatures n, the choice of b and r depends on value s calculated by using formula (2), following the algorithm:

1. Prepare the signature matrix SIG for a given value of MinHash n.
2. Determine the similarity threshold t.
3. Establish the proportions in the form of weights w_{fp} and w_{fn} between the number of *false positive* and *false negative* samples among the candidate pairs. The following condition needs to be met $w_{fp}, w_{fn} \in (0, 1)$ and $w_{fp} + w_{fn} = 1$.
4. For each possible pair combination b, r find the optimal pair b_t, r_t for which the weighted total of the probability value of *false positive* and *false negative* samples:

$$p_{fp}(t, b, r) = \int_0^t 1 - \left(1 - s^r\right)^b ds \qquad (4)$$

and

$$p_{fn}(t, b, r) = \int_t^1 1 - \left(1 - s^r\right)^b ds \qquad (5)$$

will be the smallest:

$$b_t, r_t = \underset{\substack{b = 1, \ldots, n \\ r = 1, \ldots, n/b}}{\mathrm{argmin}} \left(w_{fp} p_{fp}(t, b, r) + w_{fn} p_{fn}(t, b, r)\right) \qquad (6)$$

In the proposed algorithm the fingerprint parameters need to be divided into the stable and unstable ones (see Sect. 2.2). The algorithm is created following the steps presented below:

1. Prepare two sets of parameters: stable ones f_s and unstable ones f_n.
2. Determine the number of signatures for stable and unstable n_s and n_n respectively.
3. Determine the similarity thresholds t_s and t_n.
4. Create two signature matrixes: SIG_s and SIG_n.

In order to find fingerprints similar to fingerprint f_q the following steps need to be carried out:

1. Start the LSH algorithm using the stable parameters to find similar candidate pairs f_{qs}:

$$f_{qs} = \text{LSH}\big(SIG_s(f_q), SIG_s(f_s), t_s\big) \qquad (7)$$

where: $SIG_s(f_q)$, $SIG_s(f_s)$ – signature matrix values for stable parameters obtained for the parameters of fingerprint f_q and f_s.

2. Having found fingerprints f_{qs} do one more search for similar fingerprint, but this time using unstable parameters:

$$f_{qn} = \text{LSH}\big(SIG_n(f_q), SIG_n(f_s), t_n\big) \qquad (8)$$

where: $SIG_n(f_q)$, $SIG_n(f_s)$ – signature matrix values for unstable parameters obtained for the parameters of fingerprints f_q and f_s.

3. Return obtained similar fingerprints f_{qn}.

4 Study Results

The study was carried out on the authentic data collected by a specially prepared script run in the browser during the visits made to the website. The script collected data from 26 websites of various types (Internet shops, loan companies, advertising companies, banks and others) for 3 months. During this period of time several hundred thousand data of different browsers were collected. Using cookies it was possible to identify further visits made by the same users. Thanks to this, it was possible to monitor the changes in the parameters of the browsers. For the study, the data were selected from those persons where the changes occurred in 6, 7 or 8 cases during all the visits made. The most frequent changes occurred in the parameters listed in Table 1 as the second group.

According to the algorithm presented in Sect. 3, for the first group of parameters f_s (the stable ones) the search for similar parameters using the LSH algorithm working on the values of the SIGs matrix with the number of signatures $n_s = 128$ and the similarity threshold $t_s = 1$ were applied. For the obtained candidates f_{qs} the LSH algorithm was applied once again in the second group of parameters f_n (the unstable ones). In this step of the algorithm a number of experiments were carried out where the number of signatures n_n of the MinHash algorithm and the similarity threshold t_n were changed. Precision and recall measures were used as a measure of the effectiveness of the conducted studies [14]. Precision is the ratio of the number of correctly classified data to the total number of irrelevant and relevant data classified:

$$precision = \frac{tp}{tp + fp}$$

and recall is the ratio between the number of data that are correctly classified to the total number of positive data:

$$recall = \frac{tp}{tp + fn}$$

where tp – true positive, fp – false positive, fn – false negative and they can be derived from a confusion matrix [14]. The effectiveness of the algorithm performance was analyzed on 100 randomly selected users. The test consisted in determining whether despite the changes occurring in the fingerprint parameters assigning a particular visit to the user that had actually made it (repeat visits) was correct. The obtained precision and recall values are presented in Tables 2 and 3.

For the same data, the method of generating the hash from the acquired parameters was also used. The search for identical devices is therefore a search for identical hash values. In this experiment the obtained values were: precision $= 0.53$ and recall $= 0.13$.

In Tables 2 and 3 the results with better precision and recall values than those obtained using only hashes were marked in bold. When analyzing the results one can see that the best results of the comparison of the devices can be obtained for $t_n = 1, 0.9$ or 0.8 and $n_n = 8$.

Table 2. Precision for different probabilities of similarity t_n and MinHash value n_n.

t_n	n_n									
	2	4	8	16	24	32	48	64	96	128
1	0.50	0.52	**0.56**	**0.56**	**0.57**	**0.58**	**0.58**	**0.58**	**0.59**	**0.59**
0.9	0.50	0.52	**0.56**	**0.56**	**0.54**	**0.54**	**0.54**	**0.54**	**0.54**	**0.55**
0.8	0.50	0.52	**0.55**	0.53	0.51	0.52	0.52	0.51	0.51	0.51
0.7	0.50	0.52	0.51	0.49	0.49	0.47	0.48	0.50	0.50	0.50
0.6	0.50	0.46	0.47	0.48	0.47	0.47	0.47	0.46	0.46	0.46
0.5	0.47	0.46	0.46	0.46	0.45	0.46	0.46	0.45	0.46	0.45

Table 3. Recall for different values of probability t_n and value of MinHash n_n.

t_n	n_n									
	2	4	8	16	24	32	48	64	96	128
1	**0.19**	**0.14**	**0.14**	0.13	0.13	0.13	0.13	0.13	0.13	0.13
0.9	**0.19**	**0.14**	**0.14**	0.13	0.13	0.13	0.13	0.13	0.13	0.13
0.8	**0.19**	**0.14**	**0.14**	**0.14**	**0.14**	0.13	0.13	0.13	0.13	0.13
0.7	**0.19**	**0.14**	**0.14**	**0.14**	**0.14**	**0.14**	**0.14**	**0.14**	**0.14**	**0.14**
0.6	**0.19**	**0.24**	**0.17**	**0.14**	**0.15**	**0.14**	**0.15**	**0.14**	**0.15**	**0.17**
0.5	**0.27**	**0.24**	**0.25**	**0.20**	**0.22**	**0.16**	**0.19**	**0.19**	**0.19**	**0.20**

5 Conclusion

The paper presents a quick method of comparing device fingerprint using the LSH algorithm. It requires creating hashes using the MinHash method and saving them to the database. Proper selection of parameters of the LSH algorithm requires creating several columns in a table. Indexing these columns will then allow for an easy comparison of the values of subsequent fingerprints.

The algorithm can be extended by using neural networks [11, 15, 18] with an appropriate network structure [10, 13], the big data algorithms [9], fuzzy methods [12, 16] and other [17]. There are also plans for using such parameters as: IP number, Internet Service Provider (ISP), geolocation and additional parameters that can be obtained from the browser of a given device. The problem of similarity of the same mobile phone models whose browsers return exactly the same parameters remains yet to be solved.

References

1. Kobusińska, A., Pawluczuk, K., Brzeziński, J.: Big Data fingerprinting information analytics for sustainability. Future Generation Comput. Syst. **86**, 1321–1337 (2018)
2. Leskovec, J., Rajaraman, A., Ullman, J.D.: Mining of Massive Datasets. Cambridge University Press, Cambridge (2014)
3. Boda, K., Földes, Á.M., Gulyás, G.G., Imre, S.: User Tracking on the Web via Cross-Browser Fingerprinting. In: Laud, P. (ed.) NordSec 2011. LNCS, vol. 7161, pp. 31–46. Springer, Heidelberg (2012). https://doi.org/10.1007/978-3-642-29615-4_4
4. Mowery, K., Shacham, H.: Pixel perfect: Fingerprinting canvas in HTML5. In: Proceedings of W2SP, pp. 1–12 (2012)
5. Acar, G., Eubank, C., Englehardt, S., Juarez, M., Narayanan, A., Diaz, C.: The web never forgets: persistent tracking mechanisms in the wild. In: Proceedings of the 2014 ACM SIGSAC Conference on Computer and Communications Security, pp. 674–689, November 2014
6. Laperdrix, P., Rudametkin, W., Baudry, B.: Beauty and the beast: Diverting modern web browsers to build unique browser fingerprints. In: 2016 IEEE Symposium on Security and Privacy (SP), pp. 878–894. IEEE, May 2016
7. https://github.com/Valve/fingerprintjs2. Accessed 06 Feb 2020
8. Englehardt, S., Narayanan, A.: Online tracking: a 1-million-site measurement and analysis. In: Proceedings of the 2016 ACM SIGSAC Conference on Computer and Communications Security, pp. 1388–1401, October 2016
9. Koren, O., Hallin, C.A., Perel, N., Bendet, D.: Decision-making enhancement in a big data environment: application of the K-means algorithm to mixed data. J. Artif. Intell. Soft Comput. Res. **9**(4), 293–302 (2019)
10. Shewalkar, A., Nyavanandi, D., Ludwig, S.A.: Performance Evaluation of Deep Neural Networks Applied to Speech Recognition: RNN, LSTM and GRU. J. Artif. Intell. Soft Comput. Res. **9**(4), 235–245 (2019)
11. Ludwig, S.A.: Applying a neural network ensemble to intrusion detection. J. Artif. Intell. Soft Comput. Res. **9**(3), 177–188 (2019)
12. D'Aniello, G., Gaeta, M., Loia, F., Reformat, M., Toti, D.: An environment for collective perception based on fuzzy and semantic approaches. J. Artif. Intell. Soft Comput. Res. **8**(3), 191–210 (2018)
13. Liu, J.B., Zhao, J., Wang, S., Javaid, M., Cao, J.: On the topological properties of the certain neural networks. J. Artif. Intell. Soft Comput. Res. **8**(4), 257–268 (2018)
14. Leskovec, J., Rajaraman, A., Ullmanm, J.D.: Mining of Massive Datasets. Cambridge University Press, Cambridge (2014)
15. Bilski, J., Wilamowski, Bogdan M.: Parallel levenberg-marquardt algorithm without error backpropagation. In: Rutkowski, L., Korytkowski, M., Scherer, R., Tadeusiewicz, R., Zadeh, L.A., Zurada, J.M. (eds.) ICAISC 2017. LNCS (LNAI), vol. 10245, pp. 25–39. Springer, Cham (2017). https://doi.org/10.1007/978-3-319-59063-9_3

16. Korytkowski, M., Senkerik, R., Scherer, M.M., Angryk, R.A., Kordos, M., Siwocha, A.: Efficient image retrieval by fuzzy rules from boosting and metaheuristic. J. Artif. Intell. Soft Comput. Res. **10**(1), 57–69 (2020)
17. Wróbel, M., Starczewski, Janusz T., Napoli, C.: Handwriting recognition with extraction of letter fragments. In: Rutkowski, L., Korytkowski, M., Scherer, R., Tadeusiewicz, R., Zadeh, L.A., Zurada, J.M. (eds.) ICAISC 2017. LNCS (LNAI), vol. 10246, pp. 183–192. Springer, Cham (2017). https://doi.org/10.1007/978-3-319-59060-8_18
18. Gabryel, M., Grzanek, K., Hayashi, Y.: Browser fingerprint coding methods increasing the effectiveness of user identification in the web traffic. J. Artif. Intell. Soft Comput. Res. **10**(4), 243–253 (2020)

Gradient Boosting and Deep Learning Models Approach to Forecasting Promotions Efficiency in FMCG Retail

Joanna Henzel[✉] and Marek Sikora[✉]

Department of Computer Networks and System, Faculty of Automatic Control,
Electronics and Computer Science, Silesian University of Technology,
ul. Akademicka 16, 44-100 Gliwice, Poland
{joanna.henzel,marek.sikora}@polsl.pl

Abstract. In the paper, different approaches to the problem of forecasting promotion efficiency are presented. For four defined indicators of promotion effect, prediction models using Gradient Boosting method and Deep Learning methods were trained. The comparison of the results is provided. The experiments were performed for three groups of products from a large grocery company.

Keywords: Forecasting · Gradient boosting · Deep learning

1 Introduction

Fast-moving consumer goods (FMCG) are products that are sold very quickly. Among this category, food can be distinguished. In order to encourage customers to buy in a specific store or shop chain, retailers propose multiple promotions of the products. Very often in one shop many promotions are happening at the same time and sale from the promotions may make a big part of a total sale as it was mentioned in [7]. Because of this, the problem of a proper planning and forecasting the efficiency of the promotions is an important issue in the FMCG sector.

There are different methods used to plan and forecast the promotion effect. Sometimes, a simple baseline statistical forecast with a judgmental adjustment [10] is used. However, the authors of [16] have indicated that using judgmental forecasting may bring bias to the predictions.

In the marketing research literature the problem of the effectiveness of promotions was raised many times e.g. in [3] or [7], however, they focus on domain knowledge and do not use data mining techniques for solving this task.

The Machine Learning (ML) methods are more advanced and their results are based mostly on historical data and therefore they can give more precise forecasts. In [2], the authors showed that for periods with promotions more advanced prediction methods need to be used when simple statistical methods perform well for data without promotions. Multiple models for forecasting the

© Springer Nature Switzerland AG 2020
L. Rutkowski et al. (Eds.): ICAISC 2020, LNAI 12416, pp. 336–345, 2020.
https://doi.org/10.1007/978-3-030-61534-5_30

demand during promotion periods were compared in [19] and in the paper [8]. The use of PCA and pooled regression was presented in the paper [18] in order to predict sales in the presence of promotions. In [14] the authors proposed an extension of the Multiple Aggregation Prediction Algorithm (MAPA) to forecast number of heavily promoted products. The authors of [12] have proposed a new methodology based on a SARMA approximation for forecasting in order to indicate the timing of future promotional activities.

The finding presented in [15] showed that boosting algorithms got the best results regarding sales-forecasting of retail stores. The best results were obtained for the GradientBoost algorithm and the XGBoost implementation has been used in order to increase the accuracy. Therefore the authors of this paper assumed that it is possible that its usage will also be successful in case of forecasting the efficiency of promotions. Its comparison to the Deep Learning models can also bring insight into the effectiveness of those methods.

The objective of this paper is to present and compare the abilities of forecasting promotion effect using the gradient boosting method with Deep Learning approach. Four different indicators are presented in order to forecast the efficiency of the promotions. The paper describes the data preparation process and the experiments, which were conducted on three groups of products from retail stores. The paper is organised as follows: the next section describes problem statement and the data preparation process. Afterwards, the experiments explanation is presented. The paper ends with some conclusions.

2 Problem Statement

As it was mentioned in the Introduction, promotions are an important part of the retail sector. It is one of the techniques that increase market share and profit.

2.1 Indicators

In the paper [13] 6 indicators were described in order to capture the efficiency of the promotions. Each of them is a *gain measures*, so the higher the value, the better the promotion was. The authors chosen 4 of those indicators and they are examined in this paper:

- AVERAGE VALUE OF A BASKET CONTAINING THE PROMOTED PRODUCT (shortcut: AVG. BASKET) – This indicator says what an average value of a basket was where the promoted product appeared. The indicator says how much money they spent in total.
- AVERAGE VALUE OF A BASKET CONTAINING THE PROMOTED PRODUCT BUT DISREGARDING THE VALUE OF THE PROMOTED PRODUCT (shortcut: AVG. BASKET W/O ITEM) – It shows what an average value of a basket was where the promoted product appeared but the value of the promoted product was not taken into account. It means that this indicator is equal to 0 if the customer buys only the promoted product.

- AVERAGE NUMBER OF UNIQUE PRODUCTS IN THE BASKET (shortcut: AVG. NB. UNIQUE ITEMS) – It says how varied the basket is. The higher the value of the indicator, the better – it means that the customer not only bought a specific product but also many others.
- AVERAGE NUMBER OF THE BASKETS (shortcut: AVG. NB. CLIENTS) – The indicator shows how many, on average, transactions were performed each day during the promotion. It does not matter if the customer bought a promoted product or not.

Each promotion can be described by each indicator. As a group, they can be used to evaluate past promotions in order to identify the best or the worse of them. In case of forecasting, these indicators can be used to plan future promotions and can be helpful in the process of predicting which promotion will give the best results. Sufficiently good promotion can be defined in various ways e.g. the acceptable promotion can be the one for which the value of each indicator do not fall below a fixed threshold.

In order to forecast the values of the indicators for future promotions, models for each of them had to be proposed. The authors decided that a separate model would be created for each indicator and each group of products separately. The reason for this is that creating the models for one indicator and all products that are available in the stores can be too general and would have too much bias. The models could be created for each product separately but for not all of them the historical data were sufficient. For this reason, it was decided that the models will be created among predefined groups of products. The authors expected that products within this same category can have similar characteristic of promotions effect. The advantage of this approach is the fact that such models can be used to forecast promotion effect of a product that has never been on sale.

To summarize: in the experiments presented in this paper models for each of the 4 indicators and for each predefined category (group) of products were created and evaluated.

2.2   Data Sets

For the experiments three groups of products were chosen: dairy products, fruits and vegetables. For each group data set was prepared. One record of data described one promotion in one store. Data set for a specific category of products (e.g. vegetables) included promotions for all products that were within this category (cucumbers, carrots, cabbage etc.) and from all the stores. Therefore, the exemplary data set could look like this presented in the Table 1. The promotions that were not included in the datasets:

- the promotions that happened before or during holidays,
- for the products which price was reduced due to the approaching best-before date,
- the promotions that applied only when some specific condition was met (e.g. promotion of a type "buy 2 pay for 1").

Data used in the experiments came from a large grocery retail company (more than 500 stores).

Table 1. Example of data set before preparation

Store ID	Product	Start date	End date	Conditional attributes	Value of indicator
10	Cabbage	2018-01-22	2018-01-25	...	123.56
11	Cabbage	2018-01-24	2018-01-27	...	188.34
...	...	...	...	...	...
12	Carrot	2018-01-15	2018-01-17	...	109.35
13	Carrot	2018-01-15	2018-01-17	...	120.89
...	...	...	...	...	...
10	Cucumber	2018-01-18	2018-01-19	...	98.45
14	Cucumber	2018-01-29	2018-01-31	...	103.11

Matching Periods Without Promotions. In the data, promotions and matching periods without promotions were included. The matching period had to: consider the same product as the promotion, be in the same store as the promotion, last as many days as the considered promotion, start on the same weekday as the promotion, occur maximum 4 weeks and minimum 1 week before the promotion. Due to the lack of meeting the requirements, the matching periods were not found for all promotions. The illustration of finding the matching periods was shown in Fig. 1.

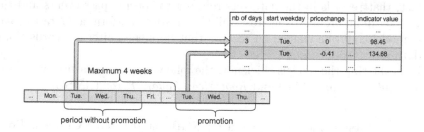

Fig. 1. Finding matching record without promotion

Matching periods without promotions were included only in training data sets and they were added in order to capture the characteristics of products in the group (e.g. what can be the range of a price). In the final data sets, records connected with periods without promotions were distinguished from promotions by having 0 value in an attribute describing the change of a price.

Attributes. Main categories of the conditional attributes that were included in the data sets were:

- connected with price (the price of a product and a change of the price),
- connected with the time and duration of the promotion (number of days of the promotion; weekday of the first day of the promotion; season etc.),
- describing the advertisement media (promotions advertised on TV, on the radio, on the Internet etc.),
- describing the store and its surroundings (number of inhabitants within 1 km; number of inhabitants per 1 square km; number of inhabitants within a 5-minute driving range; unemployment rate; number of cars per 1,000 inhabitants; average monthly salary; tourism ratio, etc.),
- describing the impact of other promotions (number of all promotions in a store; number of all promotions that were advertised on TV, radio or internet; number of all promotions that were advertised on TV, radio, internet or in a different way).

3 Experiments

The experiments were performed for three groups of products: dairy products, fruits and vegetables. For each of the selected indicator, each category of products and each investigated method, a separate forecasting model was trained. The experiments were conducted with train and test data sets. The train data sets had records with promotions and matching records without promotions from 2015–2017. The test data sets consisted only of promotions from 2018. Cross-validation was not used in a process of testing the model. The reason for this is a fact, that records in the data sets referred to specific past events and they could be set in an order. Using cross-validation would perform a "data leakage", so the model could be trained on records that happened after a records from a test data set.

For evaluating the models efficiency, the following error measures were used: *Mean Absolute Error* (MAE) and *Root Mean Square Error* (RMSE).

XGBoost. First models were based on XGBoost (eXtreme Gradient Boosting) [4] algorithm. Implementation from the R package `xgboost` [5] was used for this task. In the experiments presented in the paper [15], this algorithm has given the best results for forecasting sales in retail stores, so the authors believed that this Gradient Boosting algorithm will give satisfactory results also for forecasting the promotion effect.

In the experiments, process of the optimisation of hyperparameters was included. A *grid search* method was used for this task. The RMSE measure was the optimisation criterion. Six hyperparameters were considered in the process:

- *nrounds* – maximum number of boosting iterations; range: $[1, \infty)$.
- *base_score* – the initial prediction score of all instances; range: $(-\infty, \infty)$.

- *eta* – boosting learning rate; range: $[0, 1]$.
- *gamma* – minimum loss reduction required to make a further partition on a leaf node of the tree; range: $[0, \infty)$.
- *max_depth* – maximum depth of a tree; range: $[1, \infty)$.
- *subsample* – subsample ratio of the training instance; range: $(0, 1]$.

A detailed description of the above parameters can be found in [5]. The Table 2 shows values that were tested in the process of finding the initial best combination of the hyperparameters. After having this combination, the neighbourhood of the examined hyperparameters values were searched in order to find even better values for them. The optimisation was performed based on created validation data sets that were extracted from the training data sets.

Table 2. Values of XGBoost hyperparameters used in optimisation process.

Hyperparameter	Tested values
nrounds	1, 21, 41, 61, 81, 101, 121, 141, 161, 181, 201
base_score	Depending on indicator values. Calculated as 11 quantiles from indicator values with the following probabilities: 0.0, 0.1, 0.2, ..., 0.9, 1.0
eta	0.0, 0.1, 0.2, 0.3, 0.4, 0.5, 0.6, 0.7, 0.8, 0.9, 1.0
gamma	0, 1, 2, 3, 4, 5, 6, 7, 8, 9, 10
max_depth	1, 4, 7, 10, 13
subsample	0.0001, 0.1001, 0.2001, ..., 0.9001

Sequential Deep Learning Models. Deep Learning models were created for each indicator and each group of products. These were the Sequential models created in Python language with the usage of the `Keras` library [6]. The optimisation of hyperparameters was also performed. For this task `Hyperas` library [17] was chosen. This library helps to create template for search spaces of Keras hyperparameters in order to find the best combination of their values. For example, different sizes of the output spaces from a Dense layers were checked, fractions of the input units to drop from Dropout layers were optimised, different activation functions were considered and the number of layers was changing. The Table 3 shows values that were tested by `Hyperas` library. In this process the validation data sets, extracted from the training data sets, were also used.

Deep Learning Models from H2O. At the end, Deep Learning models obtained from running automodel (AutoML) from a H2O platform were tested. For this task `h2o` (R Interface for H2O) was used [1]. H2O's AutoML can be used for finding the best model with the best set of hyperparameters for a specific task. In the presented experiments H2O Deep Learning models were investigated.

Table 3. Values of hyperparameters used in optimisation process of Deep Learning models.

Layers and hyperparameter	Tested values
First Dense layer – sizes of the output space	64, 256, 512, 1024
First Dropout layer – fractions of the input units to drop	From 0 to 1
Second Dense layer – sizes of the output space	64, 256, 512, 1024
Second Activation layer – activation function	*relu, sigmoid*
Second Dropout layer – fractions of the input units to drop	From 0 to 1
Conditional additional layers – Dense layer – sizes of the output space	10, 50, 100
Conditional additional layers – Dropout layer – sizes of the output space	From 0 to 1
Optimizer	*rmsprop, adam*

3.1 Results

The results of the models obtained for each category of products, each indicator and each tested method are presented in the Tables 4 and 5. The Table 4 shows the values of RMSE and the Table 5 shows the values of MAE. Bolded are the smallest errors obtained for each indicator and each group of products.

Table 4. RMSE of results obtained in the experiments for the XGBoost models (*xgboost*), for Deep Learning models made with Keras library (*DL*) and H2O Deep Learning models obtained from AutoML (*h2o*).

	Dairy products			Fruits			Vegetables		
Indicator	xgboost	DL	h2o	xgboost	DL	h2o	xgboost	DL	h2o
AVG. BASKET W/O ITEM	20.32	24.51	**19.09**	**21.78**	27.41	22.96	**21.65**	27.49	22.40
AVG. BASKET	**20.14**	24.52	20.25	**22.44**	28.19	22.77	**21.56**	27.80	23.79
AVG. NB. CLIENTS	**177.15**	295.45	190.18	**164.49**	325.09	172.92	178.51	376.57	**122.36**
AVG. NB. UNIQUE ITEMS	**2.72**	3.54	2.79	**2.60**	3.54	2.70	**2.71**	3.35	3.32

4   Conclusion

Promotions are an important part of the retail sector. They need to be planned with the same precision as a regular sale. One of the aspect that can help in this process is reliable set of models. It is crucial not to focus only on the forecasting the sale but also try to focus on different meaningful aspects of customers behaviour during the promotions. Machine Learning models can help to forecast these behaviours and therefore help to plan future promotions in the best possible way.

This study has attempted to present different approaches to creating models for predicting promotion efficiency. Four different indicators were taken into

Table 5. MAE of results obtained in the experiments for the XGBoost models (*xgboost*), for Deep Learning models made with Keras library (*DL*) and H2O Deep Learning models obtained from AutoML (*h2o*).

Indicator	Dairy products			Fruits			Vegetables		
	xgboost	DL	h2o	xgboost	DL	h2o	xgboost	DL	h2o
Avg. Basket w/o Item	**14.26**	19.15	14.42	14.73	20.65	**14.41**	**14.63**	20.80	14.87
Avg. Basket	**13.93**	19.18	14.81	15.29	21.35	**14.83**	**14.39**	21.06	16.35
Avg. NB. Clients	**129.75**	224.55	136.16	125.15	291.60	110.94	135.57	335.44	**93.77**
Avg. NB. Unique Items	**2.04**	2.81	2.14	1.84	2.75	**1.74**	**1.89**	2.57	2.02

consideration and each of them can be used in a process of planning future promotions. The comparison of the results for different algorithms was performed.

From Tables 4 and 5 we can see that for most of the cases XGBoost gave the best results. Focusing on the measure that was optimised – RMSE – the best results were obtained for this algorithm in 10 out of 12 cases. Only for 2 cases Deep Learning models from a H2O AutoML were the best. Deep Learning models made in Keras and optimised by **hyperpot** library had visible lower results than the two other approaches. It is possible that this was due to the fact that too small search space for additional layers was considered.

From the results obtained, it can be concluded that for the problem of forecasting the promotion efficiency XGBoost is a better algorithm than Deep Learning methods. It is possible that this method can give better results than Deep Learning approach in most cases when dealing with tabular data, but further research would have to confirm this hypothesis. Very little has been written about a comparison of XGBoost with Deep Learning methods, but in the paper [9] the author conducted the comparison of artificial intelligence techniques for cost prediction and also got the best results for XGBoost which outperformed artificial neural networks.

The obtained results offer practical usage as well. As it was mentioned before, trained models can help in the process of planning future promotions. Let say, that the person in charge would want to start a new promotion in the future with a certain set of features. Using trained models user can check if a proposed combination of characteristics will give satisfactory results of the evaluated indicators. For example, using R library **iBreakDown** [11] for a new, planned promotion (one record of data) with a settled set of attribute values we can plot a contribution of every variable to a final prediction. The person in charge can see if the predicted value is acceptable and if not they can see which attributes have the biggest impact on the prediction.

The Fig. 2 shows a sample plot that was obtained for the model AVG. BASKET W/O ITEM for the vegetables category. The plot presents the results for the artificial new promotion. The final prediction for this record of data is 77.84. Now, for example, a price change could be manipulated in order to get bigger value for the predicted indicator. Someone could change its value and monitor how the contribution of this and different attributes changes. It can be a helpful tool in the process of optimising future promotions. Additionally, some more metrics for the model can be calculated. For the model presented as an example (Fig. 2) we can calculate Mean Absolute Percentage Error (MAPE), which value is 0.16. It means that, on average, model makes mistakes of about 16%. This additional information may help user to decide, if the obtained prediction will match his acceptable threshold taking into account error of the model.

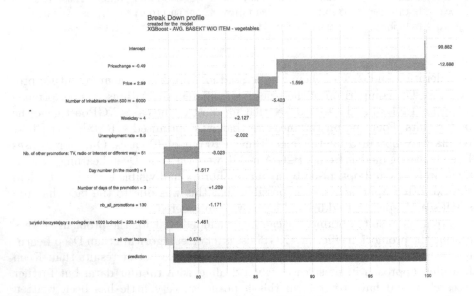

Fig. 2. Plot of variables contribution to a final prediction for an exemplary promotion. The predicted value is AVG. BASKET W/O ITEM (vegetables category).

In conclusion, this paper shows different approaches to creating models for the purpose of forecasting promotion efficiency. Results for XGBoost, custom Deep Learning models made with Keras and Deep Learning models from H2O created with AutoML were compared. In most cases, the best results were observed for XGBoost models. Practical usage of the obtained models and results is also presented in the paper.

Acknowledgment. This work was partially supported by the European Union through the European Social Fund (grant POWR.03.05.00-00-Z305). The work was carried out in part within the project co-financed by European Funds entitled "Decision Support and Knowledge Management System for the Retail Trade Industry (SensAI)" (POIR.01.01.01-00-0871/17-00).

References

1. h2o: R Interface for H2O, March 2020. http://www.h2o.ai. R package version 3.30.0.5

2. Ali, Ö.G., Sayin, S., van Woensel, T., Fransoo, J.: SKU demand forecasting in the presence of promotions. Expert Syst. Appl. **36**(10), 12340–12348 (2009). https://doi.org/10.1016/j.eswa.2009.04.052

3. Blattberg, R.C., Levin, A.: Modelling the effectiveness and profitability of trade promotions. Mark. Sci. **6**(2), 124–146 (1987). https://doi.org/10.1287/mksc.6.2.124

4. Chen, T., Guestrin, C.: XGBoost: a scalable tree boosting system. In: Proceedings of the 22nd ACM SIGKDD International Conference on Knowledge Discovery and Data Mining, KDD 2016, pp. 785–794. ACM (2016). https://doi.org/10.1145/2939672.2939785, http://doi.acm.org/10.1145/2939672.2939785

5. Chen, T., et al.: xgboost: Extreme Gradient Boosting (2019). https://CRAN.R-project.org/package=xgboost, r package version 0.90.0.2

6. Chollet, F., et al.: Keras (2015). https://keras.io

7. Cohen, M.C., Leung, N.H.Z., Panchamgam, K., Perakis, G., Smith, A.: The impact of linear optimization on promotion planning. Oper. Res. **65**(2), 446–468 (2017). https://doi.org/10.1287/opre.2016.1573

8. Cui, G., Wong, M.L., Lui, H.K.: Machine learning for direct marketing response models: Bayesian networks with evolutionary programming. Manage. Sci. **52**(4), 597–612 (2006). https://doi.org/10.1287/mnsc.1060.0514

9. Elmousalami, H.H.: Comparison of Artificial Intelligence Techniques for Project Conceptual Cost Prediction (2019). https://arxiv.org/abs/1909.11637

10. Fildes, R., Goodwin, P., Önkal, D.: Use and misuse of information in supply chain forecasting of promotion effects. Int. J. Forecast. **35**(1), 144–156 (2019). https://doi.org/10.1016/j.ijforecast.2017.12.006

11. Gosiewska, A., Biecek, P.: Do Not Trust Additive Explanations (2019). https://arxiv.org/abs/1903.11420

12. Guidolin, M., Guseo, R., Mortarino, C.: Regular and promotional sales in new product life cycles: Competition and forecasting. Comput. Ind. Eng. **130**, 250–257 (2019). https://doi.org/10.1016/j.cie.2019.02.026

13. Henzel, J., Sikora, M.: Gradient boosting application in forecasting of performance indicators values for measuring the efficiency of promotions in FMCG retail. In: Preproceedings of the 2020 Federated Conference on Computer Science and Information Systems, pp. 59–68 (2020)

14. Kourentzes, N., Petropoulos, F.: Forecasting with multivariate temporal aggregation: the case of promotional modelling. Int. J. Prod. Econ. **181**, 145–153 (2016). https://doi.org/10.1016/j.ijpe.2015.09.011

15. Krishna, A., Akhilesh, V., Aich, A., Hegde, C.: Sales-forecasting of retail stores using machine learning techniques. In: 2018 3rd International Conference on Computational Systems and Information Technology for Sustainable Solutions (CSITSS 2018), pp. 160–166. IEEE (2018). https://doi.org/10.1109/CSITSS.2018.8768765

16. Makridakis, S.: The art and science of forecasting an assessment and future directions. Int. J. Forecast. **2**(1), 15–39 (1986). https://doi.org/10.1016/0169-2070(86)90028-2

17. Pumperla, M.: Hyperas (2016). https://maxpumperla.com/hyperas/

18. Trapero, J.R., Kourentzes, N., Fildes, R.: On the identification of sales forecasting models in the presence of promotions. J. Oper. Res. Soc. **66**(2), 299–307 (2015). https://doi.org/10.1057/jors.2013.174

19. Van Donselaar, K.H., Peters, J., De Jong, A., Broekmeulen, R.: Analysis and forecasting of demand during promotions for perishable items. Int. J. Prod. Econ. **172**, 65–75 (2016). https://doi.org/10.1016/j.ijpe.2015.10.022

A Fuzzy Multi-Agent Problem in a Conceptual and Operational Depiction

Krystian Jobczyk[✉] and Antoni Ligęza

AGH University of Science and Technology, Kraków, Poland
krystian_jobczyk@op.pl

Abstract. In the paper a Fuzzy Multi-Agent Problem (FMAP) is discussed both in a conceptual and a programming-wise depiction. In particular, it is illustrated how FMAP stems from a Nurse Job Rostering Problem-based formulation of MAP. Finally, a workable subcase of FMAP is explored by means of PROLOG-solvers.

Keywords: Multi-Agent Problem · Fuzzy multi-agent problem · PROLOG · Nurse job scheduling problem

1 Introduction

A Fuzzy Multi-Agent Problem (FMAP) constitutes a fuzzified version of the Multi-Agent Problem, where the 'direction' of fuzzification is specified in some way. A Multi-Agent Problem (MAP) is usually identified with a class of different problems of in Artificial Intelligence (see: [1]) involved in a multiple of interacting and intelligent agents.

MAP remains close-related to Constraints Satisfaction Problems (CSP) – it forms a unique correlate of a simplified temporal variant of CSP – the so-called *Simple Temporal Problem* (STP) – introduced and broadly discussed together with its extensions (STPU and STPP[1]) in such works of Dechter-Khatib's school as: [2–9]. In practice, different combinations of MAP with CSPs have been elaborated under the banner of 'Multi-Agent Approaches to CSP' – as described in [10–13]. These (usually sophisticated) synergy combinations have either a nature of asynchronous solvers, such as: *Asynchronous Backtracking* (ABT) or *Asynchronous Weak-Commitment Search* (AWCS) – due to [13] or a character of distributed local search methods, such as: *Distributed Breakout Algorithm* (see: [13]) or *Environment, Reactive rules and Agents* (ERA) approach (see: [10]). Finally, an idea of the combination of MAP with CSP found its reflection in a synergy definition of *Distributed Constraint Satisfaction Problem* (DisCSP) as an algebraic foundation of the Multi-Agent CSP approach.

Although a conceptual provenance of different problems under the banner MAP should be found in a class of different optimizations problems, such as:

---

[1] STPU forms an abbreviation from 'Simple Temporal Problem under Uncertainty' and STPP – from 'Simple Temporal Problem with Preferences'.

© Springer Nature Switzerland AG 2020
L. Rutkowski et al. (Eds.): ICAISC 2020, LNAI 12416, pp. 346–356, 2020.
https://doi.org/10.1007/978-3-030-61534-5_31

the so-called *Nurse Job Scheduling Problem* (NJSP)[2] – intensively explored in such works of Nottingham's school as: [15–19]. Meanwhile, an inherent nature of NJSP – as a conceptual foundation of MAS – sometimes required a piece of fuzziness because of a need to grasp vagueness of information (for example, about the hospital objectives or personal preferences). Thus, a kind of a fuzzified MAP (FMAP) seems to be expected in order to provide a high quality scheduling tasks. A new step towards a fuzzification of NJSP involved in fuzzy goal programming (GP) models has recently been proposed in [20, 21].

Anyhow, it seems that fuzziness may be introduced to MAS – as based on NJSP – by different (sometimes unknown) degrees of ability of agents to perform their tasks. This comprehension of FMAP is just proposed in this paper.

1.1   The Paper Motivation

Independently of a visible success of the operational depiction of MAP some difficulties with NJSP and FMAP – as based on it – may be easily detected.

A NJSP – as a basis of MAP should be rather seen a basis *reservoir* of possible, more specified formulations and it still waits for a more advanced fuzzy complement. In particular,
  – Admittedly, Ernst's approach in [17] is mathematically general, but it refers to some simplified situations.
  – In contrast, Lepegue's approach to NJSP from [22] is pretty detailed, but formalization of possible temporal constraints in it seems to be too excessive and it is contr intuitive.
  – Finally, a fuzzification from [21] more predicts some results than puts forward them in detail.
B It is not completely clear how to relate MAP to the simplified temporal CSP in terms of STP and its different extensions – as defined in [2, 3, 7, 8].
C It seems that a fuzzy and multi-valued logic-based approach to combining CSP with other 'entities' of fuzzy temporal-reasoning, such as preferences – due to [9, 23–26] – does not indicate any appropriate method to grasp MAP in their contexts.
D It also seems – due to author's best knowledge – that no explicit approach to fuzziness has been proposed in the contact of MAP on the conceptual level.
E Finally, an expressive power of PROLOG and its solvers has not yet been completely explored with respect to any fuzzified version of MAP – independently of a variety of modern alternative tools (such as GP, ADOPT) used for a fuzzified NJP or Multi-Agent Constraints Satisfaction (see: [10, 20, 21].)

---

[2] This problem is also called *Nurse Rostering Problem*. NSP constitutes a classical optimization problem. Its objective is to determine the rotating shifts of the nursing shifts over a scheduled period (weekly or monthly)- see: [14].

1.2   The Novelty and Objectives of the Paper and its Organization

According to these requirements and needs and slightly against the tendency of the technology-oriented research on Constraints Satisfaction – the paper forms a unique return to the conceptual foundation of the considered issues.

In fact, this paper objective is to elaborate a fuzzy extension (FMAP) of Multi-Agent Problem in a NJSP-based depiction. FMAP will be also referred to STPU as its conceptual correlate in order to detect some important similarities and discrepancies between them. Finally, some workable subcases of FMAP will be solved by means of PROLOG machinery.

Novelty of the paper with respect to earlier approaches consists in:

N1 proposing a fuzzy modification of MAP – both in a practical and in a slightly general depiction,

N2 describing both MAP and FMAP as a synergy synthesis of planning and scheduling components,

N3 considering the PROLOG-solvers for some workable fuzzy subcases of FMAP.

The proper analysis refers to the concepts of *Simple Temporal Problem* (STP) and *Simple Temporal Problem under Uncertainty* (STPU). We assume that the reader is familiar with them[3].

The rest of the paper is organized as follows. Section 2 contains a practical depiction of FMAP as stemming from an arithmetic-based depiction of MAP. Section 3 is devoted to the programming-wise aspects of FMAP with respect to some workable subcases. Section 4 contains conclusions.

2   Fuzzy Multi-Agent Problem as an Extension of Multi-agent Problem

In this chapter, FMAP as a unique extension of MAP is put forward – in a depiction motivated by Nurse Rostering Problem. In order to make it, let us note that each well-founded depiction of MAP must satisfy the following general criteria.

C1 A finite (non-empty) of agents should be given,

C2 Agents should be involved in some activities in some time periods and sub-periods (for examples: days and shifts),

C3 There are some hard constraints (**HC**) imposed on agent activities that must be absolutely satisfied to perform the task,

C4 There are some soft constraints (**SC**) imposed on agent activities that may be satisfied.

Taking into account these general criteria, one can formulate the following generic Fuzzy Multi-Agent Problem as follows:

---

[3] The detailed definitions of them in different variants may be easily found in [2,3,7,8].

2.1 Fuzzy Multi-Agent Problem (FMAP)

In our conceptual framework, *Fuzzy Multi-Agent Problem (FMAP)* will be introduced as *Multi-Agent Problem* equipped with additional fuzzy requirements imposed on the task performing. An exemplary, paradigmatic formulation – in terminology of the NJSP entities – is given as follows (See: [27]).

Definition 1. *Consider a factory with n-agents working in a rhythm of the day-night shifts: D–the day shift and N–the night shift. Generally – each day at least one person must work at the day shift and at least one – at the night one. Each agent has "working shifts" and "free shifts". These general rules of scheduling is constrained in the following way.*

HC1 *The charm of the shift organization should be fair: each agent must to have equally: 2 day-shifts and 2 night-shifts.*
HC2 *Each agent can be associated to at most one shift,*
HC3 *Some shifts are prohibited for agents,*
HC4 *Length of the shifts sequences associated to each agent is restricted,*
HC5 *Quantity of the shifts in a scheduling period is restricted,*
HC6 *Quantity of the shifts per a day is restricted.*

Assuming also an agent $n_k \in N$ and the chosen (real) parameters m, M and α Different soft constraints and preferences of a general form are also considered in the scheduling procedure.

SC7 *A quantity of shifts in a scheduling period is established,*
SC8 *A scheduling charm's covering by shifts in a scheduling period is established,*
SC9 *A length of the shifts sequence associated to an agent is fixed,*
Fuzz1 *A number of degrees of agent ability to perform actions is a natural number from the set $1, 2 \ldots, m$,*
Fuzz2 *An agent n_k prefers to perform an action a with a degree $\alpha \in 1, \ldots M$.*

The FMAP consists in a construction of a scheduling diagram, which respects all these hard and soft constraints and the fuzzy requirements.

Although the list of possible fuzzy requirements might be enlarged, let us underline that both **Fuzz1** and **Fuzz2** rather constitute a *scheme* or a class name for different particular fuzzy constraints: **Fuzz2** – for the constraints introduced by preferences, but **Fuzz1** – for fuzzy constraints defined without them. Thus, both classes have a whiff of a paradigmatic generality.

2.2 Types of Constraints of FMAP and their Arithmetic Representation

Different approaches to a representation of both hard and soft constraints and preferences has been proposed. Majority of them grasps an arithmetic representation based on a calculus of characteristic functions – due: [20–22], but a multitude of different additional indexed parameters (c.a. 20) in their arithmetic depiction often makes an idea of representation only partially elusive.

Thus, a restricted set of parameters is introduced for a mathematical representation of temporal constraints imposed on (F)MAP. Instead of agent skills we will consider agent roles (contracts)[4]:

- $N = \{n_1, n_2 \ldots, n_k\}$ as set of agents (agents),
- $R = \{r_1, r_2, \ldots, r_k\}$ as a set of roles (contracts)
- $D = \{d_1, d_2, \ldots, d_k\}$ as a set of days in a week,
- $Z = \{z_1, z_2\}$ as a set of admissible shifts during days from D,
- $\mathcal{A} = \{a_1, a_2, \ldots, a_k\}$ as a set of actions.

It enables of representing MAP by its formal instances in the form of the triple

$$(N, D, Z, A, HC, SC), \tag{1}$$

where N, D, Z are given as above and HC denotes a set of hard constraints imposed on actions from A and their performing. Similarly, FMAP may be given by the n-tuple of the form:

$$(N, D, Z, A, HC, Fuzz), \tag{2}$$

where N, D, Z and HC are given as above and SC and $Fuzz$ denote a set of soft constraints and fuzzy requirements (*resp.*) Introducing SC to the n-tuple (1) follows from the adopted hierarchy of constraints. The hard constraints cannot be violated, the soft ones may be violated, but they should be satisfied before fuzzy constraints.

This notation allows us to elaborate the following representation of hard and soft constraints (we give some examples only). Since their list is not exhaustive[5], it might be relatively naturally extended. A formal representation of each constrain is based on a characteristic function $X_{n,d,z}$ defined as follows[6]:

$X_{n,d,z} = 1$ if an agent n works a shift z in a day d, and $X_{n,d,z} = 0$ otherwise.

HC 1: The charm of the shift organization should be fair: each agent must to have equally 2–day shifts and 2–night shifts. Assume that Z_{day} denotes a set of day-shifts and Z_{night} – a set of night-shifts. It enables the following formal representation:

$$\sum_{z \in Z_{day}} X_{n,d,z} = 2 \wedge \sum_{z \in Z_{night}} X_{n,d,z} = 2. \tag{3}$$

---

[4] All of these constraints are typical for scheduling problems of this type to be known as (usually) NP-hard – see: [15].

[5] This fact plays no important role as the main objective of this juxtaposition consists in the *quantitative representation* alone, which will be later combined with qualitative temporal constraints (of Allen's sort) for a use of further investigations.

[6] This binary representation can be also exchanged by a classical one: $X_{n,d} = z$ as presented in [15].

HC 2: Each agent can be associated to at most one shift.

$$\sum_{z \in Z} X_{n,d,z} = 1. \tag{4}$$

HC 5: Quantity of shifts in a scheduling period. It defines the minimal and the maximal quantity of shifts during a given scheduling period (day) – associated to a single agent n. If s is the minimal and S – the maximal quantity of shifts possibly associated to the agent in the scheduling period, then we get:

$$s \le \sum_{d \in D} X_{n,d,z} \le S, \tag{5}$$

where $X_{n,d,z}$ is defined as above.

Obviously, all the constraints listed above are not exhaustive and their list may be naturally enlarged. However, we interrupt their presentation in this point for a cost of a new presentation of FMAP in a more general depiction.

3 Programming-Wise Aspects of Fuzzy Multi-Agent Problem

In this section, the programming-wise aspects of FMAP will be discussed by means of SWI-PROLOG-solvers for two workable subcases of FMAP. Due to the earlier arrangements – fuzziness will be introduced by degrees of agent abilities (to work).

3.1 A Specification of the Requirements for the Solver Construction

In order to illustrate this method of the solver construction, let us assume that a non-empty set $N = \{X, Y \ldots\}$ of agents and a non-empty set $D = \{1, 2, 3, 4, 5\}$ of working days (for simplicity we omit shifts during a day) are given.

In such a framework, the PROLOG-solver task is to give a schedule respecting the temporal constrains imposed on a task performing and the corresponding agent activity. The achieved solutions will be represented by lists of the form:

$$X = [X1, X2, X3, \ldots, Xk], \tag{6}$$
$$Y = [Y1, Y2, Y3, \ldots, Yl], \tag{7}$$

where $X(i), Y(j)$ are characteristic functions representing activity of agents X and Y during i-day and j-day (*resp.*) for $k, l \in \{1, 2 \ldots, 7\}$.

Obviously, we are interested in *fuzzy*[7]-type situations, when $X(i)$ and $Y(j)$ take more than two values for $i, j \in \{1, 2, \ldots, 7\}$, for example: 0, 1, 2, 3, 4. We adopt natural numbers because of restrictions of PROLOG-syntax, which is not capable of representing values from $[0, 1]$. Nevertheless, we intend to think about these values as about normalized values. Namely, we will interpret 1 – taken from a sequence $1, 2 \ldots, k$ – as $\frac{1}{k}$, 2 as $\frac{2}{k}$, k as $\frac{k}{k} = 1$, etc.

---

[7] More precisely: multi-valued situations.

3.2   A General Specification of the PROLOG Code

SWI-PROLOG solvers will be exploited to find solutions for scheduling tasks of FMAP. As mentioned above, each admissible solution will have a form of the appropriate list of natural numbers. The required constraints imposed on the given scheduling tasks will define the appropriate 2 - argument predicate schedule(X,Y), where variables X, Y represents a pair of operating agents. The proper body of the predicate definition will contain the following components:

1. *a general specification of each agent* as a list of its working days in a scheduling period, for example, X = [X1, X2, X3, X4],
   Y = [Y1, Y2, ..., Y10], etc.
2. *an association the admissible degrees of ability* to agents – introduced by the code of the form: X ins 0...1, X *ins* 0,..., 5, etc.
3. *an arithmetic restrictions on agent during a scheduling period*, for example, sum(X, #<, 3),
4. *a logical restriction on the agents interaction*, for example: $X1\#/Y1$, $Y1\#/Y1$ (the first working day of X is not a working day for Y and conversely).

3.3   A Workable Subcase of FMAP

In the current cases, the following list of values is admitted:

- 0 – to represent the fact that an agent A is absent (on a shift),
- 1 – to represent a physical absence of the agent A, but a real disposition to be present.
- 2 – to represent a physical presence of A, which is only in a partial disposition to work.
- 3 – to represent a full disposition of A to work[8].

Let us begin with an exemplary case of two agents: A1 and A2 working 5 days in a week and having four degrees of disposition denoted by 0, 1, 2 and 3 as above.

MAP(2, 5, 4)^{Fuzz}. This situation is defined by the following requirements:

- 2 agents: A1, A2 operating during a 5-day scheduling period,
- 4 degrees of ability to work are associated to the agents: 0, 1, 2, 3.
- a summary number of admissible degrees of A1-disposition is <12,
- a summary number of admissible degrees of A2-disposition is <9,
- a summary restriction on the admissible number of the disposition degrees for both A1 and A2 (together) in the first day is smaller than 4, for A1 (alone) is greater than 1, what excludes a degree of A2-activity greater than 2,

---

[8] As mentioned, we rather prefer to think about these values as normalized to [0,1] – as $\frac{1}{3}$, $\frac{2}{3}$ etc. instead of 1, 2, or 3. We use values 0, 1, 2, 3 because of restrictions imposed on PROLOG-syntax.

- a summary restriction on the admissible number of the disposition degrees for both A1 and A2 (together) in the second, the third, the 4th and in the 5th day (D1, D2, D3, D2, D5) is smaller than 4, for A1 (alone) – is greater than 2, what excludes a degree of A2-activity greater than 2,
- a summary activity of A1 in the day triples: (D1, D2, D3) and (D3, D4, D5) is smaller than 6,
- a summary activity of A2 in the day triples: (D1, D2, D3) and (D3, D4, D5) is smaller than 7,
- a summary activity of A1 in a day triple (D2, D2, D4) is smaller than 7,
- a summary activity of A2 in a day triple (D2, D3, D4) is smaller than 5.

This situation may be reflected in the following PROLOG-program (As earlier, the sense of lines of the PROLOG-code is explained on the right side of the program):

```
schedule2(A1,A2) :- A1 = [A1D1,A1D2,A1D3,A1D4,A1D5],
-          /* Days of agent A1*/
A2 = [A2D1,A2D2,A2D3,A2D4,A2D5], - /* list of days of agent A2 */
A1 ins 0..3, /* Fuzzy degrees of A1-disposition */
A2 ins 0..3, /* Fuzzy degrees of A2-disposition */
sum(A1, #<, 12), - /* Restriction on a week activity of A1 */
sum(A2, #<, 9),
-        /* Restriction on a week activity of A2 */
sum([A1D1, A2D1], #<, 4), (A1D1 #> 1) # / (A2D1 #> 2),
-              /* Restriction on D1 */
sum([A1D2, A2D2], #<, 4), (A1D2 #> 2) # / (A2D2 #> 2),
-              /* Restriction on D2 */
sum([A1D3, A2D3], #<, 4), (A1D3 #> 2) # / (A2D3 #> 2),
-              /* Restriction on D3 */
sum([A1D4, A2D4], #<, 4), (A1D4 #> 2) # / (A2D4 #> 2),
-              /* Restriction on D4 */
sum([A1D5, A2D5], #<, 4), (A1D5 #> 2) # / (A2D5 #> 2),
-              /* Restriction on D5 */
sum([A1D1, A1D2, A1D3], #<, 6),
sum([A1D2, A1D3, A1D4], #<, 7),
sum([A1D3, A1D4, A1D5], #<, 6),
sum([A2D1, A2D2, A2D3], #<, 7),
sum([A2D2, A2D3, A2D4], #<, 5),
sum([A2D3, A2D4, A2D5], #<, 7),
-      /* Restrictions on the next 3 days*/
label([A1D1,A1D2,A1D3,A1D4,A1D5,
A2D1,A2D2,A2D3,A2D4,A2D5]).
```

In this case, the PROLOG-solver returns us the following solution-lists:

A1 = [2,3,0,3,0], A2 = [0,0,3,0,3] and
A1 = [2,3,0,3,0], A2 = [1,0,3,0,3].

It is noteworthy that in a case $\mathbf{MAP(2,5,5)}^{Fuzz}$. with five values: 0, 1, 2, 3, 4 as admissible fuzzy disposition degrees of A1 and A2, the PROLOG-solver returns us the following (slightly longer) list of solutions:

A1 = [0, 3, 0, 3, 0], A2 = [3, 0, 3, 0, 3] ;
A1 = [2, 3, 0, 3, 0], A2 = [0, 0, 3, 0, 3] ;
A1 = [2, 3, 0, 3, 0], A2 = [1, 0, 3, 0, 3].

It may be an intriguing fact that exchanging a number of admissible degrees of agent ability (4 for 5) only slightly exchanges the number of solutions – (2 for 3). In fact, we only get 2 solutions (pairs) for $MAP(2,5,4)^{Fuzz}$ and 3 for $MAP(2,5,5)^{Fuzz}$. Obviously, a similar linear relationship holds between each of the input parameters and the number of solutions. Simultaneously, if we admit 6 degrees instead of 5 and exchange 4 for 5 in each place of the program for $MAP^{Fuzz}(2, 5, 5)$ – (without any further modification) the number of solutions radically increases – as 16 new solutions are returned. Meanwhile, a slight relaxation of the conditions: sum(A1, #<, 10) for sum(A1, #<, 13) and sum(A2, #<, 10) for sum(A2, #<, 13) – preserves the same number of solutions (16). Further relaxation of temporal constrains usually changes a combinatorial explosion of the algorithm relatively quickly. For example, if exchange also a requirement sum([A1D1, A1D2, A1D3], #<, 6) for sum([A1D1, A1D2, A1D3], #<, 13), one gets more than 60 solutions.

4   Conclusion

It has already been shown how FMAP may be put forward as a unique extension of a Nurse Job Scheduling Problem-based formulation of MAP. The initial approximation of FMAP enables an arithmetic representation of different constraints imposed on FMAP, whereas the second depiction illustrates how FMAP stems from MAP in a more general way. Both of the depictions allow us to relate FMAP to STPU and DisCSP. Finally, some workable subsaces of FMAP were solved by means of SWI-PROLOG solvers. Nevertheless, it appears that PRO-LOG only approximates a kind of fuzziness in the context of MAP. In fact, considering different degrees of agent ability introduces a kind of a multi-valency to different workable subcases of FMAP. In this perspective, Bousi-PROLOG could lay claim to the role of the more adequate language to grasp different FMAP.

References

1. Traverso, P., Ghallab, M., Nau, D.: Automated Planning: Theory and Practice, vol. 2004. Elsevier, Amsterdam (1997)
2. Dechter, R., Meiri, Pearl, J.: On fuzzy temporal constraints networks. Temp. Constr. Netw. **49**(1–3), 61–95 (1991)
3. Khatib, L., Morris, P., Morris, R., Rossi, F.: Temporal reasoning about preferences. In: Proceedings of IJCAI 2001, pp. 322–327 (2001)
4. Shostak, R.: Deciding linear inequalities by computing loop residues. J. ACM **28**(4), 769–779 (1981)
5. Liao, Y., Wong, C.: An algorithm to compact a VLSI symbolic layout with mixed constraints. IEEE Trans. Comput. Aided Des. Integr. Circuits Syst. **2**(2), 62–69 (1983)
6. Leierson, C., Saxe, J.: A mixed-integer linear programming problem which is efficiently solvable. In: Proceedings 21st Annual Alerton Conference on Communications, Control, and Computing, pp. 204–213 (1983)
7. Vidal, T., Fargier, H.: Handling contingency in temporal constraints networks: From consistency to controllabilities. J. Exp. Tech. Artif. Intell. **11**(1), 23–45 (1999)
8. Rossi, F., Yorke-Smith, N., Venable, K.: Temporal reasoning with preferences and uncertainty. In: Proceedings of AAAI, vol. 8, pp. 1385–1386 (2003)
9. Jobczyk, K., Ligeza, A.: Towards a new convolution-based approach to the specification of STPU-solutions. In: FUZZ-IEEE, pp. 782–789 (2016)
10. Liu, J., Jing, H., Tang, Y.: Multi-agent oriented constraints satisfaction. Artif. Intell. **136**(1), 101–144 (2002)
11. Modi, P., Shen, W., Tambe, M., Yakoo, M.: Asynchronous distributed constraint optimization with quality guarantees. Artif. Intell. **161**(2), 149–180 (2005)
12. Mailler, R., Lesser, V.: Asynchronous partial overlay: a new algorithm for solving distributed constraints satisfaction problems. J. Artif. Intell. Res. **25**, 529–576 (2006)
13. Yokoo, M.: Distributed Constraints Satisfaction. Foundation of Cooperation in Multi-Agent System. Springer, Heidelberg (2001). https://doi.org/10.1007/978-3-642-59546-2
14. Felici, G., Gentile, C.: A polyhedral approach for the staff rostering problem. Manage. Sci. **50**(3), 381–394 (2004)
15. Cheang, B., Li, H., Lim, A., Rodrigues, B.: Nurse rostering problems-a bibliographic survey. Eur. J. Oper. Res. **151**(3), 447–460 (2003)
16. Burke, E.K., Curtois, T., Qu, R., Berghe, G.V.: A scatter search approach to the nurse rostering problem. J. Oper. Res. Soc. **61**, 1667–1679 (2010)
17. Ernst, A.T., Jiang, H., Krishnamoorthy, M., Sier, D.: Staff scheduling and rostering: a review of applications, methods and models. Eur. J. Oper. Res. **153**(1), 3–27 (2004)
18. Qu, R., He, F.: A hybrid constraint programming approach for nurse rostering problems. Technical report, School of Computer Science, Nottingham (2008)
19. Metivier, J.-P., Boizumault, P., Loudni, S.: Solving nurse rostering problems using soft global constraints. In: Proceedings of the 15th international conference on Principles and practice of constraint programming, CP 2009, pp. 73–87 (2009)
20. Cetin, E., Sarucan, A.: Nurse scheduling using binary fuzzy goal programming. In: Proceedings of ICAMSAO, pp. 1–6 (2014)
21. Selim, H., Topaloglu, S.: Nurse scheduling using modeling approach. Fuzzy Sets Syst. **161**(11), 1543–1563 (2004)

22. Lepegue, T., Prot, D., Bellenguez-Morineau, O.: A tour scheduling problem with fixed jobs: use of constraint programming. Practice and Theory of Automated Timetabling, pp. 29–31 (2012)
23. Jobczyk, K., Ligeza, B.M.A.., Karczmarczuk, J.: Fuzzy integral logic expressible by convolutions. In: Proceeding of ECAI 2014, pp. 1042–1043 (2014)
24. Jobczyk, K., Ligeza, A.: Dynamic epistemic preferential logic of action. ICAISC **2**, 243–254 (2017)
25. Jobczyk, K., Ligeza, A.: Multi-valued Halpern-Shoham logic for temporal Allen's relations and preferences. In: Proceedings of the annual international conference of Fuzzy Systems (FuzzIEEE) (2016, to appear)
26. Jobczyk, K., Ligęza, A., Bouzid, M., Karczmarczuk, J.: Comparative approach to the multi-valued logic construction for preferences. In: Rutkowski, L., Korytkowski, M., Scherer, R., Tadeusiewicz, R., Zadeh, L.A., Zurada, J.M. (eds.) ICAISC 2015. LNCS (LNAI), vol. 9119, pp. 172–183. Springer, Cham (2015). https://doi.org/10.1007/978-3-319-19324-3_16
27. Jobczyk, K.: Temporal planning with fuzzy constraints and preferences. Normandy University (2017)

Generating Descriptions in Polish Language for BPMN Business Process Models

Krzysztof Kluza[✉], Maciej Znamirowski, Piotr Wiśniewski, Paweł Jemioło, and Antoni Ligęza

AGH University of Science and Technology, al. A. Mickiewicza 30, 30-059 Krakow, Poland
{kluza,wpiotr,pawljmlo,ligeza}@agh.edu.pl

Abstract. Business Process Model and Notation (BPMN) is a widely used standard for modeling and managing process knowledge among organizations. In this paper, we present a concept of a natural language description generator for business process models. Such a generator is expected to reduce the time it takes to describe a process work manually. It may also lower the risk of making a mistake during this task, especially when working on more complex models. The outcome of executing the proposed program is a description of the given business process written in the form of understandable sentences in the Polish language. Our results show that the generated descriptions reflect the original model of the given process, which means that its potential conversion back to the BPMN model will result in a model close to the original one.

1 Introduction

A business process is often understood as a workflow performed in an organization. As work is performed in every company, a business process is carried out in every company. Awareness of processes within a company, as well as the analysis of existing business processes, can help people find a solution that allows to increase the quality of work, reduce its duration or reduce costs. Business process models constitute one of the sources of companies' knowledge [1]. Many different models allow a clear description of business processes. However, business experts do not necessarily have the knowledge of business process notations or modeling skills to read BPMN models easily. So sometimes natural language description may be easier for such domain specialists, and after suitable repair may serve as guidance for business executives [2,3]. This is also the case of all kinds of documentation or norms and specifications created by ISO (International Organization for Standardization). Moreover, the generated textual representations in natural language may also be useful in testing and improving tools which use textual process description like ModelJudge [4] for learning the modeling notation or compliance checkers [5].

The paper is supported by the AGH UST research grant.

L. Rutkowski et al. (Eds.): ICAISC 2020, LNAI 12416, pp. 357–368, 2020.
https://doi.org/10.1007/978-3-030-61534-5_32

This paper presents a natural language description generator for business process models in BPMN. The result of executing the proposed generator is a description of the given business process written in the Polish language. It is important that the sentences generated are unambiguous, grammatically, inflexionally (correct word form) and stylistically correct (especially in the field of repetition of words). In addition, the produced natural language description has to be human-readable so that the user can be guided by it as effectively as using the original BPMN model.

The evaluation of the obtained results consisted in comparing them with the descriptions created manually by a group of volunteers based on the same input models. The group subjectively assessed the level of difficulty of understanding, unambiguity, linguistic correctness and rich vocabulary of descriptions generated in natural language, descriptions written by volunteers, and original models saved in BPMN. These assessments were analyzed to see how much the corresponding descriptions differ in readability and to establish correlations between how business processes are written and how easy they are to understand.

The rest of this paper is structured as follows. Section 2 presents an overview of business process modeling, with particular emphasis on the BPMN notation on which the approach described in this work is based. In Sect. 3, the created system is presented. Its overview includes the used technologies, an outline of the proposed algorithm, as well as an illustrative example. Section 4 covers the evaluation of the obtained results, including the correctness assessment of the performed generator, as well as empirical research conducted on a group of volunteers. In the final Sect. 5, we summarize the work done and outline possible directions for the further development of the approach.

2   Business Process Models and Their Representations

In recent years, a lot of effort has been put into creating specifications and standards for modeling business processes. Various consortia and organizations, as well as individual software developers and academic groups proposed their own metamodels and business process formats.

BPMN (Business Process Model and Notation) [6] is a standard developed by OMG (Object Management Group) for business process modeling. The popularity of BPMN models stems from the fact that this standardized graphical notation can be easily used by business analysts to document and share business processes both within companies and with external business partners.

The main goal of BPMN is to provide a notation that is easy for anyone to understand, starting with the already mentioned business users, through the programmers implementing this standard, and ending with the staff deploying and monitoring business processes at companies [6].

There are four types of main graphical elements in BPMN process models:

- Flow Objects – represent all actions that can happen in a business process, especially determining the behavior of the process. There are three main types of flow objects: events, activities, and gateways.

- Connecting Objects – give the possibility to connect different objects to each other in various ways, mostly using a sequence flow or a message flow.
- Swimlanes – are used to group other elements in diagrams using pools and lanes to depict the places of execution.
- Artifacts – provide additional information that does not affect the process. The main artifacts are: data objects, groups, and annotations.

2.1 Textual Representations of Process Models

There are many challenges concerning natural language processing in business process management [7]. There has been several approaches to generating natural language sentences based on business process models represented in S-BPM [8], Petri net [9] or BPMN [10]. For generating the textual description, various intermediate representations may be used, e.g. sentence templates [11], Semantics of Business Vocabulary and Rules (SBVR) [12], Refined Process Structure Tree (RPST) [10] or Extended Process Structure Tree (EPST) [13].

In general, the approaches which generates textual description in the English language consist of three phases: text planning, sentence planning and realization [10,14,15]. Generating such description is often used for validation of models [10], checking process compliance against the natural language specification [5], aligning [16,17] or synchronizing [14] the textual and process model representation. Integrating textual description and model representation may also be used for comprehensive process search [18].

Comparing the process models with the textual description is an up-to-date research topic. There exists tools, like ModelJudge [4,19], which help to teach modeling from textual representation. Thus, the generated textual representations may help in testing and improving such tools.

Moreover, as there still exist organizations which maintain textual process descriptions for their stakeholders, it is desired to provide methods for such description generation [20,21].

2.2 Representation of a BPMN Model in Python

For the implementation of our method, we provide the model representation in Python which is stored in the `BPMNModelAdapter` class object. The structure of the loaded model is presented in Fig. 1.

The model is simplified, so it stores only the necessary subset of elements. Each node in the presented diagram consists of name and type, separated by a colon. The whole model is located in an `BPMNModelAdapter` object. It contains a dictionary of `nodes`, which stores process nodes (activities, events, and gates) in the `Node` type objects. Such objects store pieces of information about themselves and the references to the previous and the following nodes.

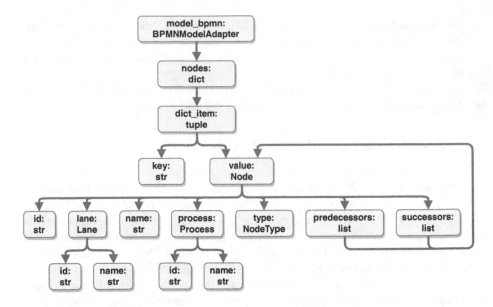

Fig. 1. The basic structure of the BPMN model representation.

3   Proposed Application

This section describes the application that was built to implement the proposed approach, as well as a detailed presentation of the algorithm that was used to generate a textual description of a BPMN model.

3.1   Used Technologies

The application was built in Python 3.6. Two external libraries for the Python language were used in the system:

1. `bpmn_python` library
   It is a library used to import and export BPMN diagrams (from and to XML files). It also provides the ability to easily visualize these diagrams in a graphic form. Figure 2 shows the structure of a model returned by this library. It consists of the following elements:
   - bpmndi_namespace – namespace for BPMN Diagram Interchange.
   - collaboration – stores a list of message exchange participants, each of them is a separate BPMN process.
   - diagram_attributes – contains basic information about the diagram: ID and name.
   - diagram_graph – stores a list of transitions between subsequent parts of the process, and also this parts, e.g. tasks, subprocesses or gateways, i.e. all flow objects of the diagram.

- id_prefix – identifier prefix for process elements.
- plane_attributes – BPMN DI object parameters, i.e. its ID and BPMN collaboration object ID.
- process_elements – contains a list of collaborating processes, as well as their parameters and included swimlanes.
- sequence_flows – a list of connections between flow objects that define the sequence flow.

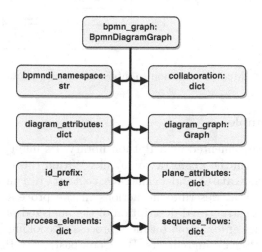

Fig. 2. Structure of a process model in bpmn_python library.

2. Morfeusz 2 (Morpheus 2)

Morpheus 2 is a complex morphological analyzer for the Polish language. In addition to analysis, it also allows the generation (synthesis) of words that are a variation of the given lemma based on the desired morphosyntactic markers. In the analysis mode, the input is a string, while the output is a list of interpretations of the segments found in this string.

3.2   Algorithm for Generating Process Description

The algorithm of constructing descriptions in natural language of a business process in BPMN (stored in an XML file) is presented in Figs. 3, 4, 5 and 6.

The process of converting the model to the intermediate representation is presented in Fig. 4. Figures 5 and 6 present the algorithm for generating sentences consists in choosing one of the prepared sentence templates, appropriate for the given node and context. Next task is to insert into this template the extracted data from the node, which should be previously recognized as parts of a sentence and changed according to the template.

Fig. 3. General process of generating the description

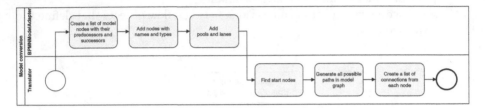

Fig. 4. Model conversion to intermediate representation

3.3 Usage Example

The generator is implemented as a Python library. Its main component is the `Translator` class from the `translator.py` file. Within this class, two available methods exist: `translate()` and `translate_to_text()`. The former generates a list of sentences that describe the actions in the process, while the latter produces a complete structured description of the analyzed process.

Figure 7 presents an example business process of cooking pasta. It consists of four tasks: A – Prepare ingredients, B – Cook pasta, C – Prepare sauce, D – Add sauce to the pasta. Tasks B and C are executed in parallel.

The result of executing the `translate_to_text()` method for the example process (Fig. 7) is as follows:

```
1. Opisywany proces rozpoczyna się następującymi zadaniami.
Poniższy proces rozpoczyna się od przygotowania składników.
Kolejne zadania opisane zostały w punktach 2 oraz 3.
Należy je wykonać równolegle.
2. Pierwszym zadaniem w tym punkcie jest ugotowanie makaronu.
Kolejne zadania opisane są w punkcie 4.
3. W tym punkcie należy przygotować sos.
Następnie należy przejść do punktu 4.
4. Po zakończeniu punktów 2 i 3 należy przejść do dalszej
części opisu. Kolejnym zadaniem jest dodanie sosu
do makaronu.
Tym zadaniem proces zostaje zakończony.
```

English translation: *1. The described process begins with the following tasks. The following process begins with the preparation of ingredients. Next tasks are described in points 2 and 3. They should be done in parallel. 2. The first task at this point is to cook pasta. Next tasks are described in Sect. 4. 3. The sauce should be prepared at this point. Then go to step 4. 4. After completing points 2 and 3, proceed to the further part of the description. another the task is to add sauce to the pasta. This task completes the process.*

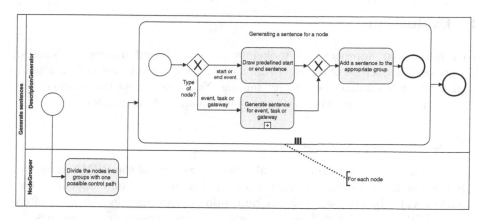

Fig. 5. Generating description algorithm

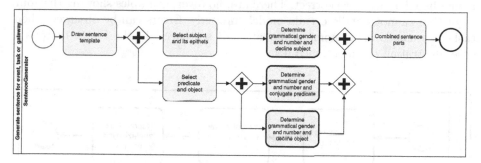

Fig. 6. Generating sentences for the algorithm

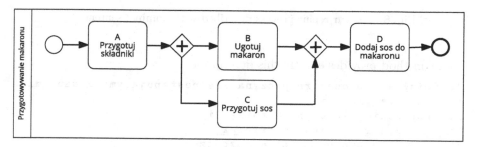

Fig. 7. The example process of cooking pasta.

The obtained result shows the division of the description into four main groups, which can be easily identified in the source process. On the other hand, the `translate()` method produces sentences that define separate groups of actions in the source process. Although writing a process description in this way makes it incomprehensible for the reader, the `translate()` method is the most useful if the generated sentences are to be further processed by the user.

4   Evaluation

To evaluate our approach, we took into account several different processes. We present the outputs of the algorithm based on a selected process of car repair, each of which has a different activity naming. Next, we present the results of the survey that was conducted to assess the performance of our method.

4.1   Correctness Assessment

The implemented system supports only selected aspects of the BPMN standard – it has not been designed to work with all elements that may appear in the model provided by the user. The program supports elements that are most often used in BPMN notation [22], such as tasks, gateways, events and swimlanes.

Most of descriptions generated based on example models including the elements listed above were correct. There are, however, examples showing that our algorithm cannot handle certain models properly. Errors can be observed when tasks are named using nominal (equational) sentences. In the Fig. 8, there is a case illustrating the mentioned defect.

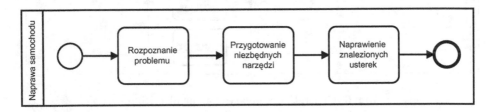

Fig. 8. The car repair process described with nominal sentences.

Our method provides exactly this description:

```
1. Opisywany proces rozpoczyna się następującymi zadaniami.
Rozpoznanie problemu.
Przygotowanie niezbędnych narzędzi.
Naprawienie znalezionych usterek.
Tym zadaniem proces zostaje zakończony.
```

English translation: *1. This process begins with the following tasks. Diagnosing the problem. Preparation of necessary tools. Repair the defects found. This task completes the process.*

In this example, nominal sentences were just extracted from the model and put to the description without any modification or transformation. Errors were underlined in the provided summary.

The output of our method can also be considered faulty when a particular task is described in a peculiarly complex way. It is presented in Fig. 9 and in the attached listing.

Fig. 9. The car repair process described with long and complex sentences.

Our method provides exactly this description:

```
1. W tym miejscu poniższy proces ma swój początek.
Poniższy proces rozpoczyna się od otworzenia maski samochodu,
której dostarczył klient i obejrzenia silnika z bliska.
Potem następuje znajście narzędzi koniecznych do naprawy
i ułożenie je w pobliżu.
Następnie trzeba naprawić znalezioną usterkę.
Tym zadaniem proces zostaje zakończony.
```

English translation: *1. This process begins here. The following process starts from opening the hood of the car, which the customer delivered and watching the engine up close. Then follows finding the tools necessary for repair and placing them nearby. Then fix the problem found. This task completes the process.*

In the description above, all misused words are underlined. The form 'której' should be replaced with 'który'. In this case, the algorithm was wrong determining the word gender. Similarly, the form 'je' should be replaced with 'ich', since in Polish, there is a necessity to decline personal pronouns. Finally, the word 'znajście' was put in the description. It is an archaism. 'Znalezienie' is far more contemporary, unfortunately, it has a different word base.

The mentioned examples prove that our method is not 100% accurate. However, it does not mean that even such faulty descriptions are useless. They can not be considered flawless, yet they can shorten the process of preparing the proper text. What is more, the risk of errors in descriptions generated using the algorithm decreases when the contents of a model are concise.

4.2 Survey Study

In order to assess the generated description, we created a survey. Every item of survey was rated using 5 element Likert's scale, with:

1 = *I agree the least*, and
5 = *I agree the most.*

The survey concerned four aspects of the provided texts, namely:

– Ease of understanding.
– Explicitness.

– Linguistic correctness.
– Quality of the vocabulary.

Respondents were obliged to use the survey and assess three types of model's description for 2 examples: BPMN, generated by our method and created in our pilot study. 42 persons took part in the survey. All of them were non-IT students aged 19–26, who had never before seen BPMN notation. Means and standard deviations are presented in accumulated form in Table 1.

Table 1. Survey results.

Descriptions	Ease of understanding		Explicitness		Linguistic correctness		Quality of the vocabulary	
	Mean	STD	Mean	STD	Mean	STD	Mean	STD
Graphical (BPMN)	4.02	0.91	–	–	–	–	–	–
Generated by our algorithm	4.12	0.93	4.44	0.78	3.25	1.15	2	0.98
Written by volunteers	3.98	0.89	3.39	1.19	4.46	0.65	3.76	0.83

Table 2. Statistical analysis for first and second example.

Descriptions	Ease of understanding		Explicitness		Linguistic correctness		Quality of the vocabulary	
	First	Second	First	Second	First	Second	First	Second
p value	–	–	.767	.000	.351	.000	.000	.000

We performed statistical analysis for each of the two examples separately (Table 2). We used the t-Student test for dependent groups. In terms of *Explicitness* and *Linguistic correctness* for the first example presented to subjects, there is no statistically significant difference between the text generated by our algorithm and the one written in the pilot study. Such a difference can be observed when talking about *Quality of vocabulary* for both examples and in terms of *Explicitness* and *Linguistic correctness* for the second example. Therefore, the descriptions provided by volunteers consist of richer vocabulary than those generated by our method. For some models, they seem pretty understandable and linguistically correct. However, further investigation in this matter is needed.

Similarly, we used GLM (General Linear Model) for establishing if the difference in terms of *Ease of understanding* is statistically significant. Received values ($p < 0.05$) point that descriptions generated by our method are more easily understandable than those written by volunteers and in BPMN.

5 Summary

The main aim of this paper was to propose a description generator for business process models in Polish language. Our solution was implemented in Python and evaluated in a survey study. We investigated the results and established that our method provided better outcome in terms of some indicators when comparing to descriptions generated by humans. The proposed algorithm can help in reducing the risk of making a mistake when preparing descriptions and significantly reduce the time needed for the task. To the best of our knowledge, this is the only algorithm that generates descriptions in Polish language for given BPMN models.

In the future, we want to focus mostly on adding support for other languages similar to Polish language. Additionally, we plan to extend functionality in order to handle all elements of the BPMN standard. It would be also beneficial to improve the clarity and quality of generated descriptions. Finally, we reckon that implementing the generator within the model editing tool with Graphical User Interface could enhance user experience.

References

1. Bitkowska, A., et al.: Business process management centre of excellence as a source of knowledge. Bus. Manag. Educ. **16**(1), 121–132 (2018)
2. Zeng, Q., Tang, X., Ni, W., Duan, H., Li, C., Xie, N.: Missing procedural texts repairing based on process model and activity description templates. IEEE Access **8**, 12999–13010 (2020)
3. Ferrari, A., Witschel, H.F., Spagnolo, G.O., Gnesi, S.: Improving the quality of business process descriptions of public administrations. Bus. Process Manag. J. **24**(1), 49–66 (2018)
4. Sànchez-Ferreres, J., et al.: Supporting the process of learning and teaching process models. IEEE Trans. Learn. Technol. **13**, 552–566 (2020)
5. van der Aa, H., Leopold, H., Reijers, H.A.: Checking process compliance against natural language specifications using behavioral spaces. Inf. Syst. **78**, 83–95 (2018)
6. Chinosi, M., Trombetta, A.: BPMN: an introduction to the standard. Comput. Stand. Inter. **34**(1), 124–134 (2012)
7. Van der Aa, H., Carmona Vargas, J., Leopold, H., Mendling, J., Padró, L.: Challenges and opportunities of applying natural language processing in business process management. In: COLING 2018: The 27th International Conference on Computational Linguistics: Proceedings of the Conference, Santa Fe, New Mexico, USA, 20–26 August 2018, pp. 2791–2801. Association for Computational Linguistics (2018)
8. Sneed, S.H.: Exporting natural language: generating NL sentences out of S-BPM process models. In: Fleischmann, A., Schmidt, W., Singer, R., Seese, D. (eds.) S-BPM ONE 2010. CCIS, vol. 138, pp. 163–179. Springer, Heidelberg (2011). https://doi.org/10.1007/978-3-642-23135-3_9
9. Meitz, M., Leopold, H., Mendling, J.: An approach to support process model validation based on text generation. EMISA Forum. **33**, 7–20 (2013)

10. Leopold, H., Mendling, J., Polyvyanyy, A.: Supporting process model validation through natural language generation. IEEE Trans. Software Eng. **40**(8), 818–840 (2014)
11. Aysolmaz, B., Leopold, H., Reijers, H.A., Demirörs, O.: A semi-automated approach for generating natural language requirements documents based on business process models. Inf. Softw. Technol. **93**, 14–29 (2018)
12. Mickeviciute, E., Butleris, R., Gudas, S., Karciauskas, E.: Transforming BPMN 2.0 business process model into SBVR business vocabulary and rules. Info. Technol. Control **46**(3), 360–371 (2017)
13. Qian, C., Wen, L., Wang, J., Kumar, A., Li, H.: Structural descriptions of process models based on goal-oriented unfolding. In: Dubois, E., Pohl, K. (eds.) CAiSE 2017. LNCS, vol. 10253, pp. 397–412. Springer, Cham (2017). https://doi.org/10.1007/978-3-319-59536-8_25
14. Azevedo, L.G., Rodrigues, R.D.A., Revoredo, K.: BPMN model and text instructions automatic synchronization. In: ICEIS, no. 1, pp. 484–491 (2018)
15. Rodrigues, R.D.A., Azevedo, L.G., Revoredo, K.C.: BPM2text: a language independent framework for business process models to natural language text. iSys-Revista Brasileira de Sistemas de Informação **9**(4), 38–5638–5656 (2016)
16. Sànchez-Ferreres, J., van der Aa, H., Carmona, J., Padró, L.: Aligning textual and model-based process descriptions. Data Knowl. Eng. **118**, 25–40 (2018)
17. Carmona, J.: The alignment of formal, structured and unstructured process descriptions. In: van der Aalst, W., Best, E. (eds.) PETRI NETS 2017. LNCS, vol. 10258, pp. 3–11. Springer, Cham (2017). https://doi.org/10.1007/978-3-319-57861-3_1
18. Leopold, H., van der Aa, H., Pittke, F., Raffel, M., Mendling, J., Reijers, H.A.: Integrating textual and model-based process descriptions for comprehensive process search. In: Schmidt, R., Guédria, W., Bider, I., Guerreiro, S. (eds.) BPMDS/EMMSAD -2016. LNBIP, vol. 248, pp. 51–65. Springer, Cham (2016). https://doi.org/10.1007/978-3-319-39429-9_4
19. Delicado Alcántara, L., Sánchez Ferreres, J., Carmona Vargas, J., Padró, L.: The model judge: a tool for supporting novices in learning process modeling. In: BPM-Tracks 2018: BPM 2018 Dissertation Award, Demonstration, and Industrial Track: proceedings of the Dissertation Award, Demonstration, and Industrial Track at BPM 2018 co-located with 16th International Conference on Business Process Management (BPM 2018), Sydney, Australia, 9–14 September 2018, pp. 91–95. CEUR-WS. org (2018)
20. Zaheer, S., Shahzad, K., Nawab, R.M.A.: Comparing manual-and auto-generated textual descriptions of business process models. In: 2016 Sixth International Conference on Innovative Computing Technology (INTECH), pp. 41–46. IEEE (2016)
21. Shahzad, K., Zaheer, S., Adeel Nawab, R.M., Aslam, F.: On comparing manual and automatic generated textual descriptions of business process models. J. Softw. Evol. Process **31**(11), e2204 (2019)
22. Muehlen, M., Recker, J.: How much language is enough? Theoretical and practical use of the business process modeling notation. Seminal Contributions to Information Systems Engineering, pp. 429–443. Springer, Heidelberg (2013). https://doi.org/10.1007/978-3-642-36926-1_35

Machine Learning Application in Energy Consumption Calculation and Assessment in Food Processing Industry

Piotr Milczarski$^{(\boxtimes)}$, Bartosz Zieliński , Zofia Stawska , Artur Hłobaż ,
Paweł Maślanka , and Piotr Kosiński

Faculty of Physics and Applied Informatics, University of Lodz, Pomorska str. 149/153,
90-236 Lodz, Poland
{piotr.milczarski,bartosz.zielinski,zofia.stawska,artur.hlobaz,
pmaslan,pkosinsk}@uni.lodz.pl

Abstract. In the paper, the application of the machine learning methods in the food processing industry is presented to validate the quality of the production process and its parameters. These parameters e.g. raw products' carbon footprint, energy resources and their carbon footprint usually may vary from day-to-day production because of meters' instrumental errors or human random errors. One of the human factor is false accounting of the production in the system that sometimes happen. One of the instrumental errors can be the malfunction of the meters. In the authors' project, the main goal is to optimize the production process so as to limit the carbon footprint. The problem that aroused is the trustworthiness of the data read from meters or provided by people operating the production line. That is why we applied the set of machine learning methods to validate the processes in order to choose the trustworthy ones. In the paper, we compare the results of processes classification k-Nearest Neighbors, Neural Network, C4.5, Random Forest and Support Vector Machines.

Keywords: Carbon footprint · Process assessment · K-nearest neighbors · Neural network · C4.5 · Random Forest · Support Vector Machines

1 Introduction

The food demand is expected to grow significantly in the coming years e.g. due to the demography. On the other hand, the food industry is heavily dependent on fossil fuels. Hence, developing energy efficiency strategies and limit the carbon footprint for this sector is crucial. In the middle of the 20th century, due to the rapid social and industrial development, a series of environmental problems have appeared, that in the 21st century are more visible. One of the most worrying problems is the increase of greenhouse emissions to the atmosphere. An increase in their concentration causes a rapid increase in the average global temperature. Nowadays, climate change is considered one of the biggest threats to our planet.

L. Rutkowski et al. (Eds.): ICAISC 2020, LNAI 12416, pp. 369–379, 2020.
https://doi.org/10.1007/978-3-030-61534-5_33

United Nations Framework Convention on Climate Change (UNFCCC) [1], the Kyoto Protocol [2] and the Paris Agreement [3] are well-known examples that our world and governments are trying to divert climate changes. The climate changes have taken place several times in the Earth history also in the recent eon e.g. 10000 years in the northern hemisphere.

Nowadays, the climate changes are regarded as one of the greatest environmental, social and economic threats facing our planet. It is a result of the industrial revolution and statistically shows a rapid increase in the average global temperature due to the increase in the atmospheric Greenhouse Gas (GHG) concentration, weather changes, draught, etc.

The growing population also needs more food especially processed food due to increased urbanization [4, 5]. That needs more supplies, raw materials and resources e.g. energy ones. Hence, not only governments or institutions e.g. the EU commission impose higher demands on lowering the usage of the energy resources (coal, fuels, electricity and gas) but also companies e.g. the food processing ones.

The companies in their food processes are interested in implementing low-carbon technologies or solutions for economic reasons i.e. the less energy the cheaper product. It must be connected with the keeping-up the food standards [5, 6].

The problem of process optimization is widely known. In the agricultural and especially food processing industry different techniques are used starting from human-based experience through expert systems to implementing artificial intelligence [5]. The whole agricultural industry can use the whole variety of standards and good-procedures in their business. The example of such standards might be:

- PAS 2050 [7] - Specification for the assessment of the life cycle greenhouse gas emissions of goods and services;
- ISO/TS 14067:2018 [8] - Greenhouse gases - Carbon footprint of products - Requirements and guidelines for quantification;
- ISO14040:2006 [9] - Environmental management-life cycle assessment: principles and framework;
- ISO14064-1:2018 [10] - Greenhouse gases - Part 1: Specification with guidance at the organization level for quantification and reporting of greenhouse gas emissions and removals.

In the CFOOD project, the research is aimed at estimating carbon footprint (CF) for a basic basket of frozen vegetable food by applying developed method and software (CF expert system, called CFexpert) as well as to develop innovative technologies for CF reduction by utilization of vegetable outgrades into valuable products. In the CF calculation task, we take into account PAS 2050 and ISO/TS 14067:2018 to calculate/estimate CF and later on in the following optimization task of the food processing. For individuals that are curious about how to evaluate the CF in their deeds, we can recommend using CF calculators that can be found on the Internet e.g. in [11].

In several papers [12–17], the problem of using the machine learning methods in the production processes is shown. The authors point out that these methods can not only help to limit the energy consumption but also refer to the data verification that is acquired in the processes.

In the paper, the application of the machine learning methods in the food processing industry is presented to validate the quality of the production process and its parameters. These parameters e.g. raw products' carbon footprint, energy resources and their carbon footprint usually may vary from day-to-day production because of meters' instrumental errors or human random errors. One of the human factor is false accounting of the production in the system that sometimes happen. One of the instrumental errors can be the malfunction of the meters. In the authors' project, the main goal is to optimize the production process so as to limit the carbon footprint. The problem that aroused is the trustworthiness of the data read from meters or provided by people operating the production line. That is why we applied the set of machine learning methods to validate the processes so as to choose the trustworthy ones. In the paper, we compare the results of processes classification k-Nearest Neighbors, Neural Network, C4.5, Random Forest and Support Vector Machines.

In the paper, we analyze the production stages of the frozen vegetables. We discuss how different production stages contribute to energy consumption as well as how they vary for similar processes. These variations of the energy per product unit on the different stages make the optimization of the production difficult.

2 Methodology of Carbon Footprint Assessment

The product's carbon footprint refers to the emissions of various greenhouse gases over the product's life cycle. These gases, as defined in IPCC 2007 [18], include carbon dioxide (CO_2), methane (CH_4), nitrous oxide (N_2O), and families of gases such as hydrofluorocarbons (HFCs), perfluorocarbons (PFCs) and fluorinated ethers.

The carbon footprint is usually calculated taking into account carbon emission factors and activity data that can be assessed using a Life Cycle Assessment (LCA). LCA is a method of assessing the environmental impact of a product's creation process associated with all stages of a product's life, from the extraction or production of raw materials to material processing, production, distribution, use, repair and maintenance, to disposal and/or recycling. Using this approach helps assess products for their harmful greenhouse gas emissions throughout their life cycle. LCA also helps to avoid a narrow view of the problem and analyze the actual environmental impact of the product.

LCA is based on the life cycle inventory (LCI), which takes into account data on resource and energy consumption and greenhouse gas emissions to the environment throughout the product's life cycle. LCA is a widely used approach to assess the actual environmental impact of a product due to its production and use [19–22]. The product carbon footprint assessment standards in LCA are mainly PAS 2050 [7] and ISO/TS 14067 [8]. Different approaches to the optimization problem are used for the carbon footprint, e.g. expert systems, machine learning, or artificial intelligence [12–14, 16].

The carbon footprint of a product (or energy consumed in the unit of the product) should be calculated taking into account all the stages necessary for its production, i.e. not only production but also transport, storage, utilization, etc. In some cases, e.g. when the relevant data is lacking, a smaller scope of analysis is allowed regarding e.g. only the production process.

3 Production Stage Life Cycle Analysis in the CFOOD Project

In Table 1 below we can compare the results of average energy utilization in kWh per one tonne of onion product at five subsequent process stages marked S1, S2, ..., S5. Each of the process stages is connected to electric meter units. The measurements were taken from April to June 2020. The process stages stand for:

- S1 – initial cooling of the raw materials before the processing;
- S2 – the raw material preparation for the production;
- S3 – raw material pre-processing on the production line;
- S4 – product freezing in the cold tunnel;
- S5 – product preparation to coldstore;

Similar stages are for the spinach production as well as the other frozen products e.g. broccoli, cauliflower, etc. The spinach production technology lacks the initial cooling, that is why the first stage starts from the raw material preparation, which is denoted as stage one S1 for spinach. Then, correspondingly S2 stands for raw material pre-processing, S3 stands for product freezing and S4 stands for product preparation to coldstore.

Each of the stages consists of one or more devices connected to the same measurement point, an electric meter. For example, stage S3 for the onion production consists of a raw materials basket and two conveyors. At the end of the process, we achieve the same or similar products. In our case, this frozen onion cut in different size cubes or spinach balls. The product lines for the onion and spinach production are the same.

In can be easily deducted from Tables 1 and 2 as well as from Figs. 1 and 2 that the final energy values depend mainly on the cooling/freezing substages. The final carbon footprint depends on the electric energy consumption. Because carbon footprint of one kWh or MWh depends on the power production structure (water, wind, solar or atomic versus carbon power plant) the classification of the processes shown below takes into account power consumption. In Poland, the equivalent for power energy of CO_2 that recalculates how much CO_2 is generated in 1 kWh is equal to 0.765 $kgCO_2/kWh$.

The aim of the project is also the process optimization. But as it can be seen the problem solution is not straightforward. It needs to take into account many factors that can happen during the production process e.g. low-quality raw materials, weather conditions; the high or low season. Figures 1 and 2 show that the same product processing on the same production lines can lead to different energy consumption structure. Some stages show meaningful but stable energy consumption e.g. S1 and S3 for the onion. In stage S5 for the onion, the energy can be meaningful but might vary from almost 0 to 0.9 kWh/t. In the stages S1 and S4 for the onion and S3 for the spinach that are connected with cooling processes, the energy used for the same stage and similar production can differ even 25–40%. That is why the main goal of the project that is energy optimization in the production can be very demanding if the data is not trustworthy.

That is why to prepare the set of verified data and to assess the trustworthiness of the production data we have compared the results of processes classification using 5 classifiers: k-Nearest Neighbors, Neural Network, C4.5, Random Forest and Support

Table 1. Average energy utilization for the onion as a raw material and similar final products.

Process ID	Average energy utilization at the process stage [kWh/t]						Weight [t]
	S1	S2	S3	S4	S5	S1-5	
149	16,54	0,24	1,06	33,79	1,43	53,07	43,93
150	12,22	0,23	1,03	30,90	1,27	45,64	44,62
171	6,78	0,07	1,17	28,32	0,26	36,60	50,04
172	8,93	0,15	0,96	29,25	0,21	39,50	70,72
175	12,22	0,19	1,24	36,10	0,05	49,79	80,41
179	21,70	0,38	0,92	31,16	0,37	54,52	26,77
201	34,95	0,15	0,94	32,31	0,02	68,37	52,84
202	22,24	0,09	0,94	28,05	0,04	51,36	45,77
207	20,16	0,09	1,17	32,73	0,03	54,18	31,17
Avg	**17,30**	**0,18**	**1,05**	**31,40**	**0,41**	**50,34**	**49,59**
Var	**8,63**	**0,10**	**0,12**	**2,65**	**0,55**	**9,32**	**17,10**
MIN	**6,78**	**0,07**	**0,92**	**28,05**	**0,02**	**36,60**	**26,77**
MAX	**34,95**	**0,38**	**1,24**	**36,10**	**1,43**	**68,37**	**80,41**

Table 2. Average energy utilization for the spinach as a raw material and similar final products.

Process ID	Average energy utilization at the process stage [kWh/t]					Weight [t]
	S1	S2	S3	S4	S1-4	
187	33,82	7,99	20,47	0,88	63,15	41,99
193	32,95	8,22	16,44	1,00	58,62	44,20
194	35,15	7,85	19,08	1,05	63,13	43,27
196	31,74	6,90	17,38	0,94	56,96	45,88
197	30,94	8,08	16,84	0,89	56,75	39,66
198	34,31	9,24	18,54	1,05	63,12	39,00
204	33,63	7,79	17,60	0,98	60,01	63,63
206	34,22	8,42	17,45	0,99	61,08	39,34
208	34,52	8,36	18,54	1,10	62,52	41,36
210	1,19	0,20	1,07	0,00	2,46	46,13
Avg	**29,85**	**7,23**	**15,88**	**0,89**	**53,85**	**44,72**
Var	**10,83**	**2,71**	**5,62**	**0,34**	**19,43**	**7,60**
MIN	**1,19**	**0,20**	**1,07**	**0,00**	**2,46**	**39,00**
MAX	**35,15**	**9,24**	**19,08**	**1,10**	**63,13**	**63,63**

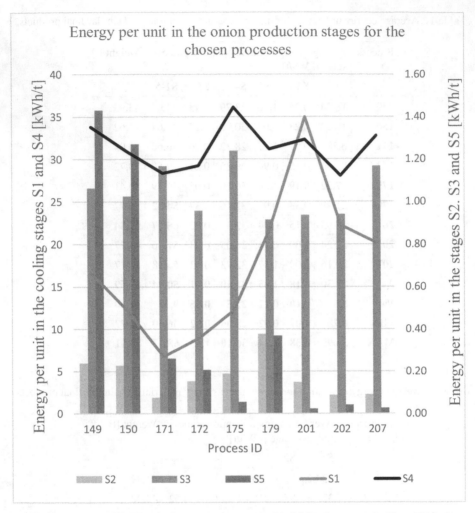

Fig. 1. Energy utilization in the processing stages S1–S5 for the processes from Table 1

Vector Machines with a radial basis kernel function [23]. The binary classifiers have the same input data that is the energy consumption per ton at each of the stages.

In Tables 3 and 4 there are classification results of the production processes using the following classifiers:

– 3NN (kNN) 3-Nearest Neighbors;
– Multilayer Perceptron (NN) with a hidden layer with 11 nodes for the onion and 10 nodes for the spinach production with a learning rate equal to 0.79 and momentum equal to 0.39;
– binary tree C4.5 with a confidence factor equal to 0.25, with a minimum number of instances per leaf equal 2;

– Random Forest (RF) with the bag size percent equal to 100, with maximum depth unlimited, number of execution slots equal to 1 and 100 iterations;
– Support Vector Machine (SVM) with two radial basis functions (RBF):

$$\text{Onion RBF Kernel: } K(x, y) = exp\left(-0.05 * (x - y)^2\right) \tag{1}$$

$$\text{Spinach RBF Kernel: } K(x, y) = exp\left(-0.0015 * (x - y)^2\right) \tag{2}$$

We took into account 55 distinct onion production processes and 31 for spinach. It is connected with a shorter period of the spinach production and gathered data.

The confusion matrix parameters are defined according to the following formulas:

$$ACC = (TP + TN)/N \tag{3}$$

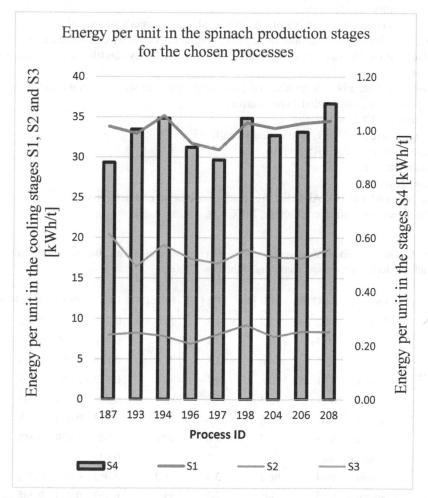

Fig. 2. Energy utilization in the processing stages S1–S4 for the processes from Table 2

$$TPR = TP/(TP + FN) \tag{4}$$

$$FPR = FN/(FP + TN) \tag{5}$$

$$Prec = TP/(TP + FP) \tag{6}$$

$$F1 = 2TP/(2TP + FP + FN) \tag{7}$$

$$MCC = (TP * TN - FP * FN)/\sqrt{(TP + FP)(TP + FN)(TN + FP)(TN + FN)} \tag{8}$$

where:

- N - a number of all cases;
- true positive, TP – a number of positive results i.e. correctly classified cases;
- true negative, TN – a number of negative results i.e. correctly classified cases;
- false positive, FP – a number of negative results i.e. wrongly classified cases as positive ones;
- false negative, FN – a number of positive results i.e. wrongly classified cases as negative ones, also called Type II error;
- accuracy, ACC;
- true positive rate, TPR, also called Recall;
- false positive rate, FPR;
- precision, Prec.;
- score test F1;
- the area under curve, AUC for the receiver operating characteristic curve, ROC;
- Matthews correlation coefficient, MCC;

Table 3. The confusion matrix parameters for the cross-validation with 10-folds of the onion and spinach production processes, according to the Eqs. (3)–(8).

Classifier	Product	ACC [%]	TPR [%]	FPR [%]	Prec. [%]	F1	MCC	AUC ROC
3NN	Onion	78.2	92.3	34.5	70.6	0.8	0.594	0.832
	Spinach	90.3	100	33.3	88.0	0.936	0.766	0.851
SVM (RBF)	Onion	85.5	84.6	13.8	84.6	0.846	0.708	0.854
	Spinach	87.1	100	44.4	84.6	0.917	0.686	0.778
NN	Onion	89.1	92.3	13.8	85.7	0.889	0.784	0.925
	Spinach	87.1	95.5	33.3	87.5	0.913	0.674	0.848
C4.5	Onion	96.4	92.3	0.0	100	0.96	0.929	0.948
	Spinach	90.3	95.5	22.2	91.3	0.933	0.76	0.952
RF	Onion	96.4	96.2	3.4	96.2	0.962	0.927	0.992
	Spinach	93.5	100	22.2	91.7	0.957	0.844	0.965

Table 4. The confusion matrix parameters for the classification with the split of the production results' sets into train (66%) and test sets (34%), according to the Eqs. (3)–(8).

Classifier	Product	ACC [%]	TPR [%]	FPR [%]	Precision [%]	F1	MCC	AUC ROC
3NN	Onion	84.2	100	27.3	72.7	0.842	0.727	0.864
	Spinach	**90.9**	**100**	**25.0**	**87.5**	**0.933**	**0.810**	**1.0**
SVM (RBF)	Onion	**94.7**	**100**	**9.1**	**88.9**	**0.941**	**0.899**	**0.955**
	Spinach	81.8	100	50.0	77.8	0.875	0.624	0.750
NN	Onion	89.5	100	18.2	80.0	0.889	0.809	0.966
	Spinach	72.7	100	75.0	70.0	0.824	0.418	0.536
C4.5	Onion	89.5	75.0	0.0	100	0.857	0.797	0.855
	Spinach	81.9	85.7	25.0	85.7	0.857	0.607	0.804
RF	Onion	**94.7**	**87.5**	**0.0**	**100**	**0.933**	**0.896**	**0.983**
	Spinach	**90.9**	**100**	**25.0**	**87.5**	**0.933**	**0.810**	**1.0**

From Tables 3 and 4 it can be concluded that:

- the best classifier for both products seems to be Random Forest;
- the onion production classification shows more concise results than the spinach production. This is because of 55 distinct data for the onion and 31 for the spinach.
- Apart from 3NN, all other classifiers used in the onion case show also good results.

4 Conclusions

The introduction of low-carbon economy assumptions, and in particular the corporate social responsibility strategy, is beginning to cause changes in the awareness of entrepreneurs. Providing the value of the carbon footprint of the product is not obligatory for entrepreneurs, but they are increasingly seeing the benefits of calculating it.

The processes depend on many factors and even in the same conditions, the results can differ by around 25% as it can be seen from Tables 1 and 2. However, the energy consumption on different stages can be even eight times bigger for the production unit. In some energy-demanding stages (S2 and S4 for the onion production) connected with cooling processes the energy used for the same stage and similar production can differ even 25–40%. That is why the main goal of the project that is energy optimization in the production can be very demanding. In the analyzed production stages the final carbon footprint depends on the level of the electricity consumption.

In the paper, we have shown that machine learning methods can be helpful in the assessment of the production processes. We have shown that using the Random Forest algorithm gave us the best results of processes classification for two products. The classification will help us choose and access production processes and pick the best production parameters.

Acknowledgments. The paper is written as a part of the project CFOOD that is supported by The National Centre for Research and Development, Poland, grant number BIOSTRATEG3/343817/17/NCBR/2018.

References

1. United Nations Framework Convention on Climate Change, 1 July 2019
2. Kyoto Protocol to the United Nations Framework Convention on Climate Change. UN Treaty Database, 27 June 2019
3. Paris Agreement. United Nations Treaty Collection, 27 June 2019
4. European Environment Agency, Increasing energy consumption is slowing EU progress in the use of renewable energy sources and improving energy efficiency (in polish), 22 March 2019
5. Godfray, H.C.J.: Food security: the challenge of feeding 9 billion people. Science **327**, 812–818 (2010)
6. Meyfroidt, P.: Trade-offs between environment and livelihoods: bridging the global land use and food security discussions. Glob. Food Secur. **16**, 9–16 (2018)
7. PAS 2050: The Guide to PAS2050-2011, Specification for the assessment of the life cycle greenhouse gas emissions of goods and services. British Standards Institution (2011)
8. ISO/TS 14067: Greenhouse gases - Carbon footprint of products - Requirements and guidelines for quantification. International Organization for Standardization, Geneva (2018)
9. ISO14040: Environmental management-life cycle assessment: principles and framework. International Organization for Standardization, Geneva (2006)
10. ISO14064-1: Greenhouse gases - Part 1: Specification with guidance at the organization level for quantification and reporting of greenhouse gas emissions and removals. International Organization for Standardization, Geneva (2018)
11. Shrink That Footprint. http://shrinkthatfootprint.com/electricity-emissions-around-the-world. Accessed 11 Aug 2019
12. Lauer, T., Legner, S.: Plan instability prediction by machine learning in master production planning. In: 15th International Conference on Automation Science and Engineering (CASE), Vancouver, Canada, pp. 703–708. IEEE (2019)
13. Clairand, J., Briceño-León, M., Escrivá-Escrivá, G., Pantaleo, A.M.: Review of energy efficiency technologies in the food industry: trends, barriers, and opportunities. IEEE Access **8**, 48015–48029 (2020)
14. Pittino, F., Puggl, M., Moldaschl, T., Hirschl, C.: Automatic anomaly detection on in-production manufacturing machines using statistical learning methods. Sensors **20**, 2344 (2020)
15. Was, L., Milczarski, P., Stawska, Z., Wiak, S., Maslanka, P., Kot, M.: Verification of results in the acquiring knowledge process based on IBL methodology. In: Rutkowski, L., Scherer, R., Korytkowski, M., Pedrycz, W., Tadeusiewicz, R., Zurada, J.M. (eds.) ICAISC 2018. LNCS (LNAI), vol. 10841, pp. 750–760. Springer, Cham (2018). https://doi.org/10.1007/978-3-319-91253-0_69
16. Ali, S.A., Tedone, L., De Mastro, G.: Optimization of the environmental performance of rainfed durum wheat by adjusting the management practices. J. Clean. Prod. **87**, 105–118 (2015)
17. Bagchi, D., Biswas, S., et al.: Carbon footprint optimization: game theoretic problems and solutions. ACM SIGecom Exchanges **11**(1), 34–38 (2012)
18. J IPCC Guidelines for National Greenhouse Gas Inventories (2006). http://www.ipcc-nggip.iges.or.jp/public/2006gl/index.html. Accessed 27 June 2019

19. Cuixia, Z., Conghu, L., Xi, Z.: Optimization control method for carbon footprint of machining process. Int. J. Adv. Manuf. Technol. **92**, 1601–1607 (2017). https://doi.org/10.1007/s00170-017-0241-1
20. Kulak, M., Nemecek, T., Frossard, E., Gaillard, G.: Eco-efficiency improvement by using integrative design and life cycle assessment. The case study of alternative bread supply chains in France. J. Clean. Prod. **112**, 2452–2461 (2016)
21. Renouf, M.A., Renaud-Gentie, C., Perrin, A., Kanyarushoki, C., Jourjon, F.: Effectiveness criteria for customised agricultural life cycle assessment tools. J. Clean. Prod. **179**, 246–254 (2018)
22. Perez-Neira, D., Grollmus-Venegas, A.: Life-cycle energy assessment and carbon footprint of peri-urban horticulture. A comparative case study of local food systems in Spain. Landscape Urban Plann. **172**, 60–68 (2018)
23. Harrington, P.: Machine Learning in Action. Manning Publications, New York (2012)

Job Offer Analysis Using Convolutional and Recurrent Convolutional Networks

Jakub Nowak[1], Kamila Milkowska[1], Magdalena Scherer[2],
Arkadiusz Talun[3], and Marcin Korytkowski[1](✉)

[1] Department of Intelligent Computer Systems,
Częstochowa University of Technology,
al. Armii Krajowej 36, 42-200 Częstochowa, Poland
{jakub.nowak,marcin.korytkowski}@pcz.pl
[2] Faculty of Management, Częstochowa University of Technology,
al. Armii Krajowej 19, 42-200 Częstochowa, Poland
magdalena.scherer@wz.pcz.pl
[3] Emplocity Ltd., Warszawa, Poland
http://kisi.pcz.pl

Abstract. We present the possibilities of using convolutional and convolutional recurrent network structures to classify large text sets on the example of job offer descriptions. In the case of recruitment agencies and job offer web pages, it is essential to have a consistent database of offers. Unfortunately, different employers use very different names for the same positions and various descriptions. In this article, we classify job offer texts using feedforward and recurrent convolutional neural networks. We present also two ways to input text data for neural networks. The research was based on five randomly selected work positions. Based on the analyzed texts, the considered neural networks can recognize the type of position with relatively high accuracy.

Keywords: Convolutional neural networks · LSTM · GRU · Recurrent neural networks

1 Introduction

Currently, the most popular way to look for a job is to use specialized internet portals. The basic criterion enabling a candidate to search for a position quickly is the category in which the advertisement is placed. In the case of large databases of advertisements, the assignment of a specific position to an offer becomes problematic, which is why this article presents a method that allows automatic classification [17,19] of job offers based on the advertisement content. Classification in such a dynamic market as the labour market requires that the system learns as quickly as possible and at the same time enables verification of its operation. Therefore, it is essential to be able to modify the structure of the neural network [2,4,5,20] and adapt it to a specific case. The problem of text classification is already well known in the literature: among others, thanks

© Springer Nature Switzerland AG 2020
L. Rutkowski et al. (Eds.): ICAISC 2020, LNAI 12416, pp. 380–387, 2020.
https://doi.org/10.1007/978-3-030-61534-5_34

to works such as [7, 24]. The disadvantage of the presented solutions is that the structures of these networks cannot be modified without re-learning. It should be remembered that the training process itself is unfortunately very computationally complex and thus takes much time. Once trained, a structure can only be used to work with a precisely defined problem.

Convolutional neural networks were used initially in computer vision [1, 6, 11, 18]. The great advantage of convolutional networks and deep learning [3, 22] is the possibility to present the input text using characters in the same way as they were written by the person creating the advertisement. Thanks to the use of one-hot encoding at the character level [12, 13], no additional data encoding process is required, and in combination with convolutional networks, text classification is more resistant to human errors when typing the text, such as typos or spelling errors. The conducted research is also intended to indicate the possibilities of network optimization by limiting the amount of space at the network input. When designing a network, we consider two variants with limiting the maximum amount of space for convolutional networks or by limiting the space for one word for recurrent networks. Neural networks work very well in recruitment processes, they help the recruiter choose a position for the indicated person [16, 21]. But none of the proposed solutions can be modified after the neural network is trained. The rest of the paper is structured as follows. Section 2 presents datatests and neural network models. Section 3 shows the results of experiments and the last section concludes the paper.

2   Data and Methods

The research was carried out on the basis of job advertisements from Emplocity Ltd (https://emplocity.com/) in five categories listed in Table 1. The entire database contained 37.3 MB of uncompressed text. All ads were previously anonymized so that they did not contain any personal data. Each job advertisement had a job title and job description. In each tested network model, one-hot character-level text encoding was used for the alphabet with 35 characters: a, ą, b, c, ć, d, e, ę, f, g, h, i, j, k, l, ł, m, n, ń, o, ó, p, q, r, s, ś, t, u, v, w, x, y, z, ź, ż,, /, -. The advertisements were converted lowercase characters and there were no characters other than those from the alphabet in the entire database. Table 1 presents the statistics of the data used for each category.

2.1   Models of CNN and RCNN Networks

Two network models were proposed in the research, namely a convolutional network for text classification consisting of six convolution layers and three fully connected layers, and a recurrent network with Long Short-Term Memory (LSTM) [10] and the Gated Recurrent Unit GRU [23] cells with a convolutional input layer. In the first variant, the convolutional network input was designed for 1024 characters from the alphabet. If the job offer description was larger than the assumed input size (the number of characters), the remaining characters were

Table 1. The number of entries broken down into individual categories.

Category name	Number of job offers
Customer advisor	6 712
Production worker	5 719
Warehouseman	1 971
Courier	1 813
Programmer	962

not taken into account. The structure of the network is described in Table 2. A different approach was used when designing the recurrent network. In this solution, the job description was fed word by word in the order it was written. This procedure is to simulate reading an advertisement on the Internet in the same way as humans do. The convolutional part encodes the written word for the needs of recurrent cells, and we expect one input vector at the output of the convolutional part. Therefore, all feature maps are combined into one dimension given to the recurrent cells. The final classification remains with the LSTM and GRU. The number of calls to the recurrent cells was dynamic and depended on the number of words for each case in the base. The limitation was placed on the number of letters in one word and was 16 characters. In both cases, the input quantity was adjusted to the network model so that it was possible to carry out the most efficient convolution between the layers of the convolutional network. The database contained only 868 advertisements exceeding the assumed area of the CNN network and 2,831 words longer than 16 characters. The structure of the network is described in Table 3. In addition to these places, the SELU activation function was used throughout the structure [9]. As an alternative to the widely used RELU function, the SELU function can give negative values, which accelerates the process of convolutional network training (Fig. 1).

$$SELU(x) = scale * (max(0, x) + min(0, \alpha * (exp(x) - 1))) \tag{1}$$

2.2 Training

The networks were implemented with PyTorch library [15]. The best results were obtained using the Adam algorithm [8] used with the Cross Entropy loss function [14]. The minibatch was set to 64 and dropout to 0.5 throughout the whole learning process. For the convolutional network, the learning coefficient was set to 0.001 and was halved after every 5 learning epochs. The total learning for this task lasted 40 epochs (each lasting approximately 25 s using GPU). For RCNN, the learning coefficient is 0.0001 and it is halved after every 8 learning epochs. The total training for this task was 60 epochs, each lasting approximately 20 s for LSTM and 19 for seconds for GRU using GPU implementation (Fig. 2).

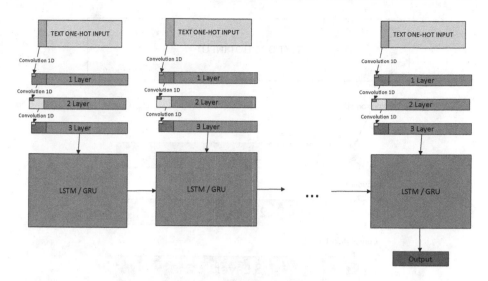

Fig. 1. Architecture of the convolutional recurrent network model used in the paper.

Table 2. Description of layers used in the convolutional network. FM denotes the number of Feature Maps

	Layer	Description
1	Input Text one-hot input	1024x35
2	Convolution - Layer 1	kernel 7x35 str. 1 256 FM, SELU activ.
3	Convolution - Layer 2	kernel 7x256 str. 1 256 FM, SELU activ.
4	Convolution - Layer 3	kernel 7x256 str. 1 256 FM, SELU activ.
5	Convolution - Layer 4	kernel 7x256 str. 1 256 FM, SELU activ.
6	Convolution - Layer 5	kernel 7x256 str. 1 256 FM, SELU activ.
7	Convolution - Layer 6	kernel 7x256 str. 1 256 FM, SELU activ.
8	Fully Connected 1	output 256, SELU activ.
9	Fully Connected 2	output 256, SELU activ.
10	Fully Connected	output 5 activ. Softmax

3   Results

The database was randomly split five times into training and testing data in a proportion of 80% and 20%. The first tests carried out on a convolutional network showed the accuracy of the best model 87.3%. For the LSTM network the error in the best implementation was 84.7% and for GRU 86.5%. A mention should be made of the difference in networks speed. The test data of 20% of all data was tested within 7.2 s for the convolutional network and 6.9 s for the network with the LSTM cell and 6.5 s for the network with the GRU cell.

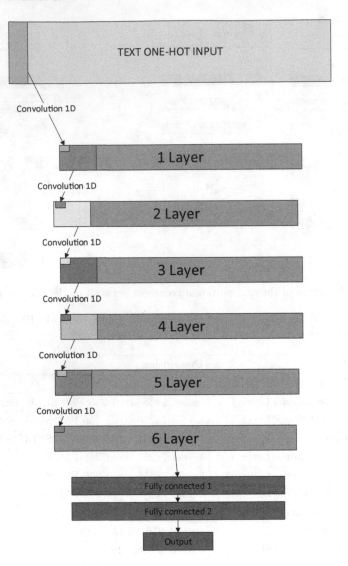

Fig. 2. Architecture of the CNN network used in the paper.

It shows the advantage in speed of the convolutional network over the recurrent networks in the presented case. The course of the training is presented in Fig. 3 (Table 4).

Table 3. Description of layers in recurrent convolutional networks. FM denotes the number of Feature Maps

	Layer	Description
	Glial and CNN	
1	Input Text one-hot input	16x35
2	Convolution - Layer 1	kernel 3x35 str. 1 36 FM, SELU activ.
3	Convolution - Layer 2	kernel 2x256 str. 1 128 FM, SELU activ.
4	Convolution - Layer 3	kernel 2x256 str. 1 128 FM, SELU activ.
5	RNN cell	LSTM or GRU
6	Fully Connected	output 5 activ. Softmax

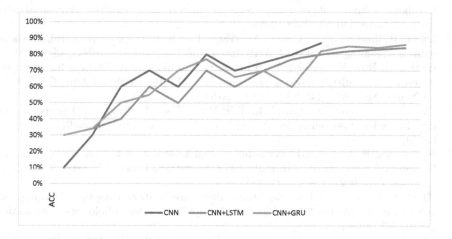

Fig. 3. CNN and recurrent CNN training (accuracy over epochs).

Table 4. Classification accuracy of convolutional networks.

No	Network	Training time [s]	Testing time [s]	Accuracy [%]
1	CNN	25.1	7.2	87.3
2	RNN + LSTM	20.1	6.7	84.7
3	RNN + GRU	19.6	6.5	86.5

4   Conclusions

The presented research proves the vast possibilities of using convolutional networks in text data classification tasks. Based on the conducted experiments, the advantage of the convolutional recurrent GRU networks over CNN in terms of time can be stated, but at the cost of a more significant error. This difference is also due to the way the input data is provided to the network. Recurrent networks require data to be given over time; therefore, the input data is divided intuitively as the words are produced by humans. Moreover, unlike in the CNN network, we do not assume a constant sentence size, which translates into the network accuracy.

Acknowledgements. This work is a part of the project number POIR.01.01.01-00-0912/18-00 "Development of an automated system using artificial intelligence for multi-channel recruitment advertising and Real-Time-Bidding operations using recurrent neural networks and generative opposing networks" funded by the National Centre for Research and Development.

References

1. Dirvanauskas, D., Maskeliūnas, R., Raudonis, V., Damaševičius, R., Scherer, R.: Hemigen: human embryo image generator based on generative adversarial networks. Sensors **19**(16), 3578 (2019)
2. Duda, P., Jaworski, M., Cader, A., Wang, L.: On training deep neural networks using a streaming approach. J. Artif. Intell. Soft Computi. Res. **10**(1), 15–26 (2020)
3. Hazra, S., Roy, P., Nandy, A., Scherer, R.: A pilot study for investigating gait signatures in multi-scenario applications. In: The International Joint Conference on Neural Networks (IJCNN). IEEE (2020)
4. Javaid, M., Abbas, M., Liu, J.B., Teh, W.C., Cao, J.: Topological properties of four-layered neural networks. J. Artif. Intell. Soft Comput. Res. **9**(2), 111–122 (2019)
5. Kamimura, R.: Supposed maximum mutual information for improving generalization and interpretation of multi-layered neural networks. J. Artif. Intell. Soft Comput. Res. **9**(2), 123–147 (2019)
6. Khan, M.A., et al.: Multimodal brain tumor classification using deep learning and robust feature selection: a machine learning application for radiologists. Diagnostics **10**(8), 565 (2020)
7. Kim, Y.: Convolutional neural networks for sentence classification. In: Proceedings of the 2014 Conference on Empirical Methods in Natural Language Processing (EMNLP), pp. 1746–1751 (2014)
8. Kingma, D.P., Ba, J.: Adam: a method for stochastic optimization. arXiv preprint arXiv:1412.6980 (2014)
9. Klambauer, G., Unterthiner, T., Mayr, A., Hochreiter, S.: Self-normalizing neural networks. In: Advances in Neural Information Processing Systems, pp. 971–980 (2017)
10. Liu, P., Qiu, X., Huang, X.: Recurrent neural network for text classification with multi-task learning. arXiv preprint arXiv:1605.05101 (2016)
11. Najgebauer, P., Scherer, R., Rutkowski, L.: Fully convolutional network for removing DCT artefacts from images. In: The International Joint Conference on Neural Networks (IJCNN). IEEE (2020)
12. Nowak, J., Holotyak, T., Korytkowski, M., Scherer, R., Voloshynovskiy, S.: Fingerprinting of URL logs: continuous user authentication from behavioural patterns. In: Krzhizhanovskaya, V.V., et al. (eds.) ICCS 2020. LNCS, vol. 12140, pp. 184–195. Springer, Cham (2020). https://doi.org/10.1007/978-3-030-50423-6_14
13. Nowak, J., Korytkowski, M., Scherer, R.: Convolutional recurrent neural networks for computer network analysis. In: Tetko, I.V., Kůrková, V., Karpov, P., Theis, F. (eds.) ICANN 2019. LNCS, vol. 11730, pp. 747–757. Springer, Cham (2019). https://doi.org/10.1007/978-3-030-30490-4_59

14. Pang, T., Xu, K., Dong, Y., Du, C., Chen, N., Zhu, J.: Rethinking softmax cross-entropy loss for adversarial robustness. In: International Conference on Learning Representations (2020)
15. Paszke, A., et al.: Pytorch: an imperative style, high-performance deep learning library. In Wallach, H., Larochelle, H., Beygelzimer, A., d'Alché-Buc, F., Fox, E., Garnett, R. (eds.) Advances in Neural Information Processing Systems 32, pp. 8024–8035. Curran Associates, Inc. (2019)
16. Rocabert, F.I., et al.: Artificial neural network system applied to human resource management. B.S. thesis, Universitat Politècnica de Catalunya (2017)
17. Scherer, R.: Multiple Fuzzy Classification Systems. Springer, Heidelberg (2012). https://doi.org/10.1007/978-3-642-30604-4
18. Scherer, R.: Computer Vision Methods for Fast Image Classification and Retrieval. SCI, vol. 821. Springer, Cham (2020). https://doi.org/10.1007/978-3-030-12195-2
19. Scherer, R., Rutkowski, L.: Neuro-fuzzy relational classifiers. In: Rutkowski, L., Siekmann, J.H., Tadeusiewicz, R., Zadeh, L.A. (eds.) ICAISC 2004. LNCS (LNAI), vol. 3070, pp. 376–380. Springer, Heidelberg (2004). https://doi.org/10.1007/978-3-540-24844-6_54
20. Shewalkar, A., Nyavanandi, D., Ludwig, S.A.: Performance evaluation of deep neural networks applied to speech recognition: RNN, LSTM and GRU. J. Artif. Intell. Soft Comput. Res. 9(4), 235–245 (2019)
21. Thorat, S.G., Bhagat, A.P., Dongre, K.A.: Neural network based psychometric analysis for employability. In: 2018 International Conference on Research in Intelligent and Computing in Engineering (RICE), pp. 1–5. IEEE (2018)
22. Wang, W., Zhao, X., Gong, Z., Chen, Z., Zhang, N., Wei, W.: An attention-based deep learning framework for trip destination prediction of sharing bike. IEEE Trans. Intell. Transp. Syst. 1–10 (2020). Early Access
23. Wang, X., Jiang, W., Luo, Z.: Combination of convolutional and recurrent neural network for sentiment analysis of short texts. In: Proceedings of COLING 2016, the 26th International Conference on Computational Linguistics: Technical papers, pp. 2428–2437 (2016)
24. Zhang, X., Zhao, J., LeCun, Y.: Character-level convolutional networks for text classification. In Cortes, C., Lawrence, N.D., Lee, D.D., Sugiyama, M., Garnett, R. (eds.) Advances in Neural Information Processing Systems 28, pp. 649–657. Curran Associates, Inc. (2015)

Team Up! Cohesive Text Summarization Scoring Sentence Coalitions

Inez Okulska[(✉)] [iD]

NASK National Reserach Institute, Warsaw, Poland
inez.okulska@nask.pl

Abstract. According to Aggarwal [6] the extractive summarization is solely about scoring sentences to maximize the topical coverage and minimize redundancy, while coherence and fluency are to be considered only in the case of abstractive summaries. It is a rather strong opinion that this paper aims to argue with by introducing different functions of text summarization, the notion of text coherence and cohesion, and last but not least by offering new methods allowing for both sentence extraction and text fluency (to a certain level). This article aims at offering a model that will be as simple as possible (but no simpler, as would Einstein put that) to satisfy the goal of informative extractive summary with a certain level of cohesion determined by sentence connectives. This abstract has been generated with the algorithm proposed in the paper.

Keywords: Extractive text summarization · Natural language processing · Coherence and cohesion

1 Introduction

Since text summarization is usually defined as a task focused on generating a short text that is considered to be the best possible (within the length limits) semantic representation of the main document (or multiple documents), the abstract of this paper included above has been automatically generated with the text summarization method proposed here - an extractive one. As a matter of facts in terms of creation process there are two different types of text summaries - abstractive and extractive ones. While the first require full text comprehension and generation of new paragraphs, the extractive one is a much simpler task of choice, where the best, most informative and therefore important sentences are extracted from the original text and put together in order to create the final summary.

Aggarwal [6] has devoted the entire chapter of his book on Machine Learning for NLP to the text summarization methods. On the very beginning of this chapter he also introduces this categorization on extractive and abstractive approach and clearly draw their differences. According to Aggarwal the extractive summarization is solely about scoring sentences to maximize the topical coverage and minimize redundancy, while coherence and fluency are to be considered

ⓒ Springer Nature Switzerland AG 2020
L. Rutkowski et al. (Eds.): ICAISC 2020, LNAI 12416, pp. 388–399, 2020.
https://doi.org/10.1007/978-3-030-61534-5_35

only in the case of abstractive summaries. It is a rather strong opinion that this paper aims to argue with by introducing different functions of text summarization, the notion of text coherence and cohesion, and last but not least by offering new method allowing for both sentence extraction and text fluency (to a certain level). There is clearly a gap in expected quality of extractive summaries which this article hopes to fill at least partially.

1.1 Related Work

Extractive summarization can be traced back to the late 1950s, as there a method based on word and phrase frequency [7] was proposed. Sentence scoring was performed with three indicators: appearance of word cues, similarity with the title, and the location of a sentence (based on the assumption that the closer to the beginning of a text or paragraph the more important becomes a sentences). An extension to this method, based on word representation of topics, was proposed by [1]. In addition to word frequency he used log likelihood ratio tests (known as topic signatures). Sentences were scored based on how many topic signatures they contain or how concise they are (which means that this method preferred shorter sentences with a higher number of topic signatures).

In general, the approach based on word or term frequency is still very popular while preparing the intermediate representation [2] of a text, used as a first step for scoring sentences. It is like PID controller in automation - there are already a lot of more complex predictive controllers available, but the relatively simple old invention is still working very well on a whole range of tasks, if not outperforming the novelties. And due to its lower complexity it is often more comfortable to apply. And so is the word or term frequency. This is why the algorithm offered in this paper also builds upon this legacy (more about it in the Sect. 3).

Extractive text summarization is a rather popular field within natural language processing, which has already resulted with a whole range of different methods and techniques that are to be found in the literature. Beside the mentioned chapter on text summarization offering a detailed view on some of them [6], there are also another comprehensive reviews and surveys of text summarization methods available (See [2,3,10]). Most common and interesting methods are TF-IDF, Centroid based method [15], Latent Semantic Analysis [12,14], graph-based methods [8], Bayesian models [5,19] or unsupervised machine learning techniques like Skip-Thoughts [20]. However, while they all are offering more and more sophisticated scoring approaches they also seem to share their perspective: focusing on single sentence and scoring it independently. They perform different types of clustering that aims at extracting most different topics, hence what is actually maximized here is the distance between chosen sentences. This way the goal of maximal topic coverage with minimal redundancy - as put by Aggarwal - is essentially preventing the resulting summary from textual fluency called cohesion.

Due to the limited size of this article only the graph-based method called TextRank will be shortly outlined here. To what does the method owe the pleasure? The summaries generated using Python implementation of TextRank will serve as competitors for the evaluation of the method proposed in this article, as shown in Sect. 4.

Graph-Based TextRank Algorithm. A graph-based approach called TextRank [13] is in fact the web page-ranking invented for search engines (PageRank) algorithm, adapted for the purpose of text summarization. Instead of modelling relations (links) between web pages, relations between sentences within single or multiple documents are represented here with the graph. Each pair of sentences are compared and if their similarity is grater than a threshold, an edge is being created. The graph is undirected but the edges are weighted with cosine similarity of sentences represented in the nodes. The resulting similarity matrix has a form of transition matrix (i.e. denotes the transition probability from one node to another) and its left dominant eigenvalues are used for sentence scoring. It means that the nodes with most (valued) edges build the set of k-top sentences for the summary.

This approach is widely used for the summarization task and easy accessible since a user-friendly python implementation called Gensim offers the TextRank based module for summarization [21].

1.2 A Further Purpose-Based Classification of Extractive Summaries

Since there has been many improvements and novel approaches offered in the literature, many further classifications of summaries methods and outputs has also been proposed [10]. The purpose behind the text summarization (and accordingly its expected output form) seems to be one of the most crucial aspects while choosing the algorithm. To illustrate the problem the differences between indicative, informative, critical and query-based summaries will be discussed here.

- **Indicative summaries** can be compared to movie trailers. Usually a trailer contain the most interesting and representative scenes (in order to present the whole range of topics discussed in the movie), mostly in original order, but with no attention to smooth transitions between them. A broken, fragmentary narrative is allowed. The main goal of an indicative summary is to draw attention of the audience (in case of texts the readers) and to persuade them to approach the full version. Thus, the shorter form and the wider spectrum of ideas the better. One of the most common application is web search engine that summarizes the web content.
- **Informative summaries** are in turn designed to serve as a handy replacement of the main text which enables the reader to safe reading time and still get the main idea(s) conveyed by the text. Ideally it should not only contain the most important topics but also provide cohesion and readability. An informative summary is supposed to be only semi-dependent and may be expected to exist as well autonomously. This kind of summary may encourage the reader to look deeper into the topic or may just help him to get a bit

familiar with the topic. Hence, the more dense and readable the summary, the better. The potential autonomy is crucial - the text should read well.

- **Critical or evaluative summaries** are subjective by design, their choice of topics, the optics of their description is influenced by the opinions included in the text that is to be summarized. The purpose of this kind of summary is kind of pervasive, it is not just conveying the facts but also the attitude about them. Automatic critical summaries are mostly extracting sentiment-related sentences – for example to build an opinion about a hotel or product based on multiple reviews. Therefore not texts as such are being summarized here, but the entire range of existing opinions are put together in order to draw the biggest possible picture [xxx]. Fluency is less important since it will contain multiple different, rather unrelated thoughts.
- And the last one, a **query-based summary**, is often used as a tool for completing automated text comprehension tasks like question answering or document classification. As such these summaries are mostly task-driven and evaluated in terms of a this particular task. Thus, their coherence or readability has much lower importance than their ability to identify and extract the desired information.

While the classification above seems reasonable and clear, a lot of papers on novel or improved methods of text summarizing seems to lack the transparency regarding their intended purpose.

The ambiguity occurs mostly between indicative and informative summaries and depends on the interpretation of proposed application or examined text corpora. For example the method of summarizing websites for search engines is rather to be thought as aiming at indicative summaries, where the output is only an eye catcher luring the user into clicking the link and reading the full text (the website). Although a summary from Wikipedia or other sources presented at the top when searching for specific term should offer the possibility of not looking deeper if the reader is satisfied with a quick and shallow definition (a brief understanding of the term). Hence even the application environment (web searching engines) is not unambiguous. And omitting the intended purpose of text summarization while proposing a method may lead to incomplete evaluation of this method. This is mostly the case when considering the informative summaries where the method focus on sentence scoring algorithms or topic relations but neglect the grammatical and syntactical fluency of the output.

As already mentioned almost every method to be find in the literature focuses on the number of topic signatures or relation between them, on the highest level of information density or on reducing redundancy, and then eventually considers some types of intratextual relations called coherence. As far as the indicative or query-based summaries are to be achieved with such a method, it is appropriate. But when designing an algorithm for generation of informative summaries, which - let's recall - are expected to replace the main text, the cohesion should not be forgotten. And to best of my knowledge none of the mentioned methods prioritize or even really consider text cohesion (beside [17], but for Spanish only, and with rather small generalization potential). What is exactly text cohesion and why coherence is not enough?

2   Text Cohesion

Cohesion is a linguistic "glue" that holds the sentences together, while coherence means how well the ideas are linked with each other. The first one is more grammatical or structural and the second one relates to the mental picture that a reader is creating in his mind by reading a text - a mind map of the ideas. However, both these features go often together - if a text lacks cohesion it will also probably be hard to follow and thus understand it. Although, a text may be coherent in terms of topic and key words distributions but not cohesive because the sentences are repetitive, not linked to each other and the entire paragraph is rather choppy. The reader will be able to understand the ideas eventually but the reading experience will be very poor. What "glues" the sentences and helps to avoid the mentioned "choppiness" is mostly conjunctions, referring words, pronouns and synonyms.

Institute for Intelligent Systems from Memphis University has been working on a project called Coh-Metrix. One of its results is an online platform for advanced text analysis. Their main focus was text coherence and cohesion (hence the 'Coh' prefix in their name). For more explanation on the necessity of both coherence and cohesion for text production or analysis see their book summarizing the projects results [11]. The Coh-metrix tool distinguishes between conceptual cohesion (ability to build mental coherent representations), performed using optimized Latent Semantic Analysis), co-reference (argument overlap), causal cohesion (if an object falls on the floor in one sentence it should probably lay on the floor in the following one, and not remain on the table as if nothing has happened) and the use of connectives.

While the coherence has lived to its own metrix and formulas for evaluating the output of automatic summarization methods [4,9], evaluating cohesion is facing an empty space. Lacking any cohesion metrics for text summaries the results of proposed summarization method will be evaluated with the values yielded by the Coh-metrix analysis, particularly by the analysis of connectives incidences.

Connectives are words or phrases that help reader to understand or infere relations between ideas in texts [16] There are mainly four types of connectives to be named: causal (because, this is why, therefore, hence, etc.), additive (also, as well, further, etc., temporal (before, after, then, etc.) and clarification (for example, including, etc.) [18].

As already mentioned for informative summaries measuring the information density or refining the choice while looking for graph-based coherence is not enough, because a certain level of connectivity between chosen sentences should also be provided. An example of this issue can be observed in following sentence generated with Gensim TextRank. While summarizing a blog article about FOMO (the Fear of Missing Out, a social phenomenon) the algorithm ranked the

sentence as highly informative and representative because of the highest value
of its summed edges:

> Therefore FOMO is not just the sense that there might be better things
> that you could be doing at this moment, but it is the feeling that you
> are missing out on something fundamentally important that others are
> experiencing right now.

The sentence does score well with cue words and topic signatures (it basically delivers the definition for the main topic) indeed, but it also does a very
poor job as an opening line for the entire summary, which was the case in this
experiment. A sentence starting with "Therefore", a causal connective, requires
at least one former sentence in order to get semantically fulfilled, to enable the
desired coherence. Without it the reader received only the information that there
is a cause for the content carried by the sentence shown in the summary but is
denied the necessary context for it.

3   The Algorithm for Cohesive Text Summarization

Beside pointing out to the necessity of including cohesion into extractive summarization I would like to offer a - may it be a bit rough - solution. This paper
aims at offering a model that will be as simple as possible (but no simpler, as
would Einstein put that) in order to satisfy the goal of informative extractive
summary with certain level of cohesion determined by sentence connectives.

As a matter of facts the intended simplicity of the model was possible to
achieve with intuitions coming from text linguistics. Before even started to experiment with different summarization methods, some important question has been
raised about how texts are been produced, how are they structured, what indicators of content and inner structure they include and how can they be detected or
made useful for this task. This is why the entire chains of thoughts are scored and
the coalition of sentences are chosen for the summary instead of single sentences.
The common histogram of word frequencies is also used differently - 30 most frequent words build a subset that provides reference for information importance
but the threshold of desired keyword number is changed dynamically and the
order of the original ranking doesn't count any more. This way two sentences
may gain the same score but contain a completely different set of words (say
each of them include 8 of the top 30 words, but these are different ones).

3.1   Let's Score the Entire Coalition Instead of Single Sentence

Let W be a dictionary, a finite set that collects all N words that can be used to
build a sentence, including an additional empty word (of length equal to zero)
denoted as $0 \in W$. If we are to consider only sentences of a finite length, then
any sentence S consisting of at most L words can be viewed as an element of
the Cartesian product of dictionaries:

$$S \in W \times W \times \cdots \times W = W^L. \tag{1}$$

Given the above definition, $S = (w_1, ..., w_l, 0, 0, ..., 0)$ represents an ordered sequence of $l < L$ words that build sentence S. For the sake of clarity, the set of nonempty words that form the sequence S will be denoted as $\bar{S} = \{w_1, ..., w_l\}$.

In a somewhat similar manner it is possible to define a finite length document D as an element of the Cartesian product of finite products of dictionaries:

$$D \in W^L \times \cdots \times W^L = W^{LM}. \tag{2}$$

Any document $D = (S_1, ..., S_m, 0, 0, ..., 0)$ is therefore an ordered sequence of $m < M$ sentences. The set of sentences used in document D will be denoted as $\bar{D} = \{S_1, ..., S_m\}$.

The key idea behind the algorithm is to select from a document at hand the sentences that contain words that are used in the document and can be interpreted as a reasonable description of the document topics. The selected sentences are next used to construct coalitions of sentences that form a basis for the summary generation.

The set of characteristic $n \leq N$ words will be denoted as:

$$T_n \subset W. \tag{3}$$

Suppose that set T_n is known for document D and we wish to find a sentence S that gives an important idea behind document D, an idea expressed by a subset of words used in D. A straightforward way to do that is to look for nonempty intersections:

$$\bar{S} \cap T_n. \tag{4}$$

The proposed summary generation algorithm takes the above operation to evaluate sentences. Namely, each sentence $S \in \bar{D}$ is evaluated by the sentence scoring function μ that counts a number of characteristic words from T_n that have been used in sentence S:

$$\mu(S) = |\bar{S} \cap T_n|. \tag{5}$$

As mentioned in the Sect. 1 there are other scoring functions described in the literature. A rather standard approach is to define score as a probabilistic measure modeling distribution of topic related information across the document. The proposed scoring function can be viewed as a generalization of this approach, introducing a general word choice operator T_n. In case of the algorithm being considered, the operator will select top n most frequent words in document D.

The sentence scoring procedure allows to identify in the document D all those subsets of sentences that may prove valuable for summary construction. Those subsets will be referred to as coalitions of sentences:

$$C \subseteq \bar{D}. \tag{6}$$

The coalition scoring function used in the presented algorithm evaluates each subset of sentences based on their total length:

$$\varphi(C) = \sum_{S \in C} |\{w : w \in S\}|, \tag{7}$$

where $|w| \in \mathbb{N}$ is the number of characters in word $w \in W$. In order to provide the desired cohesion a particular set of words or phrases (the connectives) has been build that may appear at the beginning of the sentence. When choosing sentences for the coalition the algorithm examine them in terms of the connectives. If any of them is detected the former sentence is attached to the chosen one. The attaching repeats as long as any further connectives are present in the first sentence of such a chain of thoughts. Then the coalition extended by the attached sentences is evaluated again for the set summary length.

Consider the coalition built of sentences that have their score at least at level $\alpha \in \mathbb{R}$:

$$C_\alpha = \{S \in D : \mu(S) \geq \alpha\}. \tag{8}$$

The proposed summary generation algorithm finds the coalition of sentences that all have been assigned score bounded from below by some $\hat{\alpha}$ and in total have length bounded from above by $p \geq 0$. In other words, the summary is given by the coalition:

$$C_{\hat{\alpha}} = \arg\max_{\alpha \geq 0} \{\varphi(C_\alpha) : \varphi(C_\alpha) \leq p\}. \tag{9}$$

3.2 Let the Document Speak for Itself

The latent semantic methods, like LSA, non-negative factorization or Centroid summarization, are often described as revealing the latent information hiden in the text. However, they return the exactly preset k-number of sentences, which means forcing the algorithm into clustering the document in the specific k-number of groups and then choosing their representatives, regardless the actual number of topics or thoughts that the document contain. Thus, the structure of the text to be summarized is not mined or identified, but pre-determined. Both the dynamic threshold of the information index and individual identification of cohesive thought-chains offered by the approach presented in this paper actually lets the document speak by itself. It adjusts parameters instead of imposing them. It is also possible for the user to set the desired length of the summary too (word or characters number) - but neither of them will determine the number of thoughts or topics been shown in the summary. The output will contain a cohesive and coherent set of sentences discussing the most important ideas from the text within the preset length constrains. It is likely that an idea will not make it to the summary in order to safe place for a thought-chain regarding a topic that scored higher.

3.3 POS Tagging - Parts of Speech Classes Need Some Update

POS-Tagging is a tool that allows to detect and label part of speech in examined text sequences. There are already multiple libraries and packages available for the task dedicated to different programming and natural languages (for example a built-in method for Matlab or POS-tagging library by Stanford NLP Group [22]). However, for this particular task of detecting connectives the main problem of English language is the rather fuzzy categorization of speech parts. Few of the connectives fall into category "coordinating conjunction" or "subordinating conjunction", but a lot of them are categorized simply as "determiners". The latter group is much too wide and include also articles ("the", "a"), present in almost every sentence. Therefore for English version of the algorithm there was a high need to define new task-driven set of speech parts to be detected in the document. These included the entire range of all possible word and phrases with the function of connectors.

4   Evaluation

The method presented in the article aims to generate informative summaries (as defined in the Subsect. 1.2) that will be possibly more cohesive than these offered with common algorithms. Apart from the obvious differences that can be easily observed and correctly identified by human readers - i.e. summaries openings starting with unresolved references (such as 'because', 'they', 'on the other hand', etc.) the summaries generated by the coalition algorithm and Gensim TextRank differ in the cohesion metrics computed with Coh-metrix (as explained in the Sect. 1.1). 50 articles from Scientific American, Medium.com and Wired.com have been summarized using both methods and the outcome size differed between 200 and 250 words. The results shows that in 87% of all cases the coalition method allowed to reduce the cohesion incidence (which means to improve the general cohesion) by 4,3% in average. The articles that scored worse with Coalition than with Gensim were visibly distinct in their structure as they covered more stories, quotations and dialogues. Resulting difference in the performance of the Coalition algorithm proves that this method is mostly designed for generating informative summaries of argumentative texts, not narrative or literary ones (Table 1).

Table 1. Summaries generated by Gensim and the Cohesive Coalition Algorithm compared in terms of all connectives incidence index by Coh-Metrix. An excerpt of the results.

The original article	Summary by Gensim TextRank	Summary by Cohesive Coalition	Source of the article
75,426	66,879	64,626	Scientific American
93,325	91,525	82,192	Scientific American
97.774	135,135	129,353	Wired.com
86.817	80,573	75,676	Medium.com
101.931	108,844	78,125	Medium.com

5   Conclusion

The argued book by [6] may be considered a trustworthy mirror of the discourse related to text summarization. It can both influence the readers (it has more than 60 000 downloads so far) and reflect the already existing opinions. Therefore the discussed claim that an extractive summarization method does not need to bother with text cohesion in order to offer a fluent, readable output, may be considered representative for the discourse. Motivated by possible alternative this paper intended to present a summarizing method that beside looking for information would also examine the syntactical connections between sentences that are to be chosen. However, the proposed method is not to be considered an innovation in terms of breaking through mathematics formulas. I am fully aware of the shortcomings of this solution. There is still a lot of further work to be done: the scoring function could be refined, the cohesion index reformulated, the cohesion definition extended, just to name a few. The results could also be evaluated with other metrics to prove the cohesive style (although the usual, well-known stylometric tools may be not enough for the job, so identifying own set of attributes to count would be probably necessary). Anyway, the main ambition of this paper is to draw attention to both the possible cohesion of extractive summary and the common habit of using very complex models for small but domain specific tasks. As this case has proved there is no need to use a sledgehammer if you need to just crack a nut. The text linguistics provided domain specific insight useful enough to design simple model. A model which seems to deliver satisfactory outcome, since the results obtained with this method outperformed the Gensim TextRank in the cohesion index. TextRank is much more complex than the Coalition Algorithm and offers a lot more metainformation, but they are neither used or ever useful for this task - TextRank does not look into syntactic structure between scored sentences and scores sentences independently.

Remember the abstract at the beginning of the paper? Below is the alternative abstract produced by Gensim. Shall the reader judge his or her reading experience with this one:

It is a rather strong opinion that this paper aims to argue with by introducing different functions of text summarization, the notion of text coherence and cohesion and last, but not least, by offering new method allowing for both sentence extraction and text fluency (to a certain level). This is mostly the case when considering the informative summaries where the method focus on sentence scoring algorithms or topic relations but neglect the grammatical and syntactical fluency of the output. This article aims at offering a model that will be as simple as possible (but no simpler, as would Einstein put that) in order to satisfy the goal of informative extractive summary with certain level of cohesion determined by sentence connectives. The method presented in the article aims to generate informative summaries that will be possibly more cohesive than these offered with common algorithms.

References

1. Dunning, T.: Accurate methods for the statistics of surprise and coincidence. Comput. Linguist. **19**(1), 61–74 (1993)
2. Allahyari, M., et al.: Text summarization techniques: a brief survey. Int. J. Adv. Comput. Sci. Appl. **8**(10) (2017). https://doi.org/10.14569/IJACSA.2017.081052
3. Moratanch, N., Chitrakala, S.: A survey on extractive text summarization. In: IEEE International Conference on Computer, Communication, and Signal Processing (2017)
4. Indu, M., Kavitha, K.V.: Review on text summarization evaluation methods. In: International Conference on Research Advances in Integrated Navigation Systems (2016)
5. Daume III, H., Marcu, D.: Bayesian query-focused summarizing. In: Proceedings of the 21st International Conference on Computational Linguistics and the 44th Annual Meeting of the Association for Computational Linguistics, pp. 305–312. Association for Computational Linguistics (2006)
6. Aggarwal, C.C.: Machine Learning for Text. Springer, Cham (2018). https://doi.org/10.1007/978-3-319-73531-3
7. Luhn, H.P.: The automatic creation of literature abstracts. IBM J. Res. Dev. **2**(2), 159–165 (1958)
8. Parveen, D., Ramsl, H.-M., Strube, M.: Topical coherence for graph-based extractive summarization. In: Proceedings of the 2015 Conference on Empirical Methods in Natural Language Processing. Association for Computational Linguistics (2015)
9. Parveen, D., Strube, M.: Integrating importance, non-redundancy and coherence in graph-based extractive summarization. In: Proceedings of the 24h International Joint Conference on Artificial Intelligence (2015)
10. Saziyabegum, S., Sajja, P.S.: Literature review on extractive text summarization approaches. Int. J. Comput. Appl. **156**(12), 28–36 (2016)
11. McNamara, D.S., Graesser, A.C., McCarthy, P.M., Cai, Z.: Automated Evaluation of Text and Discourse with Coh-Metrix. Cambridge University Press, Cambridge (2014)
12. Deerwester, S.C., Dumais, S.T., Landauer, T.K., Furnas, G.W., Harshman, R.A.: Indexing by latent semantic analysis. JASIS **41**(6), 391–407 (1990)
13. Mihalcea, R., Tarau, P.: TextRank: bringing order into texts. In: Proceedings of the 2004 Conference on Empirical Methods in Natural Language Processing. Association for Computational Linguistics (2014)
14. Gong, Y., Liu, X.: Generic text summarizing using relevance measure and latent semantic analysis. In: Proceedings of the 24th Annual International ACM SIGIR Conference on Research and Development in Information Retrieval, pp. 19–25. ACM (2001)
15. Radev, D.R., Jing, H., Styś, M., Tam, D.: Centroid-based summarization of multiple documents. Inf. Process. Manag. **40**(6), 919–938 (2004)
16. Halliday, M.A.K., Hasan, R.: Cohesion in English. Longman Group Limited, London (1976)
17. Alonso i Alemany, L., Fort, M.F.: Integrating cohesion and coherence for Automatic Summarization (2003). https://www.aclweb.org/anthology/E03-3002.pdf. Accessed 28 Jan 2020
18. McNamara, D.S., Louwerse, M.M., McCarthy, P.M., Graesser, A.C.: Coh-metrix: capturing linguistic features of cohesion. Discourse Process. **47**(4), 292–330 (2010). https://doi.org/10.1080/01638530902959943

19. Wang, D., Zhu, S., Li, T., Gong, Y.: Multidocument summarization using sentence-based topic models. In: Proceedings of the ACL-IJCNLP 2009 Conference Short Papers, pp. 297–300. Association for Computational Linguistics (2009)
20. Kiros, R., et al.: Skip-Thought Vectors (2015). https://arxiv.org/abs/1506.06726. Accessed 28 Jan 2020
21. Barrios, F., Lopez, F., Argerich, L., Wachenchauzer, R.: Variations of the Similarity Function of TextRank for Automated Summarization (2016). https://arxiv.org/abs/1602.03606. Accessed 28 Jan 2020
22. Kristina Toutanova, K., Klein, D., Manning, Ch., Singer, Y.: Feature-rich part-of-speech tagging with a cyclic dependency network. In: Proceedings of HLT-NAACL (2003)

New Surrogate Approaches Applied to Meta-Heuristic Algorithms

Joel A. Oliveira[1], Matheus Santos Almeida[2], Reneilson Y. C. Santos[1], Rene Pereira de Gusmão[2], and André Britto[2](✉) ⓘ

[1] Post-Graduation Program on Computer Science,
Federal University of Sergipe, São Cristóvão, Brazil
joel.alves.oliver@gmail.com, reneilson1@gmail.com
[2] Computation Departament, Federal University of Sergipe, São Cristóvão, Brazil
{matheusssa,rene,andre}@dcomp.ufs.br

Abstract. Surrogate can be defined as a mechanism capable of learning the behavior of a given objective function. As it is a regression problem, machine learning (ML) models are natural candidates to solve it. However, there is a lack of works comparing different machine learning techniques employed as surrogates. Thus, this paper proposes new surrogate approaches applied to meta-heuristic algorithms, as well as evaluate different machine learning models. It is proposed a new framework that embodies different ML models as surrogates, like decision trees, random forest, and SVR, and explores different mechanisms to train the models. An experiment set is performed to evaluate the framework.

Keywords: Surrogates · Evolutionary algorithms · Machine learning

1 Introduction

Optimization problems require that the algorithm evaluates a great number of inputs to find the optimal solution of a given problem. When the algorithm is applied to real-world problems, some limitations are faced, such as an objective function cannot be defined in an algebraic form, calculations of the objective function are computationally expensive or the problem has few feasible solutions [5]. Problems which have some of those characteristics can be classified as Expensive Optimization Problems.

To solve those problems, some approaches, like parallel computing, the use of a surrogate, and similarity of neighbors, have been proposed [5]. Surrogate is a technique that learns the behavior of the objective function and can be used to predict the objective values of a given solution. The problem faced by surrogate can be mapped to a regression problem. Some approaches can be used as surrogates such as Machine Learning (ML), Linear Regression, and Gaussian regression. Surrogates are based on the principle of replacing one or more objective functions with a prediction mechanism. For expensive problems, that mechanism is computationally cheaper than the replaced objective function. Thus, through

L. Rutkowski et al. (Eds.): ICAISC 2020, LNAI 12416, pp. 400–411, 2020.
https://doi.org/10.1007/978-3-030-61534-5_36

the application of surrogates, it is possible to execute a smaller number of calls to the objective functions and consequently reduce the execution time.

In meta-heuristics algorithms, such as evolutionary algorithms, particle swarm optimization, among others, surrogates can used to substitute the objective function during the search. In literature, the interest in applying surrogates on those algorithms has grown. Related works, like [4,5,11], present the central idea of this area in last years. In those studies, meta-modeling techniques, such as neural networks (NN), radial-basis function (RBF), support vector machines (SVM) and Kriging method, and the main surrogate methodologies are addressed.

Although the approach of applying surrogates with meta-heuristic algorithms is promising, related works have only tested these approaches with few ML techniques. Besides, commonly only evolutionary algorithms are explored. Finally, it is yet possible to explore new methodologies used for surrogate training aiming to improve the quality of the regression process.

This paper proposes new surrogate approaches applied to meta-heuristic algorithms, as well as evaluates different machine learning models as surrogates. Here, it is proposed a new surrogate framework applied to meta-heuristic algorithms that have an emphasis on the training mechanism of the machine learning models. The proposed framework is characterized by a combination of optimization algorithms and machine learning models.

The framework has the characteristic of training the models during the search. In the framework, the algorithms' search is defined by two phases. The first corresponds to the generation of initial solutions that will be used for training the surrogate. The second phase is characterized by the end of training and the replacement of the objective function. Thus, in the framework, the algorithms will start the search with the real objective function, while training the surrogate, and then they will use the surrogate.

Here, three training mechanisms are used to train the learning models. Two new approaches proposed in our work, called S_Online and S_Batch, and one approach adopted from literature, called M1 [5]. As machine learning models, the framework applies Decision Trees (DT), Random Forest (RF) and SVR, an extended version of SVM applied to regression problems [3]. Moreover, two well-known metaheuristics with good results in continuous problems, Particle Swarm Optimization, and Differential Evolution are evaluated.

A set of experiments was conducted to evaluate the proposed approach looking for the best framework configuration. Thus, different configurations of the proposed framework were confronted, considering the training mechanism, learning model, and optimization algorithm. Those configurations were applied to 5 benchmarking optimization problems. Similar to related works [13,14], in our work, the surrogate approaches will be analyzed through the quality of the obtained solutions.

This paper is organized as follows. In Sect. 2 it is presented the theoretical concepts and related works. Section 3 brings the new approaches of surrogate and the proposed framework. Section 4 presents the procedures of the experimentation and discussion of the results. Finally, Sect. 5 shows the main contributions, the conclusions of the paper as well as possible future works.

2   Background Theory

In recent years, several problems with high complexity degrees have arisen. Most of those are real-world problems and the difficulties faced by the algorithms are mainly due to three reasons [15]:

1. The objective function can not be defined in an algebraic form;
2. When the calculation of objective functions is computationally expensive;
3. The problem has a few feasible solutions.

The second reason is common in problems in which there is an objective function that represents the problem well, but the calculation of that function requires a high computational capacity or a long time for calculating (e.g. simulation). Surrogates are an approach to solve such problems. Surrogate is a technique used to build very simple and cost-effective models, which seeks to replicate the relationships that are observed when examples of a more complicated model or simulation are built [10].

In the optimization context, surrogate is a technique that will learn the objective function $(f(x))$, and then that will be used to predict the value of $f(x)$ given a solution x. There are numerous approaches that can be used as surrogates such as machine learning algorithms and linear regression algorithms. Those approaches need training. In the training process $x(x1...xn)$ solutions, as well as the fitness $f(x)$ values associated with each training solution respectively are provided. With those values, the approaches seek to build a pattern that makes the relation among the inputs and their respective output values.

Once trained, the surrogate will be applied in place of the objective function, that is, given a x solution as input, the surrogate will return a $f(x)$ value. It is noteworthy that surrogate corresponds to an approximation of the objective function, so the value predicted by it does not correspond to the actual value that would be returned by the real objective function.

The substitution of the objective function can happen in two different ways [7]. In the first, the objective function is replaced before the optimization algorithm is executed. For this, the surrogate is built using solutions generated by sampling methods. The main advantage of this method is that objective functions are rarely used, nonetheless, as a consequence, surrogates have poor accuracy.

In a second way, the objective function is iteratively replaced during the execution of the optimization algorithm. The iterative process is performed by alternating between making evaluations using an objective function and a surrogate. Evaluations using the objective function (also called full-cost) are used to train, update, or retrain a surrogate. The number of full-cost evaluations can often be reduced substantially, while high accuracy is reached yet. This is the main advantage of this type of approach.

Another advantage is that the trained meta-model can represent important information about the problem in a simple and easy to interpret way. In addition, the fact that the examples are not randomly generated, but chosen, results in training sets that will contain highly correlated data.

2.1 Related Work

In the study [7] a set of new surrogates approaches for evolutionary algorithms has been implemented. Those approaches are classified from M1 to M6, being directly associated with the number of surrogates used. M1 and M2, a surrogate to learn the behavior of each objective function is created. M3 and M4 classifications use surrogate combinations to learn the behavior from different objective functions. A procedure for the scalarization of parameters is used to combine all objective functions in a single objective function in M5 approach. Finally, M6 approach applies the KKT Proximity Measure (KKTPM) [6] metric, which identifies a solution domination degree.

Another recent work that brings new contributions is the study of [13]. In that work, a new algorithm is proposed, using different surrogates (Kriging, polynomial response surface method (RSM) and RBF) to approximate the objective function values. In the proposed algorithm, two sets of reference vectors (VR) are used and the solutions are assigned to the RF sets separately. The set that presents the best diversity metric is chosen as the winning reference vector. Furthermore, a local search is applied. The algorithm is evaluated using a set of benchmarking problems DTLZ, WFG, C1_DTLZ1, C2_DTLZ2, C3_DTLZ3, and compared to ParEGO, MOEA/D-EGO, CSEA, K-RVEA algorithms. It can be concluded that the proposed algorithm can obtain the best results.

In [4], a surrogate-guided differential evolution algorithm is proposed, called S-JADE. S-JADE builds two surrogates, a global surrogate built in the whole design space and a local one built in the neighbor region around each current population and adds optimum information provided by both. Furthermore, it performs a surrogate-guided selection strategy. The proposed algorithm is confronted with other non-surrogate-assisted and surrogate-assisted metaheuristic algorithms. The results show that S-JADE outperforms the compared algorithms for almost all problems. Also, in [11], it is proposed a new selection which employs a hierarchical structure of surrogate models. That approach can automatically choose a modeling technique during the optimization process.

3   Proposed Framework

The proposed framework explores surrogates in meta-heuristics algorithms. The framework varies in the way it trains the models, it also enables different optimization algorithms execution and particular machine learning techniques application. The framework incorporates the jMetal framework [9], responsible for the optimization algorithms, with machine learning models, using scikit-learn, a machine learning library for Python.

It employs two different meta-heuristics algorithms, a basic Differential Evolution algorithm (DE) and SMPSO. The DE scheme used in this algorithm version is called $rand/1/bin$, because the vectors are chosen randomly (rand), it used only 1 vector difference and the crossover strategy used to mix the test information and the target vectors was a binomial intersection. SMPSO is the basic version available in jMetal.

The machine learning algorithms embedded are SVR, Random Forest, and Decision Tree. SVR is applied to the regression problem by determining a ϵ radius tube, which should contain all points in the training set. The Decision Tree is based on the CART algorithm (Classification and Regression Tree). The RF technique combines decision trees with aggregation. In trees, all aggregation samples are distributed identically. This process of distributing the samples makes the average hope of B trees equal to the hope of each tree.

3.1 General Schema

The main characteristic of the proposed framework relies on training mechanisms. In our proposed approach, the surrogates are trained during the search of the meta-heuristic algorithms. As solutions are generated and evaluated using the real objective function, they are used in training the models. When a stop criteria is reached, the training is finished, and the surrogate substitute the real objective function. Here, the defined stop criteria is a maximum number of solutions selected to train the surrogate, t_max. Since every solution generated during the training phase of the framework is evaluated using the real objective function, t_max also represents a number of objective function evaluations until the end of the training. The different training mechanisms explored by the framework are defined by the way the framework selects solutions as the input of the models. Here, two training mechanisms are proposed, called S_Online, S_Batch. Furthermore, the framework also implements the M1 model present in the literature [14].

Thus, to configure an execution of the framework it is necessary to select the training mechanism, the meta-heuristic algorithm, and the machine learning model. With those three components, the framework executes the following procedures: first, the algorithm is initialized and the search is started, using the real objective function; then, as the search is performed, following the selected training mechanism, the generated solutions are used to training the surrogate; after, when the training is finished, the real objective function is replaced by the surrogate and the algorithm finish the search using the approximated function.

Considering the main framework procedure, an aspect must be further explored: how to select solutions as input to train the surrogates and when to finish the training. This aspect is defined by the training mechanisms and will be discussed in the following section.

3.2   Training Mechanisms

This section presents the training mechanisms adopted by the framework. First, the two proposed approaches, S_Online and S_Batch will be discussed. Finally, this section will discuss how M1 approach is applied to the framework.

The S_Online method trains the surrogate at the final of each evolutionary loop, therefore, training as each population update. For the S_Batch framework, the solutions are stored in a file and, when t_max is reached, the surrogate is trained.

The framework using S_Online performs the basic steps of the search algorithms. During the evolutionary loop, after the generation of the new population the surrogate is trained. Then, the machine learning model is trained with the new generated solutions. This procedure is repeated until t_max is reached. Thus, in this approach the learning model is trained several times, using as input data sets as large as the size of the population. When t_max is reached, the surrogate replaces the real objective function.

Different from S_Online, S_Batch trains the surrogate only one time, when t_max is reached. In this approach, the search algorithm executes until a maximum t_max objective function number of evaluations is reached. At the end of the evolutionary loop, every new solution is archived in a file. When t_max is reached, the learning model is trained with a data set with t_max solutions, and then, the surrogate replaces the real objective function.

M1 approach is based on the work proposed in [14]. This approach uses Latin Hypercube Sampling (LHS) [2] process to initialize the initial population. A sequence of steps is performed to train the surrogate and optimize the problem, finding the best solutions. In M1 approach, the training is performed at every t running. Different from the previous approaches, as soon as the population is initialized, the surrogate is trained and replaces the real objective function. At every t iterations, the new population is used to update the surrogate. At every surrogate update, the algorithm calculates the real objective values of the solutions.

4   Experiments

To achieve the objective of evaluating the new surrogate approach, an in vitro experiment was executed. The experiment considered five mono-objective optimization problems taken from [16]. To do so, the experiment objective formalization, following GQM model (Goal Question Metric), proposed by [1], can be stated as: to **analyze** new surrogates approach, **for the purpose** of evaluating them **according to** the performance metric hypervolume, **from the viewpoint of** researchers and developers of algorithms **in the context of** optimization.

To identify which proposed training mechanism is better and if there is some machine learning model, used as a surrogate, which can improve algorithm's performance, the planning and execution of the experiments have been defined and are described as follows.

4.1 Planning

Context Selection: The experiment is *in vitro* and makes use of mono-objectives optimization problem benchmarks, according to their mathematical modeling, Python and Java are the used programming languages. Moreover, five different problems are used [16]: Ackley, Griewank and Rastrigin (multi-modal problems), Ellipsoid (continuous, convex and unimodal), and Rosenbrock (uni-modal, and the global minimum lies in a narrow, parabolic valley). Besides that, three machine learning algorithms are used as surrogates: SVR, Decision Tree, and Random Forest. Those techniques were applied in two metaheuristic algorithms: Differential Evolution (DE) and Speed-constrained Multi-objective PSO (SMPSO).

Dependent Variables: Hyper-parameters of each classification and optimization algorithms, objective values.

Independent Variables: Optimization problems used (Ackley, Ellipsoid, Griewank, Rastrigin and Rosenbrock), decision variables of the problems and the algorithms themselves (SVR, Decision Tree and Random Forest).

Hypotheses Formulation: The research question for this paper is: Which is the best combination of machine learning and surrogate approach to learn and substitute the objective function of some optimization algorithms applied to optimization problems?

For the question, the objective values achieved by the algorithms was considered to compare the results.

Objective Selection: The experiment uses benchmark optimization problems. As the algorithm executes, the search for evaluated solutions and their respective fitness values are stored and used to train machine learning models.

Experiment Project: In both Surrogate Batch and Surrogate Online approaches, it is assumed that a surrogate is trained when the algorithm achieves fifty thousand (50.000) evaluations of the objective function, i.e, they will be trained with 50.000 solutions. At that moment, the algorithm stops using the real problem objective function and starts using the surrogate to evaluate the solutions. The algorithms are executed until they have evaluated one hundred thousand (100.000) input solutions. The first 50.000 already used in the learning process, plus new 50.000 solutions generated by the algorithm, now using the surrogate. The selection of those numbers will be further discussed in Sect. 4.2.

Instrumentation: The machine learning models were obtained from Python libraries, version 3.5.1 [12], optimization algorithms and benchmark problems were obtained through jMetal [9]. The execution was performed on a Dell laptop, with 8 GB of RAM, Intel i5-3470S (2.9 GHz) cpu, running Ubuntu 12.04.5 LTS operational system.

4.2 Preparation

Two meta-heuristic algorithms, DE and SMPSO, were applied to solve the benchmark problems. SVR, Decision Tree, and Random Forest machine learning models were applied as surrogates. IDs were created as a way of identifying the different compositions of algorithms and surrogates employed. IDs obey the following order: name of the algorithm plus surrogate approach plus machine learning algorithm. The following algorithms are considered in experiments: DEOnlineSVR, DEBatchSVR, DEM1SVR, DEOnlineRF, DEBatchRF, DEM1RF, DEOnlineDT, DEBatchDT, DEM1DT, SMPSOBatchSVR, SMPSOOnlineSVR, SMPSOM1SVR, SMPSOOnlineRF, SMPSOBatchRF, SMPSOM1RF, SMP-SOOnlineDT, SMPSOBatchDT, SMPSOM1DT. Furthermore, as a basis, original versions of both SMPSO and DE algorithms were executed without the interference of the surrogate approaches.

The hyperparameters for each algorithm were defined as follow. For SMPSO, population size $= 100$, mutation probability $= 0.05$ and mutation distribution $= 20$; for DE, population size $= 100$, crossover: cr $= 0.5$, f $= 0.5$ and variant $=$ rand/1/bin. For the algorithms ML, the Grid-search methodology was used to obtain the hyperparameters. The ML hyperparameters were: for RF, number of estimators $= 200$, minimum samples split $= 2$, random state $= 0$ and criterion of error $=$ mse; for SVR kernel $=$ rbf, C $= 1e3$, gamma $= 0.1$, tolerance error $= 0.01$; finally, for DT, maximum depth $= 500$, minimum samples split $= 2$, random state $= 0$, criterion of error $=$ mse. For the benchmarking problems, were used the default values defined in [16]. The problems were configured with 20 decision variables. The optimum objective value for every problem was $f(x) = 0$.

4.3 Execution

As presented before, it was assumed that a surrogate is trained when the algorithm reaches fifty thousand ($t\_max = 50,000$) objective function evaluations. This value was experimentally defined.

To achieve that number, initially, different values were employed. This analysis was performed as a way of identifying the best moment to finish the training process and to start the use of a surrogate. In this analysis, the algorithms were executed considering a total of 100,000 objective function evaluations. Considering this total, different values of t_max explored. Thus, if a specific t_max was chosen, the algorithms used t_max solutions in training phase, and then, executed $100,000 - t\_max$ evaluations using the trained surrogate. t_max was defined with $10,000$, $20,000$, $30,000$, $40,000$ and $50,000$ objective function evaluations.

Overall, SMPSO could converge quickly to the optimum value for some problems. This is a characteristic of PSO algorithm, although, the algorithm can often be stuck in a local optimum. However, for DE, it was noticed that the algorithm starts to get close to the optimal values after fifty thousand evaluations of the objective function. Thus, since the input data set is important to obtain a good surrogate, it was adopted $t\_max = 50,000$. Although high, considering a total of 100,000 objective function evaluations, adopting that value of t_max represents an economy of half of the objective function calls.

4.4 Quality Measure

As presented before, the research question will be answered using as a quality metric the value of the objective function, achieved by the algorithm at the end of the search. Each algorithms' configuration was executed twenty times. The means and standard deviations of those twenty best fitness values were analyzed.

Furthermore, to confirm or refute the hypothesis, Wilcoxon [8] statistical test was applied. Through that, it was possible to identify configurations whose results did not have similarities and, therefore, indicate those which had the best results. The criteria used to choose the best results was the p-value. For configurations with p-value lower than $0,05$, it is possible to infer statistically the difference among them.

4.5 Results

Tables 1 and 2 show the mean hyper-volume values and standard deviation (between brackets) of twenty executions for each configuration, for SMPSO and DE respectively. The bold highlighted results are the ones with the higher mean value and in which the Wilcoxon test did not compute statistical differences. If more than one cell is marked for a given problem, the algorithms are statistically tied. All the configurations were confronted in the experiment, except the base algorithm configuration. However, those values are shown, to make a comparison between mean values from base algorithm configuration and configurations using a surrogate, relativizing how close or far are those values from each other.

Table 1. Average results of different surrogate configurations for SMPSO algorithm

	Ackley	Ellipsoid	Rastrigin	Rosenbrock	Griewank
SMPSO	4.4409e-16 (0.0)	0.0 (0.0)	0.0(0.0)	13.43(4.5)	0.0(0.0)
SMPSOOnline SVR	2.45(0.67)	244.02(102.13)	283.97 (48.71)	823.08(217.50)	56.4277(12.31)
SMPSOBatch SVR	10.88(2.47)	3608.10(1364.61)	616.18(136.36)	7795.35(2772.36)	20.61(4.75)
SMPSOM1 SVR	0.01(0.99)	377.69(140.00)	386.30 (32.73)	1489.24(448.80)	46.23(11.9469
SMPSOOnline RF	**9.5e-08(2.9e-07)**	**6.7e-09(1.17e-08)**	**1.4e-08(2.5e-08)**	**14.07(6.58)**	**6.8e-09(2.5e-08)**
SMPSOBatch RF	**0.0001(6.3e-06)**	**8.1e-05 (5.4e-06)**	**7.4e-05(6.5e-06)**	**17.38(0.54)**	**7.5e-05(6.5e-06)**
SMPSOM1RF	0.4329(0.70)	0.0751(0.15)	0.9827(2.27)	1572.8443(466.03)	4.0e-03(6.8e-03)
SMPSOOnline DT	**4.4e-16(0.0)**	**0.0(0.0)**	**0.0 (0.0)**	**14.46(6.11)**	**0.0(0.0)**
SMPSOBatch DT	**9.3e-05(2.0e-05)**	**5.5e-05(3.7e-05)**	**7.4e-05(1.4e-05)**	**13.76(6.89)**	**6.8e-05(1.6e-05)**
SMPSOM1DT	0.70(0.80)	0.37(0.45)	1.25(2.88)	17.86(4.09)	0.03(0.06)

By observing the results from Table 1, *S_Online* and *S_Batch* approaches, using DT and RF, have obtained the best average results. Still from Table 1, it is possible to notice that those settings with the best results have mean fitness values close to mean values of the base algorithm. Also, those configurations could reach the best results, regardless of the characteristics of the problems. M1 approach could not achieve the best results in any problem. Considering the ML models, SRV was not able to achieve good results, even when applied along *S_Online* and *S_Batch*. Thus, that shows that those machine learning

Table 2. Average results of different surrogate settings for DE algorithm

	Ackley	Ellipsoid	Rastrigin	Rosenbrock	Griewank
DE	6.2e-10 (1.5e-10)	4.2e-19 (2.0e-19)	51.61 (6.61)	13.288 (0.53)	2.1e-12 (8.6e-12)
DEOnline SVR	**0.0003 (4.573e-05)**	0.704 (0.88)	121.59 (11.08)	165.84 (22.45)	0.045 (0.08)
DEBatch SVR	0.03 (0.01)	1933.23 (579.90)	**65.26 (6.57)**	10725.20 (3854.97)	45.920 (15.36)
DEM1SVR	2.89 (0.11)	27.10 (2.60)	198.20 (39.05)	196.85 (18.52)	0.245 (0.01)
DEOnline RF	**0.00032 (6.4e-05)**	4.5e-05 (5.5e-05)	124.09 (5.47)	**15.60 (0.14)**	**0.035 (0.084)**
DEBatch RF	6.0e-04 (5.98e-05)	1.0e-04 (4.6e-06)	85.79 (5.66)	**15.55 (0.16)**	**9.8e-03 (0.01)**
DEM1RF	3.212 (0.09)	**6.5e-07 (2.2e-07)**	134.93 (7.33)	216.11 (15.55)	0.193 (0.016)
DEOnline DT	**3.5e-04 (5.9e-05)**	**7.2e-07 (1.8e-07)**	**66.45 (6.49)**	**15.347 (0.177)**	**0.009 (0.021)**
DEBatch DT	6.0e-04 (6.3e-05)	7.2e-05 (5.8e-05)	**65.55 (8.80)**	**15.38(0.18)**	**2.7e-03 (4.0e-03)**
DEM1DT	3.076 (0.111)	18.293 (2.95)	117.81 (8.48)	169.89 (23.46)	0.173 (0.02)

techniques (DT and RF) associated with *S_Online* and *S_Batch* could learn the objective function behavior.

By analyzing the results obtained for the configurations using the DE algorithm, in Table 2, again, DT and RF models have obtained the best results when associated with *S_Online* and *S_Batch* configurations. However, when comparing to SMPSO analysis, despite the same conclusion, the analysis of DE results was not so clear. First, considering the comparison to the basic algorithm, the surrogate approaches applied to DE could get similar results. However, the framework faces some difficulties in Rastringin and Rosembrock problems. It worth noting that DE could not reach the global optimum for these problems. Considering the training approach, there wasn't an approach that stood out on all the problems. S_Online obtained the best results in Ackley, regardless of the ML model. It also had the best results for the other problems, however on those problems, it was often combined with DT and RF models. S_Batch could obtain the best results in 4 out of 5 problems, especially when combined to DT model. M1 approach only stood out on Ellipsoid, a unimodal problem. Considering the ML model, SVR only obtained the best results on Ackley and Rastringin. However, for Ackley, the training mechanism seems responsible for this achievement. RF obtained the best results on 4 out of 5 problems. DT stood out on all problems, combined to *S_Online* and *S_Batch*.

Summarizing, *S_Online* and *S_Batch* were the best surrogate approaches. Random Forest and Decision Trees were the best ML models used as surrogates. Furthermore, it was possible to reach results close to the optimum, replacing the real objective function by a surrogate trained during the search. In our study, the framework took half the objective function evaluations then the basic algorithm and could get similar results than the basic meta-heuristic, especially for SMPSO algorithm.

5   Conclusions and Future Works

Surrogate-assisted evolutionary algorithms have gained greater attention in recent years. Such a scenario has led researchers to refine previously used surrogate approaches. In this paper, a surrogate-based framework was proposed and a set of experiments was developed to test the approach. Here, three different machine learning models were used as surrogates and the framework had been applied to mono-objective problem classes.

The results were promising, showing that the proposed approaches obtained good results, when associated with DT and RF machine learning techniques. Besides, both techniques show good potential in learning the objective function. However, there is evidence that the training process of the surrogates is an essential step to achieve good results in the search process.

The main contribution of this paper was to validate the use of new surrogate feeding methods, as well as to validate the efficiency of machine learning models previously unused as surrogates. Among the limiting factors of this article, we can highlight the use of mono-objective problems, classified as low complexity problems. Thus, it was not possible to analyze in terms of the execution time of the algorithms, only analysis of effectiveness. In the end, it is expected to validate if different surrogate settings reduce the algorithm's execution time. This validation will be done in future work using complex optimization issues.

Future challenges include new experiments using the approaches here proposed and tested on multi-objective problems and problems with many objectives. To achieve that, KKTPM technique will be added to those approaches, to make those more general, enabling their use in such a class of problems. In this context, in addition to the techniques used in this article experiments, it is intended to apply Neural Network with regressor MLP training, Gaussian processes, Kriging (the most commonly used surrogate method in literature) and Recurrent Neural Networks (deep learning).

References

1. Basili, V.R., Caldiera, G., Rombach, H.D.: The goal question metric approach. Encycl. Softw. Eng. **2**(1994), 528–532 (1994)
2. Beachkofski, B., Grandhi, R.: Improved distributed hypercube sampling. In: 43rd AIAA/ASME/ASCE/AHS/ASC Structures, Structural Dynamics, and Materials Conference, p. 1274 (2002)
3. Branke, J., Deb, K., Miettinen, K., Słowiński, R. (eds.): Multiobjective Optimization: Interactive and Evolutionary Approaches. LNCS, vol. 5252. Springer, Heidelberg (2008). https://doi.org/10.1007/978-3-540-88908-3
4. Cai, X., Gao, L., Li, X., Qiu, H.: Surrogate-guided differential evolution algorithm for high dimensional expensive problems. Swarm Evol. Comput. **48**, 288–311 (2019). https://doi.org/10.1016/j.swevo.2019.04.009. http://www.sciencedirect.com/science/article/pii/S2210650218304590
5. Coello, C.A.C.: Recent results and open problems in evolutionary multiobjective optimization. In: Martín-Vide, C., Neruda, R., Vega-Rodríguez, M.A. (eds.) TPNC 2017. LNCS, vol. 10687, pp. 3–21. Springer, Cham (2017). https://doi.org/10.1007/978-3-319-71069-3_1
6. Deb, K., Abouhawwash, M.: An optimality theory-based proximity measure for set-based multiobjective optimization. IEEE Trans. Evol. Comput. **20**(4), 515–528 (2016)

7. Deb, K., Hussein, R., Roy, P.C., Toscano, G.: A taxonomy for metamodeling frameworks for evolutionary multi-objective optimization. IEEE Trans. Evol. Comput. **23**(1), 104–116 (2018)
8. Derrac, J., García, S., Molina, D., Herrera, F.: A practical tutorial on the use of nonparametric statistical tests as a methodology for comparing evolutionary and swarm intelligence algorithms. Swarm Evol. Comput. **1**(1), 3–18 (2011)
9. Durillo, J.J., Nebro, A.J.: jMetal: a Java framework for multi-objective optimization. Adv. Eng. Softw. **42**, 760–771 (2011). https://doi.org/10.1016/j.advengsoft.2011.05.014. http://www.sciencedirect.com/science/article/pii/S0965997811001219
10. Knowles, J., Nakayama, H.: Meta-modeling in multiobjective optimization. In: Branke, J., Deb, K., Miettinen, K., Słowiński, R. (eds.) Multiobjective Optimization. LNCS, vol. 5252, pp. 245–284. Springer, Heidelberg (2008). https://doi.org/10.1007/978-3-540-88908-3_10
11. Lu, X., Sun, T., Tang, K.: Evolutionary optimization with hierarchical surrogates. Swarm Evol. Comput. **47**, 21–32 (2019). https://doi.org/10.1016/j.swevo.2019.03.005. Special Issue on Collaborative Learning and Optimization based on Swarm and Evolutionary Computation
12. Pedregosa, F., et al.: Scikit-learn: machine learning in Python. J. Mach. Learn. Res. **12**, 2825–2830 (2011)
13. Portelli, G., Pallez, D.: Image signal processor parameter tuning with surrogate-assisted particle swarm optimization. In: Idoumghar, L., Legrand, P., Liefooghe, A., Lutton, E., Monmarché, N., Schoenauer, M. (eds.) EA 2019. LNCS, vol. 12052, pp. 28–41. Springer, Cham (2020). https://doi.org/10.1007/978-3-030-45715-0_3
14. Roy, P., Hussein, R., Deb, K.: Metamodeling for multimodal selection functions in evolutionary multi-objective optimization. In: Proceedings of the Genetic and Evolutionary Computation Conference, pp. 625–632. ACM (2017)
15. Santana-Quintero, L.V., Montaño, A.A., Coello, C.A.C.: A review of techniques for handling expensive functions in evolutionary multi-objective optimization. In: Tenne, Y., Goh, C.-K. (eds.) Computational Intelligence in Expensive Optimization Problems. ALO, vol. 2, pp. 29–59. Springer, Heidelberg (2010). https://doi.org/10.1007/978-3-642-10701-6_2
16. Surjanovic, S., Bingham, D.: Virtual library of simulation experiments: test functions and datasets. http://www.sfu.ca/~ssurjano. Accessed 20 Oct 2018

A Novel Explainable Recommender for Investment Managers

Tomasz Rutkowski[1,2(✉)] [iD], Radosław Nielek[2] [iD], Danuta Rutkowska[4] [iD],
and Leszek Rutkowski[3,4] [iD]

[1] Vandenroot Institute, 135 Montgomery St., Apt. 2J, Jersey City, NJ 07302, USA
tomasz.rutkowski@senfino.com, institute@vandenroot.com
[2] Polish-Japanese Academy of Information Technology,
Koszykowa 86, 02-008 Warsaw, Poland
[3] Institute of Computational Intelligence, Czestochowa University of Technology,
Al. Armii Krajowej 36, 42-200 Czestochowa, Poland
[4] Information Technology Institute, University of Social Sciences, Lodz, Poland

Abstract. This paper presents a novel recommendation system for investment managers using real data from asset management companies. The recommender can be viewed as a fuzzy expert system. As a matter of fact, this is an explainable recommender that works as a one-class classifier with an explanation. The inference rules, explanations, and visualizations of the recommender's results are illustrated.

Keywords: Recommender system · Asset management · One-class classification · Fuzzy sets · Fuzzy IF-THEN rules · Explainable AI

1 Introduction

A recommendation system (also called recommender system or simply - recommender) provides personalized recommendations to end-users based on their profile of preferences [1,6,8]. Over last two decades, researchers proposed three main approaches for designing recommender systems [13–17]:

- Content-based techniques – the recommender attempts to recommend items similar to those a given user preferred in the past [2,13]. In this case, the recommendations are based on information on the content of a given item, not on other users' opinions. These techniques are vulnerable to overfitting, but their great advantage is not needed for data on other users [27].
- Collaborative filtering – it is the most commonly implemented technique [9, 22]. Such systems recommend items by identifying other users with similar tastes. Recommendation for new items is based on user-user, user-item, or item-item similarities. The major problem with this technique is known under the name "cold start" - the system cannot draw any inferences for users or items about which it has not collected enough information.

© Springer Nature Switzerland AG 2020
L. Rutkowski et al. (Eds.): ICAISC 2020, LNAI 12416, pp. 412–422, 2020.
https://doi.org/10.1007/978-3-030-61534-5_37

- Hybrid approach – it relies on a combination of many different recommendation methods [4]. The final goal of this approach is to obtain the most accurate list of predictions and, as a result, a more precise specification of the user's profile.

Many real-life problems do not have well-balanced data for positive and negative examples. Very often, by observation, we can collect data that represent objects that a user acted on as opposed to objects that a user considered but decided not to act on. One of the example of such datasets is the stock market trading journal.

In the United States of America, every investment fund that manages over 100 million dollars has an obligation to submit a form with all transactions quarterly to the Securities and Exchange Commission (SEC). The form is called 13F and all data from this form are publicly available [5]. Based on all of those transactions it is possible to infer what to recommend next. Using 13F filings, we have only access to positive examples – things or actions that people have done. Hence, such problems can be treated as a one-class classification (see e.g. [10,24,25]). Based on some observations, it is possible to recommend new things (objects, actions).

The process of generating recommendations, in this paper, is based on the approach presented in [17,18]. The dataset for the investment domain includes values of attributes that characterize the companies. It should be emphasized that it contains only "Add" and "New Buy" actions. This means that only positive labels are taken into account. Why? Because the reasons for "Reduce" and "Sold Out" actions are not known, so for those cases the system cannot infer the decision "not recommend". Investors sell for several different reasons, not only because they do not like the stock. Maybe they profited enough and they want to move on, or they want to free some capital, or they are short-sellers, so they actually profit when stocks' price decreases. Nevertheless, they buy only when they think that it fits their strategy. In this case it is possible to analyze buy actions and recommend new stocks that are worth buying. Therefore, the recommendation problem is treated as a one-class classification.

In the next sections, the problem is formulated, and it is described how to design and implement the explainable fuzzy recommender. Then, explanations and visualizations of the recommender's results are illustrated.

2 Description of the Recommender System

The one-class recommender, considered in this paper, produces recommendations based on the data of past transactions of users (investors), by means of fuzzy IF-THEN rules. The fuzzy rules and fuzzy sets included in these rules are presented in the following subsections.

2.1 Fuzzy Sets

More than twenty attributes are applied in the recommendation problem. Let us choose one of these attributes, called "currentRatio", for the illustration. The

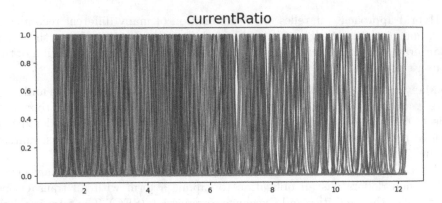

Fig. 1. Fuzzy sets for attribute: currentRatio - one fuzzy set for each past transaction

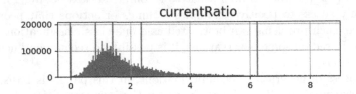

Fig. 2. Reference points for regions of attribute: currentRatio (5th, 25th, 50th, 75th and 95th percentile)

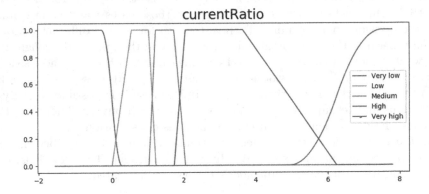

Fig. 3. Fuzzy sets for attribute: currentRatio

data points that represent the past investments are viewed as fuzzy points in the attribute space. The fuzzy points are fuzzy sets defined by the Gaussian membership functions, as shown in Fig. 1, for the single attribute. The points of the (5th, 25th, 50th, 75th and 95th percentile), depicted in Fig. 2, have been determined, in order to construct the appropriate fuzzy sets, portrayed in Fig. 3.

2.2 Recommendation Rules

Let us call the rules created by the individual fuzzy points (past transactions) depicted in Fig. 1—recommendation rules, and the rules formulated by use of the fuzzy sets depicted in Fig. 3—explanation rules. The former rules are employed in order to produce recommendations while the latter are applied for explaining the system's decisions. Rules used in the presented system are typical fuzzy rules as described in [3, 7, 23, 28].

For a particular user (investor), $u = 1, 2 \ldots, H$, and his past transactions, $t = 1, 2, \ldots, M_u$, let us present the recommendation rules, $R_t^{(u)}$, in the following, general form:

IF x_1 is $G_1^{(u,t)}$ **AND** x_2 is $G_2^{(u,t)}$ **AND** $\ldots$ x_n is $G_n^{(u,t)}$ **THEN** *Recommend* (1)

where x_i are linguistic variables, $G_i^{(u,t)}$ are Gaussian membership functions, $i = 1, 2, \ldots, n$, $u = 1, 2 \ldots, H$, $t = 1, 2, \ldots, M_u$, defined for every attribute of the past transactions for each user; n denotes the number of attributes, H – the number of users, M_u – the number of transactions of user u. It is obvious that $M_1, M_2, \ldots, M_H \leq M$ that is the number of data items in the dataset, composed of the past transactions of particular users $u = 1, 2, \ldots, H$; of course more than one user could realize the same transactions.

A specific example of a recommendation rule, derived from past transaction no. 364, can be presented as follows:

IF   currentRatio   IS   *currentRatio*364
AND   earningsPerShareGrowth   IS   *earningsPerShareGrowth*364
AND   revenueGrowth   IS   *revenueGrowth*364
AND   currentAssets   IS   *currentAssets*364
AND   profitMargins   IS   *profitMargins*364
AND   debtToEquity   IS   *debtToEquity*364
AND   dividendYield   IS   *dividendYield*364
AND   ebitda   IS   *ebitda*364
AND   enterpriseToEbitda   IS   *enterpriseToEbitda*364
AND   fiftyTwoWeekHigh   IS   *fiftyTwoWeekHigh*364
AND   fiftyTwoWeekLow   IS   *fiftyTwoWeekLow*364
AND   freeCashflow   IS   *freeCashflow*364
AND   grossProfits   IS   *grossProfits*364
AND   operatingMargins   IS   *operatingMargins*364
AND   payoutRatio   IS   *payoutRatio*364
AND   priceToBook   IS   *priceToBook*364
AND   priceToEarningsToGrowth   IS   *priceToEarningsToGrowth*364
AND   returnOnAssets   IS   *returnOnAssets*364
AND   returnOnEquity   IS   *returnOnEquity*364
AND   totalDebt   IS   *totalDebt*364
AND   totalDebtToCurrentAsset   IS   *totalDebtToCurrentAsset*364
THEN   *Recommend*

In this rule, the statement, e.g. "IF currentRatio IS *currentRatio*364" means: "IF the value of the currentRatio of a recommended stock matches the fuzzy set with linguistic label *currentRatio364* (one of the fuzzy sets illustrated in Fig. 1, assigned to past transaction no. 364)". The rule (no. 364) is represented by the multidimensional Gaussian membership function created by use of *currentRatio364* and other fuzzy sets (with labels referring to no. 364) for particular attributes.

2.3 Explanation Rules

The explanation rules, R^k, for $k = 1, 2, \ldots, N$, are formulated as follows:

$$\textbf{IF } x_1 \text{ is } A_1^k \textbf{ AND } x_2 \text{ is } A_2^k \textbf{ AND} \ldots \textbf{ AND } x_n \text{ is } A_n^k \textbf{ THEN } Recommend \quad (2)$$

where N denotes a number of the rules, and A_i^k are fuzzy sets defined by the membership functions of the shapes as shown in Fig. 3.

A specific example of an explanation rule can be presented as follows:

IF currentRatio IS Low AND earningsPerShareGrowth IS Low AND revenueGrowth IS Low AND currentAssets IS High AND profitMargins IS Medium AND debtToEquity IS Low AND dividendYield IS Very low AND ebitda IS High AND enterpriseToEbitda IS Medium AND fiftyTwoWeekHigh IS High AND fiftyTwoWeekLow IS High AND freeCashflow IS Low AND grossProfits IS Very low AND operatingMargins IS Very high AND payoutRatio IS Very low AND priceToBook IS Low AND priceToEarningsToGrowth IS Very low AND returnOnAssets IS Medium AND returnOnEquity IS Very high AND totalDebt IS Low AND totalDebtToCurrentAsset IS Low **THEN** *Recommend*

For each user, his past transactions are analyzed in order to produce new recommendations by the recommender. Every new data item that occurs is recommended to the user if there is a rule (one or more) activated by this data item with a sufficient degree. Therefore, the rule activation level should be determined. It is worth noticing that the recommendation not always refers to higher values of particular attributes but to the values close to those of the past transactions.

Usually, the rule activation level, also called the rule firing level, is calculated by the use of a T-norm operation - most often the "product" or "min" T-norm is applied [11]. However, with regard to the recommender considered in this paper, and the described problem, a different way of determining the rule firing level is proposed. Instead of the T-norm, the arithmetic average is employed; also a weighted arithmetic average is suitable for this recommender.

When rules are used with the "AND" operations in their antecedent part, the T-norm functions work very well to determine the rule firing level, in most cases of fuzzy systems applications [26]. With regard to some problems, fuzzy IF-THEN rules can be formulated in a different way, e.g. with "OR" operators in the antecedent part. In such cases, the T-norm is not appropriate. The one-class recommender, considered in the application as an investment adviser, needs another way of aggregating particular terms in the antecedent part of the fuzzy IF-THEN rules, in spite of the fact that the "AND" operation is employed.

This is because the similarities of new recommendations to the past transactions do not necessarily require exact similarity with regard to every attribute. Therefore, the arithmetic average is proposed instead of the T-norm.

For example, in the case when a new recommendation is very similar to a past transaction (or almost the same) with regard to 20 attributes, and differs much only in one attribute (assuming 21 attributes considered), the T-norm operator results in very low (or almost zero) value of the rule firing level. In such a situation, this new candidate for the recommendation will be rejected, and not recommended, despite the similarity with regard to the rest attributes. Therefore, the arithmetic average is more adequate. Hence, the following formula is applied in order to determine the rule firing levels:

$$\tau_t^{(u)} = \frac{1}{n} \sum_{i=1}^{n} G_i^{(u,t)}(\overline{x}_i) \tag{3}$$

where $\overline{x}_i$, $i = 1, 2, \ldots, n$, for rules $R_t^{(u)}$; $u = 1, 2 \ldots, H$, $t = 1, 2, \ldots, M_u$, formulated as (1).

In the same way, the rule firing levels for rules R^k, $k = 1, 2, \ldots, N$, are calculated as follows:

$$\tau_k = \frac{1}{n} \sum_{i=1}^{n} A_i^k(\overline{x}_i) \tag{4}$$

The main idea for the proposed one-class recommender is the application of the rule firing levels as a measure of similarity of the new candidate for a recommendation to the past transactions of the user for whom the recommendation is generated.

3   Explanation and Visualization of the Recommender's Results

It should be emphasized that the recommender that performs by use of this new method is transparent and explainable, which is crucial for the chosen domain [19,20]. By definition, systems based on fuzzy rules are interpretable [12]. Fuzzy sets and fuzzy rules have been applied in recommender systems before but usually for the collaborative approach, e.g. [14]. Previous attempts described in the literature included a reduction of the number of rules to achieve better interpretability, e.g. [16]. With the approach presented in this paper, rules reduction can be useful for explanation rules but is not needed for recommendation rules.

The recommender described in this paper offers a new recommendation for a user, if it is similar to his past transactions.

Let us consider a new data point that is a candidate for a recommendation for a user (investor). Figure 4 portrays this point as a yellow dot at the center. All other data points that represent past transactions of this user are illustrated in this figure. Every past transaction, as well as the new candidate for the recommendation, are multidimensional points. The visualization of these points in the

2D space, in Fig. 4, shows only how far nearest neighbors are located from the yellow point. However, the real distances are not depicted. Speaking in different words, this visualization reflects similarities to the past transactions.

As mentioned earlier, the similarities are measured by the use of the rule firing levels. Every point at this figure, representing a past transaction of the user, is viewed as a fuzzy point defined by Gaussian membership functions in particular attribute domains. Each of the past transactions refers to one fuzzy IF-THEN rule. Firing levels of these rules, calculated by Eq. (3), where $\bar{x}_i$, for $i = 1, 2, \ldots, n$, corresponds to the new candidate for the recommendation (the yellow point), determine the similarities.

For better visualization, an adjustment function $f(x) = 0.2421 * \ln(x) + 1.1242$ has been proposed and applied, resulting in the corrected (adjusted) visualization of the same points. Hence, the points portrayed in Fig. 4 a), after the adjustment are presented as Fig. 4 b) illustrates. Of course, this transformation has been introduced only for better visualization. The distances, in fact, have not been changed. The points located beyond those gathered at the circle are far away, so definitely not considered as neighbors.

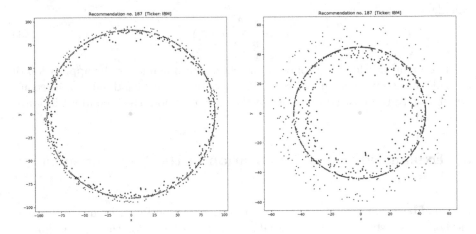

Fig. 4. a) Recommendation 187 - not adjusted, b) Recommendation 187 - adjusted (Color figure online)

As we see in Fig. 5, the candidate for the recommendation no. 363 has one close neighbor (similar point – denoted as green).

The new recommendation should be similar to the past transactions of the user. However, there is a difference between the situation like in the case of recommendation no. 363, where only one neighbor with a very high firing level exists (Fig. 5 a)), and the case illustrated in Fig. 5 b) with recommendation no. 1545 where the is a group of neighbors surrounding the recommendation. From the recommendation point of view, it is important to take into account a group of neighbors (past transactions) even less similar to the yellow point.

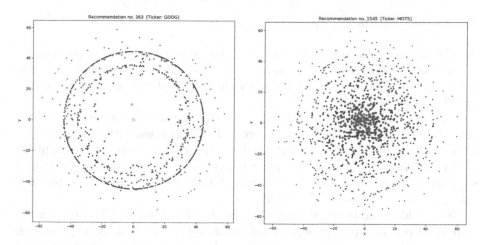

Fig. 5. Comparing recommendation: a) no. 363, b) no. 1545 (Color figure online)

Therefore, the alignmentWithStrategy function is proposed, expressed as follows:

$$alignmentWithStrategy =$$
$$\mathbf{max}(allFiringLevelsAboveAlignmentThreshold)$$
$$+numberOfNeighbors/100 - 0.01$$

(5)

where $allFiringLevelsAboveAlignmentThreshold$ is a number of all data points (past transactions of a single user) with values of the firing levels above the threshold that is set for this algorithm. The $numberOfNeighbors$ denotes the number of neighbors; for example 1 in the case of recommendation no. 363, and 35 for the group of neighbors of recommendation no. 1545 presented in Fig. 5 a) and b), respectively. The $alignmentWithStrategy$ function (5) defines the similarity of a candidate point for the recommendation to the past transaction points of a considered user (investor), taking into account a number of similar points (neighbors). Based on the calculated alignment, degrees of membership for each feature, and the distance between the closest neighbors, it is possible to automatically generate explanations that are easy to understand by a user, like in the following example:

"This stock might be interesting for you since the operating margin is very high and return on assets is medium. Moreover, the return on equity is very high, and the current ratio is low. Here are your most relevant past transactions that helped comprise this recommendation: LVS in December 2017, SYY in March 2017, LVS in March 2018."

4   Conclusions

As the one-class classifier, the recommender presented in this paper can be viewed as a special case of neuro-fuzzy recommenders [21], that is the rule-based system. The fuzzy IF-THEN rules are generated from data by the use of the Wang-Mendel method [28].

The explanation of the performance of the proposed recommender is very important, and possible based on the fuzzy IF-THEN rules, with fuzzy sets associated with linguistic labels having semantic meanings. In this way, the explainable recommenders, along with their recommendations, also produce insightful explanations, and the system itself is from A to Z transparent and interpretable (as opposed to a "black-box" model).

It should be emphasized that the visualization presented in Fig. 5 is an important part of explanation proposed in this approach which allows presenting the similarity between a recommendation and past examples of multidimensional data, on a 2D canvas.

In future research we plan to implement several clustering techniques, see e.g. [15], for rules generation.

References

1. Adeniyi, D.A., Wei, Z., Yongquan, Y.: Automated web usage data mining and recommendation system using K-Nearest Neighbor (KNN) classification method. Appl. Comput. Inf. **12**(1), 90–108 (2016)
2. Bagher, R.C., Hassanpour, H., Mashayekhi, H.: User trends modeling for a content-based recommender system. Expert Syst. Appl. **87**, 209–219 (2017)
3. Bologna, G., Hayashi, Y.: Characterization of symbolic rules embedded in deep DIMLP networks: a challenge to transparency of deep learning. J. Artif. Intell. Soft Computi. Res. **7**(4), 265–286 (2017)
4. Burke, R.: Hybrid recommender systems: survey and experiments. User Model. User-Adap. Inter. **12**(4), 331–370 (2002). https://doi.org/10.1023/A:1021240730564
5. Brown, S.J., Schwarz, C.: Do Market Participants Care about Portfolio Disclosure? Evidence from Hedge Funds' 13F Filings (2013)
6. Conforti, R., de Leoni, M., La Rosa, M., van der Aalst, W.M.P., ter Hofstede, A.H.M.: A recommendation system for predicting risks across multiple business process instances. Decis. Support Syst. **69**, 1–19 (2015)
7. D'Aniello, G., Gaeta, M., Loia, F., Reformat, M., Toti, D.: An environment for collective perception based on fuzzy and semantic approaches. J. Artif. Intell. Soft Comput. Rese. **8**(3), 191–210 (2018). https://doi.org/10.1515/jaiscr-2018-0013
8. Meehan, K., Lunney, T., Curran, K., McCaughey, A.: Context-aware intelligent recommendation system for tourism. 2013 IEEE International Conference on Pervasive Computing and Communications Workshops (PERCOM Workshops), pp. 328–331 (2013)
9. Ekstrand, M.D., Riedl, J.T., Konstan, J.A.: Collaborative filtering recommender systems. Found. Trends Hum.-Comput. Interact. **4**(2), 81–173 (2011)

10. Khan, S.S., Madden, M.G.: A survey of recent trends in one class classification. In: Coyle, L., Freyne, J. (eds.) AICS 2009. LNCS (LNAI), vol. 6206, pp. 188–197. Springer, Heidelberg (2010). https://doi.org/10.1007/978-3-642-17080-5_21

11. Klir, G.J., Yuan, B. (eds.): Fuzzy Sets, Fuzzy Logic and Fuzzy Sytems: Selected Papers by Lotfi A. Zadeh. Advances in Fuzzy Systems - Applications and Theory 6 (1996)

12. Liu, H., Gegov, A., Cocea, M.: Rule based networks: an efficient and interpretable representation of computational models. J. Artif. Intell. Soft Comput. Res. **7**(2), 111–123 (2017)

13. Pazzani, M.J., Billsus, D.: Content-based recommendation systems. In: Brusilovsky, P., Kobsa, A., Nejdl, W. (eds.) The Adaptive Web. LNCS, vol. 4321, pp. 325–341. Springer, Heidelberg (2007). https://doi.org/10.1007/978-3-540-72079-9_10

14. Prasad, M., Liu, Y.-T., Li, D.-L., Lin, C.-T., Shah, R.R., Kaiwartya, O.P.: A new mechanism for data visualization with TSK-type preprocessed collaborative fuzzy rule based system. J. Artif. Intell. Soft Comput. Res. **7**(1), 33–46 (2017)

15. Rastin, P., Matei, B., Cabanes, G., Grozavu, N., Bennani, Y.: Impact of learners' quality and diversity in collaborative clustering. J. Artif. Intell. Soft Comput. Res. **9**(2), 149–165 (2019). https://doi.org/10.2478/jaiscr-2018-0030

16. Riid, A., Preden, J.-S.: Design of fuzzy rule-based classifiers through granulation and consolidation. J. Artif. Intell. Soft Comput. Res. **7**(2), 137–147 (2017)

17. Rutkowski, T., Łapa, K., Jaworski, M., Nielek, R., Rutkowska, D.: On explainable flexible fuzzy recommender and its performance evaluation using the akaike information criterion. In: Gedeon, T., Wong, K.W., Lee, M. (eds.) ICONIP 2019. CCIS, vol. 1142, pp. 717–724. Springer, Cham (2019). https://doi.org/10.1007/978-3-030-36808-1_78

18. Rutkowski, T., Łapa, K., Nielek, R.: On explainable fuzzy recommenders and their performance evaluation. Int. J. Appl. Math. Comput. Sci. **29**(3), 595–610 (2019)

19. Rutkowski, T., Romanowski, J., Woldan, P., Staszewski, P., Nielek, R.: Towards interpretability of the movie recommender based on a neuro-fuzzy approach. In: Rutkowski, L., Scherer, R., Korytkowski, M., Pedrycz, W., Tadeusiewicz, R., Zurada, J.M. (eds.) ICAISC 2018. LNCS (LNAI), vol. 10842, pp. 752–762. Springer, Cham (2018). https://doi.org/10.1007/978-3-319-91262-2_66

20. Rutkowski, T., Łapa, K., Nowicki, R., Nielek, R., Grzanek, K.: On explainable recommender systems based on fuzzy rule generation techniques. In: Rutkowski, L., Scherer, R., Korytkowski, M., Pedrycz, W., Tadeusiewicz, R., Zurada, J.M. (eds.) ICAISC 2019. LNCS (LNAI), vol. 11508, pp. 358–372. Springer, Cham (2019). https://doi.org/10.1007/978-3-030-20912-4_34

21. Rutkowski, T., Romanowski, J., Woldan, P., Staszewski, P., Nielek, R., Rutkowski, L.: A content-based recommendation system using neuro-fuzzy approach. In: 2018 IEEE International Conference on Fuzzy Systems (FUZZ-IEEE), pp. 1–8. IEEE (2018)

22. Schafer, J.B., Frankowski, D., Herlocker, J., Sen, S.: Collaborative filtering recommender systems. In: Brusilovsky, P., Kobsa, A., Nejdl, W. (eds.) The Adaptive Web. LNCS, vol. 4321, pp. 291–324. Springer, Heidelberg (2007). https://doi.org/10.1007/978-3-540-72079-9_9

23. Sadiqbatcha, S., Jafarzadeh, S., Ampatzidis, Y.: Particle swarm optimization for solving a class of Type-1 and Type-2 fuzzy nonlinear equations. J. Artif. Intell. Soft Comput. Res. **8**(2), 103–110 (2018). https://doi.org/10.1515/jaiscr-2018-0007

24. Tax, D.M.J.: One class classification: concept-learning in the absence of counterexamples. Ph.D. thesis, Delft University of Technology (2001)

25. Tax, D.M.J., Duin, R.P.W.: Uniform object generation for optimizing one-class classifiers. J. Mach. Learn. Res. **2**, 155–173 (2001)
26. Yager, R.: Fuzzy logic methods in recommender systems. Fuzzy Sets Syst. **136**(2), 133–149 (2003)
27. Yera, R., Martinez, L.: Fuzzy tools in recommender systems: a survey. Int. J. Comput. Intell. Syst. **10**(1), 776–803 (2017)
28. Wang, L.-X., Mendel, J.M.: Generating fuzzy rules by learning from examples. IEEE Trans. Syst. Man Cybern. **22**(6), 1414–1427 (1992)

Is Chaotic Randomization Advantageous for Higher Dimensional Optimization Problems?

Roman Senkerik[1]($\boxtimes$) (iD), Adam Viktorin[1] (iD), Tomas Kadavy[1] (iD), Michal Pluhacek[1] (iD), and Ivan Zelinka[2] (iD)

[1] Faculty of Applied Informatics, Tomas Bata University in Zlin, T. G. Masaryka 5555, 760 01 Zlin, Czech Republic
senkerik@utb.cz
[2] Faculty of Electrical Engineering and Computer Science, Technical University of Ostrava, 17. Listopadu 15, Ostrava, Czech Republic
ivan.zelinka@vsb.cz

Abstract. The focus of this work is the deeper insight into arising serious research questions connected with the growing popularity of combining metaheuristic algorithms and chaotic sequences showing quasi-periodic patterns. This paper reports analysis on the performance of popular and CEC 2019 competition winning strategy of Differential Evolution (DE), which is jDE, for optimization problems of higher dimensions. Experiments utilize ten chaos-driven quasi-random schemes for the indices selection and chaotic-driven crossover operations in the DE. All important performance characteristics are recorded and analyzed with simple descriptive statistics, Friedman rank tests and target-based comparisons analyzing distribution of hitting $p\%$ best minimum values over all versions and runs of jDE. The test suite was CEC 2015 in $50D$.

Keywords: Differential Evolution · jDE · Chaos-driven heuristics · CEC 2015 benchmark · Higher-dimensional problems

1 Introduction

Ongoing intensive research in metaheuristic algorithms is undoubtedly focused on hybridizations, extensive tuning, implementing learning strategies, and self-adaptive mechanism [1].

The basic operation in the metaheuristic algorithms is randomness. Thus deterministic chaos, which is considered somewhere between stochastic and deterministic systems, was many time addressed as original/unconventional randomization techniques for metaheuristics. Its properties like unique quasi-random sequencing and dynamics, quasi-stochasticity, self-similarity, fractal properties, and attractor density gained popularity as a simple technique for improving the metaheuristic algorithms performance without changing/adding any specific functionality of particular algorithm.

The importance of randomization within metaheuristics run has been profoundly investigated in several research papers, with the main focus either on describing different

© Springer Nature Switzerland AG 2020
L. Rutkowski et al. (Eds.): ICAISC 2020, LNAI 12416, pp. 423–434, 2020.
https://doi.org/10.1007/978-3-030-61534-5_38

techniques for modification of the randomization process [2] or to influence of stochastic operations to the control parameters propagation [3].

The first study investigating the chaotic dynamic characteristics in swarm intelligence algorithms [4] and [5], that was later expanded in [6] and quickly followed by the general concept of chaos-driven genetic/evolutionary/swarm algorithms with embedded chaotic pseudo-random number generator (CPRNG) in [7]. These and most of the later works use either directly scaled or normalized quasi-periodic sequences or a wide spectrum of different chaotic maps replacing the traditional uniform pseudo-random number generators (PRNGs). CPSO representing Particle Swarm Optimizer algorithm (PSO) with chaotic components [8], together with enhanced DE [9, 10], and inertia weight based PSO [11] laid the foundations of the popularity of the chaos embedded metaheuristics concept.

Nowadays, it is very frequently used, especially in real problem optimizations, where it is necessary to achieve a fine result quickly, mostly with simpler algorithms. Recently published research utilizes chaotic swarm algorithms [12–15] and also DE [16, 17]. Further, chaotic patterns in discrete dynamics of swarms have been investigated [18].

The next sections are focused on the motivation for this work, and differences with previous research papers, the background of the DE algorithm, a simple method for embedding CPRNG into DE, experiment setup, and detailed conclusions.

2   Related Work

The metaheuristic algorithm used in this research is Differential Evolution (DE) [24], specifically its frequently used simple, yet very powerful adaptive variant jDE, which is a winning algorithm of recent CEC 2019 100 digits competition [30].

The focus of this paper is the deeper insight into arising serious research questions connected with the analysis of chaos-enhanced algorithms performance and population dynamics. The research reported here is linking elements like distribution of the results and target-based analysis in terms of reaching minimum values.

However, the most important message of this research paper is that despite the still-growing popularity of the fusion of metaheuristic algorithms and unconventional randomization schemes (mostly with chaos), the majority of research papers do not explain, as to why those schemes have been used in the first place for enhancing the evolutionary operators like selection, mutation, crossover, or others (in swarms).

This paper represents an incremental follow up of results and conclusions related to the population diversity analyses in chaotic DE published in [19–22] and completes a recent work partially presented in [22]. The motivation, the difference from previously published works, thus the originality of this paper are listed below:

- jDE, as the CEC 2019 competition winner, is investigated here in the dimensional settings of $50D$. The most related works have utilized lower-dimensional settings.
- The frequency of hitting target of the $p\%$ best (minimum values) throughout all DE versions and runs is reported here together with distributions over different benchmark functions. This paper, extending the research in [19–22], could help navigate in differences between chaotic CPRNGs when embedded into self-adaptive DE schemes.

- Here, advanced results analysis, which includes detailed descriptive statistics, distribution plots, and statistical rankings, is supporting conclusions.

3 Discrete Chaotic Systems as CPRNGs

The principle of applying the CPRNG is given by a simple exchange of the default algorithm/programming language PRNG with the deterministic chaotic system (preferably discrete one). This research is using the very same portfolio of chaotic maps as in [19–22]. With the definitions and internal parameters settings, as in [23], systems show expected chaotic dynamics and requested features. The example of discrete chaotic map definition is given in (1), representing the very popular and experimentally utilized Lozi map. The chaotic sequences of different length for the Lozi map is depicted in Fig. 1. These two plots show the presence of self-similarity within the chaotic sequence. Thus supporting the claim that the metaheuristics may be forced to the neighborhood-based selection of individuals for evolutionary operators (or similarly, for neighborhood-based dynamics for spreading of information in swarms).

$$X_{n+1} = aX_n - Y_n^2$$
$$Y_{n+1} = bY_n + X_nY_n \tag{1}$$

The CPRNG workflow is as follows:

- Generating (by default algorithm/language PRNG) the starting position (X_0, Y_0) of the discrete chaotic map.
- Generating a chaotic sequence. The next iteration positions (X_{n+1}, Y_{n+1}) are obtained using their current positions (X_n, Y_n).
- Selection of particular sequence (x or y value, or combination of both) and re-normalization according to (2). When only the solo sequence is used (from two available), such a technique results in the folding of the chaotic attractor around the axis.

$$rndreal_n = \left| \frac{X_n}{maxval} \right| \tag{2}$$

Where the $rndreal_n$ is the re-normalized CPRNG value within the range of 0–1, here, we selected x-axis, and $maxval$ is the max. value from the whole chaotic series.

4 Differential Evolution

The generic DE [24] has several control parameters that remain static during the run and user setting dependent. The improved variants jDE and SHADE, which have been evolved from the generic DE algorithm, on the other hand, adapts the scaling factor F and crossover rate CR during the optimization (evolution process).

jDE is based on the propagation of two control parameters F_i and CR_i assigned to each i-th individual of the population. The basic idea of jDE lies in the "survival" of this parameter ensemble together with a successful solution. If an individual is transferred to the new generation, so is the parameter ensemble. If the newly generated solution is not successful; the control parameters pair disappears together with the lower quality solution. The above-mentioned pair of DE control parameters may be subject to random mutation based on user-defined probability. The detailed description of essential operations in simple not-adaptive original DE is given in [24, 25], for the jDE, please see [26]. Due to the limited space, it is not here.

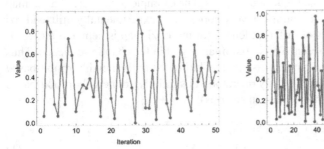

Fig. 1. Examples of two different CPRNG sequences, with significant patterns of self-similarity for Lozi map (50 iterations – left, and 150 iterations – right).

5   Results

All executed instances (51 repetitions per instance) used the established CEC 15 test problems suite [27] with dimension D set to 50. The budget of *FES* was set to the value of 500 000 (10,000 × D), according to the general rules given in the technical report for benchmark suite [27]. The performance features were recorded for all executed variants of DE: generic jDE; and for nine chaotic versions of C_jDE. The parameter setting for all algorithms is following: population size (NP) = 50, initial values for mutation and crossover $F = 0.5$, $CR = 0.8$, max. number of generations = 10000.

The identical set (as in [19–22]) of nine discrete dissipative chaotic maps was used here as the CPRNGs.

Statistical results for the comparisons are shown in comprehensive Tables 1 and 2. Table 1 shows the mean results, with the following highlighting: the bold values depict the best-obtained results (based on the simple descriptive statistics - mean values, without paired tests). Table 2 depicts the minimum values, also here, the bold values represent the best results (the minimum found). Rankings of the algorithms are presented in Fig. 2, evaluated based on the *Friedman test with Nemenyi post hoc test*. For the better understandability and visibility of differences, we have added rankings for dimensional settings of 30D, from previously reported research [22]. The data in Tables 1 and 2 are also supported by distribution plots for all 51 runs (see Fig. 3).

Table 1. Results comparisons for the mean results of jDE and C_jDE; CEC 2015 Benchmark set, 50D, 51 runs

System/f	1	2	3	4	5	6	7	8	9	10	11	12	13	14	15
jDE	247405	0.	**20.3818**	72.8258	4106.66	25676.4	43.5924	9453.66	104.074	**1836.95**	504.846	108.195	181.435	65774.1	**100.**
Arnold C_jDE	**227689**	0.	20.3919	71.3704	4106.84	28613.8	**40.6136**	8129.81	104.097	1871.76	511.492	**108.134**	181.725	**65235.9**	**100.**
Burgers C_jDE	626264	$2.65*10^-8$	20.399	81.5446	4297.16	66612.9	50.8545	22450.3	104.881	2474.34	769.129	109.12	184.145	67284.3	100.196
DeLo C_jDE	399535	0.	20.3939	76.3412	4155.48	38957.7	46.0491	17224.9	104.354	2176.81	596.917	108.756	182.648	67593.6	**100.**
Dissipative C_jDE	304684	0.	20.3844	69.7078	4105.32	**24466.4**	41.5155	10623.5	104.155	1888.66	524.184	108.376	182.056	67587.7	**100.**
Henon C_jDE	235567	0.	20.3886	**70.1469**	4140.89	25490.	42.5377	13885.	104.1	1938.43	**502.09**	108.303	182.18	66309.1	**100.**
Ikeda C_jDE	263932	0.	20.3825	70.9207	**4007.7**	31424.	40.928	10097.1	104.068	1948.94	522.25	108.294	182.22	65436.	**100.**
Lozi C_jDE	278606	0.	20.3843	71.8383	4026.17	29837.6	42.6603	**7802.79**	104.115	1934.92	516.184	108.359	**181.185**	65532.1	**100.**
Sinai C_jDE	260362	0.	20.3877	75.6142	4101.57	27938.6	42.1283	10693.8	**104.065**	1933.22	503.526	108.407	181.377	67689.	**100.**
Tinkerbell C_jDE	477178.	$2.8*10^-9$	20.3836	75.5185	4181.02	52001.5	46.7729	21866.7	104.609	2341.32	713.484	108.954	184.486	66104.4	100.03

The bold values in Table 1 depict the best-obtained results (based on the simple descriptive statistics - mean values); *Wilcoxon sum-rank test* with the significance level of 0.05 was not performed for each pair of original jDE and C_jDE; Instead, *Friedman test with Nemenyi post hoc test* is in Fig. 2).

Table 2. The best (minimum found) results for jDE and C_jDE; CEC 2015 Benchmark set, 50*D*, 51 runs

System\f	1	2	3	4	5	6	7	8	9	10	11	12	13	14	15	Total
jDE	55564.6	0.	20.2933	46.9814	3335.56	5776.6	39.3382	**1170.89**	103.738	991.231	410.39	107.235	173.473	49527.2	**100.**	3
Arnold C_jDE	58581.	0.	20.3046	52.9127	3195.97	2653.73	39.1312	1268.88	103.663	1218.49	301.128	106.931	172.163	49531.1	**100.**	2
Burgers C_jDE	147285.	0.	20.3308	57.8893	3448.77	6845.35	**8.99386**	2845.81	104.324	1443.01	525.391	107.742	173.198	49531.1	**100.**	3
DeLo C_jDE	90789.	0.	**20.2603**	50.8336	3153.81	5122.86	10.98	2726.32	103.765	1426.42	453.372	107.231	169.4	49531.1	**100.**	3
Dissipative C_jDE	41086.6	0.	20.3306	**45.1046**	3071.23	5577.46	38.9555	1238.52	103.715	1040.76	432.442	107.377	168.824	49531.1	**100.**	3
Henon C_jDE	**29634.**	0.	20.3201	48.689	3132.73	7354.98	38.9887	1204.63	103.717	1274.24	301.396	107.143	173.258	49527.2	**100.**	3
Ikeda C_jDE	67868.3	0.	20.2807	55.7903	**2741.65**	5785.85	39.471	1418.56	**103.641**	1300.68	**300.622**	107.007	169.784	49531.1	**100.**	5
Lozi C_jDE	42904.6	0.	20.292	49.1949	3200.89	**3408.78**	39.0236	1465.88	103.742	1085.19	301.001	**106.805**	164.805	**49525.4**	**100.**	5
Sinai C_jDE	75172.	0.	20.3089	48.7203	3415.6	3960.52	38.7491	1182.99	103.805	**940.449**	301.021	106.94	**166.687**	49525.6	**100.**	5
Tinkerbell C_jDE	96128.4	0.	20.2995	47.9458	3259.51	16687.9	10.84	2590.81	103.95	1618.55	555.486	107.502	169.735	49527.3	**100.**	2

The bold values in Table 2 depict the best-obtained results (based on the min. values).

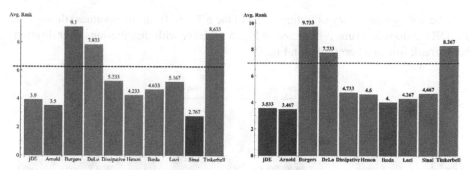

Fig. 2. Ranking of all jDE versions (30*D* – left [22], 50*D* – right), 51 runs, 15 functions of the CEC2015. The dashed line represents the Nemenyi Critical Distance.

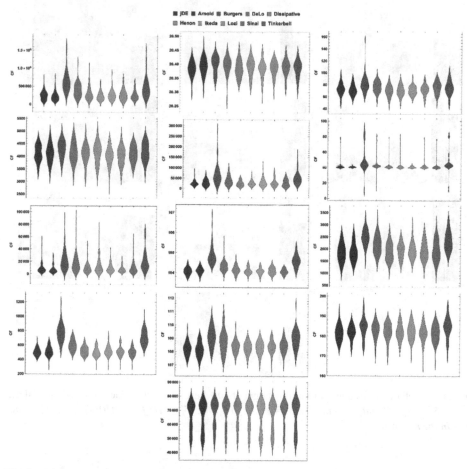

Fig. 3. Distribution Plots for all versions of jDE, CEC15 (*except f2 and f15 – i.e. f1, f3, f4 in the first row; f5, f6, f7; f8, f9, f10; f11, f12, f13; and f14 in the next rows.*

The average frequency of hitting target of the $p\%$ best (minimum values) throughout all jDE versions and runs is depicted in Fig. 5 together with distributions over different benchmark functions presented in Fig. 4.

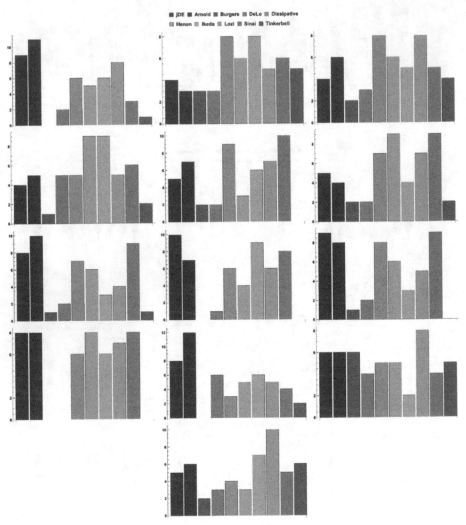

Fig. 4. Barcharts for frequency of hitting target of 10% best minimum values; all versions of jDE, CEC15 *(except f2 and f15 – i.e. f1, f3, f4 in the first row; f5, f6, f7; f8, f9, f10; f11, f12, f13; and f14 in the next rows.*

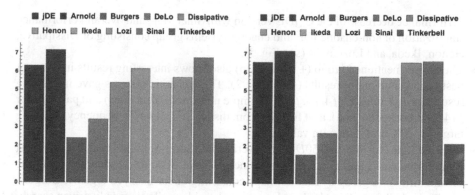

Fig. 5. The average frequency of hitting target of 10% best minimum values (sorted first 51 best results); all versions of jDE and all runs (510 runs in total), CEC15; 30*D* – left [22], 50*D* – right.

6 Conclusion

This paper completes related research reported in [19–22], with higher dimensional settings ($D = 50$) and different detailed processing of results.

Is Chaotic Randomization Advantageous for Higher Dimensional Optimization Problems? The answer may be Yes and No. There is no significant difference in performance between non-chaotic and most of the chaotic versions. However, the cluster of Arnold, Lozi, Sinai, Henon, and Dissipative maps has shown relatively stable and statistically balanced results compared to the non-chaotic jDE version. For the group of simple multimodal and composite functions, these chaotic systems secured finding minimum results. This can be advantageous especially in real-life engineering problems. Most of the C_jDE versions have proven to be very effective in finding a minimum of test functions. Moreover, such a phenomenon may be the answer to the popularity of chaos in simpler algorithms/swarm systems.

Overall, research and experiments with population dynamics and randomization schemes have been addressed as of high importance and advantageous. Therefore, descriptive statistics, detailed distribution plots, rankings, and detailed target-hitting based comparisons of all used jDE versions represent here a deeper investigation into the population dynamics and selection of individuals inside the self-adaptive jDE algorithm under the influence of different types of quasi-random (chaotic) sequences.

The findings below may reveal alternative ways of developing new ideas and more effective metaheuristics. The findings are suggested based on the CEC 2015 testbed. Under other settings, of course, these might turn out different.

- Distribution plots in Fig. 3 and data in Tables 1 and 2 support the claim that the selection of the best CPRNGs is problem-dependent task. By using the CPRNG inside the heuristic, its performance is (significantly) different: either better or worse against other compared versions.
- According to the rankings, the not-chaotic jDE was the 2nd, the C_jDE version with Arnold Cat Map was the best performing (but there is no significant difference between these two versions). Also, increase of the dimension from 30 to 50 reveal (mean)

performance decrease of the C_jDE version with Sinai Map, and overall performance stabilization of non-chaotic jDE and chaotic systems group consisting of Dissipative, Henon, Ikeda, and Lozi maps (see Fig. 5).

- The above-mentioned group (+ Sinai Map) also shows interesting results in terms of best found (minimum) results (see Table 2). These chaotic systems gave interesting results for functions $f3, f4, f5, f6, f7$ (simple multimodal functions) and partially for $f14$ (composite function), as it follows from distribution plots for frequency of hitting target of 10% best minimum values.
- Both diagrams for $30D$ and $50D$ of the average frequency of hitting target of 10% best minimum values (Fig. 5) confirms statements above. Also, these charts confirm the unsuitability of a group of chaotic maps consisting of for Delayed logistic, Burgers, and Tinkerbell for solving higher-dimensional problems. Their greedy driven searching towards function extreme (with premature population stagnation) was partially advantageous in lower dimensions.

The results presented here can help build new approaches for improving exploration abilities and support the development of advanced randomization mechanisms (multi-chaotic generators [28]) or ensemble randomization systems [29], providing the combined/selective population diversity for effective controlling of exploration/exploitation during the run of metaheuristic algorithm.

The popular self-adaptive DE version has been tested here, and we can observe, that besides the controlling of parameter adaptation, other simple approaches can be effectively used to achieve better/desired DE performance.

Acknowledgement. Authors RS, AV, TK and MP acknowledge the support by COST Action CA15140 (ImAppNIO), and the resources of A.I.Lab at the Faculty of Applied Informatics, TBU in Zlin (ailab.fai.utb.cz). Author TK also acknowledges the Internal Grant Agency of Tomas Bata University under project No. IGA/CebiaTech/2020/001. Finally, Author Ivan Zelinka acknowledges the support of grant SGS 2020/137, VSB-Technical University of Ostrava.

References

1. Karafotias, G., Hoogendoorn, M., Eiben, Á.E.: Parameter control in evolutionary algorithms: trends and challenges. IEEE Trans. Evol. Comput. **19**(2), 167–187 (2014)
2. Weber, M., Neri, F., Tirronen, V.: A study on scale factor in distributed differential evolution. Inf. Sci. **181**(12), 2488–2511 (2011)
3. Zamuda, A., Brest, J.: Self-adaptive control parameters' randomization frequency and propagations in differential evolution. Swarm Evol. Comput. **25**, 72–99 (2015)
4. Meng, H.J., Zheng, P., Mei, G.H., Xie, Z.: Particle swarm optimization algorithm based on chaotic series. Control Decis. **21**(3), 263 (2006)
5. Liu, H., Abraham, A., Clerc, M.: Chaotic dynamic characteristics in swarm intelligence. Appl. Soft Comput. **7**(3), 1019–1026 (2007)
6. Liu, H., Abraham, A.: Chaos and swarm intelligence. In: Kocarev, L., Galias, Z., Lian, S. (eds.) Intelligent Computing Based on Chaos. Studies in Computational Intelligence, vol. 184, pp. 197–212. Springer, Heidelberg (2009). https://doi.org/10.1007/978-3-540-95972-4_9

7. Caponetto, R., Fortuna, L., Fazzino, S., Xibilia, M.G.: Chaotic sequences to improve the performance of evolutionary algorithms. IEEE Trans. Evol. Comput. **7**(3), 289–304 (2003)
8. Coelho, L., Mariani, V.C.: A novel chaotic particle swarm optimization approach using Hénon map and implicit filtering local search for economic load dispatch. Chaos Solit. Fractals **39**(2), 510–518 (2009)
9. Davendra, D., Zelinka, I., Senkerik, R.: Chaos driven evolutionary algorithms for the task of PID control. Comput. Math Appl. **60**(4), 1088–1104 (2010)
10. Ozer, A.B.: CIDE: chaotically initialized differential evolution. Expert Syst. Appl. **37**(6), 4632–4641 (2010)
11. Pluhacek, M., Senkerik, R., Davendra, D.: Chaos particle swarm optimization with Eensemble of chaotic systems. Swarm Evol. Comput. **25**, 29–35 (2015)
12. Wang, G.-G., Deb, S., Gandomi, A.H., Zhang, Z., Alavi, A.H.: Chaotic cuckoo search. Soft. Comput. **20**(9), 3349–3362 (2015). https://doi.org/10.1007/s00500-015-1726-1
13. Fister Jr., I., Perc, M., Kamal, S.M., Fister, I.: A review of chaos-based firefly algorithms: perspectives and research challenges. Appl. Math. Comput. **252**, 155–165 (2015)
14. Alatas, B.: Chaotic bee colony algorithms for global numerical optimization. Expert Syst. Appl. **37**(8), 5682–5687 (2010)
15. Metlicka, M., Davendra, D.: Chaos driven discrete artificial bee algorithm for location and assignment optimisation problems. Swarm Evol. Comput. **25**, 15–28 (2015)
16. Zhang, J., Lin, S., Qiu, W.: A modified chaotic differential evolution algorithm for short-term optimal hydrothermal scheduling. Int. J. Electr. Power Energy Syst. **65**, 159–168 (2015)
17. Mokhtari, H., Salmasnia, A.: A Monte Carlo simulation based chaotic differential evolution algorithm for scheduling a stochastic parallel processor system. Expert Syst. Appl. **42**(20), 7132–7147 (2015)
18. Das, S.: Chaotic patterns in the discrete-time dynamics of social foraging swarms with attractant–repellent profiles: an analysis. Nonlinear Dyn. **82**(3), 1399–1417 (2015). https://doi.org/10.1007/s11071-015-2247-2
19. Senkerik, R., Viktorin, A., Pluhacek, M., Kadavy, T., Zelinka, I.: How unconventional chaotic pseudo-random generators influence population diversity in differential evolution. In: Rutkowski, L., Scherer, R., Korytkowski, M., Pedrycz, W., Tadeusiewicz, R., Zurada, J.M. (eds.) ICAISC 2018. LNCS (LNAI), vol. 10841, pp. 524–535. Springer, Cham (2018). https://doi.org/10.1007/978-3-319-91253-0_49
20. Senkerik, R., Viktorin, A., Pluhacek, M., Kadavy, T., Oplatkova, Z.K.: Differential evolution and chaotic series. In: 2018 25th International Conference on Systems, Signals and Image Processing (IWSSIP), pp. 1–5. IEEE, June 2018
21. Senkerik, R., et al.: Population diversity analysis in adaptive differential evolution variants with unconventional randomization schemes. In: Rutkowski, L., Scherer, R., Korytkowski, M., Pedrycz, W., Tadeusiewicz, R., Zurada, J.M. (eds.) ICAISC 2019. LNCS (LNAI), vol. 11508, pp. 506–518. Springer, Cham (2019). https://doi.org/10.1007/978-3-030-20912-4_46
22. Senkerik, R., Viktorin, A., Kadavy, T., Pluhacek, M., Zelinka, I.: Insight into adaptive differential evolution variants with unconventional randomization schemes. In: Zamuda, A., Das, S., Suganthan, P.N., Panigrahi, B.K. (eds.) SEMCCO/FANCCO -2019. CCIS, vol. 1092, pp. 177–188. Springer, Cham (2020). https://doi.org/10.1007/978-3-030-37838-7_16
23. Sprott, J.C.: Chaos and Time-Series Analysis. Oxford University Press, Oxford (2003)
24. Price, K.V., Storn, R.M., Lampinen, J.A.: Differential Evolution: A Practical Approach to Global Optimization, Berlin. Springer, Berlin (2005). https://doi.org/10.1007/3-540-31306-0
25. Das, S., Mullick, S.S., Suganthan, P.: Recent advances in differential evolution – an updated survey. Swarm Evol. Comput. **27**, 1–30 (2016)
26. Brest, J., Greiner, S., Boskovic, B., Mernik, M., Zumer, V.: Self-adapting control parameters in differential evolution: a comparative study on numerical benchmark problems. IEEE Trans. Evol. Comput. **10**(6), 646–657 (2006)

27. Chen, Q., Liu, B., Zhang, Q., Liang, J.J., Suganthan, P.N., Qu, B.Y.: Problem definition and evaluation criteria for CEC 2015 special session and competition on bound constrained single-objective computationally expensive numerical optimization. Computational Intelligence Laboratory, Zhengzhou University, China and Nanyang Technological University, Singapore, Technical report (2014)

28. Viktorin, A., Pluhacek, M., Senkerik, R.: Success-history based adaptive differential evolution algorithm with multi-chaotic framework for parent selection performance on CEC2014 benchmark set. In: 2016 IEEE Congress on Evolutionary Computation (CEC), pp. 4797–4803. IEEE, July 2016

29. Wu, G., Mallipeddi, R., Suganthan, P.N.: Ensemble strategies for population-based optimization algorithms–A survey. Swarm Evol. Comput. **44**, 695–711 (2019)

30. Price, K.V., Awad, N.H., Ali, M.Z., Suganthan, P.N.: Problem definitions and evaluation criteria for the 100-digit challenge special session and competition on single objective numerical optimization. Technical report, Nanyang Technological University, Singapore, November 2018

FastText and XGBoost Content-Based Classification for Employment Web Scraping

Arkadiusz Talun[2], Pawel Drozda[1,2]($\boxtimes$) (ID), Leszek Bukowski[2],
and Rafał Scherer[3] (ID)

[1] Faculty of Mathematics and Computer Science,
University of Warmia and Mazury in Olsztyn, Olsztyn, Poland
`pdrozda@matman.uwm.edu.pl`
[2] Emplocity Ltd., Warszawa, Poland
[3] Department of Intelligent Computer Systems,
Częstochowa University of Technology, Częstochowa, Poland
`rafal.scherer@pcz.pl`

Abstract. The purpose of this paper is to present the design and results of experiments that focus on universal, autonomous data extraction (web scraping) system fed by publicly available online job listings. In particular, methods of automated crawling, preprocessing and classifying data from job offers will be presented together with the aggregation of the acquired data stored in large-scale, structured databases. We tested two models to classify the content of job portals: fastText and XGBoost. We obtained promising results in the experimental phase, with 88% accuracy by both methods.

Keywords: Web content extraction · Classification · XGBoost · fastText · Web scraping

1 Introduction

One of the main challenges that companies face all over the world is the difficulty of finding appropriate candidates for available work positions. Typical recruitment processes are very time consuming, expensive and require a lot of work time from the recruiters. One of the possible solutions for accelerating the recruitment process is the automated analysis of the contents of recruitment ads presented on the job listing sites and encoding their content in a structured way in order to enable automated matching of the job seekers with open positions. To prepare an appropriate, structured database of job offers, firstly the problem of obtaining, preprocessing and assessing particular job description needs to be addressed – especially taking into account the size of the potential datasets (just in Poland, there are hundreds of thousands of job offers available every day).

The first task necessary to create such a database is to prepare an appropriate crawler which will be able to extract shared job offers in selected portals. The

L. Rutkowski et al. (Eds.): ICAISC 2020, LNAI 12416, pp. 435–444, 2020.
https://doi.org/10.1007/978-3-030-61534-5_39

literature provides many solutions for dealing with web crawling. Vijayarani et al. in [18] describe state-of-the-art crawling techniques. The first method which should be mentioned is Breadth-First Search [13]. It starts from the root URL and checks all neighbour URLs. Next, the Depth First Search algorithm, described in [15], searches websites in depth. The author also cites the following solutions: Best First Search, Page Rank Algorithm, Shark Search, Online Page Importance Calculation (OPIC) Algorithm and HITS. In our case, the choice of crawling technique is secondary. This is due to the fact that it is not necessary to determine the relevance of individual websites in the context of the requirement process. Based on the team's experience, leading job portals were selected; therefore, it was not necessary to crawl other sources.

The second important part of the solution is designing algorithms that allow intelligent selection of the pages containing job offers from the whole dataset of crawled websites. There is ongoing work on the topic of extracting interesting information from the WWW. For example, in [5], the authors use the Support Vector Machines algorithm classifying a large collection of web content implementing a hierarchical structure. A different approach has been applied in [1]. The research focuses on classifying web pages to block URLs containing inappropriate content based on contextual and visual features. Another approach [16] defines metrics significant for content classification based on the lexical, structural and functional attributes. Authors use Logistic Regression, Decision Trees, Bagging and Boosting for Web genre prediction. Of course, there are other classifiers, such us kNN [11], neural networks [14], fuzzy logic [12] or even population algorithms [6,17], that can be applied for natural language processing. The content can be also converted to a semantic hash for easier jandling, for example by autoencoders or the Locality-Sensitive Hashing (LSH) algorithm [8]. Research on the classification of web content still touches upon many different aspects; however, none of them deals with the problem of extracting job offers from the Web.

This work is a part of the Emplobot project [4] and describes algorithms that allow automatic crawling of recruitment portals and separating recruitment ads from other content of a given portal. In particular, following supervised classification, we used two algorithms: fastText [2,10] and XGBoost [3]. These are leading classification algorithms used in natural language processing and were examined to achieve optimal results in terms of accuracy with various parameter configurations. Moreover, different feature sets for text representation were tested, which, according to the authors, could differentiate classified objects. The collected documents from the largest portals offering job offers were classified into one of the classes: job advertisement, a list of job offers and application forms. Classification using fastText and XGBoost algorithms examining the level of accuracy in capturing job advertisements from the analyzed portals achieved a very high accuracy of 88%. To the best of the authors' knowledge, this is the only work dealing with the problem of structuring information from recruitment advertisements.

The rest of the paper is structured as follows. The next section describes the system architecture. The third section briefly presents the whole classification process with data preprocessing. In Sect. 4 the proposed approach is evaluated. Finally, in the last section the conclusions and future directions are made.

2   System Architecture

This section presents the system architecture. The general overview of the system is presented in Fig. 1. The scheme shows the elements of the system and interaction between them. In the beginning, raw HTML files are gathered in the database with the use of web crawler. It is represented in the picture by the interaction between Module 1 and Module 2. Thereafter, the process of labelling data with class names is performed. It is worth mentioning that part of the data is labelled automatically, while the other part is labelled manually. This results in the training dataset for supervised classification. In Module 3, we perform HTML and javascript preprocessing. This allows removing non-essential elements from documents, such as javascript codes. The detailed description of this process is presented in the next section. Next step of the classification process is the preparation of the training set representation for individual classification algorithms. The feature generation module is responsible for this task marked as Module 4. It should be mentioned that the generation of features is performed automatically, and for each of the algorithms, the vector representation of samples in the training set contains different elements. The detailed vector representation is described in Sect. 3. The main module of the system is the classification algorithm. It consists of two state-of-the-art algorithms: fastText and XGBoost. It performs classification in order to separate job advertisements from other website content. The results are briefly described in Sect. 4.

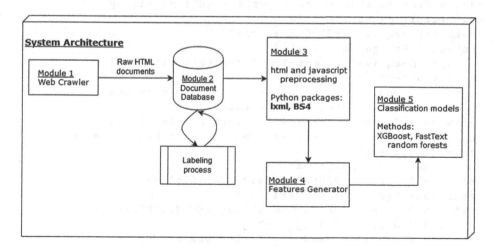

Fig. 1. Architecture of the website classification system.

3   Implementation of Methods

This section presents the main contribution of this paper, that is methods for job ads classification. The goal of the derived solutions is to automatically extract job offers during crawling web pages. We implemented state-of-the-art algorithms, namely fastText and XGBoost. We also performed initial experiments with a random forests algorithm, but it showed very low effectiveness.

3.1   Dataset Definition

As there are no studies dealing with automatic selection of job advertisements from the content of recruitment portals, there are no annotated publicly available datasets on which it will be possible to test methods for classifying portal content. For this reason, the first stage of the proposed solutions includes preparation of a training dataset for classification. The collection has three types of the most frequently appearing content on recruitment websites. The following have been identified: job listings, individual job offers and application forms. These are the most common content within thematic portals and in the first tests, distinguishing this content turned out to be crucial. To build a training set, specialized crawlers were used, which collected the necessary data from the following recruitment portals: www.pracuj.pl, www.praca.pl, www.absolvent. pl, www.gowork.pl, pl.indeed.com, www.monster.com. The example of gathered data is presented in Listing 1.1.

```
<head>
<!-- begin CMS part metatags -->
<meta name="description" content="Monster is your source for
jobs and career opportunities. Search for jobs,read career
advice from Monster's job experts, and find hiring
and recruiting advice." />
<meta http-equiv="X-UA-Compatible"
content="IE=edge,chrome=1" />
<meta http-equiv="Content-Type" content="text/html;
charset=utf-8" />
<meta http-equiv="cache-control" content="no-cache" />
<meta http-equiv="Expires" content="0" />
<meta name="viewport" content="width=device-width,
initial-scale=1.0, maximum-scale=1.0, minimum-scale=1.0,
user-scalable=no" />
<meta name="msvalidate.01"
content="DF8DBA23FC2A85B0C89741819C478E36" />
<meta name="google-site-verification"
content="hdRwRevikG3Zl1Ju07n-CT4cHgNgEBwY1J0h6mFcmv4" />
<!-- end CMS part metatags -->
<!-- begin CMS part head --><title>Monster Jobs -
Job Search, Career Advice & Hiring Resources |
Monster.com</title>      <meta charset="utf-8">
...
```

Listing 1.1. Job offer example from www.monster.com

The most important task in training dataset definition is the preprocessing data so that each algorithm can achieve a high level of accuracy. For individual methods, the data preparation process was different, as the fastText algorithm accepts the entire document as input, while the second of used algorithms, XGBoost, should have the dataset supplied in a vectorized form. Moreover, for both algorithms each of the documents was labeled with one of the categories: job offer, form and list of job offers.

For the fastText algorithm, in the beginning, each training sample consists of a whole document crawled from the website. Then, we use the Cleaner function from the lxml package (https://lxml.de/) to clean the document of unnecessary elements. In our case, we identified all JavaScript and style code as useless content. Removing them significantly reduced the size of the processed data and accelerated the execution of algorithms several times. The sample preprocessed document with class labels for fastText algorithm is presented on Table 1. On the other hand, the process of preparing the training dataset for the XGBoost algorithm required more effort and additional testing. Finally, each sample was encoded using a vector with the numbers of selected HTML tags through an experimental session and other document features. The following HTML elements and parameters proved to be the most significant in the classification of recruitment portals: length of the document, number of characters in documents without HTML tags, number of <div> containers, number of lists elements

Table 1. Sample of documents preprocessed for the fastText Algorithm

Text of data sample	Label
PRINCIPAL SEARCH ENGINEERS & SENIOR SOFTWARE ENGINEERS and DATA SCIENTISTS Shipt, Inc. San Francisco, CA 1 day ago Senior Data Scientist CyberCoders New York, NY Posted today Data Scientist Takeda Pharmaceuticals USA Cambridge, MA 1 day ago Principal Data Scientist American Bankers Life Assurance Company of Florida Atlanta, GA 1 day	List
Embedded Software Engineer - Active Security Clearance Required at CyberCoders Sterling Heights, MI Back to Job Detail Already a member? Sign in Personal information First name Last name Career level Education level Email Country US Zip code I am authorized to work for any employer in US:Yes No	Form
Radar Systems Software Engineer (S3)* at Odyssey Systems Colorado Springs, CO Skip to search results Details Highlights Company Title*: Space Surveillance Radar Systems Software Engineer Job Location: Peterson AFB, Colorado Springs, CO The Space Domain Awareness Division (USSF SMC/SPG) executes system acquisition and sustainment program management, sustaining engineering, maintenance and supply support, and modification execution for ground-based Space Situational Awareness (SSA) sensors and command and control (C2) systems	Offer

<li>, number of images <img>, number of input fields <input>, number of forms <form>, number of buttons <button> and existence of head tag. Moreover, additional combined elements increased the quality of classification using XGBoost, which are: percent of characters without HTML in the whole document and quotient of the number of container elements and length of text without HTML elements. A sample of the training set is presented in Table 2.

Table 2. Sample of dataset preprocessed for XGBoost

No	page_l	text_l	link_n	containers_n	image_n	input_n	...	Label
10191	277892	14361	3	149	12	56		Form
12075	80784	12154	171	411	37	29		Offer
14960	83328	15097	291	320	60	18		offer
4181	408834	10634	181	418	4	16		List
10565	32698	4363	35	48	3	0		Form
744	35301	316	9	38	0	1		List

3.2 FastText

FastText is one of the most popular and best-performing algorithms in text classification. This is confirmed by the number of applications of this method in many different fields. Moreover, the fastText text classification paper [10] gathered a huge number of citations since the first publication in 2016. The architecture of fastText is shown in Fig. 2. As an input, the algorithm gets a text which is divided to N n-gram features represented by $x_1, \ldots, x_N$ with the of bag-of-words [7,9] encoding. This encoding is the input for the linear classifier after averaging into a text representation. For the computation of probability distribution over the classes, the hierarchical softmax function is used, which significantly reduces computational complexity. This leads to minimizing the negative log-likelihood over the classes

$$\frac{1}{N} \sum_{n=1}^{N} \log(f(BAx_n)) \, . \tag{1}$$

Moreover, the stochastic gradient descent is introduced during the training. This allows obtaining similar accuracy to the best algorithms with a significant decrease of training and test time. In the experiment, we used the Python library fasttext version 0.9.2 (https://pypi.org/project/fasttext/).

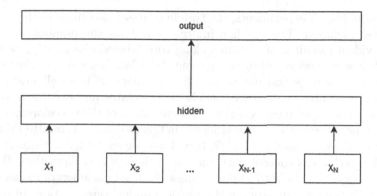

Fig. 2. Architecture of the fastText algorithm.

3.3 XGBoost

The second algorithm used in the experimental session is XGBoost [3]. It is used in many machine learning challenges and is based on tree boosting. The high effectiveness of the solution has been confirmed by a large number of publications, and the number of citations of the paper describing XGBoost has exceeded six thousands. Among the areas in which XGBoost works, especially well web text classification, should be mentioned. In particular, XGBoost is based on a tree ensemble model where prediction sums up the predictions for individual trees. It uses K additive functions for the output prediction (Eq. 2)

$$\hat{y}_i = \Phi(x_i) = \sum_{k=1}^{K} f_k(x_i), f_k \in F , \tag{2}$$

where $F = \{f(x) = w_{q(x)}\}$ is the space for regression trees. The algorithm assumes the minimization of regularized objective Eq. 3.

$$L(\Phi) = \sum_i l(\hat{y}_i, y_i) + \sum_k \Omega(f_k), \; where \; \Omega(f) = \gamma T + \frac{1}{2}\lambda||w||^2, \tag{3}$$

where l is the convex loss function which specifies the difference between $\hat{y}$ and y.

The algorithm, similarly to fastText, achieves similar effectiveness to the leading classification algorithms, but significantly reduces training time due to a number of solutions optimizing its execution. Examples include the optimization of tree boosting speed when the data are provided in a sparse form. The detailed description of this algorithm can be found in [3].

4 Experimental Results

The main aim of the experiments was to examine the possibility of automatic job offers extraction from websites. For this reason, two machine learning algorithms were taken into account in order to examine the quality of website content classification. For all experiments, the training dataset described in the previous section was prepared. The detailed information about the number of samples from individual recruitment websites along with labeled classes is presented in Table 3. It is worth paying attention to some of the data belonging to the list class from the ceneo.pl page and not to job offers webpage. It is a deliberate procedure aimed at making the learned models more versatile and capable of broader application. The experiments consist of the execution of the two aforementioned methods. One of the algorithms considered in this research was omitted since the accuracy results were far from satisfactory. First, we examined the classification of job offers webpages content with the use of the fastText algorithm. We performed the experiments with various values of initial parameters to determine the best collection of indicators in the problem under consideration. In particular, we performed the experiments with the following numbers of epochs: 20, 50, 100, and 200 and the size of word vectors: 10, 20, 50, 100, and 200. Moreover, the learning rate was set to 0.1. The accuracies of the algorithm, presented in Table 4, show that the initial parameters such as the number of epochs and the size of word vectors (dimensions) affected to a slight extent the level of accuracy. It can be seen that with different combinations of parameters the algorithm reaches a good level of accuracy of 88%.

Table 3. Training dataset content

No	Website	No of job offers	No of forms	No of lists
1	www.pracuj.pl	1200	1000	800
2	www.praca.pl	700	800	950
3	www.absolvent.pl	400	500	250
4	www.gowork.pl	1000	800	450
5	www.ceneo.pl	0	0	150
6	pl.indeed.com	2000	1800	2050
7	www.monster.com	700	1100	500
	Sum:	6000	6000	5150

In the case of the second algorithm, exactly the same dataset was taken into account except that the data provided was preprocessed and encoded in vectors. XGBoost was also launched with different initial parameter values: the minimum sum of instance weight (Hessian) needed in a child: 1, 2, 3, 4, 5 and the maximum depth of tree: 4, 5, 6, 7, 8, 9, 10, as the booster algorithm the gbtree was chosen and the learning rate was initiated with the value of 0.3. As in the case of fastText, the parameters had a negligible impact on the final accuracy of the classification. The results are presented in Table 5.

As in the case of fastText, XGBoost achieves results around 88%. Although the speed of execution of both algorithms was not tested in the experimental session, it should be mentioned that XGBoost performed the classification clearly faster, which should be considered as the advantage of this algorithm. However,

Table 4. Accuracy of the fastText algorithm

Number of epochs	Size of word vectors				
	10	20	50	100	200
20	88.04	88.05	88.05	88.05	88.06
50	88.20	88.23	88.24	88.24	88.24
100	88.12	88.09	88.44	88.08	88.11
200	88.17	88.18	88.21	88.14	88.17

Table 5. Accuracy of XGBoost execution

Max depth	Minimum child weight				
	1	2	3	4	5
4	87.89	87.83	87.71	87.65	87.89
5	87.56	87.74	87.71	87.95	87.74
6	87.86	88.15	88.09	87.82	87.80
7	88.09	88.21	87.91	87.71	87.95
8	88.24	88.09	88.15	87.86	87.83
9	88.21	88.27	88.15	88.24	88.03
10	88.06	87.83	87.95	88.03	88.18

in the case of fastText, it was not necessary to properly encode the input dataset, which first is time consuming and, secondly, the selection of encoded parameters significantly affected the accuracy of the classification.

5 Conclusions and Future Work

In this paper, the first attempt of the content classification of job offer websites in Polish was proposed. In particular, the training set was prepared along with the adjustment of the representation to individual algorithms and two state-of-the-art classification methods were implemented for automatically selecting job offers. The experimental results demonstrated that the proposed approach reached a high level of accuracy, approximately 88% and proved the ability to automatically single out job offers from major recruitment websites.

The next step of our research will address the extraction of different kinds of information from individual recruitment ads in an automatic way. In particular, we plan to extract the following features: requirements, benefits and responsibilities from job offers. Moreover, our research will focus on the automatic matching of job offers and candidate curriculum vitae.

Acknowledgements. This work is a part of the Emplobot project number POIR.01.01.01-00-1135/17 "Development of autonomous artificial intelligence using the learning of deep neural networks with strengthening, automating recruitment processes" funded by the National Centre for Research and Development.

References

1. Ahmadi, A., Fotouhi, M., Khaleghi, M.: Intelligent classification of web pages using contextual and visual features. Appl. Soft Comput. **11**(2), 1638–1647 (2011)
2. Bojanowski, P., Grave, E., Joulin, A., Mikolov, T.: Enriching word vectors with subword information. Trans. Assoc. Comput. Linguist. **5**, 135–146 (2017)
3. Chen, T., Guestrin, C.: XGboost: a scalable tree boosting system. In: Proceedings of the 22nd ACM SIGKDD International Conference on Knowledge Discovery and Data Mining, pp. 785–794 (2016)
4. Drozda, P., Talun, A., Bukowski, L.: Emplobot - design of the system. In: Proceedings of the 28th International Workshop on Concurrency, Specification and Programming, Olsztyn, Poland, 24–26th September 2019 (2019)
5. Dumais, S., Chen, H.: Hierarchical classification of web content. In: Proceedings of the 23rd Annual International ACM SIGIR Conference on Research and Development in Information Retrieval, pp. 256–263 (2000)
6. Dziwiński, P., Bartczuk, Ł., Paszkowski, J.: A new auto adaptive fuzzy hybrid particle swarm optimization and genetic algorithm. J. Artif. Intell. Soft Comput. Res. **10**(2), 95–111 (2020)
7. Gabryel, M.: The bag-of-words method with different types of image features and dictionary analysis. J. UCS **24**(4), 357–371 (2018)
8. Gabryel, M., Grzanek, K., Hayashi, Y.: Browser fingerprint coding methods increasing the effectiveness of user identification in the web traffic. J. Artif. Intell. Soft Comput. Res. **10**(4), 243–253 (2020)
9. Gabryel, M., Przybyszewski, K.: The dynamically modified BoW algorithm used in assessing clicks in online ads. In: Rutkowski, L., Scherer, R., Korytkowski, M., Pedrycz, W., Tadeusiewicz, R., Zurada, J.M. (eds.) ICAISC 2019. LNCS (LNAI), vol. 11509, pp. 350–360. Springer, Cham (2019). https://doi.org/10.1007/978-3-030-20915-5_32
10. Joulin, A., Grave, E., Bojanowski, P., Mikolov, T.: Bag of tricks for efficient text classification. arXiv preprint arXiv:1607.01759 (2016)
11. Koren, O., Hallin, C.A., Perel, N., Bendet, D.: Decision-making enhancement in a big data environment: application of the k-means algorithm to mixed data. J. Artif. Intell. Soft Comput. Res. **9**(4), 293–302 (2019)
12. Korytkowski, M., Senkerik, R., Scherer, M.M., Angryk, R.A., Kordos, M., Siwocha, A.: Efficient image retrieval by fuzzy rules from boosting and metaheuristic. J. Artif. Intell. Soft Comput. Res. **10**(1), 57–69 (2020)
13. Kumar, R., Jain, A., Agrawal, C.: Survey of web crawling algorithms. Adv. Vis. Comput.: Int. J. (AVC) **1**(2/3) (2014)
14. Ludwig, S.A.: Applying a neural network ensemble to intrusion detection. J. Artif. Intell. Soft Comput. Res. **9**(3), 177–188 (2019)
15. Mahdi, D.A.F., Ahmed, R.K.A.: A new technique for web crawling in multimedia web sites. Int. J. Comput. Eng. Res. **4**(2) (2014)
16. Malhotra, R., Sharma, A.: Quantitative evaluation of web metrics for automatic genre classification of web pages. Int. J. Syst. Assur. Eng. Manag. **8**(2), 1567–1579 (2017)
17. Tambouratzis, G., Vassiliou, M.: Swarm algorithms for NLP - the case of limited training data. J. Artif. Intell. Soft Comput. Res. **9**(3), 219–234 (2019)
18. Vijayarani, S., Suganya, M.E.: Web crawling algorithms–a comparative study. Int. J. Sci. Adv. Res. Technol. **2**(10) (2016)

Supervised Classification Methods
for Fake News Identification

Thanh Cong Truong[1](✉) [iD], Quoc Bao Diep[1] [iD], Ivan Zelinka[1] [iD],
and Roman Senkerik[2] [iD]

[1] Faculty of Electrical Engineering and Computer Science,
VSB-Technical University of Ostrava,
17. listopadu 2172/15, 708 00 Ostrava-Poruba, Ostrava, Czech Republic
{cong.thanh.truong.st,ivan.zelinka}@vsb.cz, diepquocbao@gmail.com
[2] Faculty of Applied Informatics, Tomas Bata University in Zlin,
T. G. Masaryka 5555, 760 01 Zlin, Czech Republic
senkerik@utb.cz

Abstract. Along with the rapid increase in the popularity of online
media, the proliferation of fake news and its propagation is also rising.
Fake news can propagate with an uncontrollable speed without verification and can cause severe damages. Various machine learning and deep
learning approaches have been attempted to classify the real and the
false news. In this research, the author group presents a comprehensive
performance evaluation of eleven supervised algorithms on three datasets
for fake news classification.

Keywords: Fake news · Supervised classification · Machine learning ·
Deep learning

1   Introduction

In recent times, information from social media has grown at an unprecedented
pace, and gradually the number of people consuming daily news to meet their
information needs is increasing. Nevertheless, not all sources of news on online
media are reliable. As a consequence, the problem of spreading fake news is
becoming more severe.

"Fake news" is a term that refers to the news that is purposely and verifiably
false, and could deceive readers [2]. The issues of false news have existed since the
appearance of the printing press. Nevertheless, during the age of social media,
the untruthful news problem gains a lot of momentum and visibility because of
the simple access and fast distribution mechanism of social media.

Conventional techniques for confirming the authenticity of news that rely on
human specialists, do not scale well to the massive volume of news nowadays.
Hence, automatic detection of false news on social media is a critical problem,
alluring much attention from both the academic and communities.

Machine learning (ML) and Deep learning (DL) approaches have been proven
very effective in solving many cyber security problems from network detection to

L. Rutkowski et al. (Eds.): ICAISC 2020, LNAI 12416, pp. 445–454, 2020.
https://doi.org/10.1007/978-3-030-61534-5_40

malware analysis [10–12] as well as identification spam email, which is one type of misinformation. Hence, this study aims to present a comparative performance analysis of well-known supervise classification methods by implementing each one on three of the available publicity datasets. More precisely, the author group investigates the performance of five traditional ML, three ensemble, and three DL-based methods on the publicity datasets.

The rest of this manuscript proceeds as follows. Section 2 presents briefly the previous works in fake news detection. Section 3 introduces the methodology. Section 4 describes the experiment environment. Section 5 presents and analyses the result of competing algorithms. Section 6 discusses the results obtained from the current work. Finally, Sect. 7 concludes the paper.

2   Related Works

This section presents existing and related in the field of ML and DL to analyse about Fake News Detection.

The authors in [3] proposed a model to classification news into different groups. In this research, they utilised Term Frequency-Inverse Document Frequency (TF-IDF) for feature extraction and Support Vector Machine (SVM) for classification. The authors reported that their model obtained promising results on category news into groups.

A research conducted by Granik and Mesyura [5] focused on implementation of the Naïve Bayes Classifiers for fake news detection. Their model was evaluated on a Facebook dataset and obtained approximately 74% of accuracy.

Shu et al. [8] performed a thorough review of detecting fake news on social media. In their study, they characterised fake news based on psychology and social theories. What is more, they lited existing algorithms from a data mining aspect, evaluation metrics, and typical datasets.

The authors in [6] proposed to combine speaker profiles into a Long Short-Term Memory (LSTM) model for fake news detection. Empirical results showed that their method improved the LSTM detection model.

An other approach [1] presented an n-gram model to detect automatically fake contents. In this study, they adopted two different features of extraction techniques and six machine learning classification techniques for fake news and fake reviews identification.

3   Methodology

This section presents details of the suggested models to identify fakes news. First, the data are pre-processing by filtering the redundant terms or characters such as special characters, numbers, stop-words and others. Next, the feature selection & extraction process has been applied for reducing the dimension of feature space; in this process, two techniques are used. Finally, the supervised classifiers are computed on the fake news data set.

3.1   Data Preprocessing

This phase transforms the raw text into an understandable format for further processing. Furthermore, real-world data is usually inadequate, inconsistent, and lacking in particular behaviour, and it is possible to contain various faults. Pre-processing data assist in resolving such matters. In our study, the pre-processing data phase consists of the following steps:

- Text cleaning: remove tags, HTML, punctuation, special characters, and any other kind of characters.
- Lowercase: This step involves converting the entire text into lowercase because of the computer interpret capitalise letter as different terms.
- Tokenisation: This is a process of splitting the strings into a list of words or pieces based on a specified pattern.
- Remove stop words: Stopwords are the words that are used very frequently, such as "i", "me", "my", "myself", "we", "you", "he,", "his". Remove stopwords improve the performance of the model.
- Stemming & Lemmatizing: return the word to root form. For example "cars", "car's", "cars"' get reduced to a root term "car".

After pre-processing data, the cleaned data needs to be converted into a numerical format for further tasks.

3.2   Feature Selection and Extraction

This phase aims to transform the text into numerical data so that the ML & DL algorithms can compute. Vectorisation of text is a method that allows the conversion of text into numerical representation, or in other words, numeric vector.

To transform the text into a numeric format for further processing, the text needs to encode. Multiple encoding techniques are being leveraged to extract the word-embeddings from the text data such techniques are bag-of-words [13], Term Frequency - Inverse Document Frequency (TF-IDF) [7], word2vec [4]. In this study, the author group utilise the TF-IDF with bigram and word2vec techniques to vectorise the data for the purpose of classification.

3.3   Supervised Artificial Intelligence Algorithms

The author group investigated the performance of eleven supervised algorithms on three datasets. More precise, five traditional machine learning algorithmics, three ensemble models and three deep leaning approaches had been examined as follows:

- Traditional ML models: Logistic regression, Naive Bayes, Support Vector Machine (SVM), K-Nearest Neighbours (KNN), and Decision tree.
- Ensemble models: Random forest, Extremely randomised trees (Extra trees), and Adaptive Boosting (AdaBoost).
- DL-based models: Feedforward neural network (FNN), Long short-term memory (LSTM), Bidirectional Long short-term memory (BiLSTM).

3.4   Performance Evaluation Metrics

Evaluation metrics measure the performance of a model. An essential aspect of evaluation metrics is their capability to distinguish among model results. The Confusion matrix is one of the most common and most straightforward metrics used for deciding the correctness and accuracy of the model. It is frequently used for the classification issue where the output can be of two or more types of classes. In fact, many performance metrics are calculated basing on the confusion matrix and the values inside it. To evaluate the performance of fake news classification, a confusion matrix has been utilised as shown in Table 1.

Table 1. Confusion matrix

		Actual values	
		Positive (1)	Negative (0)
Predicted values	Positive (1)	True Positive (TP)	False Positive (FP)
	Negative (0)	False Negative (FN)	True Negative (TN)

Terms associated with this confusion matrix:

- True Positive (TP): The sample is fake news, and the model predicts it fake.
- True Negative (TN): The sample is real news, and the model predicts it real.
- False Positive (FP): The sample is real news, and the model predicts it fake.
- False Negative (FN): The sample is fake news, and the model predicts it real.

In this study, we utilized the performance evaluation criteria derived from the confusion matrix [9] as following:

$$Accuracy = \frac{TP + TN}{TP + TN + FP + FN}$$

$$Precision = \frac{TP}{TP + FP}$$

$$Recall = \frac{TP}{FN + TP}$$

$$F1 - score = 2 * \frac{Precision * Recall}{Precision + Recall}$$

The accuracy is the rate of precisely predicted news to all of the samples. Precision metric measures the fake news, which is correctly predicted from the total predicted news in fake class. Recall value shows the ratio of the untruthful news, which is correctly predicted over the total number of fake news. F1-score is the harmonic mean value of the recall value and precision.

4 Experiment Setup

4.1 Execution Environment

The experiments were performed on the Intel Core i7 8750 H computer with 16GB RAM, using Python (3.7.1), deep-learning frameworks Keras (2.3.1) and TensorFlow (2.1.0).

4.2 Datasets

We used three datasets to measure the performance of different methods. The characteristics of these datasets are described here. Table 2 summarises the datasets that we used to measure the performance of the algorithms.

Liar

Liar [14] is a publicly available dataset, which comprises over 12000 labelled short statements from politifact.com. The dataset encompasses six types of labels: pants-fire, false, barely-true, half-true,mostly-true, and true—these labels based on the of truthfulness ratings. In our work, we mainly focused on classifying news as real and fake. For the binary classification, we modified these labels into two labels. Pants-fire, false, barely-true were regarded as counterfeit and half-true, mostly-true and true statements are as authentic. Consequently, we had a total of 10240 statements with 4488 labelled as fake, and the rest 5752 labelled as real.

Getting Real About Fake News

This dataset was comprising news of 2016 USA election cycle. In this dataset, the real articles received from the official news site while the fake news gathered from the Kaggle's[1] "Getting Real about Fake News". The dataset consists of 15, 712 real-labelled articles and 12, 999 fake-labelled articles, totalling 28, 711 records.

ISOT

ISOT dataset [1] has two types of articles, fake and real news, which was obtained from real-world sources. The actual news articles were gathered from Reuters.com, while the fake one was collected from various unreliable websites that were flagged by Politifact and Wikipedia. The dataset consists of 21, 417 real-labelled articles and 23, 481 fake-labelled articles, totalling 44, 898 records.

Table 2. Datasets used for measuring

Name	Properies			Notes
	Real	Fake	Total	
Liar, Liar pants on fire	5,752	4,488	10,240	
Fake or real news	15,712	12,999	28,711	
ISOT fake news	21,417	23,48	44,898	

---

[1] https://www.kaggle.com/mrisdal/fake-news.

5   Experimental Results and Analysis

In this section, the author group report the results and in-depth performance analysis of ML models and DL models when adopting to the fake news identification.

Tables 3, 4, 5 demonstrate the performance of these algorithms on three datasets, respectively. We measure the accuracy, precision, recall, and f1-score for fake and real class, then obtain the average and report an average score of these metrics. In each table, the highest scores achieved in each dataset are shown in bold.

Table 3. Performance on Liar dataset

Classifiers	Feature	Performance metrics				Time (seconds)
		Accuracy	Precision	Recall	F1 - score	
Logistic regression	Bigram TF-IDF	0.60	0.60	0.60	**0.60**	0.24
Naive bayes		0.58	**0.61**	0.58	0.48	**0.02**
SVM		**0.61**	0.60	**0.61**	**0.60**	0.28
KNN		0.57	0.56	0.57	0.53	1.38
Decision tree		0.56	0.55	0.56	0.55	10.03
Random forest		0.58	0.56	0.57	0.55	2.35
Extra trees		0.57	0.57	0.58	0.56	3.67
AdaBoost		0.59	0.57	0.56	0.4	7.08
FNN	Word embedding	0.57	0.54	0.57	0.42	20
LSTM		0.60	0.60	**0.61**	0.59	238
BiLSTM		**0.61**	0.60	**0.61**	0.59	667

In Table 3, we have reported the performance of various traditional ML and DL classifiers in identifying fake news on Liar the dataset. From this table, it can be seen that in terms of accuracy, precision, and recall, the distinction is not much between models. More precisely, with the accuracy metric, the SVM and BiLSTM models have performed the best for the data set with an accuracy of 0.61. In this data set, the worst accuracy of 0,56 has been achieved using the Decision tree. In terms of precision, the Naive Bayes algorithm has the highest precision among the eleven approaches, while the FNN has the lowest precision. On recall metric, SVM, LSTM, and BiLSTM have the highest performance with a recall of 0.61. In terms of F1-score, the highest value has been achieved by Logistic Regression and SVM (0.60), while the lowest value has been achieved by AdaBoost (0.4). On the other hand, the Naive Bayes model has the shortest training time of 0.02 s, while BiLSTM has the most extensive training time with 667 s.

Table 4 presents the obtained results for the different supervised classifications on the Getting Real about Fake News data set. In terms of all metrics,

Table 4. Performance on getting real about fake news dataset

Classifiers	Feature	Performance metrics				Time (seconds)
		Accuracy	Precision	Recall	F1 - score	
Logistic regression	Bigram TF-IDF	**0.96**	**0.96**	**0.96**	**0.96**	55.22
Naive bayes		0.62	0.78	0.62	0.53	**1.15**
SVM		0.95	0.95	0.95	0.95	8.82
KNN		0.48	0.66	0.48	0.34	72.66
Decision tree		0.85	0.85	0.85	0.85	257.59
Random forest		0.79	0.79	0.79	0.79	13
Extra trees		0.80	0.81	0.8	0.8	44.95
AdaBoost		0.76	0.76	0.76	0.76	824.93
FNN	Word embedding	0.82	0.82	0.82	0.82	34.53
LSTM		0.90	0.91	0.90	0.91	1142
BiLSTM		0.92	0.92	0.92	0.92	2427

the Logistic Regression classifier has the highest value among the eleven classifiers with a score of 0.96 for each measured metric. The second place belongs to SVM, with a score of 0.95 for all metrics. The worst classifier is KNN with a score of $0.48, 0.66, 0.48, 0.34$ for accuracy, precision, recall, and F1-score, respectively. Additionally, the Naive Bayes model continues the fastest training time of 1.152 s, while BiLSTM is again the slowest training time classifiers with 2427 s.

Table 5. Performance on ISOT dataset

Classifiers	Feature	Performance metrics				Time (seconds)
		Accuracy	Precision	Recall	F1 - score	
Logistic regression	Bigram TF-IDF	0.99	0.99	0.99	0.99	28.75
Naive bayes		0.96	0.96	0.96	0.96	0.94
SVM		0.99	0.99	0.99	0.99	5.2
KNN		0.85	0.87	0.85	0.85	106.48
Decision tree		0.99	0.99	0.99	0.99	200.9
Random forest		0.95	0.95	0.95	0.95	19.78
Extra trees		0.94	0.94	0.94	0.94	46.52
AdaBoost		**1.00**	**1.00**	**1.00**	**1.00**	731.34
FNN	Word embedding	0.96	0.96	0.96	0.96	50
LSTM		0.99	0.99	0.99	0.99	1411
BiLSTM		0.99	0.99	0.99	0.99	3724

The performance measurement for the different supervised methods on the ISOT Fake News data set is indicated in Table 5. The author group observes that the AdaBoost model is superior to other algorithms with an absolute score of 1.0 for all metrics measurements. In addition, SVM, Logistic Regression, Decision tree, LSTM, and BiLSTM also have an outstanding score of 0.99 for accuracy, precision, recall, and F1-score, respectively. KNN is the worst classifier with the score of 0.85, 0.87, 0.85, 0.85. In the training time perspective, Naive Bayes continually has the fastest training time of 0.94 , while BiLSTM no surprisingly has the longest training time of 3724 s.

6   Discussion

Table 6 indicates the mean performances of all supervised classifiers concerning to all evaluation metrics for three data sets. Figure 1 illustrated the mean performances in terms of accuracy, precision, recall, and F1-score. According to the empirical results, the best mean values in terms of all metrics have been obtained from the Logistic Regression and SVM models with the scores of 0.85. The worst model is KNN with a score of 0.63, 0.70, 0.63, 057 for accuracy, precision, recall, and F1-score, respectively. SVM and Logistic Regression (with bigram and TI-IDF) model has shown the best performance among the traditional ML models, while Bi-LSTM with word embedding vector is the most promising one amongst the DL based models (Fig. 1). Among the ensemble models, the AdaBoost classifier seems to be the superior one when adopting on a larger dataset. This leads to a research direction in the future.

Table 6. Mean performance on three datasets

Classifiers	Feature	Mean accuracy	Mean precision	Mean recall	Mean F1-score
Logistic regression	Bigram TF-IDF	**0.85**	**0.85**	**0.85**	**0.85**
Naive bayes		0.72	0.78	0.72	0.66
SVM		**0.85**	**0.85**	**0.85**	**0.85**
KNN		0.63	0.70	0.63	0.57
Decision tree		0.80	0.80	0.80	0.80
Random forest		0.77	0.77	0.77	0.76
Extra trees		0.77	0.77	0.77	0.77
AdaBoost		0.78	0.78	0.77	0.72
FNN	Word Embedding	0.78	0.77	0.78	0.73
LSTM		0.83	0.83	0.83	0.83
BiLSTM		0.84	0.84	0.84	0.83

We discover that the performance of the SVM (with bi-gram) model is equivalent and sometimes better than the performances of these DL models. Hence, SVM with 2-gram is our recommended model for a small dataset because of its training time is a great advantage compared to DL models.

The FNN model sustains a moderate performance on three datasets. On the other hand, LSTM-based models show gradual improvement when the size of the dataset rises from LIAR to ISOT. Additionally, when the articles in the dataset cover more information, the models will perform better. To sum up, DL-based models may show high performance on a larger dataset, but to avoid computational overhead and time complexity, SVM is the right choice for a smaller dataset.

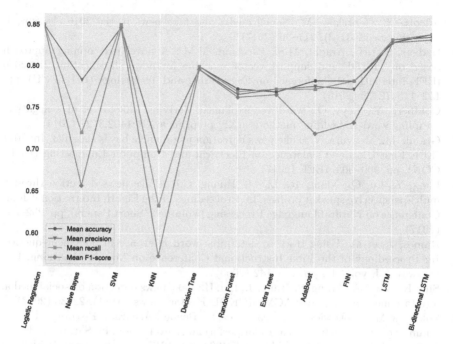

Fig. 1. Mean of performance

7   Conclusion

In this paper, the author group presented an overall performance analysis of different approaches on three different datasets to detect fake news in social media by combining text mining methods and supervised classifiers. Eleven classification models have been evaluated on three different real-world data set and measured according to accuracy, recall, precision, and F1-score values. The mean performances of all supervised artificial intelligence algorithms concerning all evaluation metrics within three data sets have been measured. According to the empirical results, the best mean values in terms of accuracy, precision, and F-measure have been obtained from the SVM and Logistic Regression with bigram TF-IDF. On the other hand, LSTM-based models with word embedding vector show a promising result in larger datasets.

Acknowledgement. The following grants are acknowledged for the financial support provided for this research: Grant of SGS No. SP2020/78, VSB Technical University of Ostrava.

References

1. Ahmed, H., Traore, I., Saad, S.: Detecting opinion spams and fake news using text classification. Secur. Priv. **1**(1), e9 (2018)

2. Allcott, H., Gentzkow, M.: Social media and fake news in the 2016 election. J. Econ. Perspect. **31**(2), 211–36 (2017)
3. Dadgar, S.M.H., Araghi, M.S., Farahani, M.M.: A novel text mining approach based on TF-IDF and support vector machine for news classification. In: 2016 IEEE International Conference on Engineering and Technology (ICETECH), pp. 112–116. IEEE (2016)
4. Goldberg, Y., Levy, O.: word2vec explained: deriving Mikolov et al.'s negative-sampling word-embedding method. arXiv preprint arXiv:1402.3722 (2014)
5. Granik, M., Mesyura, V.: Fake news detection using naive bayes classifier. In: 2017 IEEE First Ukraine Conference on Electrical and Computer Engineering (UKR-CON), pp. 900–903. IEEE (2017)
6. Long, Y., Lu, Q., Xiang, R., Li, M., Huang, C.R.: Fake news detection through multi-perspective speaker profiles. In: Proceedings of the Eighth International Joint Conference on Natural Language Processing (Volume 2: Short Papers), pp. 252–256 (2017)
7. Ramos, J., et al.: Using tf-idf to determine word relevance in document queries. In: Proceedings of the First Instructional Conference on Machine Learning, Piscataway, NJ, vol. 242, pp. 133–142 (2003)
8. Shu, K., Sliva, A., Wang, S., Tang, J., Liu, H.: Fake news detection on social media: a data mining perspective. ACM SIGKDD Explor. Newsl. **19**(1), 22–36 (2017)
9. Sokolova, M., Japkowicz, N., Szpakowicz, S.: Beyond Accuracy, F-score and ROC: a family of discriminant measures for performance evaluation. In: Sattar, A., Kang, B. (eds.) AI 2006. LNCS (LNAI), vol. 4304, pp. 1015–1021. Springer, Heidelberg (2006). https://doi.org/10.1007/11941439_114
10. Thanh, C., Zelinka, I.: A survey on artificial intelligence in malware as next-generation threats. MENDEL **25**(2), 27–34 (2019). https://doi.org/10.13164/mendel.2019.2.027
11. Truong, T.C., Diep, Q.B., Zelinka, I.: Artificial intelligence in the cyber domain: offense and defense. Symmetry **12**(3), 410 (2020). https://doi.org/10.3390/sym12030410
12. Truong, T.C., Zelinka, I., Plucar, J., Čandík, M., Šulc, V.: Artificial intelligence and cybersecurity: past, presence, and future. In: Dash, S.S., Lakshmi, C., Das, S., Panigrahi, B.K. (eds.) Artificial Intelligence and Evolutionary Computations in Engineering Systems, pp. 351–363. Springer, Singapore (2020). https://doi.org/10.1007/978-981-15-0199-9_30
13. Wallach, H.M.: Topic modeling: beyond bag-of-words. In: Proceedings of the 23rd International Conference on Machine Learning, pp. 977–984 (2006)
14. Wang, W.Y.: "Liar, Liar pants on fire": a new benchmark dataset for fake news detection. arXiv preprint arXiv:1705.00648 (2017)

Visual Hybrid Recommendation Systems Based on the Content-Based Filtering

Piotr Woldan[1], Piotr Duda[1(✉)] [ID], and Yoichi Hayashi[2] [ID]

[1] Czestochowa University of Technology, Czestochowa, Poland
{piotr.woldan,piotr.duda}@pcz.pl
[2] Department of Computer Science, Meiji University, Kawasaki, Japan

Abstract. In light of access to a huge amount of data and ever-changing trends, it is necessary to use recommendation systems to find information of interest to us. In this paper, a new approach to designing recommendation systems is proposed. It is designed to recommend images based on their content. To this end, the convolutional neural network and the Bahdanau attention mechanism are combined. In consequence, the method makes it possible to identify areas that were particularly important for a given image to be recommended. The algorithm has been tested on the publicly available Zappo50K database.

Keywords: Image recommendation · Recomender system · Attention mechanizm

1 Introduction

The amount of content available on the Internet has been steadily increasing in recent years. The number of materials shared by users on social media, such as Facebook or Instagram, video content on websites such as YouTube or Netflix, and messages on Tweeter are just some examples. All these services are characterized by the fact that a single user would not be able to trace their entire content, and thus it would be difficult for him to choose materials that interest him. Consequently, services must offer special systems that will offer to the user the items that will be selected specifically for him. Such systems are called recommendation systems [27]. Another example of the application of recommendation systems is an online store, where the system is designed to show the user those products that the user may be interested in buying. Often, apart from the recommendation itself, the user may also be interested in why the recommendation system considers these products to be of interest to him. We call this type of system an explainable recommendation system [32,33].

There are several approaches to designing recommendation systems. One of the most popular is collaborative filtering. Its operation can be described as

This work was supported by the Polish National Science Centre under grant no. 2017/27/B/ST6/02852.

ⓒ Springer Nature Switzerland AG 2020
L. Rutkowski et al. (Eds.): ICAISC 2020, LNAI 12416, pp. 455–465, 2020.
https://doi.org/10.1007/978-3-030-61534-5_41

follows. Based on the ratings that the user has given a certain number of items, other users who have similarly rated these products are selected. Based on the assessment of those items that the selected subgroup rated, and which the user has not had contact with, a recommendation is given. This approach can be successfully used e.g. for movie recommendations [34]. This approach also has several disadvantages. One of them is the so-called cold-start problem. It consists of the fact that at the time of the first contact with the system, the user has not yet rated any product, thus it is impossible to select a group of users with similar preferences. What is worse, this problem also applies to new products introduced to the offer. As this is a new product, no user could rate it, and hence it will not be recommended to anyone. A different approach to designing recommendation systems, content-based filtering, avoids these problems. Instead of comparing user ratings, the products themselves are compared, e.g. by analyzing product descriptions, their parameters, or photos. Both approaches are used in practice, and they are combined to form the so-called hybrid recommendation systems.

Evaluating the operation of the recommendation system is a non-trivial task. While in the case of a collaborative filtering approach, we can create a system that approximates user ratings as much as possible; even the best fulfill this criterium does not ensure us a good recommendation [10]. The only practical approach is to try the system in action. If the recommendations proposed by one system are chosen more often than by another, then it can be considered that the system works well. Various machine learning techniques, such as decision trees [13,28–31], density estimators [8], regression [6,7,12], ensemble methods [20,22,23] and neural networks [1,14–16] can be used to design recommendation systems. Along with the development of deep learning methods [5,11,21], image processing algorithms and natural language processing (NLP) [17,36] have found particular applications in these systems. However, these are often black-box models and the explanation of their operation requires further research.

Together with the significant increase in collected data, the field of Big Data analysis [18] was created. It was noticed that one of the problems in training models on data from various, often unverifiable sources, is the veracity of the collected data. An example of such data can be e.g. content shared by users on social networks. Lack of credibility with the training set may be due to several reasons. Incomplete data, noisy data (e.g. blurred photos), wrongly classified data (e.g. incorrectly tagged photos) are only some examples. These problems can be caused by system errors, user errors, and intentional behavior. An additional difficulty may be the difference in the proportion of data (e.g. fraction of one class data can be significantly higher than another class). All these factors negatively affect the design of recommendation systems and must be taken into account when creating such a system.

Because of the above challenges, we have proposed a new algorithm for creating content-based filtering recommendation systems to recommend similar images from the database. This algorithm uses the attention-based mechanism used mostly in NLP. It is designed to indicate areas in the proposed images that point out to similarity to the original image.

The rest of the work is divided into the following sections. Section 2 shows recent papers on image recommendations. The proposed algorithm is presented in Sect. 3. The simulation results are shown in Sect. 4. Finally, the conclusions are given in Sect. 5.

2   Related Works

Both the issues of searching for similar images and creating recommendation systems are often undertaken by researchers. Combining these fields and applying them in the field of online shopping is still a niche topic [3]. The collaborative variational autoencoders for recommender systems are applied in [19]. The author proposed the Bayesian probabilistic generative model that unifies the collaborative and content information. Graphical and deep learning models leads to a robust recommendation. The hierarchical Bayesian model was applied to the recommender system in [37]. In [4] the authors analyze the application of wide and deep models for recommendation systems. They conclude that wide models can effectively memorize sparse features interactions, and deep models can generalize to previous unseen features interactions through low dimensional embeddings. The smart shopping recommender for image search is proposed in [3]. The authors compared different neural network models (AlexNet and VGG), and SVM model and various methods to measure similarities (L_2 norm, cosine distance, and Jaccard similarity). A combination of the attention method with a convolutional neural network was applied to NLP in [35]. The attention layer was put after the word embedding layer and before the convolutional layer. The issue of image recommendation is considered in [9]. The image representation network was designed to learn an image by aggregating the semantic features of image objects with the application of an object-level attention network. More about deep learning-based recommender systems can be found in [38].

3   Attention-Based Images Recommender System

This section describes the proposed Attention Based Image Recommender system (ABIS). An important element of the proposed algorithm is the mechanism indicating what is characteristic of a given product that it has been recommended to us. To be more specific, the attention mechanism was used to determine significant areas in the image. The mechanism used here is called the Bahdanau attention algorithm (BA) [2]. It allows us to create a seq2seq model that, based on the received photo, returns attention areas in the image relative to the value of attention weights. An example of obtained features is given in Fig. 1. The proposed procedure can be summarized in the following steps.

1. Create and train a convolutional neural network to classify images.
2. Pass the image through the network.
3. Create an image descriptor from the values of outputs of the last hidden layer neurons.

Fig. 1. Original image and selected important area

4. Enter image descriptor to the BA algorithm.
5. Combine the attention weights from the BA algorithm with the input image.

The first step of the algorithm is to train the image classifier. This is a key point for further consideration. There is no single network structure that will allow us to get the best result. It must be tailored to a specific problem. Besides, it must take into account factors such as the noise in the training set or class imbalance. After training the network, the descriptors are generated by taking a values from the last hidden layer. Next, the image descriptor is entered to the encoder to ensure the fixed input size for the BA algorithm. Then, the *alignment scores* are calculated as the value of the hyperbolic tangent of the previous state of decoder and encoder state. In this step, the encoder output is concatenated with a sequence of class labels. In the classical approach, the class is a single value, but in some cases, when a class has defined subcategories, the single value can be replaced by a sequence of values (see Fig. 1, the class shoes have subclass heels). Each sequence of class labels ends with the word *<end>*. All *alignment scores* are concatenated in a single vector and subsequently fed to soft-max function. Created attention weights are multiplied with encoder outputs and create a context vector. The previous hidden state of decoder and context vector are merging to produce an output.

4 Experimental Results

This section presents a case study of shoe image recommendations. For this purpose, the Zappos50K dataset has been used. It is a collection of 50 025 pictures of shoes. On the whole, the Zappos50K dataset is divided into four main classes (Boots, Sandals, Shoes, Slippers), and each of them is divided into subcategories. In consequence, we have to deal with 21 subcategories. The data were split into 40 000 element subset, a training set, and 10 025 test set. The number of images per subcategory varies significantly, from 2 to 12 856. Moreover, some of the images are placed in the wrong category, which makes analyzes of those data even harder.

The first step is to create the best classifier. As a result of the experiments, a 13-layers convolutional neural network was selected. The convolutional layers were placed as first, second, fourth, sixth, seventh, ninth, and tenth layers. They consist of 64, 32, 32, 32, 64, 32, 32 filters, respectively. The third, fifth, and eighth layers are average-pooling with filter 2 on 2. The last three layers are fully connected. They consist of 32, 128, and 21 neurons, respectively. Apart from the last layer, the soft-max layer, the elu activation function was used in all other layers. The network model is shown in Fig. 2.

Layer (type)	Output Shape	Param #
conv2d (Conv2D)	(None, 136, 136, 64)	4864
conv2d_1 (Conv2D)	(None, 132, 132, 32)	51232
average_pooling2d (AveragePo	(None, 66, 66, 32)	0
conv2d_2 (Conv2D)	(None, 64, 64, 32)	9248
average_pooling2d_1 (Average	(None, 32, 32, 32)	0
conv2d_3 (Conv2D)	(None, 30, 30, 32)	9248
conv2d_4 (Conv2D)	(None, 28, 28, 64)	18496
average_pooling2d_2 (Average	(None, 14, 14, 64)	0
conv2d_5 (Conv2D)	(None, 14, 14, 32)	18464
conv2d_6 (Conv2D)	(None, 12, 12, 32)	9248
flatten (Flatten)	(None, 4608)	0
dense (Dense)	(None, 32)	147488
dense_1 (Dense)	(None, 128)	4224
dense_2 (Dense)	(None, 21)	2709

Fig. 2. Description of the convolutional neural network used in the experiments

To compare the classifier performance on the Zappo50K set, the network was trained in two ways. The first approach treated each instance as equally important (classic approach). In the second approach, each data element was equipped with weight being the inverse of the class frequency in the training set (weighted approach). Binary-cross entropy was used as the loss function. The networks were trained with the SGD optimizer.

To compare the accuracy of both neural networks for a single class, measures such as precision and recall were used. Suppose we consider only one particular class. If TP is a number of data elements correctly classify by a network, FT is a number of elements wrongly classify as a considered class, and FN is number of elements wrongly classified despite that it is, in fact, a considered class, then the measures are given by the following equations:

$$precision = \frac{TP}{TP + FP} \tag{1}$$

$$recall = \frac{TP}{TP + FN} \tag{2}$$

The larger values of these measures indicate the better performance of the classifier.

The network has been trained for 50 epochs. Changes in precision and recall are shown in Fig. 3. It can be easily seen that all results of the weighted approach

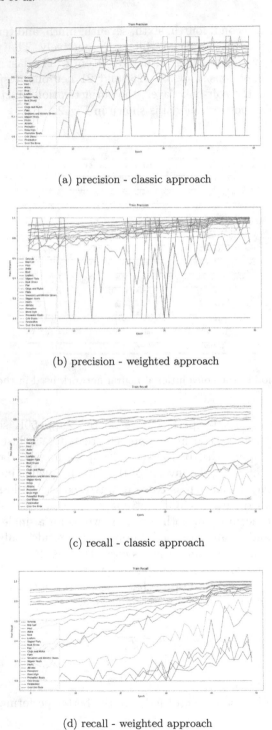

(a) precision - classic approach

(b) precision - weighted approach

(c) recall - classic approach

(d) recall - weighted approach

Fig. 3. Precision and recall for each subcategory, for the classic and weighted approach

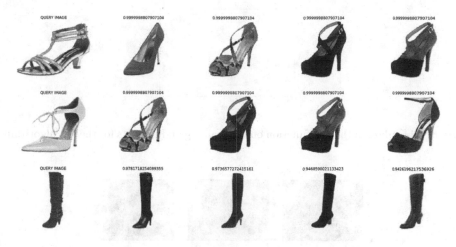

Fig. 4. The examples of shoe recommendations

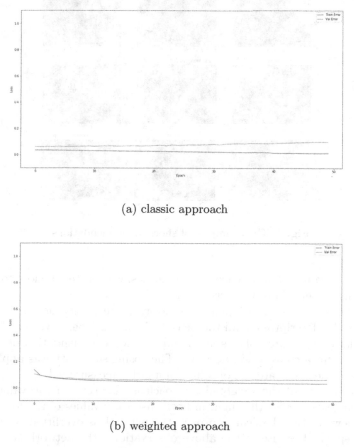

(a) classic approach

(b) weighted approach

Fig. 5. Changes in the value of the loss function on the training and test set

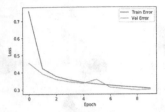

Fig. 6. The values of the loss function on the training and test sets for the BA algorithm

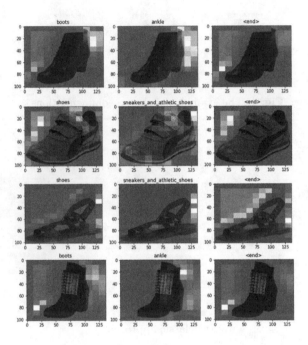

Fig. 7. The examples of shoes recommendations

reached higher values. For only few subcategories, values are not close to 1, which is due to insufficient data numbers in those classes.

The neuron values in the penultimate layer can create photo descriptors. Comparing the descriptors of all the pictures in the database, we can choose the most similar one. Figure 4 shows an example of a recommendation obtained by descriptors from a convolution network. The cosine similarity was applied. The values above the shoes are the obtained similarity measure values.

The advantage of the weighted approach is also seen in the values of the loss function, see Fig. 5. Although, in both cases, the values of the loss function remained low, in the classical approach the network is overfitted from around the 20-th epoch. Because of the above observations, the network trained with the weighted approach is selected for further analysis.

In the BA algorithm, the size of the coder output was set to 256. The network was trained by 10 epochs. The values of the loss function on the training and test sets can be seen in Fig. 6.

Examples of recommended images, with the most important areas marked for brighter color, are presented in Fig. 7. It can be seen that the recommendation system, in the case of recommendations due to one of 4 classes, pays special attention to the contours of the footwear. However, in the case of subcategories, the designated areas are not as intuitive for the user.

5   Conclusions

In this article, we have proposed a new content-based recommendation system. It aims to recommend similar images. The algorithm combines the features of a convolutional neural network, and attention mechanism. Its key feature is to indicate areas that were most important to recommend a given image. By choosing the right type of classifier, we can apply the proposed approach to various types of data sets. In the example in Sect. 4, it is shown that the areas indicated for one of the four classes are interpretable and intuitive for the user. The algorithm performance in the case of the sub-category needs further improvement. The example of the application shown in the paper can be extended to other areas, like control systems [25,26]. This approach can also be helpful in object detection [24].

References

1. Akdeniz, E., Egrioglu, E., Bas, E., Yolcu, U.: An ARMA type pi-sigma artificial neural network for nonlinear time series forecasting. J. Artif. Intell. Soft Comput. Res. 8(2), 121–132 (2018)
2. Bahdanau, D., Chorowski, J., Serdyuk, D., Brakel, P., Bengio, Y.: End-to-end attention-based large vocabulary speech recognition. In: 2016 IEEE International Conference on Acoustics, Speech and Signal Processing (ICASSP), pp. 4945–4949. IEEE (2016)
3. Chen, L., Yang, F., Yang, H.: Image-based product recommendation system with convolutional neural networks. Technical report, Stanford University (2017)
4. Cheng, H.-T., et al.: Wide & deep learning for recommender systems. In: Proceedings of the 1st Workshop on Deep Learning for Recommender Systems, pp. 7–10 (2016)
5. de Souza, G.B., da Silva Santos, D.F., Pires, R.G., Marananil, A.N., Papa, J.P.: Deep features extraction for robust fingerprint spoofing attack detection. J. Artif. Intell. Soft Comput. Res. 9(1), 41–49 (2019)
6. Duda, P., Jaworski, M., Rutkowski, L.: Convergent time-varying regression models for data streams: tracking concept drift by the recursive Parzen-based generalized regression neural networks. Int. J. Neural Syst. 28(02), 1750048 (2018)
7. Duda, P., Jaworski, M., Rutkowski, L.: Knowledge discovery in data streams with the orthogonal series-based generalized regression neural networks. Inf. Sci. 460, 497–518 (2018)

8. Duda, P., Rutkowski, L., Jaworski, M., Rutkowska, D.: On the Parzen kernel-based probability density function learning procedures over time-varying streaming data with applications to pattern classification. IEEE Trans. Cybern. **50**(4), 1683–1696 (2020)

9. Guo, G., Meng, Y., Zhang, Y., Han, C., Li, Y.: Visual semantic image recommendation. IEEE Access **7**, 33424–33433 (2019)

10. Herlocker, J.L., Konstan, J.A., Terveen, L.G., Riedl, J.T.: Evaluating collaborative filtering recommender systems. ACM Trans. Inf. Syst. (TOIS) **22**(1), 5–53 (2004)

11. Hou, Y., Holder, L.B.: On graph mining with deep learning: introducing model R for link weight prediction. J. Artif. Intell. Soft Comput. Res. **9**(1), 21–40 (2019)

12. Jaworski, M.: Regression function and noise variance tracking methods for data streams with concept drift. Int. J. Appl. Math. Comput. Sci. **28**(3), 559–567 (2018)

13. Jaworski, M., Duda, P., Rutkowski, L.: New splitting criteria for decision trees in stationary data streams. IEEE Trans. Neural Netw. Learn. Syst. **29**(6), 2516–2529 (2017)

14. Jaworski, M., Duda, P., Rutkowski, L.: On applying the restricted Boltzmann machine to active concept drift detection. In: 2017 IEEE Symposium Series on Computational Intelligence (SSCI), pp. 1–8. IEEE (2017)

15. Jaworski, M., Rutkowski, L., Duda, P., Cader, A.: Resource-aware data stream mining using the restricted Boltzmann machine. In: Rutkowski, L., Scherer, R., Korytkowski, M., Pedrycz, W., Tadeusiewicz, R., Zurada, J.M. (eds.) ICAISC 2019. LNCS (LNAI), vol. 11509, pp. 384–396. Springer, Cham (2019). https://doi.org/10.1007/978-3-030-20915-5_35

16. Kamimura, R.: Supposed maximum mutual information for improving generalization and interpretation of multi-layered neural networks. J. Artif. Intell. Soft Comput. Res. **9**(2), 123–147 (2019)

17. Ke, Y., Hagiwara, M.: An english neural network that learns texts, finds hidden knowledge, and answers questions. J. Artif. Intell. Soft Comput. Res. **7**(4), 229–242 (2017)

18. Koren, O., Hallin, C.A., Perel, N., Bendet, D.: Decision-making enhancement in a big data environment: application of the k-means algorithm to mixed data. J. Artif. Intell. Soft Comput. Res. **9**(4), 293–302 (2019)

19. Li, X., She, J.: Collaborative variational autoencoder for recommender systems. In: Proceedings of the 23rd ACM SIGKDD International Conference on Knowledge Discovery and Data Mining, pp. 305–314 (2017)

20. Ludwig, S.A.: Applying a neural network ensemble to intrusion detection. J. Artif. Intell. Soft Comput. Res. **9**(3), 177–188 (2019)

21. Javaid, M.A.M., Liu, J.-B., Teh, W.C., Cao, J.: Topological properties of four-layered neural networks. Journal of Artificial Intelligence and Soft Computing Research **9**(2), 111–122 (2019)

22. Pietruczuk, L., Rutkowski, L., Jaworski, M., Duda, P.: A method for automatic adjustment of ensemble size in stream data mining. In: 2016 International Joint Conference on Neural Networks (IJCNN), pp. 9–15. IEEE (2016)

23. Pietruczuk, L., Rutkowski, L., Jaworski, M., Duda, P.: How to adjust an ensemble size in stream data mining? Inf. Sci. **381**, 46–54 (2017)

24. Rafajłowicz, E., Rafajłowicz, W.: Testing (non-) linearity of distributed-parameter systems from a video sequence. Asian J. Control **12**(2), 146–158 (2010)

25. Rafajłowicz, E., Rafajłowicz, W.: Iterative learning in repetitive optimal control of linear dynamic processes. In: Rutkowski, L., Korytkowski, M., Scherer, R., Tadeusiewicz, R., Zadeh, L.A., Zurada, J.M. (eds.) ICAISC 2016. LNCS (LNAI), vol. 9692, pp. 705–717. Springer, Cham (2016). https://doi.org/10.1007/978-3-319-39378-0_60

26. Rafajłowicz, E., Rafajłowicz, W.: Iterative learning in optimal control of linear dynamic processes. Int. J. Control **91**(7), 1522–1540 (2018)

27. Resnick, P., Varian, H.R.: Recommender systems. Commun. ACM **40**(3), 56–58 (1997)

28. Rutkowski, L., Jaworski, M., Pietruczuk, L., Duda, P.: The CART decision tree for mining data streams. Inf. Sci. **266**, 1–15 (2014)

29. Rutkowski, L., Jaworski, M., Pietruczuk, L., Duda, P.: Decision trees for mining data streams based on the Gaussian approximation. IEEE Trans. Knowl. Data Eng. **26**(1), 108–119 (2014)

30. Rutkowski, L., Jaworski, M., Pietruczuk, L., Duda, P.: A new method for data stream mining based on the misclassification error. IEEE Trans. Neural Netw. Learn. Syst. **26**(5), 1048–1059 (2015)

31. Rutkowski, L., Pietruczuk, L., Duda, P., Jaworski, M.: Decision trees for mining data streams based on the McDiarmid's bound. IEEE Trans. Knowl. Data Eng. **25**(6), 1272–1279 (2013)

32. Rutkowski, T., Łapa, K., Jaworski, M., Nielek, R., Rutkowska, D.: On explainable flexible fuzzy recommender and its performance evaluation using the akaike information criterion. In: Gedeon, T., Wong, K.W., Lee, M. (eds.) ICONIP 2019. CCIS, vol. 1142, pp. 717–724. Springer, Cham (2019). https://doi.org/10.1007/978-3-030-36808-1_78

33. Rutkowski, T., Łapa, K., Nielek, R.: On explainable fuzzy recommenders and their performance evaluation. Int. J. Appl. Math. Comput. Sci. **29**(3), 595–610 (2019)

34. Sadeghian, M., Khansari, M.: A recommender systems based on similarity networks: Movielens case study. In: 2018 9th International Symposium on Telecommunications (IST), pp. 705–709. IEEE (2018)

35. Seo, S., Huang, J., Yang, H., Liu, Y.: Interpretable convolutional neural networks with dual local and global attention for review rating prediction. In: Proceedings of the Eleventh ACM Conference on Recommender Systems, pp. 297–305 (2017)

36. Shewalkar, A., Nyavanandi, D., Ludwig, S.A.: Performance evaluation of deep neural networks applied to speech recognition: RNN, LSTM and GRU. J. Artif. Intell. Soft Comput. Res. **9**(4), 235–245 (2019)

37. Wang, H., Wang, N., Yeung, D.-Y.: Collaborative deep learning for recommender systems. In: Proceedings of the 21th ACM SIGKDD International Conference on Knowledge Discovery and Data Mining, pp. 1235–1244 (2015)

38. Zhang, S., Yao, L., Sun, A., Tay, Y.: Deep learning based recommender system: a survey and new perspectives. ACM Comput. Surv. (CSUR) **52**(1), 1–38 (2019)

Short-Term Traffic Flow Prediction Based on the Intelligent Parameter Adjustment K-Nearest Neighbor Algorithm

Xuan Zhao[1], Ruixuan Bi[1], Ran Yang[1], Yue Chu[1], Jianhua Guo[2],
Wei Huang[2], and Jinde Cao[1(✉)]

[1] School of Mathematics, Southeast University,
Nanjing 210096, Jiangsu, People's Republic of China
{xuanzhao11,jdcao}@seu.edu.cn
[2] Intelligent Transportation System Research Center, Southeast University,
Si Pai Lou #2, Nanjing 210096, People's Republic of China
seugjh@163.com, hhhwei@126.com

Abstract. Short term traffic flow prediction is important as it supports proactive traffic control and management. A new intelligent parameter adjustment k-nearest neighbor algorithm (IPA-KNN) is proposed for the short-term traffic flow prediction. Two fundamental parameters, the nearest neighbor number k and the predicted sequence length n, are adjusted by an intelligent parameter adjusting method. In addition, the distance measure, including the similarity of fluctuation trend is adopted. Furthermore, a new error measurement method is designed to test the performance of the proposed IPA-KNN model. Compared with the improved KNN method, which is proposed by Habtemichael and Cetin (2016), the data experiments show that the error is reduced by more than 23%.

Keywords: KNN algorithm · Short-term traffic prediction · Intelligent parameter adjustment · Hyperopt module

1 Introduction

Accurate short-term traffic flow prediction is the key to proactive traffic control, which is applied to provide reliable travel information for travelers, optimize traffic signals, deploy emergency management system and so on. Because of the importance of short-term traffic forecast, a large number of studies are focused on this topic [1,2,16] currently. There are three existing categories of short-term traffic prediction methods: traditional methods, parametric methods and nonparametric methods [1]. Traditional methods based on mathematical and physical models are difficult to predict effectively and accurately. In contrast, the prediction accuracy of Kalman filter [4,6,11,14], ARIMA [12] and other parameter models [13] is higher. However, since most traffic flow data is mostly stochastic [10], it is hard to generalize a lot of time to adjust the parameters, and

© Springer Nature Switzerland AG 2020
L. Rutkowski et al. (Eds.): ICAISC 2020, LNAI 12416, pp. 466–477, 2020.
https://doi.org/10.1007/978-3-030-61534-5_42

its portability is poor. Thus, the data-driven nonparametric model [7,8,12,13] is promising to solve this kind of problems. The k-nearest neighbor (K-NN) algorithm [5,9] is one of the most classical nonparametric algorithms.

This paper proposes a short-term traffic flow forecast model based on intelligent parameter adjustment k-nearest neighbor algorithm. Firstly, locally estimated scatterplot smoothing (loess) [3] is used to preprocess the original data, so as to remove the noise data and supplement the missing data. Considering that the weighted Euclidean distance is only to measure the absolute distance, this study will use the distance measure proposed in [15] to consider the trend of neighbors In addition, the selection of the nearest neighbor number k and the predicted sequence length n is also the focus of discussion. In this study, the hyperopt module in Python is applied to optimize hyperparameters k and n. After getting the k nearest neighbors, time weights are added to get the prediction results. Finally, the forecast results of the porposed algorithm are compared with the existing ones, which show that the proposed short-term traffic flow prediction method is accurate and transferable.

The remainder of this paper is organized as follows. Section 2 presents the methodology in detail including K-nearest neighbor nonparametric regression algorithm, data preprocessing, distance measure, intelligent parameter adjustment algorithm and the prediction function. The comparisons between the IPA-KNN and the improved KNN are illustrated in Sect. 3. The paper ends in concluding remarks in Sect. 4.

2 Methodology

2.1 K-Nearest Neighbor Nonparametric Regression Algorithm

K-NN is a nonparametric pattern recognition technique commonly used for classification and regression. It is widely used in various fields because of its distinct virtues such as simple calculation and high accuracy. In this paper, K-NN is used as the basic algorithm to identify similar traffic conditions.

The basic process of K-NN prediction model is shown as follows:

1. Calculate the similarity between the subject object and candidates. In general, there are many method to measure distance, such as Euclidean distance, Manhattan distance, Mahalanobis distance, and some complex ones like dynamic time warping (DTW distance).
2. Compare the similarity between the object to be predicted and the candidates. Sort candidates according to the similarity calculated, then select k candidates (called k nearest neighbors) with the highest similarity to the object.
3. Predict the label of the subject object. The prediction function is used to process the labels of k nearest neighbors, and then assign a label to the subject object based on the nature of the k nearest neighbors.
4. Repeat the above steps until all objects are labeled.

2.2 Data Preprocessing

The data from the monitoring stations is stochastic, which is inevitable to get noise data. In order to get effective and regular historical datasets, it is necessary to preprocess the data. The method of data preprocessing is locally estimated scatterplot smoothing (loess).

Loess can effectively reduce noise and smooth data. Compared with the global linear regression, loess is superior as it takes the trend and fluctuation in to consideration, which can capture the data pattern more accurately [1]. Figure 1 shows the data preprocessing results of station 10 on March 1 using loess with a span of 0.2.

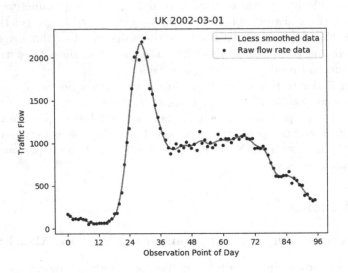

Fig. 1. Data preprocessing results using loess

2.3 Improved Distance Measurement

The commonly used distance measurements are Euclidean distance and dynamic time warping distance (DTW). Euclidean distance is proved to have better performance when the sequence length is equal, while dynamic time warping can effectively measure the distance between sequences when the sequence length is different. In this paper, the length of the traffic flow sequence is equal, so we design a new distance measurement based on Euclidean distance.

In order to reflect the fluctuation trend of the traffic flow rate, a new distance measurement [15] will be used to measure the absolute distance, which is defined as (1):

$$d(X, Y) = w_1 \sqrt{\sum_{i=1}^{n} |z_i|^2} + w_2 \sqrt{\sum_{i=1}^{n} |z_i - \bar{z}|^2} \qquad (1)$$

where $\bar{z}$ is the average value of z_i and w_1, w_2 are weights, which satisfy $w_1 + w_2 = 1$. Equation (1) consists of two parts. The first part is the traditional Euclidean distance, which is used to measure the absolute distance. The second one is to measure the similarity of the fluctuation trend. Once the predicted value is close to the real value, the second term value will be small, indicating that the fluctuation trend is relatively stable.

2.4   Evaluation Criterion

In general, three methods are utilized to error evaluation: mean absolute error (MAE), mean absolute percentage error (MAPE) and root mean square error (RMSE). Let the predicted value $X = (x_1, x_2, \cdots, x_n)$, the real value $Y = (y_1, y_2, \cdots, y_n)$, and $z_i = x_i - y_i, i = 1, 2, \cdots, n$, then

(1) MAE is defined as (2):

$$MAE(X, Y) = \frac{1}{n} \sum_{i=1}^{n} |z_i| \qquad (2)$$

(2) MAPE is defined as (3):

$$MAPE(X, Y) = \frac{1}{n} \sum_{i=1}^{n} |\frac{z_i}{y_i}| \times 100\% \qquad (3)$$

(3) RMSE is defined as (4):

$$RMSE(X, Y) = \frac{1}{n} \sqrt{\sum_{i=1}^{n} |z_i|^2} \qquad (4)$$

The above three error evaluation methods essentially measure the distance between the predicted value and the real value. Considering the improved distance measurement, a new error measurement method is developed to measure both the absolute distance and trend similarity between the predicted value and the real value.

(4) The new error measurement method is shown as (5):

$$Error(X, Y) = w_1 \sqrt{\sum_{i=1}^{n} |z_i|^2} + w_2 \sqrt{\sum_{i=1}^{n} |z_i - \bar{z}|^2} \qquad (5)$$

where $\bar{z}$, w_1 and w_2 take the same values corresponding to those in the improved distance measure Eq. (1).

2.5   Intelligent Parameter Adjustment Algorithm

Hyperopt Module. Hyperopt is a python library for hyperparameter optimization and model selection, which supports discrete, continuous and conditional variable tuning. Tree structures are used to represent the space of hyperparameters in stead of vector, which define search space conveniently.

Selection of Search Algorithm. Tree-of-Parzen-Estimators (TPE) algorithm and random search algorithm are usually used in the built-in algorithm of hyper-opt. Random search algorithm randomly selects hyperparameters from search space. In TPE algorithm, random algorithm is used to get n groups of samples randomly, and the nonparametric probability density function, which will be used for the next sampling, is generated through these n groups of samples. The optimal values is obtained after several cycles of the above algorithm.

The Establishment of Search Space. The size of the search space plays an important role in parameter adjustment, which is directly related to the predic-tion algorithm. In this study, we need to limit the range of two hyperparameters: the nearest neighbor number k and the length of prediction sequence n.

We preliminarily restrict the range of two parameters through pre-experiments. To determine the range of k, we set both w_1 and w_2 to 0.5 in the improved distance measure (3), and fix n to 5. Figure 2(a) shows the relationship between the forecast accuracy and the value of k.

Obviously, when k ranges from 1 to 15, the loss function can be controlled under 80, while the loss function is significantly larger when k is greater than 15. Therefore, we define the range [1, 15] as the search space of k.

To define the range of n, similarly, we set both w_1 and w_2 to 0.5 in the improved distance measure (3), and fix the value of k to 10. Results in Fig. 2(b) show that n's range should be [2, 10]. Accordingly, the search space is specified as k with the range [1, 15] and n in the range [2, 10].

(a) Effects of value of k on prediction accu-(b) Effects of value of n on prediction accu-racy   racy

Fig. 2. Effects of value of k and q on prediction accuracy

2.6   Prediction Method

Damping the Effect of Extreme Candidate Values. Because of the ran-domness of traffic flow data, it is necessary to reduce noise data and dampen the effect of such extreme values. Winsorization (Habtemichael et al. [17]) is used to replace the smallest and largest values with the values closest to them.

Prediction Function. In most of the existing studies, the average value of k nearest neighbors is directly used as the prediction result. In order to get better prediction results, time-dependent weights need to be added to the algorithm. In recent years, Rank-Exponent method (Habtemichael et al. [17]) has better performance than average-weight method. In this study, Rank-Exponent method is used. The weight calculation formula is shown as (6):

$$w_i = \frac{(k - r_i + 1)^2}{\sum_{i=1}^{k}(k - r_i + 1)^2} \tag{6}$$

where
r_i is the rank of the i-th nearest neighbor.
k is the number of nearest neighbors.
the prediction function is shown as (7):

$$\hat{y}_i = \sum_{i=1}^{k} w_i c_i \tag{7}$$

where
$\hat{y}_i$ is the predicted value.
c_i is the real value of the i-th nearest neighbor.

3 Data Experiments

3.1 Data Description

The data used in this study are collected from different cities and different road sections. This includes 12 datasets from United Kingdom (UK) and 24 datasets from freeways within the United States (Maryland (MD), Minnesota (MN) and Washington (WA) each with 6, 12 and 6 datasets, respectively). These datasets are collected under various driving environments and traffic conditions, having a certain amount of randomness. According to [4], these data are aggregated into 15-min data. The missing data is supplemented by locally estimated scatterplot smoothing (loess). A brief description of the dataset is shown in Table 1.

Similar to searching method in [5], when searching for nearest neighbors for any subject day, the entire dataset (except the topic day) is used, including past and future dates, which has been demonstrated reasonable in [5].

In addition to time, place and other factors, the datasets can be divided according to the traffic flow of each lane in an hour, where the dividing nodes are 0, 500, 1000, 1500, 2000 (unit: veh/h/ln), as shown in Table 2.

3.2 Determination of Distance Measure Weight

The default weights of the new distance measure are both set to 0.5. The experiment results within search space are shown in Fig. 3, where the optimal weights are set as $w_1 = 0.67$ with $w_2 = 0.33$. It can also be seen that the absolute distance and the similarity of the fluctuation trend are both vital to forecast accuracy since when w_1 is near 0 and 1, the loss function is much larger.

Table 1. Brief description of the datasets used (adopted from Guo et al. [4])

Region	Highway	Station	No. of lanes	Start	End	No. of months
UK	M25	4762a	4	9/1/1996	11/30/1996	3 months
UK	M25	4762b	4	9/1/1996	11/30/1996	3 months
UK	M25	4822a	4	9/1/1996	11/30/1996	3 months
UK	M25	4826a	4	9/1/1996	11/30/1996	3 months
UK	M25	4868a	4	9/1/1996	11/30/1996	3 months
UK	M25	4868b	4	9/1/1996	11/30/1996	3 months
UK	M25	4565a	4	1/1/2002	12/31/2002	12 months
UK	M25	4680b	4	1/1/2002	12/31/2002	12 months
UK	M1	2737a	3	2/13/2002	12/31/2002	11 months
UK	M1	2808b	3	2/13/2002	12/31/2002	11 months
UK	M1	4897a	3	2/13/2002	12/31/2002	11 months
UK	M6	6951a	3	1/1/2002	12/31/2002	12 months
MD	I270	2a	3	1/1/2004	5/5/2004	4 months
MD	I95	4b	4	6/1/2004	11/5/2004	6 months
MD	I795	7a	2	1/1/2004	5/5/2004	4 months
MD	I795	7b	2	1/1/2004	5/5/2004	4 months
MD	I695	9a	4	1/1/2004	5/5/2004	4 months
MD	I695	9b	4	1/1/2004	5/5/2004	4 months
MN	I35W-NB	60	4	1/1/2000	12/31/2000	12 months
MN	I35W-SB	578	3	1/1/2000	12/31/2000	12 months
MN	I35E-NB	882	3	1/1/2000	12/31/2000	12 months
MN	I35E-SB	890	3	1/1/2000	12/31/2000	12 months
MN	I69-NB	442	2	1/1/2000	12/31/2000	12 months
MN	I69-SB	737	2	1/1/2000	12/31/2000	12 months
MN	I35W-NB	60	4	1/1/2004	12/31/2004	12 months
MN	I35W-SB	578	3	1/1/2004	12/31/2004	12 months
MN	I35E-NB	882	3	1/1/2004	12/31/2004	12 months
MN	I35E-SB	890	3	1/1/2004	12/31/2004	12 months
MN	I69-NB	442	2	1/1/2004	12/31/2004	12 months
MN	I69-SB	737	2	1/1/2004	12/31/2004	12 months
WA	I5	ES-179D_MN_Stn	4	1/12004	6/29/2004	6 months
WA	I5	ES-179D_MS_Stn	3	1/12004	6/29/2004	6 months
WA	I5	ES-130D_MN_Stn	4	4/1/2004	9/30/2004	6 months
WA	I5	ES-179D_MS_Stn	4	4/1/2004	9/30/2004	6 months
WA	I405	ES-738D_MN_Stn	3	7/1/2004	12/29/2004	6 months
WA	I405	ES-738D_MS_Stn	3	7/1/2004	12/29/2004	6 months

3.3   Determination of the Value K and N

Set distance measure weight $w_1 = 0.67, w_2 = 0.33$. The value range of k is 1 to 15, and the value range of n is 2 to 10. TPE search algorithm is adopted in the search algorithm, and the loss function of hyperopt module is set as MAE. Then the improved K-NN algorithm is run automatically to obtain the optimal k and n values of each station. The results of station 8 and station 9 are shown in Fig. 4.

Table 2. Definition of traffic levels or traffic volume groups (adopted from Guo et al. [4])

Volume groups	Group description	Approximate level of service (LOS)
Group 1	≥ 0 and <500 veh/h/ln	LOS A
Group 2	≥ 500 and <1000 veh/h/ln	LOS B
Group 3	≥ 1000 and <1500 veh/h/ln	LOS C
Group 4	≥ 1500 and <2000 veh/h/ln	LOS D
Group 5	≥ 2000 veh/h/ln	LOS E

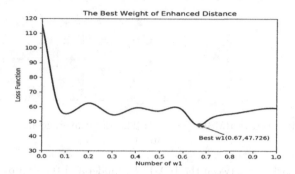

Fig. 3. Effect of w_1 on prediction accuracy

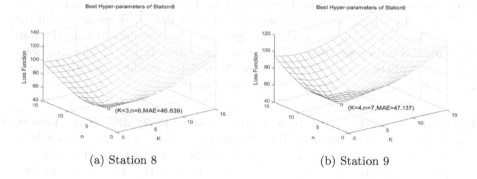

(a) Station 8   (b) Station 9

Fig. 4. Optimal parameters of stations 8 and 9

3.4 Prediction Error Analysis

In order to show the effectiveness of IPA-KNN, the comparison between the IPA-KNN and the improved KNN in reference [5] based on the same traffic data will be shown in this subsection. The MAE, MAPE, RMSE and the new measure of performance of traffic forecasts are used to present the results.

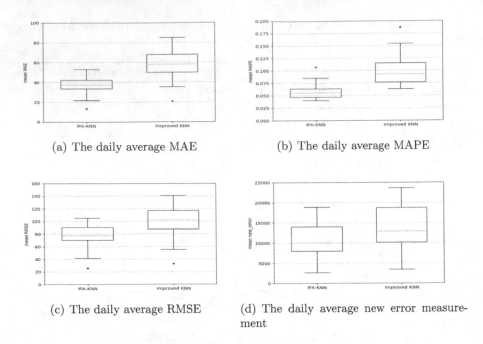

(a) The daily average MAE

(b) The daily average MAPE

(c) The daily average RMSE

(d) The daily average new error measurement

Fig. 5. The comparisons between the IPA-KNN model and the improved KNN model

Comparison of Daily Mean Error Values. The IPA-KNN and the improved KNN model are compared from the perspective of daily average error. All the data in 36 stations are used. The prediction results are measured by the four evaluation criteria respectively. The results are shown in Fig. 5, which indicate that the prediction error of the IPA-KNN model is smaller than that of the improved KNN model under the four evaluation criteria.

Comparison of Error Values Under Different Traffic Flow Levels. According to the provisions in Table 2, the traffic flow of each station will be divided into five groups according to 0, 500, 1000, 1500, 2000 (unit: veh/h/ln). The prediction results are shown in Fig. 6. It is obvious that the prediction error of the proposed model is always lower than that of the improved KNN model. Among the groups with low traffic flow, the advantages of the proposed model are particularly prominent.

Comparison of Error Values Under Different Different Hours Per Day. Considering the practical application of traffic flow, it is also very important to predict traffic flow in different time periods. Therefore, the comparisons of the prediction results of IPA-KNN and improved KNN models grouped by hour are conducted. MAPE and the new error measurement are used to measure the accuracy of prediction. Results are shown in Fig. 7, which also show the effectiveness of IPA-KNN.

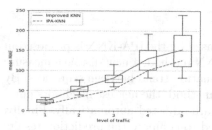

(a) The MAE under 5 traffic flow levels

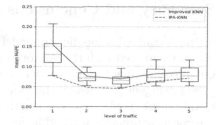

(b) The MAPE under 5 traffic flow levels

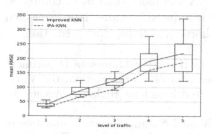

(c) The RMSE under 5 traffic flow levels

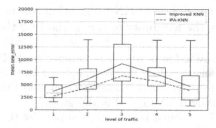

(d) The new error measurement under 5 traffic flow levels

Fig. 6. The comparison between the IPA-KNN and the improved KNN model under different traffic flow levels

(a) The MAPE in different hours per day

(b) The MAPE in different hours per day

(c) The MAPE in different hours per day

(d) The new error measurement in different hours per day

Fig. 7. The comparisons between the IPA-KNN and the improved KNN in different hours per day

4   Summary and Conclusions

A short-term traffic flow prediction model based on the IPA-KNN is proposed in this paper. Compared with the improved KNN method, a new distance measure is adopted considering the similarity of fluctuation trend between sequences. By using the intelligent parameter adjustment method, the nearest neighbors number k and the predicted sequence length n are adjusted automatically. Finally, a new error measurement method is designed to compare the prediction results of the IPA- KNN and the improved KNN model. The results of the data experiments show that the accuracy of the IPA- KNN is more than 95%, compared with the improved KNN algorithm, the error is reduced by more than 4%, which shows the feasibility of the method for the short-term traffic flow prediction.

Acknowledgements. The authors would like to thank the Minnesota Department of Transportation, the Washington State Department of Transportation, the Maryland Department of Transportation, and the United Kingdoms Highways Agency for providing the data used in this study.

The research is supported in part by the National Natural Science Foundation of China (Nos.11701081, 11861060), the Fundamental Research Funds for the Central Universities (No. 2242020K40236), the Jiangsu Provincial Key Laboratory of Networked Collective Intelligence (No. BM2017002), Key Project of Natural Science Foundation of China (No. 61833005) and ZhiShan Youth Scholar Program of SEU.

References

1. Van Lint, J., Van Hinsbergen, C.: Short term traffic and travel time prediction models. In: Artificial Intelligence Applications to Critical Transportation (2012)
2. Vlahogianni, E.I., Karlaftis, M.G., Golias, J.C.: Short-term traffic forecasting: where we are and where we are going. Transp. Res. Part C Emerg. Technol. **43**(1), 3–19 (2014)
3. Cleveland, W.S., Devlin, S.J.: Locally weighted regression: an approach to regression analysis by local fitting. J. Am. Stat. Assoc. **83**, 596–610 (1988)
4. Guo, J., Huang, W., Williams, B.M.: Adaptive Kalman filter approach for stochastic short-term traffic flow rate prediction and uncertainty quantification. Transp. Res. Part C Emerg. Technol. **43**, 50–64 (2014)
5. Habtemichael, F.G., Cetin, M.: Short-term traffic flow rate forecasting based on identifying similar traffic patterns. Transp. Res. Part C Emerg. Technol. **66**, 61–78 (2016)
6. Wang, Y.B., Papageorgiou, M., Messmer, A.: RENAISSANCE - a unified macroscopic model-based approach to real-time freeway network traffic surveillance. Transp. Res. Part C Emerg. Technol. **14**(3), 190–212 (2006)
7. Zhang, W.B., Yu, Y.H., Qi, Y., Shu, F., Wang, Y.H.: Short-term traffic flow prediction based on spatio-temporal analysis and CNN deep learning. Transp. A: Transp. Sci. **15**(2), 1688–1711 (2019)
8. Zheng, L.J., Yang, J., Chen, L., Sun, D.H., Liu, W.N.: Dynamic spatial-temporal feature optimization with ERI big data for short-term traffic flow prediction. Neurocomputing, **38**, 10–11 (2020)

9. Cai, P., Wang, Y., Lu, G., Chen, P., Ding, C., Sun, J.: A spatiotemporal correlative k-nearest neighbor model for short-term traffic multistep forecasting. Transp. Res. Part C Emerg. Technol. **62**, 21–34 (2016)
10. Shi, Y., Deng, M., Yang, X., Gong, J.: Detecting anomalies in spatio-temporal flow data by constructing dynamic neighbourhoods Computers. Environ. Urban Syst. **67**, 80–96 (2018)
11. Huang, W., et al.: Real-time prediction of seasonal heteroscedasticity in vehicular traffic flow series. IEEE Trans. Intell. Transp. Syst. **19**(10), 3170–3180 (2017)
12. Kirby, H.R., Watson, S.M., Dougherty, M.S.: Should we use neural networks or statistical models for short-term motorway traffic forecasting? Int. J. Forecast. **13**(1), 43–50 (1997)
13. Li, Y., Shahabi, C.: A brief overview of machine learning methods for short-term traffic forecasting and future directions. SIGSPATIAL Spec. **10**(1), 3–9 (2018)
14. Mihaylova, L., Boel, R., Hegyi, A.: Freeway traffic estimation within particle filtering framework. Automatica **43**(2), 290–300 (2007)
15. Wang, Z., Ji, S., Yu, B.: Short-term traffic volume forecasting with asymmetric loss based on enhanced KNN method. Math. Probl. Eng. **2019**(722), 1–11 (2019)
16. Williams, B.M., Hoel, L.A.: Modeling and forecasting vehicular traffic flow as a seasonal ARIMA process: theoretical basis and Empirical results. J. Transp. Eng. **129**(6), 664–672 (2003)
17. Habtemichael, F.G., Cetin, M., Anuar, K.A.: Incident-induced delays on freeways: quantification method by grouping similar traffic patterns. Transp. Res. Record **2484**(1), 60–69 (2015)

Agent Systems, Robotics and Control

Some Technical Challenges in Designing an Artificial Moral Agent

Jarek Gryz$^{(\boxtimes)}$

York University, Toronto, Canada
jarek@cs.yorku.ca

Abstract. Autonomous agents (robots) are no longer a subject of science fiction novels. Self-driving cars, for example, may be on our roads within a few years. These machines will necessarily interact with the humans and in these interactions must take into account moral outcome of their actions. Yet we are nowhere near designing a machine capable of autonomous moral reasoning. In some sense, this is understandable as commonsense reasoning turns out to be very hard to formalize.

In this paper, we identify several features of commonsense reasoning that are specific to the domain of morality. We show that its peculiarities, such as, moral conflicts or priorities among norms, give rise to serious challenges for any logical formalism representing moral reasoning. We then present a variation of default logic adapted from [5] and show how it addresses the problems we identified.

Keywords: Moral agents · Artificial life

1 Introduction

When we evaluate software tools and systems with respect to fairness, accountability, and transparency, we engage in their moral evaluation. We assume, at least for now, that such an evaluation is performed by a human, that is, the system itself is not capable of moral reasoning. However, with the rapid progress in the design and development of autonomous agents this assumption may no longer be true. Not only do we need to evaluate software systems from a moral perspective, these very systems will very soon need to perform moral reasoning themselves. One can imagine a self-driving car facing an inevitable collision in which either a pedestrian or an occupant of the car will be killed. Assume furthermore that the only thing the driving agent can do is to maneuver so that only one of them dies. This is a moral decision and it has to be made instantaneously by the agent itself.

The urgency of the design of moral agents has not been lost on AI community. In 2017 at PRIMA a full day was devoted just to the topic: "Can we, and should we, build ethically-aware agents?" As should be clear from the previous paragraph, we believe that this is no longer a question of *whether* but *how*. We need a formal mechanism that will allow an autonomous agent perform moral

© Springer Nature Switzerland AG 2020
L. Rutkowski et al. (Eds.): ICAISC 2020, LNAI 12416, pp. 481–491, 2020.
https://doi.org/10.1007/978-3-030-61534-5_43

reasoning and reach the same (or at least very similar) decisions that a human being would reach in the same circumstances.

There are generally two approaches to design such a mechanism: bottom-up or top-down [12]. In the bottom-up approach, we try to mimic child development: human beings do not enter the world as competent moral agents yet learn enough of that competency within a few years. There have been several projects to simulate artificial life or emergence of social values and one would hope that similar approach would work in developing/simulating morality. There are many unresolved issues with this approach, however. First, psychologists disagree how much influence nature vs. nurture play in developing a theory of morality in children. Second, they disagree what the guiding principle in this development is: reason or empathy. Third, children are subjected to reward and punishment (approval-disapproval) from the society when learning moral behavior; it is not clear what would correspond to those in a machine. In the top-down approach, ethical principles and rules are explicitly stated and an agent simply follows them via an algorithm. Although this approach has its own problems – which we discuss in Sect. 2 – we believe it is more likely to succeed than the bottom-up approach.

The paper is organized as follows. In Sect. 2, we point out several technical challenges in designing and implementing a formalism for moral reasoning in an autonomous agent. In Sect. 3, we present a variation of default logic extended to moral reasoning, which addresses most of the problems we identified. This formalism has been adapted from [5] where it was developed as a solution to practical problem of justifying one's actions, that is, providing reasons for these actions. We conclude with a discussion in Sect. 4 where we point out that default logic still falls short of adequately representing human reasoning as it fails to capture the holistic and open-ended character of such reasoning. We need an empirical study of an actual implementation of a moral agent to determine how serious this issue is. We leave it, however, as an open question in this paper.

2   Challenges

2.1   Choice of Ethics

The first decision a designer of an artificial moral agent faces is the choice of an appropriate theory of normative ethics. Such a theory provides foundations for moral reasoning of the agent. There have been numerous proposals for ethical theories in the history of moral philosophy but the majority of them fall into one of just three categories: consequentialism, deontological ethics, and virtue ethics. Consequentialism emphasizes the consequences of moral actions; deontology emphasizes duties or rules, and virtue ethics virtue or moral character of an agent. The vocabularies used in each of these theories are different too. The language of consequentialism talks of "benefits", "outcomes", "pleasures" and "pains" and they refer to the result of a moral act. The terms from the second set serve in the prescriptive function of a moral code. This function consists in providing answers to questions like: What am I (morally) required to do?

Answers to such questions usually have the grammatical form of an imperative and are called 'prescriptions', 'moral norms', 'rules', 'precepts', or 'commands'. They are expressed by means of such terms as 'right', 'obligation', 'duty', etc. The third class contains terms used for a moral evaluation of an action (or an actor). Terms used for evaluations include 'good', 'bad', 'blameworthy', 'praiseworthy', 'virtuous', etc. Consider how an obligation to keep promises is justified within each of these ethics. A consequentialist might say that keeping promises increases trust in society, which benefits everyone. A deontologist would point out to a duty – stemming from some higher-level rule (e.g. "Do unto others as you would be done by") or perhaps from some religious authority – that we as humans are obliged to observe. A virtue ethicist will emphasize the good character of a person and say that keeping promises is something that a virtuous person would do.

The three theories tend to agree – in most cases – when evaluating moral decisions as right or wrong; after all, they have to agree with our moral intuitions to be acceptable. Still, we should assert again that a designer of an autonomous moral agent faces a critical decision in choosing the theory. The transparency requirement stipulates that we explain why an agent chose a particular course of moral action. So even though all three theories might tell the agent to do the same thing, the reasons for doing so would be radically different. Whether or not these explanations are acceptable by the humans interacting with the agent may thus very well depend on the choice of a theory.

All three theories have been formalized using appropriate logics thus allowing moral reasoning for each ethics (most recently in [2–4]). Pros and cons for each of these three theories have been debated in philosophy for ages. Needless to say, we are not going to engage in this discussion here. In fact, to keep the focus in the paper, we are going to discuss only the deontic ethics as the one, which is the most appropriate for implementation for a moral agent. We have two brief arguments against the competing theories. First, virtue ethics seems out of place in a realm of non-humans: how can one talk about a "good character" or "virtue" of a robot? These terms seem to be strictly reserved for humans; we do not even ascribe them to animals (other than in metaphors). Second, although consequentialism seems the easiest to formalize, computing and ranking utilities or benefits of all possible actions seems hopeless (in fact, incommensurability of the outcomes of actions was one of the main arguments against consequentialism). Thus, in the rest of the paper we discuss the possible implementation of the deontologic ethics only. Still, our choice is somewhat arbitrary so the first challenge is: what ethical theory should an autonomous agent use?

2.2 Deontic Logic and Moral Dilemmas

Historically, the most popular way of formalizing deontological ethics has been via deontic logic. The formalism introduces two operators O and P, which represent obligation and permission respectively. Thus, a statement $O(A)$ means that it is obligatory that A (or it ought to be the case that A). One can also talk about conditional obligations: $O(A/B)$ means that under the circumstances B, it ought to be the case that A.

Although deontic logic has been widely used to formalize moral reasoning, it has a surprising weakness: it rules out the possibility of moral dilemmas. Yet it seems that we often face such dilemmas in our life. Sartre [9] tells of a student whose brother had been killed in the German offensive of 1940. The student wanted to avenge his brother and to fight forces that he regarded as evil. However, the student's mother was living with him, and he was her one consolation in life. The student believed that he had conflicting obligations. Yet when we formalize these obligations in deontic logic as $O(A)$ and $O(\neg A)$, we derive - by standard semantics of that very logic - a statement $O(A \wedge \neg A)$ which is unsatisfiable.

There is still disagreement among moral philosophers whether moral dilemmas might arise. Some of them would claim (we discuss this position in the next section) that what we see as conflicting obligations can always be prioritized; after all, we always manage to choose one over another. Still, it seems an awkward decision to build a philosophical position on moral dilemmas into the logic itself.

Thus, the second challenge is: if we believe that moral dilemmas are real and unavoidable, we need a formalism that represents them (deontic logic cannot).

2.3   Priorities Among Obligations

One can take a strong philosophical position and deny the validity (or at least likelihood) of moral dilemmas. Consider two such norms: "Keep promises" and "Save human lives" and imagine you are walking to teach a class and you see a drowning child in a nearby river. On one hand, you made a promise to your students and university administration that you will teach the class, on the other hand you should try saving the child. You cannot do both. Nevertheless, one can argue that this example does not really represent a moral conflict. Indeed, most likely everyone would agree that saving a child trumps keeping a promise (of any kind). Thus, we can introduce preference order between prima facie oughts and mark it as $A \leq B$ with the meaning that B is more important than A. Does the preference order have a property of strong connectivity, that is, either $X \leq Y$ or $X \geq Y$ for any arbitrary obligations X and Y? This strong connectivity would allow a convenient resolution of any moral conflict. Unfortunately, there is no agreement among moral philosophers whether all obligations are comparable. Some philosophers claim that any moral conflict can be resolved while others think that moral dilemmas are real and unavoidable. Most of us faced moral choices where it was not clear at all which obligation was stronger so our ordinary intuitions tell as that at least some obligations are incomparable.

However, even if we believe that all obligations are comparable, we can still face a moral conflict of two obligations that cannot be satisfied at the same time. Think of a single norm that is a source of two obligations. In the example of the self-driving car, there is one such norm, "Save human life" that is a source of two distinct obligations "Save person X" and "Save person Y". How do we handle this problem for an autonomous agent? The agent can either make no choice between the two obligations (do nothing) or choose randomly between them (toss a coin). Neither of these options seems satisfactory. The first option may simply be not available to an agent. In our example the self-driving car has to choose who dies - it does not have an option of not deciding. On the other hand, if the agent chooses randomly, its moral reasoning is, legally speaking, deplorable and unacceptable. We do not leave moral decisions to chance. It seems then, that we must rank all obligations in a strict order so that an agent always has a clear choice of action.

An interesting aspect of our moral life is that we are able to offer reasons why we give preference to one obligation over another. And often, due to these higher-level reasons, we reverse previously held preferences. For most of us, the obligation "You shall not kill" is likely to have the highest priority among all moral obligations. However, even that one – again, for most of us – loses its status at the time of war or in self-defense. So perhaps, we should allow the strict preference among obligations to be dynamic as well, that is, allow some flexibility with respect to the context in which an agent operates.

Thus, the third challenge is: how do we (or can we) arrange all obligations an agent may encounter in a strict preference order that can be dynamically adjusted in different contexts?

2.4 Moral Reasoning Is Defeasible

One of the most interesting features of moral reasoning is its defeasible character. Consider again the example when I walk through campus to teach a class. I have not reached the river yet and the only obligation I am under now is to keep the promise to start my lecture on time. When I reach the river, I notice that a child is drowning. I redo the moral reasoning, reach a new conclusion that my obligation is to save the child and withdraw the conclusion about the obligation to keep the promise to teach the class. In other words, adding a new premise to my reasoning (a proof) made me abandon the previous conclusion. We use this type of reasoning almost every day; we may hold a certain moral opinion about some event only to change it in light of new facts.

There is yet another way our reasoning can be defeasible. The general rule describing the obligation to save human lives clearly has some exception (this is precisely why this is a general rule and not a hard obligation). When I walk by a drowning child and I see the police already at the scene I am no longer obliged to assist. I should also not save the child when I will put my own life in danger or when I cannot physically get to the river due to a physical barrier, etc. Every moral norm has exceptions. We are obliged to follow a norm unless and until we learn that an exception to the norm applies.

This is rather unusual for logic. The consequence relation of a classical logic is monotonic: if a formula p is a consequence of a set of formulas S, then p is also a consequence of $S \cup \{r\}$, for an arbitrary formula r. In other words, the set of conclusions we can draw from the premises grows monotonically with an addition of new formulas to the premises. In particular, a proof of a formula cannot be invalidated by adding a new formula to the derivation. But this is not the case in common sense reasoning, in particular, moral reasoning. This type of reasoning cannot be captured by classical or even modal logic, which is often taken as a foundation of deontic logic. We need a different type of logic where monotonicity no longer holds.

Of course, we can avoid this challenge when the world of the autonomous agent is completely static, that is, no updates take place in the database describing the world around the agent. Clearly, this is not a realistic assumption for most applications.

Thus, the fourth challenge is: how do we formalize defeasibility of moral reasoning?

2.5   Ought Implies Can

One cannot expect anyone to do something impossible. Kant formulated this principle in the context of ethics as: "The action to which the "ought" applies must indeed be possible under natural conditions". In other words, if I am obliged to save a drowning child, I must be able to do so in a particular situation. It is surprisingly difficult, however, to specify what conditions have to be satisfied to make me able to save the child. For example, I cannot be handicapped, I have to have access to the river, I have to be able to swim well, the river should be slow moving rather than a torrent, etc. It is pretty much impossible to tell when this list is complete. Indeed, this problem has been identified many years ago in the context of planning in AI as the qualification problem [6]: to plan an action we need to know what initial conditions have to be satisfied for this action to succeed. The famous example in that context was the problem of necessary conditions to start a car: the battery is charged, there is gas in the tank, the exhaust pipe is not blocked, nobody has stolen the engine at night, etc. Ordinary logic could not solve that problem for actions in general and it is unlikely that it could do so for moral actions in particular.

Thus, the fifth challenge is: what practical conditions have to be satisfied to say that an agent is under a moral obligation to perform a certain action?

3   Default Logic to the Rescue

3.1   Default Logic

Default logic was originally proposed in [7] to solve planning problems in classic AI. The idea behind default logic was to account for some aspects of our commonsense reasoning. We tend to learn about the relationships in the world by making sweeping generalizations, such as all swans are white or all birds fly. And then, when we see a black swan or learn about ostriches, we retract or qualify our previous claims. In this sense, common sense reasoning is non-monotonic: a conclusion set need not grow monotonically with the premise set. If we could formalize this type of common sense reasoning, then we might be able to account for intricacies of moral reasoning.

In addition to standard rules of inference, default logic adds default rules, which represent defeasible generalizations. A default rule has the form $\alpha \rightarrow \beta$, where α is a premise and β is the conclusion. The meaning of the rule is: if α has been already established, one can add β to the set of conclusions assuming that this set is consistent with β. A default theory is a pair $\Delta = <W, D>$, in which W is a set of ordinary formulas and D is a set of default rules. Consider again the generalization "all birds fly". This can be represented as a default rule, such that $\sigma = B(x) \rightarrow F(x)$ with the meaning if x is a bird, then x flies unless we have information to the contrary. Thus, if all we know about *Tweety* that it is a bird, we conclude that *Tweety* flies. Once we learn, however, that *Tweety* is an ostrich (hence does not fly, formally, $\neg F(Tweety)$), we cannot draw a conclusion that *Tweety* flies, as it is inconsistent with what we already know. Within AI, default rules were designed to address the qualification problem, the problem of formulating useful rules for commonsense reasoning amidst a sea of qualifications and exceptional circumstances. Going back to the example from Sect. 2.5, we want to be able to say that turning the key starts the car without having to specify all the exceptions to the rule. If any of these exceptions do occur, they will simply block the application of the default (just like *Tweety's* being an ostrich blocks the rule that it flies).

To accommodate new rules of inference, the standard concept of logical consequence has to be modified.

Definition 1. *The conclusion set Γ associated with a default theory $\Delta = <W, D>$ is called an extension and is defined as a fixed point:*

$$\Gamma = \sum_{n=1}^{\infty} \Gamma_i$$

where:

$$\Gamma_0 = W$$
$$\Gamma_i = Th(\Gamma_i) \cup \{B | A \rightarrow B \in D, A \in Th(\Gamma_i), \neg B \notin \Gamma\}$$

and Th(i) is a set of standard logical consequences of i.

The idea behind this definition is that we first conjecture a candidate extension for a theory, Γ, and then using this candidate define a sequence of approximations to some conclusion set. If this approximating sequence has Γ as its limit, Γ is indeed an extension of the default theory.

A default theory can have multiple sets of conclusions, that is, extensions. A famous example [8] of this case is called the Nixon Diamond: Nixon is a republican but he is also a Quaker. Republicans tend not to be pacifists and Quakers tend to be pacifists. As a default theory, these facts can be stated as: $W_1 = \{Q(Nixon), R(Nixon)\}$ and $D_3 = \{\sigma_1 : Q(x) \rightarrow P(x), \sigma_2 : R(x) \rightarrow \neg P(x)\}$. This theory has two extensions, one with $P(Nixon)$ and one with $\neg P(Nixon)$. Both conclusions are equally valid, yet they cannot be both entertained at the same time. This seems like a natural description of commonsense reasoning which cannot be captured in classical logic.

This formalism can be enriched by adding priorities between defaults. If we believe that being a republican is an extremely strong indication of being non-pacifist (at least much stronger than being a Quaker is an indication of being a pacifist), then we can state that $\sigma_1 < \sigma_2$ with the meaning that if these two default rules apply at the same time, only the second will fire. Our extension will contain only the fact that Nixon is not a pacifist.

3.2   Obligations in Default Logic

How exactly do we represent formally obligations in default logic? Let $O(A)$ be an obligation "You should do A".[1] This can be represented as a default rule $\sigma : \mathbf{T} \to A$ (**T** stands for tautology which means that the obligation is unconditional).

Definition 2. *Let* $\Delta = <W, D>$ *be a default theory and the default,* $\sigma : \mathbf{T} \to A \in D$ *represents an obligation. Then* $O(A)$ *follows from* Δ *just in case* $A \in \Gamma$, *for some extension* Γ *of this theory.*

Default logic can represent conflicts between obligations in a straightforward way. Consider again the example of encountering a drowning child on the way to a lecture. We can represent two relevant obligations as default rules $\sigma_{life} = O(L)$ and $\sigma_{promise} = O(P)$ with the meaning respectively "you should save human lives" and "you should keep promises". We are assuming here, of course, that these two obligations are logically incompatible in this particular context, which can be expressed as $O(P) \Rightarrow O(\neg L)$ and $O(L) \Rightarrow O(\neg P)$.[2] If we do not prioritize between these two default rules our theory will have two incompatible extensions (just like in the Nixon example), one telling us to save the child, $O(L)$, the other one telling us to walk to the lecture, $O(P)$. On the other hand, if we prioritize between these two default rules by saying that saving human lives is more important than keeping promises, that is, $\sigma_{promise} < \sigma_{life}$, then we will only have one extension containing the statement that you should save the child.

We assumed so far that the priority relations among default rules representing obligations are fixed in advance. As discussed in Sect. 2.3, however, we would like to have some flexibility in setting these priorities, that is, to be able to adjust the order depending on a context. Default logic offers a straightforward mechanism to do just that. Instead of stating $\sigma_1 < \sigma_2$ as a matter of fact, we can add it as a default rule to the set of other defaults. Formally, we would express it as $\mathbf{T} \to \sigma_1 < \sigma_2$ with the meaning "Obligation σ_2 has a higher priority than obligation σ_1 unless we have the information to the contrary" .

Default logic allows us to represent defeasibility of moral reasoning in two different ways. First, an obligation may be blocked by exceptions. I am under an obligation to save a drowning child unless I know that an exception to that rule applies, for example, the police are already at the scene. The concept of default extension from Definition 1 ("the rule applies unless I have information to the

---

[1] We rely on [5] for ideas and formalism of this section.
[2] We use '$\Rightarrow$' for standard logical implication.

contrary") conveys exactly that intuition. The second type of defeasibility arises through a dynamic change of applicable obligations (default rules). Consider again the scenario described in Sect. 2.4. Initially, $\sigma_{promise}$ is the only default rule that applies (we have not yet seen the drowning child) and we keep walking to the lecture. Then, when our database of facts gets updated and σ_{life}, which has a higher priority than $\sigma_{promise}$ applies as well, we retract the obligation that we should walk to the lecture from and introduce instead the obligation of saving the child.

To summarize, under the interpretation of obligations in default logic, we can account for:

1. Moral conflicts (challenge 2): incompatible obligations lead to multiple incompatible extensions.
2. Priorities among obligations (challenge 3): they are represented as priorities among default rules.
3. Defeasibility of moral reasoning (challenge 4): exceptions will prevent a default rule from firing a default rule with a higher priority will invalidate (make it inapplicable) another default rule with a lower priority.
4. Qualification problem (challenge 5): default logic was originally introduced to handle this problem (we assume an action is doable unless we have information to the contrary).

4 Discussion and Open Issues

Default logic is not a perfect solution to codifying commonsense reasoning. It solves many problems that classical logic could not, yet it leads to some counterintuitive results in other cases. Consider the following example that illustrates the famous *multiple extension problem*. Tom is a spy. As a human being, he ought to tell the truth. However, he is also a spy and spies routinely lie (or at least are not expected or required to tell the truth). Common sense would tell us that Tom is not required to tell the truth. The fact that he is a spy is more relevant to what we expect him to do than the fact that he is human. According to default logic, however, both extensions (one with Tom required to tell the truth and the one without this obligation) are equally valid. What was considered an advantage in the case of Nixon Diamond (both extensions seemed reasonable) is clearly a flaw here. Default logic in the form described above does not distinguish between extensions unless we put priorities between defaults. Thus, consider prioritizing between these two defaults by making lying more important to spies than telling the truth to humans. But is it always more important? Should Tom lie to his physician about his health or to his wife about picking up their son from school? Clearly, priorities between defaults/obligations do not hold universally but *depend* on context. We need to be able to tell when Tom's being a spy – hence his non-obligation to tell the truth - is relevant for each context. But the concepts of context or relevance cannot be codified in logic and implemented in a software system.

Let us take stock. We proposed default logic as a way of implementing moral reasoning. This formalism accounts for a number of features typical of moral reasoning that other types of logic, such as deontic logic, cannot handle. Yet we also discovered that the conclusions reached via default logic are sometimes counterintuitive and only an appeal to a context or relevance can provide an intuitive and correct result. So how do we, the humans, discover the relevant context? Most of it we probably learn from experience, some of it may be innate. The crucial question for AI is how this knowledge is stored and processed. In great majority of our actions, we do not consciously think through our plans. In fact, the relevant knowledge rises to the surface only when we make mistakes and need to reconsider our course of action or plan an entirely novel action. But even in these cases, introspection is not of much use. We do not ponder upon facts one by one; we are somehow capable to pay attention only to the relevant ones. Also, our information processing is so fast that it cannot involve drawing thousands of interim conclusions. We operate on a portion of our knowledge at any moment and that portion cannot be chosen by exhaustive consideration. A great discovery of AI is the observation that a robot (a computer) is the fabled tabula rasa [1]. For it to operate in a real world, it must have all the information explicitly specified and then organized in such a way that only the relevant portion of it is used when it is time to act. So far, we have no idea how to do that. The problem, in a nutshell, is this: "How is it possible for holistic, open-ended, context-sensitive relevance to be captured by a set of propositional, language like representation of the sort used in classical AI?" [10].

What then are the chances of building a moral machine? We believe that the conclusions should not be all negative. AI faces the problem of the holistic and open-ended reasoning only for the holistic and open-ended environment. However, when it restricts its attention to microworlds, that is, well defined and fully described cuts or aspects of the world it works very well. In fact, recent successes in areas such as face or voice recognition systems are already a source of much anxiety because they work so well. Our conjecture then is this: if we restrict the domain of an autonomous agent to a well-defined environment, it has a good chance of working correctly in that environment. In particular, if we specify the relevant knowledge necessary for moral reasoning in that environment one may expect to circumvent the multiple extensions problem. Nonetheless, only an empirical evaluation of an actual system implementing default logic can tell how close we are to building a moral machine.

References

1. Dennett, D.: Cognitive wheels: the frame problem in AI. In: Pylyshyn, Z. (ed.) The Robot's Dillema, pp. 41–64. Ablex Publishing Corporation (1987)
2. Oesterheld, C.: Formalizing preference utilitarianism in physical world models. Synthese **193**(9), 2747–2759 (2015). https://doi.org/10.1007/s11229-015-0883-1
3. Gabbay, D., Horty, J., Parent, X., et al.: Handbook of Deontic Logic and Normative System. Blackwell, Oxford (2013)

4. Govindarajulu, N., Bringsjord, S., Ghosh, R., Sarathy, R.: Toward the engineering of virtuous machines. In: AIES Conference (2019)
5. Horty, J.: Reasons as Defaults, Oxford (2012)
6. McCarthy, J.: Applications of circumscription to formalizing commonsense knowledge. Artif. Intell. **28**, 86–116 (1986)
7. Reiter, R.: A logic for default reasoning. Artif. Intell. **13**, 81–132 (1980)
8. Reiter, R., Criscuolo, G.: On interacting defaults. In: Proceedings of IJCAI (1981)
9. Sartre, P.: Existentialism is a Humanism. Meridian, New York (1957)
10. Shanahan, M.: The frame problem. plato.stanford.edu/entries/frame-problem. Accessed 7 Mar 2020
11. Touretzky, D.S.: Implicit ordering of defaults in inheritance systems. In: AAAI Conference (1984)
12. Wallach, W., Allen, C.: Moral Machines. Oxford University Press, Oxford (2009)

Hierarchical Intelligent-Geometric Control Architecture for Unmanned Aerial Vehicles Operating in Uncertain Environments

Mikhail Khachumov[1,2]([⊠]) (iD)

[1] Federal Research Center "Computer Science and Control" of RAS,
44/2 Vavilova St, 119333 Moscow, Russian Federation
khmike1986@gmail.com
[2] Peoples' Friendship University of Russia (RUDN University),
6 Miklukho-Maklaya St, 117198 Moscow, Russian Federation
khachumov_mv@rudn.university

Abstract. This paper considers the cutting-edge scientific problem of controlling unmanned aerial vehicles (UAVs) in unstable conditions based on intelligent-geometric theory that combines geometric control methods (methods of optimal control, complex motion control and stabilization, trajectory tracking, differential pursuit-evasion games, etc.) with intelligent control methods using tools of artificial intelligence (productions, semantic networks, fuzzy logic, frame-based behavioral microprograms and operations, methods of knowledge acquisition, etc.). Such integration provides reliable and high-performance control techniques for operating in uncertain environments under wind disturbances. Hierarchical architecture of intelligent-geometric control system is proposed, designed for joint application of precise geometric and adaptive intelligent control methods as parts of a single robotic system. In accordance with the proposed architecture, the solution to the problem of controlling a UAV group taking into account mathematical models of an aircraft and wind loads was simulated in MATLAB Simulink system.

Keywords: Geometric control · Intelligent control · Unmanned aerial vehicle · Hierarchical architecture · Trajectory tracking · Pursuit-evasion · Productions · Behavioral microprograms · Uncertain environment

1 Introduction

1.1 Motivation

Studies in the field of control and automation of robotic systems, including UAVs, are conducted in many research centers around the world. Currently there is a

This research was supported by RFBR, projects No. 17-29-07003 (strategic control level); No. 18-07-00025 (tactical control level) and by the "RUDN University Program 5-100" (conducting experiments).

L. Rutkowski et al. (Eds.): ICAISC 2020, LNAI 12416, pp. 492–504, 2020.
https://doi.org/10.1007/978-3-030-61534-5_44

strong need for the development of theory, algorithms, and programs to solve the most challenging problem—to provide control autonomy when performing complex missions under imposed restrictions in an unstable environment. Despite the existence of a considerable number of papers concerning state-of-the-art approaches to the synthesis of control algorithms, the problem has not yet been resolved. The complexity of the problem lies in the fundamental impossibility to obtain accurate enough mathematical models of aerial vehicles as well as an external dynamic environment, low precision of data coming from sensors under disturbances. The analysis of the up to date achieved results showed that proposed methods are scattered and manage to cope with separate tasks.

In this paper, a novel concept of an intelligent-geometric control system is proposed, designed for joint application of accurate geometric and flexible intelligent control methods complementing each other within a single robotic system.

1.2   Related Works

Main features of an intelligent system are a high degree of autonomy, the ability to sustainably maintain or achieve necessary system states (goal) under external factors that perturb these states or prevent their achievement.

One of the promising areas in the field of intelligent robotics and group control is a fuzzy rule-based knowledge representation paradigm. In papers [1,2] the authors consider intelligent motion control approach for UAVs based on fuzzy rules, which can rapidly react to changes in the real dynamic environment. Despite the advantages of these methods, in order to successfully implement them onboard, much more attention should be given to accounting for the real external conditions, in particular, wind loads. There is a strong need for developing intelligent and adaptive control algorithms for aerial vehicles with limited computing resources operating in disturbed environment.

The development of a model of knowledge representation and processing in a general form, irrespective of a specific subject area, is considered to be one of the major challenges of creating intelligent UAVs able to perform goal-seeking actions under uncertainty [3]. The need for such a knowledge representation arises with regard to the complexity in forming a detailed model of an undetermined environment. In that respect, vehicles have to adapt to the current operating conditions, which is impossible to ensure without presenting knowledge in a general form. In other words, it is required to present knowledge model in a manner that would enable UAV to adapt to the current environmental conditions through clarifying this model in the process of goal-seeking activity.

Geometric control theory is a cutting-edge field that recently has been actively developing. A major contribution to the theory was made in papers [4,5]. It solves one of the major problems of control theory - the controllability problem, which implies finding a control function to drive the state of the system to a prescribed target state at a finite time. Admissible trajectories and reachable sets are closely related to the group of geometric transformations formed by dynamical systems. In relation to UAV control problems, a geometric control approach is applied to optimize trajectory tracking [6], solve stabilization [7], cooperation [8] and other group control problems.

Reviewing the related works on geometric control architectures shows that most up-to-date approaches require detailed information about the system dynamics. Considering that UAV dynamics is nonlinear and complex, the mathematical statements of control problems and existing exact and approximate methods of their solutions are time-consuming. In addition, dynamics uncertainties and external disturbances affect the system, and given the limited computing resources of small autonomous UAVs, the development of simple in realization, but effective control algorithms becomes of paramount importance. We expect that onboard intelligent control algorithms in conjunction with accurate geometric control methods can provide an acceptable accuracy of solutions to control problems for vehicles operating in non-deterministic environments.

An essential and actively researched issue is to design an efficient architecture for intelligent robotic systems. Multilevel architectures, as a rule, inherit the principles stated in paper [9], which describes functional elements and interaction protocols for a three-level control system. The SOAR cognitive architecture is an example of a multilevel approach [10] that has been used to design intelligent agents with rational behavior operating in a dynamic environment. A modern approach to designing three-level architecture of an intelligent aircraft control system, combining various methods and models for solving applied problems, is considered in [11].

In this paper, as an extension of these studies, a new hierarchical architecture of an intelligent-geometric control system is proposed designed to operate in cluttered environments accounting for uncertain external conditions and vehicle's limitations.

1.3 Main Contributions

The proposed theory integrates state-of-the-art achievements of geometric control methods (in terms of controlling and stabilization of complex UAV motions taking into account its mathematical model and geometric calculations for predicting and optimizing motion paths) with artificial intelligence methods (in terms of dynamic planning and controlling in unstable operating conditions). We believe such integration can significantly contribute to solving complex dynamic problems, including challenging applied tasks for UAVs, such as dynamic planning, trajectory optimization, pursuit and tracking dynamic goals in a non-deterministic perturbed environment.

The scientific novelty of the study is determined by new models and methods developed in the framework of intelligent-geometric control theory for the representation and replenishment of knowledge (sets of production rules, frame-based behavioral microprograms and frame-based operations), motion planning and controlling. The achievements in the field of geometric control theory are used to formulate and solve optimization problems and to implement complex trajectory motion of vehicles.

We expect that the proposed architecture, novel models, and methods can significantly increase the autonomy, reliability, and control efficiency for unmanned vehicles functioning in uncertain conditions.

2   The Principles of Intelligent-Geometric Control

2.1   The Purpose of Intelligent-Geometric Control

Geometric control theory explores the possibilities of applying differential geometric methods to dynamical systems control. The prerequisites for its study are linear algebra, vector calculus, differential geometry, and non-linear control theory. The term "geometric" suggests important system concepts, for example, controllability, as geometric properties of the state space or its subspaces.

Suppose that M is a smooth manifold, and U an arbitrary subset of R^m. An optimal control problem in geometric theory, as usual, is formulated as follows [4]: *minimize the cost functional J among all admissible controls $u = u(t), t \in [0; t_1]$, for which the corresponding solution $q_u(t)$ of Cauchy problem*

$$\dot{q} = f_u(q), \ q \in M, \ u \in U \subset R^m,$$
$$q(0) = q_0, \ q(t_1) = q_1, \tag{1}$$

satisfies the boundary condition $q_u(t_1) = q_1$, where

$$J(u) = \int_0^{t_1} \varphi(q(t), u(t))dt \rightarrow \min \tag{2}$$

A solution u of this problem is called an optimal control, and the corresponding curve $q_u(t)$ is an optimal trajectory.

In the present paper, the concept of "geometric control" also has a slightly different meaning. It is associated with solving several trajectory optimization problems for UAVs (as physical or virtual control objects). One of them deals with an accurate geometric calculation of heading to meet with the target. Because the pursued object can arbitrarily change its direction, the problem is solved by using the parallel approach strategy. A similar problem with imposed time constraints takes place in a pursuit-evasion game [12].

The problem is even more complicated if one considers external disturbances, and, in our opinion, it can be solved by integrating geometric and intelligent control methods. Of significant interest are multi-point path tracking, under disturbances and control restrictions, when the task is to optimize time, path length, and deviation. In such conditions to track "ideal" trajectories obtained by solving optimization problem, it's advisable to apply intelligent control methods (in particular, production rules that imitate the actions of a human operator). Such a combined principle, covering all hierarchical control levels of an autonomous UAV, is called in the present paper as "intelligent-geometric control".

The problem is to develop a unified theory of intelligent-geometric control, and to create within it:

- conceptual architecture of an intelligent-geometric control system;
- accurate geometric methods for calculation of heading vectors and points of convergence;
- adaptation and stabilization methods that provide the required control quality in a dynamic environment with disturbances;
- knowledge representation and acquisition methods under uncertainty;
- control methods aimed at solving practical problems of situational modeling and trajectory planning for UAVs.

2.2 Hierarchical System to Control a Dynamic Object

The principle of hierarchy assumes the presence of three levels of abstraction to solve various-scale control problems (see Fig. 1).

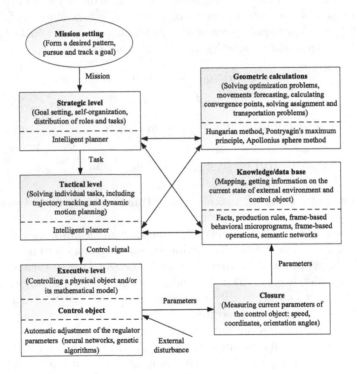

Fig. 1. Block diagram of an intelligent-geometric control system

Strategic level solves the issues of choosing global goals (goal-setting), control modes, and distribution of tasks and roles. Tactical level solves the tasks given by strategic level to an individual UAV, in particular, tracking a given trajectory under wind disturbances, static and dynamic motion planning under uncertainty, and pursuing a target. At this level, specific control signals are generated, which are transmitted to the executive level for processing by a control object.

The integrated database contains necessary facts, current model parameters, and variable values. The knowledge base stores production rules (that define the conditions under which the particular controls are generated in compliance with the current goal), frame-based behavioral microprograms, frame-based operations, semantic networks. Knowledge acquisition is carried out by a special intelligent technology in the process of UAVs functioning.

The low-level control unit changes the settings to transit the dynamic system into a new state. System's response time (transients) limits the time to measure and analyze current state parameters and timely update of the database. It is assumed that the intelligent control loop operates in integration with the geometric control loop. Geometric control methods are aimed at accurate calculation of motion trajectories, while intelligent control methods at planning the behavior and tracking the trajectories to cope with conditions of uncertainty and significant external disturbances.

To improve dynamic properties and stabilize the motion of the controlled object (UAV), we introduce a special module for adaptive tuning of PID controller coefficients. The combined control approach is implemented in the framework of a single hierarchical control system.

2.3   Strategic Control Level

At a strategic level, we propose a new knowledge representation model, which allows specifying knowledge presented in a general way for adaptation to environmental conditions. We propose a model for the representation and processing of procedural knowledge of an intelligent UAV in the form of typical frame-based behavioral microprograms (FMPs), which could overcome disadvantages of some well-known logic models [13]. The developed procedural knowledge model is based on the logic of conditional predicates [3].

In general, the area of allowable values of variable $y_i(X_i) \in Y$, $Y = \{y_i(X_i)\}$, $i = \overline{1, m}$ is determined by a set of features X_i that defines valid constants (specific objects and events). If we describe each object or event $O = \{o_j(X_j)\}, j = \overline{1, m_1}$ by its features X_j then substitution of objects or events $o_j(X_j) \in O$ for variables $y_i(X_i) \in Y$ is valid if and only if the condition "$X_i \subset X_j$" is met. In conditionally dependent predicates logic, an arbitrary multiple variable formula $M[y_1(X_1), \ldots y_k(X_k), \ldots y_n(X_n)]$ is true if and only if all constants $a_k(X_{a_k})$ substituted for variables $y_k(X_k) \in M$ meet the conditions "$(X_k \subset X_{a_k})$".

Thus, an intelligent solver in the current environment is able to verify an arbitrary statement. Let us form a standard FMP Q^* "Perform an operation b_j on a given object $y_i(X_i)$". We extend this procedure with:

- environmental conditions that must be met to successfully perform operations included in FMP;
- references for the transition to typical elements of procedural knowledge, that contain operations allowing to achieve necessary conditions;
- formalized description of the result obtained after completing corresponding operations.

Frame-based microprogram has the following structure: "Identifier" "Procedures" "Exit". The identifier allows one to select appropriate FMP by the structure of binary relations between UAVs and environmental objects. Such structure can change while performing operations included in a microprogram. FMP procedures contain conditions that must be fulfilled to successfully perform operations included in those procedures. The output of an FMP is given in the form of a semantic network labeled with connection values between environmental objects and UAVs that are obtained when operations included in its procedures are processed. The structure of FMP Q^* can be represented in the form of a logic scheme as follows:

$$P_1^* \overset{1}{\uparrow} b_1(y_i(X_i)) \overset{2}{\downarrow} P_2^* \overset{34}{\uparrow\downarrow} b_2(y_i(X_i)) \overset{51}{\uparrow\downarrow} Q_1^* \overset{23}{\uparrow\downarrow} Q_2^* \overset{45}{\uparrow\downarrow} \rightarrow \text{objective is achieved,} \quad (3)$$

where Q^* is the microprogram identifier;

P_1^* is the operator that checks the condition "if there are any obstacles preventing UAV from getting close to object $y_i(X_i)$";

$b_1(X_i)$ is the operator "get close to object $y_i(X_i)$";

P_2^* is the operator that checks the condition "if object $y_i(X_i)$ is located within visibility zone";

$b_2(X_i)$ is the operator "perform operation b_2 on object $y_i(X_i)$";

Q_1^* is the microprogram "plan and track trajectories to approach the object $y_i(X_i)$ in the presence of obstacles";

Q_2^* is the microprogram "ensure fulfillment of condition P_2^*".

Labeled arrows indicate the direction of the transition between operators when the conditions P_i^* given before initial operator are not met.

The automatic planning of advisable behavior in an uncertain environment comes down to:

1. Replacement of subject variables with real objects. Such variables are treated as slots functions in conditionally dependent predicates forming the structure of FMP-body. This model allows the vehicle to concretize general purpose knowledge for planning advisable activities in current operating conditions.
2. Planning advisable activity through verification of corresponding conditions that determine whether operations included in FMP-structure can be efficiently performed. As a result, a chain of operations is formed allowing the vehicle to achieve its objective under specific operating conditions.

Thus, to provide an intelligent UAV with the necessary functional scope, the knowledge model can be given in the form of a set of FMPs. Such a model allows a vehicle to significantly reduce the search space of fairly complex tasks by selecting effective operations at each step of behavioral planning.

2.4   Tactical Control Level

At a tactical level, to track a given trajectory (or target), we propose geometric methods to forecast and calculate the points of convergence between UAV and pursued object (in particular, with a reference target), as well as production rules that allow UAV to form behavior strategies under uncertainties. One of the effective methods of intelligent-geometric theory to solve trajectory tracking problem is associated with introducing of a so-called "pseudo-target" or a set of dynamic pseudo-targets that imitate a "reference" trajectory motion and solving the optimization problem of pursuing these targets.

Let the state $Q_{p_i}(t)$ of each UAV $p_i \in P = \{p_1, \ldots, p_n\}$ at time instant t is described by the following variables: coordinates $(x_i(t), y_i(t), z_i(t))$, speed $v_i(t)$ and orientation angles of pitch $\theta_i(t)$, and yaw $\psi_i(t)$. Suppose that an ideal trajectory of each p_i is given by the motion of a "pseudo" target $c_i \in \{c_1, \ldots, c_n\}$ and is represented by a sequence of reference points (x_{ij}, y_{ij}, z_{ij}), $i = \overline{1, n}$, $j = \overline{1, m}$. Pseudo-targets c_i simulates ideal motions along the given paths by passing from one reference point to the neighbor one. Each UAV pursues its target guided by the selected strategy and the ability to control the velocity and direction. As a result of wind perturbations, aerial vehicles could deviate, even appreciably, from the required routes. The desired time of passing through the reference points t_{ij}, $i = \overline{1, n}$, $j = \overline{1, m}$ and that of traveling the whole path T_i are known. We assume for the simplicity that each UAV have two speed modes $v_{p_i}^{(1)} > v_{c_i}$ and $v_{p_i}^{(2)} = v_{c_i}$. The angles of pitch θ_i and yaw ψ_i are established within the permissible limits $[\theta_{min}, \theta_{max}]$ and $[\psi_{min}, \psi_{max}]$, respectively. Suppose that $P_i(t)$, and $C_i(t)$ are the coordinates of UAV p_i and pseudo-target c_i and $d(P_i(t), C_i(t))$ is the distance between them at the instant t. We consider a geometric model of a vehicle as a sphere of radius R (with some safety margin). Safety distance between two vehicles is determined by the value $d(P_i(t), P_j(t)) \geq 2R$.

The problem consists in synthesizing the control $U_{p_i}(t) = (v_i(t), \theta_i(t), \psi_i(t))$ for each UAV p_i on the time interval $[0, T_i]$ under control constraints, such that

$$\sum_{i=1}^{n} \left(\int_{t=0}^{T_i} d(P_i(t), C_i(t)) dt \right) \to \min, \tag{4}$$

where $\forall i, j,\ i \neq j,\ d(P_i(t), P_j(t)) \geq 2R$.

An approach to solving the problem is based on applying geometric methods (analysis of the location of scene participants; analysis and forecasting of their movements, determination of the point of convergence) in combination with intelligent control methods (strategies imitating behavior of the pilot realized by sets of rules) taking into account imposed control restrictions and disturbances.

The problem of forecasting the point of pursuer and target convergence can be solved geometrically by constructing spheres of Apollonius [14]. In the case when the target changes its direction, we use "parallel approach" [12] strategy based on replanning pursuer's heading by calculating new orientation angles. The proposed method of calculating the point of convergence and the "parallel approach" strategy can be applied to solve the problem of dynamic target tracking in a perturbed environment for a group of UAVs.

Algorithm 1. Pseudo-code of the strategy for pursuing a pseudo-target

---

Require: Variable parameters—$Q_{i,t}$ (UAVs states, formed by $p_{i,t}$ = $(x_{i,t}, y_{i,t}, z_{i,t})$ (location), $v_{i,t}$ (speed), $\theta_{i,t}, \psi_{i,t}$ (pitch and yaw angles)), $vw_i = (vw_i^{(x)}, vw_i^{(y)}, vw_i^{(z)})$ (wind vector), strategy_approach (*true* corresponds to approach strategy, *false* - to tracking strategy), d_i (distance between UAV p_i and its pseudo-traget), $d_{i,j}$ (distance between UAVs p_i and p_j); constants — n (number of UAVs), $angle\_constraints_i = (\theta_{i min}, \theta_{i max}, \psi_{i min}, \psi_{i max})$ (permissible range of pitch and yaw angles), v_i', v_i'' (speed modes), $Qc_{i,t}$ (pseudo-target states, formed by $c_{i,t} = (xc_{i,t}, yc_{i,t}, zc_{i,t})$ (location), $vc_{i,t}$ (speed), $\theta c_{i,t}, \psi c_{i,t}$ (pitch and yaw angles)), T (mission time), Δt (duration of one clock period (step)); ε (the minimum distance at which the task of approaching the pseudo-target is accomplished), R (safety margin).

Ensure: $\mathbf{U_i} = (v_i, \theta_i, \psi_i)$ that minimize $\mathbf{d_i}$ in a time period $[0, T]$ under given constrains.

1: Initialize current UAVs states:
2: **for** each $i = 1$ to n (all vehicles p_i in a group) **do**
3:    $x_{i,0} = xc_{i,0}$; $y_{i,0} = yc_{i,0}$; $z_{i,0} = zc_{i,0}$;
4:    $v_{i,0} = vc_{i,0}$, $\theta_{i,0} = \theta c_{i,0}$, $\psi_{i,0} = \psi c_{i,0}$;
5: **end for**
6: **for** simulation time $t = 0$ to T **do**
7:    **for** iteration loop $i = 1$ to n **do**
8:       **for** iteration loop $j = 1$ to n **do**
9:          $d_{i,j} = get\_distance(p_{i,t}, p_{j,t})$;
10:       **end for**
11:    **end for**
12:    **for** each $i = 1$ to n (all vehicles p_i in a group) **do**
13:       preprocessing of the data required for further calculations:
14:       $vw_i = generate\_wind\_load(Q_{i,t})$;
15:       $(\theta_i^{(1)}, \psi_i^{(1)}) = approach\_angles(d_i, Q_{i,t}, Qc_{i,t})$;
16:       $(\theta_i^{(2)}, \psi_i^{(2)}) = tracking\_angles(d_i, Q_{i,t}, Qc_{i,t})$;
17:       transition of the system into a new state, which is triggered by a control impulse with the step Δt:
18:       $x_{i,t+1} = x_{i,t} + v_{i,t} \cos(\theta_{i,t}) \cos(\psi_{i,t}) + vw_i^{(x)}$;
19:       $y_{i,t+1} = y_{i,t} + v_{i,t} \cos(\theta_{i,t}) \sin(\psi_{i,t}) + vw_i^{(y)}$;
20:       $z_{i,t+1} = z_{i,t} + v_{i,t} \sin(\theta_{i,t}) + vw_i^{(z)}$;
21:       selecting allowable controls in accordance with the current task:
22:       **if** $(\exists j, \; d_{ij} < 2R \text{ or } d_i > \varepsilon)$ **then**
23:          strategy_approach = true;
24:       **end if**
25:       **if** $(\forall j, \; d_{ij} \geq 2R \;\&\; d_i \leq \varepsilon)$ **then**
26:          strategy_approach = false;
27:       **end if**
28:       **if** $(strategy\_approach = true)$ **then**
29:          $v_{i,t+1} = v_i'$, $\theta_{i,t+1} = \theta_i^{(1)}$, $\psi_{i,t+1} = \psi_i^{(1)}$;
30:       **else**
31:          $v_{i,t+1} = v_i''$, $\theta_{i,t+1} = \theta_i^{(2)}$, $\psi_{i,t+1} = \psi_i^{(2)}$;
32:       **end if**
33:    **end for**
34: **end for**
35: **return** $\mathbf{U_i} = (v_i, \theta_i, \psi_i)$;

A simplified pseudo-code (Algorithm 1) is given below for solving the problem (4) based on a set of production rules (expert knowledge) that determine pursuers' strategy [15]. Here, *generate_wind_load* is the function that generates wind loads depending on a UAV location, *approach_angles* calculates angles of approach $(\theta_i^{(1)}, \psi_i^{(1)})$ to the pseudo-target by using approximate point of convergence, *tracking_angles* calculates angles $(\theta_i^{(2)}, \psi_i^{(2)})$ to track ideal trajectory taking into account wind loads. This algorithm forms the basis of the UAV control system and is experimentally tested in the MATLAB Simulink system.

2.5 Simulation Scheme and Experiments

The general simulation scheme implemented in MATLAB Simulink system for controlling motion of each UAV in the group that takes into account wind loads and the mathematical model of UAV dynamics is shown in Fig. 2 [14].

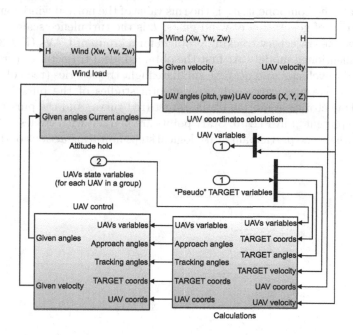

Fig. 2. Simulation scheme for controlling the motion of a UAV.

Block "*Attitude hold*" as an input receives orientation angles to be held under perturbations. The block outputs current $\theta_i(t)$ and $\psi_i(t)$ UAV angles.

Block "*UAV coordinates calculation*". In this model, the position of each UAV at time instant t depends on its coordinates at the previous time instant $t - 1$ and the following parameters: UAV given velocity, angles $\theta_i(t)$, $\psi_i(t)$, wind velocity $vw_i(t)$. This block outputs current velocity $v_i(t)$ and coordinates $(x_i(t), y_i(t), z_i(t))$ of the UAV.

Block "*Wind load*" simulates longitudinal and normal wind loads.

Block "*Pseudo TARGET variables*" outputs current $(x_{c_i}(t),\ y_{c_i}(t),\ z_{c_i}(t))$ coordinates, angles $\theta_{c_i(t)}$, $\psi_{c_i}(t)$, and velocity $v_{c_i}(t)$ of the pseudo-target c_i.

Block "*Calculations*" outputs approach angles $\theta_i^{(1)}(t)$, $\psi_i^{(1)}(t)$ and tracking angles $\theta_i^{(2)}(t)$, $\psi_i^{(2)}(t)$.

Block "*UAV control*" synthesizes particular controls according to the current state of the system.

Block "*UAVs state variables*" allows one to predict collisions in a group of UAVs and to avoid them by applying special rules.

We use MATLAB Simulink to simulate mission execution for a UAV group operating in a perturbed environment. The model of UAV motion is defined by the transfer functions that describe a double-circuit control system with an autopilot [15]. The longitudinal and normal wind actions are modeled by the correlation functions: $R_t(\tau) = \sigma_t^2 \exp^{-|V|\tau/L}$, $R_n(\tau) = \sigma_n^2(1 - 0.5|V|\tau/L)\exp^{-|V|\tau/L}$, where $|V|$ is the mean airspeed; σ_t is the rms value of the longitudinal wind component; σ_n is the rms value of the normal wind component; τ is the period of generation of wind gusts; L is the turbulence scale.

We solve the trajectory tracking problem for a group of UAVs (Fig. 3a) using the above mentioned models. At first the obtained ideal trajectories (grey color) are assigned to vehicles and next we simulate flight trajectories (red color) under disturbances. We also carry out experimental studies of the pursuit-runaway problem. Trajectories of motion of the target (red curve) and the pursuers (grey curves) are presented in Fig. 3b. Start points are marked with circles. The figure shows that the scene participants take logical steps imitating actions of the pilots.

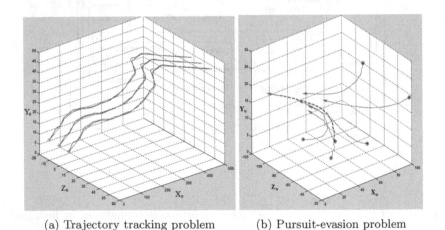

(a) Trajectory tracking problem   (b) Pursuit-evasion problem

Fig. 3. Simulation of mission execution.

The figures demonstrate the effect of wind loads on motion trajectories. As one can see, control rules enable UAV to respond promptly to changes in the environment and successfully cope with the tasks.

3 Conclusion

This paper describes methods and models of intelligent-geometric control theory applied to autonomous UAVs operating in a disturbed environment. We propose a hierarchical architecture of intelligent-geometric control system combining the methods of geometric and intelligent control theories as parts of a single robotic system. At a strategic level, we propose original approaches and tools for organizing advisable behavior of a UAV group and a new knowledge representation model, adaptable to current operating conditions. At a tactical level, to track a given trajectory (or target), we propose geometric methods to forecast and calculate the points of convergence between UAV and pursued object (in particular, with a pseudo-target), as well as production rules that allow UAV to form behavior strategies under uncertainties. The conducted experimental studies confirm the feasibility and prospects of the developed theory.

References

1. Sabo, C., Kelly, C.: Fuzzy logic unmanned air vehicle motion planning. Adv. Fuzzy Syst. **2012**, 1–14 (2012)
2. Liu, Z., Zhang, Y., Yuan, C., Ciarletta, L., Theilliol, D.: Collision avoidance and path following control of unmanned aerial vehicle in hazardous environment. J. Intell. Robot. Syst. **95**(1), 193–210 (2018). https://doi.org/10.1007/s10846-018-0929-y
3. Melekhin, V.B.: Model of representation and acquisition of new knowledge by an autonomous intelligent robot based on the logic of conditionally dependent predicates. J. Comput. Syst. Sci. Int. **58**(5), 747–765 (2019). https://doi.org/10.1134/S1064230719050101
4. Agrachev, A., Sachkov, Y.: Geometric Control Theory. FIZMATLIT, Moscow (2005)
5. Andrew, D.: Fundamental problems in geometric control theory. In: IEEE Conference on Decision and Control, pp. 1–18 (2012)
6. Lee, T., Leok, M., McClamroch, N.: Geometric tracking control of a quadrotor UAV for extreme maneuverability. IFAC Proc. Vol. **44**, 6337–6342 (2011)
7. Goodarzi, F.: Self-tuning geometric control for a quadrotor UAV based on lyapunov stability analysis. Int. J. Robot. Autom. **5**(3), 1–15 (2016)
8. Lee, T., Sreenath, K., Kumar, V.: Geometric control of cooperating multiple quadrotor UAVs with a suspended payload. In: IEEE Conference on Decision and Control (2013)
9. Albus, J.: 4D/RCS: a reference model architecture for intelligent unmanned ground vehicles. In: Proceedings of SPIE. Unmanned Ground Vehicle Technology IV, The International Society for Optical Engineering (2012)
10. Laird, J.: The Soar Cognitive Architecture. MIT Press, Cambridge (2012)

11. Emelyanov, S., Makarov, D., Panov, A., Yakovlev, K.: Multilayer cognitive architecture for UAV control. Cogn. Syst. Res. **39**, 58–72 (2016)
12. Pontryagin, L., Mishchenko, A.: The linear differential game of pursuit (analytic theory). Math. USSR-Sbornik **59**(1), 131–158 (1986)
13. Khachumov, M., Melekhin, V., Pankratov, A., Andreychuk, A.: The use of frame-based microprograms for planning the behavior of an intelligent unmanned aerial vehicle in an uncertain environment. In: The 1st Workshop (Summer Session) in the framework of the Conference on Information and Telecommunication Technologies and Mathematical Modeling of High-Tech Systems, pp. 79–86 (2018)
14. Khachumov, M.V.: Solution of the problem of group pursuit of a target under perturbations (spatial case). Sci. Tech. Inf. Process. **45**(6), 435–443 (2018). https://doi.org/10.3103/S0147688218060047
15. Abramov, N., Makarov, D., Khachumov, M.: Controlling flight vehicle spatial motion along a given route. Autom. Remote Control **76**(6), 1070–1080 (2015)

Challenging Human Supremacy: Evaluating Monte Carlo Tree Search and Deep Learning for the Trick Taking Card Game Jass

Joel Niklaus[1]([✉]) [iD], Michele Alberti[1], Rolf Ingold[1] [iD], Markus Stolze[2] [iD], and Thomas Koller[3] [iD]

[1] Document, Image and Video Analysis Research Group (DIVA),
University of Fribourg, Fribourg, Switzerland
{joel.niklaus,michele.alberti,rolf.ingold}@unifr.ch
[2] User-Interface Software Technology Lab (UIST-Lab),
University of Applied Sciences Rapperswil, Rapperswil-Jona, Switzerland
markus.stolze@hsr.ch
[3] Algorithmic Business Research Team (ABIZ),
University of Applied Sciences Lucerne, Luzern, Switzerland
thomas.koller@hslu.ch

Abstract. Despite the recent successful application of Artificial Intelligence (AI) to games, the performance of cooperative agents in imperfect information games is still far from surpassing humans. Cooperating with teammates whose play-styles are not previously known poses additional challenges to current state-of-the-art algorithms. In the Swiss card game Jass, coordination within the two opposing teams is crucial for winning. Since verbal communication is forbidden, the only way to transmit information within the team is through a player's play-style. This makes the game a particularly suitable candidate subject to continue the research on AI in cooperation games with hidden information. In this work, we analyse the effectiveness and shortcomings of several state-of-the-art algorithms (Monte Carlo Tree Search (MCTS) variants and Deep Neural Networks (DNNs)) at playing the Jass game. Our key contributions are two-fold. First, we provide a performance overview for state-of-the-art algorithms, thus, setting a strong foundation for further research on the subject. Second, we implement and open-source (https://gitlab.enterpriselab.ch/jass/info) a platform where different agents (both humans and AI) can play Jass in an automated fashion, effectively reducing the overhead for other researchers who want to perform further experiments.

Keywords: Jass · Schieber · Card game · Artificial Intelligence (AI) · Machine Learning (ML) · Monte Carlo Tree Search (MCTS) · Information set · Determinization · Convolutional Neural Network (CNN) · Deep Neural Network (DNN) · Rule-based

J. Niklaus and T. Koller—Equal contribution.

© Springer Nature Switzerland AG 2020
L. Rutkowski et al. (Eds.): ICAISC 2020, LNAI 12416, pp. 505–517, 2020.
https://doi.org/10.1007/978-3-030-61534-5_45

1   Introduction

In recent years, numerous breakthroughs have taken place in the field of research for AI in games. In particular, in the perfect information games division, where all players are familiar with the entire game state at all times, computers prevail over skilled human players on various occasions, such as Chess [4], the Atari games [6] or Go [9].

When it comes to imperfect information games, where players do not know some of the facts, such as in card games, there is a thin line separating AI from people who still have the upper hand over state-of-the-art bots. Hidden information is also present in many real-world scenarios, such as business, negotiations, physics, surgery, and others. Many of these situations can be formalized as games that, in turn, can be solved using the methods developed in the card games testbed.

Recent work has shown that the distance between humans and AI is becoming smaller in constrained situations. This is particularly evident when considering developments on Texas hold'em no-limit poker [2] and the StarCraft II computer game[1]. The multiplayer computer game Dota 2 includes hidden information and team play. Although OpenAI Five won against world champions in a 5 vs. 5 game, collaboration remains as an open research area in AI[2].

To instill AI systems with collaboration, card games may be a very suitable testbed since they a) include hidden information, b) frequently have a collaborative aspect, and c) are computationally easy to simulate because they have a finite set of actions.

Motivation

Jass is a trick-taking card game featuring hidden information. In the 4-player Schieber variant, good coordination within the team is crucial for achieving victories in top tournaments.

DeepMind introduced the Hanabi Challenge, opening a new frontier in AI research using the fully cooperative card game Hanabi [1]. In Hanabi, the players need to lay down cards in order having only the knowledge of the other players' cards. Therefore, the players need to work together to be able to win the game. Jass combines both a cooperative and a competitive aspect as it includes two competing teams of two cooperating players.

Since Schieber has approximately $1.16e28$ states after the cards have been dealt (see Sect. 2.2) and additionally it is not known in what state the player is because of the hidden cards, the game is computationally complex.

Jass is a very popular Swiss card game and is closely associated with Swiss culture. It is also similar to other games like the American Spades, the British Bridge, and the German Skat. Thus research in Jass is valuable for many other domains.

---

[1] https://deepmind.com/blog/article/alphastar-mastering-real-time-strategy-game-starcraft-ii.

[2] https://openai.com/blog/how-to-train-your-openai-five.

In contrast to Bridge, Skat, or Hearts, in Schieber, it is always allowed to play trump, even when the player can still follow suit, increasing the branching factor. Additionally, in Schieber there are 3 players with hidden cards and not only 2 (no dummy player). Finally, not only the number of tricks taken matter, but the points of the cards taken in the trick count for the final score (e.g. the Ace is worth 11 and the 7 is worth 0 points). These properties make the card play phase of Schieber harder than the one of Bridge. This also makes the implementation of a Rule-Based (RB) solver on open cards challenging.

Contributions

1. We perform an analysis of the most promising state-of-the-art methods for AI in card games (Determinized MCTS (DMCTS), Information Set MCTS (ISMCTS), DNN and RB).
2. We lay the groundwork for further research on AI in Jass.
3. We release public open-source software infrastructure (see Sect. 5.2) and an API, so anyone can quickly connect their bots and test them both against other bots as well as against human via a GUI.

2   The Jass Game

Jass is a traditional Swiss card game that is trick-taking and often played at social events. It involves hidden information, both a cooperative (cooperation within the team) and a non-cooperative aspect (two opposing teams), is sequential, finite, and constant-sum (since in each game there are always 157 points).

2.1   The Schieber Variant

The Schieber variant, our testbed, is one of the most widely played variants of Jass in Switzerland. It is played with two opposing teams of two players each. Each round consists of a trump selection phase and a consecutive card play phase. Since choosing a trump is a significant advantage, tournaments are played by a fixed number of rounds (divisible by 4) so that each player can choose trump an equal number of times. Trump selection implies that the selecting player can determine one of the four suits as trump or alternatively no trump with the card precedence top down or bottom up respectively. The player can also decide to pass the decision on to his teammate. This is called "schieben" and gave the name to the game. The Swiss Intercantonal Lottery provides a guide for general Jass rules[3] and for the variant Schieber specifically[4].

---

[3] https://swisslos.ch/en/jass/informations/jass-rules/principles-of-jass.html.
[4] https://swisslos.ch/en/jass/informations/jass-rules/schieber-jass.html.

Terminology. 4 played cards are called a *trick*, 9 tricks are a *round* (all 36 cards played) and a *game* lasts for 1000 points, or in tournaments for a number of rounds. When a player *passes* in trump selection, the partner can nominate the trump.

2.2 Complexity

In Schieber, the number of possible paths through the game tree is $36! = 3.72e41$ since there are 36 cards in the game because every card is only played once, and the order matters.

At the beginning of the game the cards are being dealt randomly to the players. There are $\binom{36}{9}\binom{27}{9}\binom{18}{9}\binom{9}{9} = 2.15e19$ possibilities to distribute the 36 cards to 4 stacks. After the cards have been dealt, each player knows their cards, so the possible distributions of the other cards are $2.28e11$.

To estimate the number of possibilities that a round can be played, we gathered empirical evidence from 1.8 million played rounds to determine the number of valid plays permitted by the rules for each of the 36 cards played. We found $5.1e16$ possible playouts, so the number of states that an algorithm has to deal with after receiving the cards is in the order of $5.1e16 \cdot 2.28e11 = 1.16e28$.

3 Related Work

In this section, we provide a short overview of the research done in AI development for card games with hidden information and cooperative elements.

[8] applied Upper Confidence Bound for Trees (UCT) to Doppelkopf reaching par-human (on par with average humans) performance. We compare the performance of UCT with a DNN implementation at the example of the similar trick-taking card game Jass. Applying DMCTS to the multiplayer games Spades and Hearts, [10] reported similar performance to the state-of-the-art at that time in Spades and slightly better performance in Hearts. He noted that random rollouts outperformed RB rollouts. Similarly, we investigate the effectiveness of random rollouts in comparison to RB rollouts and also the output of the value function of a DNN trained on data obtained from human games. [12] applied DMCTS and ISMCTS to Dou Di Zhu reaching comparable performance. In this work, we compare different DMCTS configurations with different ISMCTS configurations and additionally with DNNs and RB baseline algorithms. Using ISMCTS, [11] presented a high-human (on par with the best humans) AI for the Italian card game Scopone consistently beating strong RB players.

[7] provided an overview of current state-of-the-art methods and discussed them from a theoretical point of view. In our work, we implement the most prominent methods (DMCTS, ISMCTS, DNN, and RB) and show their different strengths and shortcomings in a new setting.

Super-human performance has not yet been achieved in the current state-of-the-art in AI for card games with hidden information and cooperative aspects. In none of these games, a complete analysis of the relevant methods has been carried out. To the best of our knowledge, there has not yet been presented any general AI capable of achieving high performance in more than two of these games.

4   Methods

4.1   Monte Carlo Tree Search

In their literature review, [7] found MCTS variants to be the most promising methods for trick-taking card games like Jass. MCTS is a successful algorithm for perfect information games [3]. It incrementally builds a search tree for the next few actions and estimates the value of a new node by simulating the game to the end using a rollout policy. Over time, the value of a node becomes the average of all the simulations that passed through it. The decision which part of the tree to extend uses a tree policy that balances exploration and exploitation, guided by the exploration hyper parameter c.

[3] provide a detailed MCTS family overview. MCTS cannot directly be applied to imperfect information games. DMCTS (Sect. 4.2) and ISMCTS (Sect. 4.3) are two major extensions addressing this problem.

4.2   Determinized Monte Carlo Tree Search

A common approach for imperfect information games is to assign values to the unobservable variables and then apply perfect information search methods. For MCTS this sampling is called *determinization*, leading to DMCTS. By sampling and searching multiple states, a more accurate evaluation can be performed. For each sampling, MCTS is performed using a number of iterations. DMCTS shows the most promising results for imperfect information trick-taking card games according to the literature [7].

4.3   Information Set Monte Carlo Tree Search

Another possibility to adapt MCTS to imperfect information games is ISMCTS [5]. In ISMCTS only a single tree is used for all determinizations and each node in the tree represents an *information set*. The information set captures all states of the games that are indistinguishable for the current player based on his knowledge of the game. This results in a tree where the children are determined not by a single determinization, but by all possible determinizations encountered so far.

To incorporate ISMCTS in the MCTS algorithms, first a determinization is calculated like in DMCTS. Then in the selection phase of MCTS, only children valid with the current determinization are considered.

An advantage of ISMCTS is that only a single tree is used so that in later determinization, we expect parts of the tree to be reused, whereas DMCTS starts with a new tree each time. On the other hand, the branching factor of the tree in ISMCTS gets much larger, making it harder to obtain a deeper search tree.

4.4 Deep Neural Network

In contrast to search based methods, Supervised Learning (SL) methods use data from played games to directly learn the best actions or to determine the expected result from an action. For SL we use a DNN, explained in more detail in Sect. 6.2.

5 General Setup

5.1 Data Sets

Data for training and evaluation was taken from Swisslos' online platform, where users can play the game both registered and anonymously. The data has been collected over a period of 6 months, starting in October 2017 and consists of about 1.8M played rounds. It is split into training, validation, and test sets with a ratio of 0.6:0.2:0.2 by random selection. Since plays from the same round are correlated, we further split the files into records for single card plays and shuffle them randomly. From this data set, we filtered out plays by all players that performed less than average, i.e., did not get an average score of 78.5 points. The resulting data set contains about 14M card plays in the training set and about 4.8M card plays in the test and validation sets.

5.2 Technical Infrastructure

We publish repositories for a Jass server (deployment[5] and sources[6]) that can run games and tournaments and display the results, as well as a Python development kit to implement algorithms. Any bot implementing a REST API[7] can be connected to the Jass server. We also provide a GUI[8] allowing humans to play on the Jass server[9].

5.3 Tournament Setup

Friendly Jass matches are played until an agreed number of points is reached. Tournaments, however, are usually played for a number of rounds, and the number of points over all rounds are accumulated.

In many card games like Jass, Bridge and Skat, cards are dealt at random in the beginning, and it is much easier to get more points with a good hand than with a bad one. This randomness makes it hard to compare the absolute strength of players. We address this issue in our experiments by dealing the cards dealt to the North/South pair in the first game to the East/West pair in the second

---

[5] https://jass-server.abiz.ch.
[6] https://gitlab.enterpriselab.ch/jass/info.
[7] https://github.com/JoelNiklaus/JassTheRipper/blob/master/JassInterface.pdf.
[8] https://github.com/JoelNiklaus/jass-server.
[9] https://jassteppich.abiz.ch.

round, which we call a *double round*. We compare the performance of two bots against each other by playing 10 times 100 rounds (= 50 double rounds) and report the mean and the Standard Deviation (STD) of the accumulated score over the 100 rounds. The p-value has been calculated with an unpaired t-test.

6   Implementation

6.1   Monte Carlo Tree Search

We implemented both a time-based and an iteration-based version of DMCTS. Unless specified otherwise we used random simulators for the rollouts. We call non-random rollouts *heavy rollouts* (e.g. RB or DNN).

The Time-based DMCTS (T-DMCTS) uses a time budget as a termination criterion for the search, so it can easily be compared to other bots with the same resources. Its implementation is publicly available on Github[10]. It uses a ranked RB trump selection passing if no trump surpasses a given threshold.

The Iteration-based DMCTS (I-DMCTS) uses a configurable number of determinizations and MCTS iterations, independent of the time budget, to enable testing of different configurations. Results for different numbers of determinizations and iterations are given in Sect. 8.1. Our ISMCTS implements Single Observer ISMCTS (SO-ISMCTS) using the same framework as the I-DMCTS.

6.2   Deep Neural Network

Card Play Network. We trained a DNN to perform 3 different tasks using SL. We a) predict the action a, i.e. the card played by a player as a policy function $p(a|s_o)$, b) the value function $v(s_o)$ and c) the card distribution probability $p_{card}(\text{player} = i|c)$ that the card c was in the hand of player i at the beginning of the game. s_o describes the current state of the game observable by the player.

A single single Convolutional Neural Network (CNN) was used with 3 different heads and loss functions. The input to the DNN is a 4×9 matrix of 43 channels containing all the information available to the player. This consists of the cards that have been played so far and in which trick and by which player, the cards in the hand of the current player and the valid cards to play, as well as who declared trump, how many cards have been played so far and how many points has each team achieved.

Training was done for 200 epochs using an Adam optimizer achieving an accuracy of 0.78 for the policy, 0.77 for the card distribution and Mean Squared Error (MSE) of 0.016 for the value function.

We use the card-distribution prediction in variants of the search algorithms as Probability DMCTS (P-DMCTS) and Probability ISMCTS (P-ISMCTS) to draw cards according to the predicted distribution during determinization (see Sect. 8.3). The value function is used as a card play algorithm by evaluating all valid cards and selecting the one with the highest value.

---

[10] https://github.com/JoelNiklaus/JassTheRipper.

Trump Selection Network. Trump selection was trained by a different DNN that uses only the cards in the hand of a player as input, as well if the player is the first or second player of the team to be asked to declare trump. The network consists of two fully connected layers with 592 channels followed by a fully connected layer with 7 channels. The accuracy of the network reached 0.82 on the validation set.

7   Value Estimation Comparison

In this section we compare different methods to estimate the value of a current game state. We assume that estimating the value better leads to a better overall card play performance.

Setup. After DMCTS samples a determinization, the algorithm is in a perfect information game situation, so all the cards are known. To evaluate algorithms in this setting, we omit the sampling and give them the perfect information of the card distribution. The experiment is performed on the validation set.

The DNN Max Policy is used to compute a heavy rollout, resulting in a score of the game at the end of the round. The DNN Value gets the value directly by taking the output of the value head. We also list Flat Monte Carlo (MC) with different numbers of random simulations. Finally, different numbers of MCTS iterations with random rollouts are shown.

Results. Figure 1 shows the results of the different investigated methods. While the improvement from Flat MC with 10 simulations to 25 is evident, the improvement of 25 to 1 K simulations is only marginal. The DNN policy rollout does not give significantly better results than using Flat MC with 1 K simulations or 100 MCTS iterations. The DNN value function seems to be comparable to 5K MCTS iterations in the first 8 cards. Later in the round, its performance drops in comparison. The accuracy of the MCTS based value estimation improves continually with the number of iterations.

Analysis. Flat MC does not seem to scale as well in accuracy as MCTS. Overall, already 100 MCTS iterations outperform both Flat MC with 1 K random simulations and the DNN Max Policy rollout. The DNN Value function is comparably strong in the beginning of the round but then drops in relative accuracy. The difference between the investigated methods is particularly evident in the first few tricks (0 to 24 cards played). Our analyses show that this phase is also the most crucial time in a round. The further the round progresses, the easier it becomes to play optimally and thus the difference between different bots becomes smaller.

8   Experiments Between Bots

In Sect. 8.1 we describe experiments with DMCTS hyper parameters. Since Jass consists of two distinct phases (trump selection and card play) we can also separately evaluate our bots in these two phases, explained in detail in Sect. 8.2

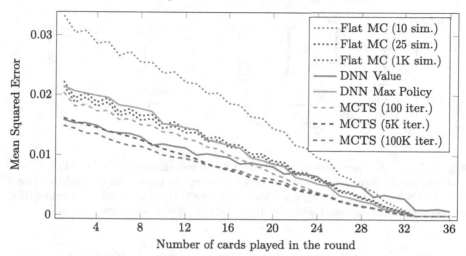

Fig. 1. We calculated the MSE between the estimated value from the algorithm and the actual outcome at the end of the round. Since the validation set contains 4.8M card plays in total it contains 133K card plays per game stage (number of cards played) on average. Each data point therefore represents the mean of the MSEs of these 133K card plays.

and 8.3 respectively. In all of these experiments between bots we used double rounds (as described in Sect. 5.3) to reduce randomness. Note that already a small difference in points between two teams can lead to a victory in a Jass game.

8.1   Hyper Parameters for DMCTS

We conducted several experiments to find the best hyper parameters for DMCTS. Given a specified number of iterations to be performed, or a specific time constraint, we investigate if it is better to have a larger number of determinizations, thus exploring many different card configurations, or if it is better to devote more resources to the MCTS giving a more accurate result for the cards.

Determinizations and Iterations. Figure 2 shows an overview of the performance of DMCTS with different allocations of a fixed budget against DNN Max Policy. The budget is 800K iterations (e.g., 20K determinizations with 40 iterations each, or 500 determinizations with 1600 iterations each). We find that an increase in the number of determinizations is beneficial up to a certain point ($p = 0.015$ for 1K × 800 and 500 × 1600). However, further increasing the number of determinizations to over 1K shows no improvement.

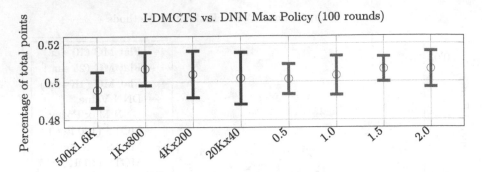

Fig. 2. Different configurations of I-DMCTS playing against DNN Max Policy. The first four results (blue) show different ratios between the number of determinizations d and MCTS iterations i ($d \times i$), while the last 4 results (red) show different exploration parameters c each executed with $d = 1000$ and $i = 1000$. (Color figure online)

Scalability. In Sect. 7 we saw that a bigger number of MCTS iterations can increase the accuracy of estimating the value at the end of the game. In this paragraph we present an experiment that checks if more iterations and more determinizations really are beneficial to the overall card play strength (measured in percentage of total points).

Table 1 shows different combinations of iterations and determinizations of DMCTS against DNN which allows us to interpret the scalability properties of DMCTS. With 25 determinizations there is a strong improvement from 25 to 100 iterations ($p < 0.01$). However, our data does not clearly support an improvement from 100 to 10 K iterations ($p = 0.29$). Yet, for 100 determinizations, there is an increase from 100 to 10 K iterations ($p = 0.023$). Increasing both the determinizations and the iterations clearly has a positive effect on the overall card play strength ($p < 0.0001$ for 25×25 to $1K \times 1K$). When the number of determinizations or iterations are high though ($1K \times 1K$ to $10K \times 1K$ and to $1K \times 10K$), our data does not support clear claims. It would be very interesting to see how the card play strength changes from 1Kx1K to $10K \times 10K$ and further to $1M \times 1M$. However, running experiments in these dimensions are very costly ($10K \times 10K$ would take 600h (25 days) on a 8 core machine running 16 threads).

8.2   Trump Selection Phase

Setup. To evaluate the trump selection methods, we let four different trump selection methods play against each other while using the same deterministic card play algorithm DNN. The four trump selection methods we tested were the following: First, the *Random* chooses the trump completely randomly. The *Simple RB* method tries to estimate the number of certain tricks that can be won. The *Ranked RB* implements a ranking algorithm and is used in T-DMCTS. The *MCTS* method considers the trump selection as just another move in the

Table 1. Percentage of total points of I-DMCTS playing against DNN with different number of determinizations and iterations and exploration constant 1.5.

Iterations	Determinizations			
	25	100	1K	10K
25	48.07 ± 0.85	48.76 ± 1.58	49.45 ± 1.00	50.02 ± 1.34
100	49.53 ± 1.10	49.92 ± 0.66	49.89 ± 1.21	49.55 ± 0.97
1K	50.11 ± 1.27	50.30 ± 0.93	50.65 ± 0.66	50.75 ± 1.34
10K	49.98 ± 0.71	50.79 ± 0.89	50.38 ± 1.02	Very costly

tree to be searched. Finally, the *DNN* performs trump selection as described in Sect. 6.2.

Results. The results are shown in the Table 2 for playing 100 rounds 10 times as described in Sect. 5.3. DNN achieves the best results, while the more elaborate RB algorithm based on the ranking is only slightly worse ($p = 0.063$ for DNN and Ranked RB).

Analysis. Trump selection is important, since even a simple algorithm is much better than random selection, so a good bot must combine good trump selection and card play. MCTS based trump selection method and rarely passes, which may be a reason for it to perform worse than the DNN method ($p = 0.012$).

We analyzed the choices of the MCTS based trump selection method and noticed that it rarely passes. This may be a reason for it to perform worse than the DNN method ($p = 0.012$).

Table 2. Percentage of total points of different trump selection algorithms playing against DNN trump selection.

Bot	Result (%)
Random	34.19 ± 2.02
Simple rule-based	47.69 ± 0.82
Ranked rule-based	49.26 ± 1.11
MCTS	48.23 ± 1.98

8.3   Card Play Phase

Setup. To evaluate the different card play algorithms, we let them play against each other with the settings described in Sect. 5.3. The DMCTS and ISMCTS are the bots as described in Sect. 4. The RB bot[11] is a baseline bot and builds on

---

[11] https://github.com/Murthy10/pyschieber/tree/master/pyschieber/player/challenge_player.

the Jass Challenge environment released by the Software Engineering company Zühlke[12]. It won the Zühlke Jass Challenge Competition in 2017. The T-DMCTS RB rollouts uses RB rollouts instead of random rollouts. The random bot selects a random card while using DNN for trump selection, the Max Value bot evaluates the value network for each valid card out of 1000 card distributions and plays the card with the highest value. The P-DMCTS and P-ISMCTS bots use the probability distributions of the cards from the DNN and draw cards according to this distribution instead of random cards. The cheating MCTS has access to the hidden information (the cards of the other players) and is added as an upper bound.

Results. Table 3 displays the results of the different bots against both the DNN and the T-DMCTS method. The bots are configured with their best settings; comparisons between different settings have been explored in Sect. 8.1.

Analysis. As expected, knowledge of the unknown cards is precious, which can be seen in the big jump in strength by the cheating MCTS player. However, surprisingly, having access to the probability distributions of the cards does not improve the card play strength compared to just sampling random cards ($p = 0.046$ for P-DMCTS and I-DMCTS and $p = 0.17$ for P-ISMCTS and ISMCTS). Rather, the variance increases, suggesting that there are both occasions where the DNN guessed the distribution of the cards correctly and others where it did not.

Table 3. Percentage of total points of different bots against T-DMCTS and DNN Max Policy respectively. The dash represents an incompatibility in the testing infrastructure.

Bot	Against T-DMCTS	Against DNN
Random	34.06 ± 1.05	33.77 ± 0.92
RB	41.45 ± 1.15	–
DNN Max Value (1000)	–	40.50 ± 1.00
DNN Max Policy	49.84 ± 0.76	50.07 ± 0.68
ISMCTS	48.46 ± 2.09	45.33 ± 0.80
P-ISMCTS	–	44.62 ± 1.37
T-DMCTS RB Rollouts	49.18 ± 0.93	–
I-DMCTS	50.19 ± 1.67	50.65 ± 0.95
P-DMCTS	–	49.52 ± 1.36
Cheating MCTS	59.00 ± 0.64	59.70 ± 1.05

---

[12] https://github.com/webplatformz/challenge.

9   Conclusion and Outlook

We provide a comparison of the most widely used methods in trick-taking card games at the example of the Schieber variant of the Swiss card game Jass. In the trump selection phase, empirical evaluation suggests that the DNN slightly outperforms the ranked RB method. In the card play phase, we found that the similarly strong DMCTS and DNN outperform the random baseline, a robust RB bot and also ISMCTS. Future work could take the challenging task of recruiting strong human teams for a detailed evaluation of the bots against humans.

References

1. Bard, N., et al.: The Hanabi challenge: a new frontier for AI research. CoRR abs/1902.00506 (2019)
2. Brown, N., Sandholm, T.: Superhuman ai for multiplayer poker. Science **365**(6456), 885–890 (2019). https://doi.org/10.1126/science.aay2400
3. Browne, C.B., et al.: A survey of Monte Carlo tree search methods. IEEE Trans. Comput. Intell. AI Games **4**(1), 1–43 (2012). https://doi.org/10.1109/TCIAIG.2012.2186810
4. Campbell, M., Hoane, A.: hsiung Hsu, F.: Deep blue. Artif. Intell. **134** (2002). https://doi.org/10.1016/S0004-3702(01)00129-1
5. Cowling, P.I., Powley, E.J., Whitehouse, D.: Information set monte carlo tree search. IEEE Trans. Comput. Intell. AI Games **4**(2), 120–143 (2012). https://doi.org/10.1109/TCIAIG.2012.2200894
6. Mnih, V., et al.: Human-level control through deep reinforcement learning. Nature **518**(7540), 529–533 (2015)
7. Niklaus, J., Alberti, M., Pondenkandath, V., Ingold, R., Liwicki, M.: Overview of artificial intelligence for card games and its application to the swiss game JASS. In: 2019 6th Swiss Conference on Data Science (SDS), pp. 25–30. IEEE, Bern (2019). https://doi.org/10.1109/SDS.2019.00-12
8. Hölldobler, S., Krötzsch, M., Peñaloza, R., Rudolph, S. (eds.): KI 2015. LNCS (LNAI), vol. 9324. Springer, Cham (2015). https://doi.org/10.1007/978-3-319-24489-1
9. Silver, D., et al.: Mastering the game of Go with deep neural networks and tree search. Nature **529**(7587), 484–489 (2016). https://doi.org/10.1038/nature16961
10. Sturtevant, N.R.: An analysis of UCT in multi-player games. In: van den Herik, H.J., Xu, X., Ma, Z., Winands, M.H.M. (eds.) CG 2008. LNCS, vol. 5131, pp. 37–49. Springer, Heidelberg (2008). https://doi.org/10.1007/978-3-540-87608-3_4
11. Watanabe, M.N., Lanzi, P.L.: Traditional wisdom and monte carlo tree search face-to-face in the card game scopone. IEEE Trans. Games **10**, 317–332 (2018)
12. Whitehouse, D., Powley, E.J., Cowling, P.I.: Determinization and information set Monte Carlo tree search for the card game Dou Di Zhu. In: 2011 IEEE Conference on Computational Intelligence and Games (CIG 2011), pp. 87–94. IEEE (2011). https://doi.org/10.1109/CIG.2011.6031993

How Motivated Are You? A Mental Network Model for Dynamic Goal Driven Emotion Regulation

Nimat Ullah[✉] [iD] and Jan Treur[iD]

Social AI Group, Vrije Universiteit Amsterdam, Amsterdam, The Netherlands
nimatullah09@gmail.com, j.treur@vu.nl

Abstract. Emotions drive our lives in one direction or another. It not only defines our psychological health but also shades light on one's goals in the external world. This paper introduces a mental network model to demonstrate how motivation states go together with emotion goals and goals in external world. The network model also deals with the variation in choice of strategies for regulating emotions to achieve the emotion goals. Moreover, it elaborates one example where anger, being a negative emotion, proves to be the right emotion goal to achieve goals in the external world. Simulation results are reported for the example scenario whereby the priority of emotion goals vary with the dynamic context.

Keywords: Emotion regulation · Emotion goals · Distraction · Rumination · Motivation · Anger · Adaptivity

1 Introduction

Emotions are considered as an adaptive response which helps in coping with the threats in the environment and demands of the situation (Frijda 1988; Izard 2009). Its regulation takes place by a causal path through motivation (Tamir et al. 2019) which means that a person must first get enough motivation to regulate his emotions. Moreover, activation of pre-hedonic goals are also considered to be as effective in downregulating negative emotions as could be the means for pursuing those emotions (Tamir et al. 2019). Activation of emotion goals automatically triggers the strategies and means that one already has at his/her disposal for changing one's emotions (Fishbach and Ferguson 2007). Emotion goals are considered as a "causal factor in emotion regulation" (Tamir 2016; Tamir and Millgram 2017). Goals and means are essential for each other to be pursued and emotion regulation strategies can independently affect emotion regulation in different ways. It's context that defines the efficacy of specific emotions i.e. each of the pleasant or unpleasant emotions can be beneficial in specific context (Izard 1990; Keltner and Gross 1999). This also means that a person can be motivated to increase his unpleasant emotions for achieving some goals such as anger in case of confrontational tasks (Tamir et al. 2008; Tiedens 2001). Moreover, the implications of anger are also dependent upon the context in which it's felt (Bonanno 2001).

© Springer Nature Switzerland AG 2020
L. Rutkowski et al. (Eds.): ICAISC 2020, LNAI 12416, pp. 518–529, 2020.
https://doi.org/10.1007/978-3-030-61534-5_46

Goals are defined as the end results that people want to achieve from self-regulation (Gollwitzer and Moskowitz 1996; Thrash and Elliot 2001) and emotion goals are, therefore, defined as the emotion states that people aim at achieving while undergoing emotion regulation (Mauss and Tamir 2014; Tamir 2016). While undergoing emotion regulation, people aim at increasing or decreasing their emotions and for that they need to select some emotion regulation strategies (Gross 2015) as a mean to change their emotional experiences (Gross 1998).

A huge body of literature can be found about goals, emotions, motives and emotion regulation and their interactions. Thus, an important question is how these are related to each other and how they work together in different contexts. To investigate this computationally in a detailed manner, a dynamic modeling approach is required, where the dynamic (and cyclic) interaction between different mental states can be addressed in order for the person to dynamically adapt to the dynamic environment. The Network-Oriented Modeling approach described in (Treur 2016; Treur 2020) and used here fulfils this requirement.

This paper proposes a mental network model for goal driven emotion regulation. This study takes distraction and rumination regulation strategies into account as both these strategies focus on the same early stage in emotion generation wherein distraction attenuates while rumination amplifies attention to the emotion inducing a stimulus (Lewis et al. 2015; Thiruchselvam et al. 2011). In the rest of the paper, Sect. 2 discusses literature on the question under investigation, Sect. 3 presents the network model and its mathematical representation. Section 4 gives scenario for the simulation and insight into the simulation results of the model. Section 5 concludes the paper.

2 Background

The occurrence of impairments in emotion regulation strategies in depression has long been an established fact (Joormann and Siemer 2014) and is attributed to dysfunctional strategies. However, recently it has been found that such impairments can also be attributed to dysfunctional emotion goals (Millgram et al. 2015). Therefore, (Tamir et al. 2019) suggest that intervention in emotion regulation should somehow focus on activation of adaptive emotion goals so that it may activate the adaptive means by emotion regulation strategies to achieve those goals (Millgram et al. 2019). Preferences for emotions depends on the goals that are intended to be achieved (Tamir et al. 2007; Tamir 2005). There can be situations where people are motivated to just increase unpleasant emotions rather than decreasing pleasant emotions (Wood et al. 2003) or maintain unpleasant emotions (Heimpel et al. 2002). These findings suggest that individuals can also be motivated for experiencing bad or unpleasant emotions if it helps in achieving some goals. Two types of goals play a role here, one refers to emotion goals and the other refers to more general goals (e.g., task-related) that are intended to be achieved, where emotion goals can be supportive for that.

According to (Tamir 2016), emotion regulation serves a specific motive and its nature and consequences are solely dependent on the motives that the emotion regulation is intended to serve. The first motive in emotion regulation should either direct or take a person away from specific goals and the second motive may specify the way in which emotion goals and their attainment are pursued. To sum it up, it can be said that "the stronger the motive, the greater the likelihood of pursuing the emotion goal that is expected to serve it" (Tamir 2016). Contrary to (Carver and Scheier 1998; Locke and Latham 1990), who are of the view that goals are deliberately activated via conscious or intentional thoughts, (Bargh et al. 2001; Shah and Kruglanski 2003) suggest that it's the perception of stimulus that, if it has some association with the goals, should alone be able to activate the goals. The perception doesn't need to be conscious (Greenwald et al. 1996; Greenwald 1992), and even if it's conscious, the person may not be aware that the perception has activated an entire array of associated memories and goal constructs (Ferguson and Bargh 2004).

According to (Suri et al. 2015), like all other behaviors, people can be motivated for emotion regulation if it has some cost effectiveness. Motives activate behavior that helps in achieving specific desired goals (Elliot and Niesta 2009), which, in case of emotions, means that motives influence or help in selection of specific emotion goals (Tamir 2016). For instance, runners amplify their anger if they feel it helps in running faster (Lane et al. 2011). People increase their anger before a confrontational task to the level that they feel will help in performing better (Tamir and Ford 2012). Similarly, people prefer to feel sadder while trying to perform better at analytical tasks (Cohen and Andrade 2004). Relations between motives, emotion goals and outcomes have been very nicely summed up in (Tamir 2016):

'For a motive to give rise to a specific emotion goal, people must associate the emotion with the desired outcome. People are likely to vary both in the nature and in the strength of associations they form between specific emotional states and desirable or undesirable outcomes. The stronger the associations between an emotion and the outcome, the more likely it is that people would pursue that emotion to satisfy the related motive.' Similarly, (Lane et al. 2011) elaborate it by an example as under: 'two athletes may be equally motivated to win a competition, but the emotions they pursue to satisfy this motive can differ dramatically depending on which emotion they expect would promote performance' (Tamir 2016), p. 215.

Apart from satisfaction of the motives, flexibility in mapping emotion goals also defines psychological health (Kim et al. 2015). Less flexibility in matching strategies to goals has been marked as emotional dysfunction (Millgram et al. 2019). Moreover, "what people want to feel can determine how they regulate emotions" (Millgram et al. 2019). For instance, if a person is motivated to decrease his emotional intensity, he may go for distraction and for rumination if the person is motivated to increase his emotional intensity.

As emotion regulation strategies, distraction and rumination are two attention-deployment strategies having an inverse effect on emotion when compared to each other, as distraction is considered to decrease emotion (Shafir et al. 2015) by decreasing the amount of attention directed towards the emotion inducing stimulus (Naragon-Gainey et al. 2017) while rumination is considered to increase emotions (Nolen-Hoeksema et al. 2008) by increasing attention towards the emotion inducing stimulus (Naragon-Gainey et al. 2017). Selection of one of these strategies is subjected to whether the person is motivated to increase or decrease his emotional experience; i.e. people should, more likely, turn to distraction when motivated to decrease the intensity of their emotions and rumination when motivated to increase the intensity of their emotions (Millgram et al. 2019).

3   The Mental Network Model

The proposed computational network model is inspired and based on the vast body of literature summarized above and developed using the Network-Oriented Modeling approach described in (Treur 2016; Treur 2020). Here networks of states are used that are dynamic based on temporal-causal connections between them: the state values change over time by the causal impact of a number of states on another state over time. It uses labels for network characteristics Connectivity, Aggregation and Timing as given below:

- **Connectivity.** Nodes X and Y, interpreted as states, are connected to each other with *connections* $X \rightarrow Y$ defining causal impact; each connection carries *a connection weight* $\omega_{X,Y} \in [-1, 1]$.
- **Aggregation.** For each state Y, a combination function $\mathbf{c}_Y(..)$ is chosen to defi*ne the aggregated* incoming causal impact from various other states
- **Timing.** Each state Y has a speed factor η_Y which shows how fast state Y changes because of the causal impact exerted on it by the other states

This Network-Oriented Modeling approach has been shown to be quite effective in modeling highly dynamic and interactive mental and social processes, which often involve dynamic and cyclic interactions of mental and social states. Also adaptive networks of different orders can be modeled; then some of the above labels for network characteristics become adaptive; see (Treur 2020). The mental network model shown in Fig. 1 was developed based on the above Network-Oriented Modeling approach. Table 1 provides a description of the states of the model. The mental network in Fig. 1 describes the process of activation as well as regulation of emotions motivated by some kind of goals. The goals refer to both emotion as well as goals (e.g., task-related) in the real world. The red connections represent negative connections. In this network model, the causal pathway from stimulus s leads to the activation of goal state for emotion goals gs_{em}, goal state for task gs_t in the real world and the motivation state ms_{motv} for achieving the emotion goals. The emotion goal then activates preparation for the suitable emotional state, i.e., anger $ps_{b.ang}$ in case of the example scenario for this model, for achieving the goals in real world gs_t. Regulation of this "perceived suitable emotional state" (i.e., anger) is further up- or down-regulated using emotion regulation strategies (rumination cs_{rmnt} and distraction cs_{dstr}, respectively) in a flexible way. Here the choice of strategies is dependent on the context. Similarly, the choice to increase or decrease the intensity of the emotional state (i.e. anger) is also dependent on the context. For instance, in case of the above mental network model, it's perceived that if anger is increased the person will be able to meet a certain deadline in his work. So, the person increases his anger by using rumination cs_{rmnt}.

On the other hand, the same emotional state (i.e., anger) is decreased using distraction cs_{dstr} when interrupted by another external stimulus; for example, a daughter srs_{ds} in

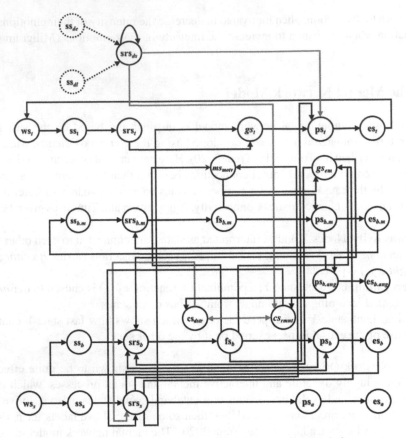

Fig. 1. Computation model for goal driven emotion regulation

case of this model. In the latter case, distraction suits the context as the person wants to deal with his daughter with love, for which he needs to decrease his anger. In contrast, in the former case, rumination is more suited to achieve the intended emotional state as it amplifies attention to the stimulus.

Transformation of the above conceptual representation of a temporal-causal network model into numerical representation takes the steps given below; these steps are automated by a dedicated software environment described in (Treur 2020), Ch. 9:

1. Every state X, at a given time point t, has a value $X(t)$ between 0 and 1.
2. The causal impact of state X on Y at time point t is computed as $\mathbf{impact}_{X,Y}(t) = \omega_{X,Y}X(t)$ where $\omega_{X,Y}$ represents the weight of the connection $X \rightarrow Y$.
3. Impact of multiple incoming causal connections to Y from $X_1...X_k$ is aggregated as:

$$\mathbf{aggimpact}_Y(t) = \mathbf{c}_Y\big(\mathbf{impact}_{X1,Y}(t), \ldots, \mathbf{impact}_{Xk,Y}(t)\big) \qquad (1)$$

$$= \mathbf{c}_Y\big(\omega_{X1,Y}X_1(t), \ldots, \omega_{Xk,Y}X_k(t)\big) \qquad (2)$$

where $\mathbf{c}_Y(...)$ represents combination function of state Y.

Table 1. States and their explanation.

Name	Description	Name	Description
$ws_{(s, t)}$	World state for stimulus s, task t	ms_{motv}	Monitoring state for motivation $motv$
$ss_{(s, b, b.m, t, de, dl)}$	Sensor state for stimulus s, body state b, body state for motivation $b.m$, task t, daughter enters de, daughter leave dl	$es_{(a, b, b.ang, b.m, t)}$	Execution state for action a, body state b, body state for anger $b.ang$, body state for motivation $b.m$, task t
$srs_{(s, b, b.m, t, ds)}$	Sensory representation state for the stimulus s, body state b, motivation $b.m$, task t, daughter status ds	$ps_{(a, b, b.ang, b.m, t)}$	Preparation state for physical action a, body state b, body state for anger $b.ang$, body state for motivation $b.m$, task t
$fs_{(b, b.m)}$	Feeling state for body b, motivation $b.m$.	gs_{em}	Goal state for emotions em
$cs_{(dstr, rmnt)}$	Control state for distraction $dstr$, rumination $rmnt$	gs_t	Goal state for task t

4. Timing of the impact of **aggimpact**$_Y(t)$ on Y is determined by speed factor η_Y as below:

$$Y(t + \Delta t) = Y(t) + \eta_Y\left[\textbf{aggimpact}_Y(t) - Y(t)\right]\Delta t \tag{3}$$

$$\text{or } \textbf{d}Y(t) / \textbf{dt} = \eta_Y\left[\textbf{aggimpact}_Y(t) - Y(t)\right] \tag{4}$$

5. Thus, the difference and differential equations obtained are given as under:

$$Y(t + \Delta t) = Y(t) + \eta_Y\left[\textbf{c}_Y\left(\omega_{X_1,Y}X_1(t), \ldots, \omega_{Xk,Y}X_k(t)\right) - Y(t)\right]\Delta t \tag{5}$$

$$\text{or } \textbf{d}Y(t) / \textbf{dt} = \eta_Y\left[\textbf{c}_Y\left(\omega_{X_1,Y}X_1(t), \ldots, \omega_{X_k,Y}X_k(t)\right) - Y(t)\right] \tag{6}$$

4 Settings and Simulation Results for an Example Scenario

Besides giving deeper insight of the network model, this section of the paper makes this model easily reproducible. Table 2 shows all the connections' weight values of the network model. Table 3 provides the values for combination functions and speed factors of the various states. Providing these connection values along with the values provided in Table 3 to the model, will yield the results shown in Figs. 2 and 3.

In Table 3 below, the identity function $\mathbf{id}(V) = V$, has been used for the states with only one incoming connection that do not have any value for steepness σ and threshold τ. The advanced logistic sum combination function Eq. (7) has been used for the states with more than one incoming connection. World state ws_s has an initial value 1. Similarly, srs_{ds} has initial value 0.11 for the case of $\tau = 0.2$, and 0.9 as initial value for the case of $\tau = 0.8$; this is to make the external context factor (daughter) appear or disappear in the middle of the process.

Table 2. Connection weights for getting the desired results

Connection	Weight	Connection	Weight	Connection	Weight
$\omega_{wss,\ sss}$	1	$\omega_{psb,\ esb}$	0.8	$\omega_{psb.m,\ srsb.m}$	0.4
$\omega_{sss,\ srss}$	0.5	$\omega_{esb,\ ssb}$	0.6	$\omega_{psb.m,\ esb.m}$	0.8
$\omega_{srss,\ psa}$	0.4	$\omega_{csdstr,\ srss}$	−0.45	$\omega_{esb.m,\ ssb.m}$	0.8
$\omega_{srss,\ psb}$	0.6	$\omega_{csdstr,\ csrmnt}$	−1	$\omega_{msmotv,\ psb.m}$	0.5
$\omega_{srss,\ msmotv}$	0.4	$\omega_{csrmnt,\ srss}$	0.5	$\omega_{gsem,\ srsb}$	0.2
$\omega_{srss,\ gsem}$	0.2	$\omega_{csrmnt,\ csdstr}$	−1	$\omega_{gsem,\ psb.ang}$	0.8
$\omega_{srss,\ gst}$	0.6	$\omega_{psb.ang,\ srsb}$	0.1	$\omega_{wst,\ sst}$	0.6
$\omega_{psa,\ esa}$	0.4	$\omega_{psb.ang,\ csdstr}$	1	$\omega_{sst,\ srst}$	0.7
$\omega_{ssb,\ srsb}$	0.1	$\omega_{psb.ang,\ csrmnt}$	1	$\omega_{srst,\ gst}$	0.2
$\omega_{srss,\ fsb}$	0.8	$\omega_{psb.ang,\ esb.ang}$	0.8	$\omega_{gst,\ pst}$	0.1
$\omega_{fsb,\ psb}$	0.2	$\omega_{ssb.m,\ srsb.m}$	0.4	$\omega_{pst,\ est}$	0.8
$\omega_{fsb,\ msmotv}$	0.25	$\omega_{srsb.m,\ fsb.m}$	0.6	$\omega_{est,\ wst}$	1
$\omega_{fsb,\ gsem}$	0.2	$\omega_{fsb.m,\ psb.m}$	0.2	$\omega_{srsds,\ csrmnt}$	−1
$\omega_{fsb,\ pst}$	0.6	$\omega_{fsb.m,\ gsem}$	0.4	$\omega_{srsds,\ pst}$	−0.8
$\omega_{psb,\ srsb}$	0.2			$\omega_{srsds,\ srsds}$	1

The advanced logistic sum combination function is defined by:

$$\mathbf{alogistic}_{\sigma,t}(V_1, \ldots, V_k) = \left[\left(1 / \left(1 + e^{-\sigma(V_1 + \ldots + V_k - \tau)} \right) \right) - 1 / \left(1 + e^{\sigma\tau} \right) \right] \left(1 + e^{-\sigma\tau} \right) \tag{7}$$

4.1 Example Scenario Used for Simulation

The following example scenario, based on findings from literature in Psychology, has been simulated using the proposed model:

Table 3. Values of steepness, threshold and speed factor of each state

State	σ	τ	η	State	σ	τ	η
ws_s	0	0	0	$ss_{b.m}$	8	0.5	1
ss_s	0	0	1	$srs_{b.m}$	8	0.3	1
srs_s	8	0.4	0.2	$fs_{b.m}$	8	0.3	1
ps_a	0	0	0.5	$ps_{b.m}$	8	0.3	1
es_a	0	0	0.5	$es_{b.m}$	8	0.3	1
ss_b	8	0.3	1	ms_{motv}	8	0.3	0.8
srs_b	8	0.3	1	gs_{em}	8	0.3	0.8
fs_b	8	0.3	1	ws_t	8	0.3	0.5
ps_b	8	0.3	1	ss_t	8	0.3	0.5
es_b	8	0.3	1	srs_t	8	0.3	0.5
cs_{dstr}	8	0.4	0.4	gs_t	8	0.3	0.5
cs_{rmnt}	8	0.2	0.5	ps_t	8	0.3	0.5
$ps_{b.ang}$	10	0.4	1	es_t	8	0.3	0.5
$es_{b.ang}$	10	0.6	0.8	srs_{ds}	18	0.2, 0.8	0.02

While working from home, Mr. Fahad gets angry at his colleagues' progress, as he is the only one yet to complete the assigned task. He ruminates his anger to stay focused and complete the task but his daughter interrupts him in between. So, he distracts his attention away from his colleagues' progress to deal with her with love and gets free from the assigned task which he wants to pursue while being angry as it increases his efficiency.

Figure 2 illustrates a situation where the person achieves one emotion goal (i.e., anger) but then his emotion goal changes as a result of an external factor (interrupting daughter). In the figure it can be seen that the daughter srs_{ds} is not present yet but the stimulus srs_s has already happened and the person's motivation state ms_{motv}, goal state for emotion gs_{em} and goal state for task gs_t in the external world already were activated. Here the person's emotion goal is to get angry, modeled by emotional response $ps_{b.ang}$. The emotion goal activates the strategy which helps in achieving the emotional state that the person is motivated to achieve (i.e. anger) represented by response state $ps_{b.ang}$ so that he can achieve his goal in the external world es_t. So, it activates the control state for increasing rumination cs_{rmnt} which increases attention towards the emotion inducing stimulus srs_s (progress of his colleagues in their assigned tasks). Rumination helps the person to get angry and hence stay more focused to working on his task. After a certain time, it can be seen that srs_{ds} gets activated which means that the daughter of the person enters the room which changes his emotion goal because he wants to deal with her with love. So, the emotion goal, now, is to reduce anger $ps_{b.ang}$. As per findings from Psychology, the emotion goal activates the means to achieve the corresponding

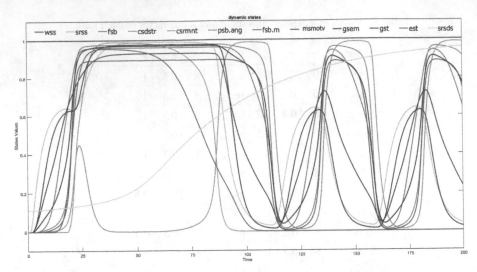

Fig. 2. Contextual switching from rumination to distraction

emotional state, i.e., it activates the control state for distraction cs_{dstr}. Activation of distraction reduces the intensity of srs_s and the associated states like ms_{motv}, gs_t but just like a more realistic situation, the intensity of the stimulus still keeps fluctuating and takes the person's attention. That's why the pattern will keep repeating itself until his daughter leaves and he gets busy in the task or he has completed the task.

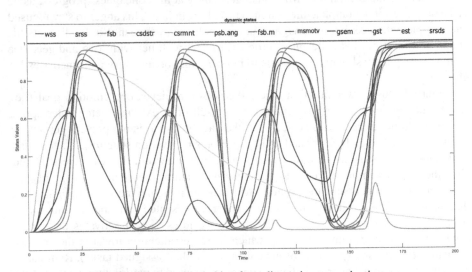

Fig. 3. Contextual switching from distraction to rumination

Figure 3 shows a situation where a person is delaying an intended emotional state by distracting his attention away from the primary stimulus srs_s to a secondary stimulus srs_{ds}. Here, the person's emotion goal is to keep his anger reduced as he wants to deal with his daughter with love. At the same time, he also has the primary stimulus in his mind which he thinks can be coped with by achieving a different emotional state, i.e. anger. To deal with the secondary stimulus srs_{ds}, the current emotion goal activates the control state for distraction cs_{dstr} to move his attention away from the primary stimulus srs_s. the fluctuation of the curves indicates the intensity of the srs_s and the person's eagerness to complete the task. After a while, as his daughter leaves (srs_{ds} decreases), the emotion goal changes from reducing anger to increasing anger $ps_{b.ang}$. The new emotion goal now activates a different strategy for achieving the new emotional state, and, therefore, switches from distraction cs_{dstr} to rumination cs_{rmnt}. It can be observed in the figure that as soon as srs_{ds} decreases enough, all the states automatically start getting higher to some extent, even before the activation of the cs_{rmnt}. This phenomenon is exactly in line with the findings from Psychology which state that the stimulus itself (unintentionally) activates an entire array of processes. Those processes also include activation of the means to achieve emotion goals, i.e. some emotion regulation strategy. That phenomenon can be observed here.

5 Conclusion

This paper presents a computational mental network model for goal driven emotion regulation. It is based on the findings from social sciences and psychology. This network model, with the help of simulation results, in a graphical way explains how some (negative) emotional state can prove adaptive in certain situations and help in achieving certain goals in the real world. It, on one hand explains the adaptivity of negative emotional states (dependent on the context); on the other hand, this model also demonstrates the contextual switching between emotional states. Bringing theoretical knowledge from social sciences and Psychology into computational science, this model shows how goals (emotional as well as other goals) activate the means to achieve those goals. This mental network model has been made possible by the dynamicity and wide applicability of network-oriented modeling approach (Treur 2016); see (Treur 2020) for a more updated and extended version of the approach.

References

Bargh, J.A., Gollwitzer, P.M., Lee-Chai, A., Barndollar, K., Trotschel, R.: The automated will: nonconscious activation and pursuit of behavioral goals. J. Pers. Soc. Psychol. **81**(6), 1014–1027 (2001)

Bonanno, G.A.: Emotion self-regulation. In: Emotions: Currrent issues and future directions, pp. 251–285. Guilford Press, New York (2001)

Carver, C.S., Scheier, M.F.: On the Self-regulation of Behavior. Cambridge University Press, New York (1998)

Cohen, J.B., Andrade, E.B.: Affective intuition and task-contingent affect regulation. J. Consum. Res. **31**(2), 358–367 (2004). https://doi.org/10.1086/422114

Elliot, A.J., Niesta, D.: Goals in the context of the hierarchical model of approach—avoidance motivation. In: The Psychology of Goals, pp. 56–76. Guilford Press, New York (2009)

Ferguson, M.J., Bargh, J.A.: How social perception can automatically influence behavior. Trends Cogn. Sci. **8**(1), 33–39 (2004). https://doi.org/10.1016/j.tics.2003.11.004

Fishbach, A., Ferguson, M.J.: The goal construct in social psychology. In: Social Psychology: Handbook of Basic Principles, 2 edn., pp. 490–515. The Guilford Press, New York (2007)

Gollwitzer, P.M., Moskowitz, G.B.: Goal effects on action and cognition. In: Social Psychology: Handbook of Basic Principles, pp. 361–399. Guilford Press, New York (1996)

Greenwald, A.G.: New look 3: unconscious cognition reclaimed. Am. Psychol. 47(6), 766–779 (1992). https://doi.org/10.1037/0003-066X.47.6.766

Greenwald, A.G., Draine, S.C., Abrams, R.L.: Three cognitive markers of unconscious semantic activation. Science 273(5282), 1699–1702 (1996). https://doi.org/10.1126/science.273.5282. 1699

Gross, J.J.: The emerging field of emotion regulation: an integrative review. Rev. Gener. Psychol. 2(3), 271–299 (1998). https://doi.org/10.1037/1089-2680.2.3.271

Gross, J.J.: Emotion regulation: current status and future prospects. Psychol. Inq. 26(1), 1–26 (2015). https://doi.org/10.1080/1047840X.2014.940781

Frijda, N.H.: The laws of emotion. Am. Psychol. 43(5), 349–358 (1988). https://doi.org/10.1037/ 0003-066X.43.5.349

Heimpel, S.A., Wood, J.V., Marshall, M.A., Brown, J.D.: Do people with low self-esteem really want to feel better? Self-esteem differences in motivation to repair negative moods. J. Pers. Soc. Psychol. 82(1), 128–147 (2002)

Izard, C.E.: The substrates and functions of emotion feelings: William James and current emotion theory. Pers. Pers. Soc. Psychol. Bull. 16(4), 626–635 (1990). https://doi.org/10.1177/014616 7290164004

Izard, C.E.: Emotion theory and research: highlights, unanswered questions, and emerging issues. Ann. Rev. Psychol. 60(1), 1–25 (2009). https://doi.org/10.1146/annurev.psych.60.110 707.163539

Joormann, J., Siemer, M.: Emotion regulation in mood disorders. In: Handbook of Emotion Regulation, 2 edn., pp. 413–427. Guilford Press, New York (2014)

Keltner, D., Gross, J.J.: Functional accounts of emotions. Cogn. Emot. 13(5), 467–480 (1999). https://doi.org/10.1080/026999399379140

Kim, M.Y., Ford, B.Q., Mauss, I., Tamir, M.: Knowing when to seek anger: psychological health and context-sensitive emotional preferences. Cogn. Emot. 29(6), 1126–1136 (2015). https:// doi.org/10.1080/02699931.2014.970519

Lane, A.M., Beedie, C.J., Devonport, T.J., Stanley, D.M.: Instrumental emotion regulation in sport: relationships between beliefs about emotion and emotion regulation strategies used by athletes. Scand. J. Med. Sci. Sports 21(6), 445–451 (2011). https://doi.org/10.1111/j.1600-0838.2011. 01364.x

Lewis, K.L., Taubitz, L.E., Duke, M.W., Steuer, E.L., Larson, C.L.: State rumination enhances elaborative processing of negative material as evidenced by the late positive potential. Emotion 15(6), 687–693 (2015). https://doi.org/10.1037/emo0000095

Locke, E.A., Latham, G.P.: A Theory of Goal Setting & Task Performance. Prentice Hall, Englewood Cliffs (1990)

Mauss, I.B., Tamir, M.: Emotion goals: how their content, structure, and operation shape emotion regulation. In: Handbook of emotion regulation, 2 edn., pp. 361–375. Guilford Press, New York (2014)

Millgram, Y., Joormann, J., Huppert, J.D., Tamir, M.: Sad as a matter of choice? Emotion-regulation goals in depression. Psychol. Sci. 26(8), 1216–1228 (2015). https://doi.org/10.1177/ 0956797615583295

Millgram, Y., Sheppes, G., Kalokerinos, E.K., Kuppens, P., Tamir, M.: Do the ends dictate the means in emotion regulation? J. Exp. Psychol. Gen. 148(1), 80–96 (2019). https://doi.org/10. 1037/xge0000477

Naragon-Gainey, K., McMahon, T.P., Chacko, T.P.: The structure of common emotion regulation strategies: a meta-analytic examination. Psychol. Bull. **143**(4), 384–427 (2017). https://doi.org/10.1037/bul0000093

Nolen-Hoeksema, S., Wisco, B.E., Lyubomirsky, S.: Rethinking Rumination. Perspect. Psychol. Sci. **3**(5), 400–424 (2008). https://doi.org/10.1111/j.1745-6924.2008.00088.x

Shafir, R., Schwartz, N., Blechert, J., Sheppes, G.: Emotional intensity influences pre-implementation and implementation of distraction and reappraisal. Soc. Cogn. Affect. Neurosci. **10**(10), 1329–1337 (2015). https://doi.org/10.1093/scan/nsv022

Shah, J.Y., Kruglanski, A.W.: When opportunity knocks: bottom-up priming of goals by means and its effects on self-regulation. J. Pers. Soc. Psychol. **84**(6), 1109–1122 (2003)

Suri, G., Whittaker, K., Gross, J.J.: Launching reappraisal: it's less common than you might think. Emotion **15**(1), 73–77 (2015). https://doi.org/10.1037/emo0000011

Tamir, M.: Don't worry, be happy? Neuroticism, trait-consistent affect regulation, and performance. J. Pers. Soc. Psychol. **89**(3), 449–461 (2005). https://doi.org/10.1037/0022-3514.89.3.449

Tamir, M.: Why do people regulate their emotions? A taxonomy of motives in emotion regulation. Pers. Soc. Psychol. Rev. **20**(3), 199–222 (2016). https://doi.org/10.1177/1088868315586325

Tamir, M., Chiu, C.-Y., Gross, J.J.: Business or pleasure? Utilitarian versus hedonic considerations in emotion regulation. Emotion **7**(3), 546–554 (2007). https://doi.org/10.1037/1528-3542.7.3.546

Tamir, M., Ford, B.Q.: When feeling bad is expected to be good: emotion regulation and outcome expectancies in social conflicts. Emotion **12**(4), 807–816 (2012). https://doi.org/10.1037/a0024443

Tamir, M., Halperin, E., Porat, R., Bigman, Y.E., Hasson, Y.: When there's a will, there's a way: disentangling the effects of goals and means in emotion regulation. Pers. Soc. Psychol. Rev. **116**(5), 795–816 (2019). https://doi.org/10.1037/pspp0000232

Tamir, M., Millgram, Y.: Motivated emotion regulation: principles, lessons, and implications of a motivational analysis of emotion regulation. In: Advances in Motivation Science, pp. 207–247. Elsevier Academic Press (2017)

Tamir, M., Mitchell, C., Gross, J.J., Tamir, M., Mitchell, C., Gross, J.J.: Hedonic and instrumental motives in anger regulation. Psychol. Sci. **19**(4), 2–6 (2008). https://doi.org/10.1111/j.1467-9280.2008.02088.x

Thiruchselvam, R., Blechert, J., Sheppes, G., Rydstrom, A., Gross, J.J.: The temporal dynamics of emotion regulation: an EEG study of distraction and reappraisal. Biol. Psychol. **87**(1), 84–92 (2011). https://doi.org/10.1016/j.biopsycho.2011.02.009

Thrash, T.M., Elliot, A.J.: Delimiting and integrating achievement motive and goal constructs. In: Trends and Prospects in Motivation Research, pp. 3–21. Kluwer Academic Publishers, Dordrecht (2001)

Tiedens, L.Z.: Anger and advancement versus sadness and subjugation: the effect of negative emotion expressions on social status conferral. J. Pers. Soc. Psychol. **80**(1), 86–94 (2001). https://doi.org/10.1037/0022-3514.80.1.86

Treur, J.: Network- Oriented Modeling: Addressing Complexity of Cognitive, Affective and Social Interactions. Springer, Heidelberg (2016). https://doi.org/10.1007/978-3-319-45213-5

Treur, J.: Network-Oriented Modeling for Adaptive Networks: Designing Higher-Order Adaptive Biological, Mental and Social Network Models. Springer, Heidelberg (2020)

Wood, J.V., Heimpel, S.A., Michela, J.L.: Savoring versus dampening: self-esteem differences in regulating positive affect. J. Pers. Soc. Psychol. **85**(3), 566–580 (2003). https://doi.org/10.1037/0022-3514.85.3.566

Author Index

Printed in the United States
by Baker & Taylor

nted in the United States
Bookmasters